The Parting of the Gods

The Parting of the Gods

Paul and the Redefinition of Judaism

David A. Brondos

Comunidad Teológica de México
Ciudad de México

Theological Community of Mexico
Mexico City

2021

THE PARTING OF THE GODS: PAUL AND THE REDEFINITION OF JUDAISM

Comunidad Teológica de México/Instituto Internacional de Estudios Superiores
Av. San Jerónimo 137
San Ángel
01000 México, CDMX
México

Cover image: Lynn Alker, *Passage* (detail), © 2020
Image photographer: Christopher Ciccone

Cover design: Rui Pereira

Interior design: Joel Friedlander

Primera edición/First edition: 2021

ISBN: 978-607-98034-7-6

Printed in the U.S.A./Impreso en los Estados Unidos de Norteamérica

Contents

Presentación de la Obra

> *Cristo es "el fin de la Ley" (Rom 10,4).*
> *El antiguo eón ha alcanzado con él su término; se alza el nuevo eón.*
> *Que esto sea una afirmación paradójica no se manifestó*
> *claramente en un principio al cristianismo primitivo.*
> *En primer lugar, es una proposición mitológica.*
> *Pues el cristianismo primitivo se representaba el fin del mundo como*
> *un acontecimiento dramático cósmico y lo esperaba en lo inmediato.*
> *Tal acontecimiento no se produjo.*
> *La fe cristiana, por cuanto se consistía*
> *en la espera del fin próximo del mundo,*
> *se convirtió en la religión cristiana, constituida en Iglesia.*
> *Pero, ¿la fe cristiana es idéntica a esa espera mitológica?*
> *¿O ésta no es más que una envoltura bajo la cual*
> *se oculta el sentido propio de la fe?*
> **– Rudolf Bultmann**

The Parting of the Gods: Paul and the Redefinition of Judaism es el flamante libro de David Brondos con el que la Comunidad Teológica de México se engalana al presentar.

Con su estilo dialéctico ya clásico, el Dr. Brondos nos presenta su posición frente al actual debate respecto de la bifurcación entre el judaísmo del siglo primero y el surgimiento de las comunidades cristianas. Este debate se da precisamente en el punto de inflexión que separa ambos caminos religiosos y que se hace presente en la literatura del Segundo Testamento, particularmente en los escritos y teología paulina.

La figura retórica que marca este debate es "the parting of the ways." ¿Fue el cristianismo un ejercicio de continuidad o un movimiento de ruptura con el judaísmo? Si bien David Brondos considera la continuidad del cristianismo en relación al judaísmo, su argumento central es precisamente el que se vuelve necesario repensar lo que era el judaísmo en el pensamiento de Pablo, así como su representación en los pensamientos y posturas de los creyentes en Cristo del primer siglo y de la era sub-apostólica.

Pablo parece sostener una evaluación positiva de los valores religiosos. El cristianismo no pretende reemplazar al judaísmo; por el contrario, procura redefinirlo o resignificarlo en torno a su perspectiva de Jesús ("Cristo") como "Hijo de Dios."

Esta obra de David Brondos, que reconoce la importancia de la *lingua franca*, se presenta en inglés por la importancia de compartir su contenido con una audiencia más amplia (principalmente angloparlante) y con la actual academia global de biblistas. En *The Parting of the Gods*, seguramente encontraremos perspectivas diferentes sobre los temas que ya se discuten en la academia, pero que también están en diálogo con ese contexto.

La perspectiva del contexto eclesial que se percibe en *The Parting of the Gods* permite apreciar de maneras diferentes el tema de la comunidad, pues su perspectiva presenta a Pablo como el apóstol que busca integrar a personas de diferentes orígenes y espacios en un espacio incluyente, una comunidad caracterizada por la solidaridad, la igualdad, la equidad, y la paz (todo junto construyendo una forma de representación del *shalom* de Dios en Cristo)—una comunidad donde personas de diferentes trasfondos y tradiciones convivirían como iguales en lugar de permanecer divididos por sus tradiciones y costumbres.

¡Enhorabuena por este formidable esfuerzo del Dr. David Brondos, a quien reconocemos su esfuerzo y dedicación al entregarnos este maravilloso trabajo!

Pablo hizo muy bien en poner por escrito una de
las fórmulas bautismales que se pasaba de boca en boca:
"En Jesucristo ya no hay más discriminación entre judío y griego,
ni entre hombre y mujer."
– Eliseo Pérez Álvarez

Dan González-Ortega
Rector
Comunidad Teológica de México
Enero de 2021

INTRODUCTION

In the wake of the systematic murder of over six million Jews in what has come to be known as the Holocaust or *Shoah*, both Jews and Christians horrified at the atrocities committed have recognized the urgent need to reconsider the ways in which their two faiths relate to one another. While those who orchestrated those atrocities for the most part did not explicitly justify their actions on the basis of Christian beliefs concerning Jews and Judaism, there can be no doubt that the negative portrayals and caricatures of Jews and Judaism and the inflammatory rhetoric directed against the Jewish people by Christians for nearly two millennia contributed significantly to the crimes and violence perpetrated against them.

Since the time of the Protestant Reformation, it has been common among biblical scholars and theologians to portray Judaism as the antithesis of Christianity.[1] Whereas Christianity proclaimed a God of grace and mercy who forgave and accepted repentant sinners freely by virtue of Christ and his death, Judaism supposedly presented God as a demanding judge whose favor had to be earned by the strict observance of his commandments and the accumulation of good works. While at times Jews were said to live under the intolerable burden of having to produce a sufficient number of good works to outweigh their transgressions and the constant anxiety of never knowing whether they had actually done so, at other times they were criticized for boastfully and arrogantly claiming that they had in fact earned God's grace and salvation through the pious life they led. In contrast, because Christians knew that salvation was a gracious divine

---

1. On what follows, see especially E. P. Sanders, *Paul and Palestinian Judaism: A Comparison of Patterns of Religion* (Philadelphia: Fortress, 1977), 33-59; William S. Campbell, *Paul and the Creation of Christian Identity* (London: T & T Clark, 2008), 15-32; Francis Watson, *Paul, Judaism, and the Gentiles: Beyond the New Perspective*, rev. ed. (Grand Rapids: Eerdmans, 2009), 27-43. As Watson notes, many of these ideas are especially associated with the thought of Ferdinand Christian Baur (1792-1860), widely regarded as the most important biblical scholar of the nineteenth century; see William Baird, *History of New Testament Research*, vol. 1: *From Deism to Tübingen* (Minneapolis: Fortress, 1992), 262-66.

gift given by faith alone, they could be at peace, fully assured of God's forgiveness in Christ and boasting only of God's grace. Because Christianity was a universal religion concerned with lofty spiritual values such as love for neighbor and even for one's enemies, it was far superior to Judaism, which was characterized by a narrow particularism and a petty legalism that was devoid of any spirituality and focused on the meticulous observance of endless rules, regulations, and rituals that had no real purpose or meaning. The hypocrisy, Pharisaism, and "eye for an eye" mentality of Judaism was set in stark contrast to the gospel of mercy, kindness, generosity, humility, and forgiveness proclaimed by Jesus and the church he had founded. In addition, as the New Testament made clear, the Jews were a rebellious and disobedient people who stubbornly refused to acknowledge the truth and had even put to death the Son of God whom God had graciously sent into the world for the salvation of all.

On the basis of views such as these regarding Judaism and the Jewish people, it was claimed that God had rejected the Jews and no longer regarded them as his chosen people.[2] Because Judaism had been superseded by Christianity, it no longer had any purpose and might simply be made to disappear as an obsolete relic of the past. The church had taken the place of Israel as God's people and the old covenant had been abolished in order to give way to the new covenant established through Christ. Observance of the law of Moses was not only pointless but even contrary to God's will, and was therefore to be rejected as well. These ideas were especially associated with Paul, who had regarded life under the Jewish law as "loss" and "rubbish" and called on both gentiles and Jews to abandon the observance of the Mosaic law as sinful in that it led to the type of boasting and works-righteousness that God detested.[3] Believers in Christ had been redeemed from their slavery and subjection to the law, which brought only death and condemnation. Any who rejected Paul's law-free gospel and insisted on clinging to the observance of the law were denying God's grace and thus remained under his wrath and curse.

It is not at all difficult to see how easily and readily these negative portrayals of Judaism fed into the conclusion that Judaism and the Jews should be eradicated, as the National Socialist regime in Germany sought to do under the direction of Adolf Hitler.[4] In his infamous treatise "On the Jews

----

2. On this idea in the history of Christian thought, see especially Michael J. Vlach, *The Church as a Replacement of Israel: An Analysis of Supersessionism* (EI 2; Frankfurt am Main: Peter Lang, 2009). On the concept and types of supersessionism, see Terence L. Donaldson, "Supersessionism and Early Christian Self-Definition," *JJMJS* 3 (2016): 1-32.

3. See Rom 2:17-23; 3:27; Gal 2:16; Phil 3:3-9.

4. On this subject, see Susannah Heschel, "From Jesus to Shylock: Christian Supersessionism and 'The Merchant of Venice'," *HTR* 99 (2006): 407-31.

and Their Lies," Martin Luther himself had advocated violence toward the Jews of his day on the basis of the same type of portrayal of Judaism.[5] It is also not difficult to understand why, when the full horrors of the Holocaust had come to light, so many Christian biblical scholars felt the urgent need to reappraise from a critical perspective the interpretations of their foundational texts that had served as a basis for the views of Jews and Judaism just considered, and to do so in dialogue with Jewish scholars, many of whom took up alongside their Christian peers the study of the New Testament and other early Christian writings.[6]

Among these scholars were figures such as David Daube (1909-1999), W. D. Davies (1911-2001), Geza Vermes (1924-2013), Krister Stendahl (1929-2008), and E. P. Sanders (1937–), whose 1977 book *Paul and Palestinian Judaism* was particularly influential in calling into question many of the traditional Christian assumptions regarding Second Temple Judaism.[7] In particular, Sanders and others argued that the concept of grace was central to the ancient Jewish worldview and that the idea that it was necessary to earn one's salvation by means of a legalistic works-righteousness was foreign to Jewish thought. On the contrary, both the Mosaic law and the covenant with Israel were seen as expressions of God's love. Rather than demanding perfect obedience to the law, God simply expected his people to respond to his grace by committing themselves to obeying his commandments and making atonement for any sins they committed by means of the sacrificial offerings he had prescribed in the law. Increasingly, Christianity came to be viewed as an *expression* or *offshoot* of Judaism rather than its antithesis. Jesus and Paul had been faithful, law-observant Jews who had never intended to abandon Judaism or replace it with something else, especially not a new religion called Christianity. Jesus' earliest followers simply expected and assumed that their fellow Jews who came to faith in Jesus would continue to observe the law as they themselves did. They valued and upheld that law rather than claiming that it was obsolete and should be abolished.

In the last few decades, this reevaluation and increased appreciation of the Jewish background and roots of the Christian faith has continued.

---

5. Martin Luther, "On the Jews and Their Lies," in *Luther's Works*, ed. Helmut T. Lehmann (Philadelphia: Fortress; St. Louis: Concordia, 1971), 47:121-306.

6. On the history of this development in biblical interpretation, see especially Terence L. Donaldson, *Jews and Judaism in the New Testament: Decision Points and Divergent Interpretations* (London: SPCK, 2010), 1-29.

7. Among the most influential works of these scholars were: David Daube, *The New Testament and Rabbinic Judaism* (London: University of London Press, 1956); W. D. Davies, *Paul and Rabbinic Judaism: Some Rabbinic Elements in Pauline Theology*, 4th ed. (Philadelphia: Fortress, 1980); Geza Vermes, *Jesus the Jew: A Historian's Reading of the Gospels* (Philadelphia: Fortress, 1973); Krister Stendahl, *Paul among Jews and Gentiles, and Other Essays* (Philadelphia: Fortress, 1976).

Many New Testament scholars now insist that Paul can only be understood properly *within* Judaism rather than in *contradistinction* to it.[8] Because widespread use of the term "Christian" post-dates Paul, to apply that term to him or the communities he sought to establish is regarded as anachronistic. Even the term "church" has connotations and conveys ideas that would have been foreign to Paul's understanding of his apostolic mission.[9] For that reason, many scholars now choose to avoid using the term "Christian" when speaking of the first believers in Christ and to transliterate the Greek term *ekklēsia* rather than translating it as "church," as I will do here.

According to many of the reconstructions of the scholars who work from this perspective, in the years immediately following Jesus' death, those Jews who came to faith in Christ continued to live in relative peace and harmony with other Jews as members of the Jewish community and to meet in Jewish synagogues and spaces. Only when large numbers of gentiles began to be incorporated into the communities of Jesus' followers did tensions and conflicts begin to arise. Most of these tensions and conflicts were primarily the result of the full acceptance and inclusion of uncircumcised gentiles who did not observe the Jewish law within those communities, which to some extent was an unexpected by-product of the proclamation of the gospel to audiences that were largely Jewish. While initially the conflicts were among Jewish believers in Christ who had different perspectives on the conditions upon which gentile believers were to be received into the *ekklēsia*, eventually tensions arose between the communities of Jesus' followers and the Jewish community at large. This led to a "parting of the ways" between the two groups. Although this parting of the ways took place at different times and in different ways in the places where Jews and Christians had previously lived alongside one another in relative peace, most agree that it would be inaccurate to speak of a parting of the ways between the two communities any earlier than the late first century. According to some scholars, in fact, any parting of the ways between the two groups was much later or never even took place at all.[10]

---

8. See Mark D. Nanos, introduction to *Paul within Judaism: Restoring the First-Century Context to the Apostle*, ed. Mark D. Nanos and Magnus Zetterholm (Minneapolis: Fortress, 2015), 1-29 (1-11).

9. On these points, see especially Anders Runesson, "The Question of Terminology: The Architecture of Contemporary Discussions on Paul," in *Paul within Judaism: Restoring the First-Century Context to the Apostle*, ed. Mark D. Nanos and Magnus Zetterholm (Minneapolis: Fortress, 2015), 53-77.

10. On the scholarly discussion regarding the "parting of the ways" between Judaism and Christianity, see Annette Yoshiko Reed and Adam H. Becker, "Introduction: Traditional Models and New Directions," in *The Ways that Never Parted: Jews and Christians in Late Antiquity and the Early Middle Ages*, ed. Annette Yoshiko Reed and Adam H. Becker (Minneapolis: Fortress, 2007), 1-33 (1-24); Paula Fredriksen, "What Parting of the Ways?: Jews, Gentiles, and the Ancient Mediterranean City,"

Needless to say, these new proposals and reconstructions regarding the origins of Christianity and its relationship to Judaism have presented a considerable challenge for those New Testament scholars accustomed to the traditional views on these subjects. While many scholars simply reject or dismiss those proposals and reconstructions and continue to adhere to the traditional views, others have recognized the need to rethink some of the most basic questions regarding the beliefs and self-understanding of those who came to identify themselves as Jesus' followers in the decades immediately following his death, including both those who were Jewish and those who were not.

Obviously, what set Jesus' earliest followers apart from those Jews who were not was their belief that the crucified and risen Jesus was Israel's Messiah and in some sense the Son of God. Yet if this was what Jesus' earliest Jewish followers proclaimed, on what basis did they attempt to convince their fellow Jews that they too should come to faith in Jesus? If Jesus' followers agreed with other Jews that a commitment to obey the Mosaic law was sufficient in order to be accepted by God as righteous and that God did not expect or demand perfect obedience of anyone, what need was there for law-observant Jews to follow Jesus as well? Why did the people of Israel need a savior in Jesus if they could already be saved by observing the commandments God had given to his people? If in the sacrificial rites prescribed in the Mosaic law the Jewish people already had a means by which they could make atonement for their sins, of what use to them was Jesus' atoning death? It might be argued that it was not Jews but only gentiles who needed the salvation and atonement offered through Jesus.[11] Yet if that was the case, why did Jesus' earliest followers also call on their fellow Jews to believe in Jesus and the gospel? What could they offer to their fellow Jews that was not already theirs independently of Jesus?

If Jewish believers in Christ were to continue to observe the Mosaic law, what was the meaning and purpose of that law-observance? Did not the full acceptance of uncircumcised gentiles within the *ekklēsia* and the insistence that in God's eyes gentile believers in Christ were just as righteous as

---

in *The Ways that Never Parted: Jews and Christians in Late Antiquity and the Early Middle Ages*, ed. Annette Yoshiko Reed and Adam H. Becker (Minneapolis: Fortress, 2007), 35-63; James H. Charlesworth, "Did They Ever Part?," in *Partings: How Judaism and Christianity Became Two*, ed. Hershel Shanks (Washington, DC: Biblical Archaeological Society, 2013), 281-300.

11. See, for example, Pamela Eisenbaum, *Paul Was Not a Christian: The Original Message of a Misunderstood Apostle* (New York: HarperOne, 2009), 242, 251-52; John G. Gager, *Reinventing Paul* (Oxford: Oxford University Press, 2000), 146. On this discussion, see Terence L. Donaldson, "Jewish Christianity, Israel's Stumbling and the *Sonderweg* Reading of Paul," *JSNT* 29 (2006): 27-54.

those Jews who observed the law render such observance superfluous and pointless? If Jews as well as gentiles were justified by faith in Christ rather than by works of the law and gentiles could be saved without observing the law, did not the ongoing observance of the law among Jewish believers in Christ imply that in their case faith in Christ was *not* in fact sufficient for justification and salvation? Given that many of the commandments established distinctions that set Jews apart from gentiles, was it not only acceptable but even good for Jewish believers in Christ to set aside observance of the law in order to enjoy full fellowship with gentile believers? In fact, if God had always intended to save people through Christ and faith in him, why had God even given the law in the first place? And why was it good and necessary for Jewish believers in Christ to continue to live in accordance with the law but bad and wrong for gentile believers to become circumcised and submit to the law?

The gospel proclaimed by Jesus' first followers also raised questions regarding the identity of God's people. Were God's people now to be defined on the basis of faith in Christ rather than on the basis of their observance of the Mosaic law? If so, where did that leave Israel? Were uncircumcised gentiles who came to faith in Christ without observing the law now to be regarded as members of Israel? Did those Jews who rejected Christ continue to form part of Israel? How did the *ekklēsia* relate to Israel? Had the *ekklēsia* now taken the place of Israel as God's people? Or did God now have two chosen peoples, namely, Israel and the community of believers in Christ? Was the covenant God had given to Israel through Abraham and Moses now to be abolished so that the new covenant established through Christ might take its place? Could Jews be saved simply by living under the old covenant, or was it necessary for them to live under the new covenant in Christ? If so, were they still to live under the old covenant as well? Now that Christ had come, what did God intend to happen to Judaism? Was Judaism to continue unchanged, to be replaced by the new faith that revolved around Christ and the gospel, or to be altered in some way in light of faith in Christ? Was there something wrong with Judaism that had necessitated the coming of Christ? If so, exactly what had been wrong? And if there was nothing wrong with Judaism, why had it been necessary for God to establish the *ekklēsia* by not only sending his Son into the world but also handing him over to death on a cross?

While some of these questions would have arisen as a result of the inclusion of uncircumcised gentiles within the community of believers in Christ, many of them would have been raised even prior to that time. Most of the New Testament writings indicate or suggest that both before and after the incorporation of gentiles into the *ekklēsia* Jesus' followers proclaimed the gospel concerning him to their fellow Jews and called on them to believe in him. The fact that those Jews who had believed in Jesus met as a distinct community, practiced baptism in Jesus' name as an entry rite into the community, and celebrated together the Lord's Supper even before they began to accept non-Jewish believers in Christ as equals within their midst makes it clear that, even though they continued to identify as Jews and to congregate with their fellow Jews in the same synagogues, they must also have identified themselves in some way that distinguished them from other Jews. While they may not initially have used the term "Christian" to describe themselves, in some way their identity revolved around their relation to Christ. Their faith in Christ and membership in his community of followers, therefore, set them apart from other Jews from the very start. When they began to accept gentiles as members of their community, the distinction between that community and the Jewish community at large would have become even more marked and noticeable.

For this reason, even if it is claimed that there was no parting of the ways between the community of believers in Christ and the community of those Jews who did not believe in Jesus until at least the latter part of the first century, from the very beginning these two communities would not have been regarded simply as one and the same. Furthermore, because what distinguished Jesus' earliest followers from other Jews was their conviction that in Jesus God had sent his Son into the world, handed him over to the death of the cross, and subsequently raised and exalted him as Lord, it must be recognized that in some sense the God of whom they spoke was no longer simply the same God in whom they and their fellow Jews had believed previously. From the perspective of those Jews who did not believe in Jesus, none of these claims regarding what the God of Israel had done in relation to Jesus were true. For that reason, they would have concluded that the God being proclaimed by Jesus' followers was distinct from the God in whom the Jewish people had believed from time immemorial.

No matter when any parting of the *ways* took place between the two communities, therefore, a parting of the *Gods* can be said to have occurred from the time that Jesus' earliest followers began to proclaim the crucified, risen, and exalted Jesus as God's Son and Israel's Messiah. To whatever extent they regarded Jesus in these terms prior to his crucifixion, it might be said that some type of parting of the Gods had already taken place during Jesus' lifetime. What would have distinguished the God of Jesus from the God in whom Jews had traditionally believed, however, would not merely have been the belief that he had sent Jesus to speak and act on his behalf as his Son and Israel's Messiah. Given the opposition and conflict that Jesus' message and ministry had generated among a good number of his fellow Jews and the fact that many had rejected him and the God he proclaimed, his earliest followers must have associated him with a vision regarding God's intentions for Israel, Judaism, and the Jewish people that was in some ways distinct from that of other Jews. This means that, in one way or another, Jesus had sought to redefine not only God and God's will but Judaism as well.

Because we do not have direct access to the historical Jesus, it is impossible to reconstruct with any certainty precisely how Jesus understood God and God's will for Judaism or to know how he would have responded to questions such as those just raised above. Many scholars and historians would argue that Jesus would never even have considered such questions since he did not foresee the establishment of what came to be known as the *ekklēsia* or anticipate any kind of outreach to non-Jews among his disciples following his death. Furthermore, we cannot assume that the message that his followers proclaimed in the days and years following his death was precisely the same message that Jesus himself had proclaimed. There can be little doubt that their understanding of Jesus, God, and God's will was transformed in important ways as a result of the events surrounding his death in Jerusalem, including especially the experiences of the risen Jesus that some of them claimed to have. Subsequently, their proclamation of the gospel regarding Jesus and the expansion of the *ekklēsia*, especially among non-Jews, would have transformed even more their understanding of Jesus, God, and God's will.

If we wish to grasp more fully what Jesus' earliest followers believed regarding God and Jesus and ascertain the ways in which they would have answered questions such as those raised above, the only reliable source to which we can turn is the New Testament itself. Yet because none of the writings that make up the New Testament date back to the period in which the *ekklēsia* originally began to take shape, if we wish to reconstruct the beliefs of his earliest followers, we must choose between two options. The first of these is to sift through those writings in an attempt to ascertain the traditions and beliefs that go back furthest in time and then seek to trace the manner in which those traditions and beliefs evolved. The problem with such an approach is that it requires a great deal of speculation and argumentation that would be highly subjective rather than yielding solid, objective results upon which most scholars and historians could agree.

For that reason, throughout the present work I have chosen a second approach. Rather than attempting to go back to the period immediately following Jesus' death to attempt to reconstruct the thought of his first followers, I will limit myself to examining the earliest sources at our disposal to examine the beliefs expressed in those sources themselves. Those sources, of course, are the epistles of Paul, and in particular the seven epistles whose Pauline authorship is generally not disputed: Romans, 1 and 2 Corinthians, Galatians, Philippians, 1 Thessalonians, and Philemon. According to the current scholarly consensus, these writings were all composed approximately twenty to twenty-five years after Jesus' crucifixion.[12] For our purposes here, it is not necessary to consider any further the precise dates of each of those letters or attempt to determine the order in which they were written. Nor is it necessary to enter into discussions regarding their original contexts, their place of composition, or the audience and purpose for which they were written, since the focus will be on broader questions related to the general context in which Paul lived and the ideas that run throughout his letters rather than the particular contexts to which he addressed each of those letters.

The argument of the present work is that, if we take the approach just outlined, we can obtain a picture of the self-understanding of Jesus' earliest followers in relation to Judaism that is able to resolve many of the questions raised by recent scholarship on that subject while at the same time avoiding the caricatures and distortions of past scholarship. While there was of course a great deal of continuity between the beliefs and practices of Jesus' first followers and the Jewish matrix out of which those beliefs and practices arose, Paul's letters provide strong evidence for the conclusion that the understanding of God and God's will that existed among Jesus' earliest followers was in important regards fundamentally distinct from anything found in the other expressions of first-century Judaism known to us. Paul and those with whom he worked were well aware that the God whom they were proclaiming was in certain ways *not* simply the same God in whom other Jews believed, yet at the same time they insisted that the God they announced *was* the God of Israel of whom the Hebrew Scriptures spoke. This is not to say, of course, that they understood the God of Jesus to be distinct from the God of Israel in a literal or ontological sense, but only that they came to view and conceive of the God of Israel in ways that distinguished them from other Jews. While they in no way understood themselves to be founding a new *religion*, they did see themselves as proclaiming a new *faith*, since the content of the faith they proclaimed on the basis of their convictions regarding Jesus had not been known previously. What distinguished this faith from that of other Jews, however, was not that the God of Jesus was gracious, merciful, and forgiving in a way that the God in whom Jews had traditionally believed was not, or that the God of Jesus saved people by faith alone instead of demanding that they earn their salvation through good works. Both of these Gods were loving and

---

12. Most scholars regard 1 Thessalonians as the earliest of Paul's epistles and date the epistle around the year 50, some twenty years before the composition of Mark, which is generally held to be the earliest of the canonical Gospels. On the chronology of Paul's ministry and his epistles, see Calvin Roetzel, *Paul: The Man and the Myth* (Minneapolis: Fortress, 1999), 178-83; G. Roger Greene, *The Ministry of Paul the Apostle: History and Redaction* (Lanham, MD: Lexington/Fortress Academic, 2019), 173-207.

merciful and saved people by pure grace and through faith. They were also the same in that they justified people on the basis of their commitment to living in accordance with their will as they had made it known, understanding that commitment as the *essence* of faith rather than something that was merely to follow upon it. Likewise, both of these Gods regarded Judaism as a very good thing and, far from condemning or abolishing it, wanted it to continue and prosper. What made the God of Jesus' followers and Paul different from the God of other Jews was that he was now to be defined and understood primarily on the basis of his relation to Jesus his Son and wanted to see Judaism not merely *reaffirmed* or *reinforced* but *redefined* and *resignified* around Jesus.

One of the central premises of the argument to be developed here is that, in order to resolve the type of questions raised above and address in a satisfactory manner many of the issues associated with the subject of "Paul and Judaism," a profound and thoroughgoing rethinking of certain aspects of the theologies underlying both Judaism and Paul is necessary. This rethinking involves changes in our understanding of some of the most basic beliefs that can be identified in Second Temple Jewish thought in general and in the writings of Paul in particular. These beliefs have to do with questions such as God's intentions for Israel and the nations, the purpose of the Mosaic law and its observance, and the nature of righteousness, justification, and salvation. In the case of Paul, at the heart of his thought are also beliefs regarding the role of Christ and his death in the salvation of human beings and the basis upon which they are justified and forgiven by God.

Many biblical scholars, of course, would reject from the outset the notion that such a rethinking is necessary. From their perspective, in general terms we already possess an adequate and accurate understanding of the core theological beliefs found in Second Temple Judaism and the thought of Paul, including those just mentioned. According to this line of thought, while particular aspects of each of the two belief systems remain open to debate and certain refinements in current views regarding one or both are still necessary, our understanding of those systems as a whole is satisfactory and thus does not require any major adjustments or significant rethinking.

To undertake the task of subjecting to critical analysis common views regarding a number of the core elements of Second Temple Jewish thought and the teaching of Paul is problematic for other reasons as well. It is not easy to rethink suppositions and points of consensus that are long-established and ideas that have become deeply ingrained in the thought of biblical scholars and theologians, even if one is open to doing so. It also involves exploring questions for which the biblical texts and Second Temple Jewish writings do not offer clear or explicit answers. Those texts never discuss in detail or at length questions such as God's intentions for Israel and the world, the purpose and meaning of the Mosaic law and its observance, or (in the case of the New Testament) the precise manner in which human beings are saved and justified through Christ and his death. Answers to such questions are generally presupposed and assumed, not only in the biblical texts but also among biblical scholars, and to attempt to bring them to the surface in order to analyze and rethink them is indeed a challenge. Nevertheless, I believe that by posing the right questions and examining the relevant texts on the basis of those questions, the type of rethinking that I am proposing can lay the foundation necessary for offering fresh and convincing answers to many of the questions associated with the subject of Paul and Judaism.

The reconstruction of Paul's thought presented here will make it evident that we may also speak of a second "parting of the Gods" that took place, not in the period immediately following Jesus' death, but in later centuries with the development of Christian thought. Over time, the God of whom Paul spoke was replaced by a God who is distinct in that this God displays certain traits that were thought to characterize the pagan gods of antiquity rather than the God of Israel. As a result, Paul's teaching on justification and his allusions to the salvific significance of Jesus' death came to be interpreted in ways that were no longer in accordance with his thought.

Because the present work is aimed purely at historical reconstruction, it does not attempt to address the theological and practical questions and concerns raised by the reconstruction offered. Thus, for example, when considering Paul's understanding of the salvific significance of Jesus' death, questions such as whether it was possible for God to save human beings without sending his Son to die on a cross or whether Paul is guilty of glorifying violence or idealizing suffering will not be discussed. Similarly, while the argument of the present work undoubtedly has important implications for relations between Jews and Christians today, those implications will not be considered here.

To the extent that it approaches the biblical texts from a historical perspective and focuses on beliefs held by Jews in the Second Temple period, including especially Paul, this work can be considered as lying squarely within the realm of biblical studies and biblical theology. At the same time, however, in some ways it represents a departure from current models and methods of biblical research. Due to the increased specialization in present-day research, for the most part biblical scholarship today focuses on questions that are very precise and concrete, having to do with narrowly-defined topics or specific passages and portions of the biblical texts rather than underlying assumptions and broader questions such as many of those that will be discussed here. This difference in approach limits the extent to which it is possible to engage with the work of other biblical scholars, since in most cases they are simply not focused on the same type of questions.

The need to engage much of the scholarly literature on the texts to be considered here is also limited a great deal by the fact that throughout much of the work I will avoid as much as possible entering into discussions regarding particular aspects of those texts on which biblical interpreters are in disagreement, often simply noting the various possibilities of interpretation without arguing in favor of one or the other. Thus, for example, when considering Phil 2:6-7, it will be sufficient to note that there Paul speaks of Christ not clinging to equality with God but instead emptying himself to be found in human form and likeness without asking exactly what he meant when he spoke of Christ in those terms or whether he was ascribing some type of preexistence to Christ. For my purposes here, questions such as the identity of the weak and strong in Romans 14 and 1 Corinthians 8–10, the precise nature of the issues behind the conflict in Antioch between Paul and Simon Peter described in Gal 2:11-16, and the group of people that Paul has in mind when he refers to "all Israel" being saved in Rom 11:26 can also be left unaddressed when considering those passages. As I hope to demonstrate throughout the present work, we do not need to resolve questions such as these in order to answer the kinds of questions raised above. At the same time, of course, I hope that my familiarity with those discussions will be evident to readers who are acquainted with them.

Rather than following any particular English translation of the Bible, throughout the present work I have elected to translate directly from the Hebrew and Greek biblical texts as well as other Second Temple Jewish writings. Such an approach makes it possible to focus more clearly and accurately on certain aspects of those texts in their original languages that may not be evident in translations that are designed to make those texts accessible, fluid, and comprehensible for English readers in the general public today.

Although I am well aware of the problems raised by the use of pronouns that are exclusively masculine to refer to God when engaging in theological reflection and biblical interpretation, I have nevertheless chosen to adhere to that practice here, in contrast to some of the other writings that I have published in the area of theology and biblical studies. Because it is aimed at historical reconstruction, in the present work I do not pretend to address questions related to the manner in which we should speak and conceive of God in our contemporary contexts but instead seek to reflect accurately the manner in which Paul and other Jews in antiquity spoke and conceived of the God of Israel. I believe that this objective can be accomplished best when we respect and replicate the language used to refer to God in the biblical tradition rather than modifying that language through the persistent use of circumlocutions aimed at avoiding the masculine pronouns used by the ancients to speak of God in response to present-day theological concerns, even though I certainly consider those concerns to be valid and important. Such circumlocutions can often be awkward and tedious and at times make it impossible to allude to God with the same freedom, directness, spontaneity, and clarity that is evident in the language used for God in the biblical texts.

Among the New Testament scholars whose feedback on the contents of the present work I have found extremely valuable, I would especially like to thank Mark Nanos for graciously taking the time to share with me his comments on a portion of Chapter 5. From my perspective, it is difficult to overstate the significance of the contributions made to the study of Paul by scholars such as Mark, Paula Fredriksen, and others who have stressed the need to interpret Paul from within the Judaism(s) of his day, rather than regarding him as a proponent of a new religious movement that was in some way opposed to Judaism or sought to constitute an alternative to it. I am deeply indebted to all of these scholars for having opened my eyes to a Paul who cherished greatly his Jewish identity and traditions throughout his life and, far from rejecting Judaism and the Torah, continued to embrace them firmly while at the same time discovering new meanings in them in light of his faith in Christ.

I would also like to thank the institution at which I teach, the Theological Community of Mexico, and especially its Rector, the Rev. Dr. Dan González, for making the publication of this work possible. No matter how much historical research has gone into any work of this kind, ultimately it is the interaction and exchange of ideas with students and colleagues that allows one to define and refine one's views on the subject matter and to articulate those views in ways that are comprehensible and conducive to further dialogue, as I hope to have done here. It is precisely that type of interaction, exchange, and dialogue that this work is intended to foster and further with others as well.

CHAPTER 1

REDEFINING THE GOD OF ISRAEL

There can be no doubt that for the first believers in Christ, including Paul and his fellow apostles, the God of Israel and the God of Jesus Christ were one and the same. For those Jews who did not believe in Jesus as the Christ, however, this was not the case. In their minds, the God of Israel had *not* sent Jesus as his Son, raised him from the dead three days after he had been crucified, or exalted him at his right hand as Lord and Christ. To refer to God as "the God and Father of our Lord Jesus Christ,"[1] as Paul did, was therefore to speak of a God who was distinct from the one true God, the God of Israel.

In a sense, of course, due to the diversity of beliefs regarding God that existed among Jews during the Second Temple period, it could be said that Jews in Paul's day believed in a variety of different Gods, even though in another sense they could all be said to believe in the same God. According to the New Testament and Flavius Josephus, for example, the God in whom the Pharisees believed would one day raise the dead, whereas the Sadducees rejected such a God.[2] The members of the community at Qumran believed in a God who had sent the Teacher of Righteousness to provide the proper interpretation of the law.[3] This God was profoundly displeased with the worship being offered to him at the Jerusalem temple and did not want his people to participate in that worship until it might be carried out properly.[4]

---

1. See Rom 15:6; 2 Cor 1:3; cf. 2 Cor 11:31.

2. See Matt 22:23; Mark 12:18; Luke 20:27; Acts 23:8; Josephus, *J. W.* 2.163-65; *Ant.* 18.14-16.

3. On the beliefs at Qumran regarding the Teacher of Righteousness, see Johann Meier, "The Judaic System of the Dead Sea Scrolls," in *Judaism in Late Antiquity*, part 2: *Historical Syntheses*, ed. Jacob Neusner, HdO 1.17 (Leiden: Brill, 1995), 84-108 (95-97).

4. See Eyal Regev, *The Temple in Early Christianity: Experiencing the Sacred*, AYBRL (New Haven: Yale University Press, 2019), 9-11.

For most Jews, however, these things were *not* true of God. The God in whom they believed *was* pleased with the worship being offered him at the temple and called on his people to continue to draw near to him there.[5] At different moments, charismatic figures such as Judas the Galilean, Theudas, the "Egyptian," and John the Baptist convinced large numbers of Jews that they had been designated by Israel's God to speak and act on his behalf as his representatives, yet many Jews regarded those figures as false prophets who had *not* been sent by God and therefore were proclaiming a false God who was *not* truly the God of Israel.[6]

In spite of the diversity of beliefs that existed among Jews regarding the God of Israel, however, most scholars today would probably affirm that members of each of these groups and of the Jewish community at large would have agreed that, in the end, all Jews ultimately worshiped the same God, despite the different ways in which they conceived of that God and his will. It is by no means clear, however, that they would have believed that the God being proclaimed by Jesus' earliest followers was the same God in whom they and other Jews had always believed. Had God revealed anything radically new and important about himself in recent times that he had never made known previously? Had the Jewish law or Torah ceased to be the definitive and supreme expression of God's will? Had the God of Israel sent any new prophet of the stature of Moses to speak on his behalf or established alongside himself any descendant of David comparable to David in greatness as king, ruler, or lord over Israel and the other nations of the world? Had God done anything that might oblige those who read the Scriptures of Israel to interpret them any differently than they had in previous generations stretching back for centuries? Had God of late come to relate to his people and act among them in a manner that was fundamentally distinct from the manner in which he had related to them and acted among them previously? Was it now God's desire that his people also come to relate to him in a different way and approach him through a mediator who transcended Aaron and the high priests that Israel had known up to that point throughout its history? Did God now call on his people to live under a new or renewed covenant that went beyond the covenant he had made with Israel in the days of the patriarchs and Moses? Had God determined that uncircumcised gentiles who did not submit fully to the commandments of the Torah yet lived under that new or renewed covenant could be just as pleasing and acceptable to him as those Jews who lived faithfully as members of his people Israel in accordance with the Torah?

---

5. See Regev, *Temple*, 7-9, 12-14.

6. On these figures, see Richard A. Horsley, "'Messianic' Figures and Movements in First-Century Palestine," in *The Messiah: Developments in Earliest Judaism and Christianity. First Princeton Symposium on Judaism and Christian Origins*, ed. James H. Charlesworth (Minneapolis: Fortress, 1992), 276-95.

I would maintain that, with one exception, we know of no Jewish group or community of antiquity, including the ancient Jewish community at large, whose members would have responded to any of the questions just posed with anything but a categorical and resounding "No!" That exception, of course, was the community of Jesus' followers, whose response of "Yes!" to each of those questions would almost certainly have been equally categorical and resounding. In both cases, however, those responses would have arisen out of deeply-seated convictions that were extremely cherished, precious, and meaningful to each.

THE GOD OF ISRAEL IN SECOND TEMPLE JEWISH THOUGHT

In recent decades, scholars have increasingly stressed that it is improper to speak of Second Temple Judaism as if it were a monolithic entity.[7] Even if we instead use the plural "Judaisms" to refer to the different types, expressions, or currents of Judaism that existed in the Second Temple period, however, it is still necessary to define the common characteristics that make it proper to use the same designation for all of them. It therefore seems appropriate to speak of a "common Judaism" during that period, as E. P. Sanders and other scholars have chosen to do.[8]

Many scholars would agree with James Dunn that the principal "pillars" of Second Temple Judaism were the beliefs that there is one God, that this God had elected Israel as his people and had given them the Torah, and that this God was to be worshiped at the temple dedicated to him in Jerusalem.[9] Others such as Lester Grabbe would add other elements to

---

7. See Jacob Neusner, *Judaism When Christianity Began: A Survey of Belief and Practice* (Louisville: Westminster John Knox, 2002), 5-6; Lester L. Grabbe, *An Introduction to First Century Judaism: Jewish Religion and History in the Second Temple Period* (Edinburgh: T & T Clark, 1996), 111-12.

8. E. P. Sanders is generally credited with proposing the use of the phrase "common Judaism" in his book *Judaism: Practice and Belief, 63 BCE–66 CE* (Philadelphia: Trinity Press International, 1992). According to Wayne O. McCready and Adele Reinhartz, since the publication of Sanders's work, "the idea that there existed a common Judaism that transcended the well-known parties and sects has become widely accepted" among biblical scholars ("Introduction: Common Judaism and Diversity within Judaism," in *Common Judaism: Explorations in Second Temple Judaism*, ed. Wayne O. McCready and Adele Reinhartz [Minneapolis: Fortress, 2008], 1-10 [1]). For further discussion and references on the subject, see the other essays in that same volume, as well as a number of the essays in *Redefining First-Century Jewish and Christian Identities: Essays in Honor of Ed Parish Sanders*, ed. Fabian E. Udoh et al. (Notre Dame: University of Notre Dame Press, 2008).

9. James D. G. Dunn, "Judaism in the Land of Israel in the First Century," in *Judaism in Late Antiquity*, part 2: *Historical Syntheses*, ed. Jacob Neusner, HdO 1.17 (Leiden: Brill, 1995), 229-61 (251-57). See also Dunn, *The Partings of the Ways between*

the list, including the prohibition of idolatry, the practice of circumcision, a shared set of sacred texts, and the belief that God had given to Israel the land it considered holy and himself dwelled in that land.[10] What brings all of these different aspects of Judaism together is the interpretation of history that we find in the Hebrew Scriptures: God had created the world, chosen Abraham and his descendants through Isaac and Jacob as his special covenant people, delivered them from their slavery in Egypt, given them his commandments through Moses, and introduced them into the land he had promised them. He had continued to be active throughout their history into the present to bless them when they were obedient and to chastise them in various ways when they needed to be corrected and purified. Most Jews expected that God would pour out his blessings on his people in even greater measure in the future so as to bring to fulfillment all of the promises he had made to them.[11]

Although Israel's God was believed to have a unique relationship with his people as a whole, he was also thought to have related in a special and more intimate manner to certain individuals in the past. These individuals included figures such as Adam and Eve, Enoch, the patriarchs and their spouses, and the great prophets and kings of whom Israel's Scriptures spoke. In particular, God had chosen Moses as the one through whom he had made his will known most fully and clearly in the Torah.[12] While these figures from Israel's history were held in extremely high esteem by all Jews of the Second Temple period, some Jews also believed that God had sent certain individuals to speak or act on his behalf or provide them with guidance and direction in their own day, including a number of teachers and political leaders. Certain passages from the Hebrew Scriptures led many Jews to expect that God would send a royal Messiah figure or "son of David" who would deliver Israel from its enemies, although this expectation may not have been as widespread as was previously thought.[13] Other passages from those Scriptures were interpreted

<hr>

Christianity and Judaism and their Significance for the Character of Christianity (London: SCM, 1991), 18-36.

10. Lester L. Grabbe, *Judaism from Cyrus to Hadrian*, vol. 2: *The Roman Period* (Minneapolis: Fortress, 1992), 527-28.

11. See Sanders, *Judaism: Practice and Belief*, 279-303.

12. On the increased importance that came to be ascribed to Moses in Second Temple Jewish thought, see Timothy B. Savage, *Power through Weakness: Paul's Understanding of the Christian Ministry in 2 Corinthians*, SNTSMS 86 (Cambridge: Cambridge University Press, 1996), 108-9.

13. See James H. Charlesworth, "From Messianology to Christology: Problems and Prospects," in *The Messiah: Developments in Earliest Judaism and Christianity. First Princeton Symposium on Judaism and Christian Origins*, ed. James H. Charlesworth (Minneapolis: Fortress, 1992), 3-35.

as foretelling the coming of a successor to Moses, a second Elijah, and perhaps other prophetic figures as well.[14]

In the centuries immediately preceding the Common Era, a number of beliefs about God that are not found in the Hebrew Bible or are scarcely mentioned there became common among many Jews.[15] God was often thought to dwell in heaven in the midst of a cohort of angelic beings who had names such as Michael, Gabriel, Raphael, and Uriel. Satan, who was also called by other names, was said to be active in the world promoting sin, evil, and injustice together with other supernatural beings who also stood in opposition to God. Many Jews believed that God would act to bring the present age to an end and inaugurate a new age in which the righteous would attain a blessed existence upon a renewed and transformed earth, while the unrighteous would perish forever. According to some, those who had died prior to the inauguration of this new age would be raised from the dead in order to take part in it, though the unrighteous might also be raised with the righteous so that all might first be judged together. These ideas are especially associated with Jewish apocalyptic thought, according to which God had determined that a period of intense suffering and trials precede his dramatic intervention in human history.[16]

Beliefs regarding the Jewish law or Torah also developed during this period. At least some Jews seem to have taught that the Torah had existed even before creation and had served as a kind of blueprint for God when he created the world.[17] Because the Torah constituted the supreme and definitive expression of God's will for his people, and perhaps for other people as well, it was generally expected that it would remain in force indefinitely, even into the age to come.[18] Many Jews came to maintain that, in addition

---

14. See Deut 18:15-18; Mal 4:5; Matt 16:14. On Jewish beliefs regarding these figures in the Second Temple period, see Richard N. Longenecker, *The Christology of Early Jewish Christianity*, SBT 2/17 (London: SCM, 1970), 32-39.

15. On the following, see especially Albert L. A. Hogeterp, *Expectations of the End: A Comparative Traditio-Historical Study of Eschatological, Apocalyptic, and Messianic Ideas in the Dead Sea Scrolls and the New Testament*, STDJ 83 (Leiden: Brill, 2009), 43-114, 362-82; Hartmut Stegemann, *The Library of Qumran on the Essenes, Qumran, John the Baptist, and Jesus* (Grand Rapids: Eerdmans, 1998), 201-10.

16. On this belief in Second Temple Jewish writings, see Brant Pitre, *Jesus, the Tribulation, and the End of the Exile*, WUNT 2/24 (Tübingen: Mohr Siebeck, 2005), 41-130.

17. On this idea in Second Temple Jewish writings and early rabbinic thought, see Werner Förster, *Palestinian Judaism in New Testament Times*, trans. Gordon E. Harris (Edinburgh: Oliver & Boyd, 1964), 184-86; Jacob Neusner, *Torah: From Scroll to Symbol in Formative Judaism* (Philadelphia: Fortress, 1985), 118-19; Michael F. Bird, *An Anomalous Jew: Paul among Jews, Greeks, and Romans* (Grand Rapids: Eerdmans, 2016), 151 n144.

18. In his landmark study on the subject, W. D. Davies argued that the common Jewish expectation was that "the Torah in its existing form would persist into the

to giving Israel the written Torah, God had provided through Moses a body of teachings and prescriptions that had been passed down orally from one generation of Israelites to the next and were therefore equally binding on God's people.[19] Of course, different Jewish groups and teachers disagreed with regard to the way in which many of the commandments of the Torah were to be interpreted and applied, yet these disagreements would not have led most Jews to question the notion that ultimately all Jews believed in and worshiped the same God.

THE GOD OF JESUS CHRIST IN THE EPISTLES OF PAUL

For Paul, one cannot speak of God without also speaking of Jesus. The two are inseparable. So close and intimate is the relation between God and Jesus that it is impossible to know God fully independently of Jesus. It is through Jesus that God acts in relation to human beings, and it is in and through Jesus that human beings are to relate to God. In Paul's thought, as a result of what God has done and will continue to do through Jesus his Son, God is no longer to be known primarily as the God of Israel. Rather, he is the God and Father of Jesus Christ. In a sense, it may even be said that the God of Israel has been transformed into a *different* God, since the God who has revealed himself to be the God of Jesus Christ had never been known as such previously and was therefore *not* simply the same God that the Jewish people had believed in and worshiped prior to Jesus' coming. In another sense, of course, he was *not* a different God, since even though the Jewish people had not known the God they worshiped to be the God of Jesus Christ, he had always been that God. For Paul, however, now that Jesus had come and God had revealed Jesus to be his Son, it was not possible to know and believe in God fully and completely without knowing and believing in Jesus as well.

The God of Israel as the God of Jesus

Perhaps the clearest evidence in favor of the claim that for Paul God is inseparable from Jesus is that there are only a handful of passages in Paul's epistles in which he mentions God repeatedly without also referring to Jesus in the same immediate context. Three of these appear in Paul's Epistle

---

Messianic Age when its obscurities would be made plain. . . ." (*Torah in the Messianic Age and/or the Age to Come*, JBLMS 7 [Philadelphia: SBL, 1952], 84). On these ideas, see also Richard N. Longenecker, *Paul: Apostle of Liberty*, 2nd ed. (Grand Rapids: Eerdmans, 2015), 116-20.

19. While such an idea was clearly held by the rabbis, Jacob Neusner argues that it was already characteristic of the Pharisees in Jesus' time; see *The Rabbinic Traditions about the Pharisees before 70*, part 3: *Conclusions* (Leiden: Brill, 1971), 163-64.

to the Romans. In Rom 1:18–3:20, Paul describes the sins of those who fail to acknowledge God and affirms that both Jews and gentiles will be subject to God's judgment before concluding that both Jews and Greeks are under sin. The single allusion to Jesus appears in 2:16, where Paul states that, according to his gospel, God will judge the hidden things of human beings through Jesus. While Paul scarcely mentions Jesus in this passage, the reason is that his argument regarding the sinfulness of both Jews and Greeks does not require it. By speaking of Christ as the one through whom God will judge all people, however, Paul in effect subjects all human beings to Christ, who will stand over them as judge rather than standing alongside them in order to be judged by God together with them. Furthermore, Paul's argument in this passage is designed to point to Christ as the one through whom God has acted to resolve the problem he describes (3:21-26). Even though Paul scarcely mentions Jesus in Rom 1:18–3:20, then, the passage as a whole ultimately revolves around him.

Immediately following this passage, in Romans 4 Paul discusses the faith of Abraham in order to argue that Abraham was accepted as righteous by God on the basis of that faith rather than on the basis of his own works or his observance of the Mosaic law, which had not yet been given. Paul makes no mention of Christ until the very end of the chapter, where he concludes that, just as Abraham's faith was reckoned to him as righteousness, so also will faith be reckoned as righteousness to those who "believe in the one who raised from among the dead Jesus our Lord, who was handed over because of our transgressions and raised on account of our justification" (4:24-25). Here again, the fact that Paul does not mention Christ when speaking of God throughout most of the passage provides no basis for the notion that here he is conceiving of God independently of God's relationship to Christ. On the contrary, he is reading the story of Abraham on the basis of his conviction that the faith and justification of Abraham anticipated the faith and justification of those who would come to believe in God as the one who raised Jesus from the dead as Lord. It is therefore in Christ that the story of Abraham finds its fulfillment

Explicit allusions to Christ appear in only a few verses of Romans 9–11. There, after arguing that God has hardened many within Israel in order to show mercy to the nations and bring about in them his righteousness, Paul argues against the idea that this means that God has rejected Israel as his people. At the very heart of this passage, however, Paul points to Christ as the one through whom the law and the righteousness of which it speaks find fulfillment (10:4-17). Rather than being secondary to the plan of God to which Paul alludes, therefore, Christ and the gospel concerning him lie at its very heart. For Paul, God's dealings with Israel have the objective of bringing all to confess Christ as Lord so that they may attain through him the righteousness and salvation God desires for them.

Outside of these passages from Romans, the only other passage in which Paul makes mention of God repeatedly without alluding to Christ is 1 Cor 13:1–14:40. Most of this passage is dedicated to a discussion of glossolalia in the context of worship. There appears to be no evidence that this constituted a topic of debate among Jews in antiquity, and much less one that had anything to do with their concept of God. Furthermore, Paul addresses this subject in the context of a discussion regarding spiritual gifts given particularly to the members of the body of Christ (1 Cor 12:1-31). In this passage, then, Paul can hardly be said to conceive of God in a way that divorces God from Christ or does not take Christ into account.

The fact that the God of whom Paul writes is inseparable from his Son Jesus Christ and that it is that Son who defines God's identity is especially evident from the way in which Paul relates to both God and Christ the key terms and concepts of his proclamation. In a word, what Paul proclaims is the gospel. Yet he refers to that gospel alternatively as the gospel of God and the gospel of Christ or God's Son.[20] Furthermore, for Paul the *content* of this gospel is that God declared Jesus to be his Son by raising him from the dead (Rom 1:1-4). Paul calls the word he speaks both the word of God and the word of Christ as Lord.[21] Through that word Paul announces a truth that he refers to as the truth of God as well as the truth of Christ.[22] Paul's objective is that all come both to the knowledge of God and to the knowledge of Christ, which is also the knowledge of the glory of God in the face of Christ (2 Cor 4:6).[23] According to Paul, believers come to know or have the mind of God as well as the mind of Christ.[24] The power Paul possesses and proclaims is both the power of God and that of Christ, who is himself the power of God (1 Cor 1:24).[25] For Paul, both the apostles as well as believers in Christ in general are servants or slaves of both God and Jesus.[26] The obedience to which Paul calls those to whom he writes is not merely obedience to God but obedience to Christ and the gospel as well.[27] They are to submit to a law and to commandments that Paul calls both God's and Christ's.[28]

---

20. See Rom 1:1; 15:16; 2 Cor 11:7; 1 Thess 2:2, 8-9; alternatively, Rom 1:9; 1 Cor 9:12; 2 Cor 2:12; 9:13; 10:14; Gal 1:7; Phil 1:27; 1 Thess 3:2; cf. 2 Cor 4:4.

21. See Rom 9:6; 1 Cor 14:36; 2 Cor 2:17; 4:2; Phil 1:14; 1 Thess 2:13; alternatively, Rom 10:17; 1 Thess 1:8; 4:15.

22. See Rom 1:25; 3:7; 15:8; alternatively, 2 Cor 11:10; cf. Rom 9:1.

23. See 1 Cor 1:21; 2 Cor 10:5; Gal 4:8-9; alternatively, 1 Cor 2:2, 14; Phil 3:8-10.

24. See Rom 11:34; alternatively, 1 Cor 2:11, 16; Phil 2:5.

25. See Rom 1:16; 1 Cor 1:18; 2:5; 6:14; 2 Cor 6:7; 13:4; alternatively, 1 Cor 5:4; 2 Cor 12:9; Phil 3:21.

26. See Rom 1:9; 6:22; 2 Cor 6:4; 1 Thess 1:9; alternatively, Rom 1:1; 14:18; 1 Cor 4:1; 7:22; 2 Cor 11:23; Phil 1:1.

27. See Rom 1:5; 15:18; 2 Cor 9:13; 10:5.

28. See Rom 7:25; 8:7; 1 Cor 7:19; alternatively, 1 Cor 7:25; 9:14, 21; Gal 6:2.

The grace and peace Paul desires for his readers at the beginning of each of his letters come not only from God the Father but from the Lord Jesus Christ as well.[29] At the end of those letters, while Paul often shares God's peace with his readers, the blessing Paul pronounces on them is that of the grace of the Lord Jesus Christ.[30] Paul speaks of the love of Christ and the love of God as if they were essentially synonymous, associates the two with each other by referring to the love of God in Christ, and at times sees the love of one as the love of the other as well.[31] He points not only to the mercy of God but also to the mercy of Jesus,[32] and presents both God and Jesus as blessing and accepting believers.[33] Believers are to place their hope, trust, and faith not only in God but also in Christ.[34] In a manner that many Jews would have found surprising, Paul speaks of interceding not only to God but to Christ as well and affirms that he himself has prayed to Christ for help and healing.[35]

For Paul, believers are to strive to please Christ as well as God and to offer up their lives to both God and Christ.[36] The reason for this is that, just as they belong to God, so also do they belong to Christ as his own.[37] As such, they are simultaneously heirs of God and heirs of Christ.[38] In fact, according to Paul, both God and Christ dwell in believers in some sense.[39] This indwelling takes place particularly through the Holy Spirit, whom he calls not only the Spirit of God but the Spirit of Christ as well.[40] The *ekklēsia* of God is also the *ekklēsia* of God in Christ as well as the body of Christ.[41]

Finally, Paul ascribes to Christ virtually all of the same salvific activities that he ascribes to God. Together with the Spirit, both God and Christ give

---

29. See Rom 1:7; 1 Cor 1:3; 2 Cor 1:2; Gal 1:3; Phil 1:2; 1 Thess 1:1; Phlm 3.

30. See Rom 15:33; 16:20; 1 Cor 14:33; 16:23; 2 Cor 13:13; Gal 6:18; Phil 4:7, 9, 23; 1 Thess 5:23, 28.

31. See Rom 5:5, 8; 8:35-39; 2 Cor 5:14-21; 13:13; Gal 2:20.

32. See Rom 11:32; 15:9; alternatively, 1 Cor 7:25.

33. See Rom 4:6; 14:3; alternatively, Rom 15:7, 29.

34. See Rom 4:24; 2 Cor 1:9-10; 1 Thess 1:8; alternatively, Rom 9:33; 14:10; 15:12; 1 Cor 15:19; Gal 2:16; Phil 1:14; 2:19, 24; 1 Thess 1:3; Phlm 5.

35. See 1 Cor 1:2; 2 Cor 12:8-9; cf. Rom 10:12-14.

36. See Rom 6:10-13; 12:1; Gal 2:19; 1 Thess 4:1; alternatively, Rom 14:7-8; 1 Cor 7:32; 2 Cor 11:2.

37. See Rom 1:6; 8:9; 1 Cor 3:23; 2 Cor 6:19; 10:7; Gal 3:29; 5:24.

38. See Rom 8:17; Gal 4:7.

39. See 1 Cor 3:16; 2 Cor 6:16; alternatively, 2 Cor 13:5; Gal 2:20.

40. See Rom 8:9, 11, 14; 1 Cor 2:14; 3:16; 6:11; Phil 3:3; alternatively, Rom 8:9; Gal 4:6; Phil 1:19.

41. See 1 Cor 1:2; 10:32; 11:22; 15:9; 2 Cor 1:1; Gal 1:13; alternatively, Rom 12:5; 16:16; 1 Cor 12:27; cf. Gal 1:22; 1 Thess 1:1; 2:14.

gifts, ministries, and abilities.[42] The revelations that Paul and other believers receive come not only from God but from Christ as well.[43] While it is God who comforts believers, he does so through Christ (2 Cor 1:3-7). Just as God gives authority to human beings, so does Christ.[44] Both believers in general and the apostles in particular have been called by Christ as well as by God to be Christ's.[45] As already noted above, Paul affirms that God will judge human beings through Christ and even presents Christ as the one who will judge all.[46] In addition to affirming that Christ has been made by God wisdom, righteousness, sanctification, and redemption for believers, Paul attributes their salvation, liberation, and redemption to both God and Christ.[47] For Paul, it is not only God who will raise the dead and effect their transformation, but Christ as well.[48]

This conception of God as inseparable from Christ is unprecedented in the Hebrew Scriptures and Second Temple Jewish literature. In those writings there is no figure, be it earthly or heavenly, who is consistently mentioned alongside God in the same way that Paul mentions Jesus.[49] Nor are the activities and attributes of God consistently ascribed to any other figure, and especially not to a man who had been crucified only a couple of decades earlier.

God as Jesus' Father and Jesus as God's Son

The passages in which Paul expresses most clearly his understanding of the intimate relationship between the God of Israel and Jesus are those in which he uses the language of Father and Son.[50] Although Paul speaks

---

42. See Rom 12:3-8; 1 Cor 12:4-11.

43. See 1 Cor 2:10; 2 Cor 12:1; Gal 1:12, 16; Phil 3:15.

44. See Rom 13:1; 2 Cor 10:8; 13:10; cf. 1 Thess 4:2.

45. See Rom 8:28, 30; Gal 1:15; Phil 3:14; 1 Thess 2:12; 4:7; alternatively, Rom 1:4-6; 1 Cor 1:1; 2 Cor 1:1; 11:13; Gal 1:1, 6; 1 Thess 5:24.

46. See Rom 2:16; 1 Cor 4:5; 2 Cor 5:10.

47. See Rom 5:9-10; 6:16-18; 7:24; 8:2-4; 1 Cor 1:21, 30; 2 Cor 1:10; 5:21; Gal 1:4; 3:13; 4:4-7; 5:1; 1 Thess 1:10.

48. See Phil 3:20-21; cf. 1 Cor 15:45; 1 Thess 4:16-17.

49. Undoubtedly, as Larry W. Hurtado has shown, many Jews in the Second Temple period believed in an array of heavenly or divine beings that existed alongside God (*Ancient Jewish Monotheism and Early Christian Jesus-Devotion: The Context and Character of Christological Faith* [Waco, TX: Baylor University Press, 2017], 163-84). In Jewish thought, however, none of these figures is ascribed anywhere near the importance that Paul ascribes to Jesus in his epistles.

50. On Paul's allusions to God as the Father of Jesus, see Marianne Meye Thompson, *The Promise of the Father: Jesus and God in the New Testament* (Louisville: Westminster John Knox, 2000), 116-32. Thompson notes that, while of course Paul often speaks of God as the Father of believers, "what one never finds is a dual reference to God as the Father of Jesus Christ and of believers" (119).

of God as the Father of Jesus in only three of the twenty-five passages in which he applies the term "Father" to God,[51] he mentions Jesus alongside of God in eleven of the twelve passages in which he speaks of God as the Father of believers. In each case, he calls Jesus "Lord" or *"our* Lord" at the same time that he calls God "our Father."[52] In the ten passages in which Paul refers to God as Father without specifying of whom he is Father, he refers to Jesus explicitly, generally calling him "Lord" or "our Lord" once more or else affirming that through him or his Spirit believers can now approach God as their Father or "Abba."[53] It is noteworthy that many of these passages appear in the introductions of Paul's letters, where they occupy a place of prominence and can therefore be seen as representing a central element in his thought and proclamation. They summarize concisely how Paul conceives of the God he serves, associating him inseparably with Jesus as his Son. In fact, while in some of the introductions and conclusions of his letters Paul invokes a blessing from Christ upon the believers to whom he writes, *not once does he ever invoke such a blessing from God without mentioning Christ conjointly.* According to Paul's letters, when God blesses, he does so together with Christ.

Paul refers to Jesus as God's Son fifteen times in his epistles.[54] In contrast, only on nine occasions does he call believers sons and daughters of God.[55] Of course, the Hebrew Scriptures and other Jewish writings of antiquity frequently refer to God as the Father of certain individuals, of Israel, and of human beings as a whole, who are also considered God's sons or sons and daughters. Perhaps the most similar usage of Father and Son language in the Hebrew Scriptures is that used to refer to the relationship between God and David. For Paul, however, the relationship between Jesus and God far transcends any relationship God has had with any other human persons or people, including David.[56] In the Hebrew Bible, neither during David's rule

---

51. See Rom 15:6; 2 Cor 1:3; 11:31.

52. See Rom 1:7; 1 Cor 1:3; 2 Cor 1:2; Gal 1:3-4; Phil 1:2; 4:19-20; 1 Thess 1:1, 3; 3:11, 13; Phlm 3. The only passage in which Paul speaks of God as Father without mentioning Jesus is 2 Cor 6:18, where he is citing Hos 1:10 and therefore using language that is not his own.

53. See Rom 6:4; 8:15; 1 Cor 8:6; 15:24; Gal 1:1, 3; 4:6; Phil 2:11; 1 Thess 1:1.

54. See Rom 1:3, 4, 9; 5:10; 8:3, 29, 32; 1 Cor 1:9; 15:28; 2 Cor 1:19; Gal 1:16; 2:20; 4:4, 6; 1 Thess 1:10.

55. See Rom 8:14-15, 19, 23; 9:26; 2 Cor 6:18; Gal 3:26; 4:5-6.

56. While David and the kings descended from him are undoubtedly spoken of as sons of God in the Hebrew Scriptures and Second Temple Jewish literature, it can be somewhat misleading to compare the relation that David and the Davidic rulers were thought to have with God with Paul's understanding of Jesus' relation to God as his Son in the way that Paula Fredriksen does, as if it were essentially the same (*When Christians Were Jews* [New Haven: Yale University Press, 2018], 109-11, 118, 122-23). Neither David nor any of the other kings descended from him, including Solomon, are

nor following it is God repeatedly referred to as the God of David, David's Father, or the one who has David as a son. This stands in stark contrast to Jesus as Paul presents him: for Paul, God's relationship to Jesus is not secondary, incidental, or non-essential to God's being and identity, but rather primary and definitive for Paul's understanding of who God is. This can hardly be said of David.

While the Hebrew Scriptures at times speak of the God of Abraham, Isaac, and Jacob or the God of Israel as if these designations defined God's identity, they hardly compare in number or importance to Paul's allusions to God as the God and Father of Jesus Christ, his Son. Outside of Genesis, Exodus, and Deuteronomy, the three patriarchs are mentioned together by name in only seven passages in the Hebrew Bible.[57] While Paul mentions Abraham and Isaac in his epistles—primarily in Romans 4 and 9 and Galatians 3 and 4—, never does he refer to God as the God of Abraham, Isaac, and Jacob or even the God of Israel; nor does he define God in terms of God's relationship to the patriarchs or Israel. While Paul does speak of the "Israel of God" in Gal 6:16, nowhere does he use the phrase "the God of Israel."[58]

Of course, throughout his epistles, Paul also relates God to Jesus his Son in other ways. In 1 Cor 11:3, for example, Paul affirms that "Christ is the head of every man, and the man is the head of a woman, and God is the head of Christ." It is not entirely clear whether "every man" here refers to every human male or only to those who are believers in Christ, and what it means to be "head" of another person is also a matter of debate among Pauline interpreters.[59] Clearly, however, Paul here is positing an extremely intimate relationship between God and Christ at the same time that he ascribes to Christ an exalted, transcendent position above other human beings.

There can be no question, then, that in speaking of God as Jesus' Father and of Jesus as God's Son, Paul describes God as relating to Jesus in a way that is unparalleled in the Hebrew Scriptures and in Second Temple Jewish literature. Not even the most important figures from Israel's past were ever

seen as defining the identity of God in the way that Jesus does in Paul's epistles and the other New Testament writings; nor are they ascribed the type of central and prominent role that Paul and the New Testament ascribe to Jesus.

57. Outside of the Pentateuch, only in 1 Kgs 18:36, 1 Chron 29:18, and 2 Chron 30:6 is God referred to as the God of Abraham, Isaac, and Jacob. The sole allusion to God as the God of Abraham appears in Ps 47:9. Elsewhere the three patriarchs are mentioned together only in Josh 24:3-4, 2 Kgs 13:23, and 1 Chron 16:16-17.

58. In the New Testament, the phrase "the God of Israel" occurs only in Matt 15:31 and Luke 1:68.

59. On these questions, see Joseph A. Fitzmyer, *First Corinthians: A New Translation with Introduction and Commentary*, AB 32 (New Haven: Yale University Press, 2008), 409-11.

thought to be in a relationship with God that was comparable to the relationship between God and Jesus as it is described by Paul. It can hardly be doubted that the conviction that God and Jesus enjoyed a relationship with one another that was special, unique, and extremely intimate was a central element not only in the thought of Paul but in the proclamation of Jesus' first followers as well, and that they conceived of that relationship in much the same way that Paul did.

God as the One Who Raised Jesus and Exalted Him as Lord

Outside of referring to God as Jesus' Father and to Jesus as God's Son, the most frequent way in which Paul alludes to God is as the one who raised Jesus up from among the dead.[60] Paul begins his letter to the Romans by alluding to the gospel of God "concerning his Son, Jesus Christ our Lord, who came to be of David's seed according to the flesh and was ordained God's Son in power according to the Spirit of holiness by his resurrection from the dead. . . ." (Rom 1:1, 3-4).[61] Here Paul summarizes the content of his apostolic proclamation in terms of God's having sent and raised Jesus his Son as Christ and Lord in power through his Spirit. Further on in the same letter, Paul affirms that righteousness is reckoned "to those who believe upon the one who raised Jesus our Lord from among the dead, who was handed over on account of our transgressions and was raised on account of our justification" (Rom 4:24-25). Seen in the context of Romans 4 as a whole, Paul here is arguing that the fact that God raised Jesus from

---

60. The Greek phrase *ek tōn nekrōn* literally means "from among the dead" and conveys the idea of being raised not only from a condition of being dead but also from the realm of the dead to which Jesus had descended following his death.

61. I would question Paula Fredriksen's claim that in Rom 1:4, Paul is referring to the general resurrection rather than Jesus' own resurrection when he affirms that Jesus was "declared to be Son of God with power according to the spirit of holiness by resurrection from the dead" (*Paul: The Pagans' Apostle* [New Haven: Yale University Press, 2017], 141-45). Undoubtedly, Fredriksen is correct in affirming that resurrection from the dead in itself does not lead to a person being designated God's Son and that Jesus' risen condition was revealed only to a small number of his followers rather than being made known in the eyes of all. However, because Jesus' followers would have believed that his resurrection confirmed a claim that was made (whether explicitly or implicitly) prior to his crucifixion, namely, that he was God's Son in a unique sense, Jesus' resurrection would have been interpreted as divine confirmation of that claim. Even though only a small handful of his followers claimed to have received that confirmation by encountering the risen Jesus personally, their proclamation would make it known publicly that Jesus had been designated God's Son in power by his resurrection, as Paul claims. The Greek phrase *ex anastaseōs nekrōn* also suggests that Jesus was proclaimed God's Son *as a result* of being raised from the dead. On the reasons why the possessive pronoun *autou* ("his") does not appear in the verse, see Arland J. Hultgren, *Paul's Letter to the Romans: A Commentary* (Grand Rapids: Eerdmans, 2011), 49.

among the dead confirms and consolidates God's identity as the one who restores life to the dead, thus making that identity primary to God's being as one of God's defining characteristics (cf. 4:19).

Elsewhere in Romans, Paul also places Jesus' resurrection at the center of his understanding of the identity of the God in whom believers are to deposit their faith. In chapter 6, Paul writes that "Christ was raised from the dead by the glory of the Father" (6:4) before exhorting the Roman believers to regard themselves as "those who have been brought from death to life" (6:13). This core belief is to define believers as those who are dead to sin and "alive to God in Christ Jesus" together with Christ (6:12; see 6:6-23). For Paul, the Spirit of God of whom the Hebrew Scriptures speak is now to be known as "the Spirit of the one who raised Jesus from among the dead" (8:11). What leads to salvation is confessing with one's mouth that Jesus is Lord and believing with one's heart that God raised him from among the dead (10:9).

Among the things Paul says he handed on to the Corinthians "as of first importance" is that Christ "was raised on the third day according to the Scriptures" (1 Cor 15:3-4). What matters for Paul is that Christ be "proclaimed as raised from among the dead" and that no one deny as false the testimony that God was the one who raised him up (1 Cor 15:12, 15). So central is this belief for Paul's understanding of God and the gospel that he tells the Corinthians: "If Christ has not been raised, your faith is in vain; you are still in your sins" (1 Cor 15:17; cf. 15:20). As in Romans, in his Corinthian correspondence Paul sees God's identity as the one who raised up Jesus as inseparable from his identity as the one who raises up the dead in general, both literally and metaphorically: "But God who raised up the Lord will also raise us up through his power" (1 Cor 6:14).[62] While many of Paul's fellow Jews also believed in a God who would raise the dead, for Paul this aspect of God's identity has come to the fore; and it has done so *precisely because of what he has done in and through Jesus his Son.*[63]

Of course, in Paul's thought God not only raised Jesus up from among the dead but also exalted him to his right side as Lord (Phil 2:9-11).[64] In

---

62. See also 2 Cor 1:8-9; 4:14; 13:4.

63. As Steven J. Kraftchick notes, "the God who raises the dead" is "not initially a Christian predicate, but an ancient Jewish description of God," yet "clearly this belief is understood in a different way after Paul's experience of the risen Christ" ("Death's Parsing: Experience as a Mode of Theology in Paul," in *Pauline Conversations in Context: Essays in Honor of Calvin J. Roetzel,* ed. Janice Capel Anderson, Philip Sellew, and Claudia Setzer, JSNTSup 221 [London: Sheffield Academic Press, 2002], 144-66 [161]).

64. On the significance of Paul's allusions to Jesus as Lord and his understanding of Jesus' role as Lord, see especially Gordon D. Fee, *Jesus the Lord according to Paul the Apostle: A Concise Introduction* (Grand Rapids: Baker Academic, 2018), 117-71. A helpful background on the subject is also found in David B. Capes, *The Divine Christ:*

this way, God has given believers assurance that the one he raised will come again from heaven to deliver them from the wrath to come and bring them to be with God.[65] For Paul, then, what defines God is not merely that he has a Son, the Lord Jesus Christ, but that God is "the Father who raised him from among the dead" so that believers might attain the salvation he desires for all (Gal 1:1; 1 Thess 1:9-10).

As Paul's words in Rom 1:3-4 and Phil 2:9-11 make clear, for Paul Jesus' resurrection is in essence a single event with his exaltation to God's side as Lord. In fact, the purpose of Jesus' resurrection was precisely "that he might be Lord of both the dead and the living" (Rom 14:9). It is therefore no coincidence that, whenever Paul mentions God raising Jesus, he tends to refer to Jesus as Lord at the same time, as he does in these three passages.[66]

In Jewish thought, of course, "Lord" had long been used as a designation for God (Hebrew *adonay*; Greek *ho kyrios*).[67] It is natural, therefore, for Paul to refer to God in that way in his letters. What is surprising, however, is that virtually the only instances in which Paul uses *ho kyrios* to refer unambiguously to God are those in which he is citing passages from the Hebrew Scriptures that employ that designation for God.[68] These passages constitute only eleven of the approximately 180 passages in which Paul speaks of God or Christ as *kyrios*. The vast majority of these—around 100—are unquestionably allusions to Christ, while another sixty-five almost certainly refer to Christ, even though in many cases it could be argued that they refer to God instead. As James Dunn notes, throughout Paul's epistles "the normal rule is that outside scriptural quotations 'the Lord' is Christ."[69] While there may be some exceptions to that rule, most Pauline scholars would agree that these are few and far between. It is also significant that Paul nowhere refers to God as the Lord of Jesus, in contrast to the rest of human beings or believers in particular, of whom he *does* consider God to be Lord.

What is particularly noteworthy is that, in at least a couple of passages, Paul seems to apply to Jesus passages from the Hebrew Scriptures in which "Lord" unquestionably referred originally to the God of Israel.[70] In Rom 10:9-13, after affirming that those who confess that Jesus is Lord and believe

---

Paul, the Lord Jesus, and the Scriptures of Israel, ASBT (Grand Rapids: Baker Academic, 2018), 47-84.

65. See 1 Thess 1:10; 4:14; cf. Phil 3:20-21.

66. See also Rom 4:24; 10:9; 1 Cor 6:14; 2 Cor 4:14; 1 Thess 4:14-15.

67. On the use of "Lord" for God in Second Temple Jewish writings, see James D. G. Dunn, *The Theology of Paul the Apostle* (Grand Rapids: Eerdmans, 1998), 249. Dunn there notes that the use of "Lord" for God in Aramaic went back at least two centuries before Paul's time.

68. See Rom 9:27-29; 11:3; 12:19; 14:11; 15:11; 1 Cor 3:20; 10:26; 2 Cor 6:16-18.

69. Dunn, *Theology*, 251.

70. On Paul's application to Christ of passages from the Hebrew Scriptures that refer to God as YHWH, see Capes, *Divine Christ*, 85-150.

that God raised him from the dead will be saved and quoting Isa 28:16, "Everyone who believes in him shall not be put to shame," Paul continues: "For the same one is Lord of all, rich to all who call upon him. For 'everyone who calls upon the name of the Lord will be saved.'" These last words are taken from the Septuagint text of Joel 2:32 (LXX 3:5), where they clearly refer to God. As Dunn observes, "Since Paul has just emphasized the confession 'Jesus is Lord' (10.9), it would be surprising if he did not mean his readers to understand the 'Lord' of 10.12 and 13 as Jesus also. To 'believe in him' (10.11) is evidently equivalent to 'calling upon him' (10.12). So the Lord whose name is called upon in 10.13 could hardly be other than the Lord Jesus."[71]

While it is possible that Paul applies to Jesus passages from the Hebrew Scriptures that originally referred to God as Lord in 1 Cor 2:13 and 2 Cor 10:17-18 as well, there can be little doubt that he does so in Phil 2:9-11. There, after stating that Jesus did not aspire or cling to equality with God, Paul in essence affirms that this is what he attained by humbling himself to the point of dying on the cross: "For that reason, God exalted him highly above all and bestowed on him the name that is above every other name, so that at the name of Jesus every knee might bow down, in heaven and on earth and underneath the earth, and every tongue confess that Jesus Christ is Lord, to the glory of God the Father." Obviously, Paul here is envisioning some day in the future when all will acknowledge Jesus' lordship over all, yet he does so with the use of a phrase taken from the Septuagint version of Isa 45:23. There Israel's God calls on the nations to abandon their false gods and idols so as to turn to him and be saved by acknowledging that he alone is God and therefore that no other god is worthy of worship and devotion (45:20-25). In that context, the prophet writes: "'As I live,' says the Lord, 'to me shall every knee bend and every tongue shall give praise to [me as] God'" (v. 23). Paul cites this same verse from Isaiah in Rom 14:11, yet there the allusion is almost certainly to God rather than Jesus.

If Paul is in fact applying Isa 45:23 to Jesus in Phil 2:9-11, he is doing something that would have astonished most Jews, namely, identifying Jesus in some way with God as the Lord of whom Isaiah speaks.[72] While this is remarkable in itself, it is even more so when one considers that the passage from Isaiah is stressing God's sovereignty as the only true God who alone can save: "There is no other god besides me, a righteous God and savior; there is none other but me. Turn to me and be saved, all the ends of the

---

71. Dunn, *Theology*, 249-50.

72. To affirm this is not necessarily to maintain that Paul is referring to Jesus simply as God in this passage; see Paul A. Holloway, *Philippians: A Commentary*, Hermeneia (Minneapolis: Fortress, 2017), 127-29. Gordon D. Fee rightly notes that "Paul's monotheism is kept intact by the final phrase, *to the glory of God the Father*" (*Philippians*, IVPNTC 11 [Downers Grove, IL: InterVarsity, 1999], 101).

earth! For I am God, and there is no other" (Isa 45:21-22). Equally remarkable is Paul's affirmation that every knee is some day to bow before Jesus and every tongue is to confess him as Lord. By clarifying that he is referring to the knees of all those in the heavens, on earth, and in the underworld, Paul makes it clear that he has in mind every human person that had ever lived. This would include all of the great figures of Israel's history, such as Abraham, Isaac, Jacob, David, and Solomon, who were thought to dwell in *sheol* or the underworld, as well as those who were believed to have been taken up by God into heaven, in particular Enoch, Elijah, and perhaps Moses as well.[73] It is difficult to conceive of any Jews in antiquity other than Jesus' earliest followers ever envisioning all of those figures bowing down and bending their knee before another human being in order to confess that human being as Lord to the glory of God. There appears to be no evidence in Second Temple Jewish literature, for example, that those Jews who believed in a Messiah expected any of those figures to pay homage to that Messiah by kneeling before him. According to Paul's affirmation here, those who would bow the knee before Christ would also have included the great figures of human history in general, including the kings of Assyria, Babylon, and Persia, Alexander the Great, Julius Cesar, and every other Roman emperor, past, present, and future. It should not be overlooked that in Phil 2:6-11 Paul appears to be citing a hymn,[74] which suggests that it was not Paul but some other follower of Jesus who had originally applied Isa 45:23 to Jesus at an earlier point in time. In that case, there were other believers in Jesus prior to Paul who were making such lofty claims about Jesus and applying to him passages from the Scriptures that originally referred to the God of Israel.

This same vision of Jesus as one who is exalted above all other human beings appears in 1 Cor 15:24-28. There, drawing on imagery he takes from Psalms 8:7 and 110:1, Paul writes:

> Then comes the end, when he will hand over the kingdom to the one who is God and Father, when he has rendered powerless every ruler and every authority and power. For it is necessary for him to reign until he places all enemies under his feet. The last enemy that he will render powerless is death. For he will subject all things under his feet. But when it is said that all things have come to be subjected, it is obvious that the one who subjected all things to him is excluded. And when all things are subjected to him, then the Son himself will subject himself to the one who subjected all things to him, so that God may be all in all.

---

73. On the beliefs regarding Moses' assumption into heaven in the Second Temple period, see Daniel A. Smith, *The Post-Mortem Vindication of Jesus in the Sayings Gospel Q*, LNTS 338 (London: T & T Clark, 2006), 75-77.

74. On the evidence that Phil 2:5-11 constitutes a hymn that predates Paul, see G. Walter Hansen, *The Letter to the Philippians*, PNTC (Grand Rapids: Eerdmans, 2009), 122-33.

While Paul does not explicitly refer to Jesus as Lord here, he does speak of him as God's Son and presents him as one to whom all will be subject but God himself. Paul's use of *panta* here, however, seems to go further: what is involved is not just bringing *all people* into subjection under his rule but *all things*.[75] While here Paul does not allude explicitly to all that is in the heavens, on the earth, and under the earth, most would agree that he has this in mind, since otherwise he would be claiming that there are many things, people, and beings—including those dwelling in the underworld—that will *not* come under God's sovereign rule at the *eschaton*. As in Phil 2:9-11, however, all of these things must first come to be subjected to Christ; only then will they be brought into subjection to God. Although the idea that God will be "all in all" is by no means inconsistent with other ancient Jewish conceptions of the age to come, what is unprecedented is the notion that everything and everyone in creation must first be brought under the rule of a man who had been crucified by the Romans only a generation earlier and subsequently exalted to heaven at God's side.

The fact that throughout the New Testament the first verse of Psalm 110 is repeatedly applied to Jesus suggests that, when Paul does the same in this passage, he is drawing on earlier tradition.[76] The words of that verse were thought to be those of David as the author of that Psalm: "The Lord said to my lord, 'Sit at my right hand until I place your enemies as a footstool under your feet.'" In Greek, both God and the one called "my lord" are called *ho kyrios*. These words can be understood as addressed not to David himself but to someone else whom David regarded as his lord. If applied to Jesus, the words attributed to David would once more be seen as placing Jesus in a position of superiority to David.

There can be no question that, as is common elsewhere in the New Testament, Paul interpreted the idea of Christ being told by God to sit at his right hand as an allusion to Jesus' exaltation into heaven. In Rom 8:34, Paul explicitly draws these two ideas together: "Who is it that condemns? It is Christ Jesus who died, yet more than that was raised, who is also at the right hand of God and intercedes on our behalf." Needless to say, such a claim regarding Jesus would also have sounded astonishing to most Jews in Paul's day.[77] Whereas Phil 2:9-11 and 1 Cor 15:24-28 anticipate Jesus' exalted position over all as something that lies in the

---

75. As Fitzmyer notes, the neuter *panta* in 1 Cor 15:27-28 would be understood as "comprehending both persons and things" (*First Corinthians*, 575).

76. On this point, see Aquila H. I. Lee, *From Messiah to Preexistent Son: Jesus' Self-Consciousness and Early Christian Exegesis of Messianic Psalms*, WUNT 2/192 (Tübingen: Mohr Siebeck, 2005), 202-16.

77. David M. Hay notes that there are "no very close parallels in Jewish literature" to Paul's use of Ps 110:1 in Rom 8:34, although "some apparent precedents exist" (*Glory*

future, in Rom 8:34 Paul speaks of Jesus as being active in the present from God's side in heaven. Because it is taken from a Psalm of David, the idea that God has made Jesus to sit at his right side would be interpreted to mean that Jesus had been made to sit upon a throne as a king like David in order to reign there alongside God. In fact, Paul seems to say precisely that in 1 Cor 15:25, where he cites the same verse from Psalm 110 to speak of Jesus reigning until he has put all of his enemies under his feet.[78] For Paul, then, Jesus has not only been exalted into heaven as Lord but made to reign over the world at present while seated on a throne at God's right hand, that is, in the highest position that exists next to God. His role as the one through whom all human beings will be judged places him in a position far above them.[79] Once again, rather than standing alongside other human beings in order to be subject to God in the way they are, he is instead presented as being seated alongside God above all other human beings.

Many scholars reject out of hand the possibility that Paul is referring to Jesus as God in Rom 9:5.[80] According to a literal translation of his words, Paul there refers to "the Christ according to the flesh, who is above all things, God blessed for all the ages." While Paul's words can be translated in ways that would not involve affirming that Paul is calling Christ "God" in this verse, it is difficult to exclude that possibility entirely.[81] If Paul is in fact referring to Jesus as God above all things, no matter what he meant by that phrase, it would have come across to other Jews in his day as highly problematic.

---

at the Right Hand: Psalm 110 in Early Christianity, SBLMS 18 [Nashville: Abingdon, 1973], 131).

78. According to Lee, the fact that the same fusion of Ps 110:1 with Ps 8:6 that appears in 1 Cor 15:25 also appears in Eph 1:20-22, 1 Pet 3:22, Heb 1:13, and Heb 2:6-9 suggests that these Psalms were already being combined by Jesus' followers in a tradition that predates Paul, even though these latter writings were composed later (*From Messiah to Preexistent Son*, 216-19).

79. Marc Turnage notes that Eusebius of Cesarea cites a Jewish writing from the first century BCE that speaks of Moses judging the world, yet he adds that the account of Moses's occupation of God's throne as judge in that writing is "unique in Jewish literature of the Hellenistic and Roman eras" ("Jesus and Caiaphas: An Intertextual-Literary Evaluation," in *Jesus' Last Week*, vol. 1 of *Jerusalem Studies in the Synoptic Gospels*, ed. R. Steven Notley, Marc Turnage, and Brian Becker, JCPS 11 [Leiden: Brill, 2006], 139-68 [153-54]).

80. Among those who have argued at length that in Rom 9:5 Paul is referring to Jesus as "God over all, blessed forever" is George Carraway, *Christ is God over All: Romans 9:5 in the Context of Romans 9–11*, LNTS 489 (London: Bloomsbury T & T Clark, 2013); see especially his conclusions at 184-91.

81. For a summary of this discussion, see Robert Jewett, *Romans: A Commentary*, Hermeneia (Minneapolis: Fortress, 2007), 566-69.

Jesus as the One through Whom God Acts

In addition to presenting God as inseparable from his Son Jesus Christ and ascribing to Christ a position of supreme transcendence alongside God in relation to all other human beings, Paul places Christ at the very heart of the story of salvation he tells. For Paul, this story revolved around Christ as God's Son from the very beginning, and as we have just seen with regard to 1 Cor 15:24-28, in him it will also find its consummation.

In Rom 8:3, Paul speaks of God "having sent his own Son in the likeness of sinful flesh and for sin." In whatever manner Paul's words are understood, they clearly indicate that God sent Christ to deliver others from sin in some sense. A similar idea appears in Gal 4:4-5, where Paul writes: "But when the fullness of time came, God sent forth his Son, born of a woman, born under the law, in order that he might redeem those under the law, in order that we might receive adoption as daughters and sons." Here again the purpose for which God is said to have sent his Son into the world is that he might save others in some fashion. Paul's allusion to God sending forth his Son "when the fullness of time came" suggests that he may have in mind some type of divine plan, according to which God had been waiting for the right moment for his Son to make his appearance in history.

According to Paul, this plan contemplated the death of his Son on a cross. God had anticipated Jesus' crucifixion long before it happened and had foretold it in the Scriptures (1 Cor 15:3). Jesus had died for others "at the right time" (Rom 5:6).[82] In 1 Cor 2:7-8, Paul writes: "But we speak the wisdom of God hidden in a mystery, a wisdom which God predestined before the ages for our glory and which none of the rulers of the present age apprehended; for if they had, they would not have crucified the Lord of glory." Here Paul intimates that God foresaw Jesus' death on a cross even before the creation of the world. In Rom 5:9 and 2 Cor 5:18-21, Paul sees God's activity through Jesus, and especially his death, as the means by which God has reconciled to himself human beings and in some sense the world in general. According to Gal 1:4, when Jesus gave himself for the sins of others in order to deliver them from the present evil age, he did so "in accordance with the will of our God and Father." Elsewhere Paul refers to Jesus' "righteous act" and his "obedience"—evidently to God—as the means by which "justification of life has come to all people" and "many have been constituted as righteous" (Rom 5:18-19). Paul also affirms that it was God himself who gave his Son up or delivered him over to death on behalf of others (Rom 8:32; cf. 4:25).

---

82. As Frank J. Matera observes, although in principle "at the right time" in Rom 5:6 may be taken in conjunction with the phrase "when we were weak," it may be preferable to understand Paul as referring to a "time appointed by God" (*Romans*, PCNT [Grand Rapids: Baker Academic, 2010], 133).

It can hardly be doubted that the vast majority of Jews in Paul's day would have been surprised to hear him proclaim that God had accomplished all of these things on behalf of them and human beings in general by sending his Son and delivering him up to death on a cross. It is perfectly understandable, therefore, that Paul would tell the Corinthians that the message he proclaims regarding a crucified Christ or Messiah is not only foolishness to gentile ears but also scandalous for those Jews who hear it (1 Cor 1:23). Paul immediately goes on to affirm that "to those who are called, both Jews and Greeks, Christ is the power of God and the wisdom of God" (1 Cor 1:24). Among most Jews, a crucified man would have been considered anything but "the power of God," and for Paul to associate such a man with the "wisdom of God" of which the Torah was generally considered the supreme expression would have sounded not only strange but perhaps even offensive.[83] This would certainly not sound like the God in whom they had always believed, nor was this the way in which that God was expected to bless and save human beings. Equally foreign to Jewish thought would be Paul's claims that God had exalted this same crucified man to his right hand as judge over all so that he might come again to raise others from the dead, deliver them from God's wrath, and bring them to dwell together with him in God's presence.[84] Many Jews expected God to do things such as these, yet they would have found it strange to be told that he had appointed a crucified and risen man as his agent to carry out these tasks on his behalf.

Many of the other affirmations that Paul makes with regard to Christ would also have sounded very odd to Jewish ears. He tells the Corinthian believers: "By his doing you are in Christ Jesus, who has been made from God for us wisdom and righteousness and sanctification and redemption" (1 Cor 1:30). In 2 Cor 1:22, he writes: "The one who establishes us in Christ together with you and anoints us is God." Further on in the same epistle he adds: "For it is the God who said, 'Let light shine out of darkness' who has shone in our hearts to give us the light of the knowledge of the glory of God in the face of Christ" (2 Cor 4:6). Paul tells his Roman readers that "we have peace with God through our Lord Jesus Christ" (Rom 5:1) and that it is through Christ that they are "alive to God" (Rom 6:11) before exclaiming: "Thanks be to God through Jesus Christ our Lord!" (Rom 7:25). In 2 Cor 3:4, he speaks of "the confidence we have through Christ toward God." When Paul affirms that through the Spirit of his Son

---

83. On the identification of the Torah with the wisdom of God in Second Temple Jewish thought, see Eckhard J. Schnabel, *Law and Wisdom from Ben Sira to Paul: A Tradition Historical Enquiry into the Relation of Law, Wisdom, and Ethics*, WUNT 2/16 (Tübingen: Mohr Siebeck, 1985), 8-226.

84. See Rom 5:8; 6:23; 7:24-25; 1 Cor 15:21-22; Phil 3:20-21; 1 Thess 1:10; 4:14-17; 5:9-10.

God enables believers to address him as "Abba," he implies that believers enter into a relationship with God that is similar to that of Christ himself and is made possible through Christ (Gal 4:6; cf. Rom 8:15). All of these passages describe a reality in which God and believers relate to each other through Christ, thus placing Christ in a mediatorial position between human beings and God.

In addition to presenting God's past, present, and future activity through Christ as something that God intended to accomplish from the very beginning, Paul seems to conceive of Christ existing in some sense alongside of God long before he was born in human flesh. In 1 Cor 8:6, he appears to speak of God acting through Christ when he created the world: "But for us there is one God, the Father, from whom all things proceed, and for whom we exist; and one Lord Jesus Christ, by means of whom are all things, and through whom we exist."[85] While it is not entirely clear how Paul understands the relationship of Jesus to God the Father here, neither the Hebrew Scriptures nor any Second Temple Jewish writings ever speak of any heavenly figure who would some day become human, die, and rise again serving as God's agent or instrument when he had created the world. Much less did they affirm that it was through that figure that human beings existed for God. Even if Paul is not actually ascribing to Christ any role in creation here, most Jews would never have spoken of any human person being in the type of relation to God that Paul attributes to Christ in this passage.

Most New Testament scholars seem to agree that in Phil 2:5-8 Paul also presents Christ as existing in some sense alongside God before being born as a human being. There Paul writes that "Christ Jesus, though existing in the form of God, did not regard equality with God as something to be grasped, but emptied himself, taking the form of a slave and being born in human likeness; and being found in human form, he humbled himself and became obedient to the point of death—even death on a cross." Once again, though Paul's words here can be interpreted in many different ways, for our purposes it is sufficient to note that there is no precedent in the Hebrew Bible or Second Temple Jewish literature for speaking of any figure existing in the form of God and being equal with God prior to being born as a human being and subsequently dying on a cross. Regardless of what this passage says about Jesus, it presents God as being in a relationship to him that far transcends any relationship between God and any other human figure in ancient Jewish thought.

While many questions remain as to how Paul conceived of Jesus' existence in relation to God prior to his birth, his words in Rom 8:28-29 leave

---

85. As Fitzmyer observes, while most commentators see in this passage an allusion to the preexistence of Christ and his role in creation, not all agree on this point (*First Corinthians*, 343).

no doubt that he believed that God intended to accomplish his purposes among human beings through his Son Jesus from the start. There, after mentioning those who have been called according to God's purpose or plan, he continues: "because those whom he knew ahead of time, he also foreordained to become conformed to the image of his Son, so that he might be the firstborn among many sisters and brothers." The language of being conformed to the image of another evokes the account of the creation of human beings in Genesis.[86] Whether or not Paul had this idea in mind here, he speaks of God's plan or purpose in terms of bringing human beings to conform, not to his own image, but to that of his Son so that they may all live as his sisters and brothers as part of a single family. Such an affirmation places Christ not only at the *center* of the story Paul tells regarding God and humanity but also at its *beginning* and its *end* as the goal toward which God intended to bring the human beings he created.

In 1 Cor 10:1-11, Paul places Christ within the Torah's narrative of Israel's sojourn in the desert under Moses. After affirming that the Israelites were "baptized into Moses in the cloud and the sea" and ate the same spiritual food, he alludes to the story of Moses bringing forth water with his rod from the rock at Meribah to claim that they also "all drank the same spiritual drink, for they drank from the spiritual rock that followed them, and the rock was Christ" (1 Cor 10:4; cf. Exod 17:1-17; Num 20:2-13). Paul appears to have in mind here not only Christ but that which God would later bring into being through him, namely, a community centered upon Christ in which all would be baptized in water and share the same spiritual food and drink. Several verses later, referring to the story of the bronze serpent found in Num 25:1-9. Paul insists that believers must "not put Christ to the test as some of them did, and were destroyed by serpents" (1 Cor 10:9). While it is possible that the text originally spoke of "the Lord" rather than "Christ," Paul seems to be affirming that the Israelites who were bitten by snakes in the desert put Christ to the test.[87] Twice in this passage, then, Paul affirms that in some way the Israelites in the desert related to Christ long before he was born, although it is not entirely clear in what sense he understood this to be true.

In all of these passages, Paul points to Christ as the one through whom God has acted and continues to act to accomplish his purposes among human beings, stressing as well that God intended to do these things through Christ as his Son from the very beginning. Although what Paul says about Christ in these passages is remarkable when viewed against the background of

---

86. See Gen 1:26-27; 5:1; 9:6. On this point, see James D. G. Dunn, *Romans 1-8*, WBC 38A (Dallas: Word, 1988), 495.

87. On the textual variant in 1 Cor 10:9, see Roy E. Ciampa and Brian S. Rosner, *The First Letter to the Corinthians*, PNTS (Grand Rapids: Eerdmans, 2010), 461-62 n145.

Second Temple Jewish thought, for our purposes here what is particularly significant is what these passages say about the God of Israel. For Paul, it is impossible to conceive of God's activity in the history of Israel and the world without speaking of Christ as the one through whom God accomplishes all of his purposes. That history therefore revolves not only around God but around Christ as well.

Paul's Treatment of Jewish Themes

When Jews in antiquity thought of God, they associated him with Israel as his chosen people, with the covenant he had made with them through Abraham and Moses, with the Torah he had given them at Sinai, with the Scriptures of Israel, and with his dwelling place at the temple in Jerusalem. In principle, therefore, one would expect that as a Jew Paul would refer to these same themes and figures with some frequency when he speaks of God. When we look at Paul's epistles, however, we find that allusions to these themes and figures are relatively sparse.

Outside of Romans 9–11 and Gal 6:16, Paul mentions Israel only four times in his epistles (1 Cor 10:18; 2 Cor 3:7, 13; Phil 3:5). In Rom 9:4, he affirms that the Israelites have been given "the adoption, the glory, the covenants, the gift of the law, the temple worship, and the promises." In the preceding verse, however, he expresses "profound grief and endless sorrow" in his heart over his kinspeople and wishes that he might be accursed and separated from Christ on their behalf (9:3). He then affirms that not all who belong to Israel actually form part of Israel and that not all who are descended from Abraham are actually his children (9:7-8). While in Rom 11:26 he contemplates the salvation of "all Israel" and a few verses later insists that they remain beloved for the sake of their ancestors on account of their election and the gifts given them, which are irrevocable (11:28-29), in the same context he hopes that at least some of his fellow Israelites will be saved (11:14). He also states that his heart's desire and his petition to God is that they attain salvation (10:1). These verses, like 9:3, imply that many who belong to Israel will *not* be saved. The same idea is at least suggested in 11:17-24, where Paul speaks of many of his fellow Israelites being cut off like branches from the trunk of an olive true due to their unbelief and states that they can be grafted back into the trunk only if they do not continue in that unbelief.

Throughout these three chapters from Romans, Paul repeatedly stresses Israel's disobedience and hardened heart, although he regards this hardening as only partial and temporary (11:25, 30-31). Citing several passages from the Hebrew prophets, he speaks of only a remnant being saved and says that those who were not God's people have now become his people (9:25-29). Whereas gentiles who did not seek righteousness have attained it through faith, Israel failed in its pursuit of that righteousness through the law rather than faith and "stumbled over the stumbling stone" (9:30-32).[88] Although he commends his fellow members of Israel for their zeal, he adds that this zeal is "not in accordance with knowledge; for being ignorant of the righteousness that is of God and seeking to establish their own, they have not submitted to God's righteousness" (10:2-3). Further on, citing Isa 65:2, Paul writes: "But concerning Israel he says, 'All day long I have held out my hands to a disobedient and obstinate people'" (10:21). While he stresses that God has not rejected his people as a whole, he says that only some have attained what they were seeking and then cites Isa 29:10 and Ps 69:22-23 to speak of them having a spirit of stupor, eyes that do not hear, ears that do not hear, and backs that are bent (11:7-10).[89] He then refers twice to their transgression (11:11-12).

Overall, then, the picture of Israel that Paul draws in Romans 9–11 is a rather negative one, though he does emphasize God's love and mercy toward Israel and the irrevocability of Israel's call. Even if his affirmation in Rom 11:26 that ultimately "all Israel will be saved" is understood in the sense that the Jewish people in their entirety will attain salvation, he is claiming that this will take place in spite of the disobedience, transgression, unbelief, obstinacy, blindness, and hardened heart that he attributes to Israel in his own day throughout the passage. Of course, the idea that Israel is a sinful and disobedient people is well-attested in both the Hebrew Scriptures and Second Temple Jewish literature. Many of the prophetic books, such as Jeremiah, Ezekiel, Hosea, and Amos, also present Israel primarily in a negative light in many passages while nevertheless holding out hope for the people's salvation, as Paul does. We cannot conclude from these passages, therefore, that Paul believed that God had rejected his people Israel because of their sin. On the contrary, the whole point of the passage is to demonstrate that God has *not* rejected his people and continues to desire their salvation due to his deep love for them.

While Paul follows Jewish tradition in speaking of Abraham as the father of all those who belong to Israel, he claims that Abraham is also the father of the gentiles who come to faith in Christ.[90] Outside of the passages in which he speaks of Abraham in those terms, however, Abraham plays no role in any of the arguments Paul develops in his epistles. In both Romans 4 and Galatians 3, the comparison Paul draws is not between Abraham and Christ but between Abraham and *believers in Christ*, who like Abraham are justified and have righteousness reckoned to them by virtue of their faith.

---

88. On this understanding of Paul's affirmation that "Israel, pursuing a law of righteousness, did not arrive at that law" in Rom 9:31, see Hultgren, *Romans*, 378.

89. On the possible meanings of the phrase "keep their backs forever bent," see C. E. B. Cranfield, *A Critical and Exegetical Commentary on the Epistle to the Romans*, 6th ed., ICC (Edinburgh: T & T Clark, 1975), 2:552.

90. See especially Rom 4:1-16; 9:7; Gal 3:6-18, 29; cf. 2 Cor 11:22; Gal 4:22.

Yet the *object* of this faith is not merely God or God's promises but the God who raised Jesus from the dead (Rom 4:22-25), as well as the promises regarding Abraham's seed that revolve around Jesus and find in him their fulfillment (Gal 3:16-18, 29; 4:21-31).

In the passage from 1 Corinthians 10 already cited above, Paul apparently sees Moses as comparable to Jesus in the sense that the people of Israel were baptized into Moses, just as believers are baptized into Christ.[91] Nevertheless, this comparison is not made explicit in 1 Corinthians. The only passage in which Paul speaks of Moses at any length is 2 Cor 3:7–4:6. There Paul contrasts the "ministration of death" and "of condemnation" given to Moses at Sinai with the "ministration of the Spirit" and "of righteousness," obviously associating the latter ministration with Christ (3:7-9). After insisting that the splendor of this second ministration far surpasses that of the first (3:9-11), Paul continues:

> Therefore, since we have such a hope, we are very bold in our speech, unlike Moses, who put a veil over his face so that the children of Israel might not gaze at the splendor of what was fading away until it disappeared completely. But their minds were hardened; for to this day, when the old covenant is read, the same veil remains in place, because only in Christ is it taken away. But to this day, whenever Moses is read, a veil lies covering their heart. When a person turns to the Lord, however, the veil is removed. Now the Lord is the Spirit, and where the Spirit of the Lord is, there is freedom. But all of us, as we behold the glory of the Lord with unveiled faces, as if looking into a mirror, are being transformed into the same image from one degree of glory to another; this is the work of the Lord, who is the Spirit (3:12-18).

It is noteworthy that the comparison Paul initially makes here is not between Moses and Christ but Moses and those who *announce* Christ, such as Paul and his co-workers.[92] He also contrasts believers in Christ with the children of Israel: because their minds were hardened, they could not gaze upon the splendor of God's glory in Moses' face. Those who do not turn to Christ continue to have a veil over their heart and eyes and therefore are unable to understand properly the Scriptures of Israel when they read them. In addition to describing unbelieving Israel as having hardened minds here, Paul presents what was given through Moses as something that leads to condemnation and death.

In this passage Paul does not explicitly mention the Torah, though it is likely that he has it in mind when he refers to tablets of stone and affirms that "the letter kills" (2 Cor 3:4, 6).[93] Elsewhere in his epistles, however, he writes a number of things that many Jews would have perceived as disparaging of

---

91. See 1 Cor 10:2; Rom 6:3; Gal 3:27.

92. On this point, see Margaret E. Thrall, *A Critical and Exegetical Commentary on the Second Epistle to the Corinthians*, ICC (Edinburgh: T & T Clark, 1994), 2:254.

93. See Thrall, *Second Corinthians*, 2:234-35.

the law. Above all, in Romans and Galatians Paul affirms that the law holds people in bondage, as if it were oppressive: "But we are discharged from the law, dead to that by which we were bound, so that we might serve in the newness of the spirit and not the oldness of the letter" (Rom 7:6). "Before faith came, we were kept in confinement under the law, held in restraint until the faith that was to come might be revealed. The law was therefore our disciplinarian to lead us to Christ so that we might be justified by faith. But now that faith has come, we no longer live subject to a disciplinarian" (Gal 3:23-25; cf. 4:3, 9). Paul speaks of dying to the law as if that were something good, and says that he himself has died to the law in order to live to God (Gal 2:19; Rom 7:4). At the very least, the notion that in order to live to God one is to die to the law would have sounded strange to most Jews, since one lived to God precisely by submitting to the law and in a sense living to it as well. In Gal 3:21, Paul denies that the law was able to give life or had ever been intended for that purpose, while in Rom 7:9-10, he writes: "I was once alive apart from the law, but when the commandment came, sin came back to life and I died; and the commandment that was to lead to life came to lead instead to death." According to Paul, the law makes sin abound in some sense and brings God's wrath and judgment.[94] Paul even claims that "the power of sin is the law" (1 Cor 15:56) and states that "all who are of the law are under a curse" (Gal 3:10).

Obviously, all of these affirmations must be read in the context of the arguments in which they appear and are open to many different interpretations. For our purposes here, however, what is important is that few Jews in Paul's day would say things such as these regarding the law. In fact, many Jews would probably have objected to them. In Jewish thought, the law did not kill people or hold them in bondage or under a curse. Nor did it restrict people in the way that a disciplinarian kept a child under restraint, produce sin in them, increase trespasses, or place those who were committed to living in conformity to it under God's wrath and judgment, except in the sense that God would lovingly act to correct them when they needed such correction.[95] It was not God's will that anyone die to the law or be discharged from it. On the contrary, the law promised life to those who kept it and had been given by God to bring about in his people the righteousness that God desired to see in all. Yet Paul repeatedly states that *this is precisely what the law did not and cannot do.* He insists that God has made known his righteousness *apart* from the law, even though the law and prophets attest to that righteousness (Rom 3:21). He also stresses on several occasions that righteousness does not result from doing the works that the law prescribes.[96] From the start, the law was incapable of giving life (Gal 3:21). For Paul, God's

---

94. See Rom 3:19-20; 4:15; 5:20; cf. Gal 2:19.
95. See Rom 4:15; 5:20; 7:6-11; Gal 3:23-25.
96. See Rom 3:20, 28; Gal 2:16, 21.

promises are not inherited through the law.[97] Whereas in Jewish thought the law was the supreme expression of God's grace and those who had faith in God were to manifest that faith by striving to live in obedience to it, Paul at times sets grace and faith *in opposition* to the law, as if they were contrary to it: "You are not under law but under grace" (Rom 6:14-15).[98] According to Paul, through Christ God has done something that the law could *not* do, namely, condemn sin in the flesh and enable those who submit to it to attain the righteousness God desired when he gave the law (Rom 8:3-4; 9:30–10:3). Paul even affirms that "Christ is the end of the law to lead to righteousness for all who believe" (Rom 10:4). Even if Paul intends these words in the sense that Christ is the law's goal rather than its termination,[99] few Jews in antiquity would have agreed with such a statement, much less made it themselves.

Elsewhere Paul affirms that "all things are lawful" (or "permitted," *exestin*), even though they may not be profitable or edifying (1 Cor 6:12; 10:23). He also states that "nothing is unclean in itself" and that "all things are clean" (Rom 14:14, 20). No matter how these statements are interpreted, it is difficult to think that any law-observant Jew in Paul's day would have agreed with them. Because the commandment regarding circumcision was one of the commandments God had given Israel, few if any Jews would have found it acceptable or even comprehensible to say, as Paul does: "Circumcision is nothing and uncircumcision is nothing, but what matters is the observance of God's commandments" (1 Cor 7:19; cf. Gal 5:6). While many Jews would have been opposed to seeking actively to make proselytes of non-Jews and pressuring the males among these non-Jews to undergo circumcision, it is by no means clear that those Jews who ascribed great value to law-observance and circumcision would have thought it a bad thing for non-Jews who wished to be circumcised and submit to the law to do so, as Paul did (1 Cor 7:18; cf. Gal 5:2-3). Many Jews would also have regarded as problematic Paul's claim that he himself is not under the law but is without the law (*anomos*) because he is under a different law, that of Christ (1 Cor 9:20-21). To be *anomos* might even be understood as living in *anomia*, that is, lawlessness, sins, or transgressions.

Undoubtedly, Paul also has positive things to say about the law. He stresses that it is holy, just, good, and spiritual, says that he delights in the law in his inmost self, and insists that he does not regard the law as abolished but instead upholds it (Rom 3:31; 7:12, 22). He claims that circumcision is of value and that it is an advantage to be a Jew (Rom 2:25; 3:1-2). In general terms, however, most Jews would probably have disagreed strongly with many of the things that Paul says about the law. Any who made the kind of

---

97. See Rom 4:13-14; Gal 3:17-22; 4:3-7.

98. See Rom 3:21-22, 28; 5:20; Gal 2:16, 21; 3:11-12, 21-25; 5:4.

99. On this discussion, see Hultgren, *Romans*, 382-83.

statements about the law that Paul does would hardly be seen as showing respect for the law. And because in Jewish thought the law was the greatest gift God had given to the world, as well as the definitive expression of God's will, any who failed to respect the law properly would be seen as disrespecting God himself.

Some scholars have argued that Paul's negative language regarding the law was addressed only to non-Jews and that, when he says that to live under the law is to be held in bondage and under a curse, he means that these things are true only for gentiles, since the law was not intended for them.[100] Even if that were the case, however, any Jews who heard Paul speaking negatively about the law to gentiles would probably have been just as upset at him as if he were addressing himself to a Jewish audience. It is also difficult to conceive of any Jew in antiquity maintaining that gentiles who had come to live under the law were being held in bondage by that law or were under its curse.

Although in 2 Corinthians 3 Paul contrasts the old covenant God made through Moses with a new one and speaks of the giving of that covenant as a ministration of death and condemnation, it would be difficult to conclude from that passage that he viewed God's covenant with Israel in purely negative terms. On the contrary, his words in Rom 9:4 suggest otherwise, since there he speaks of the covenants (plural) in a positive manner. It is significant, however, that in Galatians he argues that the promises God made to Abraham do not come to fulfillment through the covenant God established through Moses 430 years after Abraham. Instead, those promises revolved around Christ as Abraham's seed or offspring from the very beginning (Gal 3:15-18). In Gal 4:21-31, Paul associates the Sinai covenant and the present Jerusalem with slavery and the sending away of Hagar. He then contrasts that slavery with the freedom of the Jerusalem above that the Galatian believers enjoy as children of Isaac. What is particularly noteworthy in these passages from 2 Corinthians and Galatians is the way in which Paul sets the covenant God made with Israel at Sinai in contrast to another covenant, which he clearly associates in some way with Christ. It is difficult to imagine other Jews in antiquity associating the covenant given at Sinai with a life of slavery and claiming that it is by living under another covenant that people attain freedom as children of Abraham, Sarah, and Isaac.

---

100. So, for example, Fredriksen: "The Law was a curse *for gentiles*. The Law only revealed sin *for gentiles*. The Law was a service of death *for gentiles*. But for Israel the Law, God-given, was a defining privilege" (*Paul*, 165). Such an affirmation seems to overlook Gal 3:21, where Paul denies that the law could give life to anyone, as well as the context of 2 Cor 3:7-16, where Paul is speaking of the law given *to Israel* through Moses at Sinai as a ministration of death and condemnation.

In a number of passages from his epistles, Paul makes use of temple imagery. He calls believers in Christ or their bodies a temple of God or God's Spirit.[101] In Rom 12:1, he tells the Roman believers to offer their bodies up to God as a "living and holy sacrifice." Further on in the same epistle, Paul presents himself as a priest who ministers to the gospel and offers gentiles up to God (Rom 15:16). In 1 Cor 5:7, he compares Jesus to a Passover lamb that has been sacrificed. It is possible that Paul has sacrificial ideas in mind when he mentions Jesus' blood in Rom 5:9, as well as in 1 Cor 10:16 and 11:25-27.[102] His affirmation in Rom 3:25 that God put Jesus forward as an "expiation (or propitiation) in his blood through faith" clearly involves the use of sacrificial imagery. Although in a couple of passages Paul alludes very briefly to the sacrificial worship offered to God in the Jerusalem temple (Rom 9:4; 1 Cor 10:18), nowhere does he discuss that worship or the temple in any detail. While the relative lack of attention that Paul pays to this subject may not be significant, it is worth noting that in most of these passages he sees that worship as meaningful by virtue of its relation to Christ and the new reality that now exists through him rather than independently of Christ and that reality.

In light of what we have seen throughout the present chapter, then, it seems very clear that for Paul what defines God above all else is not simply his relation to Israel, the patriarchs, Moses, the Torah, and the temple, but his relation to Jesus Christ as his Son. All of Israel's history, as well as Israel's Scriptures, pointed to Christ as the one through whom God's promises and purposes would be fulfilled. While Paul certainly believed that the God of Jesus Christ was the God of Israel of whom the Scriptures of Israel spoke, those Jews who did not share his faith in Christ would hardly have recognized the God proclaimed as the Father of Jesus Christ by Paul as the same God whom they and their ancestors had confessed and worshiped since the days of Abraham, Isaac, Jacob, and Moses. Instead, they would have seen Paul as proclaiming not only a different God but a new and different faith as well, a faith characterized by innovations and claims that were foreign to their thought and therefore a faith that they did not share. In their minds, in recent times God had *not* revealed anything radically new and important regarding himself, made his will known in a way that transcended the Torah, spoken through one who was greater than Moses, established as Lord alongside himself in heaven one who was greater than David or Aaron, made a new covenant in addition to the covenant he had made with Israel at Sinai, or redefined in any fundamental way the manner in which he related to his people or the manner in which they were to relate to him. According to Paul and his fellow believers in Christ, however, all of these

---

101. See 1 Cor 3:16; 6:19; 2 Cor 6:16.
102. See Jewett, *Romans*, 363.

things were true of the God of Israel, and any who did not accept them were therefore not accepting the full truth regarding him.

To affirm these things is by no means to claim that their proclamation of a God and a faith that were in important ways new and different made it impossible for Paul and other Jews who believed in Christ to enjoy good relations with those Jews who did not come to faith in Christ and to coexist peacefully with them in a spirit of friendship and concord. Nothing in that proclamation required that believers in Christ separate themselves from other Jews or condemn them for their failure to acknowledge Christ as God's Son and Lord. On the contrary, as Paul affirms in Rom 12:14-21, it was expected that believers in Christ do everything possible to live in peace and harmony with all people, including those who did not share their faith fully, and to respond in love and kindness to any animosity they faced on the part of others. In fact, throughout his epistles Paul repeatedly condemns any type of boasting or haughtiness in relation to others. If God had temporarily hardened the heart of many of his people Israel and they had been blinded from seeing the truth of the gospel, their unbelief was not entirely their fault and in due time they too would eventually come to believe in that gospel.[103] In that case, rather than censuring them for their unbelief, it was important to show them patience, kindness, understanding, and consideration. As Paul writes in Phil 2:15, what was necessary was not to treat others with condemnation or contempt but to "shine like luminaries in the world" so that those who had not yet been enlightened by the gospel might come to see its truth.

At the same time, it is likely that most of Paul's fellow Jews who did not believe in Christ would have agreed that those who did come to faith in Jesus as the Messiah or Christ should be treated with the same type of love, kindness, and respect mentioned by Paul, given especially the fact that the Torah itself mandated these things of all of God's people. If Jews could coexist peacefully and amicably with their gentile neighbors who worshiped gods who were distinct from the God of Israel, there was in principle no reason why they could not enjoy the same type of relationship with those within their midst who associated the God of Israel with Jesus Christ in a way that they did not. Many of them probably even rejoiced at seeing the way in which the lives of gentiles were transformed in positive ways through their faith in the gospel proclaimed by Paul and received them warmly in their midst rather than condemning them for that faith. A careful reading of Paul's epistles demonstrates that this was the type of relationship that he sought to promote among the Jews and non-Jews among whom he lived and worked.

---

103. See Rom 9:18; 11:7-26; 2 Cor 3:14; 4:4.

CHAPTER 2

Redefining God's Purposes for Israel and the World

If the God of Israel had created the world and elected Israel as his special people, he must have had a purpose in doing so. That purpose might have to do either with God himself or with Israel and the other nations. If God's concern had been for himself, then he had done these things and now commanded obedience to his will because he needed or desired to receive something from human beings in general or from Israel in particular. If that were the case, his motivation would have been self-centered and he could not truly be said to have acted out of love for human beings when he did those things. Instead, he would have been motivated by self-interest, concerned primarily not for the well-being and happiness of others but only his own.

If God had instead elected Israel to be his special people for the sake of others rather than for his own sake, had he done so primarily for the sake of Israel alone or rather for the sake of all the nations of the world? In Jewish thought, there was no question that the purpose for which God had chosen Israel as his people was to bless them. Numerous passages from the Hebrew Scriptures made this very clear.[1] However, the fact that God had also created other nations meant that God must have had some purpose for them as well.[2] If this purpose was that of blessing those nations

---

1. On the wide variety of terms and metaphors used to speak of Israel's election in the Hebrew Scriptures, see Seook-Tae Sohn, *The Divine Election of Israel* (Grand Rapids: Eerdmans, 1991), 9-100, 138-82.

2. For a survey of ideas regarding the purpose of Israel's election in the Hebrew Scriptures, see Sohn, *Divine Election*, 194-98; Sigurd Grindheim, "Election and the Role of Israel," in *God and the Faithfulness of Paul: A Critical Examination of the Pauline Theology of N. T. Wright*, ed. Christoph Heilig, J. Thomas Hewitt, and Michael F. Bird (Minneapolis: Fortress, 2017), 329-46 (333-37). On the various contemporary

together with Israel, God must have elected Israel not only for Israel's sake but also for theirs. In that case, God's election of Israel had been designed to accomplish something on behalf of the other nations as well and not only on behalf of Israel.[3]

It might instead be claimed, however, that God had created the other nations and had allowed them to continue to exist primarily for the sake of Israel. If so, then the most important purpose of those nations was to serve as a means by which God might accomplish his objective of blessing Israel. If God were said to love those nations, that "love" would depend on their treatment of Israel, who constituted his first or greatest love. Of course, it might also be said that God had created the nations for their own sake and wanted them to enjoy to some extent the same type of well-being he desired for Israel. However, if God loved Israel more than any other people, his love for the other nations of the world could never match his love for Israel and his concern for their well-being was secondary to his concern for the well-being of Israel.[4]

Alternatively, it might be maintained that God wished to bless Israel and the nations equally. If this were the case, however, then in some sense every nation could be regarded as unique and special in God's sight and the object of his same love. God might also be said to have had created each nation for some unique and particular purpose in relation to the others due to the differences he had established among them. If so, God's election of each of the nations he had created would in essence be no different than his election of Israel, though the task of each nation would be distinct. Most Jews, however, would probably have regarded the idea that all nations had been elected by God to be his own as a denial of Israel's

---

Christian and Jewish interpretations of the purpose of Israel's election in biblical and Jewish thought, see Joel N. Lohr, *Chosen and Unchosen: Conceptions of Election in the Pentateuch and Jewish-Christian Interpretation*, SLTHS 2 (Winona Lake, IN: Eisenbraums, 2009), 3-91.

3. As Joel S. Kaminsky notes, the Hebrew text in Gen 12:3, 18:18, 22:18, and 26:4 can be understood either in the sense that all the families of the earth will be blessed by or through Abraham or in the sense that they will bless themselves by or through Abraham: "Neither translation of Gen 12:3 makes it absolutely clear how the families of the earth might be blessed or bless themselves through Abram and his descendants, but passages later in Genesis suggest that part of this blessing comes about through mediatorial services rendered by Abraham and Israel" (*Yet I Loved Jacob: Reclaiming the Biblical Concept of Election* [Nashville: Abingdon, 2007], 82-83).

4. Such an idea is suggested by Joel Kaminsky's reading of numerous biblical texts that speak of Israel's election and God's love for Israel, while nevertheless stressing God's love for others as well: "If God's love is like human love in any way whatsoever, then it is unlikely that God has an identical love for all nations and all individuals" ("Did Election Imply the Mistreatment of Non-Israelites?," *HTR* 96 [2003]: 397-425 [425]).

special status as God's chosen people and as contrary to the teaching of Israel's Scriptures.[5]

If God had elected Israel in a way that he had not elected other nations, then, either he had intended to bless Israel more than any other nation or else that election had been designed to fulfill some special purpose in relation to those other nations, who would come to be equally blessed as a result of God's election of Israel. According to the first of these two possibilities, whatever blessing the nations received from God ultimately had the purpose of providing a greater blessing to Israel. While God might bless the nations to some extent for their own sake, his primary motivation would be that the nations use the blessings they received from him to serve Israel or contribute in some way to Israel's well-being and prosperity. According to the second possibility, God's blessing of Israel had the purpose of enabling Israel to be a means by which the other nations might attain the same blessing that Israel did. If Israel did not fulfill that role in the way God desired, God might either withdraw his blessing from his chosen people until they began to do so or else simply treat them in the same way that he treated the other nations, since it would be pointless for him to continue to relate to them in a special and unique manner.

In principle, Israel's Scriptures could be cited in support of either of these two ideas. Many passages from those Scriptures conveyed the idea that God had chosen Israel in order to bless other nations as well. According to Gen 12:2-3, for example, from the time that God had chosen Abraham, he had told him: "I will make of you a great nation, and I will bless you and make your name great so that you will be a blessing. I will bless those who bless you and curse those who curse you, and in you will all the families of the earth be blessed." These words could be understood in two different ways. They might be interpreted in the sense that God would bless Abraham and his descendants so that through them other nations might eventually attain the very same blessing. However, it is also possible to interpret those words in the sense that whatever blessings the nations would receive through Abraham would ultimately have the purpose of enabling them to serve as his means to provide an even greater blessing for Abraham and the nation that would arise from him. Similarly, God's promise to bless those who blessed Abraham and curse those who cursed him could be understood either as an end in itself or as a means toward another end. If God's primary

---

5. As Walter Brueggemann has pointed out, there is some evidence in the Hebrew Scriptures for the idea that "God has other peoples with their own story of chosenness," most notably Isa 19:23-25, which envisions "a coming time when YHWH will have a plurality of chosen peoples and Israel will have no monopoly on that status" ("Election," in *Reverberations of Faith: A Theological Handbook of Old Testament Themes* [Louisville: Westminster John Knox, 2002], 61–64 [63]). Such an idea is extremely rare, however, both in the Hebrew Scriptures and in Second Temple Jewish writings.

purpose was to bless Abraham, then when God blessed and cursed others on the basis of their treatment of Abraham, ultimately he did so for the sake of Abraham and his descendants. If God's primary purpose was instead that of blessing all people equally together with Abraham and his descendants, then when God blessed those who blessed Abraham and cursed those who cursed him, God's objective was to ensure that Abraham and his descendants might serve as his means to make it possible for the other nations to come to enjoy the same blessing some day. The reason why God would curse any who cursed Abraham was that Abraham and his descendants were to be God's instrument to bless all the families of the earth, and therefore any who impeded or prevented Abraham and his descendants from fulfilling that role would constitute an obstacle to God's loving purposes for all and would thus need to be dealt with appropriately.

The Hebrew Scriptures also made it clear that the purpose for which God had given his people Israel the Torah was that of blessing them. Once again, this might be seen as an end in itself or as a means for blessing the nations together with Israel. According to Deut 4:6-8, for example, when God gave his commandments to Israel, he told them: "You must observe them diligently, for this will show your wisdom and discernment to the peoples, who, when they hear all these statutes, will say, 'Surely this great nation is a wise and discerning people! For what other great nation has a god so near to it as the Lord our God is whenever we call to him? And what other great nation has statutes and ordinances that are as just as this entire law that I am setting before you today?'" These words imply that, by giving Israel such wonderful commandments and having them obey those commandments, God intended to attract other nations to himself and his good commandments as well.[6] The same idea is found in the writings of several of the Hebrew prophets, who affirm that the Torah will go forth to the nations from Zion and look forward to the day when the nations will flock to Israel to worship God and be blessed by him as they serve him alongside Israel.[7]

In fact, even when Israel is commanded to remain entirely separate from other nations or to destroy certain peoples (Deut 7:3), it is possible to interpret those commands in two different ways. They can be seen as having the purpose either of making it possible for Israel to enjoy a blessing that will be Israel's alone or alternatively as enabling other nations eventually to be blessed together with Israel and through Israel. If Israel's blessing is an end

---

6. As Lohr notes, according to this passage, what will provoke wonder among the nations is not merely the law itself but in particular Israel's obedience to the law (*Chosen and Unchosen*, 151).

7. On this idea in the Hebrew Scriptures and Second Temple Jewish writings, see Donald E. Gowan, *Eschatology in the Old Testament* (Philadelphia: Fortress, 1986), 48-57.

in itself, then Israel is to retain its unique identity and when necessary subdue or destroy any who stand in the way of that blessing for its own sake. If instead, however, Israel's blessing has the purpose of eventually bringing other nations to enjoy that same blessing together with Israel, then at present Israel must remain separate so that it may be blessed in a special way, and any who might pose an obstacle to that blessing must be prevented from doing so until Israel itself attains that blessing. Only when this has happened can Israel become the means by which all others can be blessed in the same way and to the same degree. While it might be necessary temporarily to treat other nations harshly and even destroy some of them in order to enable Israel to be blessed in the present, eventually the blessing of Israel would lead to the same blessing for the other nations of the world. The affirmation that Israel will be "the most blessed of all peoples" in Deut 7:13 can similarly be understood either as the description of a final state or else as a temporary objective aimed at making it possible for all other people to attain the same blessing.

The Jewish claim that God had chosen Israel as his special people and promised to bless them, then, raised a number of questions. Had God chosen Israel for his own sake, simply for the purpose of fulfilling some desire or need on his part, such as the desire to be glorified and served? If this had not been God's purpose, then was God's election of Israel an end in itself or instead a means by which he intended to make it possible for the other nations to come to enjoy the same blessing that Israel was to receive? In either case, what did that blessing consist of, and how did God intend to bring it about? What role was Israel to play in relation to the other nations at present, and what role were they to play in relation to Israel?

Although for the most part the Hebrew Scriptures and Second Temple Jewish literature do not address these questions directly, they do provide a basis for offering answers to them. As one would expect, given the diversity of these writings, the answers that can be discerned from them vary greatly and in many cases cannot easily be harmonized with one another. For our purposes here, however, what is of interest is not merely the ways in which Jews in Paul's day answered these questions but also the ways in which Paul and his fellow believers in Christ answered them. For what purpose had the God of Jesus Christ elected Israel and promised to bless them as his special people? Was God's intention merely to bless Israel through Jesus or to bless the other nations as well through both Israel and Jesus? Had God chosen Israel and sent Jesus for his own sake or for the sake of Israel and the other nations of the world? What role were Israel and Jesus to play in God's plan, and how would God bring about through them the blessings he intended to bestow? And where did the nations fit into this plan? As we shall see here, Paul's epistles offer answers to all of these questions. More importantly, they also provide further evidence for the conclusion stated at the end of Chapter

1: the God proclaimed by Paul was in many ways very different from the God in whom most Jewish people had traditionally believed.

THE BLESSINGS OF THE TORAH

Whether God's blessing of Israel was an end in itself or a means toward eventually blessing other nations in the same way, God's first priority had to be that of doing whatever was necessary to make Israel's blessing a reality. In principle, it might be maintained that God could simply shower freely upon his people Israel all the blessings that he desired for them and in that way accomplish his purposes. In reality, however, such was not the case. The people might take the blessings that God had graciously bestowed on them and use what they had received in ways that undermined and destroyed their happiness, well-being, and prosperity. The result of those blessings would then be suffering and injustice for many of God's people, including especially the less privileged and the disadvantaged, and if any part of the people suffered injustice and oppression at the hands of their fellow Israelites, the people as a whole would be adversely affected. That injustice and oppression would make it impossible for them to experience collectively the blessing God desired for all equally. If God's purpose was also to bless the other nations together with Israel, Israel's misuse of the blessings received from God would ultimately affect those nations negatively as well, since Israel's blessing was a pre-condition to theirs.

In order to enable his people Israel to attain the blessings he sought for them, therefore, it was necessary for God to provide them with guidance and instruction, leading them in the path that was best for them and acting to bring them back into that path whenever they departed from it. In both the Hebrew Scriptures and Second Temple Jewish literature, the means by which God sought to accomplish that objective was the Torah.

Shalom, Justice, and the Torah

In all human societies, legal codes are generally regarded as having the purpose of promoting justice, equity, and the well-being of all. Such was clearly the purpose of the precepts of the written Torah or law of Moses. The justice that it prescribes requires not only that the members of God's people refrain from doing things that are harmful to one another but also that they love and care for one another. Numerous commandments insist on the need to care especially for those in greatest need, such as the widows and the orphans, and to defend the rights of the poor, the foreigners, and the underprivileged.[8] All Israelites were to show respect for their parents, the

---

8. See Exod 22:21-27; 23:9; Lev 19:13-14, 32-34; 23:6, 9; Deut 1:16-17; 15:4; 24:6-7, 10, 12-15, 17; 27:19. On this emphasis in the Hebrew Scriptures, see Christofer Frey, "The Impact of the Biblical Idea of Justice on Present Discussions of Social

elderly, and those with disabilities such as the blind and deaf.[9] The Torah sought to preserve the integrity of marriage and maintain healthy relationships within each family.[10] Young girls and women were not to be abused or exploited sexually.[11] Workers and servants were to be treated fairly and humanely, and laborers were to be paid their wages on a daily basis.[12] Fields and orchards were not to be harvested completely in order to make sure that those who might go hungry could find something to eat.[13] Judgments were to be just and equitable, and measures were to be taken to ensure that those judgments did not favor the rich and powerful.[14] For this reason, judges were prohibited from receiving any type of gifts from those under their jurisdiction.[15] The Torah mandated that scales and balances be accurate and prohibited any type of dishonesty or deception.[16] All were to practice generosity and to be willing to loan to those in need, taking special care to make sure that those burdened down by debt did not go cold at night or become destitute.[17] The people were expressly told that they must not oppress or hate anyone, seek revenge, or bear grudges.[18] Instead, they were to love not only their family members, friends, and neighbors, but even those who hated them.[19]

The laws prescribing the cancellation of debts, the liberation of slaves, and the return of property to its previous owners every seven years also had the purpose of promoting equity and avoiding poverty among the people.[20] Such measures were designed to prevent the accumulation of wealth and power by some and the gradual impoverishment of others.[21] By mandating periodic rest for all people, animals, and even the land, the Torah sought not only to promote the physical well-being of all but also to enable them

---

Justice," in *Justice and Righteousness: Biblical Themes and Their Influence*, ed. Henning Graf Reventlow and Yair Hoffman, JSOTSup 137 (Sheffield: JSOT, 1992), 91-104.

9. See Exod 20:12; 21:15, 17; Lev 19:3, 32; 20:9; Deut 5:16; 27:16, 18.

10. See Exod 20:14, 17; Lev 18:6-20; 20:10-21; Deut 5:18, 21; 22:13-30; 23:17; 27:20, 22-23.

11. See Exod 21:22; 22:16-17; Lev 19:29-30.

12. See Deut 24:15.

13. See Exod 23:10-11; Lev 19:9-10; Deut 24:19-22.

14. See Exod 21:23-25; 23:1-3, 6-7; Lev 19:15, 35; Deut 16:18-20; 25:1; 27:19.

15. See Exod 23:8; Deut 16:19; 27:25.

16. See Lev 19:11-12, 35-36; Deut 25:13-16.

17. See Lev 25:35-37; Deut 15:7-11; 24:10-13.

18. See Lev 19:13-18; 23:4-5; Deut 23:7; 24:14.

19. See Exod 23:4-5.

20. See Lev 25:1-55; Deut 15:1-16.

21. See Yairah Amit, "The Jubilee Law—An Attempt at Instituting Social Justice," in *Justice and Righteousness: Biblical Themes and Their Influence*, ed. Henning Graf Reventlow and Yair Hoffman, JSOTSup 137 (Sheffield: JSOT, 1992), 47-59 (50-53, 59).

to have the time necessary to enjoy life.[22] Commandments regarding food, sanitation, and the treatment of illnesses and diseases also contributed to their overall health and well-being.[23] Numerous passages even command that the people be joyful.[24]

Throughout the passages from the Mosaic law that prescribe things such as these, the focus is primarily on *distributive* justice, that is, forms of justice aimed at ensuring that the needs of all within the society are met and that resources are distributed as evenly as possible. While *retributive* justice is also necessary, retribution is not regarded as an end in itself but is instead to contribute in some way to *distributive* justice.[25] Punishments for violations of the law were to serve the good of all by correcting injustices, restoring equity, preventing some from oppressing others, deterring harmful behavior, and putting a stop to such behavior before it might extend further. The purpose of the talion law, "an eye for an eye and a tooth for a tooth," was to ensure that punishments for wrongdoing were just and fair rather than excessive or overly lenient.[26] Other forms of justice, such as restorative justice, also had distributive justice as their goal.

In a number of passages from the Hebrew Scriptures, the result of the observance of the commandments of the Torah is said to be shalom. While this word generally is translated as "peace," in reality shalom is a much broader concept. According to Old Testament scholar George Knight, "The verbal root from which it derives conveys the conception of being whole or being complete or sound; consequently the transitive form of the verb [*shalam*] means to make whole, to restore, to complete."[27] As Knight points out, in Hebrew thought shalom involves a total well-being in body, mind, and spirit, as well as abundance, prosperity, material security, contentment, harmony, fullness of life, and relations with others that are peaceful, constructive, and satisfying.[28] In many contexts, its closest Greek equivalent is not *eirēne*, generally translated "peace," but rather *sotēria*, which is also derived from the word for "whole" (*sōs*). This meaning of *sotēria* and its cognate verb *sōzō* is reflected in the words often ascribed to Jesus in the Synoptic Gospels,

---

22. See Exod 20:8-11; 23:12; 31:12-17; 35:2-3; Deut 5:12-15; 20:5-7.

23. See Lev 11:1–15:33; Num 5:1-4; 19:11-22; Deut 14:3-21; 24:8.

24. See Deut 12:7, 12, 18; 14:26; 16:11, 14-15; 26:11; 27:7.

25. On the centrality of distributive justice in biblical thought, see Christopher D. Marshall, *Beyond Retribution: A New Testament Vision for Justice, Crime, and Punishment* (Grand Rapids: Eerdmans, 2001), 45-53; Jeremiah Unterman, *Justice for All: How the Jewish Bible Revolutionized Ethics*, JPSEJS (Philadelphia: Jewish Publication Society, 2017), 15-84.

26. See Hans Jochen Boecker, *Law and the Administration of Justice in the Old Testament and Ancient East*, trans. Jeremy Moiser (London: SPCK, 1980), 173-75.

27. George A. F. Knight, *A Christian Theology of the Old Testament* (Richmond, VA: John Knox, 1959), 250.

28. Knight, *Christian Theology*, 250, 253.

where he tells those whom he has healed: "Your faith has saved you" or "made you well" (*hē pistis sou sesōken se*).[29] Both shalom and *sotēria* can therefore be translated as "wholeness," "completeness," or "well-being," and can be applied to individuals as well as communities and groups of people.[30] Justice was said to exist when all without exception enjoyed this shalom to the extent that this was possible, and such justice was the goal of the Torah: "There will be justice among us if we are careful to do all this commandment before the Lord our God, as he commanded us" (Deut 6:25).

Precisely because God had given the Torah to promote among his people the well-being of all, it was generally considered the most precious gift and blessing ever bestowed upon human beings. The Psalmists rejoice over the goodness of the Torah and express their delight in its precepts.[31] When both God and his commandments are said to be "righteous" or "just," this is not because they are designed to ensure that wrongdoing will be punished but rather because they promote shalom for all. In other words, the justice that they promote is primarily *distributive* rather than *retributive*. For this reason, in the Hebrew Scriptures justice is often regarded as synonymous with grace, mercy, and kindness, and to judge is generally to *save*.[32] Such would not be the case if judgment and justice were understood primarily in terms of retribution.

There can be no doubt that most Jews in antiquity viewed the Torah in these terms. Philo of Alexandria and Flavius Josephus, for example, repeatedly express their admiration for the law and speak of its goodness, excellence, and beauty.[33] Both stress that it is far superior to any other law found among human beings and affirm that people of other nations marvel at its greatness.[34] They claim that the Mosaic law promotes kindness, gentleness, and compassion for all and brings harmony, happiness, and

---

29. See Matt 9:22; Mark 5:34; 10:52; Luke 7:50; 8:48; 17:19; 18:42.

30. See Claus Westermann, "Peace (Shalom) in the Old Testament," in *The Meaning of Peace: Biblical Studies*, ed. Perry B. Yoder and William M. Smartley (Louisville: Westminster John Knox, 1992), 16-48 (19-21).

31. See especially Ps 1:2; 19:7-10; 112:1; 119:14-16, 35, 47, 70, 77, 143, 162.

32. See Deut 10:18; 32:36; 1 Chron 16:33; Ps 9:7-9; 10:17-18; 33:5; 36:5-6; 67:4; 71:2, 15; 72:2-4; 76:9; 82:3-4; 89:14-17; 96:10-13; 103:6, 17; 112:9; 116:5; 135:14; 145:17; 146:5-10; Prov 31:9; Isa 1:17; 11:4; 30:18; 45:21; 59:11; Jer 5:28; 9:24; 21:12; 22:3, 15-16; 33:15-16.

33. See especially Philo, *Creation* 1.1-3; *Moses* 2.12, 52; *Spec. Laws* 2.79; *Virtues* 113, 125, 183; Josephus, *Ant.* 1.14; 4.122-23; 16.44; 18.266; *Ag. Ap.* 2.173-88, 277-95. On this point, see Peder Borgen, "Philo of Alexandria," in *Jewish Writings of the Second Temple Period: Apocrypha, Pseudepigrapha, Qumran Sectarian Writings, Philo, Josephus*, ed. Michael E. Stone, CRINT 2 (Philadelphia: Fortress, 1984), 233-82 (234-35); Trent A. Rogers, *God and the Idols: Representations of God in 1 Corinthians 8 and 10*, WUNT 2/427 (Tübingen: Mohr Siebeck, 2016), 140.

34. See Philo, *Moses* 1.1-3; 2.25-27; Josephus, *Ant.* 3.93, 223; 4.114; 12.110-11.

countless other benefits into the lives of those who observe it. The fact that Jews who lived in the diaspora generally preferred to live according to their own law rather than the laws of the nations among whom they dwelled indicates that they held the Mosaic law in the same high esteem that Philo and Josephus did.

If the purpose of the Torah was to promote shalom for his people, it follows that the God of Israel had given its commandments out of love for them and insisted that they obey those commandments for their own good. Commandments such as those considered above had intrinsic consequences in that, in and of themselves, they contributed to the well-being of all. Communities in which all respected and cared for one another, and especially for the disadvantaged and those in greatest need, would tend to be healthy and enjoy peace and prosperity. The social fabric would remain strong and things such as injustice, violence, and oppression would be avoided as much as possible. Nevertheless, the law itself could not ensure well-being for all, since that well-being also depended on factors that were beyond the control of human beings. In order to enjoy shalom, the people needed to have good harvests, live free of plague and disease, and not be oppressed by enemy nations. Because God alone could ensure things such as these, the people depended on his loving intervention and providence.

Undoubtedly, there was a sense in which the law could be understood as a burden that made great demands on God's people. Yet this should be understood in the sense that it requires a great deal of effort and commitment to persist in doing what is good, healthy, and wholesome for oneself and others. To offer a present-day analogy, it is burdensome and demanding to get up early in the morning to do some type of exercise, to limit oneself to eating foods that are healthy and nutritious, and to refrain from drinking alcohol in excess or smoking. Yet in the long run the benefit of doing these things far outweighs the cost, dedication, and effort that they require. In Jewish thought, the law was seen in the same way: it made difficult demands on those who were committed to observing it faithfully, yet the wellness and blessings that resulted from that observance made it well worth the sacrifices involved in doing so.[35]

Once it is understood that in Jewish thought God had given the Torah to Israel for the sake of the people themselves rather than for his own sake, other ideas that appear throughout the Hebrew Scriptures and in the Jewish writings of antiquity take on new meaning. For example, the idea

---

35. On this understanding of the law, see Ed Condra, *Salvation for the Righteous Revealed: Jesus amid Covenantal and Messianic Expectations in Second Temple Judaism*, AGJU 51 (Leiden: Brill, 2002), 67; Philip S. Alexander, "Torah and Salvation in Tannaitic Literature," in *Justification and Variegated Nomism*, vol. 1: *The Complexities of Second Temple Judaism*, ed. Donald A. Carson, Peter T. O'Brien, and Mark A. Seifrid, WUNT 2/140 (Tübingen: Mohr Siebeck, 2001), 261-303 (282-83).

that God was a "jealous God" who prohibited Israel from serving other gods and practicing idolatry stresses the notion that only God and his law were able to grant fully the shalom, justice, and prosperity that he desired for his people.[36] The worship of other gods and idols led to injustice, oppression, violence, lawlessness, and all sorts of evils, undermining and destroying human well-being rather than contributing to it.[37] Because no other set of commandments, precepts, and guidelines found in the laws of other nations could promote the same wholeness that the Torah did, in and of itself it was harmful and detrimental to God's people to forsake Israel's law for the laws of other nations or to disregard the Torah partially or entirely. If God was "jealous," therefore, prohibiting his people from serving other gods and demanding that they observe carefully and faithfully the Torah he had given them, it was not for *his own* sake but for *theirs*.

The idea that God punishes or chastises Israel should likewise be understood on the basis of these same ideas. In passages such as Leviticus 26 and Deuteronomy 28, God promises to pour out blessings of different types upon his people on the condition that they obey the commandments he was giving them for their own good. At the same time, however, God tells them that he will chastise them by means of various types of afflictions and hardships if they fail to obey those commandments. This meant that there was not only an *intrinsic* relation between the people's behavior and the consequences of that behavior, but an *extrinsic* one as well. Because the law prescribed a way of life that was conducive to the people's well-being, in and of itself obedience to that law would enable them to enjoy a certain level of well-being and shalom. Nevertheless, for reasons already mentioned above, that well-being also depended on God's responding to their obedience by intervening from heaven to bless them in various ways and to protect them from suffering and misfortune. If they failed to live in the way that God had commanded them out of a loving concern for their well-being, it would be counter-productive for God to continue to shower them with blessings, since to do so would only promote further injustice and inequity, in essence adding fuel to the fire. Instead, God would need to inflict some type of hardship or suffering upon them until they might become conscious of their wrongdoing and return to him in obedience for their own good.

-----

36. See Exod 20:5; 34:14; Deut 4:24; 5:9; 6:15; Josh 24:19; Ezek 39:25.

37. On this idea, see Lev 18:21; Deut 20:18; 32:15-17; 1 Kgs 18:18; 2 Kgs 17:9-17, 29-41; 21:6-9; 2 Chron 33:4-6; Ps 106:36-38; Isa 57:1-10; Jer 7:9-10; 9:13-14; 16:11-12; 19:4-5; 22:9; 32:35; 44:8-10, 22-23; Ezek 18:6-17; 20:24-26, 31; 22:3-12; 23:37-39; 33:25-26; Wis 14:1-31; Jub. 11:3; T. Reu. 1:4; Josephus, *Ant.* 5.107-8; Philo, *Spec. Laws* 1.312. On Philo's thought on this subject, see Karl-Gustav Sandelin, *Attraction and Danger of Alien Religion: Studies in Early Judaism and Christianity*, WUNT 290 (Tübingen: Mohr Siebeck, 2012), 27-59.

Both the Hebrew Scriptures and Second Temple Jewish literature repeatedly use the language of correction and discipline to speak of the afflictions God imposed on his people in an attempt to bring them back into conformity with his good law when they had abandoned it.[38] Such correction and discipline is consistently presented as an expression of love.[39] Perhaps no passage articulates this idea as clearly as 2 Macc 6:12-16. There, after describing the terrible cruelties inflicted on many Jews by the Syrian king Antiochus when they refused to forsake their laws and adopt Greek customs as he had commanded, the author of the book writes:

> Therefore I exhort those who read this book not to be disheartened by these afflictions, but to consider that these punishments were aimed not at the destruction of our people but at their correction (*paideia*). For it is a sign of great kindness to punish the impious immediately rather than leaving them alone for long. For the Lord has determined not to treat us like the other nations. In their case he waits patiently for them to reach the full measure of their sins before punishing them, but in our case he does not wait until our sins have reached their height before inflicting punishment on us. Therefore he never withdraws his mercy from us. He does not abandon his people, but disciplines (*paideuōn*) us with afflictions (2 Macc 6:12-16; cf. 7:32-33; 10:4).

Whether God poured out his blessings on his people or subjected them to hardships, therefore, he was believed to be acting out of love for them. Although at times the sufferings inflicted by God might be so intense as to seem excessively cruel, only when Israel persistently and stubbornly refused to heed God's call to return to him in obedience did God find it necessary to treat his people so harshly and take such drastic measures. The alternative was for God simply to abandon his people and let them go their own way to their own perdition and destruction. While God might do so for a time in order to let them experience the painful consequences of their disobedience to his good law, however, his love for his people would never allow him to forsake them definitively.

Purity, Sacrifice, and the Worship of Israel's God

At first glance, many of the commandments found in the Torah do not appear to promote any type of well-being in and of themselves. This is especially true with regard to the commandments that prescribe the worship

---

38. The Hebrew word often used is *mûsar* (verb *ysr*). See, for example, Lev 26:18, 23, 28; Job 36:10; Jer 2:30; 5:3; 7:28; 17:23; 32:33. The Septuagint generally uses the term *paideia* and its cognates to express the same idea of correction, discipline, and instruction; see Wis 3:5; 11:9-16; 12:20; Pss. Sol. 3:4; 7:3, 9; 8:26, 29; 13:7-12; 14:1; 16:11; 17:5; 18:7-8; cf. 2 Bar. 1:4; 4:1.

39. See, for example, Deut 8:5; Job 5:17-18; Ps 94:12; Prov 3:11-12; Pss. Sol. 13:9-10; Josephus, *Ant.* 3.311.

of Israel's God through sacrifice, as well as many of the regulations having to do with purity. It might seem that there is no intrinsic relationship between the observance of these portions of the law and the people's well-being. If such were the case, then it would be necessary to affirm that God had given such commandments for some purpose other than that of seeking the well-being of those who obeyed them. For example, God might have prescribed sacrificial offerings simply because he wished to be served, worshiped, and glorified for his own sake or sought to keep any type of impurity or pollution at a distance from himself, perhaps because his holy nature could not allow him to tolerate being in the presence of anything impure or polluted.[40] Surprisingly, some scholars have even claimed that impurity or pollution actually *endangered* Israel's God, as if he might be harmed or affected adversely by it.[41]

There is little evidence, however, that ideas such as these were common among Jews.[42] In the Second Temple period, by far the most comprehensive consideration of the meaning of the sacrificial worship offered to Israel's God in accordance with the prescriptions of the Mosaic law is found in the writings of Philo. In the first two books of his work *Special Laws*, Philo examines in detail the various procedures, elements, objects, places, and figures associated with the sacrificial rites carried out at the Jerusalem temple in order to discern the meaning they were to have for those who participated in them.[43] According to Philo, the sacrificial rites had a didactic purpose: God had ordered the people to practice sacrifice in order to instruct them and reinforce basic truths regarding God and their relation to him.

---

40. Thus, for example, Roy Gane claims that for Israel's God to maintain his presence in the temple, "he requires the purification of his sanctuary because the people's moral and physical imperfection, which affect his dwelling place, are incompatible with his nature" (*Cult and Character: Purification Offerings, Day of Atonement, and Theodicy* [Winona Lake, IN: Eisenbrauns, 2005], 327). On the basis of this idea, it is often claimed that some of the sacrificial rites had the purpose of cleansing the sanctuary from its pollution to make it possible for God to dwell there; see, for example, Jacob Milgrom, *Studies in Cultic Theology and Terminology*, SJLA 36 (Leiden: Brill, 1983), 81-82; Michael Newton, *The Concept of Purity at Qumran and in the Letters of Paul*, SNTSMS 53 (Cambridge: Cambridge University Press, 1985), 6-7, 36; F. F. Bruce, *The Epistle to the Hebrews*, rev. ed., NICNT (Grand Rapids: Eerdmans, 1990), 230.

41. Baruch A. Levine, for example, writes: "Implicit in all expiatory rites is the assumption that ritual offenses endanger the deity in some way, since they threaten to diminish the purity of his earthly dwelling. . . . There is a reason for Yahweh's wrath. It was not mere displeasure at being disobeyed. His wrath was a reaction based on a vital concern, as it were, for his own protection" (*In the Presence of the Lord: A Study of Cult and Some Cultic Terms in Ancient Israel*, SJLA 5 [Leiden: Brill, 1974], 76, 78).

42. On what follows, see David A. Brondos, *Jesus' Death in New Testament Thought*, vol. 1: *Background* (Mexico City: Theological Community of Mexico, 2018), 125-201.

43. See especially Philo, *Spec. Laws* 1.168-302; 2.145-222.

The offering of first fruits, for example, "teaches us a high truth," namely, that "the beginnings of things both material and immaterial are found to be by God only" (*Heir* 113-14). The commandment to offer God victims without blemish was given to instruct the people regarding the need to live innocent from evil and free of moral defilement (*Spec. Laws* 1.167). The Feast of Tabernacles teaches those who celebrate it to honor equality and hate inequality and to be thankful to God as the source of all good things (*Spec. Laws* 2.204). Both Philo and Josephus also see the decorations on the temple curtain, the various ornaments in the sanctuary, the high-priestly vestments, and the sacrificial worship in general as fulfilling the same kind of didactic purpose.[44]

The purpose of sacrifice, however, was not only to offer the people instruction as to how they were to think and live but also to bring about in them that same way of thinking and living. The people's participation in the sacrificial worship offered to Israel's God served to produce and strengthen in them the spirit of love, obedience, and dedication to God that God desired to see in them for their own good. By performing the rites prescribed and participating in them, they not only learned that they should be grateful to God and obey him but were given concrete means of expressing that gratitude and manifesting that obedience. According to Philo, because the difficulties and costs involved in traveling to Jerusalem from afar to present sacrificial offerings to God there were considerable, they both required and generated greater devotion and commitment to God among those who made the journey to worship at the temple (*Spec. Laws* 1.67-70). The commandments mandating offerings for sins reiterated to the people the importance of avoiding sin and led them to reflect constantly on their behavior to see if they were living as God desired. The sacrificial rites therefore cultivated and reinforced in them the way of thinking and living that God desired to see in them for their own good.

Thus Philo, for example, repeatedly stresses that the offering of sacrifice leads the worshipers to reflect on their actions and produces a spirit of gratitude in them.[45] The sacrifices for sin, including those prescribed for the Day of Atonement, are to bring people to repentance and renew them in their obedience: "For those who have acknowledged their sin are changing their way for the better, and while they reproach themselves for their errors are seeking a blameless life as their new goal" (*Spec. Laws* 1.227). The rites involved in the sacrifices for sin also reminded the people to refrain from sinning and allowed them to "make themselves pure by curbing the

---

44. See Josephus, *J.W.* 5.212-14; Philo, *Moses* 2.93-108, 117-35, 150-51; *Heir* 221-29. On these points, see especially Jonathan Klawans, *Purity, Sacrifice and the Temple: Symbolism and Supersessionism in the Study of Ancient Judaism* (Oxford: Oxford University Press, 2006), 113-23.

45. See, for example, Philo, *Spec. Laws* 1.171, 283-95; 2.174-75, 180, 209.

appetites for pleasure" so that they might become "enamoured of continence and piety" (*Spec. Laws* 1.193). Sacrificial worship was therefore intended to induce in those who participated in it a life dedicated to practicing justice and righteousness in accordance with God's will. According to Philo, this is the ultimate purpose of all of the sacrificial worship prescribed by Israel's God.

Numerous passages from other Second Temple Jewish writings and from the Hebrew Scriptures themselves speak of sacrifice as having the purpose of reminding the worshipers of certain truths.[46] By reminding the people that both they and all they possessed belonged to God as the sovereign creator of all, the sacrificial worship of God led them to dedicate themselves wholly in body and soul to serving God and using all that they had received from him in the way he desired, in accordance with his will for justice and the well-being of all. In particular, the three great feasts of Passover, Pentecost, and Tabernacles served to bring to mind the ways in which God had been active in the events of Israel's past so that the people might remain conscious of their unique identity. By reinforcing that identity, the celebration of the feasts and the observance of special days helped bring the people to live in the way God had commanded for their own good out of love for them.[47]

When God's people offered him their sacrifices and gifts, they were understood to be offering *themselves* to God as well. Any sacrificial offering that did not represent a heartfelt and sincere offering of oneself to God was not acceptable to God. Numerous passages from the Hebrew Scriptures and Second Temple Jewish literature stress that, without a sincere commitment to doing God's will, no sacrifice is pleasing to God.[48] If those offerings were not expressions of the spirit of self-offering that God desired to see among his people for their own good, they were not fulfilling their purpose. And if that spirit was genuine, it would naturally and inevitably manifest itself in the desire to share one's life and one's possessions with God through gifts and offerings that were visible expressions of that spirit. For this reason, it was generally expected that all who approached God bring something

---

46. See, for example, Exod 20:24; Lev 2:2, 9, 16; 5:12; 6:15; Deut 16:3, 12, 16; Josephus, *J.W.* 5.212-13, 218; Let. Aris. 157-59; Philo, *Heir* 113-16; *Spec. Laws* 1.261-66; 2.145-46, 150-52, 156-60, 197-203.

47. See Exod 12:14, 26-27; 13:3-16; 31:13, 17; Lev 16:29-34; Num 10:10; Deut 5:15; 15:15; 16:3, 12; 26:1-9.

48. See, for example, 1 Sam 15:22-23; 1 Kgs 8:39; Ps 40:6-8; 50:7-18, 23; 51:16-17; Prov 15:8; 21:27; Jer 11:14-15; 14:10-12; Hos 6:6; 8:12-14; Mal 1:7-14; 2:13-15; Jdt 16:19; Sir 7:9-10; 35:1-9, 14-15; 38:9-11; 2 En. 45:3; 46:1; Philo, *Moses* 2.106-8; *Spec. Laws* 1.67-70, 171, 196, 203, 257-60, 269-85, 293; 2.35, 42; *QG* 1.61; 2.52; *Names* 240; *Unchangeable* 8-9; Josephus, *Ant.* 6.147-48. On this point, see also Everett Ferguson, "Spiritual Sacrifice in Early Christianity and its Environment," *ANRW* 2.23.2, 1151-89 (1156-60); Unterman, *Justice for All*, 93-108.

to share with him rather than drawing near to him with empty hands.[49] To express one's gratitude to God without manifesting that gratitude in a concrete way when one had the means to do so was seen as a lack of sincerity. Nevertheless, it was stressed that if for some reason one was not able to present any offering, it was equally acceptable for one to enter into his presence merely to praise and thank him with a sincere heart and acknowledge his loving sovereignty over one's life.[50] It was often repeated that those who approached God in that spirit yet for some reason were unable to present God a sacrificial offering were pleasing to God, whereas those who offered God sacrifices of great opulence and material worth without the proper inner disposition and devotion were not.

Of course, it was expected that the desire to share one's being and possessions with God through sacrificial offerings be accompanied by a desire and commitment to share one's being and possessions with others as well, especially those in greatest need. The offerings of any who were not committed to justice and equity among God's people were not acceptable to God, no matter how lavish those offerings might be.[51] By strengthening his people's love and dedication to him through his command that the people manifest their praise, honor, and adoration for him by means of sacrificial offerings, therefore, the God of Israel was understood to be reinforcing in his people their commitment to seeking the well-being of all.

One other reason why God was thought to have mandated sacrifice was that it afforded his people an opportunity to live and experience palpably their communion with God and one another. The sacrificial offerings served as means for the people to express concretely the sincerity of their petitions to God as well as sentiments such as gratitude for God's blessings or remorse for their sins. Numerous passages from the Hebrew Scriptures and Second Temple Jewish writings make it clear that to offer sacrifice was in essence to offer up prayers to God.[52] Words and actions complemented each other and gave meaning to each other. Neither was thought to be sufficient without the other. While it was a pagan philosopher who wrote, "Prayers divorced from sacrifices are only words, prayers with sacrifices are

---

49. See Exod 23:15; 34:20; Deut 16:16; Sir 35:6.

50. See Philo, *Moses* 2.106-8; *Spec. Laws* 1.271-72; Josephus, *Ant.* 6.148.

51. See, for example, Prov 21:3; Isa 1:11-17; 58:6; Jer 7:3-10; Amos 5:21-25; Mic 6:6-8; Sir 34:23-24.

52. See 2 Sam 24:25; 1 Kgs 18:24-26, 36-37; 2 Kgs 16:15; 2 Chron 20:9; Ps 4:1, 5; 20:3-6; 27:6; 69:30; 116:17; 141:2; Isa 1:15; 19:21-22; 56:7; Dan 9:20; Amos 5:22-23; Zech 8:22; Mal 1:8-9; 1 Macc 7:37; 2 Macc 1:8, 23; 10:3-4; 14:34-35; Jdt 9:1; Sir 50:5, 18-19, 22-24; Jub. 6:14; 13:9; 16:20-31; Josephus, *Ant.* 3.100; 4.243; 5.256; 6.19, 25, 102; 7.331-34; 8.108; 11.17; 14.260-61; 18.15; *J.W.* 2.197, 409; *Ag. Ap.* 2.77, 196; Philo, *Dreams* 2.299; *Drunkenness* 66; *Moses* 1.219; 2.5, 133, 147, 153-55, 159; *Spec. Laws* 1.97, 113, 167-71, 224; *Unchangeable* 8.

animated words, the word giving power to the life and the life animation to the word," his saying reflects very well Second Temple Jewish thought on the subject as well.[53] Sacrificial worship therefore fulfilled the purpose of enabling the members of God's people to manifest their innermost sentiments, beliefs, and desires in tangible and visible ways that went far beyond anything that words alone could ever articulate.

The Letter of Aristeas stresses many of these same points with regard to the purity laws given through Moses, which were intimately related to sacrificial practices:

> In his wisdom the legislator, in a comprehensive survey of each particular part, and being endowed by God for the knowledge of universal truths, surrounded us with unbroken palisades and iron walls to prevent our mixing with any of the other people in any matter, being thus kept pure in body and soul, preserved from false beliefs, and worshiping the only God omnipotent over all creation.... So, to prevent our being perverted by contact with others or by mixing with bad influences, he hedged us in on all sides with strict observances connected with meat and drink and touch and hearing and sight, after the manner of the Law. In general everything is similarly constituted in regard to natural reasoning, being governed by one supreme power, and in each particular everything has a profound reason for it, both the things from which we abstain in use and those of which we partake.... The fact is that everything has been solemnly set in order for unblemished investigation and amendment of life for the sake of righteousness.... [God] has thereby indicated that it is the solemn binding duty of those for whom the legislation has been established to practice righteousness and not to lord it over anyone in reliance upon their own strength, nor to deprive him of anything, but to govern their lives righteously.... The symbolism conveyed by these things compels us to make a distinction in the performance of all our acts, with righteousness as our aim.... I have therefore given a brief résumé of these matters, indicating further to you that all the regulations have been made with righteousness in mind, and that no ordinances have been made in Scripture without purpose or fancifully, but to the intent that through the whole of our lives we may also practice justice to all mankind in all our acts, remembering the all-sovereign God (Let. Aris. 139, 143-44, 147, 151, 168).

Like the commandments regarding sacrificial offerings, the prescriptions regarding purity in the Torah were thought to have been given to reinforce the people's unique identity as those chosen by God, as the text just cited makes very clear.[54] By doing so, those prescriptions helped to hold

---

53. Sallustius, *Concerning the Gods and the Universe* 15.16 (quoted in Ferguson, "Spiritual Sacrifice," 1156).

54. On the purpose of the purity laws in the Hebrew Scriptures and Second Temple Jewish thought, see Cana Werman, "The Concept of Holiness and the Requirements of Purity in Second Temple and Tannaic Literature," in *Purity and Holiness: The Heritage of Leviticus*, ed. Marcel J. H. M. Poorthuis and Joshua Schwartz, JCPS 2 (Leiden: Brill, 2000), 163-79. On Josephus' understanding of the relationship between

sin in check and discouraged the people from adopting the beliefs and practices of other nations, which did not contribute to shalom and well-being in the way that the Torah did. Observance of the Torah's prescriptions regarding the distinction between the pure and the impure thus promoted certain attitudes and sentiments among God's people, reminding them of who they were and what God desired to see in them. By constantly leading them to reflect on their conduct, those prescriptions strengthened their obedience to God's will for their own well-being. In addition to promoting physical health among God's people, the purity regulations helped bring about in them indirectly a life that was pure in a moral or ethical sense.

Although many of the sacrificial practices carried out among God's people Israel were similar to the practices of people from other nations who worshiped their own gods, the belief that Israel's God was fundamentally distinct from other gods led to an understanding of sacrifice that was also fundamentally distinct from that of other nations. Among the majority of those peoples, sacrifice was connected with the worship of gods and idols that made few if any moral or ethical demands on their worshipers. Those gods and idols desired sacrificial offerings *for their own sake*, either because they depended on those sacrifices to satisfy their own needs or because those offerings satisfied the passions and selfish desires of those divinities and brought them pleasure.[55] Contrary to the God of Israel, who had commanded that the people present him sacrificial offerings out of love for them with the goal of bringing about in them the type of life that was in their own best interest, most of the gods of other nations were thought not to care whether the people who worshiped them showed concern for the oppressed and needy or dedicated themselves to promoting justice, equity, and well-being for all. What was believed to anger the God of Israel, however, was not the people's failure to offer him the sacrifices he had mandated but the failure to practice the justice and righteousness he had commanded in his law for the good of all. And the reason that this angered him was precisely his love for the people, since by disobeying or ignoring him they were doing harm to themselves and others whom he also loved.

By repeatedly stressing that Israel's God had no need of the sacrificial offerings presented to him, therefore, the Hebrew Scriptures and Second Temple Jewish writings made it clear that God had instituted the sacrificial

---

purity and justice, see Steve Mason, "Pollution and Purification in Josephus's *Judean War*," in *Purity, Holiness, and Identity in Judaism and Christianity: Essays in Memory of Susan Haber*, ed. Carl S. Ehrlich, Anders Runesson, and Eileen Schuller, WUNT 305 (Tübingen: Mohr Siebeck, 2013), 183-207.

55. On the Second Temple Jewish critique of the nature and character of the gentile gods to whom sacrifice was offered, see especially Robert Goldenberg, *The Nations that Know Thee Not: Ancient Jewish Attitudes towards Other Religions*, BibSem 52 (Sheffield: Sheffield Academic Press, 1997), 51-62.

system of Israel, *not for his own sake or the sake of his own holiness and justice*, but *for the sake of the people themselves.* There were no self-interests behind the God of Israel's demand for sacrifices—not even the desire to be honored, glorified, or worshiped. What was thought to have motivated the God of Israel to command his people to worship, glorify, and honor him through sacrifice was not a concern for himself, his own ego, or his own holiness and justice, but rather his desire to reinforce the people's obedience to the commandments that he had given them for their own well-being and happiness. If that obedience was not being reinforced, the offering of sacrifice was not fulfilling its purpose and thus was not pleasing to the God of Israel.

Had God Given the Torah for His Own Sake?

Throughout the Hebrew Scriptures and Second Temple Jewish literature, the God of Israel is presented as all-powerful. It is claimed that there is nothing impossible for God and that in his sovereignty he can do all things. As creator of all things in heaven and on earth, he is subject to nothing and no one.[56] Even among those Jews who came to believe in spiritual forces of evil such as Satan during the Second Temple period, it was not thought that those forces had any power over God. He could destroy any or all of them in an instant simply by willing their destruction. Just as he had created all things with his word, so also could he destroy anything he wished simply with a word.

In Second Temple Jewish thought, this belief in the God of Israel as sovereign creator of all set him apart from all the gods of the nations as a God who was fundamentally distinct from them.[57] While there might be other gods and supernatural beings above, in, and below the earth, they were in no way comparable to the God of Israel. On the contrary, because God had created all that there is, any other spiritual beings that existed must have had their origin in him and were therefore subject to his power and authority.

One of the primary differences between the God of Israel and the other gods of antiquity is that the God of Israel needed nothing from the human beings he had created. Because he did not eat or drink, he had no

---

56. On this conception of God in Second Temple Jewish writings, see the collection of passages presented in Henry J. Wicks, *The Doctrine of God in the Jewish Apocryphal and Apocalyptic Literature* (London: Hunter & Longhurst, 1915), 27-129.

57. On what follows, see especially Unterman, *Justice for All*, 1-14; Peter Frick, "Monotheism and Philosophy: Notes on the Concept of God in Philo and Paul (Romans 1:18-21)," in *Christian Origins and Hellenistic Judaism: Social and Literary Contexts for the New Testament*, ed. Stanley E. Porter and Andrew Pitts, TENTS 10 (Leiden: Brill, 2012), 237-58 (240-44); John M. G. Barclay, "Snarling Sweetly: Josephus on Images and Idolatry," in *Idolatry: False Worship in the Bible, Early Judaism, and Christianity*, ed. Stephen C. Barton (London: T & T Clark, 2007), 73-87; Rogers, *God and the Idols*, 58-155, 216-19.

need for any of the food or libations that might be offered to him. Because he did not sleep or grow tired, he did not need to rest and could not be disturbed by human behavior. At the same time, because he had no passions, he did not depend on any of the beings he had created to satisfy any type of personal desire on his part. Undoubtedly, he wished for certain things such as the obedience and well-being of those whom he had created. Yet he wished for those things, *not for his own sake*, but only *for the sake of the human beings he loved*. To have affirmed the contrary would have been to maintain that it was possible to manipulate, coax, or pressure God into doing certain things or acting in a certain way by offering him something that he desired in and of itself for his own sake. In that case, God would have been like the gods of the nations, bestowing favors on those who gave him what he wanted, needed, and demanded out of self-interest and lashing out at those who refused to do so in order to inflict suffering on them until they did.

In ancient Jewish thought, all of these things set Israel's God apart from the gods of other nations. Because those gods cared primarily for themselves, what angered them was merely that human beings not give them what they desired, and what placated that anger and gained their favor was simply that they receive from human beings what they demanded of them for their own sake. In order to experience any blessings those gods might bestow or be spared any punishment they might inflict, it was necessary to purchase their favor and avoid arousing their wrath by doing whatever they commanded and refraining from any action or activity that displeased them. In many cases, those gods were not only unconcerned about justice among human beings but actually wanted their worshipers to subjugate and dominate others so that they might obtain from them the gifts and offerings they wanted in even greater measure. If those gods did want there to be justice, peace, or happiness among human beings, this was not an end in itself but rather was desirable in that it made it possible for those human beings to be engaged in doing whatever pleased those gods and kept them content rather than acting in ways that they found bothersome and upsetting.

In many Christian circles in the West, it has been common to teach that the purpose for which God created all things, including especially human beings, was his own glory. For this reason, what God ultimately demands of all is that they worship and glorify him. Such a teaching, however, seems to run contrary to what we find in the Hebrew Bible and Second Temple Jewish thought. If the God of Israel had created the world for the purpose of being worshiped and glorified by those he created, then any who rendered him such worship would have been pleasing to him, independently of whether they practiced justice, righteousness, mercy, and kindness to others as God had commanded in his law. In this regard, he would be essentially the same as the gods of the nations, who wished to be revered and adored by human beings for their own sake. According to ancient Hebrew and Jewish thought, however, the God of Israel was fundamentally different from those gods in that nothing could please or satisfy him if it was not accompanied by the practice of justice and goodness in conformity with his law. What ultimately concerned and interested Israel's God was not the praise and adoration of human beings or anything else they might offer him, but a life in accordance with his good and loving will as he had made that will known. If he desired that his people worship him and offer him sacrifices, then, it was not *for his own sake but for theirs*, since had it been for his own sake, their worship and sacrifices in themselves would have been sufficient to please him.[58] If instead he wished to be worshiped for the sake of his people, it was because only by acknowledging him as the good and sovereign God over all would they be able to enjoy the well-being he desired for them by living in the way he had commanded for their own well-being and happiness.

The Salvation of Israel and the Nations

Given the wide diversity that existed within Second Temple Judaism, it is not surprising that beliefs regarding the future varied greatly from one Jewish circle to another. Some biblical scholars, in fact, would even question whether it is appropriate to use terms such as "salvation" and "soteriology" to refer to those beliefs.[59] Undoubtedly, as scholars such as Michael Fuller have shown, there were groups of Jews who were not anticipating or hoping for any type of future salvation and merely expected things in the world to continue as they were indefinitely.[60] Nevertheless, those who were acquainted with the Hebrew Scriptures would have been aware that those Scriptures contained many divine promises of blessing with regard to Israel that most Jews probably regarded as yet unfulfilled. These hopes are reflected in many Second Temple Jewish writings as well.

If at present Israel was not yet experiencing the blessings of salvation that God intended for his people, then there were only two things that the people could do: strive to obey the commandments God had graciously given them to the best of their abilities and wait patiently for God to act

---

58. As Rogers has noted, this idea was particularly stressed by Philo: "Because God is sufficient in himself, it is improper to say that worship of God is for God's benefit. Rather, proper worship has as its goal the benefit of humanity. . . ." (*God and the Idols*, 132 [commenting on Philo, *Decalogue* 81]).

59. See, for example, E. P. Sanders, *Judaism: Practice and Belief, 63 BCE–66 CE* (Philadelphia: Trinity Press International, 1992), 279-80.

60. Michael E. Fuller, *The Restoration of Israel: Israel's Re-gathering and the Fate of the Nations in Early Jewish Literature and Luke-Acts*, BZNW 138 (Berlin: de Gruyter, 2006), 84-101, 184-86.

to bring about the fulfillment of his promises whenever he saw fit. Due to the intrinsic relationship between the observance of those commandments and the well-being that resulted from that observance, to some extent such observance in itself made it possible for God's people to experience the well-being and shalom that God desired for them in the present. In order for them to attain the promised blessings of salvation in their fullness, however, it would be necessary for God to intervene in history to bring those blessings to pass.

If God had not yet acted to bring about Israel's salvation in the way he had promised, it was logical to conclude that the people had not yet attained the level of obedience he desired and expected to see in them. In that case, it was necessary for them to become more diligent in their obedience to his commandments. However, just as God had given them the Torah as a gift by pure grace in order to guide and instruct them in the way that they should go for their own good, so also could the people hope and expect that God might bring about in them by pure grace the obedience to the Torah that they needed in order to experience the salvation God intended for them. There were several ways in which God might accomplish this objective. He might send them teachers and leaders to enable them to understand the Torah more clearly and help them create the conditions necessary to obey it as they should. In addition to disciplining and chastising them through suffering and rewarding them for good behavior, God might also send the people prophets to call them to repentance when they fell into sin and to enable them to understand how he was acting in history to bring them to obey him as they should.

A number of passages from the Hebrew Scriptures and Second Temple Jewish writings looked forward to the day in which God would act to transform his people's hearts.[61] By pouring out his Spirit upon them and freeing them from the sinful inclination and tendencies that characterized human existence in this world, God would give them a new heart so that they might practice the justice and righteousness necessary for them to experience his salvation. Thus, while the people needed to do their best to live in accordance with God's will and attempt to bring their fellow Jews to do so as well, at the same time they needed to continue to look to God in faith and trust, asking him to give them the obedience they needed as a gracious gift.

Because well-being and shalom cannot exist when people refuse to live in ways that make that well-being and shalom possible, in order for God's promises of salvation to be fulfilled, it would be necessary for God to judge all people in order to separate those who were committed to practicing

---

61. On this point, see Kyle B. Wells, *Grace and Agency in Paul and Second Temple Judaism: Interpreting the Transformation of the Heart*, NovTSup 157 (Leiden: Brill, 2015), 25–206.

justice and righteousness from those who were not.[62] The reason that God would reject the unrighteous and evildoers was not any lack of love for them on his part or a need to exact punishment for their sins in order to satisfy the demands of his own justice, but simply the fact that their way of thinking and behaving made it impossible for them to experience the blessings of salvation God desired for all people. Their sinful, unjust, and oppressive behavior also posed an obstacle to the well-being of others, including especially the righteous.

In biblical thought, therefore, God will judge all people, not for *his own sake* or for the sake of his perfect and immutable holiness, righteousness, and justice, but *for the sake of human beings themselves*. That judgment was seen as the means by which he would bring about the salvation of all whose way of thinking and behaving was conducive to shalom for themselves and others and thus made it possible for that salvation to be theirs. What would bring God to judge human beings was not any type of desire or demand for retribution as an end in itself, as if his concern were to satisfy an inner need related to his own holy and righteous nature, but his longing to see the human beings he loved finally be able to enjoy fully the same wholeness, well-being, and distributive justice that constituted the objective of all of his activity in history.

According to those Jews who believed in the resurrection of the dead, all who had died prior to the arrival of the new age of salvation would be raised so that God might judge them together with the living and thereby enable those who had been righteous to share in the blessings of the age to come. Because it was expected that those saved would dwell upon a renewed earth rather than in some heavenly realm, the bodily resurrection of those who had died was also necessary in order for them to partake of the salvation to come.

Among many Christian biblical scholars, it has become common to speak of an inaugurated eschatology, according to which the awaited new age was to become a reality already in the present age in some sense.[63] While those scholars claim to find this idea in a number of New Testament texts, including especially the letters of Paul, there is little if anything in the Hebrew Bible or Second Temple Jewish literature to suggest the existence of such a belief prior to Paul's day. Undoubtedly, because of the continuity that was thought to exist between the two ages, many of the blessings associated with the age to come might be experienced to some extent

---

62. On this belief in Second Temple Judaism, see Chris VanLandingham, *Judgment and Justification in Early Judaism and the Apostle Paul* (Peabody, MA: Hendrickson, 2006), 66-174.

63. So, for example, Dale C. Allison Jr., *The End of the Ages Has Come: An Early Interpretation of the Passion and Resurrection of Jesus* (Philadelphia: Fortress, 1985), 148-51; Condra, *Salvation*, 80-84.

in the present age. There is no clear evidence, however, for any widespread belief that God would bring about some mysterious transformation of the world and human beings collectively in the present age in preparation for the age to come.

Expectations regarding the fate of the nations or gentiles varied considerably among those Jews who maintained eschatological hopes.[64] Some Jews believed that the salvation to come would be for the people of Israel alone and that the nations would either be destroyed or subjected to Israel, perhaps even as slaves dedicated to serving God's people.[65] Other Jews anticipated that righteous gentiles would also be able to participate in that salvation in some way.[66] Even though these gentiles would not be fully Torah-observant in the present world, they would be accepted by Israel's God as righteous on the basis of their faithfulness to basic moral principles that were in conformity with God's will for all people. Of course, if the life of the age to come was to be characterized by the observance of the Torah, any gentiles to be saved would need to be brought to observe the Torah once that age arrived if they were to share fully in its blessings.

Numerous passages from the Hebrew Bible and Second Temple Jewish writings express such a hope. They look forward to the day in which people of other nations will come to worship the one true God and live in accordance with the Torah.[67] To most Jews, however, it seemed obvious that this would not take place as long as the present world continued as it was. All of the different nations and peoples continued to worship their own gods, and it was difficult to conceive of any major changes taking place in this regard. Scholars debate the extent to which Jews sought to proselytize non-Jews, yet to whatever degree this took place, relatively few non-Jews abandoned their own traditional faiths entirely so as to commit themselves to living in full accordance with the Jewish law.[68] In the case of males, of course, that commitment would involve becoming circumcised. It was much more common for interested non-Jews simply to attend Jewish synagogues and

---

64. See Sanders, *Judaism: Practice and Belief,* 267-70, 295; Paula Fredriksen, "Judaism, the Circumcision of Gentiles, and Apocalyptic Hope: Another Look at Galatians 1 and 2," *JTS* 42 (1991): 532-64 (544-48).

65. On these beliefs, see Fuller, *Restoration of Israel,* 102-97.

66. On the category of "righteous gentiles" in Second Temple Judaism, see Fredriksen, "Judaism," 533-43; Mark D. Nanos, *The Mystery of Romans: The Jewish Context of Paul's Letter* (Minneapolis: Fortress, 1996), 50-56.

67. On these expectations, see Terence L. Donaldson, *Paul and the Gentiles: Remapping the Apostle's Convictional World* (Minneapolis: Fortress, 1997), 69-74.

68. Most scholars now agree that active Jewish attempts to make proselytes of non-Jews were relatively uncommon in antiquity; see Stephen Spence, *The Parting of the Ways: The Roman Church as a Case Study,* ISACR 5 (Leuven: Peeters, 2004), 48-52; Scot McKnight, *A Light among the Gentiles: Jewish Missionary Activity in the Second Temple Period* (Minneapolis: Fortress, 1991), 34-77; Fredriksen, "Judaism," 537-40.

participate in the worship offered to Israel's God without abandoning entirely their previous way of life, including the fulfillment of the obligations they were believed to have in relation to their traditional divinities and to those of the state. This participation took many different forms, yet as one would expect, those who chose to worship the God of Israel without submitting to all of the precepts of the Torah were rarely if ever accepted as equals within the Jewish community or considered full members of that community.[69]

THE AIMS OF PAUL AND THE GOD OF THE GOSPEL

If there is one point on which all Pauline scholars would agree, it is that Paul was extremely passionate about the work he carried out on behalf of the gospel he proclaimed. Clearly, he believed very strongly in what he was doing, so much so that he was willing to suffer all sorts of trials and hardships, endure the hatred and animosity of many, and repeatedly put his life at risk in order to accomplish the ends he pursued.

Precisely what those ends were, however, is not as apparent as it might first appear. There can be no doubt that they had to do primarily with the salvation of others. Paul himself explicitly defines this as the goal of his ministry in a number of passages.[70] In scholarly circles, however, there have been many different views regarding what he understood that salvation to consist of and the exact manner in which he believed people could attain it.[71] There can be no question, however, that in one way or another Paul's aims had to do with the establishment of communities such as the ones to which he directed his letters. While he refers to these communities as *ekklēsiai* in the plural, he also regards them as part of a single *ekklēsia*.[72] Of course, because Paul understood himself to be in the service of God and Christ, he must have believed that the aims of his apostolic ministry were at the same time the aims of God and Christ as well. God and Christ had sent him "to bring about the obedience of faith among all the nations"

---

69. On the variety of ways in which non-Jews participated in the life of the Jewish communities in the Second Temple period, see Donaldson, *Paul and the Gentiles*, 52-69; McKnight, *Light among the Gentiles*, 78-101; Spence, *Parting of the Ways*, 52-61.

70. See especially Rom 1:16; 10:1; 11:14; 1 Cor 9:22; 10:33; 2 Cor 1:6; 1 Thess 2:16.

71. For different views regarding how Paul understood salvation, see James D. G. Dunn, *The Theology of Paul the Apostle* (Grand Rapids: Eerdmans, 1998), 461-98; Gerd Theissen, *Social Reality and the Early Christians: Theology, Ethics, and the World of the New Testament*, trans. Margaret Kohl (Minneapolis: Fortress, 1992), 159-86; N. T. Wright, *Paul and the Faithfulness of God*, vol. 4 of *Christian Origins and the Question of God* (Minneapolis: Fortress, 2013), 1043-95.

72. See 1 Cor 12:28; 15:9; Gal 1:13; Phil 3:6.

by calling them to belong to Christ and to the community of those who acknowledged him as Lord (Rom 1:4-6).

Paul's Vision for the Communities of Believers

While space does not allow us to consider here every aspect of the kind of communities that Paul envisions in his letters and presents himself as seeking to create and consolidate, for our purposes a general description of those communities will suffice. To begin with, Paul speaks of those communities bringing together on an equal basis not only Jews and non-Jews, men and women, free persons and slaves, but also people of different socioeconomic backgrounds, including both rich and poor, educated and uneducated.[73] Within these communities, there were people with many different occupations and gifts, and Paul expected all to use their gifts, talents, time, and resources to build one another up. Like a body with many different parts, each of which is necessary and vital for the others, each community was to be characterized by unity and harmony among its members, and all were to live in solidarity with one another, rejoicing with those who rejoiced and weeping with those who wept.[74]

According to Paul, what is to distinguish and identify these communities above all else is the love that all are to show not only to one another but also to those outside of the community. The exhortation to live in love appears far more than any other in Paul's letters.[75] Paul understands that love in terms of seeking the good of others together with one's own.[76] In Phil 2:1-4, he exhorts believers to show "affection and compassion" for one another, "being of the same mind, sharing the same love, united in spirit, thinking the same thoughts," acting out of humility and deference for others rather than selfishness or vanity, looking out for the interests of others and not merely their own. In 1 Corinthians 13, one of the passages most frequently cited from his epistles, Paul goes into considerable detail as to

---

73. See, for example, 1 Cor 1:17-29; 11:17-34; Gal 3:28; Phlm 10-20. On the social diversity within the Pauline communities, see Wayne A. Meeks, *The First Urban Christians: The Social World of the Apostle Paul* (New Haven: Yale University Press, 1983), 51-73; Young-Ho Park, *Paul's Ekklesia as a Civic Assembly: Understanding the People of God in their Politico-Social World*, WUNT 2/393 (Tübingen: Mohr Siebeck, 2015), 178-217.

74. See Rom 12:4-8, 15-16; 1 Cor 12:4-31. On the centrality of the notion of solidarity in Paul's thought, see William S. Campbell, *Paul and the Creation of Christian Identity*, LNTS 322 (London: T & T Clark, 2006), 35-38. Neil Elliott defines Paul's objectives in terms of forming communities of discernment, resistance, and solidarity (*Liberating Paul: The Justice of God and the Politics of the Apostle* [Minneapolis: Fortress, 2006], 189-214).

75. On the strong emphasis on love in Paul's epistles, see Wright, *Paul and the Faithfulness of God*, 1118-21.

76. See Rom 13:9; 1 Cor 10:24.

what the love or *agapē* of which he speaks involves. That love is patient and kind rather than jealous, boastful, arrogant, or unbecoming. It does not insist on its own way, irritate others intentionally, hold grudges toward them, or rejoice at their misfortunes. Instead, "it bears all things, believes all things, hopes all things, endures all things," and never falters (vv. 4-8).

Throughout his epistles, Paul repeatedly calls on believers to build up or edify one another.[77] This exhortation is especially common in the passages in which he is stressing the freedom that believers enjoy in Christ. Rather than laying down hard and fast rules of conduct, he tells his readers to follow their conscience and make decisions based on the way in which others will be affected by those decisions.[78]

In several passages from his epistles, Paul offers lists of behaviors and attitudes that believers in Christ are to avoid. These include wickedness, covetousness, malice, quarreling, deceit, slander, insolence, arrogance, animosity, boastfulness, callousness, cruelty, carousing, idolatry, sexual immorality, selfishness, conceit, dissension, and other vices.[79] Elsewhere he condemns things such as judging others, stubbornness, divisiveness, hypocrisy, self-indulgence, grumbling, and exploitation.[80] Paul contrasts these things with virtues such as perseverance, integrity, hope, generosity, sympathy, tenderness, concord, goodness, thankfulness, joyfulness, faithfulness, encouragement, consolation, self-control, gentleness, and respect.[81] Of course, all of the virtues that Paul mentions can be regarded as expressions of love, while the vices consist of behaviors that are contrary to love.

In his Epistle to the Romans, Paul exhorts the believers in Rome to do what is "good and acceptable and perfect," practicing sobriety, unselfishness, and hospitality as they serve, teach, exhort, assist, and care for each other. They are to love one another with a love that is genuine, cling to what is good, bless their enemies, associate with the lowly, refrain from paying evil for evil, seek to be at peace with all, and "not be overcome by evil, but overcome evil with good" (Rom 12:3-21). Rather than presenting their members to sin as instruments of wickedness and injustice, believers are to present themselves and their members to God as instruments of justice and righteousness (6:13, 19). All are to set their minds on things of the Spirit rather than things of the flesh (8:5-7; 13:14). They are to show respect and consideration for others, conduct themselves in love and integrity rather than following the passions of their flesh, and care especially for those who are weak rather than judging them or doing anything that might cause

---

77. See especially 1 Cor 8:1; 14:1-5, 12, 26; 2 Cor 10:8; 12:19; 13:10; 1 Thess 5:11.

78. See especially Rom 14:1–15:6; 1 Cor 8:9-13; 10:23-30; 14:1-33; 2 Cor 8:7–9:15; Gal 5:13–6:5; 1 Thess 5:21-22; Phlm 8-14.

79. See Rom 1:29-31; 13:13; 1 Cor 5:10-11; Gal 5:19-21.

80. See Rom 2:1, 5; 14:10; 1 Cor 11:17-22; Gal 2:13; 5:13; Phil 2:14; 1 Thess 4:6.

81. See Rom 5:4; 12:7-10; 1 Cor 14:3; Gal 5:22-23; Phil 4:5-6; 1 Thess 5:11-15.

them to stumble and fall (13:7–15:7). Paul exhorts his readers in Rome to welcome one another, oppose those who cause strife and friction, and be "wise in what is good and guileless in what is evil" (15:7; 16:17, 19). Above all, they are to walk in love by pursuing whatever promotes peace and builds others up (14:15, 19).

Similarly, Paul exhorts the Corinthian believers to heal the divisions that result from arrogance, immaturity, feelings of superiority, and contempt for others (1 Cor 1:10–4:21). He criticizes them for accepting blatant immorality in their midst and for taking one another to court for their affairs to be judged by unbelievers rather than resolving conflicts in their own midst.[82] According to Paul, all are to show special regard for their sisters and brothers who have weak consciences (1 Cor 8:11-13). Paul reproaches the Corinthians for being contentious in the way they conduct themselves in their worship, becoming drunk and failing to show consideration for others when celebrating the Lord's Supper, and letting themselves be deceived by others.[83] At the same time, he exhorts them to demonstrate their love for one another by using their gifts for the common good and to share what they have with those in need.[84]

Paul's primary concern in his letter to the Galatians is that the Galatian believers have turned to a "different gospel" by paying attention to those who are pressuring them to submit to circumcision and the Jewish law.[85] Throughout that letter, however, he also equates faithfulness to the gospel that he proclaims with ethical behavior that is pleasing to God. Rather than gratifying the desires of the flesh, the Galatians are to walk by the Spirit and produce the Spirit's fruit (5:16-25). They are to restore in a spirit of gentleness those who have fallen into trespasses, bear one another's burdens, not think too highly of themselves, share what they have with those who teach them, and not lose heart in doing good to all people, but especially to those who belong to the family of faith (6:1-10).

In Philippians, Paul exhorts his readers to live in love, harmony, and unity, imitating his example so as to live a life worthy of the gospel and shine brightly like luminaries in the world.[86] All are to focus their thoughts on "whatever is true, whatever is honorable, whatever is right, whatever is pure, whatever is pleasing, whatever is reputable," and everything that is virtuous and commendable (4:8). Paul's prayer for the Philippian believers is that their love "may abound more and more in knowledge and understanding" in order that they may "approve what is admirable and be pure

---

82. See 1 Cor 5:1-13; 6:1-8.
83. See 1 Cor 11:2-34; 2 Cor 11:3-21.
84. See 1 Cor 12:7; 16:1-3; 2 Cor 8:1–9:15.
85. See Gal 1:6-9; 3:1-5; 5:1-13; 6:12-13.
86. See Phil 1:3-7, 27; 2:15; 3:17; 4:9.

and blameless for the day of Christ, filled with the fruits of righteousness which come through Jesus Christ" (1:9-11).

At the outset of 1 Thessalonians, Paul thanks God for the labor of faith, love, steadfastness, and hope that the believers in Thessalonica have carried out before praising them for their welcoming spirit and expressing his desire that they walk in a manner worthy of God.[87] He then tells them: "May the Lord cause you to increase and abound in your love for one another and for all people, as we do in our love for you, so that he may establish your hearts unblemished in holiness before our God and Father at the coming of our Lord Jesus with all his holy ones" (3:12-13). In his closing to the letter, Paul writes:

> Therefore encourage one another and build one another up, just as you are already doing. But we implore you, sisters and brothers, to respect those who work among you and care for you in the Lord and instruct you, and to esteem them very highly in love because of their work. Be at peace with one another. And we exhort you, brothers and sisters, to admonish the indolent, encourage those who are disheartened, help the weak, and be patient with all. See that none of you repays evil for evil, but always seek what is good for one another and for all persons. . . . Examine everything; hold fast to what is good; keep yourselves from every form of evil (5:11-15, 21-22).

In his letter to Philemon, Paul expresses his joy and contentment at the love Philemon has shown for others and the way he has refreshed them while at the same time appealing to that love on behalf of Onesimus his slave (Phlm 4-14). In a request that many in Paul's day would have found surprising, Paul also asks Philemon to manifest his fellowship with Paul by receiving Onesimus back "no longer as a slave, but as more than a slave, a beloved brother" (15-17). At the same time, he offers to compensate Philemon for any wrong Onesimus has caused or any debt he has incurred (18-19).

In addition to all of the explicit admonitions and exhortations that appear in Paul's letters, there are countless others that are implicit. In fact, virtually every passage from those letters can be seen as having some type of ethical implication. The customary greeting that Paul uses at the outset of his letters, wishing his readers grace and peace from God the Father and Christ as Lord, implies that they should continue and grow in their relationship to God as their Father and to Christ as their Lord and that the grace and peace of which Paul speaks should be reflected in every aspect of their life. Similarly, even though Paul does not explicitly exhort his readers to live in faith in Romans 4, his discussion of Abraham's faith throughout that chapter clearly supposes that believers are to live in that same faith, fully assured that God will fulfill his promises (v. 21). When Paul explains in Romans 9–11 that many of his fellow Israelites according to the flesh

---

87. See 1 Thess 1:2-8; 2:12; 3:6.

have not believed in Christ because God has temporarily hardened their hearts, his words imply that his readers should not have hard hearts and at the same time should not judge those who belong to Israel or act arrogantly toward them (11:17-31). The warm and affectionate greetings he sends certain individuals at the conclusion of his Letter to the Romans imply that his readers should treat one another and others with the same warmth and affection (Rom 16:1-16). The explanation he provides for the Corinthians regarding how the bodies of believers will be resurrected and what those resurrection bodies will be like serves not only to provide them with knowledge or information but also to encourage them to remain "steadfast and immovable, always abounding in the work of the Lord" (1 Cor 15:35-58). Likewise, in the many passages in which Paul mentions the love of God and Christ for believers as well as his own love for them and for God, Paul is not merely making observations about love but communicating implicitly the idea that their lives are to be filled with the same type of love.

Virtually everything that Paul writes, therefore, must be seen as projecting to his readers a vision regarding the type of community that Paul is attempting to create and consolidate, and at the same time as an exhortation for them to conform to that vision. To claim that Paul merely wants his readers to believe that his message and the many things he tells them are true so that on that basis they can be saved would be to misunderstand entirely Paul's aims. Clearly, Paul does not regard belief and ethical conduct as separate and unrelated, but instead consistently presupposes that they are intimately connected and form part of a unified whole. By definition, the lives of all who truly believe in the gospel he proclaims will be radically transformed. If such a transformation does not take place, they have not comprehended that gospel or truly believed in it.

As noted above, the name that Paul gives to this community throughout his letters is the *ekklēsia*.[88] It is a community that is defined by the gospel and the characteristics just mentioned, all of which Paul associates with the gospel he proclaims. Just as Paul can refer to the gospel as both the gospel of God and the gospel of Christ, so also for Paul the community of believers in Christ is both the *ekklēsia* of God and the *ekklēsia* of Christ, as well as the *ekklēsia* of God in Christ.[89]

Salvation, Israel, and the Nations

Like many other Jews of his time, Paul looked forward to the day in which God would fulfill the promises he had made regarding Israel and the world. He regards the present age as evil and as dominated by rulers and forces

---

88. On the origin and background of this term, see Dunn, *Theology*, 537-38.

89. See Rom 16:16; 1 Cor 1:2; 10:32; 11:16, 22; 15:9; 2 Cor 1:1; Gal 1:13; 1 Thess 2:14; cf. Gal 1:22; 1 Thess 1:1.

that are opposed to God, chief among whom is the "god of this age."[90] In Rom 8:17-25, Paul affirms that one day creation will be "set free from its bondage to corruption" so as to be transformed into a condition of glory.

As one would expect, what distinguishes Paul's view of the salvation to come from that of other Jews of his day is the role that he ascribes to Christ in that salvation. Christ will return in glory and power to raise the dead and judge human beings together with God.[91] Those who are judged to be righteous will receive eternal life, that is, the life of the age to come.[92] Satan will be crushed, and all will be subjected to Christ so that he may then in turn subject all to God. In that way, from that time on all will live together with Christ in God's presence.[93]

In contrast to many contemporary interpretations of his thought, Paul never affirms that the age to come has "dawned" or been "ushered in" by Christ.[94] While he affirms in Rom 13:11-12 that "the night has advanced and the day has drawn near," his idea is merely that the awaited day of salvation is closer than it was previously: "for our salvation is nearer now than it was when we first believed."[95] He affirms essentially the same idea in 1 Cor 7:29-31, where he writes that "the time has grown short" and that "the present form of this world is passing away," as well as in 1 Cor 10:11, where he speaks of believers as "those to whom the ends of the ages have arrived."[96] His idea is not that the end has come *in part* but merely that it will come *soon*. Although in Gal 1:4 Paul says that Christ "gave himself in order to deliver us from the present evil age," strictly speaking, he does not affirm that this deliverance has already taken place, since the present age *remains* evil (cf. Rom 12:2).[97] As just noted above, Paul regards the world as continuing to lie under the domination of the rulers of this age.

---

90. See 1 Cor 2:6-8; 3:18-21; 2 Cor 4:4; Gal 1:4.

91. See Rom 2:6-16; 8:11; 1 Cor 4:5; 15:20-57; Phil 3:20-21; 1 Thess 1:10; 4:13–5:5; 5:23.

92. See Rom 2:7; 5:21; 6:22-23; 2 Cor 4:17–5:4; Gal 6:8.

93. See Rom 16:20; 1 Cor 15:24-28; 1 Thess 4:16-17.

94. See, for example, Wright, *Paul and the Faithfulness of God*, 1061-78, 1101-13.

95. This point is rightly noted by Michael Wolter: "Sie dauert noch an, und darum ist es noch »Nacht«" (*Die Brief an der Römer*, EKKNT 6 [Ostfildern: Patmos, 2014/2019], 2:340).

96. Neither in these passages nor anywhere else in his epistles does Paul affirm that "a new age had dawned and that the old age had passed away" or that believers "have been delivered or redeemed from the present age. . . ." (so Arland J. Hultgren, *Christ and His Benefits: Christology and Redemption in the New Testament* [Minneapolis: Fortress, 1987], 39).

97. As David J. Lull stresses, the tradition Paul quotes in Gal 1:4 "implies that the *present* age, even after the coming of Christ, is *still* 'evil'" and thus that "the end of 'the present evil age' has not yet come. . . ." ("Salvation History: Theology in 1 Thessalonians, Philemon, Philippians, and Galatians. A Response to N. T. Wright, R. B. Hays, and R.

There is nothing in Paul's letters, therefore, to substantiate the claim that he believed that some type of "change of ages" had already taken place through Christ or that the new age had in some sense been "inaugurated." Undoubtedly, at present believers in Christ are able to participate in many of the blessings associated with the age to come, including especially the gift of God's Spirit.[98] When Paul speaks of a "new creation" in 2 Cor 5:17 and Gal 6:15, the context indicates that he is not referring to anything that has taken place in the cosmos but only to the new existence of believers themselves as they live out their faith in Christ.[99]

According to many traditional interpretations of Paul's thought, what he ultimately sought was the salvation of others in the world to come rather than some type of salvation in the present world. While there is undoubtedly a sense in which Paul regards salvation as something that will be fully realized only at the *eschaton*, such a dichotomy between the present and the future must be considered foreign to his thought. As was noted at the outset of this chapter, in biblical thought, in order for people to experience well-being and wholeness, they must be committed to living in a way that makes that well-being and wholeness possible. Those who practice violent and destructive behavior, therefore, are unable to experience the good that God desires for all, not only in the age to come, but in the present age as well. When Paul affirms in 1 Cor 6:9-10 that those who abuse and do harm to others in various ways "will not inherit the reign of God," his words should be understood not merely in the sense that God will not allow them to enter into that reign because their behavior displeases him, but more precisely in the sense that the way of life of those who abuse and harm others will make it impossible for them to experience the life and blessings of

---

Scroggs," in *Pauline Theology*, vol. 1: *Thessalonians, Philippians, Galatians, Philemon*, ed. Jouette M. Bassler [Minneapolis: Fortress, 1991], 247-65 [264]).

98. See Rom 8:14; 2 Cor 1:22; 5:5; Gal 4:6. Whether Paul's allusions to the Holy Spirit as an *arrabōn* in 2 Cor 1:22 and 5:5 are understood in the sense of a guarantee (so Kurt Erlemann, "Der Geist als ἀρραβών, 2 Kor 5,5," *ZNW* 83 [1992]: 203-9), a pledge (so Yon-Gyong Kwon, "Ἀρραβών as Pledge in Second Corinthians," *NTS* 54 [2008]: 525-41), or a "first installment" (so Margaret E. Thrall, *A Critical and Exegetical Commentary on the Second Epistle to the Corinthians*, ICC [Edinburgh: T & T Clark, 1994], 1:158), at most Paul is affirming that in the future at the *eschaton* believers will receive in full what they have at present received only in part. When Paul affirms that the end is near and that the present age is on the verge of passing away, therefore, he is not speaking of any type of process that has begun or been "inaugurated" and will over time come to completion in the same way that dawn gradually gives way to full daylight.

99. As Moyer V. Hubbard affirms in his study on the subject, "Paul's new creation expresses a reality *intra nos* not a reality *extra nos*. . . ." (*New Creation in Paul's Letters and Thought*, SNTSMS 119 [Cambridge: Cambridge University Press, 2002], 232; see especially his conclusions at 233-41).

the age to come. In other words, what displeases God is that their lifestyle destroys their own well-being and that of others as well. If God demands that human beings practice justice and love, it is *for their sake* rather than his own. Only those who are committed to living in conformity with God's will, therefore, are able to inherit the reign of God, which for Paul consists of "justice, peace, and joy in the Holy Spirit" (Rom 14:17).

For this reason, it must be stressed that what Paul sought was not merely to bring people to faith so that they might be saved, as if faith alone were the condition for salvation. Rather, what he sought was that they come to live as part of the type of communities that he dedicated himself to establishing and strengthening so that there they might be brought to live in a way that would make their salvation and wholeness possible. To say that Paul's objective was the formation of such communities and to say that his objective was the salvation of others is to affirm, not *two different* things, but the *same* thing. By being brought to live in accordance with God's will in the present by means of their participation in Paul's communities, those who came to faith in the gospel would be enabled to experience the blessings of the age to come as well.

Although some Jews expected that one day many people of other nations would come to worship and serve the God of Israel alongside of them, Paul not only sees this inclusion of the gentiles as a present reality but also stresses repeatedly that gentile believers in Christ share the same status in relation to God as those who are Jewish. There is no difference between them with regard to righteousness, since God will judge and justify members of both groups on the same basis, independently of their observance of the Torah.[100] Through faith in Christ, gentiles are just as much Abraham's children as those who descend from Abraham physically.[101] Because the gentile believers in Christ whom Paul compares to branches taken from a wild olive tree have been grafted into the same cultivated olive tree as those who belong to Israel, they are now just as much a part of that tree as the latter are (Rom 11:17-24). Paul repeatedly uses the language of election and call that in Jewish circles was applied almost exclusively to Israel in order to claim that gentiles are also the chosen of God.[102] After speaking of those whom God has "called, not from among the Jews only but also from among the nations," Paul continues: "As he also says through Hosea, 'I will call "my people" those who were not my people, and call "beloved" her who was not beloved; and in the place where it was said to them "You are not my people," there will they be called children of the living God'" (Rom 9:24-26). It is significant that here, citing the Hebrew Scriptures themselves, Paul applies to gentile believers an adjective generally reserved for the members of Israel alone in ancient

---

100. See Rom 2:6-16; 3:28-30; Gal 2:16.
101. See Rom 4:9-12; 9:8; Gal 3:7-9, 29.
102. See Rom 1:7; 8:28-33; 1 Cor 1:2, 24; 1 Thess 1:4.

Jewish thought: "beloved." For Paul, then, believers from among the nations are loved by God just as much as those who belong to Israel.

For Paul, however, God's love for the nations of the world is manifested not merely in his full acceptance of people from among those nations within the community of believers in Christ but even more so in his active outreach to those nations in an attempt to bring them to live as his own. Contrary to many presentations of Paul's thought, such an outreach was not incidental to his understanding of the gospel, an afterthought, or something that arose merely by accident, but was instead integral to his core convictions regarding God, Christ, and the gospel.[103] While Paul and other of the earliest followers of Christ may not initially have understood the outreach to the gentiles as a central component of the gospel they proclaimed, the favorable response they received among many non-Jews—perhaps unexpectedly— soon made them realize that such an outreach was the logical consequence of that gospel and was by no means secondary to it. Instead, in their minds, that outreach constituted the very essence of the gospel initially proclaimed by Jesus himself to many who were considered to be outside of the realm of God's love. As noted above, Paul defines his task in terms of bringing people of all nations to live in obedience to God so that they may experience God's blessings both in this world and the world to come.[104] For this to happen, it is necessary for those such as Paul to go out to the ends of the earth (Rom 10:18). According to Paul, through Christ and his apostles God had the goal of reconciling the entire world to himself and bringing about the righteousness he desired among all people everywhere.[105] This mission to all of the nations so that together with Israel they might come to form part of a single people is clear evidence that in Paul's thought God loves those nations just as much as he loves Israel. If God had loved them less, rather than seeking to incorporate them into a single community or people together with Israel as his "beloved," he would have willed that they remain separate from Israel so that he might bless Israel more than them. Of course, within this new community or people, each group would maintain its own identity rather than forfeiting it. Their distinct identities would therefore constitute a *basis* for communion and fellowship rather than an *obstacle* to it.

Because in Paul's thought God's love for the nations is as great as his love for Israel, it would be a mistake to attribute to Paul the idea that the salvation of the nations has as its ultimate goal the salvation of Israel. Such

---

103. Paula Fredriksen, for example, writes that "Gentile Christ-followers were initially, in the first years of the movement, an accidental consequence of the gospel's post-crucifixion spread out to mixed pagan-Jewish cities. . . ." (*Paul: The Pagans' Apostle* [New Haven: Yale University Press, 2017], 146, emphasis removed).

104. See Rom 1:5; 5:18-19; 15:18; 16:26.

105. See Rom 5:18; 11:15; 2 Cor 5:18-19.

an idea would imply that the salvation of the nations is not an end in itself but a means toward Israel's salvation, as if the latter were more important and God cared more about Israel than he does for the nations. Undoubtedly, Paul affirms in Romans 11 that his ministry and the salvation of the gentiles are intended to provoke the members of God's people Israel to jealousy, and that "a partial hardening has happened to Israel until the fullness of the gentiles comes in, and in this way all Israel will be saved" (Rom 11:11, 14, 25-26). In the thought of both Paul and the Hebrew Scriptures, however, God not only acts in certain ways in relation to the nations in order to bless and save Israel, but he also acts in certain ways in relation to Israel in order to bless and save the nations. Therefore, for Paul to affirm that his ministry to the gentiles and their salvation is intended to provoke Israel to jealousy and thereby bring about Israel's salvation is by no means to give priority to the salvation of Israel over against that of the nations. In Paul's mind, both are equally important to God.

Although Paul stresses God's love for the nations in his letters, by no means does he maintain that, because through Christ God now considers many people from among the nations as his people, he no longer loves Israel in the same way that he has in the past. On the contrary, in Rom 11:28 he insists that Israel continues to be "beloved for the sake of the fathers; for the gifts and the calling of God are irrevocable." Like other Jews, Paul seems to have believed that the love of God for Israel is special and unique and thus that it has taken certain forms that it does not always take for the nations as well. By no means, however, does such a belief necessarily imply that God's love for Israel is greater than his love for the nations. To affirm that something is special and unique is not necessarily to affirm that it is also greater. In Paul's thought, therefore, throughout history God has related in a special way to Israel in order that his purposes both for Israel and the nations might now be accomplished through Christ, who as Abraham's seed was born under the law so that both Jews and non-Jews might live together as Abraham's sons and daughters and children of God.[106] In Paul's own words, "Christ has become a servant of the circumcised on behalf of God's truth in order to confirm the promises given to the ancestors, and so that the nations may glorify God for his mercy; as it is written, 'For this reason I will confess you among the nations and sing praises to your name'; and again he says, 'Rejoice, O nations, with his people!'" (Rom 15:8-10). Here Christ is said to have become a servant to Israel in order that the gentiles might come to live as God's people as well. According to Paul, God's purpose in calling Abraham and commanding him and his male descendants to be circumcised was "to make him the ancestor of all who believe without being circumcised so that righteousness might also be reckoned to them, as

---

106. Gal 3:16-18, 25-29; 4:4-5.

well as the ancestor of those who are not only circumcised but also follow the example of faith that our ancestor Abraham had before he was circumcised" (Rom 4:11-12). As Paul insists in Galatians as well, God had chosen Abraham and elected Israel to be his people not only so that Israel might be blessed but also so that the nations might be blessed through them (Gal 3:8-10). God's intention was that "the blessing of Abraham might come to the nations through Christ Jesus" (Gal 3:14).

Finally, it is important to stress that Paul conceives of the *ekklēsia* or community of believers as something that is by nature very distinct from Israel. Unlike Israel, the *ekklēsia* is not an ethnic or political entity, and much less a nation or a race of people. Similarly, the gospel had not been designed to govern the lives of believers in Christ in the same way that the Torah had been given to govern all aspects of the political, social, and economic life of God's people Israel. Whether they were Jewish or gentile, those who came to faith in Christ and the gospel were not expected to abandon or set aside their own ethnicity, customs, traditions, and way of life except insofar as those things might compromise or run contrary to the values and principles of the gospel and the faith associated with it. Instead, both Jews and non-Jews who came to faith in Christ were to live out that faith in the context of their own communities, customs, and cultural identity.

In essence, then, the gospel and the Torah were two very different things that had been designed for different purposes, although in some ways those purposes might overlap, just as certain aspects of the laws of other peoples overlapped with the type of life prescribed by the gospel. For that reason, Jews who came to faith in the gospel were not to abandon observance of the Torah, just as gentiles who came to faith were not to deny or abandon their own identity in order to become Jews and submit to the law and customs of Israel. Instead, as Paul insists in 1 Cor 7:17-24, all believers were to live the life to which they had been called by God and assigned by Christ as Jew, gentile, slave, or free: "Each of you, sisters and brothers, is to remain with God in the condition in which you were called." Because the *ekklēsia* was not the same type of entity as Israel and the Torah was something of a different nature and order than the gospel, in Paul's thought neither was the *ekklēsia* to replace, supplant, or supersede Israel, nor was the gospel to replace, supplant, or supersede the Torah.

CHAPTER 3

REDEFINING HOW GOD SAVES

If the Torah is the means by which God grants his people Israel the blessings of life and shalom that he desires for them, then in order for the Torah to accomplish that task, God must remain active among his people to bring them into conformity with his will as he has made it known in the Torah. As he had promised in the Torah, God was believed to act in history to bless his people when they obeyed his commandments and to discipline and correct them through chastisements when they did not. God also gave his people leaders such as priests, prophets, and teachers to enable them to live in accordance with his commandments, as well as rulers who were to help bring about the conditions necessary for his people to enjoy God's blessings in the land God had given them.

Paul's conviction that the salvation and well-being that God desires for all people is given primarily through Christ rather than through the Torah independently of Christ leads to a very different understanding of how God saves. While Paul's proclamation that Jesus is the Messiah promised to Israel is undoubtedly rooted in Jewish beliefs, that proclamation also departs from Jewish thought in ascribing to Jesus a centrality that the Messiah does not have in any forms of the Second Temple Judaism known to us. Among those Jews who believed in a Messiah, the Torah generally remained central and the Messiah was considered secondary, since the Messiah existed for the sake of the Torah and was to serve as God's instrument for establishing the conditions necessary for Israel to live in accordance with the Torah in the land God had given his people. In the thought of Paul, the Torah is to lead people to the Messiah rather than the Messiah leading people to the Torah, because it is through Jesus the Messiah rather than through the Torah that God will ultimately bring to fulfillment his promises of salvation for Israel and the nations. While everything that God has done and will continue to do through his Son contributes in various ways to that salvation, for Paul it is especially Jesus' willingness to give up his life by accepting death on a cross that has made it possible for God's saving purposes among human beings to be accomplished through him.

THE TORAH AND GOD'S SAVING ACTIVITY IN JEWISH THOUGHT

In one way or another, all of the various types of leaders and authorities that God was thought to raise up for his people were to serve as his instruments for enabling his people to attain his blessings by living in accordance with the Torah. Through their service in the temple, the priests and Levites focused the people's attention on God as their sovereign Creator, Lord, and King so that they might submit to him and the commandments he had given them out of love for them. The worship over which the priests presided served to express, maintain, and strengthen the people's commitment to offer up their lives to God so as to do his will as he had made it known in the Torah. The priests were also expected to instruct the people in the Torah and urge them to observe it faithfully.[1]

At various moments in Israel's history, but especially when the people fell into sin and injustice, God was also thought to raise up prophets to speak to the people on his behalf. In addition to calling on the people to turn back to God and his law, the prophets interpreted God's activity in history so that the people might understand the ways in which God was at work through the events they experienced to strengthen the people's relation to him and to bring them back to the path they were to follow for their own good when they had strayed from it. Although by the first century CE many Jews believed that God no longer sent his people prophets in the way that he had previously in Israel's history, there were still individuals who were seen by some Jews as fulfilling a prophetic role, such as John the Baptist.[2] Rather than looking primarily to prophetic figures to discern God's will for their lives, however, Jews in the Second Temple period increasingly came to look to teachers or rabbis to provide them with the interpretations of the Torah necessary to observe it properly. Among these

---

1. As E. P. Sanders observes, most of the Jewish priests served as teachers and magistrates when not carrying out their duties at the Jerusalem temple (*Judaism: Practice and Belief, 63 BCE–66 CE* [Philadelphia: Trinity Press International, 1992], 170-71).

2. George W. E. Nickelsburg notes that among Jews in antiquity it was commonly thought that prophecy in Israel had come to an end during the Persian period (*Ancient Judaism and Christian Origins: Diversity, Continuity and Transformation* [Minneapolis: Fortress, 2003], 96-97). On the Jewish prophetic figures during the Second Temple period, see Joan E. Taylor, *The Immerser: John the Baptist within Second Temple Judaism,* SHJ (Grand Rapids: Eerdmans, 1997), 223-34; Rebecca Gray, *Prophetic Figures in Late Second Temple Jewish Palestine: The Evidence from Josephus* (Oxford: Oxford University Press, 1993), 114-63.

teachers were figures such as Gamaliel, Shammai, Hillel, and the Teacher of Righteousness mentioned in the Dead Sea Scrolls.[3]

Although the monarchs and rulers God placed over his people were generally not viewed as religious authorities, it was nevertheless expected that they not only submit obediently to the Torah themselves but also promote and enforce obedience to its precepts among the people over whom they governed. In principle, they were to embody the type of leadership and faithfulness to God that had been characteristic of Israel's judges in the period prior to the monarchy and of kings such as David, Hezekiah, and Josiah, all of whom had fostered observance of the Torah among God's people.

Many Jews expected that God would continue to raise up military leaders for his people in order to deliver them from their enemies as he saw fit. These might include not only kings or rulers but also figures such as those who had made it possible to expel Antiochus Epiphanes from the land of Israel in the time of the Maccabees. Of course, many Jews also anticipated the coming of a Messiah through whom God would act to restore Israel's fortunes. Their hope was that they might be able to live in peace in the land God had given them, practicing the Torah so as to enjoy the blessings that came through its observance. Some Jews even expected more than one Messiah and ascribed other tasks and roles to the Messiah(s) whom God would send, such as teaching the people and carrying out priestly activities on their behalf in relation to God.[4]

In some sense, then, all of these different figures were understood as God's agents or instruments to bring salvation and shalom to his people. While these figures might fulfill different roles in that regard, ultimately they would make it possible for God's people to experience salvation and shalom by enabling them to live in accordance with the Torah. Of course, if at some point God intended to bring people from the other nations to serve and worship him alongside his people Israel, it would be necessary for some of these same salvific figures to serve as his instruments to accomplish his saving purposes among those nations as well.

---

3. On these figures and other Jewish teachers and rabbis in the first century CE, see Anthony J. Saldarini, *Pharisees, Scribes, and Sadducees in Palestinian Society: A Sociological Approach* (Wilmington, DE: Michael Glazier, 1988), 199-220. On Qumran's Teacher of Righteousness, see Hartmut Stegemann, *The Library of Qumran: On the Essenes, Qumran, John the Baptist, and Jesus* (Grand Rapids: Eerdmans, 1998), 147-57.

4. On these points, see Ed Condra, *Salvation for the Righteous Revealed: Jesus amid Covenantal and Messianic Expectations in Second Temple Judaism*, AGJU 51 (Leiden: Brill, 2002), 198-271; John J. Collins, "What Was Distinctive about Messianic Expectation at Qumran?," in *The Bible and the Dead Sea Scrolls: The Second Princeton Symposium on Judaism and Christian Origins*, ed. James H. Charlesworth (Waco, TX: Baylor University Press, 2006), 2:71-92.

SALVATION THROUGH CHRIST AND THE CROSS
IN THE THOUGHT OF PAUL

Throughout his epistles, Paul repeatedly defines his objective in terms of bringing others to live under Christ as members of the community that looks to him as their Lord, that is, the *ekklēsia*. The content of his proclamation is not only the gospel of Christ and the word of Christ, but Christ himself.[5] He tells the Corinthians: "For I determined to know nothing among you except Christ crucified" (1 Cor 2:2; cf. 1:24). What he seeks to see confirmed among them is simply the "testimony concerning Christ" (1 Cor 1:6). Through his ministry the Corinthians have been "called into fellowship with [God's] Son, Jesus Christ our Lord" (1 Cor 1:9). At the outset of Romans, Paul claims to have been "set apart for the gospel of God," which is also "the gospel concerning his Son" (Rom 1:1-3). The "word of faith" that he announces is that "if you confess with your lips that Jesus is Lord and believe in your heart that God raised him from the dead, you will be saved" (Rom 10:8-9). In Gal 4:19, Paul speaks of being in labor until Christ is formed in the Galatians, while in 2 Cor 11:2 he writes that he betrothed the Corinthians to Christ by presenting them to Christ as a pure virgin. Paul also seeks to bring others to be clothed in Christ (Rom 13:14; Gal 3:27). In Phil 3:2-9, Paul contrasts the life he previously lived under the law alone with the life that is now his through Christ, claiming that all that he valued previously is loss and rubbish in comparison with knowing and gaining Christ so as to be found in him. Rather than seeking to bring people of other nations to form part of Israel and live under the Torah, then, Paul's objective is that they come to live as Christ's own as members of his body so that they may attain salvation and life through him.

To some extent, Paul regards all that God has done through Christ as salvific. This includes not only his coming into the world and the things that he taught in word and deed during his ministry, but also his ongoing activity on behalf of believers from heaven.[6] As the one who makes known

---

5. See Rom 10:17; 16:25; 1 Cor 9:12; 1 Thess 3:12.

6. See Rom 7:24; 8:11-23, 34; 15:8; 1 Cor 7:10-11; 9:14; 2 Cor 13:3; Phil 1:6; 1 Thess 3:11-12. Following scholars such as Rudolf Bultmann, for a long time it was common to claim that Paul was either uninterested in Jesus' teaching and ministry or unacquainted with it: "Jesus' manner of life, his ministry, his personality, his character play no role at all; neither does Jesus' message" (*Theology of the New Testament*, trans. Kendrick Grobel [New York: Scribner, 1951/1955], 1:294). In more recent times, however, scholars have increasingly come to question that view. See, for example, James D. G. Dunn, *The Theology of Paul the Apostle* (Grand Rapids: Eerdmans, 1998), 189-95; David Wenham, *Paul: Follower of Jesus or Founder of Christianity?* (Grand Rapids: Eerdmans, 1995), 354-63, 380-92. On this discussion, see also Victor Paul Furnish, "The Jesus-Paul Debate: From Baur to Bultmann," in *Paul and Jesus: Collected Essays*, ed. Alexander J. M. Wedderburn, JSNTSup 137 (Sheffield: Sheffield Academic Press, 1989), 17-50.

God's word and will in definitive fashion, Christ fulfills not only the functions associated with the prophets and teachers of Israel but also the role of the Torah itself. According to Paul, Christ himself is "the power and wisdom of God" (1 Cor 1:24). For Paul, Jesus is not merely a figure of past history but a living Lord who continues to be intimately involved in the life of believers and his *ekklēsia*.[7] Paul also ascribes a central role to Christ in the consummation of the salvation that is to come at the end.[8] As the Son of God descended from David and now exalted as Lord, Christ also fulfills the expectations associated with Israel's Messiah. According to Paul, he is establishing his reign now and will one day establish God's reign definitively by overcoming every other ruler, power, and authority and subjecting all things to God (1 Cor 15:24-28). Christ also fulfills the priestly function of interceding to God on behalf of God's people (Rom 8:34).

While all that God has done and continues to do through Christ contributes to the salvation of believers, in Paul's thought it is especially Christ's death that has made that salvation possible. Paul affirms that Jesus died for others and for their sins, tells his readers that they have been justified through Jesus' blood and reconciled to God through his death, and says that Christ has redeemed them from the curse of the law by becoming a curse for them.[9] He also speaks of believers being dead and crucified together with Christ and repeatedly looks to the cross to define who believers are and how they are to live.[10]

Nowhere in his epistles, however, does Paul ever offer any type of explanation as to the precise manner in which Jesus' death leads to the salvation of believers. In an attempt to supply the explanation that is lacking in those epistles, interpreters have looked to a number of ideas. Chief among these is the notion that in his death Christ endured in the place of sinful human beings the punishment or consequences to which they were subject on account of their sins, thereby delivering them from that punishment or those consequences. Interpreters have also attributed to Paul the idea that human beings are saved by participating in Christ and his death. This participation is often understood in a mystical, ontological, or "real" sense so as to claim that believers or human beings in general actually share in the

---

7. On Paul's understanding of the ongoing presence and activity of the risen Jesus, see Chris Tilling, *Paul's Divine Christology*, WUNT 2/323 (Tübingen: Mohr Siebeck, 2012), 147-54.

8. See Rom 2:16; 5:9-10; 11:26; 1 Cor 1:8; 11:26; 2 Cor 5:10; Phil 1:6; 3:20-21; 1 Thess 1:10; 3:13; 4:14; 5:23.

9. See Rom 4:25; 5:6-10, 18-19; 8:32; 14:15; 1 Cor 8:11; 15:3; 2 Cor 5:14-21; Gal 1:4; 2:20; 3:13; 1 Thess 5:9.

10. See Rom 6:3-11; 7:4-6; 1 Cor 1:17-18, 23-24; 2 Cor 4:10; 13:4; Gal 2:19-20; 5:11, 24; 6:12, 14, 17; Phil 2:1-8; 3:18.

very same sufferings and death that Christ endured when he was crucified.[11] Paul's allusions to the salvific significance of Jesus' death have also been understood on the basis of the *Christus Victor* idea, according to which Jesus has conquered powers such as sin, death, the devil, and the law by means of his death, thereby liberating human beings from those powers.[12] It is also common to claim that in Paul's thought the way in which Jesus' death saves others is by providing them with a pattern, example, or model for them to follow and imitate.[13]

All of these interpretations of Paul's thought regarding Jesus' death are problematic for many reasons. They raise many theological problems that seem to admit of no satisfactory solution. Among these problems is the claim that all human beings have been saved objectively by Jesus' death, yet are *not* actually saved by his death unless they come to faith in him. In that case, what ultimately saves human beings is their faith in Christ and his death rather than his death itself. Supposedly, Christ's death fulfills some requirement or condition that had previously made it impossible for human beings to be saved and forgiven by God simply by looking to him in faith and trust. If faith and trust in God had been sufficient for that salvation and forgiveness to be theirs, Christ would not have had to die. What has changed as a result of Christ's death, therefore, is that those who previously could *not* be saved by faith now *can* be saved by faith. Such an idea clearly seems to run contrary to Paul's thought, especially in passages such as Romans 4, where he speaks of Abraham being justified by faith long before Christ's coming.

Each of the different interpretations of Christ's death just mentioned also involves ascribing to Paul ideas and assumptions that are not only absent from his epistles but also run contrary to what we find in the Hebrew Scriptures and Second Temple Jewish literature. Nowhere in any of those writings do we find the idea that it was impossible for God to save human beings or forgive them their sins without the death of a sacrificial victim, and much less that of a human being who would take their place as their substitute. What God wanted from his people was not the suffering and

---

11. See, for example, Albert Schweitzer, *The Mysticism of Paul the Apostle*, trans. William Montgomery (Baltimore: Johns Hopkins University Press, 1998), 101-49; E. P. Sanders, *Paul and Palestinian Judaism: A Comparison of Patterns of Religion* (Philadelphia: Fortress, 1977), 497-508, 521-23. On the history of this interpretation of Paul, see especially L. Gregory Bloomquist, *The Function of Suffering in Philippians*, JSNTSup 78 (Sheffield: JSOT, 1993), 35-49.

12. See Gustav Aulén, *Christus Victor: An Historical Study of the Three Main Types of the Idea of Atonement*, trans. A. G. Hebert (New York: MacMillan, 1969), 63-73.

13. For a survey of these different interpretations of Paul's thought regarding Jesus' death, see Stephen Finlan, *Problems with Atonement: The Origins of, and Controversy about, the Atonement Doctrine* (Collegeville, MN: Liturgical Press, 2005), 39-103.

death of an innocent victim but the practice of love, justice, and righteousness among all his people for their own sake. That alone could please him and put away his wrath.

Similarly, human beings were not thought to be in need of some representative savior figure to whom they might be united physically, mystically, ontologically, or in some other sense in order to be saved. Nor did they require that such a figure suffer and die so that they might come to participate in his suffering and death. Contrary to what many New Testament scholars have argued, nothing in Paul's epistles, the New Testament, the Hebrew Scriptures, or Second Temple Jewish writings ever presents the human plight in such a manner. For Paul, the manner in which people come to live under the lordship of the crucified, risen, and exalted Christ is simply through faith in him rather than through some type of mysterious "transfer" effected by an actual participation in him and his death.[14] While human beings need to be liberated from powers such as sin, death, and the devil, neither God nor human beings were in need of the death of a Messiah or savior figure in order for such a liberation to take place. As the sovereign and all-powerful creator of the universe, God is free to overcome and destroy any power in heaven or on earth at any moment simply with a word. In order to raise the dead and bring about the redemption of all people and things, it was not necessary for God first to send his Son into the world and have him put to death on a cross so that human beings might participate in that death in some mysterious fashion in the present. Nowhere in Paul's epistles does he ever make such a claim. Similarly, while he certainly sees the love that Christ manifested in life and death as something that others are to imitate, Paul never claims that what human beings needed in order to be saved was that God send his Son and hand him over to the cross so that they might thereby be given a model, pattern, or example that they might subsequently reproduce in their own lives.

Common to all of these understandings of Christ's work is the idea that Christ's death fulfills some requirement or condition for human salvation that could be fulfilled in no other way. His crucifixion was therefore designed, staged, or engineered by God for the purpose of fulfilling that requirement or condition and thereby making it possible for God to do something that he could not do otherwise. Christ's death is seen as salvific by virtue of some type of "effect" that it produces upon God, the devil, evil powers, human nature, or human beings themselves. Such ideas represent assumptions that have no basis in the thought of Paul or in ancient Hebrew and Jewish beliefs regarding what needed to happen in order for human beings to be saved and redeemed from the plight to which they were subject. Instead, the human plight was understood in terms of the need for people

---

14. Contra Sanders, *Paul and Palestinian Judaism*, 453-73.

to be brought to live in ways that would enable them to experience the life, salvation, and wholeness that God desires for all.

In the thought of Paul, it is this that God accomplishes through Christ. Strictly speaking, however, it is not accomplished through Christ's death but through *all* that God has done and will continue to do in human history. While this saving activity is centered upon Christ and revolves around him as the one through whom God accomplishes his purposes, it is not only what God has done in Christ and his death that saves human beings. What God did prior to Christ's coming also contributes to their salvation, as does God's pouring out of the Holy Spirit in the present and his sending out of apostles into the world to establish the *ekklēsia* through the proclamation of the gospel.

A close look at Paul's epistles makes it clear that, rather than ascribing some type of salvific effect to Jesus' death or claiming that God planned and orchestrated Jesus' death so that it might accomplish some salvific purpose, he regards it as the *consequence* of God's efforts to bring human beings back to himself so that they might attain the life and wholeness he desires for all by living in conformity with his will. According to Paul, God did not send his Son to die but to be his instrument for bringing human beings to live in love, justice, righteousness, and freedom as his children for their own happiness and well-being. It was Jesus' dedication to that objective that led to his death, yet at the same time what made it possible for him to accomplish that objective was his willingness to give up his life in order to attain it. In Paul's thought, had Jesus sought to save his life rather than surrendering it in the face of the cross, that objective would never have been accomplished. The only sense in which it can rightly be said that God sent his Son to die is that he willed that his Son enter into a context in which his efforts to bring about the new reality that God desired to see would result in his death. Even though God knew ahead of time that his Son's dedication to the task of establishing the type of community that Paul describes in his epistles would lead to a violent death, God nevertheless chose to send his Son to carry out that task rather than holding him back. It is therefore *by means* of Jesus' death and blood—that is, his willingness to give up his life rather than seeking to save it—that God's saving purposes for human beings are now accomplished.

Of course, Paul never lays out explicitly in these terms his understanding of the salvific significance of Jesus' death. In reality, however, his epistles offer ample evidence that he interpreted Jesus' death in the manner just outlined. Paul repeatedly compares his own sufferings and the death or dying that he endures as a result of his work on behalf of the gospel to the suffering and death that Jesus himself endured. In fact, in many ways Paul sees his own ministry as replicating that of Jesus himself.[15] By examining the passages in which Paul describes what he endures in his apostolic ministry and alludes to the suffering and death of Jesus himself, we can grasp quite clearly what Paul means when he affirms that Jesus gave his life for others and for their sins and says that believers have been redeemed, justified, and reconciled to God by means of Jesus' death or blood.

The Sufferings of Christ and Those of Paul

Paul's most extensive comparison between his own ministry and sufferings and those of Jesus occurs in 2 Corinthians. There Paul offers a lengthy description and defense of his own ministry in favor of the gospel. As he does so, Paul repeatedly refers to his own afflictions and suffering. At the outset of the epistle, he even refers to the sufferings he and his co-workers endure as the "sufferings of Christ":

> Blessed be the God and Father of our Lord Jesus Christ, the Father of mercies and the God of all consolation, who consoles us in all our affliction, so that we may be able to console those who are in any kind of affliction with the same consolation through which we ourselves are consoled by God. For just as the sufferings of Christ are abundant for us, so also our consolation is abundant through Christ. But if we are enduring afflictions, it is for your consolation and salvation; and if we are being consoled, it is for your consolation, which you experience when you endure patiently the same sufferings that we too are suffering. And our hope for you is unwavering, for we know that, just as you share with us our sufferings, so also you share our consolation (2 Cor 1:3-7).

The general thrust of Paul's words here is very clear. He is speaking of the suffering, hardships, and afflictions that he and his co-workers endure as a result of their work on behalf of the gospel and saying that God comforts and consoles them in the midst of those sufferings. This experience of suffering enables them to comfort and console others, in particular the Corinthian believers, who according to Paul suffer the same things. This is because they too are laboring in favor of the gospel or supporting in some way those such as Paul who are dedicated to spreading that gospel. It is in this sense that they share in Paul's sufferings, as well as his consolation. While Paul does not explicitly say *how* the Corinthians share in his consolation, his idea seems to be that, when they see Paul suffer, they also suffer

---

15. On the parallels between the ministry of Paul and that of Jesus, see Alexander J. M. Wedderburn, "Paul and Jesus: Similarity and Continuity," in *Paul and Jesus: Collected Essays*, ed. Alexander J. M. Wedderburn, JSNTSup 37 (Sheffield: Sheffield Academic Press, 1989), 117-44; Christian Wolff, "Humility and Self-Denial in Jesus' Life and Message and in the Apostolic Existence of Paul," in *Paul and Jesus: Collected Essays*, ed. Alexander J. M. Wedderburn, JSNTSup 37 (Sheffield: Sheffield Academic Press, 1989), 145-60.

due to their love for him and their solidarity with him and his ministry. When his suffering is alleviated, therefore, their suffering is alleviated as well, since they are relieved to know that he and his co-workers have been delivered from whatever hardships they were enduring.[16]

Paul appears to have the same basic idea in mind when he affirms that he and his co-workers undergo "the sufferings of Christ."[17] There is no reason to take this phrase in a literal or ontological sense, as if in some mysterious way Paul and his co-workers actually participate in the very same sufferings that Christ himself endured when he was crucified.[18] Rather, Paul's words should be understood in the sense that, because he and his co-workers are dedicated to the same task to which Christ had been dedicated and on behalf of which he also had suffered, they suffer the same type of things that Christ did.[19] Their sufferings are one and the same since they are the result of the same work that Christ carried out and in fact continues to carry out through them. There is nothing mystical or mysterious about this suffering, therefore, just as there is nothing mystical or mysterious about the Corinthian believers sharing the sufferings of Paul.[20]

---

16. Victor Paul Furnish expresses the idea thus: "When the apostles are comforted in their afflictions, this enables others in the body of Christ to be comforted in theirs" (*II Corinthians*, 2nd ed., AB 32A [Garden City, NY: Doubleday, 1984], 120).

17. On the background and interpretation of the phrase "the sufferings of Christ" in 2 Cor 1:3-7, see especially Furnish, *II Corinthians*, 118-21.

18. Such an idea is suggested by Margaret Thrall, who claims that the relationship between Paul's afflictions and the sufferings of Christ "derives from a mystical fellowship with Christ grounded in baptism" (*A Critical and Exegetical Commentary on the Second Epistle to the Corinthians*, ICC [Edinburgh: T & T Clark, 1994], 1:108). Similarly, C. K. Barrett relates the sufferings of Christ with the "messianic woes" (*A Commentary on the Second Epistle to the Corinthians*, HNTC [New York: Harper & Row, 1973], 61-62). Nothing in the context of 2 Cor 1:3-7, however, suggests that Paul has such ideas in mind.

19. As Murray J. Harris notes, Paul's idea appears to be, not that the sufferings of the Corinthians "were identical with Paul's affliction," but rather that they were "generically, not actually, 'the same'" (*The Second Epistle to the Corinthians: A Commentary on the Greek Text*, NIGTC [Grand Rapids: Eerdmans, 2005], 148). According to Paul Barnett, "These 'afflictions' arise directly from his missionary message and lifestyle, so abundantly set forth in this letter. Just as Christ suffered in his ministry and death from forces hostile to God, so, too, the apostle, in continuity with Christ, suffered in the course of his ministry and proclamation" (*The Second Epistle to the Corinthians*, NICNT [Grand Rapids: Eerdmans, 1997], 75).

20. In one of the most complete studies on 2 Cor 1:5, Kar Yong Lim argues that Paul's allusion to the sufferings of Christ "cannot be understood in itself according to any of the categories of messianic woes, mystical union, or the imitation of Christ, but can only be fully appreciated if we consider the story of Jesus in the wider context of 2 Corinthians in particular and Paul's mission theology in general. In the light of this, Paul most likely interprets the phrase *ta pathēmata tou Christou eis hēmas* as the

The simplicity of Paul's logic is evident from a similar affirmation that he makes further on in the same epistle. When he tells the Corinthian believers in 2 Cor 7:3, "you are in our hearts, to die and to live together," Paul clearly does not intend his words to be understood in a mystical, literal, or ontological sense. Paul and the Corinthians do not participate mystically in each other's death or resurrection. Instead, Paul is simply referring once more to the spirit of solidarity that exists between the Corinthian believers and himself, together with his co-workers. As he carries out his work as an apostle, Paul is constantly thinking of the Corinthians fondly, desiring their well-being and their consolidation in the faith they share. He also offers up prayers to God on their behalf and reflects on the things that he might do to assist and strengthen them. Among these things, of course, is the sending of a letter on his part. The Corinthian believers in turn share the same concern for Paul and want his work to accomplish its objectives. Because they share the same heart, mind, and purpose as Paul and his co-workers, when one group suffers, the other suffers as well. Conversely, when things go well for one of the two groups, the other also rejoices. It is in that sense that they "die and live together."[21]

Elsewhere in the same letter, Paul mentions in a couple of passages some of the things that he has suffered and endured in his work for the gospel. In 2 Cor 6:4-10, he speaks of himself and his co-workers as those who commend themselves

> in all things as servants of God, in great endurance, afflictions, hardships, tribulations, beatings, imprisonments, riots, travails, sleepless nights, and hunger; through pure conduct, knowledge, perseverance, acts of kindness, holiness of spirit, genuine love, truthful speech, and the power of God, wielding the weapons of righteousness in the right hand and the left; in honor and ignominy, in contempt and admiration. We are regarded as deceivers by some and as truthful by others; as nobodies by some and as illustrious by others. We have been given up for dead, and yet, look! We are still alive! We are castigated, yet not killed, beset by sorrows, yet always rejoicing. We are poor, yet enrich many; we possess nothing, yet everything is ours.

Many of these ideas are repeated in 2 Cor 11:23-33. There Paul compares himself to the false apostles of Christ who claim to be superior to him:

> Are they ministers of Christ? I am raving as if I were insane!—I am a better one: with far greater travails, far more imprisonments, beaten countless times, and often near death. Five times I have received the forty lashes

---

suffering he experienced in his apostolic ministry for Christ" (*'The Sufferings of Christ are Abundant in Us' [2 Corinthians 1.5]: A Narrative Dynamics Investigation of Paul's Sufferings in 2 Corinthians*, LNTS 399 [London: T & T Clark, 2009], 63).

21. As Thrall notes, in 2 Cor 7:3 Paul is referring to the "deep bond of friendship, loyalty, affection and the like" that exists between those concerned (*Second Corinthians*, 1:483).

minus one from the Jews. Three times I was beaten with rods. Once I received a stoning. On three occasions I have been shipwrecked; once I was adrift at sea for a night and a day. I have been on frequent journeys, in danger of drowning in rivers, in danger from bandits, in danger from my own people, in danger from gentiles, in danger in the city, in danger out in the wilderness, in danger while at sea, in danger from false sisters and brothers; in toil and in hardship, spending many nights sleepless, enduring hunger and thirst, often without food, cold and naked. And, besides all of that and other things, every day I bear the weight of my concern for all of the communities of believers. Who suffers weakness without my accompanying them in that weakness? Who is made to stumble without my becoming indignant? If I must boast, I will boast of the things that make my weakness evident. The God and Father of the Lord Jesus—he who is blessed forever!—knows that I am not lying. In Damascus, the ethnarch under Aretas the king placed the city of the Damascenes under guard in order to arrest me, but I was let down in a basket through a window in the wall and thereby escaped from his hands.

According to the Jesus-tradition as best we can reconstruct it, Jesus himself did not suffer most of the things Paul mentions here. As far as we know, for example, Jesus was never shipwrecked, stoned, assaulted by bandits, or adrift at sea in danger of drowning. As Paul undoubtedly knows, however, Jesus did suffer *the same type of things* that Paul mentions here: rejection, persecution, derision, hardships, hunger, thirst, sleepless nights, anguish, weakness, privation, danger, and other types of affliction.[22] Like Paul, Jesus had been despised by many and accused of being a deceiver. The reason that Jesus had endured all of these things is that he had been dedicated to proclaiming the same gospel Paul proclaims. Jesus had also borne daily the weight of his care and concern for others and the pressures of his ministry on behalf of others. He had suffered a great deal as a result of his efforts to establish what Paul now calls the *ekklēsia*. Because Paul carries on the same work on behalf of the same objective, he therefore suffers the same things that Jesus suffered.[23]

Undoubtedly, the gospel that Paul proclaims revolves around Jesus rather than around Paul himself. Even though Paul can describe his own work in terms of laying a foundation, ultimately it is Christ who constitutes the only foundation (1 Cor 3:5-15). Nevertheless, because Paul, his co-workers, and the Corinthian believers are all dedicated to the same objective to which Christ had dedicated his life, Paul can affirm that they all share the same sufferings. In fact, just as Christ had given up his life as a result of his dedication to that objective, so also Paul and his co-workers give up their lives daily in the sense that they are willing to sacrifice everything

---

22. On the parallels Paul draws between his own sufferings and those of Christ, see Wolff, "Humility," 156-59.

23. As Lim stresses, throughout 2 Corinthians 10–13, Paul sees his ministry as embodying the story of Jesus (*'Sufferings of Christ'*, 179-80).

for the same objective that had been Christ's in life and death. Ultimately, that objective is the establishment of the *ekklēsia* throughout the world in the way that Christ and his Father had envisioned from the start. In other words, Paul suffers what Jesus did because he proclaims the same gospel that Jesus did and thereby seeks the same objective that Jesus did, namely, the establishment and consolidation of communities that would live under Jesus as Lord so as to be characterized by the same love, righteousness, faithfulness, dedication, and commitment seen in Jesus himself and now reflected in Paul and others who believe in Jesus.

Like Jesus before him, Paul pays a very high price in order to attain that objective. In 2 Cor 12:15, he writes: "I will most gladly spend whatever is necessary for you and also be spent for your sake. If I love you all the more, will I be loved any less?"[24] The love for others that characterizes and drives Paul's ministry is the same love that characterized and drove Jesus' ministry. In the case of both Jesus and Paul, that love involves denouncing and opposing sin and injustice, as well as doing things that upset the status quo and affect the interests of many, including especially the rulers and powers of this age (1 Cor 2:6-8). As Jesus did, Paul calls on others to reject the predominant system or "world" in order to live in ways that are not accepted within that system and even clash with it.[25] The result of that rejection is persecution.

Of course, not everything that Jesus and Paul suffered was the result of persecution at the hands of others. Much of what they suffered was due simply to the tremendous sacrifices they made in order to carry out their itinerant ministries and serve others. In fact, as Paul indicates elsewhere in 2 Corinthians, much of his pain and anguish is caused by believers themselves. Just as Jesus' disciples at times caused him a great deal of grief, so also those who have come to live as followers of Jesus in the communities established by Paul at times cause him the same type of grief. In 2 Cor 2:1-5, after mentioning the painful visit he had made to Corinth, he continues: "For I wrote to you out of much distress and anguish of heart and with many tears, not in order to cause you pain, but to let you know how great my love for you is" (v. 4). The reason Paul endures the same type of pain and suffering that Jesus did, therefore, is that he loves others with the same type of love seen in Jesus. That love moves Paul to be willing to make the same type of sacrifices that Jesus had made, and to do so with the same joy and gladness reflected in Jesus, in spite of the grief and anguish he

---

24. Ralph P. Martin summarizes Paul's thought in this passage thus: "He is willing to extend himself to the uttermost limits of his capacity.... The point is that in 12:15 Paul will not withhold any resource he has, including himself.... Paul will spend himself— his energy, his health, if need be..., his reputation, his affections—on the Corinthians" (*2 Corinthians*, WBC 40 [Waco, TX: Word, 1986], 443).

25. See Rom 12:2; 1 Cor 1:18-31; Gal 6:14.

must bear as a result of his work. The satisfaction that Paul experiences as he contemplates the transformation of the lives of others through the faith he proclaims is the same satisfaction that Jesus had experienced when proclaiming that faith. For that reason, no matter what it costs Paul, he will not put a stop to his work on behalf of others, even if that means that he must give up or "spend" all that he has and be left totally "spent." In this regard, he is once again exactly like Jesus, whom he proclaims as the crucified and risen Lord of all.

In 2 Corinthians 4 and 5, Paul alludes repeatedly to Jesus' death in order to compare it with the death that he himself endures in a metaphorical sense. In 2 Cor 4:8-9, he affirms that he and his co-workers are "afflicted in every way, but not crushed; bewildered, but not despondent; persecuted, but not abandoned; struck down, but not destroyed." He then continues: "always carrying in our body the death of Jesus, so that the life of Jesus may also be made visible in our body. For we who are still alive are always being delivered up to death for Jesus' sake, so that the life of Jesus may be made visible in our mortal flesh. Therefore death is at work in us, but life in you" (2 Cor 4:10-12).

Here again, there is no reason to suppose that Paul has in mind any type of mystical, literal, or ontological participation in Jesus' sufferings and death, as if he carried around in his own body the past event of Jesus' death in some mysterious way.[26] Rather, the context clearly indicates that he simply has in mind the idea that, in his own ministry, he is constantly on the brink of suffering the same type of violent and untimely death that Jesus suffered.[27] At the same time, he endures hardships and afflictions of the same type that Jesus endured all the way to the cross as a result of his own work on behalf of others. Literally, Paul speaks of bearing in his body the "dying" or "deadness" (*nekrōsis*) of Jesus, that is, the *process* of dying or the *condition* of being dead.[28] While in one sense Paul's language here is

---

26. Jan Lambrecht, for example, claims that Paul has in mind "a kind of ontological union with Christ" in this passage, yet cites no evidence to support that claim ("The nekrōsis of Jesus: Ministry and Suffering in 2 Corinthians 4,7-15," in *Studies on 2 Corinthians*, ed. Reimund Bieringer and Jan Lambrecht, BETL 112 [Leuven: Leuven University Press, 1994], 309-33 [326]).

27. As Barnett argues, "The 'dying of Jesus' that takes place 'in [Paul's] body' is the affliction, bewilderment, persecution, and humiliation mentioned in vv. 8-9" (*Second Corinthians*, 235).

28. Scholars have debated extensively the meaning of *nekrōsis* in 2 Cor 4:10, including the question of whether it refers to a process or condition; see Richard I. Deibert, *Second Corinthians and Paul's Gospel of Human Mortality: How Paul's Experience of Death Authorizes His Apostolic Authority in Corinth*, WUNT 2/430 (Tübingen: Mohr Siebeck, 2017), 141-81; Thrall, *Second Corinthians*, 1:331-34. In reality, however, this distinction is not particularly important as long as it is stressed that for Paul Jesus' death was the consequence of a ministry such as his own, since in that case Paul is carrying about a

metaphorical, in another sense Paul is already experiencing a type of dying that is closely akin to that which Jesus endured. He knows that, as a result of his work on behalf of the same gospel Jesus proclaimed, he will probably die a death that is similar to that which Jesus suffered, and in a sense is already in the process of dying such a death.

Paul can also speak of Jesus' "deadness" in this passage because, in his risen condition, Jesus remains forever dead and crucified. Jesus' present condition of "deadness" is the result of his own faithful proclamation of the gospel, since that proclamation led him to be put to death on a cross before subsequently being raised by his Father. Because Paul dedicates his life to the proclamation of that same gospel, he too is constantly threatened with the same type of violent death that Jesus suffered and in a sense has already embraced that death as his own by continuing in his work despite the price he must pay. He therefore considers himself to be dead already, together with Jesus. He also experiences Jesus' same "deadness" in that he has given up his life and all that he is and has in order to proclaim the gospel, as Jesus did. In 1 Cor 15:31-32, Paul employs essentially the same logic that he does here. There, after alluding to the fact that he was forced to fight with wild beasts in Ephesus, he writes: "I die every day." In this passage, Paul obviously does not intend his words to be taken mystically, literally, or ontologically. He does not *actually* die every day. Instead, what he does every day is to endure hardships and put his life at risk for the sake of the gospel of Christ, knowing that because of his work on behalf of the gospel, there is a sense in which he is already as good as dead. Paul is willing to suffer and die for that gospel just as Jesus did. In fact, he is fairly certain that ultimately he will pay the price of his life for having proclaimed that gospel. In a sense, he is already paying that price every day by virtue of all that he suffers and his knowledge that at any moment he may die as a result of his work on behalf of Christ and the *ekklēsia*. In Paul's mind, from the moment he responded to Christ's call to be his apostle, he had already given up his life and anticipated the type of death he was going to die. In that sense, he was dead from that moment on. Of course, what spurs him on in the face of the death that he experiences daily and will endure literally at any moment is his conviction that God raises the dead (2 Cor 1:9-10).

These are the same ideas that Paul has in mind in 2 Cor 4:11, where he speaks of being delivered up to death "for the sake of Jesus" (*dia Iēsoun*). In the same context, he uses this same phrase to tell the Corinthian believers: "we proclaim Jesus Christ as Lord and ourselves as your slaves for Jesus'

---

condition that will be the result of a process: Paul will ultimately die the same type of death as Jesus due to the fact that in his ministry he is constantly giving up his life for Jesus and for others. The *nekrōsis* is therefore a future condition that is already present in Paul, as well as an ongoing process in his life and ministry.

sake" (2 Cor 4:5).[29] In Paul's thought, as a result of his own commitment to proclaiming the gospel with the aim of forming the same type of communities that Paul seeks to establish, Jesus himself had been "delivered up" (Rom 4:25; 8:32). Of course, because all of those communities are at the same time a single community, the *ekklēsia* that Paul seeks to see established throughout the world is the same *ekklēsia* that Jesus sought to establish in life and death. In Paul's mind, Jesus had died as a result of his efforts and dedication to bringing that *ekklēsia* into existence and giving it the shape it now has. Because Paul is willing to give up his life as Jesus did in order to attain the same objective that Jesus sought, he too can affirm that he is constantly being delivered up to death for Jesus' sake. Like Jesus, as he carries out his ministry on behalf of the gospel and the *ekklēsia*, he seeks to be obedient to God in everything and to do God's will rather than his own. If at some point God calls on Paul to give up his life for the sake of Jesus, the gospel, and the *ekklēsia*, he will go willingly to his death, just as Jesus himself had willingly gone to his own death rather than putting an end to his ministry so as to avoid the cross. Only in that way is it possible for the type of community that constituted the objective of the ministry of Jesus and now constitutes the objective of that of Paul to be brought into existence. For Paul, of course, this is the same community that God himself desires to see as well. If God gives Paul over to death and wills for him to give up his life, therefore, God will do so for the same reason that he gave Jesus his Son over to death and willed for him to give up his life: it is impossible to create a community in which all are willing to give up their lives for others out of love for them if one is not willing to give up one's own life or the life of the one whom one loves above all else in order for such a community to exist.

In Paul's thought, the fact that Jesus' desire to see such a community brought into existence was so strong that he was willing to give up his life so that it might become a reality means that nothing could please Jesus more than having others such as Paul dedicate their lives to that same end, in spite of the consequences. As Paul asserts in 2 Cor 5:9, whether he lives or must die as a result of his gospel proclamation, he seeks only to do what is pleasing to Jesus: "whether we are at home or away, we make it our aim to please him." Thus, when Paul speaks of being delivered up "for Jesus' sake," his words should be understood in the sense that, out of love for Jesus, he gives his life for the same gospel and community that Jesus did, pursuing the same objective that Jesus sought to the very end in obedience to God out of love for all.

---

29. As Lim observes, when Paul speaks of being handed over to death for Jesus' sake in 2 Cor 4:11, the idea is not that Jesus himself is benefited but that others are benefited in the way Jesus desires by Paul's willingness to suffer as a result of his ministry on their behalf (*'Sufferings of Christ'*, 116-17).

In 2 Cor 4:14–5:11, Paul uses similar imagery to speak of his willingness to endure suffering and death as a result of his apostolic ministry. While the outer person of those who work on behalf of the gospel is constantly wasting away, their inner person is being renewed every day (4:16). Of course, the same thing happens to those who accept that gospel. Both those who proclaim it and those who receive it favorably groan in an earthly tent, longing for their eternal dwelling to manifest itself from heaven (5:2-4). Here again Paul's language is clearly metaphorical. Believers share the hope that, just as God raised Jesus, he will also raise them to be with Jesus in his presence (4:14).[30] In order to attain the "eternal weight of glory that is far beyond any comparison" prepared for them, however, they must continue to endure the "momentary, light affliction" that is theirs in the present (4:17). While their resurrection to that glory lies in the future, at the same time they are renewed every day, not because some mysterious transformation is taking place in their inner being, but rather because they become stronger in that hope and more convinced of it daily. They have also received the Holy Spirit from God as a pledge or guarantee of the new life that awaits them (5:5). It is this hope and confidence that animate the ministry of Paul and his co-workers, who dedicate themselves to persuading others of the message they proclaim so that God's grace may continue "spreading to more and more people" (4:15; 5:6-8).[31]

In a number of passages from his other letters, Paul also refers to his work on behalf of the gospel as a struggle that he shares alongside other believers. He exhorts the Romans to struggle together with him in the love of the Spirit through their prayers on his behalf in the face of the opposition that he fears he may encounter in his trip to Jerusalem (Rom 15:30). In Phil 1:27, it is the Philippians who struggle together with Paul with one mind and one spirit "for the faith of the gospel." Further on in the letter, he uses the same verb (*synathlein*) to refer to Euodia and Syntyche as those who have "struggled alongside me in the work of the gospel" (Phil 4:3). He also thanks the Philippian believers for sharing in the gospel with him, just as they share in his imprisonment (Phil 1:5, 7). After affirming that he knows how to be content under any circumstances, including scarcity and prosperity, hunger and fullness, and necessity and abundance, he expresses

---

30. As Thrall observes, in 2 Cor 4:14 "it is best to suppose Paul is saying that God will raise him to join Jesus in the resurrection existence" (*Second Corinthians*, 1:343).

31. Throughout 2 Cor 4:16–5:5, Paul's argument seems to revolve around the idea that his sufferings serve to demonstrate his faithfulness to Christ as an apostle and his love for the Corinthians, rather than representing a sign of God's discontent with Paul or his disapproval of Paul's ministry, as some who oppose Paul may have been claiming; see Fredrik Lindgård, *Paul's Line of Thought in 2 Corinthians 4:16–5.10*, WUNT 2/189 (Tübingen: Mohr Siebeck, 2005), 106-219.

to the Philippians his appreciation for the kindness they have shown in sharing in his afflictions through their support for him (Phil 4:11-14).

All of these passages speak merely of a shared suffering as a result of a commitment to a common goal or purpose rather than any type of mystical or ontological participation in the suffering of another. The suffering that Paul endures is the result of the sacrifices he makes for the work of the gospel on behalf of others. He speaks of himself as one whose life is being poured out sacrificially as a libation or drink-offering in the service of the faith of others (Phil 2:17). After mentioning that he sent Timothy to strengthen and encourage the Thessalonians in their faith, he reminds them that he told them ahead of time that he and his co-workers would have to endure many afflictions (1 Thess 3:2-4). The Thessalonian believers should therefore know that those afflictions are not the result of God's displeasure or anger but rather of the dedication of Paul and his co-workers to the proclamation of the gospel out of love and concern for others. Similarly, in 1 Cor 9:12-27, he tells the Corinthians that he and his co-workers willingly "endure all things so as not to hinder the spread of the gospel." After affirming that he would rather die than be deprived of the pride and satisfaction he experiences in his ministry (v. 15), Paul refers to himself as a "slave of all" who has become all things to all people for the sake of the gospel (vv. 19, 22-23). Like a runner or fighter who subjects his body to intense training and even pummels it in order to subdue it, Paul gives up everything so that he may attain the imperishable prize that he associates with Christ and the gospel, not only for his own sake but for the sake of others as well (vv. 24-27).

In several passages from his other epistles, Paul draws the same type of comparison between that which Christ suffered and that which those who work on Christ's behalf must suffer. In two of these passages, he criticizes certain persons who claim to serve others in Christ's name yet in reality are "enemies of the cross" (Phil 3:18-19) and refuse to "endure persecution for the cross of Christ" (Gal 6:12). The reason he refers to them in this way is precisely that they seek their own interests and pleasures rather than being willing to suffer out of love for others, as Christ did.[32] In contrast, Paul himself is willing to endure persecution for the sake of the cross (Gal 5:11; 6:17). In Rom 15:1-3, Paul points to the manner in which Christ was willing to suffer the reproaches of those who scorned him in order to exhort the Roman believers to be willing to do the same thing, namely, embrace the suffering that inevitably results from their efforts to strengthen others and build them up rather than seeking to avoid suffering at all costs in order to

---

32. According to Stephen E. Fowl, it is likely that in both Phil 3:18-19 and Gal 6:12 Paul is referring to those who "seek to avoid suffering that might come their way as the result of their convictions about Christ" (*Philippians*, THNTC [Grand Rapids: Eerdmans, 2005], 171).

pursue their own pleasure or interests instead.[33] Paul may have the cross in mind as well in Gal 6:2, where he tells the Galatians to take upon themselves the burdens of others in order to bear those burdens on their behalf. By doing so, they fulfill "the law of Christ."[34]

Although Paul does not explicitly mention Jesus' death on the cross in 1 Cor 4:9-13, there can be little doubt that he has it in the back of his mind, together with the ministry that led to it. There he speaks of going hungry, thirsty, and homeless and being poorly clothed, roughly treated, reviled, persecuted, and slandered, yet responding in love to those who mistreat him and his co-workers. Together with those co-workers, he is "exhibited" as one "condemned to death," a "spectacle to the world," so as to become like "the scum of the earth" and "the dregs of all things." This was precisely how those whom the Romans put to death by crucifixion would be described.[35] For the sake of the gospel, Paul and his co-workers are willing to be ridiculed as "lunatics for Christ's sake." In this passage, then, Paul almost certainly has in mind the way that Jesus was exhibited on the cross as a spectacle to the world so as to be condemned, humiliated, and mocked in the same way that Paul and his co-workers are.

It is extremely important to stress, however, that for Paul *suffering is not an end in itself*. Paul is not a masochist. He does not seek to suffer. Instead, what he seeks is to enable others to experience the well-being and salvation that he associates with the gospel and to see them confirmed and strengthened in that gospel. Thus, for example, when he points to the things he has suffered and endured in 2 Corinthians 10–13 in order to boast, he is not saying that what makes him superior to the "super-apostles" whom he criticizes as "false apostles" is that he has suffered more than they have, as if suffering were good or desirable. Rather, his idea is that his willingness to suffer all sorts of afflictions, hardships, and persecutions on behalf of the gospel is proof of the tremendous love he has for the Corinthians. It is precisely that love for the Corinthians that he stresses repeatedly throughout

---

33. As Leander E. Keck points out, given that Psalm 69 "came to be associated with various elements of the Passion story," it is likely that when Paul cites Ps 69:9 in Rom 15:3, he is referring to the mocking that Jesus endured on the cross (*Romans*, ANTC [Nashville: Abingdon, 2005], 350-51).

34. John M. G. Barclay sees a parallel between Gal 6:2 and Rom 15:1-3 and on that basis suggests that the love that Paul associates with the law of Christ may be especially the love he manifested in his death (*Obeying the Truth: A Study of Paul's Ethics in Galatians*, SNTW [Edinburgh: T & T Clark, 1988], 133-34). It may also be significant that the same Greek verb that Paul uses to speak of bearing others' burdens in Gal 6:2 (*bastazein*) is used in Luke 14:27 and John 19:17 to speak of bearing the cross and by Paul himself in Gal 6:17 to allude to the *stigmata* or scars of Jesus that he bears on his body as a result of his ministry on behalf of others.

35. See B. J. Oropeza, *1 Corinthians*, NCC (Eugene, OR: Cascade, 2017), 61.

2 Corinthians.[36] In contrast, the other so-called apostles are *not* willing to suffer the same type of things on their behalf because they do not love them as Paul does. Instead, those pseudo-apostles seek to enslave and devour the Corinthians, taking advantage of them and even slapping them in the face so as to exalt themselves (11:20). Paul, however, is truly dedicated to serving the Corinthians and desires only that they be built up and made complete (11:8; 13:9-10). It is for that reason that he suffers.

In fact, after reminding the Corinthians that he and Titus did not seek to take advantage of them but instead conducted themselves in a fitting and worthy manner while working among them, he tells them: "All this time you have been thinking that we are defending ourselves to you. Actually, we have been speaking in Christ in the presence of God, and all that we have said has had the purpose of building you up" (2 Cor 12:17-19). In other words, the reason why Paul points to all that he has given up and suffered in order to carry out his ministry on behalf of the Corinthians in 2 Corinthians 10–13 is not that he wishes to defend himself to the Corinthians, as if his concern were merely for himself. Rather, it is for *their* sake that he stresses all that he has done and suffered on their behalf.[37] His hope is that, by realizing how much Paul has endured in order to build them up, they will pay attention to him instead of those who seek instead to tear them down, caring only for themselves rather than for the Corinthians (10:8-12). The jealousy that Paul has for the Corinthians is a "godly jealousy," since unlike the false apostles, he is jealous not for *his own sake* but *for the sake of the Corinthians themselves* (11:2). That jealousy is motivated only by his deep desire to present them to Christ as Christ's betrothed.[38] According to Paul, the reason why he sought to avoid being a burden to the Corinthians by not asking anything of them when he proclaimed the gospel to them is simply that *he loves them* (11:7-11; 12:13-15).

For Paul, what is true of his own ministry is also true of the ministry that Christ carried out. What Christ sought was not *to suffer* but *to serve others in love*. In Paul's words, even though he was rich, Christ became poor for the sake of others such as the Corinthians, since only by doing so could he accomplish his objective of enriching others by bringing them to live as members of his community (2 Cor 8:9). Paul seeks that same objective, and thus is also willing to endure hardships and poverty in order to make others rich (2 Cor 6:10). It is not the poverty of Christ or Paul in itself, however, that makes others rich. Rather, the only way to serve others in love is to

---

36. See 2 Cor 2:4; 6:11-12; 11:11; 12:15.

37. Thrall summarizes Paul's thought here thus: "Paul has not been speaking to obtain a judicial verdict from the Corinthians, but for the sake of their spiritual and moral welfare, and on account of his love for them" (*Second Corinthians*, 2:857).

38. As Barnett points out, it may be preferable to use the language of "zeal" rather than "jealousy" to translate Paul's thought in 2 Cor 11:2 (*Second Corinthians*, 499-500).

empty oneself in the way that Christ did in order to enter into their midst and give oneself to them by serving them (Phil 2:6-8). Paul points to the Macedonian communities as an example of those who "gave themselves to the Lord and to us by the will of God" in order to exhort the Corinthians to live lives characterized by the same type of graciousness and earnest, sincere love (2 Cor 8:5-8, 16).

Throughout his letters, Paul points to this same love for others as that which motivates him to do all that he does on their behalf. The reason he desires to go to Rome to see the believers there is to strengthen and encourage them and share some spiritual gift with them (Rom 1:11-12). He writes to the Corinthian believers and visits them because he wants them to be filled with joy and established in their faith so that they may do all things in love.[39] In Gal 4:11-20, he reminds the Galatian believers of the enormous love that led him to go to Galatia to proclaim the gospel to them and exhorts them to recall how his love for them evoked in them the same love for him. In fact, they had come to love him so much that they would have been willing to pluck out their own eyes for him if necessary (4:15).[40] Like a mother about to give birth, Paul is willing to endure the pain of childbirth if only Christ may be formed in them again (4:19). It is his love for the Galatians that provokes him to such anger at those who seek only to bewitch and enslave the Galatians and thereby do them harm, acting out of self-interest rather than any concern for the Galatians.[41]

Similarly, Paul tells the Philippians that, even though he would prefer to "depart and be with Christ" so as no longer to have to endure suffering on behalf of Christ and the gospel, he prefers to "continue in the flesh" in order to enable them to progress and grow in their faith (Phil 1:21-26). In other words, rather than seeking his own comfort, which he would obtain if he were to be taken away to live in Christ's presence, he prefers to continue to labor on behalf of the Philippians, despite the sacrifices and intense sufferings involved. Due to his concern for their well-being, he considers it to be "no trouble" to write to them from jail, yet that same concern leads him to warn them regarding the "dogs" or "evil workers" who "mutilate the flesh" and thus would do harm to the Philippians motivated by their own self-interests (3:1-2). He also tells the Philippian believers that, while he does not actively seek their gifts, he receives them because by doing so he is able to see the profit or fruit he desires brought about in them and others (4:17). His logic here is not only that the support that the Philippians provide for him enables him to continue in his ministry, but also that through their generosity

---

39. See 1 Cor 16:14; 2 Cor 1:24; 2:4.

40. According to Richard N. Longenecker, the reference to the Galatians plucking their eyes out for Paul "is probably an idiom that speaks of going to the extreme to provide for another's needs" (*Galatians*, WBC 41 [Dallas: Word, 1990], 193).

41. See Gal 2:4; 3:1; 4:17; 5:1, 7-12; 6:12-13.

and commitment to supporting Paul's ministry they are themselves enriched, since they grow in their generosity and their love for Christ. He thus accepts their gracious gifts *for their sake* and not for his alone.

In 1 Thess 2:1-12, Paul reminds the Thessalonian believers that he and his co-workers came to Thessalonica in the midst of considerable suffering, mistreatment, and opposition in order to share the gospel with them. What Paul and his co-workers sought was not their own glory but simply to care for the Thessalonians gently and tenderly, as a nursing mother cares for her children (vv. 1-7). Because the Thessalonians are very dear to them, it gave Paul and his co-workers great pleasure not only to share the gospel with "fond affection" for the Thessalonians, but also to share with them their very lives (v. 8). Paul reminds them that he treated them as a loving father treats his children, exhorting, encouraging, and pleading with them to live in the way that God desires for their own good (vv. 9-12). In the midst of their ongoing distress and affliction, Paul and his co-workers rejoice that they are able to strengthen and encourage the Thessalonian believers, establish them in their faith, and see their love abound and increase (1 Thess 3:1-12). Paul even states explicitly that he had wanted to work among the Thessalonian believers, not for *his* sake, but for *theirs* (1 Thess 1:5).

While Col 1:24 may not have been written by Paul, it expresses very well the same ideas that we have seen here. There Paul as the author of Colossians writes: "Now I rejoice in my sufferings on your behalf and I fill up in my flesh what is lacking of the afflictions of Christ on behalf of his body, which is the *ekklēsia*." This verse has confounded many interpreters because they suppose that the purpose of Christ's sufferings was to atone for sins. In that case, it is shocking to think not only that what Christ suffered on the cross was not sufficient to make full atonement for human sins but also that the sufferings of Paul should be required and accepted by God to atone for human sins as well.[42] In reality, however, this verse has nothing to do with atonement for sins. Rather, the idea is very simple: while Christ suffered a great deal to establish the *ekklēsia*, the task of consolidating and building up that *ekklēsia* and bringing it to extend throughout the world

---

42. Alexander J. M. Wedderburn's concern for "the possible implication that somehow Christ's sufferings had been deficient or insufficient" presupposes that a certain amount of suffering on the part of Christ had been necessary to atone for sins (Alexander J. M. Wedderburn and Andrew T. Lincoln, *The Theology of the Later Pauline Letters*, NTT [Cambridge: Cambridge University Press, 1993], 38). The same presupposition leads W. F. Flemington to insist that Col 1:24 must not be read as contradicting "the finished and decisive character of what God through Christ effected by means of the Cross" ("On the Interpretation of Colossians 1:24," in *Suffering and Martyrdom in the New Testament: Studies Presented to G. M. Styler by the Cambridge New Testament Seminar*, ed. William Horbury and Brian McNeil [Cambridge: Cambridge University Press, 1981], 84-90 [86]).

was far from finished when he died. For that reason, apostles such as Paul must continue to dedicate themselves to that task. Yet because for the reasons we have seen above that task inevitably entails suffering and enduring great afflictions, those such as Paul who are dedicated to it must continue to suffer the same type of things that Christ himself suffered until the day when it will finally be completed in the way God desires and intends. Like Paul himself, *the reason why Christ suffered was not to atone for the sins of anyone but to establish and build up the ekklēsia.*

Paul's Understanding of Jesus' Death

If Paul affirms that he is willing to give up his life to attain the same things that Jesus had sought in life and death, then it follows that in Paul's mind Jesus himself had suffered and died precisely because he had pursued the same objectives as Paul does in his ministry. In a number of passages from his epistles, Paul states explicitly what those objectives are.

Throughout Romans 6, for example, Paul describes the new reality that Jesus had sought to bring about when he gave up his life. There Paul affirms that there are two ways in which human beings can live. The first is to live as slaves of righteousness, justice, and obedience, which is equivalent to being "enslaved to God" (Rom 6:13). The second is to live as slaves of sin, unrighteousness, injustice, impurity, and lawlessness (6:12-22). Paradoxically, however, to be a slave to God and righteousness is in reality to be free. According to Paul, believers are "free from sin" and dead to it as they live as slaves or servants of God. Paul's words in this passage make sense only when it is understood that, in Paul's thought, *sin destroys true life and well-being.* In contrast, when one lives obediently as a slave of God, one comes to experience salvation (*sōteria*) by being made whole (*sōs*), both in this life and the life to come. The reason for this is that, when human beings submit fully to God's will rather than their own and consider their lives to be God's so that he may do what he wishes in and with them, they make it possible for God to make them whole in the way he desires. What God commands of those who live as his slaves is that they love him and one another with their whole heart for their own good, giving themselves to others as God has given himself to them in Christ. Only if they do this can they attain the well-being God desires for them and all people, since that well-being is inseparable from a life lived in love. As they submit to God in all things as his slaves, God guides them in the way that they are to go for their own good and the good of others. Thus, when one lives "enslaved" to God and sees oneself as belonging to God rather than to oneself (1 Cor 6:19), one's way of life will enable one to experience the well-being, wholeness, life, and salvation that God desires for all.

In Romans 7 and 8, Paul speaks of the two possibilities for human existence in terms of being "in the flesh" and living "in the Spirit." The flesh holds one captive to sin and does not allow one to do the good that would enable one to experience the well-being and wholeness God desires for all (Rom 7:7-24). In contrast, God's Spirit, who is "the Spirit of life in Christ Jesus," sets one free from both sin and the law and thereby allows one to experience life and peace by putting to death the deeds of the body or flesh (Rom 8:1-14). As Paul repeats in Rom 8:15-17 and Gal 4:6-7, rather than living under a spirit of slavery, believers receive a spirit (or Spirit) of adoption that enables them to live as God's children and thereby attain the true life, well-being, and wholeness that God desires for them. Whereas the flesh makes such a life impossible by virtue of the fact that it leads to the type of destructive behavior Paul describes in passages such as Gal 5:19-21, the Spirit produces fruit such as "love, joy, peace, patience, kindness, goodness, faithfulness, thoughtfulness, and self-control" (Gal 5:22-23). *In and of themselves*, these kinds of behavior enable believers to experience the joy, peace, and well-being of which Paul speaks.

In Paul's thought, *all of this is what Jesus sought in life and death*. He sought to deliver others from their slavery to sin, unrighteousness, and death and to free them to live in ways that make it possible for them to attain the well-being, joy, and peace that God desires for all. Jesus did this by reaching out to others in love for them in the same way that Paul does, instructing, exhorting, and guiding them so as to lay the foundation necessary for the *ekklēsia*, the community in which all live in Jesus' same love under his lordship—a lordship that he exercises for *their* sake rather than his own. Undoubtedly, Paul does not proclaim himself as Lord or call apostles of his own, as Jesus did. Nevertheless, he follows Jesus in reaching out to others seeking to establish the same community that constituted the objective of Jesus himself in life and death, a community in which all would share the same commitment to the well-being of all seen first in Jesus himself and now in those who call him Lord.

In the present age, however, those who seek to enable others to be freed from their slavery to sin and unrighteousness inevitably face opposition and generate conflict at the hands of those who do the enslaving. For Paul, sin, unrighteousness, and injustice are *forces* or *powers* that hold human beings in subjection and slavery and thereby *oppress* them. Those forces are found not merely in the hearts of individual human beings but especially in the structures and systems of what Paul calls the "world" or "the present (evil) age."[43] Whether they know it or not, those who do not live under Christ live instead under "the god of the present age," who "has blinded the minds of unbelievers to prevent them from seeing the light of the gospel of the glory

---

43. See Rom 12:2; 1 Cor 1:20-21, 27-28; 2:12; 3:18-19; 4:9; 5:10; Gal 1:4; 6:14. On Paul's understanding of structural sin, see Mercedes López and Carlos Mesters, "Codicia, corrupción, pecado estructural en la Carta a los Romanos," *RIBLA* 78 (2018): 103-12.

of Christ" (2 Cor 4:4). Life, joy, freedom, and well-being can be attained only by resisting sin, unrighteousness, and injustice and struggling against these things in order to overcome and vanquish them. In Rom 13:12, Paul exhorts believers to take up the "weapons of the light" (*hopla tou phōtos*).[44] He uses similar imagery in Rom 6:13 to urge believers to present their members to God as "weapons of justice" (*hopla dikaiosynēs*) rather than presenting them to sin as "weapons of injustice" (*hopla adikias*).[45] In 2 Cor 10:3-5, he speaks of using weapons that are contrary to the flesh in order to wage war and destroy "strongholds" that consist of *ways of thinking* (*logismoi*) that rise up presumptuously against the knowledge of God.[46] These ways of thinking take human beings captive and therefore must be brought into subjection. This occurs as people come to live in obedience to Christ. The "war" or "struggle" that must take place is not to be waged in some supernatural sphere, therefore, but in human hearts and minds, since what must be overcome are *ways of thinking and behaving*.

For these same reasons, Jesus' efforts to bring others to live in love and righteousness as members of his community of followers so as to attain there the well-being and wholeness he sought for all generated conflict and opposition. Those human beings who held power over others by virtue of their alliance with the forces of sin, unrighteousness, and injustice were led by those forces to seek to silence Jesus by putting him to death (1 Cor 2:7-8). They could not tolerate Jesus' efforts to free human beings from their power, just as they subsequently could not tolerate the efforts of Paul on behalf of the same objective.

From Paul's perspective, the conflict and opposition that Jesus' activity on behalf of others generated left both Jesus and God his Father with two alternatives. The first of these was to bring to an end Jesus' efforts to create the type of community that both God and Jesus desired to see by having him back down from those efforts. Were they to have done so, it might have been possible for Jesus to have been spared the cross, yet the type of community that God and Jesus had sought to establish would never have become a reality. God might also have spared Jesus the suffering of the cross by taking him up into heaven prior to his passion and death in the same way that he had taken Enoch and Elijah into heaven before they died. Had God done this, however, he could no longer have expected to create a community in which all would be willing to give up what they regarded as most precious in order to seek the well-being of all out of love for them. If God

---

44. On Paul's battle-imagery in this passage, see Søren Agersnap, *Baptism and the New Life: A Study of Romans 6.1-4* (Aarhus: Aarhus University Press, 1999), 366-78.

45. On the possibility that Paul has in mind a military metaphor in Rom 6:13, see James D. G. Dunn, *Romans 1-8*, WBC 38A (Dallas: Word, 1988), 337.

46. As Harris observes, *logismoi* here "clearly has a pejorative sense" and in the context refers not only to ways of thinking but attitudes as well (*Second Corinthians*, 681-82).

had truly wished to bring into existence a community in which all would love one another and others with no limits and hold nothing back, when faced with the suffering and death of his Son, he could hardly have placed limits on his own love and held back his Son. The only way in which he could hope to accomplish that objective was to give up the life of his Son rather than sparing him such a death. If he truly loved human beings and wished for them to live in the same love, he could do no other. Therefore, when Jesus' ministry led to the threat of a violent death, the only alternative that God and Jesus had was to have Jesus remain firm to the end without backing down and let him be handed over to such a death. Only then could the type of community that God had sought to create together with his Son be brought into existence.

Paul therefore affirms not only that Jesus died but that he "gave himself for our sins to deliver us from the present evil age, according to the will of our God and Father" (Gal 1:4). In other words, in obedience to his Father, he chose to give up his life rather than seeking to save it so that others might be delivered from their sinful ways and the present evil age. Rather than pleasing himself or pursuing his own interests, he sought the good of others (Rom 15:3; Phil 2:1-8). Because he refused to compromise with sin but remained steadfast in his struggle against it, "he died to sin" (Rom 6:10).[47] His objective was that others might be constrained by his same love and live for him by living for others as well: "For the love of Christ constrains us, because we are convinced that one has died for all; consequently, all have died. And he died for all, so that those who live might live no longer for themselves, but for him who died and was raised for them" (2 Cor 5:14-15). Paul affirms not only that Christ gave himself for others in accordance with his Father's will but also that God himself gave up his Son (Rom 8:32; cf. 4:24-25). In the same way that Paul gives up his life for others in accordance with God's will as a result of his commitment to bringing others to leave behind their sins and live under Christ so that they may find life and salvation in him, so also Christ gave up his own life in obedience to his Father with the same objective in mind. It was to that same end as well that God gave up the life of his Son. Had God acted to spare his Son from death, the *ekklēsia* of which Paul speaks throughout his epistles would never have come into existence. Much less would it have taken the shape that it had now as a community in which all were willing to give of themselves fully to and for others in the same way that God and Christ had.

It might be thought that there were other alternatives open to God. One of these might have been simply to crush the forces of sin and evil through an act of power so as to destroy them. According to the logic of

---

47. Robert Jewett argues that, when Paul speaks of Christ having died to sin, he has in mind the "murderous consequences" of the sinful human actions Christ endured (*Romans: A Commentary*, Hermeneia [Minneapolis: Fortress, 2007], 407).

Paul's thought, however, this was not an option, since what God wanted was for people to be brought to live in the type of love and solidarity that Paul associates with the community of believers. Love is not something that one can bring about in others by force, coercion, imposition, or acts of power. Rather, by its very nature, love must be voluntary and heartfelt. In order to love, one must *want* and *choose* to love, yet that can only happen when one is *brought* to love by being loved. Furthermore, because sin and unrighteousness were so deeply rooted in human beings and ingrained in their ways of thinking and behaving, for God to have acted to crush and destroy sin and unrighteousness by an act of sovereign power would by definition have involved crushing and destroying human beings themselves. Therefore, according to Paul's logic, to eradicate sin and evil in that way was not an option, at least not at present. While the day will come when God will indeed take such a measure by pouring out his wrath on sin and evil to destroy them,[48] before doing so he instead chooses to be active in the ways Paul describes to bring about in human beings the love he desires to see in them for their own good. Because the behavior of those who come to live in that love will make it possible for them to attain the peace and joy that Paul associates with the reign of God (Rom 14:17), they will be saved rather than destroyed in the day when God will do away with sin, evil, and injustice definitively. In that way, he will finally make it possible for them to live free of the pain and suffering caused by those who insist on oppressing others and destroying their lives and happiness.

In the thought of Paul, therefore, the reason that Jesus had died was not because there was no other way in which God might forgive human beings their sins or destroy the forces of evil. Nor had Jesus died in order that others might come to participate in his death in some mysterious fashion or reproduce that same death in themselves. Rather, the reason that Jesus had died was because he had dedicated himself to the establishment of the type of community of which Paul speaks throughout his epistles, a community in which all would give themselves to one another and to others with a love that knows no limits and holds nothing back. What had been impossible without Jesus' death was not the forgiveness of sins or the destruction of sin and death, but the type of community that God has now brought into existence by sending his Son and handing him over to death when his efforts to make that community a reality led to the threat of the cross.

Furthermore, according to this interpretation of Paul's thought, Jesus' death did not save or redeem anyone. Strictly speaking, it did not have a purpose or an objective. God had not designed or orchestrated Jesus' death in order to "effect" something by that death. What saves human beings is not Jesus' death but his faithfulness and dedication to the task of establishing

---

48. See Rom 2:5-10; 3:5-6; 5:9; 16:20; 1 Thess 1:10; 5:9.

the type of community of which Paul repeatedly speaks, since it is by coming to live as part of that community that believers attain the salvation or wholeness that God desires for them. Throughout his epistles, Paul never affirms that Jesus' death, his blood, or his cross saves, justifies, or redeems anyone or reconciles them to God. Instead, what he says is that believers are justified, redeemed, and reconciled to God *by means of Jesus' death or blood*, that is, by means of his unbending commitment to the creation of a community in which they might come to live under him so as to attain there through him the justification and redemption he sought for them and experience the joy of living in peace with God and one another as God's friends rather than his enemies (Rom 5:6-10).

In the thought of Paul, all of these things had constituted God's objective when he sent his Son and subsequently handed him over to death. What God had wanted was not that his Son die but that he consecrate himself fully to the task of forming the type of community Paul describes in his epistles, that is, the *ekklēsia*. However, both God and his Son had known ahead of time that Jesus' consecration to that task would result in his death. In spite of this knowledge, they had chosen for Jesus to undertake that task and thereby had embraced fully the consequences of that task at the same time. From the perspective of Paul, only by giving himself fully to human beings in love by sending his Son to bring about in them his same love could God accomplish that objective. When his Son's efforts on behalf of that objective led to conflict and the threat of the cross at the hands of the rulers of this age, according to Paul God gave up his Son rather than sparing him such a death out of love for the sinful human beings he sought to save, who were not only undeserving of such a love but actively opposed to it. By embracing the cross rather than shunning it, however, God and Jesus his Son had made it possible for a community to exist in which all now live in that same love so as to be reconciled with God and one another and to live in peace with God and others there.

It is these ideas that Paul appears to have in mind when he affirms that "God shows his love for us in that, when we were still sinners, Christ died for us," and that "when we were enemies, we were reconciled to God through the death of his Son" (Rom 5:8, 10). As Paul's use of the Greek preposition *dia* in this latter verse makes clear, what has now made that reconciliation possible was Jesus' willingness to give up his life so that the type of community that he and his Father sought to bring into existence from the start might now become a reality throughout the world.[49] It is the community of which Paul speaks in Rom 8:29, composed of those who are being conformed to the image of God's Son so as to constitute a new family

---

49. Ernst Käsemann rightly notes that the preposition *dia* here is clearly instrumental (*Commentary on Romans*, trans. Geoffrey W. Bromiley [Grand Rapids: Eerdmans, 1980], 138).

together with him. Yet, as Paul states in 2 Cor 5:18-21, it is not Jesus' faithfulness to death alone that has made such a reconciliation possible, but *all* of the saving activity that God has carried out not only through Christ but through his ambassadors such as Paul as well. Because not only God and his Son Jesus but others such as Paul willingly embrace the consequences of their efforts to bring others to live in love under Jesus in the context of that community, both that community and the type of love embodied by Jesus and God in the death of his Son have now become a reality in the *ekklēsia*. As a result of what God has done through his Son, any who are not committed to living in that same love cannot rightly claim to form part of that community or truly call Jesus their Lord. Both that community as a whole and the individuals who belong to it are now stamped forever by the cross as that which defines them above all else, just as it forever defines the Lord under whom they live.

Although Paul clearly believed that in his death Jesus had laid down an example or model that others are to follow and imitate, it must be stressed that he did not see this as the *objective* of Jesus' death. Strictly speaking, what believers are to imitate and reproduce is not Jesus' sufferings and death but his unbending love for others and his willingness to endure suffering and if necessary even death so that they might be brought to live in that same love as members of his community of followers. It is this that they also see in Paul and his co-workers.[50] Furthermore, the reason that Jesus had gone to the cross was not that he wished to lay down an example for others but rather that he had dedicated himself to establishing the type of community of which Paul speaks so that people throughout the world might be brought to attain life and salvation by living in love as members of that community.

In order to understand the difference between these two ideas, a couple of the images that Paul uses in 1 Thess 2:7-12 may prove helpful. There Paul reminds the believers at Thessalonica of the way in which he and his co-workers conducted themselves as they proclaimed the gospel to them:

> But we behaved gently among you, like a nurse tenderly caring for her own children. So deeply do we care for you that we were pleased to share with you not only the gospel of God but also our very selves, because you had become so beloved to us. For you remember, brothers and sisters, our labor and toil. We worked night and day so that we might not be a burden to any of you as we proclaimed the gospel of God among you. Both you and God are witnesses of how purely, uprightly, and blamelessly we behaved toward those of you who believed, just as you know how we treated each of you as a father does his children, exhorting and encouraging and pleading with you to lead lives worthy of God, who calls you into his own kingdom and glory.

---

50. See Rom 15:1-3; 1 Cor 11:1; Phil 2:1-8; 3:17; 1 Thess 1:6-7. On this idea in Paul's thought, see Larry W. Hurtado, "Jesus' Death as Paradigmatic in the New Testament," *SJT* 57 (2004): 413-33 (431-32).

When Paul and his co-workers behaved in this way toward the Thessalonians, what they were seeking was not merely to lay down an example for them to follow or to show them how to love others. Rather, they sought to care for them, nurture and strengthen them, and build them up, even though by doing so at the same time they undoubtedly provided them with an example to follow. Similarly, a mother who cares gently and tenderly for her children is not simply attempting to teach them something, just as a father who exhorts, encourages, and pleads to his children to live in the way he desires does not do so for the purpose of giving them a lesson in how to exhort, encourage, and plead with others to live in the same way. Rather, the activity of such a mother or father is *an end in itself* aimed at the well-being of the children. In the same way, when Jesus gave himself to and for others all the way to the end of his life, even though he laid down an example for others, this was not the purpose or objective of his death, as if he had wanted to die so that he might give others an object lesson. Rather, his death was the consequence of his dedication and efforts to nurture, strengthen, and build up others so that through them the type of community he sought to establish might become a reality.

Isaiah 53 and Christ's Death for Sins

Although in a couple of passages from his epistles Paul cites words from Isaiah 52:13–53:12 (hereafter Isaiah 53) in order to claim that the proclamation regarding Christ was foretold there,[51] nowhere does Paul ever allude to the verses from that passage that describe the sufferings of the servant of God of whom it speaks. Nevertheless, many Pauline scholars believe that Paul has this passage in mind in 1 Cor 15:3-4, where he affirms that Jesus "died for our sins" and was buried and raised "according to the Scriptures," and perhaps Rom 5:19 and Phil 2:7-8 as well.[52] In particular, his affirmation that Jesus was "handed over on account of our transgressions" in Rom 4:25 echoes the last phrase of Isaiah 53, where it is said that the servant of whom the passage speaks "was handed over on account of our sins."[53]

For centuries, Isaiah 53 has been understood on the basis of the idea of penal substitution. According to this idea, when the passage speaks of the servant bearing the infirmities and iniquities of others, being wounded

---

51. See Rom 10:16; 15:21.

52. On Paul's use of Isaiah 53, see especially Francis Watson, *Paul and the Hermeneutics of Faith*, 2nd ed. (London: Bloomsbury T & T Clark, 2016), 503-16; Craig A. Evans, "Isaiah 53 in the Letters of Peter, Paul, Hebrews, and John," in *The Gospel according to Isaiah 53: Encountering the Suffering Servant in Jewish and Christian Theology*, ed. Darrell L. Bock and Mitch Glaser (Grand Rapids: Kregel, 2012), 145-70 (159-62). On what follows, see David A. Brondos, *Jesus' Death in New Testament Thought*, vol. 1: *Background* (Mexico City: Theological Community of Mexico, 2018), 203-22.

53. See Jewett, *Romans*, 342-43.

and crushed for their transgressions, enduring the chastisement of others so that they might thereby be healed, and being handed over for their sins (vv. 4-6, 10, 12), what is meant is that the servant delivers others from the divine punishment due to their sins by enduring that punishment in their stead as their substitute.[54] In reality, however, there is no evidence that Paul or anyone else in antiquity read the passage in that way.[55] Such a reading once again is based on the presupposition that in Jewish thought and the thought of Paul, it was impossible for God to forgive human beings their sins without exacting retribution for those sins by having someone endure the penalty or consequences of those sins in their place. Nor does the passage affirm that the servant's suffering or death constituted the *basis* upon which others obtained forgiveness or healing.[56]

What the passage *does* affirm is that the transgressions of the people were the *cause* of the servant's suffering and death, that he bore the sins of others, that the chastisement that led to the people's peace was upon him, and that through his bruises, wounds, or beatings the people were healed

---

54. Shalom M. Paul, for example, writes: "The servant bears the sins of the many, and because of his afflictions the multitude is forgiven. . . ." (*Isaiah 40-66: Translation and Commentary*, ECC [Grand Rapids: Eerdmans, 2012], 398). Edward J. Young similarly affirms: "When the servant bore the guilt of our sins, we are saying that he bore the punishment that was due to us because of those sins, and that is to say that he was our substitute. His punishment was vicarious. Because we had transgressed, he was pierced to death; and being pierced and crushed was the punishment that he bore in our stead" (*The Book of Isaiah: The English Text, with Introduction, Exposition, and Notes*, NICOT [Grand Rapids: Eerdmans, 1965-1972], 3:348).

55. On the interpretations of Isaiah 53 found in Jewish writings of the Second Temple period, see Martin Hengel, "The Effective History of Isaiah 53 in the Pre-Christian Period," in *The Suffering Servant: Isaiah 53 in Jewish and Christian Sources*, trans. Daniel P. Bailey, ed. Bernd Janowski and Peter Stuhlmacher (Grand Rapids: Eerdmans, 2004), 75-146. Although Hengel finds several texts that seem to allude to the suffering of certain figures that are identified with the servant of Isaiah 53, he is forced to recognize that the motif of vicarious suffering and death scarcely appears in the writings of that period. At most, a few texts may hint vaguely at that idea.

56. Contra, for example, John Oswalt, *The Book of Isaiah: Chapters 40-66*, NICOT (Grand Rapids: Eerdmans, 1998), 386-89. David L. Allen similarly goes far beyond anything found in Isaiah 53 or the Hebrew Scriptures as a whole by affirming that "the punishment for sin in view in Isaiah 53 is not temporal punishment but spiritual (eternal) punishment" ("Substitutionary Atonement and Cultic Terminology in Isaiah 53," in *The Gospel According to Isaiah 53: Encountering the Suffering Servant in Jewish and Christian Theology*, ed. Darrell L. Bock and Mitch Glaser [Grand Rapids: Kregel, 2012], 171-89 [175]). In fact, contrary to James D. Smart, who claims that "the central theme of ch. 53 is forgiveness" (*History and Theology in Second Isaiah: A Commentary on Isaiah 35, 40-66* [Philadelphia: Westminster, 1965], 195), the passage does not even mention forgiveness, but only the peace and healing that the people attain, as well as their justification (according to the MT).

and made whole (53:4-6, 8, 10-12). All of these affirmations can be understood perfectly well without recurring to the idea of penal substitution and without attributing the forgiveness of sins to the servant's sufferings and death. In fact, the passage itself indicates that it should be read differently. It stresses the reaction of the people to the servant's ghastly appearance: those who observed the servant were astonished at his semblance, since he no longer even appeared to be human (52:14), and the powerful were left speechless upon contemplating the way he had been disfigured by all that he had endured (52:15–53:2). Many even hid their faces from him and despised him out of revulsion for him (53:3). The rest of the passage also stresses the cruel sufferings and injustices the servant endured and the unjust and violent way he was put to death, as well as his willingness to submit to these things without protesting, retaliating, or even opening his mouth.

Because the speakers in the passage refer to *"our"* transgressions, sins, and iniquities, it would also be seen as a confession of sins on the part of the speakers.[57] In this way, they acknowledge openly their sin. At the same time, the speakers affirm that the servant had done nothing to deserve the mistreatment, ordeals, and death he endured. Initially the speakers appear to have believed that God was chastising the servant for his own sins, yet while they continue to see God as the one causing his sufferings and inflicting pain on him (vv. 4, 10), they come to the conclusion that God did so because of *their* sins and perhaps those of others as well, rather than any sins of the servant himself.[58] In v. 5, what the servant is said to have suffered is a chastisement which had the goal of correction, discipline, or even instruction. Such is the meaning of both the Hebrew term *mûsar* and the Greek term *paideia* used in the Septuagint translation of this verse.[59] The irony is that God brought about the people's peace and healing by inflicting the chastisement necessary to correct the people and bring them to repent of their sins, *not on the people themselves*, but *on the righteous and innocent servant*.

Although the passage states that the servant suffered and died so that the people might attain this peace and healing, it *does not* affirm that the servant's sufferings and death *in themselves* brought peace and healing for the people. Rather, in the context of the passage as a whole, that peace and healing would have been understood as the result of the people's

---

57. Jesper Tang Nielsen rightly observes: "In the confession that the servant is slain for their sins they confess that they are sinners" ("The Lamb of God: The Cognitive Structure of a Johannine Metaphor," in *Imagery in the Gospel of John: Terms, Forms, Themes, and Theology of Johannine Figurative Language*, ed. Jörg Frey, Jan G. van der Watt, and Ruben Zimmermann, WUNT 200 [Tübingen: Mohr Siebeck, 2006], 217-56 [231]).

58. On this point, see especially Joseph Blenkinsopp, *Isaiah 40-55*, AB 19A (New York: Doubleday, 2002), 352-53.

59. See Fredrik Häggland, *Isaiah 53 in the Light of Homecoming after Exile*, FAT 2/31 (Tübingen: Mohr Siebeck, 2008), 39.

recognition and repentance of their sins, since they could hardly enjoy peace and healing if they continued unabated in their sinful and destructive behavior. According to the passage, therefore, what God had sought to accomplish through the servant was that the people attain peace and healing by acknowledging their sins and turning back to God in obedience, no longer following their own way so as to continue to go astray like sheep (v. 6). It was not the servant's sufferings and death, however, that accomplished this objective, but rather the servant's persistence to the task of bringing the people back to God in spite of all that he suffered as a result of that persistence.[60]

The notion that the sins of the people were the *cause* of God's placing his servant in their midst and having him endure violence, suffering, and death there would have been understood on the basis of these same ideas. While the passage states that *God* inflicted sufferings on the servant, crushing and striking him, the fact that it refers to his bruises, wounds, and beatings, speaks of him behaving like a lamb led to the slaughter, and affirms that he was taken away by a perversion of justice clearly communicates the idea that much of what the servant suffered was inflicted on him *by other people*. He was despised and rejected *by others*, who hid their faces from him (53:3). Even the infirmities and diseases that he is said to have borne would have been regarded as being at least to some extent the result of the injuries he suffered at the hands of others, though in some sense they were also brought about by God.

If we combine these ideas with one another, we can discern a narrative that is closely akin to narratives we find elsewhere throughout the Hebrew Scriptures and Second Temple Jewish literature, as well as a number of passages from the New Testament itself.[61] Israel's God sends his servant— usually a prophet—into the midst of a sinful people in an attempt to bring them to repent and turn back to him. At least some of the people refuse to do so, and instead respond by mistreating severely and eventually killing the servant, thus committing a grave injustice.[62] Many of the people, however, including perhaps even some who had participated in the mistreatment

---

60. In this regard, Harry M. Orlinsky comments that "the innocent prophet suffered because of his unpopular mission. And when the people were made whole again, when their wounds were healed, it was only because the prophet had come and suffered to bring them God's message of rebuke and repentance" (*The So-Called "Servant of the Lord" and "Suffering Servant" in Second Isaiah*, VTSup 14 [Leiden: Brill, 1967], 57).

61. On the traditions regarding the persecution and killing of the prophets in the Hebrew Scriptures and early Jewish literature, see Orlinsky, *So-Called "Servant"*, 56-57; Claudia Setzer, *Jewish Responses to Early Christians: History and Polemics, 30-150 C.E.* (Minneapolis: Fortress, 1994), 21; Betsy Halpern Amaru, "The Killing of the Prophets: Unraveling a Midrash," *HUCA* 54 (1983): 153-80.

62. This idea runs throughout the parable of the wicked tenants that the Synoptic Gospels and the Gospel of Thomas attribute to Jesus (Matt 21:33-46; Mark 12:1-12;

and murder of the servant, do come to acknowledge their sin, repent of it, and turn back to God in obedience.[63] As a result, they are able to experience peace, healing, and wholeness.

The claim that God himself inflicted pain and suffering on the servant, perhaps bringing upon him some type of ailment, disease, or infirmity that severely disfigured or marred him, would naturally have been understood on the basis of these same ideas in Paul's day. Although the sinful people themselves would be seen as directly responsible for the wounds, bruises, afflictions, and death of the servant,[64] God could be said to have inflicted pain and suffering on the servant *indirectly* both by sending him into the midst of a sinful and violent people, knowing that they would mistreat him harshly and perhaps even kill him, and also *by insisting that the servant remain there*, in spite of the abuse, afflictions, and violent death that the servant would endure as a result of his continuing to carry out his prophetic ministry in their midst. While the people were responsible for the servant's sufferings and violent death, in a sense God was also responsible in that he willed that the servant persist in carrying out his prophetic work among the people, attempting to bring them to abandon their sinful ways and return to God, in spite of the bloody consequences of that work.

In that case, what would have led many of the people to recognize their sin, repent of it, and change their ways was *that which they observed* in the servant. Independently of the extent to which God or the people themselves were responsible for what the servant endured, it was the people's contemplation of the bruised, battered, bloody, and disfigured servant and the unjust things done to him that brought them to repent and turn back to God. As the passage emphasizes, however, it was not only their contemplation of the servant's revolting appearance that impacted the sinful people but the servant's willingness to endure such abuse and mistreatment patiently without protesting or lashing out at those who did him harm. According to the passage, what impressed the people was the servant's perseverance and the meekness he displayed while being subjected to violence and abuse. Rather than wishing his tormentors evil or asking God to punish them, he

---

Luke 20:9-19; Gos. Thom. 65-66). It is therefore very possible that it formed part of the Jesus-tradition known to Paul.

63. David A. Sapp finds this idea especially in the LXX version of Isaiah 53: "His sufferings bring them back to their senses, for his sufferings convict them of their sins" ("The LXX, 1QIsa, and MT Versions of Isaiah 53 and the Christian Doctrine of Atonement," in *Jesus and the Suffering Servant: Isaiah 53 and Christian Origins*, ed. William H. Bellinger Jr. and William R. Farmer [Harrisburg, PA: Trinity Press International, 1998], 170-92 [186]).

64. John Goldingay and David Payne rightly stress: "Verses 7-9 make it quite explicit that the suffering the vision describes is humanly wrought" (*A Critical and Exegetical Commentary on Isaiah 40-55*, ICC [London: T & T Clark, 2006], 2:309).

not only interceded for them but even went so far as to offer up his life to God on their behalf as they put him to death, imploring God to forgive them their sins and wickedness. This perseverance, meekness, patience, and commitment to serving others in spite of the abuse and violence he endured at their hands would be seen as an expression of great love for the people. In faithfulness and obedience to God and out of love even for those who did him harm, the servant chose to remain in the midst of the sinful people due to his desire that they might be brought back to God through his efforts and willingly embraced the terrible consequences of those efforts. In essence, this involved making himself a sin-offering on their behalf, since he offered his life up to God interceding for the people, asking that God might forgive them (53:10, 12).[65] It was therefore the love of the servant for the people and his commitment to bringing them to put away their sinful behavior so as to turn back to God that led to the people's peace, healing, and justification.[66] Through the servant's patient endurance of the mistreatment and violence inflicted on him, the people were delivered from a way of life that had made that peace, healing, and justification impossible.

On the basis of this interpretation of the passage, the affirmations that the servant bore the sins, iniquities, and transgressions of the people would have been understood in several different ways. First, the servant patiently bore sins, iniquities, and transgressions that were unjustly committed *against* him. Second, he bore the people's sins by taking upon himself the task and responsibility of bringing them to leave those sins behind and instead live in the way that God commanded and desired for their own good. Of course, because God willed and ordered the servant to persevere in his prophetic work among the sinful people despite the gruesome and bloody consequences to which that perseverance led, the servant would also be regarded as having endured the chastisement of God that was aimed at correcting, not *him*, but *the people*, as the passage affirms (53:5). Nevertheless, while it might be said that the servant had suffered at God's hands what the people deserved to suffer as chastisements for their sins and did so in their place, it was *not his suffering itself* that led to peace, healing, and justification for

---

65. The intercession of the servant figure is especially stressed in *Targum Isaiah*; see Jostein Ådna, "The Servant of Isaiah 53 as Triumphant and Interceding Messiah: The Reception of Isaiah 52:13–53:12 in the Targum of Isaiah with Special Attention to the Concept of the Messiah," in *The Suffering Servant: Isaiah 53 in Jewish and Christian Sources*, trans. Daniel P. Bailey, ed. Bernd Janowski and Peter Stuhlmacher (Grand Rapids: Eerdmans, 2004), 189-224.

66. As Goldingay and Payne observe with regard to the LXX version of Isaiah 53, "the passage's concern throughout is with the servant in connection with his ministry, and thus the implications of this ministry for other people.... Through his ministry the people will grow and flourish, and thus Yhwh's plan will be fulfilled" (*Isaiah 40-55*, 322).

the sinful people. Rather, these things resulted from *the way in which the servant reacted to that suffering*, with love, patience, and steadfast persever-ance to his God-given task and without complaining, protesting, or raising his voice, as well as from the impression that the servant's patient endur-ance and steadfast love for the sinful people in the midst of the sufferings they inflicted on him produced in them. And third, by interceding for the people as he went to his death, the servant had borne the people's sins and transgressions in the sense that he had sought that God forgive them those sins and transgressions. The basis for that forgiveness, however, would not be the servant's death per se, but the change that would take place in the people as a result of the servant's commitment and dedication to bringing them to turn back to God, even to the point of dying for that objective.[67]

Rather than looking to the notion of penal substitution, therefore, which was just as foreign to the thought of Paul as it was to the Hebrew Scriptures and Second Temple Judaism, if Paul had seen Isaiah 53 as foretelling what would take place in Jesus' death, he would almost certainly have understood the passage on the basis of ideas such as those just mentioned, all of which are contained or implied in the passage itself. Out of love for others, Jesus had patiently endured the abuse and violence inflicted on him by others as he carried out his God-given task of bringing others to leave behind their sinful ways and live in his same love as members of a community charac-terized by that love. Like the servant of Isaiah 53, when Jesus had been threatened with a violent death, rather than seeking to save himself from such a death by abandoning his work on their behalf, he had patiently and steadfastly persevered in that work in an attempt to bring others back to the God he proclaimed. As a result, he too had been beaten, bruised, and killed. Because God had willed that Jesus remain in the context into which God had sent him and had willed that he continue to carry out his work there in spite of the violent consequences, it would be said that Jesus had been obedient to God to the end and also that God had handed his Son over to death out of love for others rather than sparing him the death of the cross.[68]

Such an understanding of Jesus' death would also have led Paul and other believers to affirm that Jesus had died for the sins and transgressions of others, as the servant of Isaiah 53 had, but in the same sense that the servant is there said to have done.[69] He had patiently borne the sins and transgressions that sinful human beings had committed against him, yet he had also died for their sins and transgressions in the sense that he had taken

---

67. R. N. Whybray rightly notes that "the phrase 'bear sin' (*nāśā' ḥāṭ'*), which occurs almost exclusively in the laws of Exodus and Leviticus, always refers to a person's respon-sibility for his own sin, and is never used in connexion with atoning sacrifice" (*Isaiah 40-66*, NCB [London: Oliphants, 1975], 183).

68. See Rom 4:24-25; 5:19; 8:32; Phil 2:7-8.

69. See Rom 4:25; 1 Cor 15:3; Gal 1:4.

it upon himself to bring them to leave behind those sins and transgressions. His suffering and death had been the result of his commitment to that task. Of course, by bringing them to leave behind their sins and transgressions, through his faithfulness and obedience unto death he had also made it possible for them to be saved from God's wrath at those sins and transgressions. While Paul never speaks of Jesus interceding for others in his death in the way that the servant of Isaiah 53 was said to have done, it is likely that he believed that Jesus had gone to his death asking that God forgive and accept all those who would come to live under him as their Lord. At the very least, Paul would have seen Jesus' death as an implicit petition for God's forgiveness and acceptance of all who would live as his followers. While Paul speaks of Jesus interceding on behalf of believers from heaven in Rom 8:34, he does not specify whether the content of that intercession is that God forgive believers their sins or also that God act in other ways on their behalf. Paul probably would have seen Jesus' intercession as embracing both of these things and no doubt believed that Jesus had sought the same things from God in prayer throughout his life and up to the moment of his death.

If Paul understood Isaiah 53 and Jesus' death on the basis of all of these ideas, he may also have had Isaiah 53 in mind in other passages in which he speaks of Jesus' death. Among these may have been Rom 5:6-10, already mentioned above. Just as God had manifested his love for the sinful people of whom Isaiah 53 speaks by sending his servant into their midst and having him remain there despite the abuse and violence he endured so that the people might be brought to abandon their sinful ways and return to God, so God had manifested his love for those who were living as his enemies by having his Son persist in his ministry on their behalf, even at the cost of his life, so that they might leave behind their enmity and be reconciled to him. Even while they were sinners, therefore, Christ had died for them in the sense that he had given up his life so that they might be brought back to God as a result of all that he had done and would continue to do on their behalf. Through his blood—that is, his unbending commitment to that objective, even to the point of pouring out his life—, he had brought those who had been God's enemies to live under himself in righteousness so as now to be justified by God and to be at peace with him (Rom 5:1, 9-10). His act of righteousness and his obedience had therefore led to the justification of many, not because his death in itself led God to justify anyone, but because his dedication all the way to his death to the task of bringing others to live in righteousness had now made it possible for people everywhere to be justified by God by living under him as members of the community that called him Lord (Rom 5:18-19). He had "died for all" in the sense that he had given up his life as a result of his commitment to bringing others to "live no longer for themselves but for him who died and was raised for them," thus living in the same way that he had (2 Cor 5:14-15). God had "made him sin" by handing him over to death as if he were a sinner, since only by handing him over rather than sparing him such a death could God hope to bring human beings to practice his righteousness by living in the same type of love (2 Cor 5:21).

The Exaltation of Christ as Lord and the Love of God in Christ

Although throughout his epistles Paul repeatedly alludes to the love of both God and Christ, his most extensive treatment of that subject is found in Rom 8:31-39. There he describes the love of God and Christ as something that can never be overcome and affirms that nothing can ever separate believers from that love. It is a love that gives of itself entirely and holds nothing back, not even one's Son (v. 32). According to Paul, if God loves human beings so much that he was willing to hand his Son over to death so that they might live in that same love as his own, no one can doubt that God will continue to "give us all things with him." It is this same love that Paul has in mind when he affirms that no type of tribulation, distress, persecution, or other hardships can ever separate believers from the love of Christ, and that neither death, nor life, nor the present, nor the past, nor spiritual powers, nor earthly powers can ever separate believers from the love of God that is in Christ Jesus their Lord (vv. 35-39). The idea that Jesus sought to be exalted to God's side so that he might continue to seek the salvation and well-being of others from there is implicit in Paul's allusion to Jesus' intercession on behalf of others in v. 34 of this passage. Because that intercession is an act of love on Jesus' part, it might be said that in Paul's thought Jesus' resurrection and exaltation allowed his love to be made perpetual and eternal. That same love will bring him to subject all things to God some day so that God may be "all in all" (1 Cor 15:28). For that reason, according to Paul, believers will never be separated from the love of God and Christ.

While Paul does not refer explicitly to the love of God or Christ in Phil 2:1-11, there can be little doubt that throughout the passage he has in mind the love of Christ, and probably that of God as well. There he writes:

> If then there is any encouragement in Christ, any consolation of love, any fellowship in the Spirit, any affection and compassion, make my joy complete by being united in the same mind, sharing the same love, being of the same spirit, and thinking in the same way. Let nothing you do arise from selfishness or vanity, but in humility look upon others as having priority over yourselves. Let each of you consider not your own interests but those of others. Have among yourselves the same way of thinking that was reflected in Christ Jesus: even though he existed in the form of God, he did not regard equality with God as something worth clinging to adamantly, but instead he emptied himself by taking the form of a slave and coming to exist in the same manner as other human beings; and being found in human form, he

humbled himself and became obedient to the point of death—even death on a cross. For that reason, God also highly exalted him and gave him the name that is above every name, so that at the name of Jesus every knee should bend, in heaven and on earth and under the earth, and every tongue should confess that Jesus Christ is Lord, to the glory of God the Father.

Perhaps more than any other passage in Paul's epistles, this passage explains what Paul means when he affirms that Jesus died or gave up his life for others, in spite of the fact that such an affirmation does not appear in the passage itself. For Paul, Jesus had given up his life in obedience to his Father precisely so that the type of community that Paul describes at the outset of this passage might become a reality. That kind of community could be brought into existence only if Jesus himself was willing to give up his life in obedience to his Father. Of course, it was not only God's will but that of Jesus himself that had led him to give up his life, since he would hardly have given up his life for others had he himself not loved others in the way Paul describes. As the Philippian believers were now to do, Jesus had considered others to be of the highest importance and had valued their well-being and wholeness more than he did his own life. Because this is precisely the way in which his Father wanted him to think, and because his Father wanted him to give himself to and for others to the very end, by thinking in this way and giving of himself fully, Jesus was being obedient to his Father up to the very end.

According to Paul (or the hymn he is citing here), God responded to Jesus' obedience by exalting him as Lord over all. The conjunction used in Greek (*dio*) indicates that Jesus' obedience to the cross was the *reason* why God exalted him.[70] It is extremely important to grasp the connection that exists in Paul's thought between Jesus' death and his exaltation by God as Lord. From Paul's perspective, it would be totally incoherent for Jesus in his present, exalted condition as Lord simply to desire to be acclaimed, honored, and glorified for his own sake. In that case, what he would have been seeking all along was to attain a position above all others in order to exert his dominance over them and gain their adulation and obeisance by

---

70. Michael Wade Martin and Bryan A. Nash have argued that, in contrast to Greek hymns about the gods and other exalted figures, Phil 2:6-11 is "subversive" and "startling" in that it "praises Christ neither for having high descent nor for overcoming low descent, but rather for exchanging high for low descent," thus moving "in the opposite direction" from the gods and figures generally extolled in Greco-Roman literature ("Philippians 2:6-11 as Subversive *Hymnos*: A Study in the Light of Ancient Rhetorical Theory," *JTS* 66 [2015]: 90-138 [110, 118]). In addition, the hymn points to Christ's "scandalously shameful" death as "a source of praise" (127). Thus "Christ is praised for taking up what under each topos was conventionally considered shameful, and in place of what was considered honourable. His selfless motive for doing so, moreover, is implied throughout and seems to be the source of the unconventional praise. . . . At every turn, stations of shame are refurbished as stations of honour because they were taken up selflessly, in service to others, by one 'existing in the form of God'" (135).

subjecting them to himself. In other words, Jesus would have gone to the cross, *not for the sake of others out of love for them*, but *moved and motivated entirely by self-interest*. Yet this is precisely what Paul says did *not* happen. Paul could not look to Jesus and his death on the cross to exhort others to do nothing from selfishness or a desire to satisfy their own interests over against those of others if he believed that ultimately that was what Jesus himself had sought. Nor could Paul have had the concept of God that he articulates here had he thought in those terms. A God who would exalt his Son simply because he wanted to be Lord over others for his own sake and for that reason was willing to pay any price—including the cross—to get what he wanted would not be a God of love. He would be a God just like his Son, perhaps even willing to suffer, as long as he got something for himself in exchange. His ultimate goal would have been simply to be acclaimed, adulated, revered, and worshiped. Such a God would never be truly *loved*, however, because from the start he would have been seeking only his own selfish interests rather than those of others, out of a desire to establish his dominion over them. The same would be said of his Son. Paul can only exhort believers to seek the interests of others rather than their own because he proclaims a God who does the same, together with his Son, no matter how great the cost.

If we work backwards from Paul's allusion to Jesus' exaltation as Lord over all in this passage, we can comprehend more clearly Paul's understanding of the salvific significance of Jesus' death. According to Paul, what Jesus sought, and what God sought through him, was not simply the exaltation *of Jesus* but the exaltation of *the love of God in Christ Jesus* of which Paul speaks in Rom 8:31-39. In Paul's thought, everything that God has done and continues to do through Christ was designed to bring about that same love in human beings. If what God sought from the very beginning was that all might come to be "conformed to the image of his Son" (Rom 8:29), then this must have been what God was seeking and contemplating from even before the time in which he sent his Son (Gal 4:6). Christ himself must also have been seeking that same objective when he emptied himself and took the lowliest form of human being imaginable in antiquity, namely, the form of a slave, and subsequently died the most horrific type of death that existed, death on a cross, which was a death reserved primarily for slaves. Just as importantly, however, in Paul's mind Jesus must have been seeking all of these things not only at the moment of his death but throughout his ministry and up until his very last breath. His objective from the very beginning had been to see the lives of all people transformed by that same kind of love and self-emptying, because it alone could fill them with joy and make them whole.

All of this makes it clear why in Paul's thought the salvation that God sought for all is brought about by means of Christ and the cross rather than by means of the Mosaic law. It is not through the law but through Christ and his cross that the kind of love of which Paul speaks in Phil 2:1-11 and elsewhere in his epistles becomes a reality in the lives of those who come to faith in Christ. From Paul's perspective, the Mosaic law with its commandments, prohibitions, rewards, and punishments could never have produced in human beings of all nations the same type of love that God now brings about in them everywhere through Christ. At the same time, of course, God acts to save human beings not only through Christ but also through those such as Paul who reach out to others in the same love so that they might come to live under the crucified Christ as their risen Lord. The love of those who proclaim the gospel to others in word and deed, as well as their willingness to give their life for that gospel and all that it represents, is just as indispensable to the establishment of the community brought into existence through Christ as the love for others that Christ himself manifested in life and death. Yet rather than constituting a love of their own that is separate and distinct from the love of God and Christ, the love of those such as Paul who dedicate their lives to serving others is the love of God himself poured into their hearts, as well as the love of Christ, which has taken control of the lives of believers so as to constrain them to live and love in the same way that Christ did (Rom 5:5; 2 Cor 5:14).

CHAPTER 4

Redefining God's Will

Despite their disagreements over its proper interpretation, virtually all Jews in antiquity believed that the Torah God had given through Moses constituted the ultimate and definitive expression of God's will for their lives. As such, its commandments were valid for all generations, as numerous passages from the Torah itself affirmed.[1]

When Paul exhorts the believers in Christ to whom he writes to think, act, and live in certain ways, however, he consistently bases those exhortations on what he believes and proclaims regarding Christ rather than on commandments and prescriptions found in the Torah. While Paul no doubt continued to consider the Torah a valid expression of God's will, his epistles indicate that his faith in Christ brought him to the conviction that it was through Christ rather than through the Torah that God had now made known his will in definitive fashion. Such a conviction would have forced him to redefine not only the way in which God's will was to be understood but the purpose for which God had given the Torah as well.

GOD'S WILL AND THE TORAH IN SECOND TEMPLE JEWISH THOUGHT

One of the problems with translating Torah as "law" is that, in Jewish thought, the Torah is much more than a set of commandments.[2] About half of the Torah consists of narratives that for the most part do not contain legal prescriptions. Nevertheless, many different ethical principles can be derived from those narratives and considered normative for behavior.

---

1. The idea that certain commandments given in the Torah are to be kept for all generations appears in many passages throughout the Pentateuch; see, for example, Exod 12:14, 17, 21; 27:21; 31:16; Lev 3:17; 10:9; 23:31, 41; Num 15:15; 35:29.

2. On the problems of translating Torah as *nomos* or law, see Alan F. Segal, *The Other Judaisms of Late Antiquity*, BJS 127 (Atlanta: Scholars Press, 1987), 125-37.

Paul himself does this in Romans 4, for example, where he points to certain aspects of the Genesis narrative regarding Abraham in order to encourage believers in Christ to have faith in God in the same way that Abraham did. Similarly, in 1 Cor 10:1-11, he recalls the sins of the Israelites in the desert and admonishes the Corinthian believers not to behave in the same ways. He concludes that narratives such as those to which he points there were "written down for our instruction" (v. 11). There can be no question that all Jews who looked to the Torah for guidance in antiquity considered its narratives to be as normative as its explicit commandments.[3]

In order to discern God's will from the Torah, of course, it was necessary to interpret it. Given that the text of the Torah was still somewhat fluid in the Second Temple period and the oral tradition of its interpretation was even less fixed, there was a great deal of debate and disagreement regarding what constituted proper observance of the Torah.[4] By its very nature, the Torah lent itself to ambiguities and conflicting interpretations. Precisely how the Sabbath was to be observed and what constituted a violation of the Sabbath, for example, could not be determined from the Torah alone, which merely prescribed rest in general terms without specifying precisely what particular activities were to be avoided.

Furthermore, at times one needed to disobey one commandment in order to observe another. This made it necessary to define which commandments were to be considered more important or more "weighty." Thus, for example, it was necessary to determine whether it was acceptable to break the Sabbath rest in order to circumcise a male child, carry out priestly duties at the temple, engage an enemy in battle, or remove from a well or cistern an animal that had fallen into it on that day. In the Gospels, Jesus himself is presented as becoming involved in discussions such as these. While many Jews would have considered it a violation of the Sabbath to do things such as perform healings, pluck grain to eat, and carry one's mat or pallet, others might appeal to some weightier precept found in the Torah to argue not only that such actions were justified, but even that they did not constitute a violation of the Torah at all.[5] They could claim that, given the particular circumstances involved, true obedience to the Torah made it not

---

3. As Jacob Neusner has noted, in ancient Jewish thought as it is reflected in the Mishnah, "Israel's way of life is defined by the Torah's cases and stories" (*The Emergence of Judaism* [Louisville: Westminster John Knox, 2004], 41). For examples of the use of the Torah narratives to prescribe moral conduct, see 41-55.

4. On this point, see Karin Hedner Zetterholm, "The Question of Assumptions: Torah Observance in the First Century," in *Paul within Judaism: Restoring the First-Century Context to the Apostle*, ed. Mark D. Nanos and Magnus Zetterholm (Minneapolis: Fortress, 2015), 79-103.

5. See Matt 12:1-13; Mark 2:23–3:6; Luke 6:1-10; 13:10-17; 14:1-6; John 5:1-18; 7:21-23; 9:14-16.

only acceptable but necessary to allow for the activities in question.[6] On that same basis, even those who did not follow a strict literal observance of the Torah but were more flexible in their interpretations could argue that they were in fact observing the Torah faithfully rather than violating it when they carried out activities that other Jews regarded as contrary to its prescriptions.

The idea that there were core values and principles underlying all of the commandments and narratives contained in the Torah was universally recognized in Second Temple Judaism.[7] In fact, such an idea was by no means unique to Judaism, since all peoples and societies in antiquity regarded their own laws as being based on the same type of core values and principles. In Judaism, the core values and principles that were commonly acknowledged included things such as faith and trust in God, love for God and others, and the practice of justice, righteousness, compassion, forgiveness, and solidarity with those in greatest need. At times, however, many of God's people might come to see observance of the commandments as an end in itself, forgetting or disregarding the need to observe those core values and principles. Such a problem is by no means purely or even primarily a Jewish one, since people of all faiths at times come to set aside the core values and principles associated with their laws, rules, and regulations in order to focus on obedience to those laws, rules, and regulations as an end in itself.

If insufficient weight was given to the fulfillment of the values and principles underlying the commandments God had given, some might come to the conclusion that God had mandated and prohibited certain practices and activities without asking *why* he had done so. In that case, they would believe that the observance of certain commandments pleased God for no particular reason other than that they were in conformity with his sovereign will. They might also think that by observing those commandments they could gain his favor and obtain from him the blessings they desired.

Few would doubt that there were at least some Jews in antiquity who thought in this manner. Several things in the biblical and Jewish tradition guarded against such a belief, however. First, because God was thought not to need or desire anything from human beings for his own sake due to his sovereignty and omnipotence as creator of the world, there was nothing that human beings could give him or do for him that could exert any influence over him or coerce him to grant what one sought from him. Second, in the Torah and the Hebrew Scriptures as a whole, God had made it very clear that there was one thing alone that satisfied and pleased him: the

---

6. On this point, see Markus Bockmuehl, "Halakhah and Ethics in the Jesus Tradition," in *Early Christian Thought in its Jewish Context*, ed. John Barclay and John Sweet (Cambridge: Cambridge University Press, 1996), 264-78.

7. On this point, see E. P. Sanders, *Judaism: Practice and Belief, 63 BCE–66 CE* (Philadelphia: Trinity Press International, 1992), 230-35, 257-60, 267-70.

practice of justice, righteousness, mercy, kindness, and solidarity with others. This meant that ultimately it was impossible for one to fulfill anything God had commanded if it was not an expression of sincere love for him and others. By definition, therefore, anything done purely out of selfishness or self-interest out of a desire to pressure or manipulate God could not please him or obtain his favor. Instead, such behavior would provoke God to anger.

Third and most importantly, however, the stress on God's grace and unconditional love for his people that we find in the biblical and Jewish tradition meant that, in a sense, it was impossible to merit or earn God's favor because he had already *granted* that favor to his people as a *gift*. Whether God blessed his people or acted to discipline and correct them, he was acting out of love for them and pursuing what was in their best interest. For that reason, it was impossible for obedience to his commandments to merit or obtain his love, since that love was a gracious and unconditional gift. For the same reason, disobedience to God's commandments could not put an end to his love. Strictly speaking, therefore, what his people merited through their obedience or disobedience was not God's love or rejection but rather a *particular form* which God's love for them would take in accordance with his gracious purposes. If people obeyed God by doing what he commanded, his love and favor would generally take the form of blessing. If people instead disobeyed God, his love and favor would take the form of chastisement, which had the goal of purifying and correcting those who needed to be brought back to him in obedience. Of course, at times God might continue to seek to purify even those who were obedient through suffering rather than delivering them from their suffering, yet because he did this for their own good, it was an expression of his love rather than being contrary to it. At the same time, when his persistent efforts to correct people and bring them back to himself in obedience did not produce in them the desired effect, he might have no choice but to abandon them or even destroy some of them if they were themselves destroying the lives of others. If he did these things, however, it was not due to any lack of love for them, but simply because their refusal to respond to his love left him no alternative. Only in that way could he continue to seek the well-being of his people as a whole.

The Jewish belief that the Torah had been given to Israel alone led many Jews to the conclusion that God's will for Israel was distinct from God's will for people of other nations. Although the Hebrew Scriptures anticipated a time when the other nations might come to observe the Torah, it was thought that in the present age this was simply neither feasible nor possible, primarily because the other nations were irreversibly entrenched in their worship of their own gods. Most Jews would have recognized, however, that to some extent it was possible for non-Jews to live righteously by practicing the core values and principles that Jews associated with the Torah, even if they did not abandon entirely the worship of their own gods.

The belief that the Torah constituted the ultimate and definitive expression of God's will and was the greatest gift ever given to human beings would also lead most of those who held such a belief to consider it a good thing for gentiles to commit themselves to observing the commandments of the Torah if they so chose.[8] To do so would involve becoming a proselyte and living as a Jew. While proselytes would generally wish to be regarded as full members of God's people Israel, some non-Jews might be motivated to submit fully to the Jewish law not because they wished to be considered Jews but simply because they were convinced that the Mosaic law was superior to their own laws, since its observance promoted shalom and well-being in a way that the laws of other nations did not.[9] While many Jews might avoid actively seeking to make full proselytes of non-Jews in order to avoid alienating their gentile neighbors, it is hard to imagine that any would have seen full submission to the Torah on the part of non-Jews as bad or wrong in itself, as long as it was motivated by the right reasons. If the God of Israel loved all nations and wanted them to enjoy shalom and well-being alongside Israel, and if nothing could bring about shalom and well-being in the same way and to the same degree than the Torah, why would God be upset if gentiles became proselytes and began to observe the Torah's commandments? On the contrary, God would be pleased to see such a thing, and would expect the members of his people to be pleased as well.

Problems, of course, would arise if those proselytes began claiming as their own certain rights, privileges, and responsibilities that were thought to belong only to those who were Jews by birth or to act in ways that did harm to the Jewish community. For example, if those proselytes provoked to anger those non-Jews who worshiped other gods by actively seeking to bring them to abandon those gods and serve the God of Israel alone, their actions would probably be seen as harming the Jewish community as a whole, since that anger would come to be directed at the community.[10] On that basis, those proselytes might be censured by the community, just as any Jews who provoked to anger non-Jews who worshiped other gods by attempting to convert them to Judaism might face the censure of their fellow Jews.

---

8. On this point and what follows, see Paula Fredriksen, "Judaism, the Circumcision of Gentiles, and Apocalyptic Hope: Another Look at Galatians 1 and 2," *JTS* 42 (1991): 532-64 (533-48).

9. On this belief in ancient Jewish thought, see Stanley K. Stowers, *A Rereading of Romans: Justice, Jews, and Gentiles* (New Haven: Yale University Press, 1994), 58-65.

10. On this problem, see Paula Fredriksen, "Judaizing the Nations: The Ritual Demands of Paul's Gospel," *NTS* 56 (2010): 232-52 (239-40).

It is not clear whether some Jews would have considered that it was not only undesirable but impossible for non-Jews to become Jews, as Matthew Thiessen has argued.[11] On the basis of the Animal Apocalypse, a Jewish writing from the second century BCE, Thiessen argues that many Jews believed that they were "ontologically distinct" from gentiles and that this "genealogical gap" made it impossible for any gentile to become a Jew through law-observance: "It is no more likely that a gentile could turn himself or herself into a Jew than it is that a wolf or an ass or a camel could turn itself into a kosher animal such as a cow or sheep."[12] The belief that being a Jew was understood primarily in ontological terms or in terms of possessing the right genes, "stuff," or "matter," however, would have been as problematic in antiquity as it is today.[13] Then as now, many Jews would have maintained that those who are Jewish by birth but show blatant disregard for observance of the Torah are no longer truly living as Jews or as members of Israel, even though in an ethnic sense of course they would still be regarded as such. Furthermore, if one was not exclusively of Jewish lineage, it would be necessary to define precisely how many generations might pass since the last Jewish person appeared in one's genealogy in order for one to be considered a Jew by virtue of having what we now might call a "Jewish gene."[14] There is in fact ample evidence from the Second Temple period that not only individual non-Jews but in at least one instance an entire population—the Idumeans—were believed to have become fully integrated into Israel, just as many different individuals and peoples from other nations were said to have done in the Hebrew Scriptures.[15]

---

11. Matthew Thiessen attributes this idea to Paul: "Paul not only thought that gentiles *did not need to* or *should not* convert to Judaism to be acceptable to God, but that they *could not* convert to Judaism" (*Paul and the Gentile Problem* [New York: Oxford University Press, 2016], 14). Thiessen argues that the difference between Jew and gentile was thought to be "ontological and seemingly permanent" and that "gentile identity is genealogical and irreparable. . . ." (24-25).

12. Matthew Thiessen, "Paul, the Animal Apocalypse, and Abraham's Gentile Seed," in *The Ways that Often Parted: Essays in Honor of Joel Marcus*, ed. Lori Baron, Jill Hicks-Keeton, and Matthew Thiessen, ECL (Atlanta: SBL, 2018), 65-78 (67-69, 72).

13. These are terms used by Thiessen himself ("Paul," 72-73).

14. On the problem of defining who was a Jew in antiquity, see James D. G. Dunn, "The Question of Anti-Semitism in the New Testament Writings of the Period," in *Jews and Christians: The Parting of the Ways A.D. 70 to 135. The Second Durham-Tübingen Research Symposium on Earliest Christianity and Judaism*, ed. James D. G. Dunn (Grand Rapids: Eerdmans, 1999), 177-211 (181-87); Shaye J. D. Cohen, *The Beginnings of Jewishness: Boundaries, Varieties, Uncertainties*, HCS 31 (Berkeley: University of California Press, 1999), 69-174.

15. See James Carleton Paget, *Jews, Christians, and Jewish Christians*, WUNT 251 (Tübingen: Mohr Siebeck, 2010), 149-83. As Paula Fredriksen observes, "Full assumption of a Jewish social identity—meaning, for males, circumcision—was a known, and

Even more problematic, however, is Thiessen's claim that many Jews would have thought that non-Jews who submitted fully to the law were wrongly arrogating to themselves a privilege that belonged only to those who were Jews by birth. In Thiessen's words: "The gentile who usurps the Jewish law is guilty of stealing a privilege and responsibility that is not his."[16] According to the Torah itself, possession and observance of the Torah were not to be considered the exclusive privilege of anyone. Rather, for their own well-being, *any* who desired to observe the Torah were not only entitled but also encouraged to do so, since such observance would contribute to their well-being, independently of whether or not they might be considered full members of Israel.[17] As just noted, both the Hebrew Scriptures and many Second Temple Jewish writings speak of *many* non-Jews being integrated into Israel so as to pledge to serve and worship the God of Israel alone and to observe faithfully his laws. Because observance of the law brought shalom and well-being into the lives of those who submitted fully to it, any Jew who would have been opposed to non-Jews willingly subjecting themselves to the Torah and the exclusive worship of Israel's God out of a sincere and heartfelt desire to serve him would have been regarded as having selfish motives. If God truly loved people of other nations, then his people could only rejoice with him when non-Jews came to submit fully to the Torah in order to observe it alongside them, since to do otherwise would be to desire that other peoples *not* attain the shalom and well-being that resulted intrinsically from the observance of the Torah.

CHRIST AND THE REDEFINITION OF GOD'S WILL IN THE THOUGHT OF PAUL

When one looks at the ethical exhortations that Paul makes in his letters, the core values and principles he stresses seem to be no different from those found in the Torah and Second Temple Jewish literature. All are to show love, kindness, and compassion to others, including their enemies, and to abstain from repaying evil with evil or intentionally seeking to do others harm. They are also to be fair and honest in all their dealings with others and not desire or covet anything that is not their own.

---

thus a comparatively familiar, phenomenon" (*Paul: The Pagans' Apostle* [New Haven: Yale University Press, 2017], 104).

16. Matthew Thiessen, "Paul's So-Called Jew and Lawless Lawkeeping," in *The So-Called Jew in Paul's Letter to the Romans*, ed. Rafael Rodríguez and Matthew Thiessen (Minneapolis: Fortress, 2016), 59-83 (78; see also 82-83).

17. According to Scot McKnight, "It is a consistent feature of the ancient evidence, both Jewish and Gentile and both literary and nonliterary, that the Jews favored non-Jews joining their religion. . . ." (*A Light Among the Gentiles: Jewish Missionary Activity in the Second Temple Period* [Minneapolis: Fortress, 1991], 34; see 34-43).

By looking to what God has done in and through Christ rather than the Torah in order to define the core values and principles that he associates with God's will, however, Paul claims that in some sense Christ stands above the law and transcends it.[18] While believers in Christ are to continue to observe laws, commandments, regulations, and prohibitions such as those associated with the Torah and the legal codes of other nations, according to Paul they are now to obey above all else a *person*, namely, Jesus Christ, whom they are to call their Lord, as well as a message that revolves around that person, namely, the gospel. Of course, such obedience also involves the observance of particular rules, regulations, and principles associated with Christ and the gospel, yet these are to be derived from the gospel Paul proclaims concerning Christ rather than from the Torah or some other law viewed independently of that gospel.

Paul's Use of the Law in His Epistles

There are only four passages from Paul's epistles in which he cites commandments of the Mosaic law and points to them as expressing God's will for believers in Christ. In two of them, he points to the love of neighbor as the fulfillment of the law: "Owe nothing to anyone except to love one another; for whoever loves another has fulfilled the law. For, 'You shall not commit adultery,' 'You shall not murder,' 'You shall not steal,' 'You shall not covet,' and any other commandment, is summed up in this principle: 'You shall love your neighbor as yourself.' The love of one's neighbor does not do wrong to anyone; therefore love is the fulfillment of the law" (Rom 13:8-10). "For the whole law is fulfilled in a single principle, namely, 'You shall love your neighbor as yourself'" (Gal 5:14).

While in both of these passages Paul speaks of the commandment to love one's neighbor as normative for believers in Christ, in reality his words do not represent an exhortation to his readers to fulfill that commandment. Rather, he is merely affirming that, if one fulfills the principle of loving one's neighbor, one inevitably fulfills all that the law commands.[19] In fact, his words even suggest that, as long as they live in love, they need *not* concern themselves with the observance of specific commandments of

---

18. This is not to say, however, that in Paul's thought Christ supplants or supersedes the law. As we saw at the end of Chapter 2, obedience to Christ and the gospel complements obedience to the Jewish law and the laws of other peoples that promote justice rather than replacing such obedience.

19. As James Dunn notes, "The talk of love as an obligation (v 8) and the uncontrived rendering of the love command in negative as well as positive form (vv 9-10) would strike many of his audience as characteristically Jewish. But Paul nevertheless is evidently moving beyond this characteristic emphasis drawn from the law, and he would probably expect his readers to recognize a more specific allusion to the teaching of Jesus as such" (*Romans 9-16*, WBC 38B [Dallas: Word, 1988], 782).

the law because, by loving others as they should, they will thereby fulfill all of the commandments naturally.[20] In both of these passages, then, Paul is directing his readers to live in love rather than exhorting them to submit to commandments of the Mosaic law.

The only passage in which Paul explicitly exhorts those to whom he writes to obey literally a commandment of the Mosaic law is 1 Cor 5:1-13. There he affirms that it is immoral and sinful for a man to live in union with the wife of his father, as one of the members of the Corinthian community of believers was doing. He tells the Corinthians that they are to judge such behavior as unacceptable in their midst, although he stresses that this does not involve judging outsiders: "But those who are outside, God will judge. 'Remove the wicked person from within your midst'" (v. 13). Here Paul is alluding to several passages from the book of Deuteronomy, where this commandment is presented as a general principle that applies to many different situations.[21] At the same time, he appeals to a general principle common to many peoples when he writes that such sexual immorality is "of a kind that is not found even among gentiles" (v. 1). This clearly conveys the idea that Paul's condemnation of such behavior is not based on the Mosaic law alone but on principles that even non-Jews accepted as valid. In fact, what Paul cites as binding in this passage is not a commandment condemning fornication or immorality, but only the commandment to remove the evil or wicked person from the community. Even though he takes that commandment from the Mosaic law, it is hardly unique to that law, since such a practice is common among people of virtually every society and culture.

The other passage in which Paul bases an exhortation on a commandment of the Mosaic law is 1 Cor 9:9.[22] There he cites Deut 25:4: "You shall not muzzle an ox while it is treading out grain." Paul does not, however,

---

20. According to Richard N. Longenecker, "The focus of Paul's statement in Gal 5:14, as also in Rom 13:8-10, is not on law but on love" (*Galatians*, WBC 41 [Dallas: Word, 1990], 243).

21. On these passages, see Roy E. Ciampa and Brian S. Rosner, *The First Letter to the Corinthians*, PNTC (Grand Rapids: Eerdmans, 2010), 220.

22. Paul does appeal to the Mosaic law in 1 Cor 14:34-35 in order to affirm that certain women in the Corinthian congregation are to be subject to their husbands in the contexts and under the circumstances that he has in mind in the passage. Although he does not cite any particular commandment in this regard, most would agree that the allusion in this passage is to Gen 3:16, where God tells Eve that her husband "shall rule over you." Strictly speaking, of course, this is not a commandment of the Torah but a general principle that Paul would regard as applying to Jews and non-Jews alike. On the difficulties associated with Paul's allusion to a commandment of the law in 1 Cor 14:34 and the possibility that this passage is a later addition to the epistle, see David E. Garland, *1 Corinthians*, BECNT (Grand Rapids: Baker Academic, 2003), 665-67, 672-73.

insist here that his readers observe this commandment literally. Instead, he affirms that God gave it, not simply out of a concern for oxen, but for the sake of those who would come to faith in Christ in order that they might provide support for those who work on behalf of the gospel (1 Cor 9:9-14).[23] For Paul, therefore, there is a deeper or figurative sense to that commandment that is of equal or greater importance than its literal sense.

The Basis for Defining God's Will

As we have seen in the previous chapter of this study, when Paul speaks of God's plan or purposes for human beings, he points not to the Torah but to Christ. Paul's clearest statement of that plan and God's purposes is found in Rom 8:28-30. There, after referring to those who love God and are called "according to his purpose" (*kata prothesin*, v. 28), Paul continues: "For those whom he foreknew, he also foreordained to be conformed to the image of his Son, so that he might be the firstborn among many sisters and brothers" (v. 29).[24] This passage is often interpreted on the basis of the idea that God elected or predestined particular human beings to be saved long before those human beings existed.[25] It is important to note, however, that Paul does not actually say such a thing here or elsewhere in his epistles. Instead, his words can be understood in the sense that God foreordained that a large group or family of people who would be conformed to the image of his Son would come into existence, and that he determined as well that these people would be called, justified, and glorified (v. 30). All those who now come to faith in Christ so as to be conformed to his image form part of this foreordained family of sisters and brothers and can therefore count themselves among those whom God chose before the ages. In this case, what God knew ahead of time and foreordained or predestined was not the justification and glorification of certain individuals whose names and histories he foresaw long before they came into existence, but rather the justification and glorification of the community of believers as a whole, of which all who come to faith in Christ now form part. Such a community is therefore open to *all* people rather than being open only to certain individuals predestined or chosen by God long ago.

---

23. Paul may also have in mind a more general application of Deut 25:4 to human beings in general, an idea for which there is precedent in Jewish interpretations of the verse; see Ciampa and Rosner, *First Corinthians*, 404-6.

24. As Thomas R. Schreiner observes, Paul's language in Rom 8:28-30 clearly reflects the idea of a "preordained plan of God" (*Romans*, 2nd ed., BECNT [Grand Rapids: Baker, 2018], 444-45).

25. Schreiner, for example, argues that "God foreknows not just facts about the world but specific persons. Nor is the focus here on God's foreknowledge of the church; instead, individual believers are in view. . . ." (*Romans*, 444).

Independently of the manner in which Paul's allusion to God's foreknowledge of believers is interpreted, two other points from this passage are particularly important for grasping Paul's understanding of God's purposes in history. First, from the very beginning, that which God intended to accomplish revolved around Christ as God's Son and had as its goal that of bringing human beings to be conformed to his image. And second, God's plan was not merely to bring isolated individuals to be conformed to the image of his Son but to make of them a family of sisters and brothers among whom Christ would be the firstborn. In other words, what God desired was not merely to save human beings individually but to form a people or community in which they would all live as one under Christ. For Paul, salvation is by definition *collective* and involves *a people*, though not merely a *nation*, since those who are to belong to this people come from many different nations rather than from Israel alone. Most interpreters of Paul agree that when he uses the term "mystery" in his epistles, he has these same ideas in mind: that mystery involves an eternal divine plan to be accomplished through Christ aimed at the salvation of people of different nations from all over the world.[26]

While Rom 8:28-30 is the only passage in Paul's epistles in which he speaks of God's purposes in terms of establishing a community or family in which all would be conformed to the image of his Son, the same basic idea can be regarded as standing at the center of his thought and as constituting the basis for virtually everything he says concerning the way in which believers are to think and act. In Phil 2:5-8, for example, Paul exhorts believers to have in themselves the same way of thinking that Christ had in himself when he emptied himself by taking the form of a slave rather than clinging to equality with God. Precisely what this way of thinking involves is explained in the preceding verses, where Paul speaks of things such as love, consolation, fellowship, affection, compassion, unity, humility,

---

26. See Rom 11:25; 16:25; 1 Cor 2:1-8. It is possible that Rom 16:25-27 is a later addition to Paul's epistle; see Arland J. Hultgren, *Paul's Letter to the Romans: A Commentary* (Grand Rapids: Eerdmans, 2011), 20-22, 601. On Paul's use of the language of mystery, see Donald A. Carson, "Mystery and Fulfillment: Toward a More Comprehensive Paradigm of Paul's Understanding of the Old and the New," in *Justification and Variegated Nomism*, vol. 2: *The Paradoxes of Paul*, ed. Donald A. Carson, Peter T. O'Brien, and Mark A. Seifrid, WUNT 2/181 (Tübingen: Mohr Siebeck, 2004), 393-436. As Carson notes, while the content of the mystery of which Paul speaks is not always clear, it undoubtedly refers to "something that has been hidden in times past, and now revealed" (425). The same basic ideas are associated with the idea of a mystery in Ephesians and Colossians, which develop even further and more explicitly the notion of an eternal plan embracing the nations now accomplished through Christ (see Eph 1:9-12; 3:1-12; Col 1:24–2:3). Even if these epistles were not written by Paul, they are clearly rooted in his thought and can therefore be regarded as reflecting that thought to a great extent.

a lack of selfishness, a high regard for others, and a concern for the interests of others (2:1-4). Similarly, in 1 Cor 2:16, following a lengthy discussion of "the wisdom of God hidden in a mystery, which God ordained before the ages for our glory" (2:7), Paul affirms that believers have "the mind of Christ" (see 1:17–2:16). This mind or way of thinking is theirs through the Spirit, who enables them to comprehend and discern what is truly of God so as to be subject to the scrutiny of no one else (2:10-15).[27] Given the fact that in Jewish thought God's wisdom was closely related to the Torah, it is significant that Paul instead associates God's wisdom with Christ in this same context. According to Paul, Christ has been "made for us wisdom from God" (1 Cor 1:30).[28]

In both Rom 8:28-30 and 1 Cor 1:17–2:16, and probably in Phil 2:5-8 as well, Paul points back to a time prior to the coming of Christ and perhaps even prior to creation itself. He also seems to attribute some type of preexistence to Christ in 1 Cor 8:6, where he writes that there is "one Lord, Jesus Christ, through whom are all things and through whom we exist." The Epistle to the Colossians goes one step further in affirming that all things were created not only *through* Christ but also *for* him, and that "he is before all things, and in him all things hold together" (Col 1:16-17). Although these words may not be Paul's own, it is quite possible that they are in continuity with his thought. In any case, if Paul ascribed some type of preexistence to Christ as God's Son, he probably set Christ in contrast to the Torah, given that by Paul's time at least some Jews seem to have begun to teach that the Torah had existed before all things and that the world had been created both *through* it and *for* it.[29] Such a contrast would have served to emphasize the idea that from the start God had intended his will to be defined most fully through Christ rather than through the Torah alone, independently of Christ.

When Paul affirms in Phil 2:5-8 that Christ "emptied himself" to take the form of a slave by coming to exist in human form and likeness, what he is stressing is not Christ's preexistence per se but rather the tremendous love that led him not only to leave behind his equality with God and humble himself as a slave but also to give up his life by dying the death of a slave on a Roman cross. This means that, for Paul, what defines God's

---

27. As Anthony C. Thiselton stresses, when Paul speaks of the mind of Christ here, his language suggests that he has in mind a "mode of thought" or "mindset" (*The First Epistle to the Corinthians: A Commentary on the Greek Text*, NIGCT [Grand Rapids: Eerdmans, 2000], 275).

28. On Paul's association of the wisdom of God with Christ, see James D. G. Dunn, *Christology in the Making: A New Testament Inquiry into the Origins of the Doctrine of the Incarnation* (London: SCM, 1980), 176-96.

29. See Werner Förster, *Palestinian Judaism in New Testament Times*, trans. Gordon E. Harris (Edinburgh: Oliver & Boyd, 1964), 184-86.

will and his intention for human beings from even before creation is not simply *Christ himself* but *the type of love seen in Christ*, namely, a love that is willing to give itself fully, no matter how great the cost. A similar idea seems to be present in 2 Cor 8:9. There, in the context of an exhortation for the Corinthians to be generous in contributing to the offering he is collecting for the saints in Jerusalem, Paul writes: "For you know the grace of our Lord Jesus Christ, who for your sake became poor even though he was rich so that through his poverty you might become rich."[30] Both of these passages can be seen as shedding light on Paul's words in Rom 8:29: the image of God's Son to which God had always intended human beings to be conformed was an image of one who loved human beings with the same love of God even before he became one of them. This is the love of which Paul speaks and at which he marvels in Rom 8:31-39. It is that same love, which holds nothing back and is willing to endure all things for others, that was to constitute the defining characteristic of the family of sisters and brothers of which Christ was to be firstborn.

Paul also may have in mind some type of preexistence on the part of Christ in 1 Cor 11:3, where he tells the Corinthians that "Christ is the head of every man, and the head of a wife is her husband, and the head of Christ is God." In whatever manner this passage is understood, it once again places Christ in a transcendent role alongside God and subjects human beings to Christ not only as their Lord but also as God's Son.[31] Significantly, Paul uses his understanding of the relationship of Christ to God and to believers as a basis for the exhortations he makes throughout the passage (11:3-16).

Of course, when Paul wishes to speak of the love of Christ and to exhort others to live in that same love, he tends to focus not on Christ's coming or his ministry but on his willingness to give up his life so that others might come to live as part of a community defined by the same type of love. In both Rom 14:15 and 1 Cor 8:11, Paul exhorts the believers to whom he writes to show the same love and concern for others that Christ did when he died for others, especially those who are weak, seeking that they be strengthened and built up. Believers are to follow Christ in living and if necessary even dying for others rather than living solely for themselves or their own pleasure (Rom 14:1-21; 1 Cor 8:9-13). Paul tells the Romans: "Let us all please our neighbors for their good, in order to build them up. For even Christ did not please himself; but, as it is written, 'The insults of those who insulted you fell upon me'" (Rom 15:2-3). The Roman

---

30. On the discussion as to whether Paul has in mind Christ's preexistence in 2 Cor 8:9, see Murray J. Harris, *The Second Epistle to the Corinthians: A Commentary on the Greek Text*, NIGTC (Grand Rapids: Eerdmans, 2005), 578-80.

31. According to B. J. Oropeza, "Christ's headship probably implies his preexistence and lordship as creator of all things (8:4-6)" (*1 Corinthians*, NCC [Eugene, OR: Cascade, 2017], 143).

believers are thus to "be of the same mind with one another in accordance with Christ Jesus" and to accept one another as Christ has accepted them (Rom 15:5, 7).

In many other passages, Paul also defines God's will for believers by directing them to the love that Jesus showed for others in his death, when he gave up his life so that others might be brought to live in his same love as members of his community. Because Christ has died for all, believers are constrained by the love of Christ and to live for him rather than for themselves (2 Cor 5:14-15). The basis upon which Paul exhorts the Thessalonians to "encourage one another and build one another up" is that Christ died for them so that they might live with him (1 Thess 5:9-11). To manifest the love, patience, kindness, and generosity that constitute the fruit of the Spirit is to crucify the flesh (Gal 5:22-24). Paul's identification with the crucified and risen Jesus, who loved him and gave himself for him, leads Paul to consider himself "crucified with Christ" and to claim that through Christ's cross the world has been crucified to him and he to the world (Gal 2:19-20; 6:14). Although Paul does not allude explicitly to Christ or his death in Rom 12:1-2, his exhortation for believers to present their bodies to God as a living sacrifice and to be transformed in their way of thinking rather than being conformed to the world would almost certainly have brought to mind the manner in which Christ offered himself up to God due to his own refusal to be conformed to the world.[32]

In several passages, Paul points to Jesus' willingness to give up his life for others in order to criticize the behavior of those who fail to reflect that same love. He calls those who set their minds on earthly things rather than living in the same love reflected in himself and his co-workers "enemies of the cross of Christ" (Phil 3:18). Such persons "seek after their own interests, not those of Jesus Christ" (Phil 2:21). Similarly, because those who wish to compel the Galatians to be circumcised are motivated by self-interests rather than any concern for the Galatians, Paul describes them as being unwilling to suffer for the cross of Christ (Gal 6:12). He tells the Corinthians that, when they gather to eat the Lord's Supper, their factions and lack of regard for one another are entirely contrary to the spirit of what Jesus intended when he distributed the bread and the cup to his disciples at the Last Supper as his body and blood and told them to continue to celebrate the meal in memory of him (1 Cor 11:17-25). When Paul states that to eat of the bread and drink of the cup is to "proclaim the Lord's death until he comes" (11:26), his words should be understood as referring not simply to the *event* of Jesus' death, but rather to the love for others that he manifested in giving up his

---

32. This is suggested by the close parallels between Rom 12:1-2 and Romans 6, where Paul repeatedly speaks of believers dying with Christ; see Frank Matera, *Romans*, PCNT (Grand Rapids: Baker Academic, 2010), 286-87.

life for them.[33] He responds to their lack of love for one another by reminding them that to partake together of the same bread and cup is to share in Christ's body and blood and form one body with him (1 Cor 10:16-17). Paul's insistence that it was Christ rather than Paul who was crucified for the Corinthians in 1 Cor 1:13 is also a response to the divisions and quarrels that were taking place among them.

In Rom 6:3-11, Paul appears to have in mind not only Jesus' life and death but his risen condition as well. Paul's affirmation that in their baptism believers have been buried and crucified with Christ should be understood in the sense that, when they came to faith and submitted to the rite of baptism so as to become members of the community of believers, they committed themselves to living in the way that Paul describes throughout Romans 6. Just as in his own death Christ died to sin in order to live to God, so also those who have identified with Christ and his death in their baptism are to continue to consider themselves "dead to sin and alive to God in Christ Jesus" (v. 11). In their baptism, they renounced and put off their old self or person so as to become crucified with Christ (v. 6). Their body that had previously been an instrument of sin and unrighteousness has ceased to exist as such so as to become instead a body whose members are dedicated to practicing justice and righteousness (vv. 6, 12-13, 16-22).[34] To be buried into death with Christ and "united with him in a death like his," therefore, is to follow him in refusing to live as a slave of sin and injustice, since it was precisely that refusal that led to his death (v. 10). At the same time, because in their baptism believers have identified with the risen Christ as well, they are now to live to God as he does, walking in newness of life and presenting their bodies and members to God as instruments of justice and righteousness as he did (vv. 4, 10-13). Throughout this passage, then, it is Christ in his life, death, and resurrection who defines how believers are to live rather than the Mosaic law.

In this passage and several others in his epistles, Paul refers to the teaching that his readers have received regarding God's will for their lives.[35] This teaching, of course, is not primarily the instruction that Jews identified with the Torah, but instead revolves around Christ and the way of life seen in

---

33. See Peter Lampe, "Das korinthische Herrenmahl im Schnittpunkt hellenistischrömischer Mahlpraxis und paulinischer Theologia Crucis (1 Kor 11,17–34)," *ZNW* 82 (1991): 183-213 (211-12).

34. Leander E. Keck can be said to reflect faithfully Paul's thought in Romans 6 when he claims that the old *anthrōpos* that is crucified with Christ is "not part of the self, but the whole self ruled by sin," and that the body of sin "refers to the concrete, phenomenal self, the whole actual person...." (*Romans*, ANTC [Nashville: Abingdon, 2005], 162).

35. See Rom 6:17; 16:17; 1 Thess 2:5-13; 3:2; 4:1-12; 5:12.

him.[36] Paul even tells the Thessalonians that they have been "taught by God to love one another" in the context of a reminder regarding "the instruction we gave you through the Lord Jesus" (1 Thess 4:2, 9). In several passages, Paul appears to point his readers to the teaching that Jesus gave during his ministry.[37] In particular, some of the exhortations Paul makes in Rom 12:9-21 seem to reflect Jesus' teaching as we find it in the Synoptics, especially in the Sermon on the Mount of Matthew 5–7.[38] There, as in 1 Corinthians 13, Paul not only stresses the centrality of love in the life of believers in Christ but goes into detail as to the forms which that love is to take.

Of course, for Paul, Jesus' teaching embraces not only the words he spoke but the type of life that he led. Thus, even when Paul stresses certain behaviors that are not mentioned explicitly in the teaching of Jesus as we find it in the canonical Gospels but are associated with the character of his ministry there, those behaviors can be seen as constituting part of Jesus' teaching as well.[39] Although believers are to look to Christ and his service of others as a model for their behavior, Paul also exhorts them to look to his own conduct and ministry on behalf of others. The reason for this, however, is that Paul himself models his behavior on that of Christ. In 1 Cor 10:23–11:1, after exhorting believers to seek what is beneficial to others, Paul adds: "Be imitators of me, as I am of Christ." According to Paul, those who imitate him in reality are imitating not him alone but his "ways in Christ Jesus," which are therefore not simply his own but those of Christ (1 Cor 4:16-18).[40] Similarly, he tells the Thessalonians that by becoming imitators of him and his co-workers as well as "the Lord," they too become an example for other believers (1 Thess 1:6-7). According to Phil 4:9, the Philippian believers are also to continue to do the things that they have "learned and received and heard and seen" in Paul.

---

36. As Douglas J. Moo argues, in Rom 6:17 Paul is almost certainly referring to the teaching regarding Christ and the faith associated with him rather than Jewish teaching, although according to Paul's phrasing in this verse "it is not the teaching that is handed down to believers but the believers who are handed over to the teaching" (*The Epistle to the Romans*, NICNT [Grand Rapids: Eerdmans, 1996], 401-2).

37. These passages include 1 Cor 7:10-11, 1 Cor 9:14-15, and 1 Thess 5:2; see David Wenham, *Paul: Follower of Jesus or Founder of Christianity?* (Grand Rapids: Eerdmans, 1995), 4, 305-16.

38. On these parallels, see especially Michael B. Thompson, *Clothed with Christ: The Example and Teaching of Jesus in Romans 12.1–15.13*, JSNTSup 59 (Sheffield: Sheffield Academic Press, 1991), 90-110.

39. This point is especially stressed by James D. G. Dunn, "Jesus Tradition in Paul," in *Studying the Historical Jesus: Evaluations of the State of Current Research*, ed. Bruce Chilton and Craig A. Evans, NTTS 19 (Leiden: Brill, 1994), 155-78 (168-72).

40. As Boykin Sanders has argued, when Paul appeals to the Corinthians to imitate him in 1 Cor 4:16, he especially seems to have in mind the Corinthians' life in community ("Imitating Paul: 1 Cor 4:16," *HTR* 74 [1981]: 353-63).

In order to define the way in which believers are to live, Paul particularly points to different aspects of their relation to Christ. In addition to speaking repeatedly of believers as being "in Christ," in a number of passages Paul affirms that they belong to Christ.[41] Because the price that Christ had paid to establish the community of those who would live as his own was that of his life, Paul can affirm that they have been purchased with a price (1 Cor 6:20; 7:23). As Christ's possession, believers can also be called his slaves or servants.[42] Behind affirmations such as these is the idea that believers exist in order to do, not their own will, but that of Christ as their Lord. In fact, the notion that believers relate to Jesus as their Lord can be seen as constituting the foundation for all of Paul's paraenesis. They live and die not to themselves but to the Lord, because whether they live or die, they are his (Rom 14:6-8). For Paul, however, it must never be forgotten that Jesus is not merely the Lord of believers but their *crucified* Lord, since what defines him and his lordship forever is the fact that he gave up his life so that they might live as his own by living for others. In addition, because Christ's will is that they seek what is in the interests of all and build one another up in love, to belong to Christ, do his will, and live as his slaves under his lordship is not oppressive but fulfilling and liberating. It brings well-being and wholeness.

Paul uses a variety of images to describe the intimate relationship of believers to Christ that is to define who they are and how they are to live. According to 2 Cor 11:2-3, the purpose for which Paul seeks to present the Corinthians as a pure virgin to Christ as their husband is that they might practice a "sincere and pure devotion" to him. To be clothed in Christ like a garment is to live as a child of God rather than gratifying the flesh (Rom 13:14; Gal 3:27). If Paul seeks that Christ be formed in the Galatians in the way that a mother gives birth to a child, this is obviously so that Christ might live in them as he lives in Paul (Gal 2:20; 4:19). The purpose for which believers have been called into fellowship with Christ as God's Son is that he might be active among them to strengthen them to the end (1 Cor 1:8-9). Because they have been washed, sanctified, and justified in the name of Christ their Lord, they have left behind their former life in order to be united to the Lord and live as one spirit with him (1 Cor 6:9-17). According to 1 Cor 1:30, thanks to God they are in Christ, whom God has given to them as their source of wisdom, righteousness, sanctification, and redemption.

The obedience of which Paul speaks throughout his epistles is not obedience to the commandments of the Mosaic law per se but rather obedience to Christ, the truth, and the gospel.[43] For Paul, this is also the

---

41. See Rom 7:4; 8:9; 1 Cor 3:21-23; 7:17, 20-22; Gal 3:29; 5:24; cf. 1 Cor 1:16-17.

42. See 1 Cor 4:1; 7:22; Gal 1:10; Phil 1:1.

43. See Rom 2:8; 10:16; 2 Cor 9:13; 10:5-6; Gal 2:14; 3:1; 5:7; cf. 2 Cor 7:15; Phil 2:12.

"obedience of faith" that he seeks to bring about in those whom he serves.[44] The Philippian believers are to live "in a manner worthy of the gospel of Christ," "standing firm in one spirit" and "striving together with one mind for the faith of the gospel" (Phil 1:27). Paul exhorts them to be "of the same mind in the Lord" and stand fast in him not only because this is what Christ wills but also because struggling together in the cause of the gospel requires it (Phil 4:1-4). In 2 Cor 9:6-13, Paul appeals to the Corinthians to manifest their love and concern for those served by Paul's ministry by being generous in their offering for the saints, affirming that in this way they demonstrate their "obedience to the confession of the gospel of Christ." All are to share together the same mind and purpose "by the name of our Lord Jesus Christ" (1 Cor 1:10). As they serve others, everything that believers do is to be "done in love," both for one another and also for the Lord (1 Cor 16:13-16, 22). What is to bring Philemon to share his love and faith with others is all the good that is in him for the sake of Christ (Phlm 5-6). Paul tells Philemon that, while in principle he could make his appeal to him on the basis of the duty that Philemon has in Christ, he instead chooses to make that appeal on the basis of the love that leads him to be willing even to suffer prison for Christ's sake (Phlm 8-10). The reason that Paul is confident of Philemon's obedience is that Philemon's relationship to the Lord leads him to do more than what is required (Phlm 20-21). In 1 Thess 5:14-18, Paul defines "the will of God in Christ" for the Thessalonians in terms of encouraging and helping the weak patiently, praying without ceasing, rejoicing, and giving thanks in every circumstance.

This same love for others is evident in Paul's work on behalf of the Corinthians and the Philippians, both of whom he addresses as his "beloved."[45] It is for the sake of others and Christ himself that Paul proclaims Christ as Lord (2 Cor 4:5-18). The compassion he feels for the Philippians is that of Christ himself (Phil 1:8). What pleases God and obtains his approval is precisely that one serve Christ and share the gospel.[46] Those who proclaim the gospel faithfully receive the approval and commendation of Christ (2 Cor 10:13-18). The decisions Paul makes in his life are based on considerations regarding what enhances and promotes most the gospel he proclaims (1 Cor 9:16-23). Paul defines God's will for his own life on the basis of his knowledge of Christ and his desire to gain Christ and the righteousness that comes through faith in him (Phil 3:7-11). It is the conviction that Christ has made him his own that drives him (Phil 3:12). For Paul,

---

44. See Rom 1:5; 16:25-26; cf. 15:18-19. Commenting on the phrase "the obedience of faith" in Rom 1:5, Moo rightly notes that "Paul views faith in Christ and commitment to him as Lord as inseparable and mutually interpreting" (*Romans*, 400).

45. See 2 Cor 11:11; 12:15, 19; Phil 2:12.

46. See Rom 14:18; Gal 1:10; 1 Thess 2:4.

everything is loss and rubbish in comparison to gaining Christ and being found in him (Phil 3:7-9).

Throughout his epistles, Paul also presents his ministry as something that has been entrusted to him both by God and Christ. It is both God and Christ who send him out as their apostle and entrust him with the proclamation of the gospel.[47] The authority with which Paul carries out his work on behalf of the edification of others is that of Christ himself (2 Cor 10:8; 13:10). It is therefore Christ himself who orients and directs those such as Paul in their labor on his behalf. Christ is also the one to whom they will give an account of what they have done.[48]

While much more could be said about the manner in which Paul defines God's will for believers in Christ and the basis upon which he does so, what we have seen here is sufficient to demonstrate that throughout his epistles we encounter a manner of defining God's will that is fundamentally different from that of other currents of the Judaism of his day. Rather than looking to the Mosaic law or to principles derived from that law to define how the people to whom he writes are to live, think, and act, Paul consistently looks to Christ, the gospel, and the faith that revolves around Christ. God's will is that all live under Christ as those who belong to him and acknowledge him as their Lord. Yet because what defines Christ forever is the love for all that led him to give himself fully to and for others so that they might be brought to live in the same manner as members of his community, to belong to Christ and submit to him as Lord is by definition to live and give of oneself in the same way. For Paul, this way of being and giving of oneself defines not only Christ but God as well. It is through Christ rather than through the Mosaic law, therefore, that God has revealed most fully who he is and what he desires of all. For this reason, in order to define God's will, rather than pointing others to the law, Paul consistently points them to Christ and the message, faith, and life in community that revolves around Christ.

Love, Christ, and the Law

In principle, to affirm that God's will is defined through Christ and the gospel centered on him is by no means to deny that God's will is defined through the Mosaic law as well. Nevertheless, throughout his epistles Paul not only looks to Christ and the gospel to define God's will but also insists that the Mosaic law does not constitute God's will for all people. In fact, Paul rejects not only as mistaken but as contrary to God's will the notion

---

47. See Rom 1:1; 1 Cor 1:1; 9:17; 12:28; 2 Cor 1:1; 5:19-20; Gal 1:1, 15-16; 1 Thess 2:4, 7.

48. See 1 Cor 4:4; 2 Cor 5:10; Phil 2:16.

that non-Jewish believers in Christ should submit fully to the Mosaic law, including the rite of circumcision.[49]

Of course, the idea that God had intended the Mosaic law for Israel alone was common to most Jews in antiquity, just as it is common among most Jews today. It is therefore not surprising that Paul himself affirms such an idea. Nevertheless, what sets the thought of Paul apart from that of other Jews in his day is his conviction that it is Christ rather than the Torah that constitutes the supreme expression of God's love for all as well as his will for both Israel and the nations. For Paul, the blessings of salvation and life that most Jews associated with observance of the Torah are now to be given to all people through Christ, since it is through Christ that people are brought to live in accordance with God's will in the way he desires. Paul explicitly rejects one of the central tenets of Judaism, namely, the notion that the Mosaic law and the works it prescribes can in and of themselves bring about the type of righteousness that God desires to see in all for their own good. According to Paul, "no flesh will be justified in his sight by works of the law" (Rom 3:20). "No one is justified by works of the law" (Gal 2:16). "For we hold that a person is justified by faith independently of works of the law" (Rom 3:28). "I do not nullify the grace of God; for if righteousness comes through the law, then Christ died in vain" (Gal 2:21). "For if a law had been given that could give life, then righteousness would come through the law" (Gal 3:21). Paul even affirms that it was "impossible for the law" to enable "the just requirement of the law" to be fulfilled in human beings (Rom 8:3-4). In Rom 9:30-32, he writes that, in contrast to those gentiles who have attained righteousness as a result of their faith, "Israel, pursuing a law of righteousness, did not arrive at the law." A few verses later, he continues: "For being ignorant of the righteousness of God and seeking to establish their own righteousness, they did not submit to the righteousness of God" (Rom 10:3). Here the idea is clearly that submission to the Mosaic law in itself does not bring about the type of righteousness that constitutes God's will for all people.[50] In all of these passages, Paul insists that the righteousness that God desires to see in all is given not through the law but through Christ and the faith associated with him.[51]

In order to understand the logic of Paul's thought, it is necessary to consider once again the nature of the type of community that constituted

---

49. See Rom 6:14; 1 Cor 7:18-24; Gal 5:1-4, 18; 6:12-15; Phil 3:2-3.

50. On the problems involved in translating *nomon dikaiosynēs* in Rom 9:30, see Brice L. Martin, *Christ and the Law in Paul*, NovTSup 62 (Leiden: Brill, 1989), 135-38. I would argue that the phrase should be understood in conjunction with Rom 8:3-4, where Paul affirms that the law could not bring about the righteousness it demanded; see Peter Stuhlmacher, *Paul's Letter to the Romans: A Commentary*, trans. Scott J. Hafemann (Louisville: Westminster John Knox, 1994), 152.

51. See Rom 3:20-21; 5:18-19; 9:30–10:10; 2 Cor 5:21; Gal 2:16; Phil 3:4-9.

the objective of his ministry as well as the nature of laws and commandments in general. As we have seen in the previous two chapters of this study, what Paul sought was the establishment of communities in which all would give of themselves fully to God and one another in love, holding nothing back as they would seek what is in the interests of all and dedicate themselves to building one another up. At the same time, because by its very nature genuine love is something that comes from the heart, it is not something that can be legislated. Prohibitions, for example, may help to prevent destructive behavior but do not necessarily lead to constructive behavior or love for others. Laws can regulate conduct and prescribe behaviors, yet in themselves they cannot bring about sincere, heartfelt, and committed love. Only love can produce love. People must *want* to love and be *drawn* to love in order to truly love, and for that to happen they must first be truly loved by others. A *commandment* to love does not of itself produce the *desire* to love. In fact, when that commandment is enforced merely by offering people rewards for compliance and threatening them with punishments for non-compliance, they are motivated by self-interest and fear of punishment rather than by genuine love.

For this reason, in Paul's thought, what God had done through Christ was above all else to reach out to human beings in love, holding nothing back—not even his own Son—in an effort to draw them to live in the same type of love. This is the love of which Paul speaks in Rom 8:31-39: a love that gives believers all things together with his Son so that they may be his own and never be separated from him. Obviously, if God loves believers with such a love, the love that he pours into their hearts and desires to see in them must be that same love (Rom 5:5). The only way to bring about in people a love of the type of which Paul speaks in passages such as 1 Corinthians 13 is by showering them constantly with such a love and giving oneself to them fully and unreservedly, seeking their well-being and happiness by reaching out to them in many different ways with the goal of bringing them to live in the same love as well. According to Paul, that is what God has done and continues to do through Christ, who gave up his life so that others might be constrained by his same love (2 Cor 5:14-15). If God's objective was to bring human beings to be conformed to the image of his Son so that he might be the firstborn in a large family of sisters and brothers who would reflect that same image, therefore, the law was not enough. What was necessary was that God first fill their lives with the love that he has shown in giving them all things, including the life of his Son, and bring them to form part of a community whose defining characteristic would be that same love.

Of course, it would be a mistake to claim that in Jewish thought God had sought to bring his people to love others merely through legal prescriptions and commandments. As noted at the outset of this chapter, the commandments of the Torah appear in the context of a narrative and must be interpreted within that context. That narrative speaks of a God who manifests his love by creating a world in which everything is good and by pouring out his blessings upon Israel and the world in general. God's love for Israel had taken the form of redeeming the people from their slavery and afflictions in Egypt, giving them the Torah to guide them, and granting them a land of their own in which they might live.[52] In fact, in many of the passages of the Torah in which God commands his people to show love, care, and compassion for others, he reminds them of the love, care, and compassion he showed them when he delivered them from the bondage to which they themselves had been subject in Egypt.[53] Throughout the rest of the Hebrew Scriptures as well, there are many passages that describe God's love for Israel with language that is extremely moving, tender, and affectionate in the context of exhortations to obey him and return to him.

Paul would undoubtedly have agreed with his fellow Jews that the Hebrew Scriptures spoke repeatedly of God's tremendous love for his people Israel and that the commandments he had given Israel could only be understood and interpreted properly in the context of the story of God's loving dealings with Israel. Nevertheless, Paul almost certainly would have maintained that the love God had shown by sending his only beloved Son into the world and giving him over to death on a cross went beyond anything found in the Hebrew Scriptures and the Jewish tradition, especially in that it had involved paying a price in a manner that was unknown in those Scriptures and that tradition. It had not actually cost God anything to redeem his people Israel from their slavery in Egypt or introduce them into the promised land. It might perhaps be argued that God had paid a price for loving Israel when the people had repeatedly fallen into sin and God's love had left him no choice but to inflict suffering on them in order to attempt to bring them back to him. No doubt this could be seen as having pained God a great deal, yet the price that God had paid by sending his beloved Son into the world to redeem human beings from their sinful ways was that of seeing him suffer and die the horrific death of the cross. Furthermore, the love that had led God to send his Son into the world and give him over to death in the face of the cross was not for Israel alone but for the entire world: "In Christ God was reconciling the world to himself, not counting their trespasses against them" (2 Cor 5:19). In Paul's thought,

---

52. Scott D. Mackie rightly points out that "the command to love God in Deut 6:5 should be understood as advocating, in addition to loyal obedience, an emotional response commensurate with the passionate love God has first shown Israel (Deut 1:31; 4:31, 37; 6–11)" ("The Two Tables of the Law and Paul's Ethical Methodology in 1 Corinthians 6:12-20 and 10:23–11:1," *CBQ* 75 [2013]: 315-34).

53. See, for example, Exod 22:21-24; 23:9; Lev 19:33-37; 25:39-43; Deut 4:37-40; 5:14-15; 6:20-25; 7:7-11; 15:12-15; 24:17-22.

because God's intention from the very beginning had been to bring people of all nations into that community, the love for all people that God had now made known to the world in Christ and his cross had exceeded and surpassed any of the manifestations of God's love in the past.

The Purpose of the Law

If in Paul's thought the law in itself does not fulfill the function of bringing about the way of life that Paul associates with God's love in Christ, then obviously God must not have given the law for the purpose of bringing about that way of a life. It was not designed to bring about something that, according to Paul, it was incapable of bringing about. In that case, it must have been given for some other purpose that was related in some way to what God intended to do through Christ.

In Gal 3:19, Paul himself asks and answers the question of why God had given the law. There he writes: "Why then the law? It was added on account of transgressions, ordained through angels at the hand of a mediator, until the seed to which the promises had been made might come." Here Paul clearly speaks of the law fulfilling a role related to Christ, who for Paul constitutes Abraham's "seed" to whom God had made his promises (Gal 3:15-16). Paul's allusion to the law being given through angels at the hand of a mediator also seems intended to place the law in a position of secondary importance in relation to Christ and to assign to it an auxiliary role in the fulfillment of God's promises through Christ.[54]

More importantly, however, Paul's words here point to the idea that God gave the law in response to human sin. In his Epistle to the Romans, Paul presents at greater length his understanding of the problem of sin. There he speaks of it as a power that dwells in human beings, producing sinful and covetous desires that deceive and kill them and hold them in bondage (Rom 7:5-14). Even if they wish to do what is good, the sin that dwells in them will not allow it (7:15-21). Paul writes: "For in my inner person I delight in the law of God, but in my members I see another law that wages war against the law of my mind and makes me a captive to the law of sin that is present in my members" (7:22-23). Although here Paul speaks of this existence as a bondage, at the same time he represents human beings as being complicit with sin in the sense of consciously and willfully presenting their bodies to sin as "instruments of unrighteousness" so as to make their members "slaves to impurity and ever-increasing lawlessness" and make of themselves "slaves of sin" (6:12-20). Paul especially associates this existence with the flesh. The flesh leads one to live enslaved to the law of sin and to set one's mind on the things of the flesh so as to be hostile

---

54. See Longenecker, *Galatians*, 139-41.

to God (7:25; 8:5-7). The desires of the flesh result in all sorts of destructive behavior, such as immorality, impurity, dissension, and selfishness (Gal 5:17, 19-21).

Therefore, in order for people to live in the way that God desires out of love for all and for their own good, they need to be freed from sin and the flesh.[55] According to Paul, however, the law is incapable of liberating people from their captivity to the power of sin: "the mind that is set on the flesh is hostile to God; it does not submit to God's law, for it is unable to do so, and those who are in the flesh cannot please God" (Rom 8:7-8). That liberation comes only through Christ and the Holy Spirit associated with Christ.[56]

Nevertheless, the law can hold sin in check and restrain it. Paul speaks of the law doing precisely that in Rom 7:6 and Gal 3:23. It binds and confines those who are subject to it, holding them in custody and constraint. Of course, this condition of confinement is not an end in itself, but a temporary measure until the coming of Christ, through whom people are able to be liberated from the power of sin and the flesh. Paul makes this clear in Gal 3:23-25, where he speaks of the law as a *paidagōgos*. This Greek word literally means "child-conductor" and can be translated as guardian, tutor, caretaker, custodian, or disciplinarian. Paul writes: "Before the coming of faith we were confined under the law, kept in custody until the faith that was to come might be revealed. Consequently the law was our *paidagōgos* to lead us to Christ, so that we might be justified as a result of faith; but now that faith has come, we are no longer under a *paidagōgos*." Interpreters of this passage have debated extensively whether Paul's idea here is that the law led people to Christ by serving to educate and instruct them or instead by confining them and holding them in constraint. By no means are these two interpretations mutually exclusive, however.[57] A *paidagōgos*

---

55. See Rom 6:18, 22; 7:24; 8:2.

56. If we view the activity of the Spirit in light of Paul's affirmation regarding God's plan and purposes in Rom 8:29, the reason why it had been necessary for Christ to live, die, and be raised in order for God to be at work through his Spirit in the way that he now is becomes evident. Paul never claims that, for some mysterious reason, it had been impossible for God to pour out his Spirit without his Son's death and resurrection. Rather, his thought seems to be that, in order for God to bring human beings to be conformed to the image of his Son by means of that Spirit, it was first necessary for human beings to come to see and know that image, as they now have through Christ's life, death, resurrection, and exaltation. Thanks to what God has done through his Son, therefore, that Spirit can now serve to accomplish God's purposes in a way that was not possible prior to Christ's coming.

57. As Jeffrey R. Wisdom notes, the task of the *paidagōgos* included both "instruction and discipline when necessary" (*Blessing for the Nations and the Curse of the Law: Paul's Citation of Genesis and Deuteronomy in Gal 3.8-10*, WUNT 2/133 [Tübingen: Mohr Siebeck, 2001], 150). On the task of a *paidagōgos* in antiquity and the various interpretations given to Gal 3:23-25, see Michael F. Bird, *An Anomalous Jew:*

was generally an adult slave placed over a male child to keep him from falling into destructive or dangerous behavior and at times also to guide and educate him in behavior that was considered appropriate and desirable.

The way in which a *paidagōgos* fulfilled that task was by rewarding good behavior while pronouncing threats and inflicting punishment for bad behavior.[58] In many cases, the *paidagōgos* had the responsibility of constantly watching over the child under his charge and looking over his shoulder, accompanying him wherever he went and correcting him whenever necessary. The child was never left alone outside of the home and was not free to go where he wanted or do whatever he wished. Although the child was rewarded when he behaved in the way desired, he was constantly being confined, constrained, and restricted through threats of punishment so as never to be entirely free. Even the rewards that the child received for good behavior had to be earned or merited, so that it would become tiresome and cumbersome for the child to live constantly attempting to attain the behavior necessary to receive the rewards he desired.

It is likely that Paul intended his allusion to the law as a *paidagōgos* to be understood in this same manner. Both in this passage and Rom 7:6, Paul speaks of the Mosaic law functioning in basically the same manner that it is said to do in passages such as Leviticus 26 and Deuteronomy 28. It promises that the people will be rewarded with various types of blessings when they obey the commandments of the law but threatens them with chastisements and punishments if they disobey those commandments. In this way, like the *paidagōgos*, the law is constantly compelling and constraining those who live under it to obey it. If they wish to experience God's blessings, they must do what it commands. When they fail to obey, they know that chastisements and punishments will follow. They cannot free themselves from this situation, because if they decide to abandon the law, they will be unable to attain its blessings and instead continue to be subject to its punishments. According to this understanding of the law, what motivates people to observe it is a desire for the blessings it offers as a reward for obedience and fear of the sufferings and punishments it prescribes for disobedience.

Paul appears to have these same ideas in mind in Gal 3:10-12. There, citing Deut 27:26, Hab 2:4, and Lev 18:5, he writes: "For all those who proceed from works of the law are under a curse. For it is written: 'Cursed is everyone who does not remain in all the things written in the book of the law in order to do them.' For it is evident that no one will be justified before God through the law, since 'the one who is righteous will live out of faith.' But the law does not proceed from faith, since 'the one who does these

---

Paul among Jews, Greeks, and Romans (Grand Rapids: Eerdmans, 2016), 153-55; Longenecker, *Galatians*, 146-48.

58. On this point, see especially Hans Dieter Betz, *Galatians: A Commentary on Paul's Letter to the Churches in Galatia*, Hermeneia (Philadelphia: Fortress, 1979), 177-78.

things shall live in them.'"This passage has traditionally been interpreted to mean that, because no one can obey the law perfectly or adequately, all are condemned to the curse of eternal perdition.[59] However, neither here nor in Gal 3:13, where Paul speaks of Christ redeeming believers from the curse of the law by becoming a curse on their behalf, does Paul mention eternal perdition. In fact, Paul never touches on that subject anywhere in Galatians. Nor does he ever say there or elsewhere that if one could keep the law perfectly one could earn or merit one's justification and salvation.

Because passages such as Leviticus 26 and Deuteronomy 28 describe blessings and punishments that have to do with life in the present world, it is much more likely that Paul understood the curse of the law in the same manner. In fact, the curses pronounced throughout the Pentateuch on those who disobey the commandments of the law have to do with punishments experienced in the present world inflicted not only by God directly but also by means of God's people themselves, who are to cast out offenders from the community or carry out other disciplinary measures against them. This is what took place in the Jewish communities among whom Paul worked. In effect, it is also what had taken place when Jesus was crucified. Even though the Gospel traditions affirm that it was the Roman authority that had sentenced Jesus to death, they nevertheless claim that it was the Jewish authorities who had handed him over to Pilate, seeking that he be crucified after they had condemned him as a law-breaker. When Paul speaks of Jesus having undergone the curse of the law in Gal 3:13, he may have in mind the idea that Jesus was cast out of the community as a law-breaker so as to be sentenced to a type of death that the law associated with a curse.

When Paul speaks of those who live by the law being under the law's curse in Gal 3:10-12, therefore, he may simply have in mind the idea that they are constantly being threatened by punishments and curses, not in the world to come, but in the present age.[60] These punishments might be those inflicted by God upon the sinful people as a whole, such as exile, oppression at the hands of their enemies, and other types of hardships, or they might be afflictions that God brought upon particular persons or groups in response to their sins in order to discipline and correct them. It is also possible, however, that Paul had in mind the type of exclusionary measures that the Jewish community took against its members who committed blatant and willful offenses that according to the law were not to be tolerated in the people's midst. Although relatively few members of the Jewish community were subjected to those types of measures, all were constantly subject to the

---

59. See, for example, Stephen Westerholm, *Perspectives Old and New on Paul: The "Lutheran" Paul and His Critics* (Grand Rapids: Eerdmans, 2004), 376.

60. On this point, see the texts cited in Kjell Arne Morland, *The Rhetoric of Curse in Galatians: Paul Confronts Another Gospel*, ESEC 5 (Atlanta: Scholars, 1995), 33-96, 253-300.

threat of being placed under an anathema or ban so as to be excluded from the community if they persistently refused to submit to the prescriptions of the law and instead abandoned its faithful observance.

In any case, because in Rom 7:6 and Gal 3:23 Paul speaks of life under the law prior to Christ as a type of confinement or bondage, he may have regarded such a life as a curse in itself.[61] Those under the law were constantly threatened with various types of punishments and disciplinary measures in order to compel them to continue to subject themselves to the law's commandments and thereby remain within the confines of the community rather than being expelled from it. In essence, it was as if they had been placed in confinement by being enclosed within walls, as the Greek word *sygkleiomenoi* that Paul uses in Gal 3:23 implies. In this regard, the law functioned as a type of *paidagōgos*, keeping them in custody and constraint. Those who sought to break free of this confinement were also thought to be subject to the disapproval or wrath of God himself, who would withhold his blessings from them and subject them to afflictions and hardships. Even those who remained within the community and sought to observe the law faithfully might be seen as being under a curse in that they were not only restrained by threats of punishments but also had to strive to obey the commandments diligently in order to obtain the blessings promised to obedience in the law.

Paul's affirmation that no one is justified or becomes righteous by the works of the law should be understood against the background of these ideas. It is virtually impossible to translate into English his allusion to those who are *ex ergōn nomou* in Gal 3:10 and elsewhere in his epistles.[62] Paul's meaning appears to be that they base their lives on works of the law or live "out of" those works in the sense that their daily existence is grounded in those works. The phrase Paul uses should not be understood in the sense that those who live under the law rely or depend on their works to obtain God's grace and favor, as many Pauline scholars now recognize, since God's grace and favor were considered a free gift. Both the Hebrew Scriptures and Second Temple Jewish writings do affirm, however, that by doing what the law commands one may merit the blessings associated with obedience to the law, just as disobedience merits chastisements and discipline. Nevertheless, to *merit* those blessings by one's works was not to *earn* them, since the latter term implies that one's obedience to God's commandments placed God under the obligation of granting his blessings. Such an idea was foreign to the Jewish understanding of God, who was always free in his sovereignty to respond to human behavior in any way he saw fit. It was

---

61. On the background of Paul's use of the phrase "under the law," which is unknown in ancient Jewish literature, see Joel Marcus, "'Under the Law': The Background of a Pauline Expression," *CBQ* 63 (2001): 72 83.

62. See Rom 3:20; 4:2; 9:11, 32; 11:6; Gal 2:16; 3:2, 5.

also recognized that any blessings that God granted in response to one's obedience were always a gracious and merciful gift because that obedience was always imperfect and deficient. In fact, obedience itself was a gift from God. In some cases, God's grace might lead him to discipline and test even those who were obedient in order to bring them to grow in their obedience even more. When Paul speaks of those who live *ex ergōn nomou*, therefore, he seems to have in mind those who base their lives on the works that the law prescribes and the promises it makes. In that sense, they "proceed from works of the law."

Paul repeatedly contrasts those who live *ex ergōn nomou* with those who live *ek pisteōs* or "out of faith." In Rom 9:30-32, he affirms that gentiles who did not seek righteousness have attained the righteousness that proceeds from faith (*ek pisteōs*), in contrast to those who pursued a law of righteousness but did not attain it because they did so *ex ergōn* rather than *ek pisteōs*. Similarly, in Gal 2:16 he affirms that it is those who live *ek pisteōs Christou*, "out of Christ-faith,"[63] who are declared righteous rather than those who live *ex ergōn nomou*. As just noted above, in Gal 3:12 he insists that the law does not proceed from faith or is not *ek pisteōs* because "the one who does these things shall live in them." This latter phrase has commonly been understood in the sense that one attains the life of the age to come by observing the law. As many interpreters have pointed out, such an interpretation is problematic because in Paul's thought one *does* not and *cannot* attain the life of the age to come simply by observing the commandments of the law.[64] While it is possible to interpret Paul's words in the sense that he is merely stating a theoretical possibility that in reality is unattainable, it seems more likely that Paul has in mind the idea that those who base their existence on the law's works rather than on faith must live the type of existence of which he speaks in the following verses: their life is like that of a child under a *paidagōgos* in that they live restrained and confined by the law.[65]

Other statements that Paul makes in his epistles regarding the purpose of the law can be understood on the basis of these same ideas. When he affirms that the law was given "on account of transgressions" in Gal 3:19,

---

63. On this translation of *pistis Christou*, see Chapter 7 of the present study.

64. According to Martin, for example, Paul's point in Gal 3:12 is that, because no one is able to observe the law, "it is no longer even a theoretical possibility to obtain salvation by perfect obedience to the Torah...." (*Christ and the Law*, 85-86).

65. As Martinus C. de Boer argues, the future tense in Gal 3:12 ("the one who does these things shall live in them") should be understood as determinative rather than promissory (*Galatians: A Commentary*, NTL [Louisville: Westminster John Knox, 2011], 207-8). In other words, in this passage Paul is speaking of how the lives of God's people will be determined in the present rather than referring to the promise of life in the age to come.

he may have in mind not only the idea that the law restrains people from practicing harmful behavior but also that it enables them to know what things are sinful. Transgressions are not merely sins but violations of the precepts and commandments of a law. Paul's idea seems to be that the law made it possible for the sins that human beings committed to be recognized as such, perhaps not merely to restrain them but also to guide them in their life in the way that a *paidagōgos* guides a child.[66] In Rom 3:20, Paul similarly affirms that "through the law comes the knowledge of sin." This affirmation occurs in the context of his argument that none are righteous or justified by works of the law since all are under sin and that, "whatever the law says, it speaks to those who are under the law" (Rom 3:9-19). In this case, the law indicates to human beings that they are sinners and that as such they "fall short of the glory of God," that is, the glory that God intended for human beings (Rom 3:23). While the knowledge of sin that the law gives them enables them to monitor and correct their behavior and to avoid and repress behavior that is destructive, it also leads them to look to God in faith for help so that they may receive from him what they need to overcome their sinfulness and to attain the righteousness that will enable them to enjoy the salvation and shalom that God desires for all.

Paul makes similar affirmations regarding the law in Romans 4 and 5. In Rom 4:15, he writes: "For the law brings wrath; but where there is no law, neither is there any transgression." Here the law makes known what is contrary to God's will and provokes his wrath.[67] While most interpreters have understood this wrath in eschatological terms, Paul may have in mind the ways in which God was thought to punish and discipline people in the present world. Paul himself appears to speak of God's wrath in this way in 1 Thess 2:14-16, if in fact this passage formed part of the original epistle.[68] There he affirms that God's wrath has come upon certain people in the present due to their opposition to God's will. The law may therefore be said to bring wrath in the sense that it functions like a *paidagōgos* by serving as a means and a basis for punishing wrongdoing in this world rather than the

---

66. On this idea, see Terence L. Donaldson, *Paul and the Gentiles: Remapping the Apostle's Convictions World* (Minneapolis: Fortress, 1997), 132. Scholars have debated extensively Paul's affirmation that the law was "added because of transgressions" in Gal 3:19. As Andrew H. Wakefield observes, Paul's phrase *tōn parabaseōn charin prosetethē* "is rather cryptic concerning the exact relationship between the law and transgressions" (*Where to Live: The Hermeneutical Significance of Paul's Citations from Scripture in Galatians 3:1-14*, AcBib 14 [Leiden: Brill, 2003], 191 n7).

67. On this understanding of Rom 3:20 and 4:15, see James D. G. Dunn, *Romans 1-8*, WBC 38A (Dallas: Word, 1988), 160, 214-15.

68. On the problems associated with 1 Thess 2:14-16 and its interpretation, see Didier Pollefeyt and David J. Bolton, "Paul, Deicide, and the Wrath of God: Towards a Hermeneutical Reading of 1 Thess 2:14-16," in *Paul's Jewish Matrix*, ed. Thomas G. Casey and Justin Taylor, StJC (Mahwah, NJ: Paulist, 2011), 229-57.

world to come. In Rom 5:12-13, Paul affirms that as a result of Adam's sin both sin and death were already in the world prior to the giving of the law, yet sin was not accounted as such because the law had not yet been given to define sin as transgression. A few verses later, Paul continues: "And the law came in to increase transgression; but where sin increased, grace abounded even more, so that just as sin reigned through death, so also grace might reign through righteousness for eternal life through Jesus Christ our Lord" (5:20-21). Here again Paul speaks of transgressions, which suggests that he has in mind the idea that the law enables sinful and harmful behavior to be recognized as such. It is probably best to understand Paul's affirmation that "the law came in to increase transgression" in the sense that an increase in transgressions was the *result* rather than the *purpose* of God's giving of the law.[69]

This passage, however, also seems to reflect another idea that Paul develops elsewhere. In Rom 7:5, Paul writes: "For while we were in the flesh, the sinful passions that are aroused by the law were at work in our members to bear fruit for death." A few verses later, he continues:

> I would not have come to know sin had it not been through the law. For I would not have known what it is to covet had the law not said, "You shall not covet." But sin, taking opportunity through the commandment, produced in me all kinds of covetousness, for apart from the law sin lies dead. And I was once alive apart from the law; but when the commandment came, sin came to life and I died. And this commandment that was intended to lead to life instead led to death. For sin, taking opportunity through the commandment, deceived me and through it killed me (Rom 7:7-11).

Here the law's command not only makes sin known but awakens and arouses the desire to sin. By explicitly prohibiting certain actions, it incites one who previously may not even have considered carrying out those actions to contemplate the possibility of doing so. At the same time, by using constraint in an attempt to prevent people from doing whatever is prohibited, the law may awaken and strengthen the desire to do what it prohibits. When one is held in restraint or is prevented by force from doing something, one may come to desire even more strongly to do that which is prohibited. The child who is prevented from doing certain things by a *paidagōgos* may long to do those things even more, perhaps simply out of curiosity, and the moment he can escape from the grasp of the *paidagōgos* he will seek to satisfy that desire. Paul seems to have this same idea in mind in 1 Cor 15:56, where he writes that "the power of sin is the law."

When one reaches maturity, however, one refrains from destructive behavior, not because one is obliged to abstain from that behavior by a law or a

---

69. Matera, for example, translates this phrase from Rom 5:20: "the law entered in with the result that wrongdoing increased" (*Romans*, 140).

custodian, but because one realizes that even though such behavior may appear to be attractive, in reality it is harmful and undermines true well-being. For that reason, one no longer needs to be held in constraint by punishments and threats made by a law or by a person acting as a *paidagōgos*. According to Paul, this is what has now happened to believers: "now that faith has come, we are no longer under a *paidagōgos*, for in Christ Jesus you are all children of God through faith" (Gal 3:25-26). Paul seems to develop the same idea in the following verses, where he says that believers previously lived "enslaved to the elemental principles of the universe" as minors in the same way that children are placed under custodians and caretakers until they reach the age necessary to take possession of their inheritance (Gal 4:1-3).[70] Paul then goes on to argue that, when the fullness of time arrived, Christ came to redeem believers from the law and set them free from slavery so that they might live as God's sons and daughters.[71]

The Greek verb that Paul uses in Gal 4:5 is *exagorazein*, which means to purchase something away from someone else so that it no longer belongs to them.[72] Paul's idea seems to be that Christ came in order to make believers his own so that they might no longer belong to the law as its slaves or as those it holds in custody as their *paidagōgos*. Paul uses the same Greek verb in Gal 3:13, where he affirms that Christ has bought others out from under a curse by becoming a curse on their behalf. This passage should be understood in the sense that the price Christ paid in order to make believers his own so that they might no longer be subject to the confinement of the law was that of enduring a type of death that the law associated with a curse.[73] As Paul writes in Rom 8:14-17, believers now belong to Christ and to God as his children. Because they are now led by the Spirit rather than being led by the Torah as their guide and custodian, believers are no longer subject to the law.[74] According to Paul, God's Spirit enables believers to do what the

---

70. On the continuity between Gal 3:23-25 and 4:1-3, see Wisdom, *Blessing*, 151-52.

71. See Gal 4:4-7; 5:1, 13.

72. On Paul's use of *exagorazein* in Gal 3:13 and 4:5 and his use of metaphors of purchase elsewhere to speak of deliverance from slavery, see D. Francois Tolmie, "Salvation as Redemption: The Use of 'Redemption' Metaphors in Pauline Literature," in *Salvation in the New Testament: Perspectives on Soteriology*, ed. Jan G. van der Watt, NovTSup 121 (Leiden: Brill, 2005), 247-69.

73. The idea in Gal 3:13 is similar to that which appears in 1 Cor 6:20 and 7:23, where Paul tells the Corinthians that they were "bought with a price." In other words, Christ's commitment to the objective of making it possible for others to live as his own as members of his community cost him his life, yet by paying that price he accomplished that objective.

74. See Rom 6:14; Gal 5:18, 24-25. Given that in Hebrew Torah means instruction or guidance and that this was at least in part the task of a *paidagōgos* in Greek thought, it is possible that Paul derived the idea that the Torah acts as a *paidagōgos* from the Hebrew term itself.

law could not, namely, to set their mind on the things of the Spirit rather than the things of the flesh so that they may thereby attain life and peace (Rom 8:5-13). If the law's purpose was to reveal to them their sin and hold that sin in check until Christ might come, by fulfilling that task, it has led them to Christ as the one who delivers them from their sinful way of life.

This understanding of the law as a *paidagōgos* coheres well with what was said above concerning love. While rewards and punishments can serve to encourage or discourage certain behaviors, they cannot by themselves bring people to love others. In order for any behavior to be truly loving, is must be rooted in sincere and heartfelt sentiments and a wholehearted commitment to the well-being of others. Because true love is not motivated by a desire for rewards or the fear of punishment but rather by an earnest desire for the well-being and happiness of others as an end in itself, it cannot be brought about by legal prescriptions or commandments. The only way people can come to love others with that type of love is by being loved in that way themselves. While many people were no doubt already led to love in this way within the Jewish communities of Paul's day prior to his proclamation of the gospel and independently of it, for Paul that love is now brought about in the context of the community of those who come to faith in Christ so as call him "Lord"—a community that is made up of Jews and uncircumcised gentiles alike.

The Law in the Life of Believers

Paul's affirmations that believers in Christ are no longer under the law and that the law has now fulfilled its purpose of leading them to Christ have often led Pauline scholars to conclude that Paul taught that believers in Christ are not to observe the Mosaic law and that Jewish believers are to abandon their observance of that law. A careful look at his letters, however, reveals that such a conclusion is unjustified. In a sense, of course, all believers are to continue to observe the basic principles associated with the law.[75] Yet while Paul insists that gentile believers are not to submit to the law, he never says or suggests that Jewish believers are not to observe the law in the ways that they had prior to coming to faith in Christ.

To understand Paul's thought regarding the role of the law in the life of believers, it is important to distinguish between *observing* the law and being *enslaved* to the law. The passage from Paul's epistles that is particularly helpful for grasping this distinction is Romans 14. There Paul insists that believers in Christ are free to eat all things or instead abstain from certain foods. They also have the freedom to observe distinctions between certain days or alternatively to disregard those distinctions. Because of this

---

75. For this reason, as Paula Fredriksen has argued, it is inaccurate to characterize Paul's mission to the gentiles as "law-free" (*Paul*, 108-12).

freedom, they are not to judge one another with regard to such things (vv. 1-6, 10-13). What matters is that they follow their conscience and do everything out of devotion to Christ (vv. 6-9). Above all, they are to take others into consideration, walking in love so as to build one another up and avoid anything that might prove harmful to others (vv. 15-23). In the context of these affirmations, Paul writes: "I know and am convinced in the Lord Jesus that nothing is unclean in itself, but for anyone who regards something as unclean, it is unclean" (v. 14). "Everything is indeed clean, but it is wrong for you to make others fall by what you eat" (v. 20). In this passage, Paul clearly seems to have in mind questions relating to the observance of the Jewish law, in particular the commandments regarding clean and unclean foods. Paul's words in Romans 14, therefore, communicate the idea that, at least under certain circumstances, believers in Christ are free to disregard the commandments that have to do with the distinction between clean and unclean foods and the observance of certain days, which would include the Sabbath. While Paul is probably addressing gentile believers in the passage, the principles he lays out seem to apply to Jewish believers as well, since it was they rather than gentile believers who would be particularly concerned with the type of distinctions and observances that Paul mentions.[76]

Up until recently, scholars have generally maintained that in 1 Cor 9:19-22, Paul similarly insists that by virtue of his faith in Christ he is free to disregard the observance of the commandments of the Mosaic law, at least under certain circumstances.[77] There he writes:

> For although I am free in relation to all people, I have made myself a slave to all in order that I might win over more people. To the Jews I have become as a Jew, so that I might win over Jews; to those under the law as one under the law, though I myself am not under the law, so that I might win over those under the law. To those outside the law I have become as one outside the law, even though I am not outside the law of God but subject to the law of Christ, so that I might win over those without the law. To those who are weak, I have become weak, so that I might win over the weak. I have become all things to all people so that by any means possible I might save some.

Mark Nanos has argued that, because Paul remained law-observant, in this passage he is not speaking of "lifestyle adaptability" but "explaining his

---

76. On this point, see John M. G. Barclay, "Do We Undermine the Law? Study of Rom 14:1–15:6," in *Paul and the Mosaic Law*, ed. James D. G. Dunn, WUNT 89 (Tübingen: Mohr, 1996), 287-308; William S. Campbell, *Unity and Diversity in Christ: Interpreting Paul in Context. Collected Essays* (Eugene, OR: Cascade, 2013), 48-58.

77. See, for example, C. K. Barrett, *A Commentary on the First Epistle to the Corinthians*, HNTC (New York: Harper & Row, 1968), 211-14. On the traditional interpretations of 1 Cor 9:19-22, see David J. Rudolph, *A Jew to the Jews: Jewish Contours of Pauline Flexibility in 1 Corinthians 9:19-23*, 2nd ed. (Eugene, OR: Cascade, 2016), 1-13.

evangelistic tactic of adapting rhetorically" to the context of those whom he addresses.[78] Nanos also argues that for Paul to have set aside the observance of the Torah when he was among gentiles but to observe it carefully when among his fellow Jews would have been deceptive and hypocritical.[79] However, that would be the case only if Paul were not open and transparent with everyone, including especially his fellow Jews, about his custom in this regard. He would hardly be acting hypocritically or deceiving anyone if he made it known to all, both Jews and non-Jews, that it was his policy to be observant of certain commandments under certain circumstances, including especially when he was among Jews, but to set them aside under other circumstances, at least in part. The fact that he states in writing that this is his policy, knowing that his letter would be read publicly and would sooner or later be seen by both gentiles and Jews, indicates that he had no qualms about sharing openly his practice in this regard.

Given that in Second Temple Jewish thought observance of the law was defined in different ways among different groups of Jews and that virtually all Jews recognized that it was necessary at times to set aside certain commandments in order to observe others that were considered more weighty, there is not much point in debating whether Paul remained law-observant after he came to faith in Christ. No matter what interpretation of the law he followed, some Jews would have considered Paul law-observant while others would not. Even if at times Paul set aside a strict observance of certain commandments in his work on behalf of the gospel, he would have argued that he was doing so in order to observe a principle that was of greater importance, even if this principle was that of entering into full fellowship with non-Jewish believers in Christ.[80] After all, from Paul's perspective, to enter into such fellowship was to observe what the law commanded regarding love of neighbor.[81] Such a practice is suggested in 1 Cor 6:12, where Paul writes: "All things are lawful for me, but not everything is beneficial. All things are lawful for me, but I will not be dominated by anything." Here Paul states that he is free to observe what is beneficial, profitable, or expedient, yet at the same time he insists that he will not allow anything to

---

78. See Mark D. Nanos, "Paul's Relationship to Torah in Light of His Strategy 'to Become Everything to Everyone' (1 Corinthians 9:19-23)," in *Paul and Judaism: Crosscurrents in Pauline Exegesis and the Study of Jewish-Christian Relations*, ed. Reimund Bieringer and Didier Pollefeyt, LNTS 463 (London: T & T Clark, 2012), 106–40.

79. Mark D. Nanos, "Was Paul a 'Liar' for the Gospel? The Case for a New Interpretation of Paul's 'Becoming Everything to Everyone' in 1 Cor 9:19-23," *RevExp* 110 (2013): 591-607.

80. According to Rudolph, for example, "Paul's accommodation language in 1 Cor 9:19-23 likely refers to halakhic adaptability in different table-fellowship contexts, with ordinary Jews, strict Jews and Gentiles" (*A Jew to the Jews*, 17).

81. See Rom 13:8-10; Gal 5:14.

hold him in subjection or have dominance over him. Among these things would have been the Mosaic law, at least as other Jews interpreted it. Paul therefore fulfills what the law commands without being enslaved to the law.

In 1 Cor 9:21, Paul refers to the "law of Christ." He uses similar language in Gal 6:2, where he exhorts the Galatian believers to bear one another's burdens and thereby "fulfill the law of Christ." While Paul may be using the phrase "law of Christ" in two different ways in these passages, in both instances he clearly seems to be alluding to God's will as it is defined through Christ.[82] He may also be referring to the idea that believers are to interpret the Mosaic law on the basis of their faith in Christ and perhaps in the same way that Christ himself interpreted it. This would have involved being flexible with regard to a strict literal observance of certain commandments in order to observe the weightier principles underlying those commandments and the law as a whole. In Rom 2:27-29, Rom 7:6, and 2 Cor 3:6, Paul makes a distinction between the spirit and the letter of the law. According to the second of these passages, believers "serve in the newness of the spirit and not the oldness of the letter" (Rom 7:6). In whatever manner this verse is understood, at the very least it implies that believers are at times free to set aside a strict literal observance of the law in order to observe its spirit, especially as they are led by the Spirit of God.

In light of these passages and others in his epistles, it is likely that Paul allowed himself a certain degree of freedom with regard to the observance of many of the commandments of the Mosaic law as they had traditionally been interpreted. He would have encouraged his fellow Jewish believers in Christ to practice the same type of freedom in their observance of the law. By no means would this have meant setting aside entirely the observance of the law in daily life. Instead, it would have involved observing the law in the way that Paul had prior to coming to faith in Christ under normal circumstances, yet being flexible with regard to the strict observance of certain commandments when necessary in order to have fellowship with gentile believers in Christ, promote the gospel, and do what was most beneficial for others. In light of passages such as Phil 3:4-9, where Paul affirms that he regards all things as rubbish in comparison to Christ in the context of an allusion to his former life of meticulous law-observance, it can hardly be doubted that Paul regarded the proclamation of the gospel and fellowship among Jewish and gentile believers in Christ as taking precedence over an observance of the law that was inflexible and allowed for no exceptions. The same conclusion can be drawn from his repeated affirmations that in

---

82. Michael Winger, for example, argues that the parallel between 1 Cor 9:21 and Gal 6:2 is "doubtful" ("The Law of Christ," *NTS* 46 [2000]: 537-46 [545-46]). On the meaning of the phrase "law of Christ," see especially de Boer, *Galatians*, 378-81; Graham N. Stanton, "The Law of Moses and the Law of Christ," in *Paul and the Mosaic Law*, ed. James D. G. Dunn, WUNT 89 (Tübingen: Mohr, 1996), 99-116.

Christ believers have freedom and are not under the law because they are led by the Spirit.

Although Paul nowhere states explicitly that he continued to observe the Mosaic law in the way that most Jews did, several passages from his epistles suggest that he continued to value law-observance among Jews in general and Jewish believers in Christ in particular. In Rom 3:1-2, for example, after asking what advantage the Jew has and what the value of circumcision is, he answers: "Much, in every respect." This statement comes several verses after he affirms that "circumcision is of value if you practice the law" (Rom 2:25). In both of these passages, he explicitly affirms that circumcision is good and profitable. In Rom 3:21, he affirms that the righteousness of God is "attested by the law and the prophets," thereby attributing to the law the function of witnessing to the righteousness that comes through Christ. At the end of the same section of his epistle, Paul writes: "Do we then nullify the law through faith? By no means! On the contrary, we establish the law" (Rom 3:31). In Rom 7:12-16, Paul insists that the law is holy and spiritual and that its commandments are just and good. In addition, rather than viewing in a negative light the law's role in revealing sin and leading people to Christ as a *paidagōgos*, Paul would have seen these functions of the law as a good thing. A *paidagōgos* fulfills a role that is helpful and conducive to the well-being of others rather than doing something that is harmful or negative.

If Paul viewed favorably the observance of the law on the part of Jewish believers in Christ, as these passages suggest, then in light of other passages from his epistles that we have seen previously, he would have agreed that Jewish believers are to observe the law without being enslaved by it. In that case, their observance of the law would be an act of freedom on their part and the law would no longer function as a *paidagōgos* for them, since they would follow their conscience as to what was best in every circumstance in the way that Paul recommends in passages such as Rom 14:1–15:6, 1 Cor 6:12, and 1 Cor 9:19-22. Jewish believers would be led both by the Holy Spirit and by the spirit of the law, as well as by the "law of Christ" and other considerations related to their faith in Christ, so as to determine what was most beneficial, profitable, and expedient for themselves and others in every instance. When they ate, drank, and observed special days in conformity with the law or at times abstained from some of these observances, they would do so "to the Lord," out of devotion to him and with a desire to please him, as Paul encourages all believers to do in Rom 14:6.

This understanding of the observance of the law also meant that Jewish believers in Christ such as Paul could be said to have "died to the law" together with Christ, as Paul writes in Rom 7:1-6 and Gal 2:19-20. By virtue of their faith in Christ and the fact that they had died with Christ in the sense of putting away their old self or person, they were no longer bound by the law or restrained by it in the way that they had been previously. Instead, they were free to live to God and Christ by observing the law out of love for God and others under normal circumstances, while at the same time being flexible with regard to that observance under other circumstances. Because that law had served as God's instrument to lead them to Christ, they might also be said to have "died to the law through the law so as to live to God" (Gal 2:19). Paul's allusion to dying to the law in this verse should probably be understood in terms of dying to his former relationship with the law rather than in the sense that he no longer observes the law.[83] It might even be said that he *observes* it without being *under* it in the way that he had been previously. When Paul states that he has died *to* the law *through* the law, his words should probably be understood in the sense that, once the law has led people to Christ as its end or goal (Rom 10:4), they become "dead to the law" in that they no longer relate to the law in the way that they did previously, even though they may continue to observe it in their daily life. It is therefore *through* the law, which leads them to Christ, that they die *to* the law.

At the same time, it should be stressed that the situation of gentile believers in Christ was distinct from that of Jewish believers. While in principle Paul may not have been opposed to gentile believers in Christ observing the Mosaic law, when they subjected themselves to the law and to circumcision in the way that some persons were pressuring the gentile believers in Galatia to do, they were enslaving themselves to the law and negating their freedom in Christ. In essence, they were allowing themselves to be bound and held in custody in a manner comparable to that of a grown man who has left behind his childhood so as no longer to be subject to a *paidagōgos* only to submit once again to that *paidagōgos* in order to be placed in confinement under him. Such a man would be subjecting himself once more to forms of control and discipline that were fitting only for children. For that reason, for Paul it is unthinkable that the gentile believers in Galatia might submit to the law and to circumcision in the way some within the *ekklēsia* were pressuring them to do.

In Galatians 4, a few verses after affirming that believers in Christ had been "enslaved to the elemental things of the world" when they lived as minors (v. 3), Paul continues:

> At that time, however, when you did not know God, you were enslaved to gods who by nature are not truly gods; but now that you have come to know God—or rather to be known by God—, how can you turn back to the weak

---

83. Caroline Johnson Hodge has argued that Gal 2:19 should not be understood in the sense that Paul no longer observes the law but rather in the sense that he has died to those practices or attitudes that would distance him from gentiles (*If Sons, Then Heirs: A Study of Kinship and Ethnicity in the Letters of Paul* [Oxford: Oxford University Press, 2007], 122).

and beggarly elemental things in order to be enslaved by them once more? You observe days and months and seasons and years. I am afraid for you, that I may have labored among you in vain (vv. 8-11).

Although Pauline scholars have disagreed over the interpretation of several parts of this passage, the general ideas seem clear. Before coming to faith in Christ, when the Galatians still practiced idolatry, they had not only observed certain days and times as sacred but had been a slave of those observances, probably because the gods they served were thought to demand that their worshipers submit slavishly to those observances and to punish any who failed to do so. Paul's affirmation that the Galatian believers are turning *back* to the slavish observance of the same kind of regulations indicates that, from his perspective, for them to submit to the Mosaic law would be to submit to the same type of captivity and bondage that had characterized their life previously when they worshiped their traditional gods.[84] He is simply incredulous that they might choose to return to such an existence.

In Gal 3:1-5, after asking the Galatians: "Who has bewitched you?," he reminds them that they had received from God his Spirit independently of any subjection to the law on their part, simply through faith. By pouring out his Spirit upon them, God had not only in effect declared his full acceptance of them in their uncircumcised condition but had also freed them from their previous existence and worked many wonders among them. For the Galatians now to submit to the Mosaic law and to circumcision would therefore be to go back to the fleshly existence that was theirs before they had received the Spirit.

After contrasting the freedom that is theirs in Christ with a life of slavery throughout Galatians 4, Paul tells the Galatian believers in Gal 5:1: "For Christ has set us free to live in freedom. Therefore stand fast and do not be subjected once again to a yoke of slavery." Here again, Paul regards the type of subjection to the law that some are attempting to impose on the Galatian believers as a form of slavery. By claiming that to submit to the law would involve coming to be under a yoke "once again" (*palin*), Paul suggests that life under the law is comparable to the type of existence that the Galatian believers led when they worshiped other gods prior to coming to Christ.[85]

For Paul, then, it was not only senseless but also wrong for gentile believers in Christ such as the Galatians to subject themselves to the same type

---

84. On this understanding of Gal 4:3, 8-11, see Longenecker, *Galatians*, 165-66, 178-83; James D. G. Dunn, *A Commentary on the Epistle to the Galatians*, BNTC (London: A & C Black, 1993), 212-13, 223-30.

85. As Longenecker notes, in antiquity the term "yoke" (*zygos*) was used not only by Jews to speak of life under the Torah but also among non-Jews to refer to "any disagreeable burden that was unwillingly tolerated. . . ." (*Galatians*, 224-25).

of law-observance practiced by Jews. Rather than being benefited in some way by such an observance, they would be placing themselves in bondage to commandments and regulations that for them would be onerous, enslaving, and in the case of circumcision, extremely painful. Those who were pressuring them to become circumcised were therefore doing them great harm and acting purely out of self-interest rather than out of any kind of love or concern for the Galatians themselves.

CHAPTER 5

REDEFINING JUDAISM

For those Jews who lived in accordance with their Jewish faith and traditions, Judaism was the way of life that had been mandated by the one true God for those who formed part of his chosen people Israel. Outside of believing that such a way of life was superior or preferable to the ways of life of other peoples, however, Jews in general had many different ideas regarding God's desires and intentions for the Jewish people and the Judaism they practiced. In some Jewish circles, those ideas constituted a subject of intense debate and at times even led to conflict among Jews themselves.

Like his fellow Jews, Paul also had views regarding what God desired to see take place with regard to Judaism and the Jewish people in the present age. Interpreters of Paul's letters have often claimed that he expected Judaism to be replaced by the new faith he proclaimed concerning Christ and eventually even to disappear as such. Today, however, Pauline scholars have increasingly come to regard such an idea as foreign to his thought.[1]

At the same time, however, Paul's proclamation that salvation came through faith in Christ rather than through the observance of works commanded in the Torah inevitably raised the question of *why* Jewish believers in Christ should continue to live as faithful Jews in accordance with the Torah. Now that God gave his blessings of salvation, forgiveness, and righteousness through Christ rather than the Torah alone and non-Jews who did not observe the Torah had equal access to those blessings, what sense did it make for Jews to continue to practice Judaism and submit to the commandments of the Torah God had given Israel? By comparing and contrasting Paul's vision for Judaism with that of his Jewish contemporaries,

---

1. For a summary of this discussion, see Terence L. Donaldson, "Supersessionism and Early Christian Self-Definition," *JJMJS* 3 (2016): 1-32; William S. Campbell, "Perceptions of Compatibility between Christianity and Judaism in Pauline Interpretation," *BibInt* 13 (2005): 298-316; Mark D. Nanos, *Reading Paul within Judaism*, vol. 1 of *Collected Essays of Mark D. Nanos* (Eugene, OR: Cascade, 2017), 3-59.

we can discern in general terms the way in which Paul and his fellow believers in Christ would have responded to that question.

GOD'S VISION FOR JUDAISM IN SECOND TEMPLE JEWISH THOUGHT

By the Second Temple period, largely as a result of the destruction of the northern kingdom of Israel at the hands of the Assyrians centuries earlier, the members of the people of Israel had come to be known primarily as Jews or Judeans (*Ioudaioi* in Greek), since the southern kingdom of Israel had been composed primarily of Israelites who belonged to the tribe of Judah (*Ioudas*). Their homeland likewise received the name of Judea (*Ioudaia*). For this reason, the way of life God commanded in the Torah out of love for his people could simply be called Judaism. By the time of Jesus and Paul, therefore, what God was said to expect of his people Israel was that they live as Jews and practice Judaism.[2]

Most Jews recognized, however, that the conditions under which they were living were far from the ideal conditions of which the Torah spoke. They lived under foreign domination rather than enjoying the peace and blessings of living under God's reign in the land he had given them. They also continued to suffer many types of trials and hardships rather than experiencing the shalom and well-being that according to the Torah God had intended to be theirs. Obviously, therefore, something had to happen in order for all of the promises God had made to his people to be fulfilled. In particular, it was God's desire that something happen *to Judaism* and *within Judaism*. But what exactly was it that God desired to see take place?

When we look at Second Temple Jewish literature as well as the Jewish writings composed in the decades immediately following the destruction of the Jerusalem temple in 70 CE, we find a wide variety of answers to that question. While there was a great deal of diversity of thought among Jews in general, this diversity was particularly evident among the many different groups of Jews that came into existence during the Second Temple period.[3] These included not only the four sects (*haireseis*) mentioned by Josephus, namely the Pharisees, Sadducees, Essenes, and a "fourth philosophy," but

---

2. On the background and history of the term *Ioudaios* and its cognates, see Peter J. Tomson, *Studies on Jews and Christians in the First and Second Centuries*, WUNT 418 (Tübingen: Mohr Siebeck, 2019), 141-61; Shaye J. D. Cohen, *The Beginnings of Jewishness: Boundaries, Varieties, Uncertainties*, HCS 31 (Berkeley: University of California Press, 1999), 69-106.

3. On the diversity within Second Temple Judaism, see Lester L. Grabbe, *A History of the Jews and Judaism in the Second Temple Period*, vol. 3: *The Maccabean Revolt, Hasmonean Rule, and Herod the Great (175-4 BCE)*, LSTS 95 (London: T & T Clark, 2020), 134-75; George W. E. Nickelsburg, *Ancient Judaism and Christian Origins: Diversity, Continuity and Transformation* (Minneapolis: Fortress, 2003), 9-183.

many other groups as well.[4] Many Jews identified closely with certain teachers or rabbis such as Gamaliel, Hillel, and Shammai, in contrast to those who followed charismatic leaders such as Judas the Galilean, Theudas, or the "Egyptian." While most Jews identified with the worship offered to Israel's God at the Jerusalem temple and held in high regard the priests and high priests who presided over the worship offered to the God of Israel there, many did not.[5] Some Jews believed it was good and acceptable to be assimilated into the non-Jewish population and even adopt some of the beliefs, customs, and practices of other peoples, while others condemned strongly any type of assimilation and advocated Jewish separatism. In some Jewish circles beliefs that have come to be labeled "apocalyptic" became prominent, yet many Jews rejected apocalyptic thought as foreign to Judaism and its Scriptures.[6] Even among those Jews who identified with a particular group there were differences of opinion and belief, with the result that many subdivisions and subgroups also existed within the Jewish groups of Paul's day.

As we noted at the outset of Chapter 1 of this study, due to their different understandings of God's will for the Jewish people and for Judaism, there is a sense in which each of these different Jewish leaders and groups can be said to have believed in a different God. Some Jews believed in a God who wanted them to rise up in arms against Rome or resist Roman rule in other ways, while other Jews believed in a God who wanted them to submit obediently to Rome and its emperor, at least for the time being. The God of the Essenes called on those who wished to serve him to withdraw to the desert to live apart from other Jews, yet few Jews shared their understanding of God and his will. Some Jews proclaimed a God who wanted all Jews to follow the interpretation of the Torah law given by the Pharisees, while others believed that God intended for the Torah to be observed in the way that the Sadducees taught. When some Jews began to proclaim that God had sent Jesus as his Son and as Israel's Messiah, most of their fellow Jews maintained that God had done no such thing and therefore that the God whom those Jews were proclaiming was not truly the God of Israel. In fact, some Jews were convinced that the true God had determined

---

4. See E. P. Sanders, *Judaism: Practice and Belief, 63 BCE–66 CE* (Philadelphia: Trinity Press International, 1992), 317-490; James C. VanderKam, *An Introduction to Early Judaism* (Grand Rapids: Eerdmans, 2001), 175-93.

5. On the different attitudes toward the Jerusalem temple among Jews in the Second Temple period, see Philip Church, *Hebrews and the Temple: Attitudes to the Temple in Second Temple Judaism and in Hebrews*, NovTSup 171 (Leiden: Brill, 2017), 29-198.

6. For a summary of the characteristics of Jewish apocalyptic, see John J. Collins, "What Is Apocalyptic Literature?," in *The Oxford Handbook of Apocalyptic Literature*, ed. John J. Collins (Oxford: Oxford University Press, 2014), 1-16; Lester L. Grabbe, *An Introduction to Second Temple Judaism: History and Religion of the Jews in the Time of Nehemiah, the Maccabees, Hillel and Jesus* (London: T & T Clark, 2010), 87-105.

that Jesus should be condemned to death, as the Roman authorities had done with the approval or consent of at least some of the Jewish leaders, and wanted any Jews who believed in Jesus to be censured, reprimanded, and perhaps even persecuted in some way in order to prevent them from misleading other Jews. Among these, of course, was Paul or Saul prior to his experience on the road to Damascus.

What all of these different Gods had in common, of course, was that they expected Jews to practice Judaism by living in accordance with the Torah. Yet each of these Gods had a distinct vision of what should happen *to* Judaism and *within* it. By examining these different Gods and their vision for Judaism, we can not only obtain a greater appreciation of the variety of thought that existed among Jews in the Second Temple period but also come to grasp more clearly what was unique about the understanding of God and his vision for Judaism that existed among Paul and his fellow believers in Christ.

1. The God who wanted to see Judaism reaffirmed.

Most Jews in antiquity would probably have understood God and Judaism in this way.[7] They strove to be faithful to the Mosaic law, attended a synagogue or Jewish place of prayer with at least some regularity, had their infant sons circumcised, and raised and educated their children in the Jewish faith. They also followed the laws regarding diet and purity, offered up prayers to Israel's God according to Jewish custom, celebrated the Jewish holy days, and traveled to Jerusalem for the Jewish festivals when they could or made pilgrimages there at other times, participating in the sacrificial worship at the temple.[8]

While there were undoubtedly some differences among these Jews in the way they interpreted obedience to the law, they would generally have followed other Jews with whom they associated in adopting whatever interpretations were common among them. In most cases, they would have had contact with someone trained in the interpretation of the law, such as a Jewish teacher or rabbi, who would provide them with guidance as to how the Torah should be observed in their daily life. Some of them may have accepted and followed somewhat stricter interpretations of the law than others, yet even the differences of interpretation among different Pharisees

---

7. On the following points, see especially Shaye J. D. Cohen, *From the Maccabees to the Mishnah*, 2nd ed. (Louisville: Westminster John Knox, 2006), 165-66; Sanders, *Judaism: Practice and Belief*, 241-303.

8. On the widespread participation of Jews in the worship offered at the Jerusalem temple, see Shaye J. D. Cohen, "The Temple and the Synagogue," in *The Cambridge History of Judaism*, vol. 3: *The Early Roman Period*, ed. William Horbury, W. D. Davies, and John Sturdy (Cambridge: Cambridge University Press, 1999), 298-325 (307-13).

or rabbis such as Hillel and Shammai were not great.[9] Any disagreements over the proper interpretation of the law were therefore relatively minor and did not prevent most Jews from gathering together with others whose interpretations of the commandments were different on some points.

2. The God who wanted to see Judaism reinforced.

There is evidence that some Jews actively sought to bring other Jews to practice more faithfully and fervently their Judaism. This seems to have been one of the objectives of the Pharisees, for example. Scholars continue to debate questions such as who the Pharisees were, where they were active, how they interpreted the Torah, and what objectives they pursued in relation to other Jews.[10] It seems clear, however, that they sought to convince their fellow Jews to adopt their interpretations and practices with regard to the Torah and to be more fervent in their obedience to its commandments.[11]

To some extent, the Pharisees may have had the power or authority to impose on other Jews their interpretations of the Torah. Such was especially the case with those who formed part of the Sanhedrin or Jewish council due to their ability to legislate and enforce the decisions they made on the basis of the law.[12] Many Pharisees, however, would have preferred simply to encourage greater piety and devotion among their fellow Jews by peaceful means. There were no doubt many other Jews and Jewish groups who pursued the same aim. They sought not only to *reaffirm* the practice of Judaism but also to *reinforce* it.

3. The God who wanted to see Judaism reformed.

For some Jews, it was not enough to attempt to reaffirm or reinforce Judaism. What God desired was that Judaism be *reformed*. Such a reformation would

---

9. For a comprehensive consideration of these differences, see Jacob Neusner, *The Rabbinic Traditions about the Pharisees before 70*, part 1: *The Masters* (Leiden: Brill, 1971), 184-376.

10. On these questions, see Sanders, *Judaism: Practice and Belief*, 413-57; Joachim L. W. Schaper, "The Pharisees," in *The Cambridge History of Judaism*, vol. 3: *The Early Roman Period*, ed. William Horbury, W. D. Davies, and John Sturdy (Cambridge: Cambridge University Press, 1999), 402-27.

11. N. T. Wright has referred to this objective in terms of an "intensification of Torah" (*The New Testament and the People of God*, vol. 1 of *Christian Origins and the Question of God* [Minneapolis: Fortress, 1992], 221-22, 335-36; see also 229-30, 237-38).

12. As Joan Taylor has argued, to whatever extent the Pharisees occupied positions of formal authority within Jewish society, they certainly had a great deal of power and influence over the general population (*The Immerser: John the Baptist within Second Temple Judaism*, SHJ [Grand Rapids: Eerdmans, 1997], 156-86). On this point, see also Roland Deines, "The Social Profile of the Pharisees," in *The New Testament and Rabbinic Literature*, ed. Reimund Bieringer et al., JSJSup 136 (Leiden: Brill, 2010), 111-32.

be seen as involving changes in the way in which Judaism was practiced or structured. John the Baptist, for example, called on other Jews to go beyond the mere observance of the Torah as most Jews had come to understand it in order to live out their Judaism in the ways that he prescribed, fulfilling the deeper principles of the Torah.[13] The baptism he practiced had not been commanded explicitly in the Torah, though he undoubtedly would have claimed that it was grounded in the Torah in some way. Other Jews called for reforms in the interpretation of the Torah or in the sacrificial worship that was being offered up to the God of Israel at the Jerusalem temple.[14] While some Jews would simply call for changes to be made in the way Judaism was being practiced, others would want to see the high priest ousted so as to be replaced by someone who was more deserving of the position.[15]

Bruce Chilton, for example, has argued that the rabbi Hillel was opposed to the practice of offering sacrifices that were not one's own but had been purchased.[16] Other Jews may have been opposed to the way in which the temple tax and the tithes and offerings were gathered or what was done with them *after* they were gathered.[17] There were undoubtedly many Jews who thought that the Jewish authorities should change the way in which they related to the Romans. Some wanted those authorities to become less tolerant and accommodating to Roman interests, while others wanted them to be more aggressive in resisting Roman interference in Jewish life and the

---

13. On this aspect of John's thought, see Taylor, *Immerser*, 101-54; Robert L. Webb, "John the Baptist and His Relationship to Jesus," in *Studying the Historical Jesus: Evaluation of the State of Current Research*, ed. Bruce Chilton and Craig A. Evans, NTTS 19 (Leiden: Brill, 1994), 179-229 (187-206).

14. See Cohen, *From the Maccabees to the Mishnah*, 122-29; Mark Adam Elliott, *The Survivors of Israel: A Reconsideration of the Theology of Pre-Christian Judaism* (Grand Rapids: Eerdmans, 2000), 235-43; Sanders, *Judaism: Practice and Belief*, 452-57.

15. On the opposition to the high priestly families among many Jews, see especially Jonathan Klawans, *Purity, Sacrifice, and the Temple: Symbolism and Supersessionism in the Study of Ancient Judaism* (Oxford: Oxford University Press, 2006), 147-50; Richard A. Horsley, "The Dead Sea Scrolls and the Historical Jesus," in *The Bible and the Dead Sea Scrolls: The Second Princeton Symposium on Judaism and Christian Origins*, ed. James H. Charlesworth (Waco, TX: Baylor University Press, 2006), 3:37-60 (45-50); Craig A. Evans, "Jesus' Action in the Temple: Cleansing or Portent of Destruction?," in *Jesus in Context*, ed. Bruce Chilton and Craig A. Evans, AGJU 39 (Leiden: Brill, 1997), 395-439 (408-28, 433-34).

16. Bruce Chilton, *The Temple of Jesus: His Sacrificial Program within a Cultural History of Sacrifice* (University Park: Pennsylvania State University, 1992), 101-3.

17. On Jewish views regarding the temple tax, see Ekkehard W. Stegemann and Wolfgang Stegemann, *The Jesus Movement: A Social History of its First Century*, trans. O. C. Dean Jr. (Minneapolis: Fortress, 1999), 119-23; William Horbury, "The Temple Tax," in *Jesus and the Politics of His Day*, ed. Ernst Bammel and C. F. D. Moule (Cambridge: Cambridge University Press, 1984), 265-86 (277-82).

practice of Judaism.[18] Reforms of many different types could be proposed, defended, demanded, or carried out. According to those Jews who called for reforms, the God of Israel was displeased with the way that Judaism was being practiced among many of their fellow Jews and called on his people to make significant changes of some type.

4. The God who wanted to see Judaism restored.

In the eyes of many Jews, the practice of Judaism or the Torah had become corrupted and needed to be restored to a form in which it had existed previously. At least some Jews longed for what was called "the restoration of Israel." For some, this restoration involved a return to the "glory days" of Israel under David and Solomon, even though the Hebrew Scriptures describe the time of Solomon as one of great social injustice and inequity.[19] Others understood this restoration in terms of being brought to live in the type of paradise that had existed prior to the sin of Adam and Eve.[20]

In whatever way this restoration was understood, it involved a critique of the conditions under which God's people were now living. God wanted his people to enjoy shalom and well-being rather than being subjected to the suffering and oppression that characterized their lives at present. In order for them to attain what God desired for them, the people needed to be liberated from foreign rule and brought to live in the way God desired and commanded in the Torah. Either of these two things might be seen as the condition of the other.[21]

Whether or not the Jewish people understood themselves still to be in exile in Jesus' day, no one believed that the restoration of Israel had already taken place.[22] Nor is there any clear evidence that those Jews who came to

---

18. On these ideas, see Irving M. Zeitlin, *Jesus and the Judaism of his Time* (Oxford: Basil Blackwell, 1988), 29-37.

19. On the different conceptions of Israel's restoration in the Second Temple period, see Michael E. Fuller, *The Restoration of Israel: Israel's Re-gathering and the Fate of the Nations in Early Jewish Literature and Luke-Acts*, BZNW 138 (Berlin: de Gruyter, 2006), 23-101.

20. According to Émile Puech, for example, "The Essenes' eschatology connects with the protological concept of awaiting entry to the lost paradise. They expected the restoration of mankind to the state he was in before the original fall" ("Messianism, Resurrection, and Eschatology at Qumran and in the New Testament," in *The Community of the Renewed Covenant: The Notre Dame Symposium on the Dead Sea Scrolls*, ed. Eugene C. Ulrich and James C. VanderKam [Notre Dame: University of Notre Dame Press, 1994], 235-56 [253]).

21. See Ed Condra, *Salvation for the Righteous Revealed: Jesus amid Covenantal and Messianic Expectations in Second Temple Judaism*, AGJU 51 (Leiden: Brill, 2002), 274-75.

22. On the idea that the Jewish people remained in exile in the first century CE, see N. T. Wright, "Yet the Sun Will Rise Again. Reflections on the Exile and Restoration in Second Temple Judaism, Jesus, Paul, and the Church Today," in *Exile: A Conversation*

believe in Jesus as Israel's Messiah maintained that Israel's exile had come to an end when Jesus had died and been raised, contrary to what N. T. Wright has claimed.[23] Any Jews who would have affirmed such a thing would have been told simply to look at the reality around them to see that such a restoration had not yet come to pass. The conditions under which the people of Israel were living had not changed as a result of Jesus' crucifixion. Those who longed for Israel's restoration could only obey God's commandments to the best of their abilities and wait patiently for God to intervene in history to deliver Israel from its present plight. Of course, by definition, the restoration of Israel would involve the restoration of Judaism as well, since all of God's people would be brought to practice the way of life God had commanded when that restoration took place.

5. *The God who wanted to see Judaism* redeemed.

Many Jews would have regarded the redemption of Israel and its restoration as synonymous with one another. However, while restoration is generally understood as a return to a situation that existed previously, redemption would have been understood in terms of a liberation that would bring about something entirely new, that is, a "new age" (*ha-olam haba'*; *to kainon aiōnion*). This new reality would be unlike anything Israel or human beings in general had known in the past.[24]

Hopes regarding what this new age would be like varied greatly.[25] Some imagined a radical transformation of the whole of creation and human beings in general, while others conceived of the two worlds or ages as being in close continuity with one another. Many Jews believed that a descendant of David would appear as Messiah to bring about Israel's redemption.[26] In the thought of some Jews, this redemption would be preceded by the resurrection of the dead and perhaps a final judgment as well. There were also Jews who anticipated a period of great tribulation prior to the redemption

---

with N. T. Wright, ed. James M. Scott (Downers Grove, IL: InterVarsity Academic, 2017), 19-80 (19-45).

23. Wright attributes this idea to Paul: "The end of this exile, and the real 'return', are not now future events to be experienced in terms of a cleansed Land, a rebuilt Temple, an intensified Torah. The exile came to its cataclysmic end when Jesus, Israel's representative Messiah, died outside the walls of Jerusalem, bearing the curse, which consisted of exile at the hands of the pagans, to its utmost limit" (*New Testament*, 406).

24. See Wright, *New Testament*, 320-38.

25. On the following, see Craig A. Evans, "Aspects of Exile and Restoration in the Proclamation of Jesus and the Gospels," in *Jesus in Context*, ed. Bruce Chilton and Craig A. Evans, AGJU 39 (Leiden: Brill, 1997), 263-93 (276-81); Sanders, *Judaism: Practice and Belief*, 275-303.

26. On these beliefs, see Condra, *Salvation*, 236-50.

of Israel.[27] This tribulation, however, would have a specific purpose, namely, that of weeding out those who were not truly committed to living in conformity with God's will from those who were so that the latter might enjoy fully the shalom God desired for all.[28]

Like those Jews who hoped for the restoration of Israel, those who awaited Israel's redemption often insisted that it was necessary for God's people to return to him in obedience to his law. Among some, however, it was thought that God would act to bring about in his people the obedience he desired to see by creating a new heart in them, writing his law upon their heart and pouring out his Spirit upon them in the way that the prophets Jeremiah and Ezekiel had foretold. According to Jer 31:31-34, God would also forgive all of the sins that his people had committed in the past and establish a new covenant with them. Similar ideas appear in a number of Second Temple Jewish writings.[29] Some of these writings also looked forward to a day in which God would free his people from the evil inclination that impeded them from doing his will.

Undoubtedly, those Jews who shared these ideas had different views regarding the extent to which this new life of obedience would depend on human beings themselves. Some stressed that God alone would bring about such a life in those whom he had elected previously out of sheer grace. Others stressed the free will of human beings in order to claim that only those who chose to be obedient at present would be enabled to be perfected in their obedience in the future.[30] As the Dead Sea Scrolls demonstrate, among at least some Jews it was possible to maintain both of these apparently contradictory ideas simultaneously.[31] In any case, the redemp-

---

27. See Brant Pitre, *Jesus, the Tribulation, and the End of the Exile: Restoration Eschatology and the Origin of the Atonement*, WUNT 2/204 (Tübingen: Mohr Siebeck, 2005), 41-130.

28. For this reason, it would have been senseless for Jesus' followers to claim that he had undergone the great tribulation or messianic woes in their place; see David A. Brondos, *Jesus' Death in New Testament Thought*, vol. 1: *Background* (Mexico City: Theological Community of Mexico, 2018), 598-601.

29. For references, see Kyle B. Wells, *Grace and Agency in Paul and Second Temple Judaism: Interpreting the Transformation of the Heart*, NovTSup 157 (Leiden: Brill, 2015), 25-206.

30. On the question of election and free will in Second Temple Jewish thought, see E. P. Sanders, *Comparing Judaism and Christianity: Common Judaism, Paul, and the Inner and Outer in the Study of Religion* (Minneapolis: Fortress, 2016), 108-10, 186-87.

31. See Magen Broshi, "Predestination in the Bible and the Dead Sea Scrolls," in *The Bible and the Dead Sea Scrolls: The Second Princeton Symposium on Judaism and Christian Origins*, ed. James H. Charlesworth (Waco, TX: Baylor University Press, 2006), 2:235-46; Philip S. Alexander, "Predestination and Free Will in the Theology of the Dead Sea Scrolls," in *Divine and Human Agency in Paul and his Cultural Environment*, ed. John M. G. Barclay and Simon J. Gathercole (London: T & T Clark, 2006), 27-49.

tion of Israel from its oppression at the hands of others, including perhaps the devil, was inseparable from its redemption from its sinful behavior. *One could not happen without the other.* Only those who were redeemed from their disobedience could be redeemed from the plight they endured at present as well.

Precisely what God's people were to do in preparation for the arrival of this new age was not always clear. According to some, such as the Essenes and the community associated with the Dead Sea Scrolls, faithful Jews were to abandon the cities and towns in order to live together in the desert. John the Baptist called on the inhabitants of Jerusalem and Judea to repent of their sins and undergo baptism at his hands, perhaps forming part of a community of his disciples as well. Others thought that the people had to show their faith in God by taking the initiative to rise up against the Roman oppressor, trusting that God would then come to Israel's aid to liberate his people from their yoke.[32] In their minds, Jews could hardly expect God to intervene to liberate Israel if the people did not demonstrate concretely to God that they truly believed in him by actively seeking that liberation themselves. Still other Jews maintained that the way in which all were to show their faith was simply to "watch and pray," submitting passively to God by accepting whatever he had established in his sovereign will without attempting to force his hand or make demands on him.[33]

Even though Jews generally spoke of the redemption of *Israel* rather than the redemption of *Judaism*, the latter idea was implied by the former. What was to be redeemed was not only a people but a way of life. At least some of those who lived at the community in Qumran, for example, believed that when the day of Israel's redemption came, God would vindicate their interpretation of the law as well. All Jews would come to see that they alone observed the Torah in the way that God intended. God would thus redeem not only Israel but also the form of Judaism that was truly in accordance with his will.

6. The God who wanted to see Judaism radicalized.

For many Jews, the problem with the Judaism practiced by other Jews was that it was not as *radical* as God wanted it to be. The radicalism necessary could be understood in terms of an active struggle not only against the Roman oppressors but also against those Jews who actively collaborated with Rome. The *Sicarii*, for example, believed that it was God's will that

---

32. On the different attitudes and approaches to Roman rule among Jews in this period, see especially Sanders, *Judaism: Practice and Belief,* 279-89; Fuller, *Restoration of Israel,* 148-62.

33. Lester L. Grabbe, *An Introduction to First Century Judaism: Jewish Religion and History in the Second Temple Period* (Edinburgh: T & T Clark, 1996), 115-16; Sanders, *Judaism: Practice and Belief,* 288.

they put at least some of those Jews to death.[34] The radicalism required might also be understood in terms of selling all of one's possessions in order to live out in the desert with other faithful Jews in the way that the Essenes did.[35] Such Jews were regarded as extremists by the majority Jewish population. Their understanding of Torah-observance went far beyond that of most Jews.

The effects of this radicalism could also be understood in different ways. According to some Jews, the radical type of Torah-observance that they advocated would lead God to intervene on Israel's behalf to redeem his people.[36] Others might see their understanding of Torah-observance as something that would bring about the awaited transformation of Israel in and of itself. They might even expect that such a radical observance of the Torah would finally allow Israel to illuminate the other nations and draw them not only to the one true God but also to the one true way of life that he had prescribed.[37]

7. *The God who wanted to see Judaism* revolutionized.

To affirm that some Jews believed that a revolutionized form of Judaism was to be brought about is not necessarily to maintain that they advocated some type of actual revolution in the present. Undoubtedly, there were some Jews who longed for and expected a total upheaval in the world order that could be understood in terms of a revolution. Such an idea seems to be present in the War Scroll found at Qumran, which anticipates a war between the children of light and the children of darkness (1QM). According to this scroll, an army composed of those who were true Israelites would actually go into battle. Their victory over God's enemies would bring about a new and distinct political, social, economic, and religious order or system that would finally be fully in accordance with God's will.[38]

---

34. On the *Sicarii*, see Morton Smith, "The Troublemakers," in *The Cambridge History of Judaism*, vol. 3: *The Early Roman Period*, ed. William Horbury, W. D. Davies, and John Sturdy (Cambridge: Cambridge University Press, 1999), 501-68 (506-9); Grabbe, *Introduction to Second Temple Judaism*, 72-74.

35. See Catherine M. Murphy, *Wealth in the Dead Sea Scrolls and in the Qumran Community*, STDJ 40 (Leiden: Brill, 2002), 447-55; Hartmut Stegemann, *The Library of Qumran on the Essenes, Qumran, John the Baptist, and Jesus* (Grand Rapids: Eerdmans, 1998), 176-90.

36. On this idea, see Martin Hengel, *Victory over Violence* (Philadelphia: Fortress, 1973), 31-32.

37. See Terence L. Donaldson, *Paul and the Gentiles: Remapping the Apostle's Convictional World* (Minneapolis: Fortress, 1997), 71-74.

38. On these beliefs, see Albert L. A. Hogeterp, *Expectations of the End: A Comparative Traditio-Historical Study of Eschatological, Apocalyptic, and Messianic Ideas in the Dead Sea Scrolls and the New Testament*, STDJ 83 (Leiden: Brill, 2009), 31-114.

In contrast to a reformed version of Judaism, a revolutionized Judaism would be characterized by structures and a system that would be fundamentally different from those that had existed previously among Jews. Certain passages in the Dead Sea Scrolls, for example, reflect the belief that the Jerusalem temple would be replaced by a new, eschatological temple that would be larger and better.[39] It is not a far stretch to imagine that something similar might happen as well with Judaism in general. Nevertheless, precisely because such a form of Judaism would arise out of the forms of Judaism that preceded it and would preserve certain aspects of those forms of Judaism, it would still be considered Judaism.

Similarly, rather than radicalizing Judaism by bringing it back to its roots (*radices*) so as to purify it, those who wanted to see Judaism revolutionized might long for a new reality that was unlike anything that had previously been known or imagined.[40] According to the Exodus account, for example, God himself had written the ten commandments or "words" that in some sense summarize the entire Torah on the two stone tablets that Moses had originally brought down from the mountain. When Moses saw the golden calf and threw down those tablets in anger, they broke into pieces (Exod 32:15-19). Subsequently, although God initially told Moses that he would himself write on the new tablets the words that had been on the tablets Moses had broken, the Exodus narrative affirms that it was ultimately Moses who inscribed on the tablets the things that God dictated to him (Exod 34:1, 27-28).[41] This account might lend itself in some way to the claim that the law that God had given Moses after the incident with the golden calf was in some way distinct from the law he had originally given or intended to give Moses before that incident. What had made this alteration of the Torah necessary was precisely the sinfulness that the people of Israel had manifested by building and worshiping the golden calf. In that case, the Torah that God had ultimately given through Moses had been altered from the Torah originally drawn up by God so as to contain certain concessions on account of Israel's persistent sinfulness. It might therefore be expected that God would act in some way to put an end to that sinfulness in order to enable his people to live

---

39. See David Flusser, *Judaism of the Second Temple Period*, vol. 1: *Qumran and Apocalypticism*, trans. Azzan Yadin (Grand Rapids: Eerdmans, 2007), 207-13.

40. According to Puech, for example, the eschatology of the Essenes spoke of a new creation that would be radically different from the present reality and follow upon a "universal conflagration and a total renewal" of the present world ("Messianism," 251-56).

41. In this regard, the Exodus account differs from the account found in Deuteronomy, which does claim that God himself inscribed his commandments on the second set of tablets hewn out by Moses (Deut 10:1-4).

in accordance with the first and superior version of the Torah that he had originally given or intended to give to Moses.[42]

In principle, then, it is possible that some Jews believed that God wanted the present form of Judaism to be revolutionized rather than merely reformed, radicalized, or redeemed. By definition, at present this revolutionized form of Judaism would exist only as a theoretical construct or idea. According to such a view, Judaism would undergo a drastic change, assuming qualities or attributes that it had never possessed previously. Some might claim that this new form of Judaism had been foreseen and foretold by some of Israel's prophets, such as Isaiah, Jeremiah, and Ezekiel.[43] According to this idea, in their own day these prophets had described something that lay beyond any present conceptions of what true Judaism involved. If God intended to give a new version of the Torah or perhaps even a new Torah altogether, while it might look very different from the present Torah, in most ways it might also be very much the same.[44]

Again, while we do not have any clear evidence that such views existed among Jews in the Second Temple period, it is by no means impossible that some Jews thought in such terms. For various reasons, there may have been small groups of Jews or certain individuals who were critical not only of the different interpretations of the Torah but the Torah itself and therefore hoped that God would revise or improve it in some fashion in the future. Naturally, if he did so, the Judaism that would exist under that Torah would also be different from that which existed at present.

---

42. Although this distinction between the two versions of the Torah is not found explicitly in Jewish writings of the Second Temple period, it does appear in Christian writings around the same time that the Mishnah came into being; see Marcel Simon, *Verus Israel: A Study of the Relations between Christians and Jews in the Roman Empire (135–425)*, trans. H. McKeating (Oxford: Oxford University Press, 1986), 88–91. Simon notes that the Greek term used to refer to this "second law," which was *deuterōsis*, was "applied directly to the Mishnah" and claims that the terms *deuterōsis* and Mishnah "are etymologically exact equivalents" (89). Pieter Willem van der Horst finds a similar idea in Justin Martyr's interpretation of Ezek 20:25 in his *Dialogue with Trypho*; see "'I Gave Them Laws that Were Not Good': Ezekiel 20:25 in Ancient Judaism and Early Christianity," in *Sacred History and Sacred Texts in Early Judaism: A Symposium in Honour of A. S. van der Woude*, ed. J. N. Bremmer and F. García Martínez, CBET 5 (Kampen: Kok Pharos, 1992), 93–109.

43. Donald E. Gowan lists a number of passages from these books and other writings of the Hebrew Scriptures and Second Temple Judaism that anticipate a radical transformation of Israel and humanity in general (*Eschatology in the Old Testament* [Philadelphia: Fortress, 1986], 83–95).

44. Pointing to the work of W. D. Davies, Richard N. Longenecker argues that there is some evidence in the Second Temple period for the idea that a new or renewed Torah would exist in the Messianic age: "Judaism seems to have contained this thought in at least its embryonic form. . . ." (*Paul: Apostle of Liberty*, 2nd ed. [Grand Rapids: Eerdmans, 2015], 168–70).

8. *The God who wanted to see Judaism* refrigerated.

Because in our modern world to refrigerate something is to put it inside of an electrical refrigerator, in the ears of most people today it sounds extremely odd to speak of Judaism being "refrigerated." Originally, however, the Latin verb *refrigerare* simply meant to keep something cool, especially for the purpose of preserving it. Such was the objective of many Jews in the Second Temple period. The Jewish elite who collaborated with the Romans in Palestine, for example, sought to ensure that the political situation did not "heat up" or become inflamed in any way.[45] This concern is reflected in the affirmation that the Fourth Evangelist attributes to Caiaphas in John 11:47-53. There the chief priests gather under the leadership of Caiaphas and express their concern that, if nothing is done to Jesus and he is allowed to continue doing the things he has been doing, "everyone will come to believe in him, and the Romans will come to destroy both our holy place and our nation." To whatever extent one regards as historically accurate this passage from the Fourth Gospel, there can be little doubt that it was precisely this type of ferment and convulsion that Jesus' crucifixion was intended to help avoid and prevent.

Groups such as the chief priests and the Sadducees, therefore, proclaimed that the God of Israel desired that all Jews submit obediently to the present order of things, bowing to Roman rule and continuing to present their offerings to God at the temple dutifully and peacefully. Of course, the Jewish elite profited enormously when God's will for the Jewish people was understood in these terms. They enriched themselves not only from the wealth that flowed into the Jerusalem temple but also from the business dealings they had with Rome and other peoples around the empire. For this reason, they wanted to do everything they could to see that Judaism remained as it was. They did this by presiding over a temple that had been greatly embellished since the time of Herod and by promoting the idea that both the temple and the city in which it was located were holy, since they constituted the dwelling-place of God. Those who benefited from the

---

45. On the relations between the Romans and the Jewish aristocracy in the Second Temple period, see Martin Goodman, *The Ruling Class of Judaea: The Origins of the Jewish Revolt against Rome, A.D. 66-70* (Cambridge: Cambridge University Press, 1987), 27-108; James S. McLaren, *Power and Politics in Palestine: The Jews and the Governing of their Land, 100 BC-AD 70,* JSNTSup 63 (Sheffield: JSOT, 1991), 10-27; Richard A. Horsley, "High Priests and the Politics of Roman Palestine: Contextual Analysis of the Evidence in Josephus," *JSJ* 17 (1986): 23-55. On the role of the Pharisees, Sadducees, and scribes in the Jewish political and social order in Palestine in the Second Temple period, see especially Anthony J. Saldarini, *Pharisees, Scribes, and Sadducees in Palestinian Society: A Sociological Approach* (Wilmington, DE: Michael Glazier, 1988), 79-123, 251-308.

system in place under Rome, therefore, can be said to have advocated a "refrigerated" form of Judaism aimed at preserving the status quo.

The Sadducees' rejection of the idea that God would raise up the dead so that they might participate in a new world order should be seen against this background. Such an idea could be seen as encouraging Jews to rebel against Rome, since those who might be killed in such a rebellion could rest assured that they would still be able to participate in the age to come by being resurrected so as to participate in that age when it arrived.[46] In the book of 2 Maccabees, it is precisely this idea that is said to have encouraged the scribe Eleazar and other Jews to hold out in resistance to the efforts of the Seleucid king Antiochus Epiphanes to eradicate the Jewish way of life.[47] Belief in a future resurrection of the dead, therefore, could be highly subversive and serve to encourage disobedience, rebellion, and revolt. For that reason, many of the Jewish elites would have found it problematic.

9. *The God who wanted to see Judaism* relaxed.

Both within Palestine and in the diaspora, there were unquestionably some Jews who ascribed relatively little importance to the law and the practice of Judaism.[48] At times, especially in the diaspora, this may have been because for various reasons they wanted to live as non-Jews, blend in with non-Jews, obtain some personal benefit, or avoid facing any type of discrimination or persecution on the part of non-Jews. At other times, because of their occupation or profession or the place in which they lived, they simply found it impossible to observe the law, at least to the extent that most faithful Jews did. In some cases, such Jews were branded "sinners" and regarded as lawless.[49] Even those who may have been relatively observant of the Mosaic law may have participated at times in rites, ceremonies, activities, or celebrations that were dedicated to the Roman emperor or gods other than the God of Israel, doing things that other Jews might have considered unlawful according to the Torah.

The book of 1 Maccabees, for example, affirms that many Jews were willing to give up the observance of the Torah in order to adopt Hellenistic

---

46. On this aspect of the Jewish belief in the resurrection of the dead, see Paul M. van Buren, *According to the Scriptures: The Origins of the Gospel and of the Church's Old Testament* (Grand Rapids: Eerdmans, 1998), 27-28; Richard A. Horsley, *Jesus and the Spiral of Violence: Popular Jewish Resistance in Roman Palestine* (Minneapolis: Fortress, 1993), 136.

47. See 2 Macc 7:9-14, 23, 29.

48. See Cohen, *From the Maccabees to the Mishnah*, 69.

49. On the wide range of Jews who were commonly regarded as sinners in first-century Judaism, see Elisabeth Schüssler Fiorenza, *In Memory of Her: A Feminist Reconstruction of Christian Origins* (New York: Crossroads, 1983), 128.

beliefs and customs during the reign of Antiochus Epiphanes.[50] These Jews built a gymnasium in Jerusalem, had the marks of their circumcision removed, ceased to observe the Sabbath and other Jewish festivals, and began to live as Greeks. To whatever extent this account is considered to be historically accurate, it can hardly be doubted that there were at least some Jews who did things such as these. While in some cases they may have abandoned Judaism altogether, in other cases they may simply have adopted certain beliefs, customs, and practices that other Jews regarded as contrary to the Torah and Judaism.[51] There is archaeological evidence, for example, that many Jews made considerable contributions to temples dedicated to the gods of other peoples.[52] Whether other Jews would have considered such contributions as a violation of the Torah's command that God's people serve him alone is not clear.

Philo also mentions certain Jews who apparently continued to identify as Jews yet did not observe the Jewish law.[53] These Jews may have believed that the law that God had given to Moses was archaic and obsolete. In that case, God's will was that the observance of that law be relaxed and that Jews not concern themselves with the literal observance of its prescriptions to any great extent. Nevertheless, they would probably still have maintained that God wanted them and all people to live moral and upright lives and avoid falling into any type of licentiousness or immoral behavior.

If Jews such as these continued to believe in the God of Israel and to identify themselves as Jews or members of his people Israel, therefore, some of them may even have thought that it was acceptable to him for them to worship other deities while worshiping him as well. They may even have

---

50. See 1 Macc 1:11-15, 41-53. On the assimilation of some Jews to Hellenistic practices and beliefs, see Martin Hengel, "The Interpenetration of Judaism and Hellenism in the Pre-Maccabean Period," in *The Cambridge History of Judaism*, vol. 2: *The Hellenistic Age*, ed. W. D. Davies and Louis Finkelstein (Cambridge: Cambridge University Press, 1989), 167-228 (195-96).

51. On Jewish participation in the worship and customs associated with Greco-Roman gods in the Second Temple period, see Karl-Gustav Sandelin, *Attraction and Danger of Alien Religion: Studies in Early Judaism and Christianity*, WUNT 290 (Tübingen: Mohr Siebeck, 2012), 1-26, 40-47, 135-36, 142-44, 157; Paula Fredriksen, *Paul: The Pagans' Apostle* (New Haven: Yale University Press, 2017), 46-48.

52. See Paula Fredriksen, "The Question of Worship: Gods, Pagans, and the Redemption of Israel," in *Paul within Judaism: Restoring the First-Century Context to the Apostle*, ed. Mark D. Nanos and Magnus Zetterholm (Minneapolis: Fortress, 2015), 175-201 (180-81).

53. See E. P. Sanders, "The Covenant as a Soteriological Category and the Nature of Salvation in Palestinian and Hellenistic Judaism," in *Jews, Greek and Christians: Essays in Honor of William David Davies*, ed. Robert Hamerton-Kelly and Robin Scroggs, SJLA 21 (Leiden: Brill, 1976), 11-44 (38); Daniel R. Schwartz, *Studies in the Jewish Background of Christianity*, WUNT 60 (Tübingen: Mohr, 1992), 15-19.

justified their accommodation to the religious practices of other peoples by claiming that their God did not want them to suffer persecution at the hands of their non-Jewish neighbors. Instead, God desired that they live in peace and harmony with their gentile neighbors by participating in their religious ceremonies and celebrations, at least to some extent. They might also claim that they were not actually worshiping other gods themselves but merely providing support for others to worship their own god or gods, or perhaps worshiping the God of Israel as they gathered alongside others who were worshiping their own gods at the same time.

It was also possible for some Jews to equate one or more of those gods with the God of Israel, claiming that in reality the gentiles were merely calling the one true God by other names as they worshiped him.[54] If the one true God was called "Yahweh" or "the Lord" by Jews, "Zeus" by the Greeks, and "Jupiter" by the Romans, then it might be perfectly acceptable to offer up sacrifices to that God in gentile temples and shrines outside of Jerusalem. Of course, the overwhelming majority of Jews would probably have criticized strongly such ideas.

There were also many Jews who were simply unable to observe the Mosaic law for other reasons. Perhaps they were slaves who were not allowed to rest on the Sabbath, soldiers or mercenaries who could follow neither the Sabbath commandment nor other commandments having to do with food and purity, or Jews who lived isolated from other Jews or any Jewish community. Some Jews may have had no choice but to eat food that was impure or even had been sacrificed to gentile gods. Many of the Jews who lived in circumstances such as these would still have identified themselves as Jews and believed in the God of Israel. They might also attempt simply to observe to the best of their abilities the ethical principles found in the Mosaic law, expecting that God would understand the difficult situation in which they found themselves and not hold against them their failure to observe the Torah under those circumstances. In that case, they would have claimed that it was acceptable to God that they practice a relaxed form of Judaism, at least in the circumstances in which they found themselves.

10. The God who wanted to see Judaism replaced.

As just noted, some Jews may have thought that the one true God not only desired that observance of the Torah be relaxed but also willed that the Torah be set aside entirely so as to be replaced by some other set of laws, at least in certain contexts or settings. This God not only remained indifferent to their failure to submit to the Torah under certain circumstances but actually encouraged them to adopt the customs and practices of other peoples, perhaps for one or more of the reasons just mentioned above. Some

---

54. On this point, see Hengel, "Interpenetration," 204-6.

Jews may have claimed that the world had evolved since the time of Moses and therefore that the law God had given Moses should be replaced by something newer and better. Undoubtedly, the basic principles of morality would remain the same, yet those principles were now to take the form of some type of law that was distinct from the Torah, such as the law of the Greeks or Romans.

At various times during the Second Temple period, Greek and Roman rulers sought to impose the worship of their own gods or images among Jews and even in the Jerusalem temple.[55] When such attempts were made, the majority of Jews seem to have opposed them vehemently with great fervor. Many were even willing to give up their life rather than see the temple of their God defiled or desecrated in that way. It would be naïve and simplistic, however, to think that all Jews without exception were so adamantly opposed to the placement of images and figures of other gods in the temple. Some may actually have supported such attempts, thinking that they and many of their fellow Jews would be benefited by allowing this to happen, perhaps because relations with the foreign powers who ruled over Jerusalem and Palestine would thereby be improved and strengthened.[56] They might argue that the God of Israel himself had ordained that these other powers govern over Israel and even claim that he had now come to accept the worship of other deities alongside himself in his temple under certain conditions. If Israel's God was in control of history and had subjected Israel to a foreign power, he might also be seen as wanting the people to subject themselves to the gods of that power. As noted above, the book of 1 Maccabees affirms that there were at least some Jews who thought that Judaism in its traditional forms should disappear so as to be replaced by a Hellenistic way of life. There were therefore circumstances under which some Jews might accept the worship of other gods either alongside Israel's God or in his place, especially if they identified Israel's God as the same God adored by many non-Jews.

Those Jews who believed that under certain circumstances Judaism might be replaced by some other way of life would not necessarily have rejected Judaism altogether. In many cases, they may not have regarded this replacement as something that God wished to be universal and definitive. On the contrary, they may have thought that it was willed by God only at certain times, in certain places and contexts, or under extraordinary circumstances, and that it was to be only temporary rather than permanent.

---

55. See Martin Goodman, *A History of Judaism* (Princeton: Princeton University Press, 2018), 93-96, 102-5.

56. It may be significant that the Jewish high priests for the most part remained silent in the face of Caligula's efforts to place his statue in the Jerusalem temple rather than taking an active role in the popular protest; see Horsley, *Spiral*, 112-13; N. H. Taylor, "Popular Opposition to Caligula in Jewish Palestine," *JSJ* 32 (2001): 54-70.

The idea that God wished for Judaism to be replaced by something else has long been maintained by many Christians, who have claimed to find such an idea in the New Testament. This idea is particularly associated with supersessionism, which is generally defined as the belief that God intended the church or Christianity to replace Judaism and has now adopted Christians as his chosen people in the place of Israel. Because in New Testament times neither the church nor Christianity were thought to exist as entities distinct from Judaism, it is highly doubtful that the first believers in Christ thought in those terms, which should probably be regarded as anachronistic. As we noted at the end of Chapter 2 of this study, the community of Jesus' followers or *ekklēsia* was seen as an entity that was very different from Israel, since it was not defined by ethnicity or social and political structures. Because of these differences, it would not be seen as replacing Israel as a people.

It is possible, however, that the first Jewish believers in Christ thought that other forms of Judaism should give way to theirs as the truest or most correct form of Judaism. A similar idea is found in certain passages from the Dead Sea Scrolls that appear to affirm that only those Jews who follow the interpretation of the Torah given by the Teacher of Righteousness constitute the true Israel and practice the form of Judaism that is pleasing to God. In that case, the entity that most Jews called "Israel" was in some sense to be replaced by a different entity, namely, the community mentioned in those scrolls.[57] This group or community would therefore be seen as having superseded other forms of Judaism. Only the members of this group could now rightly consider themselves God's chosen people and bear the name "Israel."

If Paul and other Jewish believers in Christ of his day believed that they alone constituted the true Israel, therefore, they would not have been unique in that regard. While in one sense such a belief might be considered anti-Jewish, in another sense it can be seen as thoroughly Jewish. Since ancient times, the question of who constitutes the true Israel has been debated continuously among Jews.[58] If there was anything unique about the way in which the earliest believers in Christ understood the identity of Israel, it probably had to do with the idea that in some sense believing gentiles were now to be considered members of God's chosen people, even if they were not thought to become part of Israel. According to such a view,

---

57. See Lawrence H. Schiffman, "Jewish Law at Qumran," in *Theory of Israel*, vol. 1 of *The Judaism of Qumran: A Systemic Reading of the Dead Sea Scrolls*, part 5 of *Judaism in Late Antiquity*, ed. Alan Avery-Peck, Jacob Neusner, and Bruce Chilton, HdO 1.56 (Leiden: Brill, 2001), 75–90 (90).

58. On the discussions regarding the definition of Israel in the Second Temple period, see Graham Harvey, *The True Israel: Uses of the Names Jew, Hebrew and Israel in Ancient Jewish and Early Christian Literature*, STDJ 70 (Leiden: Brill, 2008), 33–42.

while all those who truly belonged to Israel were God's people, not all of God's people belonged to Israel.

PAUL'S REDEFINITION OF JUDAISM

Scholars of Paul have often attempted to fit him into one or more of the types of categories just considered. While some have argued that Paul believed that God desired for Judaism to be *replaced* by what later came to be known as Christianity, others have claimed that Paul wanted to see Judaism *relaxed* in that he believed that observance of the law among Jews was no longer necessary or important. Many scholars would agree that in some sense Paul would have thought that God intended for Judaism to be reformed, redeemed, radicalized, and perhaps even revolutionized. Others would maintain that Paul proclaimed a God who simply wanted to see the practice of Judaism reaffirmed or perhaps even reinforced. A careful examination of Paul's letters, however, reveals that his understanding of God's vision for Judaism was fundamentally different from all of those just considered. For Paul, Judaism needed to be *redefined* by being *resignified* around Christ as the Son of him whom Israel had always called "God."

The Purpose of Law-Observance for Jewish Believers in Christ

If Paul continued to observe the Mosaic law in much the same way that he had before coming to faith in Christ, as many Pauline scholars now argue,[59] the question arises as to the meaning that he ascribed to that observance. His letters seem to leave no doubt that he did *not* teach that observance to the law is necessary to attain the salvation of which he speaks. If believers in Christ can be declared righteous by God without observing the Mosaic law in all its points, then they can also be saved by God independently of any such law-observance. Furthermore, for Paul, those believers who live faithfully under Christ's lordship but do not observe the Mosaic law are no less righteous in God's sight than those who do. If observance of the law does not affect one's salvation or justification before God, then if Paul taught that Jewish believers in Christ should continue to observe the law, he must have regarded that law-observance as having some purpose other than attaining salvation or justication.

Like other Jews, Paul would have thought that the observance of the law was something good in itself in that it promoted well-being and shalom in many different ways. A close look at his epistles, however, reveals another purpose of such observance: *the law pointed to Christ as its fulfillment.* If

---

59. On this discussion, see especially Nanos, *Reading Paul within Judaism*, 3-10, 41-50; Paula Fredriksen, "Paul and Judaism," in *The Jewish Annotated New Testament*, ed. Marc Brettler and Amy-Jill Levine, 2nd ed. (New York: Oxford University Press, 2017), 633-37.

Jewish believers in Christ were to abandon the observance of the law, not only would they deprive themselves of the blessings that followed intrinsically from that observance, but they would also cease to point both themselves and their fellow Jews as well as non-Jews to Christ by means of that observance so that all might acknowledge him as Lord and live under his lordship.

To understand this idea, we may begin by looking at 1 Cor 5:6-8. There, after affirming that "a little leaven causes the whole batch of dough to rise," Paul continues: "Clean out the old leaven, so that you may become a new batch, just as you are unleavened. For Christ our Passover has been sacrificed. Therefore let us celebrate the feast, not with old leaven, nor with the leaven of malice and evil, but with the unleavened bread of sincerity and truth." Here Paul clearly sees Christ's death as fulfilling in a typological sense the sacrifice of the lambs for the feast of Passover. Similarly, he regards the law's commandment that those celebrating the Passover cleanse out any old leaven from their houses in order to replace it with new leaven as prefiguring the way in which believers in Christ would come to put away malice and evil in order to live in sincerity and truth. Paul would almost certainly have believed that, from the time that God had mandated that the people of Israel and their descendants celebrate the feast of Passover in the way he prescribed, he had intended for that celebration to foreshadow what would some day come to pass when he would send his Son into the world to establish through him and his death the *ekklēsia*. In that case, those Jews who had celebrated the Passover over the centuries had unknowingly been anticipating Jesus' sacrificial death and everything that would come to pass as a result of that death, including especially the establishment of communities such as the *ekklēsia* in Corinth in which believers would cleanse out malice and evil from within their midst and come to practice sincerity and truth.

In 1 Cor 5:6-8, then, Paul interprets both the narrative of the Passover and the commandments given in relation to its celebration *typologically*. Although typology is similar to allegory in that it involves ascribing to a text a deeper or hidden meaning that goes beyond its literal sense, in typological interpretations what took place in the past is understood as prefiguring or foreshadowing what would come to take place in the future.[60] This type of typological interpretation of the Hebrew Scriptures is also found elsewhere in Paul's letters.[61] In 1 Cor 10:1-11, he regards Christ as the rock

---

60. On the distinction between typology and allegory, see Larry W. Hurtado, *Lord Jesus Christ: Devotion to Jesus in Earliest Christianity* (Grand Rapids: Eerdmans, 2003), 571-72.

61. On Paul's use of typology, see Donald A. Carson, "Mystery and Fulfillment: Toward a More Comprehensive Paradigm of Paul's Understanding of the Old and the New," in *Justification and Variegated Nomism*, vol. 2: *The Paradoxes of Paul*, ed. Donald

from which the people of Israel drank in the desert and draws comparisons between the Israelites and believers in Christ. Just as the Israelites passed through water when they were brought out of Egypt through the Red Sea and then partook of a common food and drink in the desert, so also believers in Christ have passed through water when they were baptized and now share the same food and drink when they celebrate meals, in particular the Lord's Supper. Even though in Gal 4:21-31 Paul speaks of the story of Abraham, Sarah, and Hagar as an allegory, his interpretation of that story is instead typological in that he sees Sarah and Hagar as representing two covenants, one associated with Mount Sinai and the Jerusalem of the present age, and the other with the Jerusalem above, which is free.[62] In Rom 5:18, he also calls Adam "a type of the one to come."[63]

Paul must therefore have thought that the Passover celebration that God had mandated long before Christ's death and the formation of the *ekklēsia* anticipated and prefigured what would take place through Christ in his own day. As a faithful Jew, however, Paul would almost certainly have continued to celebrate the Passover even after he came to faith in Christ. His affirmation that he would stay in Ephesus until Pentecost in 1 Cor 16:8 indicates that he continued to order his life around the Jewish feasts at least to some extent and probably that he continued to observe them as well.[64] In the passage from 1 Cor 5:6-8 just considered, he also assumes that the gentile believers in Corinth to whom he writes are acquainted with the sacrifice of the Passover lamb, the ritual of cleansing out leaven from Jewish homes, and the practice of preparing unleavened bread for the festival. While they may simply have learned about the celebration of Passover from reading the Scriptures or by hearing how Jews celebrated it in their own day, it is also possible that at some point they had themselves participated in the celebration of Passover in Jewish circles or in the company of their fellow believers in Christ.

While to some extent we can only speculate, if Paul did continue to celebrate the Passover after coming to faith in Christ, it was not because he thought that it was necessary to do so in order to attain the salvation

---

A. Carson, Peter T. O'Brien, and Mark A. Seifrid, WUNT 2/181 (Tübingen: Mohr Siebeck, 2004), 393-436 (404-10).

62. See Carson, "Mystery," 404-6. Steven Di Mattei argues, however, that Gal 4:21-31 is properly understood as allegorical rather than typological ("Paul's Allegory of the Two Covenants [Gal 4.21-31] in Light of First-Century Hellenistic Rhetoric and Jewish Hermeneutics," *NTS* 52 [2006]: 102-22).

63. Strictly speaking, Paul may be referring to Adam's sin rather than Adam himself as the type that is fulfilled in Christ; see Ryan S. Schellenberg, "Does Paul Call Adam a 'Type' of Christ?," *ZNW* 105 (2014): 54-63.

64. It is possible, however, that in 1 Cor 16:8 Paul is simply referring to a season rather than to the Jewish feast of Pentecost; see David E. Garland, *1 Corinthians*, BECNT (Grand Rapids: Baker Academic, 2003), 758.

promised by God. It is difficult to imagine any Jews in antiquity believing that the purpose of celebrating Passover was to merit or earn God's favor, attain righteousness in his sight, or avoid coming under God's wrath and punishment. Such thinking would have been as strange and foreign to Jews in antiquity as it is among Jews today. Instead, it was recognized that God had commanded that the Jewish people celebrate Passover *for their own sake*, in order to strengthen and confirm their identity as God's people and bring to mind the love that God had shown Israel in the past and continued to show them in the present. By recalling the story of the exodus from Egypt and celebrating the liberation that Israel had experienced in Moses' time, the Jewish people reflected on things such as their relation with God and one another, the meaning and purpose of their existence, the identity of their God as one who liberates from slavery, and their election by God to be his treasured possession as a kingdom of priests and a holy nation (Exod 19:5-6). Their celebration of the Passover thus reinforced all of these ideas and strengthened them in their resolve and commitment to live in accordance with his commandments as members of his covenant people.

If Paul did continue to celebrate the Passover by following the traditional rites in whatever form they had come to exist in his day, he would have recited the passages from Scripture that other Jews read at Passover and the texts that had come to form part of a Passover liturgy.[65] In light of his faith in Christ, however, he would also have *reread* and *reinterpreted* those passages and texts, understanding them as prefiguring and anticipating what would come to pass in his own day through Christ and his death. When allusion was made to the sacrifice of the Passover lamb, he would have made an explicit connection between that lamb and Christ, as he does in 1 Cor 5:7. Likewise, when the ritual cleansing of leaven from the home was carried out, he would have reflected upon the deeper meaning of that ritual, as he does in 1 Cor 5:6-8. In fact, all Jews were to do this as they celebrated Passover, not only recalling the events of the past and carrying out the prescribed rites, but also reflecting on the meaning of those events and rites and their significance for life in the present. The novelty, therefore, would not be that of finding deeper meaning in those events and rites but rather doing so by looking to what God had now done in Christ. Paul may have made other connections between the Passover rites and the new reality in Christ as well, such as associating the blood that was placed on the lintels and doorposts with the blood of Christ and recalling how Jesus at the Last Supper had also passed the bread and cup around to his disciples with the words he ascribes to Jesus in 1 Cor 11:24-25. In light of what Paul says in 1

---

65. On the Christian adaptation of the Jewish Passover Haggadah as it is reflected in the *Apostolic Tradition* of Hippolytus, see Sean Edward Kensella, "The Transformation of the Jewish Passover in an Early Christian Liturgy: The Influence of the Passover *Haggadah* in the *Apostolic Tradition*," *ScEs* 52 (2000): 215-28.

Cor 5:6-8, therefore, it is likely that both Paul and other Jewish believers in Christ made such modifications in their celebration of Passover.

However, one can also easily imagine Paul teaching gentile believers in Christ such as those at Corinth to gather together to celebrate such a modified version of the Passover meal. If so, those gentile believers would almost certainly have done this alongside Jewish believers in Christ, unless of course the community of believers of which they formed part had come to be composed exclusively of gentiles. At times, gentile believers in Christ may even have celebrated Passover with Jews who did not believe in Christ. Non-Jewish believers would probably not have followed strictly all of the rites that Jews observed carefully when preparing to eat the Passover, since there would be no need for gentiles to concern themselves about many of the purity regulations. Whether or not Paul actually modified the traditional Passover celebration, his purpose in inviting gentile believers to take part in that celebration would have been largely instructional. The rituals, readings, and recitations involved would give a deeper meaning to their faith and strengthen their identity as children of Abraham joined to Israel as wild branches grafted on to an olive tree by virtue of their faith in Christ (Rom 11:17-24). The belief that the Scriptures and the story of Israel pointed not only to Christ but *to them as well* would also be reinforced among both non-Jewish and Jewish believers in Christ who participated in this Passover celebration.

If Paul began to interpret the Torah in this way, then, he would have continued to observe it as he had previously, but he would also have ascribed to it *new and different meanings* in light of his faith in Christ. On the basis of this same logic, he might even have modified the way that he observed other commandments of the Torah. For example, when he observed the Sabbath, he may have associated it with the idea that through Christ God provides believers with rest in some deeper, spiritual sense and therefore performed some type of ritual or pronounced some type of prayer that reflected that idea.[66] If he recited traditional Jewish prayers, he could have altered these to include allusions to Christ and petitions on behalf of the *ekklēsia*. As is evident from several of the passages just considered above, when Paul read the Hebrew Scriptures, his faith concerning Christ led him to find new meanings in those texts. In fact, he states this explicitly in 2 Cor 3:1-18. According to Paul's words in this passage, when one turns to Christ, a veil is removed from one's eyes so that one may understand that the Scriptures of Israel point to the "ministry of justification" and the "greater glory" that he associates with Christ. Both the commandments and the narratives of the Torah as well as the Scriptures in general, therefore, found fulfillment

---

66. The idea that believers in Christ attain the true Sabbath rest had arisen at least by the time that the Epistle to the Hebrews was written; see Heb 4:1-11. Such an idea is also suggested in Matt 11:28-29.

in Christ and the gospel. That conviction led Paul to *resignify* what he read in the Torah, as well as the observance of many of the things it prescribed.

Paul's Reinterpretation of Jewish Sacrifice

In his epistles, Paul never addresses explicitly the question of whether he continued to participate in the sacrificial worship offered to God at the Jerusalem temple after he came to faith in Christ. Throughout those epistles, however, he repeatedly uses imagery associated with the offering of sacrifices.[67] He describes himself both as a priest and a drink-offering, refers to believers as God's temple, tells believers to offer themselves and their bodies up to God as a sacrifice, and even sees the gentiles who come to believe in Christ as a result of his ministry as his own offering to God.[68] By no means do any of these passages suggest that Paul rejected the literal observance among Jews of all that God had commanded in the Torah regarding sacrifices or the sacrificial worship offered to God at the Jerusalem temple.[69] In fact, ideas similar to those just mentioned are found in the Hebrew Scriptures, which speak of the people as a whole as priests, and the Dead Sea Scrolls, where the Qumran community is described as a temple for God.[70] All Jews were to offer themselves and their own lives up to God together with their sacrificial offerings. It is likely, therefore, that Paul thought that Jewish believers in Christ should continue participating in the sacrificial worship offered at the Jerusalem temple, not only for the same reasons that they had done so previously, but also because such participation would constantly remind them of the truths they associated with their faith in Christ and testify to their conviction that the rites and rituals carried out there pointed to Christ as their fulfillment.

Even though the gentile believers in Christ with whom Paul worked would not have been able to participate in the sacrificial worship carried out in Jerusalem in the same way that Jews did, other ways of participating in that worship would have been open to them. In fact, throughout the Second Temple period, there were many ways for non-Jews to take part

---

67. On Paul's use of sacrificial imagery, see Eyal Regev, *The Temple in Early Christianity: Experiencing the Sacred*, AYBRL (New Haven: Yale University Press, 2019), 53-95.

68. See Rom 12:1; 15:15-16; 1 Cor 3:16-17; 6:19; 2 Cor 6:16; Phil 2:17.

69. See Fredriksen, *Paul*, 154. On Paul's favorable attitude toward the Jerusalem temple, see Friedrich Wilhelm Horn, "Paulus und der Herodianische Tempel," *NTS* 53 (2007): 184-203.

70. See Exod 19:6; Isa 61:6. On the idea in the Dead Sea Scrolls that the Qumran community constitutes a metaphorical temple, see Cecilia Wassen, "Do You Have to Be Pure in a Metaphorical Temple? Sanctuary Metaphors and Construction of Sacred Space in the Dead Sea Scrolls and Paul's Letters," in *Purity, Holiness, and Identity in Judaism and Christianity: Essays in Memory of Susan Huber*, ed. Carl S. Ehrlich, Anders Runesson, and Eileen Schuller, WUNT 305 (Tübingen: Mohr Siebeck, 2013), 55-86.

in the Jewish sacrificial cult.[71] Gentiles too could pray at the time of the daily sacrifices and make monetary contributions to finance the sacrifices offered in Jerusalem. Although they could not enter into the inner courts of the temple that were reserved for Jews alone, they could always go up to Jerusalem and participate in the worship offered there, perhaps standing in the Court of Gentiles as they did so. They might even go to Jerusalem at the time of the Jewish feasts to celebrate them there. They could also pay for prayers and sacrifices to be made on their behalf. In principle, there was no reason why gentiles who came to Christ should abstain from doing any of these things. Paul may even have encouraged gentiles who wished to participate in the Jewish sacrificial worship in these ways to do so, since in that way they too could give witness to their conviction that all that God had prescribed in the Torah found its fulfillment in Christ. However, Paul would have insisted that those gentiles who participated in various ways in the sacrificial worship offered to Israel's God did not thereby become more righteous in God's sight than those who did not, because in themselves works of the law such as these did not make anyone more righteous. On this point, Paul's fellow Jews would have agreed with him entirely, since in and of themselves, such rites did not make one righteous. As we have seen in Chapter 2 of this study, those rites only helped to promote righteous living by reminding those Jews who participated in them of their history and identity and leading them to reflect on their relation to God and one another in other ways.

One of the most important days of the Jewish calendar was *Yom Kippur* or the Day of Atonement. If Paul continued to observe the Jewish festivals in some way, he probably also continued to observe *Yom Kippur* in much the same way that other Jews did. In that case, he would have encouraged his fellow Jewish believers in Christ to do so as well. It is even possible that Paul taught and encouraged non-Jewish believers in Christ to observe *Yom Kippur* in some way, such as fasting, confessing their sins, and asking God to forgive them those sins. Both Jewish and non-Jewish believers in Christ, however, would probably have gone beyond the traditional interpretations of the rites prescribed for *Yom Kippur* in order to resignify those rites on the basis of their faith in Christ. It is likely that they would have seen the mediation of the high priest and his entrance into the Holy of holies with the blood of sacrifices as prefiguring in some way what had now taken place through Christ and his death, perhaps in much the same fashion that the Epistle to the Hebrews later came to do.[72] When offering up to God their prayers of confession and petitions of forgiveness, they would have alluded to Christ in some way. In other ways as well, their

71. On the participation of gentiles in sacrificial worship at the Jerusalem temple, see Schwartz, *Studies*, 102-16.

72. See Heb 5:7-10; 9:11-14; 10:5-14, 19-22.

observance of *Yom Kippur* would revolve around their faith in Christ as well as their traditional Jewish faith.[73]

Neither Paul's epistles nor the New Testament as a whole offer any clear evidence that the earliest believers in Christ associated him with the goat for Azazel upon which the high priest symbolically laid the sins of the people before it was led out into the desert. It is possible, however, that Paul or others who came to faith in Christ made such an association. If they did, it was not because they believed that when Jesus had died God had actually laid the sins of believers or the world upon him in some literal or ontological sense so that he might endure the punishment those sins deserved in the place of those who had committed them. There is nothing in Second Temple Jewish literature to suggest that Jews in antiquity understood themselves to be inflicting God's punishment for their sins on the goat led out to the desert so that they might thereby be spared that punishment. Instead, Paul would have thought that, by giving up his life so that others might come to be saved and forgiven through him, Christ had taken away sins in some other sense. For example, it might be said that the sins of believers had been laid upon Christ and borne away by him in the sense that he had willingly offered up his life as a result of his efforts to bring others to leave behind them their sinful ways of living and no longer dedicate themselves to sin as its slaves. Just as the old person of believers could be said to have died and been crucified and buried with Christ when they came to identify with him and his death through faith and baptism, so also could it be said that the sinful actions and lifestyle to which they had previously dedicated themselves had been borne away by Christ. Of course, there is no clear evidence in Paul's epistles or the New Testament in general that Jesus' earliest followers interpreted the rite with the goat for Azazel in that manner. The earliest evidence we have of any association of that rite with Christ's death is from the second century, although the idea that the goat for Azazel prefigured the way in which Christ would bear away the sins of others in his death does not appear until later centuries.[74]

If Paul and other believers in Christ did continue to observe *Yom Kippur*, however, they would have believed that what led God to forgive and accept them anew was their commitment to living in accordance with his will as

---

73. On the possible allusions to *Yom Kippur* in Paul's epistles, the New Testament, and early Christian writings, see Daniel Stökl Ben Ezra, *The Impact of Yom Kippur on Early Christianity: The Day of Atonement from Second Temple Judaism to the Fifth Century*, WUNT 163 (Tübingen: Mohr Siebeck, 2003), 145-227. Stökl Ben Ezra cites evidence that "a number of Christians continued celebrating Yom Kippur, and other Jewish festivals, with their Jewish neighbors until at least the fourth century" (227).

74. The first explicit comparisons between Jesus and the two goats associated with the Day of Atonement appear in the second century in the Epistle of Barnabas (7:6-11) and Justin Martyr's *Dialogue with Trypho* (40:4).

it had now been redefined through Christ so as no longer to be identified solely with the observance of the Mosaic law. For them, to repent was to turn back, not simply to a more faithful observance of the law, but to Christ as the Lord of their life. It was their living relationship to Christ as their Lord that ultimately constituted the basis upon which God forgave them both their past sins and any sins into which they continued to fall.

It is worth noting that Joseph Caiaphas, the same high priest who in the Gospel tradition had declared Jesus worthy of death, remained in office until the year 36 CE.[75] Most Pauline scholars date Paul's experience on the road to Damascus prior to that year.[76] In the five years following Caiaphas's removal from the high priesthood, it was occupied by two of the sons of Caiaphas's father-in-law Annas, who according to the Fourth Gospel had also participated in the unjust condemnation of Jesus.[77] If they considered both Annas and Caiaphas to be corrupt, Jesus' first followers would probably have drawn comparisons between them and Jesus in order to portray Jesus in a much more favorable light as the one whose intercession before God truly obtained his forgiveness. In that case, Jesus would be understood as a new and better high priest. Nevertheless, Jesus' followers would probably have seen his high priesthood, not as *superseding* or *replacing* the traditional office of the high priest as defined in the Torah, but rather as *fulfilling* what was described in the Torah and as filling the rites carried out even by corrupt high priests with new meaning. In that case, Jesus' followers would have had no reason to want to see those rites abolished. On the contrary, they would have wanted to see them continue, despite the sinfulness of Israel's high priests, due to the way in which their participation in those rites pointed them and others to Christ and gave meaning to their faith in Christ.

Many New Testament scholars believe that Paul had the Day of Atonement in mind in Rom 3:25, where he affirms that God "put forward Jesus as a *hilasterion*-by-faith by means of his blood." While we will look more closely at this passage in Chapter 8, here it should be noted that in the Septuagint the word *hilastērion* is used to refer to the mercy seat of the ark of the covenant, which lay behind the inner veil in the tabernacle and first temple.[78] Even if Paul did not have the mercy seat in mind in this passage but was

---

75. On Caiaphas's time in the high priesthood of Israel, see Helen K. Bond, *Caiaphas: Friend of Rome and Judge of Jesus?* (Louisville: Westminster John Knox, 2004), 42-54, 83-92.

76. On the variety of proposals regarding the date of Paul's Damascus experience, see Rainer Riesner, *Paul's Early Period: Chronology, Mission Strategy, Theology*, trans. Doug Stott (Grand Rapids: Eerdmans, 1998), 3-28. As Riesner's survey makes clear, the majority of scholars today date Paul's Damascus experience no later than the year 35 CE.

77. See John 18:13-24. On this point, see Bond, *Caiaphas*, 146-48.

78. See Exod 25:16-21 (LXX); 31:7; 35:12; 38:5-8 (LXX); Lev 16:2, 13-15; Num 7:89.

simply referring in general terms to the idea of expiation or propitiation, his allusion to Jesus' blood in this context indicates that in one way or another he associated Jesus' death with a sacrificial offering. It is possible, of course, that Paul was using the term *hilastērion* to refer to any type of expiation or propitiation, perhaps even to Greek and Roman beliefs and not merely Jewish ones. This seems unlikely, however, given that in the same immediate context he alludes to ideas associated with Judaism, such as the law and prophets, the righteousness and glory of God, and the redemption that was to come through a Jewish Messiah (Rom 3:19-26).

Paul's allusions to the sacrificial worship offered to God by Israel in accordance with the Torah, therefore, suggest that he saw that worship as prefiguring and finding fulfillment in what had now come to take place in Christ, the community of believers in Christ, and the ministry of apostles such as Paul himself. While it is of course possible that Paul no longer participated in that worship and taught that Jewish believers in Christ should abstain from such participation, this seems highly unlikely. Instead, he probably continued to value deeply the offering of sacrifices to Israel's God not only for the same reasons he had prior to coming to faith in Christ, but also as a means by which God pointed both Jews and non-Jews to Christ so that through him they might attain the redemption, forgiveness, and righteousness that he now offered to people of all nations through his Son.

Paul's Resignification of Judaism

On the basis of what we have seen here, there are good reasons to conclude that, rather than willing that Judaism be replaced or relaxed, the God of whom Paul spoke wanted to see Judaism *resignified* as a result of what he had done and would continue to do through his Son Jesus Christ. In that case, Paul would have encouraged his fellow Jewish believers in Christ to continue to observe the Torah and live as Jews, not only for the same reasons that they had done so previously, but also because, by doing so, they pointed both themselves and others to Christ as the one in whom the Torah found fulfillment, purpose, and meaning.

Paul may have had these ideas in mind in Rom 10:4, where he writes that "Christ is the end of the law for righteousness to everyone who believes." Like the English word "end," the Greek word *telos* that Paul uses here can be understood as referring both to the termination of something and to its goal or purpose.[79] Because there is nothing in Paul's letters to indicate that he believed that Jews who came to faith in Christ should no longer observe the Torah and practice Judaism as they had previously, it is more likely

---

79. On the scholarly discussion regarding the translation of *telos* in Rom 10:4, see Robert Badenas, *Christ the End of the Law: Romans 10.4 in Pauline Perspective*, JSNTSup 10 (Sheffield: JSOT, 1985), 7-37.

that in this passage Paul is affirming that Christ is the *goal* of the Torah. Through Christ the purpose of the Torah is fulfilled, not merely because it directs and brings people to Christ, but also because by doing so it enables those who come to faith in Christ to practice the righteousness of God as it has now come to be defined and given through his Son. According to Paul, while the Torah pointed forward to that righteousness and anticipated it, it was not capable of bringing about the type of righteousness that now enabled Jews and gentiles to live as one in the same community of faith.[80] In Paul's thought, the righteous way of living God desired to see in all is brought about through faith in Christ or "Christ-faith" rather than through the observance of the Torah alone, independently of Christ. However, by serving as God's instrument to bring people to Christ, the Torah makes it possible for that righteousness to become a reality in them. Thus Christ is the goal of the law in the sense that through him God brings about in all who come to live under him as their Lord the righteousness of faith of which the law spoke and to which it pointed, together with the prophets (Rom 3:21-22).

If Paul understood observance of the Torah in this manner, he may have not only *encouraged* his fellow Jewish believers in Christ to continue to observe the Torah but even *insisted* that they do so, telling them that it would be sinful and wrong for them to *stop* observing the Torah. The reason for this insistence, however, would not be that such observance would make them more righteous in God's sight. Instead, Paul would have insisted that it was sinful and wrong for Jewish believers in Christ to stop observing the law for at least two reasons. The first of these is that which we have just seen: such observance would allow both Jews and non-Jews to be directed to Christ as the one in whom the Torah finds its fulfillment. The Torah is fulfilled in Christ not only in the sense that it anticipated and prepared the way for everything that God has now done through him, but also in the sense that the kind of righteousness that it demanded but could not bring about due to the power of sin in the flesh is now offered to all who come to faith in Christ so as to live under his lordship (Rom 7:7–8:4; 9:30–10:9).

The second reason why Paul would have insisted that Jewish believers in Christ continue to observe the Torah has to do with ideas such as those that we find in Romans 14–15 and 1 Corinthians 8–10. In these passages, Paul exhorts believers to make decisions regarding food and drink on the basis of considerations related to the edification of others. According to Second Temple Jewish thought, God had determined that his people were to keep the Torah for all generations.[81] Paul would almost certainly have agreed on this point with his fellow Jews. Because the Torah pointed people

---

80. See Rom 8:3-4; 9:30–10:10; Phil 3:6-9.

81. On this point, see Longenecker, *Paul*, 116-20.

to Christ, for any Jewish believer in Christ to cease to observe the Torah would not only be contrary to God's command that Jews of all generations keep the Torah but also constitute a lack of love for others. Rather than edifying other Jews, any Jewish believer who claimed to be living righteously yet intentionally disregarded the Torah and failed to submit to it would scandalize them, especially if that believer did so in the name of Christ. If that were Christ's desire, then both Christ and Paul himself would have been ministers of sin in that they led others to fail to show love and consideration for others by disparaging the law and denying the value of its observance.[82] In contrast, to continue to observe that law would be an act of love on the part of Jewish believers in that it would lead both Jews and gentiles to see that in Christ the law now found its fulfillment. Of course, observance of the law on the part of Jewish believers would also be seen as fulfilling the same good purposes that it always had in Jewish thought, and therefore would have been thought to be of value in and of itself as well.

In the end, then, as Paul himself insists in his epistles, he valued deeply the Torah and its observance and considered such observance on the part of Jews not only good but also important and perhaps even necessary. By no means did Paul wish to see Judaism disappear or become abolished, since it was the means by which God continued to bring to pass all of the promises he had made of old by directing people to Christ. In fact, it would probably be correct to affirm that the God proclaimed by Paul wanted Judaism to be reaffirmed and reinforced, and even to be reformed, redeemed, radicalized, and revolutionized in some sense, though not in the ways that many of his fellow Jews envisioned, advocated, or expected. For Paul, all of these things could happen in the way that God desired and intended only if Judaism as it had come to exist in his day was first *resignified* by looking to Christ as the one through whom the purpose and goal of Judaism and the Torah were now fulfilled.

---

82. See Gal 2:17; cf. Rom 3:7; 6:1, 15.

CHAPTER 6

REDEFINING GOD'S PEOPLE

In ancient Jewish thought, of all the peoples of the world, God had chosen
Israel alone to be his special and treasured possession. Although at times
God might subject his people to suffering and exile in an effort to purify
them of their sinfulness and might abandon them for a time for the same
purpose, no matter how disobedient they were, God would never reject
them entirely or abandon them definitively. Nothing could ever alter Israel's
status as God's chosen people.

According to the gospel proclaimed by Paul, uncircumcised gentiles
who lived faithfully as members of the community of believers in Christ
enjoyed the same righteous status in God's eyes that faithful Jews had traditionally believed was theirs as the people whom God had chosen as his
own above all others. Such a proclamation would inevitably raise the question of whether only those who formed part of Israel could rightly be considered members of God's people. While it was common for some Jews to
claim that others who called themselves Jews were not truly members of
Israel due to their mistaken interpretations of the Torah or their failure to
observe it properly, none of the Jewish groups known to us ever proclaimed
that uncircumcised gentiles who did not observe the Torah could be considered full members of God's people Israel.[1] Paul himself never makes this
claim explicitly, although some interpreters of his letters have ascribed such
an idea to him. What Paul does unequivocally affirm is that gentile believers in Christ have been called and chosen by God and are in some sense his
people as well.[2] Through faith in Christ they become both children of God

---

1. Stephen Spence points to evidence from antiquity that non-Jews who did not
submit fully to the law could be attached to the synagogue but could not actually belong
to it as members (*The Parting of the Ways: The Roman Church as a Case Study*, ISACR 5
[Leuven: Peeters, 2004], 58-61).

2. See Rom 1:7; 8:30; 9:24-26; 1 Cor 1:2, 24; 1 Thess 1:4.

197

and children of Abraham.[3] However, together with those Jews who came to faith in Christ, they also came to form part of a single community that was distinct from the larger Jewish community in that it was defined on the basis of their adherence to Christ as Lord.

ISRAEL AS THE PEOPLE OF GOD IN JEWISH THOUGHT

Coupled with the belief that Israel was God's chosen people in a way that distinguished Israel from all other peoples of the world was the conviction that the covenant that God had made with Israel and the commandments that he had given his people were also unique and irreplaceable. The terms of that covenant were fairly simple. God would relate to his people Israel in a special way so as to bring about among them the blessings and well-being he sought for them, yet Israel was to live under that covenant by obeying the instruction and commandments he had given them in the Torah.[4] We have previously considered the reason why Israel's blessing was understood as being inseparable from the people's obedience to the Torah: the commandments of the Torah prescribed behavior and activities that both directly and indirectly promoted the well-being of all, enabling God's people to live in ways that would make that well-being possible. Therefore, out of love for his people God demanded that they obey his good commandments and promised to act in various ways to correct and discipline them when they brought harm upon themselves by failing to observe those commandments carefully. That correction and discipline had the aim of restoring them to obedience for their own sake.

Outside of the New Testament, the only Hebrew and Jewish writings of antiquity in which the phrase "new covenant" appears are the book of Jeremiah and the Damascus Document found at Qumran. In Jer 31:31-34, God promises Israel and Judah that he will make a new covenant with them, since they have broken the covenant he made with their ancestors when he brought them out of Egypt. In this new covenant, God would put his law within them and write it upon their hearts so that they might know him and live as his people. On that basis, God also promised to forgive them their sins and remember those sins no more. Precisely what is meant by a new covenant in this passage is not entirely clear. On the one hand, it appears to be a covenant that is distinct from the covenant he made with Israel at Sinai, since that covenant is regarded as having been broken and it is said the new covenant will be unlike that one. At the same time, God

---

3. See Rom 4:11; 8:14-17; Gal 3:7, 26, 29; 4:6-7; Phil 2:15; cf. Gal 4:22-31.

4. On the various concepts of the covenant that existed in Second Temple Jewish thought, see the essays that discuss the Second Temple period in *The Concept of the Covenant in the Second Temple Period*, ed. Stanley E. Porter and Jacqueline C. R. de Roo, JSJSup 71 (Leiden: Brill, 2003).

promises to put his Torah in them and write it on their hearts. While this suggests that in some way God will bring the Torah he gave his people at Sinai to be internalized in them, if the term Torah is understood simply in a general sense, the passage can also be understood to mean that he will put his instruction in them and write it on their hearts.[5]

In several passages, the Damascus Document found at Qumran speaks of a "new covenant in the land of Damascus."[6] Nevertheless, this document never contrasts the new covenant of which it speaks with an old covenant and regards the study and observance of the Torah as central to that new covenant.[7] Furthermore, as Petrus Gräbe notes, "the new covenant in the Qumran community is not depicted as established by God himself, but as an entity instituted by persons that people may choose to join."[8] In particular, the phrase is used in connection with a group that split off from the larger community.[9] It may also refer to "a new ability to obey the covenantal stipulations," yet the basis for this ability is the interpretation of the Torah found in the community.[10] Both the Damascus Document and the other writings from Qumran speak of the covenant God originally made with Israel as if it were still valid and in force. It therefore does not replace, supersede, or modify that covenant in any way.[11]

One of the purposes of the covenant that God had made with Israel at Sinai and the Torah he had given his people there was that of keeping them separate from other nations. For their own good, they were not to worship the gods of the other nations or submit to their laws or customs but to remain faithful to their own God and his law as well. Among the commandments God had given his people to distinguish them from other nations was the commandment to circumcise the males from among the people. While the Jews were not the only people to practice circumcision in the Second Temple period, most non-Jews throughout the Roman Empire

---

5. See Serge Ruzer, *Mapping the New Testament: Early Christian Writings as a Witness for Jewish Biblical Exegesis*, JCPS 13 (Leiden: Brill, 2007), 215-16.

6. See *CD* 6.19; 8.21 (=19.33-34); 20.12.

7. See Petrus J. Gräbe, *New Covenant, New Community: The Significance of Biblical and Patristic Covenant Theology for Contemporary Understanding* (Waynesboro, GA: Paternoster, 2006), 58-61.

8. Gräbe, *New Covenant*, 59.

9. See Philip R. Davies, *The Damascus Covenant: An Interpretation of the "Damascus Document"*, JSOTSup 25 (Sheffield: JSOT, 1982), 176-81.

10. Ed Condra, *Salvation for the Righteous Revealed: Jesus amid Covenantal and Messianic Expectations in Second Temple Judaism*, AGJU 51 (Leiden: Brill, 2002), 97-99.

11. On this point, see Ellen Juhl Christiansen, "The Consciousness of Belonging to God's Covenant and What It Entails according to the Damascus Document and the Community Rule," in *Qumran between the Old and New Testaments*, ed. Frederick H. Cryer and Thomas L. Thompson, JSOTSup 290 (Sheffield: Sheffield Academic Press, 1998), 69-97 (82-84).

seem to have associated circumcision most closely with Judaism and the Jews rather than some other faith or people.[12]

In the Second Temple period, practicing Jews generally took precautions to avoid being involved in any way with the worship of the gentile gods.[13] Many of these precautions had to do with food and drink. In addition to following what the Torah prescribed in order to determine whether or not what was to be eaten or drunk was pure, many Jews took care not to eat or drink anything that might possibly have been offered to a gentile god.

On the basis of passages such as Acts 10:1–11:18, where Luke relates the encounter between Simon Peter and the Roman centurion Cornelius, it has often been argued that Jews considered gentiles impure and refused to enter into their homes or have any close contact with them. Numerous scholars and historians today, however, have argued that if there were Jews in antiquity who thought and behaved in that way, they were probably a minority.[14] In the sources we possess from antiquity, there is ample evidence of Jews entering into non-Jewish homes and buildings to eat with non-Jews and engaging in many different sorts of activities with non-Jews, including activity that required close proximity and even physical contact.[15] Many of those sources suggest that Jews in general did not regard gentiles as impure simply by virtue of their being gentiles, if at all.[16]

Of course, the Hebrew Scriptures made it clear that what was really to distinguish Israel from other peoples was not merely the practice of the rites, traditions, and customs particular to Israel but above all else the practice of

---

12. See Paula Fredriksen, *Paul: The Pagans' Apostle* (New Haven: Yale University Press, 2017), 43-44.

13. On these precautions, see Michelle Slee, *The Church in Antioch in the First Century CE: Communion and Conflict*, JSNTSup 244 (London: Sheffield Academic Press, 2003), 17-22.

14. See Spence, *Parting of the Ways*, 45-48, 52-65; Fredriksen, *Paul*, 49-60.

15. On the evidence in favor of table fellowship among Jews and non-Jews in antiquity, see Peter J. Tomson, *Paul and the Jewish Law: Halakha in the Letters of the Apostle to the Gentiles*, CRINT Section 3: Jewish Traditions in Early Christian Literature 1 (Assen: Van Gorcum; Minneapolis: Fortress, 1990), 229-36; Alan F. Segal, *Paul the Convert: The Apostolate and Apostasy of Saul the Pharisee* (New Haven: Yale University Press, 1990), 230-33. As David J. Rudolph notes, however, there is also evidence that some Jews did not eat with gentiles (*A Jew to the Jews: Jewish Contours of Pauline Flexibility in 1 Corinthians 9:19-23*, WUNT 2/304 [Tübingen: Mohr Siebeck, 2011], 125-30).

16. See Paula Fredriksen, "Paul, Purity, and the *Ekklēsia* of the Gentiles," in *The Beginnings of Christianity: A Collection of Articles*, ed. Jack Pastor and Menachem Mor (Jerusalem: Yad Ben-Zvi, 2005), 205-17 (205-10); Pamela Eisenbaum, *Paul Was Not a Christian: The Original Message of a Misunderstood Apostle* (New York: HarperOne, 2009), 100-101; E. P. Sanders, "Jewish Association with Gentiles and Galatians 2:11-14," in *The Conversation Continues*, ed. Robert Fortna and Beverly Gaventa (Nashville: Abingdon, 1990), 170-87.

the justice and righteousness that God mandated in the Torah. The purpose for which God had given his people those rites, traditions, and customs to observe was that they might serve as means to bring about in them the justice, righteousness, and love he desired to see among them for their own good and well-being. Thus, for example, several passages from the Hebrew Scriptures insisted that Israel was to be circumcised not only according to the flesh but in the people's hearts as well.[17] In other words, God had ordered them to be circumcised, not as an end itself, but so that they might constantly be reminded that they had been called to live as God's special people in the way he desired and commanded for their own good. While circumcision helped promote righteous living, therefore, in itself it was not thought to make anyone righteous in God's sight.

Virtually all Jews recognized that in some sense physical descent from Jacob alone was not sufficient to define who belonged to Israel. According to the Hebrew Scriptures, from the time of the exodus from Egypt onward, peoples who were not descended from Jacob had also come to form part of Israel.[18] Throughout the Second Temple period, people of other nations continued to be incorporated into Israel as members of God's people by submitting fully to everything commanded in the Torah, including groups such as the Idumeans who were pressured to convert to Judaism in the early first century BCE by the Hasmonean ruler Alexander Jannaeus.[19]Although converts to Judaism might not initially be fully accepted as Jews by those of Jewish ancestry, eventually as a result of integration and intermarriage any distinctions between the two groups within the Jewish community would for the most part disappear. The Torah did not assign to those who descended physically from Jacob any privileges that people of other nations who submitted fully to its commandments did not also come to possess.

At the same time, of course, those who had been born and raised as Jews might come to renounce Judaism and choose not to submit to the Torah. They might cease to observe any of the commandments particular to it and no longer have their male children circumcised. It was not always clear whether or not those who renounced Judaism were still to be considered Jews and as members of Israel. In an ethnic sense, of course, their lineage *made* them Jews or Judeans, and this was not something that they could

---

17. See Lev 26:41; Deut 30:6; Jer 4:4; 9:26.

18. In Exod 12:38, a "mixed crowd" is said to have departed Egypt with the Israelites. As Joel N. Lohr notes, the precise meaning of this phrase (*'ereb rab* in Hebrew) continues to be debated among biblical scholars (*Chosen and Unchosen: Conceptions of Election in the Pentateuch and Jewish-Christian Interpretation*, SLTHS 2 [Winona Lake, IN: Eisenbraums, 2009], 86-89).

19. It is debated whether this conversion was imposed by force; see Peter Richardson, *Herod: King of the Jews and Friend of the Romans* (Columbia, SC: University of South Carolina Press, 1996), 55-56.

change. By refusing to live as Jews and perhaps integrating into some other community, people, or ethnicity, of course, they might come to be identified as something other than Jewish as well. When ethnic Jews had children with non-Jews, and those children and their descendants then had children with spouses or partners that were not Jewish, eventually the ethnicity of those descendants would no longer be considered Jewish.

The problem of defining precisely who did and did not form part of Israel or belong to the Jewish community was therefore extremely complex. Among Jews themselves, there was disagreement on these questions.[20] It must be stressed, however, that because words such as "Israel" and "Jew" could be used in many different ways and with many different meanings, the problem was largely semantic. This is evident, for example, in Paul's affirmation in Rom 9:6, which can be translated literally: "for not all who are of Israel are Israel." Here one can be of Israel and *not* of Israel at the same time, though obviously in two different senses. On occasion, Jews or people who identified as Israel might be told by their fellow Jews and members of Israel they they were *not* truly Jews or members of Israel, generally because their behavior was considered unacceptable. At other times, Jews or members of Israel might tell gentiles who behaved righteously and showed kindness to the Jewish people: "You are truly one of us, a brother or sister and a true child of Abraham, Isaac, and Jacob." When such affirmations were made, it would not always be entirely clear whether they were to be understood literally or figuratively. Gentiles who were received in that way into the Jewish community might be regarded as part of the Jewish people or Israel in some sense even if they did not come to submit fully to all of the commandments of the law. For the most part, however, only those who submitted to the Torah in its entirety as proselytes would be considered truly Jewish.

PAUL AND THE PEOPLE OF GOD

The idea that through faith in Christ Jews and gentiles might form part of a single community on an equal basis as God's people raised numerous problems and challenges for those such as Paul who were dedicated to establishing and overseeing such communities. In addition to the many religious, social, and cultural differences that existed between the two groups and the traditional prejudices inherited by members of both groups, the fact that Jewish believers in Christ lived in accordance with the Torah and gentile believers did not made full fellowship between the two groups difficult.

In order for the two groups to eat together and share their lives closely with one another, it was necessary for both to make concessions on behalf of the other and to be willing to endure a certain amount of criticism and

---

20. On this discussion, see Eisenbaum, *Paul*, 99–115.

at times even rejection on the part of their family, friends, and peers. Full integration into the community of Jesus' followers meant altering in some ways one's relationships with those who remained outside that community and saw it as a threat to the status quo. To live as a member of Jesus' community of followers not only required a full commitment in relation to the other members of that community but also involved proclaiming a message that many Jews and non-Jews who did not form part of that community found highly problematic and objectionable.

The Challenges of Full Fellowship between Jews and Non-Jews within the Ekklēsia

Paul's account of his confrontation with Simon Peter at Antioch in Gal 2:11-16 illustrates well some of the problems and complexities that would inevitably arise as a result of maintaining that Jewish and non-Jewish believers in Christ were to relate to one another as equals within the community of Jesus' followers. No matter what reason is given for Paul's reproach of Peter in that passage, it is clear that for Jews and non-Jews to live as members of a single community and have table fellowship with one another would require that one group or the other make certain concessions. If there was to be full table fellowship, either the non-Jewish members had to abide by Jewish customs and practices or else Jewish believers had to set aside to some extent some of the traditional customs and practices that set them apart from non-Jews. Undoubtedly, both of these things occurred at times under certain circumstances.[21]

Of course, there would be many foods that were acceptable to members of both groups, such as fruits and vegetables. Meat, however, would present a problem.[22] Non-Jews could eat of meat that was clean or kosher in the eyes of Jews, but in order for Jewish believers to be sure that the meat was kosher, it would need to be supplied and prepared by Jews or under Jewish

---

21. As James G. Crossley has noted, the inclusion of non-Jews at Jewish meals "does not automatically mean that the law must be rejected in any significant way. . . . Gentiles could be present at a gathering of law-observant Jews or Jewish Christians and, naturally, keep the law at least whilst present" (*Why Christianity Happened: A Sociohistorical Account of Christian Origins (26–50 CE)* [Louisville: Westminster John Knox, 2006], 124). In contrast, Ekkehard W. Stegemann and Wolfgang Stegemann have argued that, at least in Antioch, "the practice of table fellowship meant a change in *Jewish* customs" (*The Jesus Movement: A Social History of its First Century*, trans. O. C. Dean Jr. [Minneapolis: Fortress, 1999], 271).

22. As A. Andrew Das points out, the main obstacles to table fellowship between Jews and non-Jews would have had to do with the meat and wine served: "Historically, those observing Jewish customs would abstain from meat and wine in hostile circumstances where they had no control over their diet" (*Solving the Romans Debate* [Minneapolis: Fortress, 2007], 107).

supervision. In that case, the non-Jewish believers could not supply and prepare meat for the two groups to eat together unless they were supervised by someone within the Jewish community. Naturally, each group could supply and prepare its own meat independently of the other, but then the table fellowship would not be full. Problems might also arise with regard to the purity of the utensils used. In principle, as long as non-Jews were willing to make concessions in these regards, there would be no reason why the two groups could not eat with one another. Sooner or later, however, members of one group or the other might tire of such an arrangement, and tensions and conflicts might arise. Perhaps the Jewish members of the community would grow weary of having to provide and prepare most of the food to be consumed or supervise its preparation, especially as the number of non-Jews within the community grew. Non-Jews might wish to eat of things that for some reason were not acceptable for Jews. They might even feel deprived of having the opportunity to show their generosity to their Jewish sisters and brothers by sharing with them food of their own making rather than constantly being on the receiving end of what was offered.

In order for both groups to meet and eat together, they would need to choose a place and setting that would either be Jewish, non-Jewish, or common to Jews and non-Jews alike.[23] If the setting were to be the Jewish synagogue, those Jews who were not believers in Christ would need to be taken into account. Would they be invited to the meal by their fellow Jews? Would they accept the invitation? Would they be upset that their fellow Jews were using the synagogue to have meals that involved full table fellowship with gentiles? If the synagogue had facilities for preparing food, would non-Jewish believers in Christ be allowed to make use of those facilities to help prepare the food there?[24] At the very least, non-Jews would probably

---

23. On the spaces in which the believers to whom Paul addressed his Epistle to the Romans gathered, see E. Stegemann and W. Stegemann, *Jesus Movement*, 276-79; Mark D. Nanos, *Reading Romans within Judaism*, vol. 2 of *Collected Essays of Mark D. Nanos* (Eugene, OR: Cascade, 2018), 6-8. Among others, Spence has questioned Nanos' claim that the believers in Christ in Rome continued to meet in synagogues (*Parting of the Ways*, 61-65). For our purposes here, all that matters is that Jewish and non-Jewish believers in Christ were meeting together to have table fellowship, no matter where this took place.

24. As Mark Nanos notes, whether or not the believers in Christ in Rome ate in Jewish gathering places or private homes, those spaces were probably not set aside exclusively for worship (*The Mystery of Romans: The Jewish Context of Paul's Letter* [Minneapolis: Fortress, 1996], 42-43 n4). This means that they would have had areas for preparing food. Andrew R. Krause has also pointed to evidence for food preparation and consumption in Jewish meeting places in the first century CE (*Synagogues in the Works of Flavius Josephus: Rhetoric, Spatiality, and First-Century Jewish Institutions*, AJEC 97 [Leiden: Brill, 2017], 196).

not feel entirely comfortable and at home in such a setting, given that the space was not their own.

If the community instead met and ate together at the house or property of a member, whether Jewish or non-Jewish, similar problems would arise.[25] Those who did not belong to that household would never feel entirely at home using the facilities to prepare food, overseeing and controlling access to the meeting place, and supervising the use of the space in general. If some members of the household were not believers in Christ, they might feel as if their space was being invaded by strangers and become upset not only at the visitors but also at the members of their household who were receiving and hosting those visitors.

No matter whether a particular believer in Christ was Jewish or instead belonged to some other ethnic or social group, at some point those who belonged to the same group as that believer would probably criticize him or her for identifying and associating so closely with people of a different ethnic or social group.[26] One might even be regarded as denying or betraying one's own ethnic or religious identity. Believers in Christ would also be criticized by their family and friends who were not believers for spending more time with those who previously had been strangers and paying less attention to those who had formerly been close to them. Even if they tried to avoid it, sooner or later believers in Christ would be regarded as members of an ethnic or social group that constituted a "third entity" that was neither entirely Jewish nor entirely non-Jewish, since both Jews and non-Jews who were not believers would regard some of the members of the community of believers as outsiders who did not form part of their own group. As David Rudolph has argued, this "third entity" would not be regarded as something "independent of Jews and gentiles" but rather as "a body of Jews and gentiles who believed in Jesus."[27]

When the Jewish and non-Jewish members of these mixed communities of believers in Christ sat down to eat together, it would be natural for those of the same social and ethnic group to sit with those whom they

---

25. See Paula Fredriksen, "Judaism, the Circumcision of Gentiles, and Apocalyptic Hope: Another Look at Galatians 1 and 2," *JTS* 42 (1991): 532-564 (554).

26. Mark Nanos, for example, argues that "the larger Jewish communities would have responded negatively" to Paul's reception of non-Jews as "full members of the family of Abraham, as more than guests and yet not candidates for becoming Jews." For their part, the family members of those non-Jews who abandoned their own customs to form part of the community of believers in Christ within a Jewish context would have found "incomprehensible and scandalous" their lack of respect for the family and civic cult ("The Question of Conceptualization: Qualifying Paul's Position on Circumcision in Dialogue with Josephus's Advisors to King Izates," in *Paul within Judaism: Restoring the First-Century Context to the Apostle*, ed. Mark D. Nanos and Magnus Zetterholm [Minneapolis: Fortress, 2015], 105-52 [150]).

27. Rudolph, *A Jew to the Jews*, 34-35.

knew best and associate with them rather than with those who were relative strangers. Members of any particular family would tend to sit with other members of that same family. At times, these extended families would be rather large, leading them to form a separate block, unless of course they split themselves up. Jews would naturally sit alongside other Jews, especially if they were already acquaintances of theirs, while non-Jews would seek the company of non-Jews. If members of each group were to intermingle with those of the other group rather than sitting separately from them, they would probably need to be urged or told to do so explicitly. The wealthy would associate more easily and readily with others who were wealthy, whereas those who were of a lower social class or were slaves would feel more comfortable among others of their same group. This is the reality that Paul describes in 1 Cor 11:17-22, where he criticizes the Corinthian believers for the divisions and distinctions that exist among them when they share the Lord's Supper.[28] Similarly, one can scarcely imagine how difficult it would be for slaves and their owners to eat alongside one another as if they were equals.

In order for there to be full table fellowship among believers of different backgrounds and social levels, it would be important for all those gathered to participate together in some type of common cup or bread in the way that Paul mentions in 1 Cor 10:16-17. While each particular group would therefore preserve somewhat its own identity, at the same time the different groups that came together could symbolize their unity by drinking from the same cup and eating of the same bread. This ritual eating would eventually come to take place separately from the main meal when the number of believers at the gatherings grew, since more than one table would be necessary to accommodate all those present and it would be difficult for larger groups to interact and share full table fellowship with one another.

When Paul criticizes Peter and other Jewish believers for isolating or separating themselves from gentile believers in Gal 2:11-16, therefore, their reason for sitting apart from the gentiles may have had nothing to with the purity of the food served or a concern for proper observance of the Torah.[29] It is possible that Peter and other Jewish believers were simply not interacting with the non-Jewish members of the community because they felt

---

28. On these divisions and distinctions, see E. Stegemann and W. Stegemann, *The Jesus Movement*, 283-84.

29. While the problem may have been seating arrangements that placed some above others, as Mark Nanos has argued, it may also have been simply that the Jewish believers were sitting apart from the non-Jewish ones rather than mixing with them, since this too would have implied that the two groups were not fully equal (see Nanos, *Mystery of Romans*, 347-54; Mark D. Nanos, "What Was at Stake in Peter's 'Eating with Gentiles' at Antioch?," in *The Galatians Debate*, ed. Mark D. Nanos [Peabody, MA: Hendrickson, 2002], 282-318 [296-301]).

more comfortable sitting with their fellow Jews.[30] If that was the case, Paul nevertheless accuses Peter and several other Jewish believers of hypocritical behavior because their isolation from the non-Jewish members of the community was giving the impression that they considered themselves superior to the gentiles and were rejecting them on the basis of their ethnic identity and perhaps their non-observance of the Mosaic law as well.

In order for Jewish and non-Jewish members of the communities of believers in Christ to eat together, then, it would be necessary for those of both groups not only to make concessions to those of the other group but also to make a conscious effort to interact with them. While the group that made concessions to the other might be considered inferior in that its members were subjecting themselves to the practices of the other, for the very same reason those who made the concessions might instead be considered superior if their willingness to make concessions on behalf of the members of the other group was seen as manifesting a greater love for them. Similarly, those who did not make concessions could either be regarded as superior in that their beliefs and practices prevailed over those of the other group, or instead as inferior in that they were not the ones making concessions to the other group out of love for them. Paul, of course, insists that neither of the two groups should consider itself superior or inferior to the other, no matter which of the two made concessions.

In these contexts, some of the Jewish believers in Christ may have been willing to make concessions to the non-Jewish believers by eating meat that was not pure or kosher by Jewish standards, though they may have wanted to be assured that it had not been sacrificed to idols. Other Jewish believers, however, may have been uncomfortable eating such meat. In that case, rather than insisting that the meat served be pure or kosher, these believers might simply refrain from eating meat altogether and eat only vegetables when sharing table fellowship with gentile believers.[31] This may be the

---

30. Both Paula Fredriksen and E. P. Sanders have argued that the concern of the Jewish believers in Christ had to do with interaction between the two groups rather than the observance of the law per se, whether this was because they were gathering in gentile homes (so Fredriksen, *Paul*, 96-99) or because the Jewish believers did not wish to fraternize too closely with non-Jews (so Sanders, *Comparing Judaism and Christianity: Common Judaism, Paul, and the Inner and the Outer in Ancient Religion* [Minneapolis: Fortress, 2016], 306-7).

31. As Nanos notes, "The insistence of the 'weak' on eating vegetables when with gentiles (and in many cases even when not with gentiles) rather than pagan meat is consistent with a long tradition in Diaspora cities of Jews refusing to eat meat that might have been offered to idols, or been improperly butchered so that the animal strangled or suffocated on its own blood, or simply be the meat of unacceptable animals (such as pigs, the favorite meat in Rome)" (*Mystery of Romans*, 106).

scenario described by Paul in Romans 14.[32] In that case, the Jewish believers were making a concession to the gentile believers in that they were not insisting that the meat served be kosher, yet some of the Jewish believers did not feel comfortable eating of that meat themselves. Their reluctance to eat such meat might lead them to be considered weak or "stumbling" by other believers, particularly Jewish believers such as Paul, who would see themselves as strong in comparison in that they had no qualms about eating such meat.[33] In Romans 14, however, Paul insists that rather than criticizing those who were weak and believing themselves to be superior, those believers who did eat of non-kosher meat were to show consideration and understanding for those who preferred not to eat of that meat.

The concern that non-kosher meat had been offered to idols would lead not only Jewish believers but also some gentile believers to show caution in eating meat.[34] This would not have been because they believed that something mysterious happened to the flesh of animals sacrificed to gentile gods, however, as if it had become infected by demons.[35] There is no reason to take Paul's allusion in 1 Cor 10:20-21 to partaking of the table and cup of demons and being partners with demons in that sense. Rather, love for the God of Israel and Jesus Christ dictated that believers make it clear to all, both their fellow believers and unbelievers as well, that they rejected the lifestyle and immorality that they associated with the worship of other gods. For this reason, in 1 Corinthians 8–10, Paul argues that in principle believers are free to eat of any meat, since the meat itself had not been affected by being offered to a gentile god or idol.[36] However, it was also important for believers to make it clear through their behavior that they did

---

32. On the different views regarding the interpretation of Rom 14:1–15:13 and proposals regarding the identity of the weak and strong of whom Paul speaks, see J. Paul Sampley, "The Weak and the Strong: Paul's Careful and Crafty Rhetorical Strategy in Romans 14:1–15:13," in *The Social World of the First Christians: Essays in Honor of Wayne A. Meeks*, ed. Michael L. White and O. Larry Yarbrough (Minneapolis: Fortress, 1995), 40-52; Brian J. Tucker, *Reading Romans after Supersessionism: The Continuation of Jewish Covenantal Identity*, NTAS 6 (Eugene, OR: Cascade, 2018), 197-220; Nanos, *Mystery of Romans*, 85-165; Arland J. Hultgren, *Paul's Letter to the Romans: A Commentary* (Grand Rapids: Eerdmans, 2011), 495-534.

33. On the translation of *asthenēs* as "stumbling" in Romans 14–15, see Nanos, *Mystery of Romans*, 120-39.

34. See Das, *Solving the Romans Debate*, 109-14.

35. So, for example, Mark Nanos, *Reading Paul within Judaism*, vol. 1 of *Collected Essays of Mark D. Nanos* (Eugene, OR: Cascade, 2017), 96.

36. It is possible that in 1 Corinthians 8 and 10 Paul has two distinct situations in mind, as Joop F. M. Smit has argued (*"About the Idol Offerings": Rhetoric, Social Context and Theology of Paul's Discourse in First Corinthians 8:1–11:1*, CBET [Leuven: Peeters, 2000], 47-58). Nevertheless, in some ways the issues to which Paul is responding in both of these passages would have been much the same.

not regard the worship of other gods as something that was indifferent or acceptable due to the immorality associated with the worship of those gods, whom Paul considers demons.

As Paul argues, for believers to fail to make manifest their rejection of the values and behaviors associated with the worship of other gods could only be considered a lack of love for others, since it would imply that there was nothing wrong or objectionable about those values or behaviors. Paul's argument in 1 Corinthians 8–10 should be understood against the background of these ideas. What concerns Paul there is not so much the behavior of believers in itself, but rather the effect that their behavior has on others. While they are free, they are not to do anything that might harm the conscience of others. In 1 Cor 10:1-14, what Paul criticizes is the immoral behavior of those who set aside the worship of the one true God in order to worship idols, as Israel did in the desert when the people made for themselves a golden calf. When Paul writes that believers cannot drink the cup of demons and the cup of the Lord in 1 Cor 10:21, his point is not that it is by nature impossible for one to do both, but rather that the way of life associated with the worship of idols is incompatible with the way of life of those who are committed to living as members of Christ's body the *ekklēsia*.[37]

The difficulties and conflicts that would arise for Jewish believers in Christ who wished to live in full fellowship with gentile believers in Christ can be illustrated by considering what would happen when a male child would be born to a Jewish couple who belonged to the community of believers in Christ. Such a couple would consider it unthinkable not to have their child circumcised.[38] Any who refused to do so would be strongly criticized and perhaps even ostracized by their Jewish family and friends, as well as the Jewish community at large. The circumcision of the child

---

37. According to Karin Hedner Zetterholm, in 1 Corinthians 8 and 10 "Paul seems to be saying that it is a person's religious orientation (intention toward God or toward 'idols') that determines whether or not the food should be considered an idol offering, which determines whether the Jesus-believing gentile can eat it or not. The power of idolatry, according to this way of reasoning, is not in the food, but in the attitude and intention of those who are devoted to Greco-Roman gods" ("The Question of Assumptions: Torah Observance in the First Century," in *Paul within Judaism: Restoring the First-Century Context to the Apostle*, ed. Mark D. Nanos and Magnus Zetterholm [Minneapolis: Fortress, 2015], 79-103 [99]). Paul's concern would therefore be the message one was communicating by partaking of food knowingly sacrificed to idols. Mark Nanos has argued that Paul's concern in 1 Corinthians 8–10 had to do primarily with the impact that the behavior of believers would have on polytheists rather than believers in Christ (*Reading Corinthians and Philippians within Judaism*, vol. 4 of *Collected Essays of Mark D. Nanos* [Eugene, OR: Cascade, 2017], 3-35).

38. As scholars such as Paula Fredriksen have argued, there is no reason to suppose that Paul did not continue to expect that Jewish believers in Christ circumcise their newborn male children (*Paul*, 112-14).

would almost certainly take place in the context of a traditional Jewish ceremony that would be followed by some type of celebration. In that case, the parents would need to decide whom to invite to the ceremony and celebration. If they invited their fellow believers in Christ who were gentiles to the ceremony and celebration, especially if the group of these gentile believers was somewhat large, they might face some type of criticism on the part of those Jews who were not believers in Christ, who would consider it odd that such a group of non-Jews be invited to the traditional Jewish ceremony and celebration. If they did not invite their fellow believers in Christ who were gentiles to the ceremony and celebration, however, they might face criticism within the community of believers for continuing to make distinctions that supposedly had been overcome in Christ. In fact, the Jewish parents might even feel badly for not inviting the gentile believers to whom they had grown close simply because some of their Jewish family, friends, and acquaintances might disapprove of the inclusion of gentiles in the activities associated with the ceremony and celebration. One way or the other, then, the Jewish parents would probably face criticism and would tend to feel somewhat uncomfortable with any decision they took about whom to invite.

If the parents of the child wanted to resignify the ceremony of circumcision in some way by alluding to Christ in the course of the ceremony, their fellow Jews who were not believers in Christ might object to such modifications of the traditional Jewish rite. In that case, the parents might feel pressured to suppress the witness concerning their faith in Christ that they wished to give others during the ceremony. If they did omit any allusions to their faith in Christ as a result of such pressure, they might feel as if they were failing to stand up for the truth of their beliefs as they should out of concern for how their Jewish family, friends, and acquaintances might react.

Non-Jewish believers in Christ would face similar tensions and conflicts with their own family, friends, and acquaintances who were not believers in Christ.[39] They too would be pressured to practice their traditional faith and participate in activities, practices, and ceremonies that they no longer considered to be compatible with their faith in Christ. Furthermore, if they were to have some type of personal or family celebration, they too would need to decide whom to invite and whom *not* to invite. If that celebration fell on a Jewish Sabbath or involved eating or drinking something that Jews considered contrary to their customs on the basis of their interpretation of the Torah, any Jewish believers invited would face the difficult decision of whether to act contrary to those customs. Under such conditions, all would be encouraged to act according to their conscience in the way that Paul advises in Romans 14–15 and 1 Corinthians 8–10.

---

39. On the nature of these tensions, see Larry W. Hurtado, *How on Earth Did Jesus Become a God?: Historical Questions about Earliest Devotion to Jesus* (Grand Rapids: Eerdmans, 2005), 60-62.

Both Jewish and non-Jewish believers in Christ would also face difficulties if their spouse was not a believer. Because sooner or later those believers would have to endure criticism and perhaps some type of ostracism or rejection by some of their family members and acquaintances who did not believe in Christ, a spouse who was not a believer would at times need to decide whether to side with his or her believing spouse over against those family members and acquaintances or instead stand alongside the family members and acquaintances over against his or her spouse. Inevitably, among those members of the community whose spouse was not a believer in Christ, questions such as those discussed by Paul in 1 Cor 7:10-16 would arise.[40]

Ultimately, then, believers in Christ would need to make extremely difficult and painful decisions regarding their relations to non-believers, especially those with whom they had previously enjoyed strong ties. Following Jerry Sumney, a distinction can be made between the primary and secondary identity of believers in Christ.[41] Paul's epistles, along with the other writings of the New Testament, seem to indicate that it was not acceptable for believers in Christ to regard their identity as believers as secondary to some other identity, whatever it might be. Under certain circumstances, for example, Jewish believers would be pressured to choose between giving priority to their Jewish identity or their identity as followers of Christ. The same would be true of non-Jews who came to faith in Christ, who would need to decide whether to give priority to their own ethnic, social, family, or religious identity over against their identity as followers of Christ. No matter how much they tried to avoid it, therefore, sooner or later both Jewish and non-Jewish believers in Christ would need to decide whether or not to assume their identity as believers in Christ as primary. Those who failed or refused to do so would no longer be considered members of the community of believers in good standing, since by definition membership in that community involved giving of oneself fully to others within that community and holding nothing back.[42]

It would not be long before the community of believers would be seen and see itself as a community that was distinct from all other communities.[43] What was to distinguish it was primarily the unconditional, uncompromising love

---

40. On the questions that Paul addresses in 1 Cor 7:10-16, see Roy E. Ciampa and Brian S. Rosner, *The First Letter to the Corinthians*, PNTC (Grand Rapids: Eerdmans, 2010), 289-306; Hurtado, *How on Earth*, 63-64.

41. Jerry L. Sumney, "Paul and Christ-believing Jews Whom He Opposes," in *Jewish Christianity Reconsidered: Rethinking Ancient Groups and Texts*, ed. Matt Jackson-McCabe (Minneapolis: Fortress, 2007), 57-80.

42. In this context, it was natural that the language of family and kinship came to be used among believers in Christ; see Wayne A. Meeks, *The First Urban Christians: The Social World of the Apostle Paul* (New Haven: Yale University Press, 1983), 87-89.

43. See Spence, *Parting of the Ways*, 64-65.

of all of its members for the God of Jesus Christ and for one another, as well as for all people in general. Those who were not willing to commit themselves to living in such love would therefore not be considered as full members of that community, though they could certainly be accepted as sympathizers. Once baptism had been established as an entrance rite, it would be understood precisely in terms of making such a commitment. Baptism would be administered to a believer only once because such a commitment was thought to be definitive and irreversible. Anything less was not truly a commitment.

It is not clear when the members of the community of believers in Christ came to be called by a name of their own. It seems that this had not yet occurred when Paul wrote his epistles, at least in the communities to which he addressed them. By the year 64, when the Roman emperor Nero began to target believers in Christ as "Christians," the community of believers seems to have been a group that was defined with some degree of clarity, at least in Rome.[44] It is possible, of course, that the designation "Christian" was already in use in Paul's day and that Paul simply did not use it in his letters, perhaps because he wished to avoid identifying the members of the *ekklēsia* as a group that was distinct from Israel.[45] No matter when they were given a name of their own, however, by the time that Paul wrote his letters, it seems clear that the community of believers in Christ had already assumed an identity that was distinct from that of other communities. While today it may be preferable to avoid calling these early believers "Christians" both because such a term is anachronistic and because of the many connotations which it has come to have, there is a sense in which it would be entirely appropriate to call these believers "Christians," just as it is appropriate to call the communities of believers founded by Paul as "Pauline," even though they never identified themselves in that way.

The Practice of Circumcision within the Community of Believers in Christ

At no point in his letters does Paul ever view circumcision in a negative light.[46] In Rom 2:25-29, however, he does speak of two kinds of circumcision, one which is physical or literal and a second which is "of the heart,

---

44. See Spence, *Parting of the Ways*, 119-26.

45. Mikael Tellbe, for example, has argued that the designation "Christian" (*christianos*) was already known in Eastern parts of the Roman Empire in the beginning of the decade of the forties, though many New Testament scholars would question that claim (*Paul between Synagogue and State: Christians, Jews, and Civic Authorities in 1 Thessalonians, Romans, and Philippians*, ConBNT 34 [Stockholm: Almqvist & Wiksell, 2001], 65-66).

46. There is nothing in Paul's epistles, for example, to substantiate the claim of Peter-Ben Smit that circumcision "represents a flawed or deficient ritual for Paul" ("In Search

in spirit." As we have noted above, this distinction is found in the Hebrew Scriptures themselves, which affirm that Israel should be circumcised in its heart. There, of course, this circumcision of the heart presupposes physical circumcision rather than precluding it. The logic behind circumcision is basically that which Paul mentions in Rom 4:11-12: God commanded Abraham and his descendants to be circumcised as a sign or symbol of the righteousness that was to characterize their lives as God's special, chosen people. Circumcision was therefore to serve as a reminder of Israel's identity as God's people. As Paul argues in Rom 2:25, those who were circumcised physically but did not obey the Mosaic law became uncircumcised in a sense since their behavior represented a denial of what it meant to live as members of God's people Israel and to live as Abraham's children.[47]

Scholars have debated whether or not Paul taught that those who remain uncircumcised physically but observe the Mosaic law and believe in Christ come to be considered by God as Jews and members of Israel. Paul never makes such an affirmation. When he writes in Rom 2:28-29 that "a person is a Jew who is one inwardly" (*en tō kryptō*) and that "a person is not a Jew who is one outwardly" (*en tō phanerō*), his idea seems to be that only those Jews who are Jews inwardly are truly Jews, but not that gentiles actually become Jews by living inwardly as Jews.

In Rom 2:26, however, Paul claims that believers who are physically uncircumcised are regarded by God as if they were circumcised by virtue of their faith and obedience. Similarly, in Phil 3:3, he writes: "For we are the circumcision, who worship by the Spirit of God and boast in Christ Jesus and put no confidence in the flesh." Paul's point here seems to be that those who believe in Christ are circumcised spiritually and in God's sight.[48] In neither of these passages does Paul question the value or meaning of physical circumcision for Jews or affirm that only believers in Christ are truly circumcised in God's sight. While virtually all Jews would have agreed with Paul that physical circumcision is of little or no value if it is not accompanied by a life of obedience to the Mosaic law, however, it is doubtful that Jews who did not believe in Christ would have agreed that

---

of Real Circumcision: Ritual Failure and Circumcision in Paul," *JSNT* 40 [2017]: 73-100 [74]).

47. As Nanos argues, rather than "attributing circumcision or Jewish ethnic identity to non-Jews," in Rom 2:25-29 Paul is merely claiming that Jewish circumcision is "undermined if not accompanied by circumcision of their heart" ("Question of Conceptualization," 115 n17).

48. Many scholars would agree with Markus Bockmuehl that in Phil 3:3 Paul "is not saying that uncircumcised Christians are the 'true' (allegorical) circumcision and Jews are not, or that Christianity has replaced and invalidated Judaism...," but rather that "faith in Christ places Gentile believers on the same footing before God as Jewish believers" (*The Epistle to the Philippians*, 4th ed., BNTC [London: A & C Black, 1997], 191).

those not circumcised physically could become circumcised in God's sight by believing in Christ and living under him as their Lord.

Most Jews would have regarded as a contradiction in terms the notion that an uncircumcised male could observe faithfully the commandments of the Mosaic law, since one of those commandments was precisely the commandment regarding the circumcision of males. For this reason, 1 Cor 7:19 would have sounded strange to Jewish ears: "Circumcision is nothing, and uncircumcision is nothing; but what matters is observing the commandments of God." Paul makes similar affirmations about circumcision in Gal 5:6, where he writes: "For in Christ Jesus neither circumcision nor uncircumcision matters, but faith working in love," and in Gal 6:15: "Neither circumcision nor uncircumcision is anything, but only a new creation." Taken together, these passages suggest that for Paul "keeping the commandments of God" is equivalent to "faith working in love." The new creation of which he speaks would involve both of these things.

Most scholars reject the possibility that in this last passage Paul has in mind something such as a "third race" composed of persons who are neither Jews nor Gentiles.[49] Nevertheless, certain passages from his epistles do suggest that believers in Christ are no longer to be defined primarily as Jews or gentiles but in some sense as a unique and distinct entity. In Rom 9:24, Paul affirms that believers are called *ex Ioudaiōn* and *ex ethnōn*, which can be translated as "out from among the Jews" and "out from among the gentiles."[50] For people to be called *out of* both of these groups would involve being called *into* some group that is distinct from them. In 1 Cor 12:2, he writes to the Corinthians: "You know that when you were gentiles (*ethnē*), you were led to idols that could not speak so as to be led astray." This suggests that the Corinthian believers are in some sense no longer gentiles.[51] In Gal 3:28, Paul also affirms that in some sense there is no longer Jew nor Greek in the community of believers, since all are one in Christ. It is possible, therefore, that in Gal 6:15 Paul's idea is that believers in Christ are no longer to be defined primarily as Jews or gentiles since they are "something new," a "new creation" that does not fit entirely under the category of either

---

49. As Judith Lieu has observed, there is no clear evidence for such an idea prior to the second century ("Self-Definition vis-à-vis the Jewish Matrix," in *The Cambridge History of Christianity*, vol. 1: *Origins to Constantine*, ed. Frances M. Young and Margaret M. Mitchell [Cambridge: Cambridge University Press, 2006], 214-29 [214]).

50. James D. G. Dunn rightly notes: "The *ek* indicates a calling 'out of,' with implication of separation, from a larger body...." (*Romans 9-16*, WBC 38B [Dallas: Word, 1988], 570).

51. See Carolyn Johnson Hodge, "The Question of Identity: Gentiles as Gentiles— but also Not—in Pauline Communities," in *Paul within Judaism: Restoring the First-Century Context to the Apostle*, ed. Mark D. Nanos and Magnus Zetterholm (Minneapolis: Fortress, 2015), 153-73 (156).

Jew or gentile. There is no reason to think, however, that this "something new" would have been understood in terms of a new race of human beings.

The affirmations Paul makes in 1 Cor 7:19, Gal 5:6, and Gal 6:15 have generally been understood in the sense that it is unimportant whether one is circumcised or uncircumcised. However, they can also be taken in another sense, namely, that both circumcision and uncircumcision can be meaningful in different ways.[52] This is suggested by Rom 4:11-12, where Paul writes that Abraham

> received the sign of circumcision as a seal of the righteousness of faith which was his when he was as yet uncircumcised. The purpose was that he might be regarded as the ancestor of all those who believe without being circumcised, so that they might have righteousness reckoned to them, and also the ancestor of those who are circumcised, yet who in addition to being circumcised follow in the footsteps of the faith that Abraham had when he was not yet circumcised.

On the basis of this passage, one might argue that, just as circumcision could serve as a reminder to those circumcised that Abraham was their ancestor or father, so also the condition of not being circumcised could serve to remind uncircumcised gentile believers that Abraham was their ancestor or father as well, since he too had been accepted as righteous by God when he was still uncircumcised. In Christ, therefore, they might look upon their uncircumcision as a sign or seal in the same way that circumcised Jews regarded their circumcision as a sign or seal. Paul himself insists in Rom 2:25 that circumcision is of value for those who obey the law rather than regarding it as meaningless. Similarly, in Rom 3:1-2, after asking, "What is the value of circumcision?," he answers: "Much, in every way." These passages indicate that Paul continued to regard circumcision as being of value for Jewish believers in Christ. He may therefore have seen uncircumcision as meaningful for gentile believers in a similar manner.

In his letter to the Galatians and in 1 Cor 7:18-20, however, Paul insists that gentile believers in Christ not only *need* not be circumcised but also *should* not be circumcised or seek circumcision. Whereas prior to the "new perspective on Paul" it was generally maintained that the reason for this is that for gentiles to be circumcised would involve lapsing into the type of legalism and works-righteousness that Paul supposedly condemned in

---

52. William S. Campbell, for example, affirms that Paul "does not think that to be circumcised or uncircumcised is a matter of indifference. . . . Far from being indifferent to these things, these forms of living, in circumcision or in the foreskin, are still significant factors for Paul. . . ." ("Covenantal Theology and Participation in Christ: Pauline Perspectives on Transformation," in *Paul and Judaism: Crosscurrents in Pauline Exegesis and the Study of Jewish-Christian Relations*, ed. Reimund Bieringer and Didier Pollefeyt, LNTS 463 [London: T & T Clark, 2012], 41-60 [46]). On this point, see also Rudolph, *A Jew to the Jews*, 28-33.

Judaism, today other reasons are given.[53] According to those associated with the "new perspective on Paul" such as James Dunn, the problem with circumcision and other similar works of the law was that they were "identified as distinctive marks of the Jewish nation and so in effect confined the grace of God to members of that nation."[54] Scholars such as Paula Fredriksen and Mark Nanos have rejected such an interpretation of Paul and have instead argued that, in accordance with Jewish eschatological beliefs, Paul believed that those from the nations who come to worship the God of Israel were to do so as *gentiles* and not as Jews.[55] As we have noted previously, Matthew Thiessen has even argued that Jews thought it was impossible for a gentile to become a Jew.[56]

While I would certainly agree that the issue for Paul is not Jewish legalism or works-righteousness, I doubt very much that what led Paul to insist that gentile believers not be circumcised was a belief that at the *eschaton* gentiles should still be gentiles rather than Jews or that it was impossible for gentiles to become Jews. As Terence Donaldson has argued, there is very little evidence for any Jewish belief in antiquity that gentiles needed to remain gentiles at the *eschaton* rather than becoming Jews or members of Israel.[57] On the contrary, the widespread acceptance of proselytes among Jews in the Second Temple period suggests that most Jews had no problems with gentiles becoming Jews in the present age.[58] If many gentile believers in Christ became Jewish proselytes, certainly there would still be plenty of righteous gentiles left over who did not take such a step and could therefore fulfill the role of representing the nations at the *eschaton* if this were deemed necessary. Furthermore, if Paul's concern was merely

---

53. On this discussion, see Nanos, *Reading Paul within Judaism*, 11-16; Martinus C. de Boer, *Galatians: A Commentary*, NTL (Louisville: Westminster John Knox, 2011), 145-48.

54. James D. G. Dunn, *Jesus, Paul and the Law: Studies in Mark and Galatians* (Louisville: Westminster John Knox, 1990), 11-12. The same basic understanding of works of the law in Paul's thought is found in the writings of N. T. Wright: "they are not the moral works through which one gains merit but the works through which the Jew is defined over against the pagan" (*Pauline Perspectives: Essays on Paul, 1978-2013* [Minneapolis: Fortress, 2013], 276).

55. See Fredriksen, *Paul*, 103-4, 164; Nanos, "Question of Conceptualization," 109, 124-27,

56. Matthew Thiessen, *Paul and the Gentile Problem* (New York: Oxford University Press, 2016), 14, 161-63.

57. Terence L. Donaldson, "Paul within Judaism: A Critical Evaluation from a 'New Perspective' Perspective," in *Paul within Judaism: Restoring the First-Century Context to the Apostle*, ed. Mark D. Nanos and Magnus Zetterholm (Minneapolis: Fortress, 2015), 277-301 (286-93).

58. See Scot McKnight, *A Light among the Gentiles: Jewish Missionary Activity in the Second Temple Period* (Minneapolis: Fortress, 1991), 34-48.

that uncircumcised gentiles continue to be gentiles at the *eschaton*, then ultimately what mattered to him was merely that everyone "get the script right." To maintain that this was his concern raises the question of whether he would have thought that those gentile believers who became circumcised would no longer be saved. Nothing in his epistles suggests that this was the case. If those gentile believers who did undergo circumcision did not forfeit their salvation, then ultimately it would not seem to matter if they chose to become circumcised, unless perhaps their becoming circumcised would affect themselves or others negatively in some other way.

Even if Paul and other Jews believed that it was impossible for gentiles to become Jews, as Thiessen claims, they would not necessarily have concluded on that basis that it was wrong or sinful for gentile believers in Christ or gentiles in general to submit to circumcision and all of the commandments of the Mosaic law. In principle, gentiles could do these things without expecting to be considered Jews or integrated into the Jewish community as full members of Israel. It is also difficult to see why any Jews would become upset if gentiles became Torah-observant and submitted to circumcision if they so desired. Rather than being angered, many Jews would probably have felt honored and pleased that gentiles *qua* gentiles had decided to validate the Jewish tradition by adopting it, especially if they did so without claiming that they were now equal to Jews in every way or members of Israel in the same way that Jews were.[59] It is also not clear why it would be thought that the God of Israel would become upset or angry if gentiles were circumcised and became fully law-observant. What harm would there be in that? Would he not instead be pleased?

It might be argued that some Jews would be concerned that members of the non-Jewish community around them could become upset that the Jewish community seemed to be encouraging non-Jews to become Jews by receiving favorably within their community non-Jews who were abandoning their own ancestral traditions and religious practices in order to live as Jews. If this were the problem, however, it would not make any difference whether or not the non-Jewish believers in Christ became circumcised, since in either case they would still be abandoning their own traditions and practices in order to integrate into spaces that were considered Jewish. This might upset non-Jews independently of whether the non-Jewish believers

---

59. Both Philo and Josephus maintained that it was good for non-Jews to come to live in conformity with the Jewish law; see E. P. Sanders, "The Covenant as a Soteriological Category and the Nature of Salvation in Palestinian and Hellenistic Judaism," in *Jews, Greeks, and Christians: Religious Cultures in Late Antiquity. Essays in Honor of William David Davies*, ed. Robert Hamerton-Kelly and Robin Scroggs, SJLA 21 (Leiden: Brill, 1976) 11-44 (27-29); Stanley K. Stowers, *A Rereading of Romans: Justice, Jews, and Gentiles* (New Haven: Yale University Press, 1994), 63-65; Nanos, "Question of Conceptualization," 110-19.

in Christ were becoming circumcised or not. In fact, many Jews would have preferred that such non-Jews become circumcised, since their willingness to submit to such a rite would provide a basis for claiming that they really had integrated fully into the Jewish community rather than simply claiming to be Jewish in some sense out of personal interest without fully committing themselves to living as Jews.

I would therefore argue instead that Paul's concern was primarily *practical* in nature. If gentile believers in Christ who were male were required to become circumcised in order to form part of the *ekklēsia*, the number of gentiles who would be willing to undergo the extremely painful procedure of circumcision would be very low. In that case, most non-Jewish male believers in Christ would have remained uncircumcised and simply participated in the *ekklēsia* as persons who did not fully belong to it in the same way that many pious gentiles attended a synagogue and adopted some Jewish customs without actually becoming Jews and submitting fully to the Torah. For uncircumcised male gentile believers to be denied full membership and inclusion within the *ekklēsia*, however, would involve making distinctions of the type that Paul rejected.

Furthermore, if uncircumcised gentile believers in Christ already possessed the only circumcision they needed, as Paul claims in Phil 3:2-3 and Rom 2:26, for them to undergo physical circumcision would not only be senseless but would also represent a denial of that truth. In effect, any who would become circumcised would be denying or calling into question the notion that uncircumcised believers in Christ could be regarded as "the circumcision." By their actions, they would be implying that those believers in Christ who were not physically circumcised were lacking something and that those who were circumcised only spiritually were in some way inferior to those who were circumcised not only spiritually but physically as well. Paul clearly rejects such an idea and instead insists that within the community of believers in Christ physical circumcision does not make one superior in any way to those who are circumcised spiritually but not physically. Physical circumcision is only a sign given for the sake of God's people Israel and in itself does not affect one's relation to God. Nor was it to affect one's status within the community of believers, since all were to regard one another as equals and show no favoritism on the basis of whether one was physically circumcised or not.

One can only imagine the confusion and turmoil that would begin to reign in the communities of believers in Christ that included gentiles if some of them started becoming circumcised. In addition to asking what motivation they could possibly have for doing so, everyone would begin to ask and wonder whether those gentile believers who underwent circumcision thereby became superior to the uncircumcised members of the community in some way. If not, then it would not be clear why any gentile believers would choose to undergo circumcision. For some gentile believers to do so would communicate the idea that there was some advantage to being circumcised, either because it made one more acceptable to God or because it enabled one to gain a greater status or level of acceptance within the community. If such was the case, all the male gentile believers within the community would feel pressured to become circumcised so as to belong to the group of believers that was more acceptable to God or enjoyed special status within the community of believers. In this way, the type of distinctions that Paul found so objectionable and fought against so vigorously would be introduced into the community. For any to claim that those believers who had been circumcised and were law-observant enjoyed a privileged status in God's eyes or were to be more fully accepted within the *ekklēsia* would destroy the unity among the members. Conversely, those uncircumcised were not to be considered less acceptable to God or of a lower status within the community. According to Paul, no type of favoritism was to be shown to any on the basis of whether they were circumcised or not. Circumcision or law-observance was not to be regarded as a condition for exercising greater power or influence within the community or being placed in positions of leadership or authority that were denied to the uncircumcised. Such distinctions would make it impossible for the members to live as one in full fellowship and equality with one another.[60]

For all of these reasons, Paul's gospel and his understanding of the nature of the *ekklēsia* led him to adopt the position that he articulates in 1 Cor 7:18-20: both those believers who were circumcised and those who were not should remain in the same condition that they had been in when they came to faith. For them to do otherwise would not only create serious problems within the *ekklēsia* but would also "pervert the gospel of Christ" (Gal 1:7), since it would inevitably lead to distinctions within the community that ran contrary to the gospel. The community would cease to be one in which all accepted one another fully just as they were, whether circumcised or uncircumcised, and circumcision and uncircumcision would become points of contention and division.

Only when one understands these things can one also understand why Paul is so angry when he writes to the Galatians. Those pressuring the Galatian gentile believers to be circumcised were in essence either affirming that within the *ekklēsia* there were to be two different groups, one of which was to be regarded as superior to the other, or that those uncircumcised were not to be regarded as full members of the *ekklēsia*. What upset Paul so much was not that those in Galatia were "getting the script wrong"

---

60. On Paul's stress that circumcised Jews and uncircumcised gentiles were to be regarded as equals within the community of believers, see Terence L. Donaldson, *Paul and the Gentiles: Remapping the Apostle's Convictional World* (Minneapolis: Fortress, 1997), 151-61; Nanos, *Mystery of Romans*, 348-56.

by encouraging gentiles to become Jews before the *eschaton* arrived. That would hardly have mattered to him. Instead, what enraged Paul was that divisions and distinctions were beginning to be made in the communities of believers that ran contrary to everything that those communities were to stand for and represent. In fact, those divisions and distinctions would ultimately destroy them altogether. Contrary to some contemporary portrayals of Paul, Paul was not some power-hungry despot who wanted to exert control and authority over others for his own sake in communities that he selfishly considered his own personal property.[61] What led Paul to write to the Galatians in such an aggressive tone was not any type of selfishness, jealousy, envy, or personal interest on his part. Rather, the very gospel of love, mutual acceptance, and solidarity that he had proclaimed was being not only compromised but denied, and the result would be the destruction of the type of communities Paul had worked so hard to establish. Everything for which both Christ and Paul had given up their lives would come to naught.

This same anger is evident in Phil 3:2, where Paul tells the Philippian believers: "Beware of the dogs, beware of the evil workers, beware of the mutilators," as well as 2 Corinthians 10–13, where Paul condemns the "false apostles" and "workers of deceit" who "disguise themselves as apostles of Christ" in the same way that "Satan disguises himself as an angel of light"

---

61. This is suggested by portrayals of Paul such as that of Christina Harker, who argues that what ultimately concerned Paul when he wrote Galatians was losing the type of paternalistic control that he wanted to exert over the Galatian believers: "He presents himself as an apostle by divine right, with greater authority than his rivals and a paternalistic obligation to mold the Galatians into his ideal community, such as they were. . . . As a letter, Galatians is explicitly driven by Paul's desire to control the Galatians' practices and beliefs as he first intended. . . ." (*The Colonizers' Idols: Paul, Galatia, and Empire in New Testament Studies*, WUNT 2/460 [Tübingen: Mohr Siebeck, 2018], 208-9). According to Harker, Paul was convinced "that he knew what was best for the Galatians, and that he had the authority to tell them so. . . ." (211). Similarly, Paula Fredriksen speaks of Paul "railing" against those who wanted to impose circumcision on gentile believers in Christ, "reviling" them, resorting to "intemperate name calling" against them, and employing "tirade" and "invective" in order to "berate" them, merely because he wanted to get his own way (*When Christians Were Jews: The First Generation* [New Haven: Yale University Press, 2018], 153, 157, 160; *Paul*, 99, 127). Such language suggests that Paul was lashing out at those who sought to impose circumcision on the gentile believers in Galatia purely out of a concern for his own interests rather than out of a genuine concern for those believers themselves and the type of community he had helped establish among them. The same selfish motivation is implied by Fredriksen when she writes: "Not only Paul but (much to his fury) other Jewish Christ-followers also strive to bring the good news of the coming Kingdom to non-Jews. . . ." (*Paul*, 30). As Paul himself states in Phil 1:14-19, he rejoiced when others shared the gospel, even when they did so for the wrong reasons or out of personal interest, rather than becoming enraged at them.

(2 Cor 11:13-14).[62] For Paul, what those whom he calls "dogs" and "muti-lators" were doing was truly reprehensible. In both of these passages, he insists that if any had grounds to boast in their Jewishness, it was Paul himself (2 Cor 11:22-33; Phil 3:4-6). Those who were proclaiming a different Jesus and a different gospel were serving only their own interests rather than the interests of others, since what they were doing was destroying the love and solidarity that those among whom Paul had worked had come to experience within their communities (2 Cor 11:4). According to Gal 6:12-14, they were also acting contrary to the spirit of love and self-giving that Paul associated with Jesus' death for others, which had been the result of Jesus' own efforts to establish the basis for the type of communities that Paul describes throughout his epistles. The believers at Galatia who were seeking to be justified by becoming circumcised and submitting fully to the Torah were indeed severing themselves from Christ and falling from grace (Gal 5:4). This was because they were denying everything that Christ stood for and implying that God showed preference for those who observed the Torah rather than showering his grace, mercy, and gifts equally upon the circumcised and uncircumcised, both of whom were objects of the same love on his part.

One can also understand why Paul uses the strong language he does in Phil 3:7-11 to speak of his former life as a zealous Pharisee as "loss," "rubbish," or even "excrement" (*skybala*) in comparison to knowing Christ as Lord and "gaining" him.[63] What Paul had found in Christ that he had not found in his former life in Judaism was the type of community he describes in passages such as Phil 2:1-5, that is, a community in which Jews and gentiles made a commitment to live in fellowship, affection, and compassion, "united in the

---

62. Even though in 2 Corinthians 11 Paul does not mention circumcision as a point of contention between him and the false "super-apostles," his insistence that he too is a Hebrew, an Israelite, and a descendant of Abraham in v. 22 of that chapter suggests that some aspect of Jewish identity was at the heart of the conflict and that those whom he criticizes were related in some way to those whom he opposes in Galatians and Philippians 3; see Ian J. Elmer, *Paul, Jerusalem and the Judaisers: The Galatian Crisis in Its Broadest Historical Context*, WUNT 2/258 (Tübingen: Mohr Siebeck, 2009), 165-96. Rather than pressuring gentile believers to be circumcised and submit to the Torah, however, these "false apostles" may simply have been claiming a superior status within the Corinthian community on the basis of their Jewish identity. If so, they were in effect maintaining that those who were Jewish and observed the Mosaic law were to enjoy a special or higher status within the community of believers, contrary to Paul's teaching. In any case, the conflict to which Paul alludes in all of these passages had to do with relations within the community of believers rather than relations between the community of believers and the members of the Jewish community who did not believe in Christ.

63. On the forcefulness of Paul's language in Phil 3:7-11, see Moisés Silva, *Philippians*, BECNT (Grand Rapids: Baker Academic, 2005), 179-81.

same mind, sharing the same love, being of the same spirit, and thinking in the same way," doing nothing from selfishness but rather seeking the interests of others. To establish distinctions within that community on the basis of circumcision and law-observance would utterly destroy such a community.

The New Covenant

It has become common among New Testament scholars today to claim that the concept of a new covenant did not play a central role in Paul's thought, since he uses that phrase only twice in his letters.[64] These passages are 1 Cor 11:25, where he cites the tradition he received regarding the Lord's Supper, and in 2 Cor 3:6, where he speaks of himself and his co-workers as ministers of a new covenant. It is also often maintained that, when Paul does speak of a new covenant, he does not have in mind a covenant that is distinct from the covenant God made with Israel but instead a renewed form or version of that same covenant.[65]

In Gal 4:21-31, Paul affirms that Sarah and Hagar represent two covenants, yet he does not refer to either of the two as old or new. He also uses the plural "covenants" in Rom 9:4-5, yet he speaks of these as belonging to Israel "according to the flesh." It is possible that he sees the covenant God made with Moses at Sinai as distinct from the one God had made previously with Abraham, even though in some sense he would also have seen these two covenants as one.[66] In the Hebrew Scriptures, of course, God is said to have made a variety of covenants with different people and individuals.[67] According to 2 Chron 7:18, 21:7, and 2 Sam 23:5, God had made an everlasting covenant with David according to which David would never lack a descendant to rule over Israel. In 1 Kgs 8:23-24, in fact, God's

---

64. James D. G. Dunn, for example, claims that "'covenant' was not a primary category for Paul," that "the link between his gospel and the idea of the 'new covenant' lay somewhat on the periphery of his thought," and that "talk of covenant is not central to Paul's theologizing...." ("Did Paul Have a Covenant Theology? Reflections on Romans 9.4 and 11.27," in *The Concept of the Covenant in the Second Temple Period*, ed. Stanley E. Porter and Jacqueline C. R. de Roo, JSJSup 71 [Leiden: Brill, 2003], 287-307 [297, 301]).

65. William S. Campbell, for example, questions the notion that Paul has in mind two separate covenants when he speaks of a new covenant: "Whilst a new covenant is offered in Christ, we do not see this as a second covenant, but more as a renewal so that continuity in the divine purpose is thereby assured" (*Paul and the Creation of Christian Identity*, LNTS 322 [London: T & T Clark, 2006], 131).

66. On this interpretation of Gal 4:21-31, see Dunn, "Did Paul Have a Covenant Theology?," 293.

67. On the multiplicity of covenants mentioned in the Hebrew Scriptures and Second Temple Jewish literature, see Mark Adam Elliott, *The Survivors of Israel: A Reconsideration of the Theology of Pre-Christian Judaism* (Grand Rapids: Eerdmans, 2000), 251-58.

covenant with David is mentioned together with the covenant that God had made with Israel as a whole. Obviously, the covenant that God made with David and his descendants in no way nullified the covenant he had made with Abraham and Israel previously. On the contrary, if the older covenant with Israel did not remain in force but came to an end, the newer covenant God had made with David could not be fulfilled but would also come to an end, since in that case there would be no covenant people over which David's descendants might rule.

It is important, therefore, not to jump to the conclusion that the two covenants of which Paul speaks in Gal 4:21-31 are the old and new covenants as these have traditionally been understood. Paul may have interpreted God's promise to Hagar to make a great nation of her son Ishmael in the sense of a covenant made with their descendants, for example, even though the word covenant does not appear in the narrative in Gen 21:15-18. For the same reasons, even though Paul speaks of an old and a new covenant in 2 Cor 3:6-14, it should not be assumed that he has in mind the same idea that is found in Heb 8:6-13, according to which the old covenant is obsolete and is to disappear so as to give way to a new one. A new covenant does not necessarily displace an older one, supersede it, or render it invalid, but may merely complement it, as the covenant with David complemented the covenant God had made with Israel. Even if Paul thought that Israel had broken the covenant, as the people of Israel are said to have done in Jer 31:32, there is no reason to think that a broken covenant could not be mended and renewed rather than having to be abolished.

Although the language of covenant and new covenant is relatively scarce in Paul's letters, this does not necessarily mean that the concept is not of primary importance for Paul. In the Hebrew Scriptures and Jewish thought in antiquity, a covenant involves the establishment of a relationship between two parties in which both make certain commitments and promises. One might also speak of an "arrangement" between the two parties. There can be little doubt that in Paul's thought the people of Israel related to God in a way that was different from the way in which believers in Christ had now come to relate to him. The principal difference, of course, is precisely that those who lived only under the covenant with Israel did not consciously relate to God through Christ as their Lord, in contrast to the latter. The conditions of the covenant made or confirmed at Sinai were that God would be Israel's God and Israel would live as God's people, obeying the commandments of the law God was giving them through Moses. These are not, however, the conditions under which all believers in Christ live. Instead, they live under Christ as their Lord as members of a community that is defined, not by the Mosaic law, but by the "law of Christ" and his love (1 Cor 9:21; Gal 6:2). This community is therefore distinct from Israel, though it is by no means *separate* from Israel. At the same time, the community of believers in Christ lives under a covenant that is *distinct* from the covenant God had made with Moses, although it complements and builds on that covenant rather than replacing it.

It is possible, of course, that when Paul speaks of a new covenant he has in mind a renewal of the covenant God had made with Israel previously rather than a covenant that is totally new. Even if that is the case, however, in some sense this renewed covenant would be distinct from the covenant he had made with Israel. Paul would have maintained that there is one group that lives under that renewed covenant—namely, believers in Christ—and another that does *not* live under the renewed covenant or else lives under the same covenant as it exists in a non-renewed form. Precisely what the difference would be between speaking of two different covenants and two different forms of a single covenant—one renewed and the other "unrenewed"—is by no means clear. The same observation could be made regarding the law of Christ. Even if that law is understood as a renewed version of the law of Moses or as a reinterpretation of the Mosaic law on the basis of principles associated with Christ, ultimately there is little difference between speaking of two different laws and two versions of the same law so as to claim that some live only under one or the other.[68] Just as gentile believers live under the law of Christ but not under the law of Moses (Rom 7:6; Gal 5:18), so also do they live under the new covenant of which Jesus spoke at the Last Supper rather than under the covenant God had made with Israel through Moses. Jewish believers in Christ, however, could be said to live under both, and there is no reason to suppose that in their minds to live under one covenant was incompatible with living under the other. On the contrary, they must have found life and fullness in living under both at the same time, considering each of them to be wonderful in its own way.

The tradition Paul cites with regard to the new covenant in Jesus' blood in 1 Cor 11:23-26 also suggests that Paul understood that covenant as something that did not exist prior to the Last Supper. There can be little doubt that Jews who did not believe in Christ did not partake of the Lord's Supper when it was celebrated by Jewish and gentile believers in Christ. They did not share in the cup of blessing and the bread which Paul calls the body and blood of Christ in 1 Cor 10:16-17. Nor did they undergo baptism in the name of Christ so as to be incorporated into the *ekklēsia* alongside

---

68. On the possibility that Paul is referring to the law of Moses when he speaks of the law of Christ in Gal 6:2, see Todd A. Wilson, *The Curse of the Law and the Crisis in Galatia: Reassessing the Purpose of Galatians*, WUNT 2/225 (Tübingen: Mohr Siebeck, 2007), 100-104. John M. G. Barclay suggests that in Gal 6:2 Paul has in mind the idea of obeying the law as it has been redefined through Christ and fulfilling the law in love in the way exemplified through Christ (*Obeying the Truth: A Study of Paul's Ethics in Galatians*, SNTW [Edinburgh: T & T Clark, 1988], 125-45).

Jewish and gentile believers. Thus, believers in Christ constituted a separate group that ate and drank with one another separately from those Jews who did not identify as believers in Christ, at least when they ate and drank of the same cup and bread in memory of Jesus. Jewish and gentile believers in Christ clearly understood themselves to be living under a covenant of their own that was distinct from the covenant given through Moses under which all faithful Jews lived.

More importantly, however, in Paul's thought Christ had not only established a new covenant in his blood at the Last Supper but had also defined the content and nature of that covenant through his life and death as a whole. All who partook of the Lord's Supper identified not only with Christ as Lord but also with the love that he had shown in giving up his life so that the type of community of which they now formed part might be brought into existence and assume the characteristics that it had. It was the love of which Paul spoke in passages such as Rom 8:31-39, 1 Corinthians 13, and Phil 2:1-8 that defined what it meant to live under the new covenant established through Christ.

In Rom 7:4-6 and Gal 2:19-21, Paul also alludes to Jesus' death in order to speak of a change in the way in which believers in Christ relate to the law. He tells the Roman believers that they were "made to die to the law through the body of Christ" so that they might "belong to another, to him who was raised from the dead." He then adds that they have been "released from the law" by having died to that to which they had been bound so that they may live "in the newness of the Spirit rather than the oldness of the letter." If believers have died to the law and been released from it together with Christ as members of his body, obviously they are a community that is distinct from the community of those who *do* live under the law as understood independently of Christ and do *not* form part of Christ's body. According to Paul, the latter do *not* belong to Christ or live in the newness of God's Spirit but in the "oldness of the letter," in contrast to believers in Christ. Similarly, in Gal 2:19-20, Paul writes: "For I through the law have died to the law, so that I might live to God. I am crucified together with Christ, and it is no longer I who live but Christ who lives in me." Here Paul's identification with the crucified Jesus is said to lead to a new condition in which he is dead to the law so as to live to God together with Christ. To live under a new covenant established through Christ was therefore thought to involve living in his same love in a way that went beyond simply living under the law associated with the covenant God had made through Moses. It was precisely Christ's efforts to bring others to live in that love that had led him to give up his life. To die to the law, however, should probably be understood in terms of dying to one's previous relationship to the law in order to live in a new relationship that would not necessarily involve abandoning observance of the law, at least in the case of Jewish believers in

Christ. Instead, that observance would be redefined in light of their faith in Christ as Lord.

Israel and the Ekklēsia

Although Paul refers to believers in Christ as children of Abraham and the circumcision and speaks of the Corinthian believers as former gentiles,[69] nowhere does he explicitly refer to gentile believers as Jews or as members of Israel.[70] Neither does he affirm that they come to practice Judaism. As Mark Nanos has argued, however, there is probably some sense in which Paul believed that gentile believers in Christ came to *live* and *behave* as Jews and therefore could be said to be living "Jewishly."[71] Because of the relation of their faith to Judaism as well as the ties between the community of believers in Christ and the Jewish community, many non-Jews would have seen gentile believers as persons who had adopted Judaism as a way of life and had even become Jewish in some sense. However, Paul apparently continued to associate the terms "Jew," "Jewish," and "Judaism" with those who observed the Torah faithfully and identified themselves as Jews, as well as being accepted as such by their fellow Jews.

With one possible exception, whenever Paul uses the terms "Israel" and "Israelite," he seems clearly to be referring to his "kinspeople according to the flesh" (Rom 9:3-4). In a number of passages, he contrasts Israel with gentile believers.[72] He also repeatedly contrasts Jews with Greeks and gentiles.[73] In Rom 9:25-26, Paul cites Hos 1:10 and 2:23 to affirm that God now calls "my people" those who were previously *not* his people and calls "beloved" those who were previously *not* his beloved. This passage does not affirm that those who have become God's people are now part of Israel, however. Rather, Paul seems to regard the nations or gentiles who through Christ become God's people as existing *alongside* Israel. Thus, for example, in Rom 15:10 he cites Deut 32:43 to describe what has taken place in the community of believers in Christ: "Rejoice, nations, with his people!" Here the nations or gentiles are not referred to as God's people but are seen as joining themselves to Israel so as to worship God together with Israel.

While Paul repeatedly uses the word *ekklēsia* in both the singular and the plural to refer to the communities of believers in Christ, he never speaks of the *ekklēsia* superseding or replacing Israel as God's people. Because the *ekklēsia* includes Jews and not only gentiles, it does not stand in contrast to

---

69. See Rom 4:11-25; 9:7-8; 1 Cor 12:2; Gal 3:7-9, 29; 4:21-31.

70. On this point, see Campbell, *Paul*, 48-49.

71. See Nanos, "Question of Conceptualization," 136-39; *Reading Paul within Judaism*, 128-32.

72. See Rom 9:30-31; 10:19-21; 11:11, 25.

73. See Rom 1:16; 2:9; 3:9, 29; 9:24; 10:12; 1 Cor 1:22-24; 10:32; 12:13; Gal 2:14-15; 3:28.

Israel, since many Jews or members of Israel are included within it. Some of the affirmations Paul makes with regard to Israel, however, suggest that at times he uses Israel to refer to Jewish believers in Christ, as if in some sense they constitute the true Israel. This distinction is especially evident in Rom 9:6-7, where Paul writes: "not all who are of Israel are Israel, because not all the children are the seed of Abraham, but 'through Isaac shall your seed be named.'" Here Paul explicitly affirms that some who belong to Israel at the same time do *not* belong to Israel. From the context, it seems clear that those who belong to Israel in the more restricted sense of the term are Jewish believers in Christ, yet Paul does not affirm here or elsewhere that those Jews who do not come to faith in Christ no longer form part of Israel. He almost certainly maintained, for example, that those Jews who live righteously and do not stand in opposition to the gospel continue to belong to Israel in at least one of the senses in which he speaks of Israel in this passage, even though they do not believe in Christ.

The idea that "not all who are of Israel are Israel" is reflected elsewhere in Romans 9–11 as well. In Rom 9:27, Paul cites Isa 10:22 to speak of only a remnant of Israel being saved. A few verses later, he affirms that gentiles have attained a righteousness that Israel did not attain (9:30-32). In Rom 10:1, echoing his words in 9:1-3 and 11:14, Paul expresses his deep desire that his kinspeople be saved, which suggests that many of them are *not* included among those being saved. Paul begins Romans 11 by affirming that God has not rejected his people, yet he then refers once again to a remnant chosen by grace, while claiming that those who have not been chosen are hardened and have stumbled (11:1-12). He then employs the imagery of the ingrafting and removal of branches in relation to an an olive tree to claim that some branches have been broken off due to their unbelief, while others have been grafted in through faith (11:17-24). He then concludes that "all Israel will be saved" after the fullness of the gentiles or nations has come in (11:25-26). Here the branches grafted into the olive tree are clearly gentile believers in Christ. Interpreters have debated extensively whether the root or trunk of the olive tree in this comparison refers to Israel, to the patriarchs, or to God's people in a general sense.[74] When Paul speaks of the branches that have been removed, he may not have in mind all Jews who do not believe in Christ but only those whose unbelief brings them to stand in opposition to that faith, especially since he holds out hope that many of those Jews who have not yet believed in Christ may still do so, including of course those who have not yet heard the gospel. In any case, his idea that some of the natural branches have been cut off seems to indicate that he regards at least some of the Jews who do not believe in the gospel

---

74. For a survey of views on this question, see Svetlana Khobnya, "'The Root' in Paul's Olive Tree Metaphor (Romans 11:16-24)," *TynBul* 64 (2013): 257-73 (257-62).

as no longer forming part of God's people or perhaps even part of Israel. At the same time, however, the fact that Paul speaks of some of the natural branches being grafted back into their own olive tree so that all Israel may be saved indicates that he expected that at least some Jews who had ceased to form part of God's people in the present would come to be reincorporated within that people again. His idea seems to have been that ultimately they too will come to believe in the gospel. Paul's allusion to the coming of the deliverer from Zion in 11:26 seems to suggest that he thought that this would happen at the end, when Christ comes.[75]

Paul nowhere states or implies that the *ekklēsia* displaces or replaces Israel as God's people, therefore. While in some sense he seems to regard Israel in the present as being made up of those Jews who come to faith in Christ and perhaps other Jews as well, in another sense he considers those who do not come to faith in the present as still forming part of Israel. It might be said that for Paul there is a "true Israel" that at present is distinct from Israel as a whole. As we have noted previously, this idea would be similar to that which we find in the Dead Sea Scrolls, where the members of the community at Qumran are regarded as constituting the true Israel, though they may also have thought that other Jews formed part of the true Israel with them. Unlike the Qumranites, however, Paul never asserts that those who do not form part of the true Israel at present will be destroyed in the end. On the contrary, he expects "all Israel" to be saved as a result of the reincorporation of the "natural branches" that at present have been cut off, as long as they do not "persist in their unbelief" (Rom 11:23). The remnant of which Paul speaks does not supersede or replace Israel since it never existed apart from Israel. Eventually, however, Israel will be reconstituted in some sense so as to form part of a single people of God together with those gentiles to be saved.

This reconstruction of Paul's thought would also explain what he means in Gal 6:16, where he writes: "and to all those who walk by this rule, peace and mercy be upon them and upon the Israel of God." Many interpreters regard the phrase "Israel of God" as an allusion to the *ekklēsia*, as if all believers in Christ now belong to the Israel of which Paul speaks.[76] The problem with such an interpretation is that Paul seems to be referring to two different entities in this verse when he speaks of those who walk according to the rule and the Israel of God. However, if Paul believes that "not all who are of Israel are Israel" (Rom 9:6), then it is likely that in Gal 6:16 he is making

---

75. On the different proposals regarding the interpretation of "all Israel" in Rom 11:26, see Robert Jewett, *Romans: A Commentary*, Hermeneia (Minneapolis: Fortress, 2007), 701-2; Pablo T. Gadenz, *Called from the Jews and from the Gentiles: Pauline Ecclesiology in Romans 9–11*, WUNT 2/267 (Tübingen: Mohr Siebeck, 2009), 275-80.

76. For a survey of interpretations of Paul's allusions to the "Israel of God" in Gal 6:16, see de Boer, *Galatians*, 405-8.

a distinction between the "Israel of God" or the true Israel and the larger Israel that is composed of all Jews. The Israel of God would be the remnant of which he speaks in Rom 9:6-8, 27-29, and 11:1-10. Given the nature of the conflict in Galatia, however, it is also possible that the distinction Paul is making is between the Jewish believers in Christ who accept gentile believers on equal terms without requiring that they be circumcised and those who do not. In that case, among those who do *not* form part of the Israel of God would be those who were pressuring the Galatian believers to become circumcised and submit fully to the Torah. Paul would then be greeting as the "Israel of God" those Jewish believers in Christ who stand alongside of him in opposing those who are promoting the circumcision of gentile believers.[77] This idea would be somewhat different from that which we find in Romans 9–11 in that here those whom Paul would have in mind as the Israel that is *not* of God would be Jewish believers in Christ who insist on gentile believers being circumcised and submitting fully to the Torah rather than Jews who did not believe in Christ. Nevertheless, it must be recognized that Paul's thought in all of these passages remains somewhat enigmatic and is difficult to grasp fully.

Conflicts between the Ekklēsia *and the Jewish Community*

Most of the conflicts that Paul mentions in his letters appear to have taken place among different groups within the communities of believers in Christ. There are several passages from those letters, however, that suggest conflicts between the community of believers and the Jewish community at large. At the end of his letter to the Romans, Paul asks the believers in Rome to pray for him so that when he goes to Jerusalem he may be "delivered from those who are disobedient in Judea" (Rom 15:31). While it is possible that he has in mind believers in Christ, most interpreters understand him to be referring to Jews who are not believers.[78] In 2 Cor 11:24-25, Paul mentions having received thirty-nine lashes at the hands of the Jews five times and having received a stoning once. Stoning, of course, was primarily a Jewish practice. Paul does not indicate the reason why he was disciplined with lashings, probably in the context of Jewish synagogues. Paul mentions the *ekklēsiai* in Judea enduring suffering at the hands of "the Jews" in 1 Thess 2:14-16 and appears to relate this to the outreach to gentiles. There are many questions surrounding this passage, including its authenticity, yet it clearly points to some kind of conflict between followers of Jesus and certain members of

---

77. As Das comments, in Gal 6:16 "Paul may be opposing the false 'Israel' in the Galatians' midst who were promoting gentile circumcision" (*Solving the Romans Debate*, 242).

78. See Hultgren, *Romans*, 562.

the Jewish community in Judea.[79] In 1 Cor 15:9, Gal 1:13, 23, and Phil 3:6, Paul states that prior to coming to faith in Christ he persecuted the *ekklēsia* out of a desire to destroy it, though he offers no reason for this persecution other than his zeal.[80]

While all of these passages point to some type of conflict between Jesus' earliest followers and the Jewish community at large, it is important not to assume that the causes of the conflicts of which Paul speaks were all the same. If Paul came to faith in Christ only a few years after Jesus' crucifixion, for example, it is unlikely that he initially persecuted the *ekklēsia* due to its outreach to gentiles, since the number of non-Jews within the community of believers would still have been quite small. The inclusion of a small handful of gentiles within the Jewish community would probably not have generated enough tension or conflict to spark any type of active persecution on his part or that of other Jews, although some opposition might have arisen if it were being claimed that it was necessary to accept those gentiles as equals.[81] Similarly, we should not presuppose that the lashings Paul received on five different occasions and the stoning he endured were in every instance inflicted on him for the same reasons. In fact, those reasons may have been somewhat complex rather than having to do with one issue in particular.

While it is difficult to ascertain precisely what those motives may have been, on the basis of what we have seen previously in this chapter and this study as a whole, several of the traditional explanations for the conflict between the early communities of Jesus' followers and the Jewish community at large should be ruled out. Since at least the time of the Protestant Reformation, it has been common to argue that what upset those Jews who did not believe in Christ, including Paul prior to his Damascus experience, was the disregard for observance of the law that supposedly existed among the earliest Jewish believers in Christ.[82] As we have seen repeatedly, how-

---

79. On the problems relating to the interpretation of 1 Thess 2:14-16 and the reasons why many reject its authenticity, see Earl J. Richards, *First and Second Thessalonians*, SP (Collegeville, MN: Liturgical Press, 1995), 119-27.

80. Some scholars have questioned as excessively harsh the translation of the Greek verb *diōkein* as "persecute" in 1 Cor 15:9, Gal 1:13, 23, and Phil 3:6 to characterize Paul's treatment of the *ekklēsia* prior to his Damascus experience; see especially Nanos, *Reading Paul within Judaism*, 31-32.

81. For a survey of views on the reasons why Saul or Paul persecuted the *ekklēsia*, see Claudia Setzer, *Jewish Responses to Early Christians: History and Polemics, 30-150 C.E.* (Minneapolis: Fortress, 1994), 10-16; Calvin Roetzel, *Paul: The Man and the Myth* (Minneapolis: Fortress, 1999), 38-42. Most scholars would agree with Roetzel: "Because the issue is so complex and the information is so scanty it is impossible to offer a fully satisfying explanation" (39).

82. So, for example, Peter Stuhlmacher, *Reconciliation, Law, and Righteousness: Essays in Biblical Theology* (Philadelphia: Fortress, 1986), 69.

ever, there is no reason to suppose that Jewish believers in Christ ceased to observe the law. While gentile believers would not have been expected to observe the law, in principle this would not have generated conflict, since virtually all Jews agreed that God had given the Torah to Israel alone.

As mentioned above, according to the sources from antiquity at our disposal, for most Jews fellowship and close interaction with gentiles would not have been problematic, as long as these things did not require that Jews compromise or set aside their own observance of the Torah. It is doubtful, therefore, that Jews such as Paul prior to his Damascus experience would have persecuted Jewish believers in Christ simply because they accepted gentile believers within their midst unless that acceptance affected the Jewish community negatively in some way or threatened its integrity.

There also appears to be no clear evidence that the first believers in Christ attempted to erase any distinctions between Jews and gentiles within their community. At times, Paul's affirmation in Gal 3:28 that there is no longer Jew nor gentile because believers are all "one in Christ Jesus" has been interpreted to mean that he considered all such distinctions to be abolished in Christ. Throughout his letters, however, Paul continues to distinguish not only between Jews and gentiles or Greeks but also between the other groups he mentions in Gal 3:28, namely, slaves and free persons as well as males and females. Paul's words in that passage, therefore, should be understood not in the sense that such distinctions are no longer to exist, but rather in the sense that those distinctions are not to be a cause for any type of division or to present an obstacle to full fellowship and equal acceptance among persons of those different groups.[83] Paul himself recognizes elsewhere in his epistles that the distinctions between slave and free as well as men and women still exist within the community of believers, and thus he would have thought the same regarding the distinction between Jews and gentiles.

Nevertheless, at some point the idea that "in Christ Jesus" uncircumcised gentiles could enjoy the same righteous status before God as law-observant Jews would probably have been controversial among many Jews. Even more controversial would have been the claim that those gentile believers in Christ were more acceptable to God than those Jews who did *not* come to faith in Christ, if in fact the first believers in Christ ever made

---

83. As Nanos has argued, to affirm that Jewish and non-Jewish believers in Christ shared equal status within the *ekklēsia* was by no means to claim that all distinctions between the two groups were now abolished. Commenting on Gal 3:28, Nanos writes: "Whereas here we see again the theme of oneness, Paul *cannot* mean that these different identities no longer exist among Christ-followers. There are very real biological, cultural, and socio-economic differences that are not dissolved. Slaves are not by definition freed in these groups, and Jews do not become gentiles any more than gentiles become Jews" (*Reading Paul within Judaism*, 118).

such a claim. In that case, those believers would have been maintaining that the life that resulted from faith in Christ independently of the observance of the Torah was more pleasing to God than a life lived in conformity with the Torah alone, thereby relegating the Torah to a position of secondary importance.

While many Jews would have had no problems accepting as righteous uncircumcised gentiles who lived in accordance with the basic principles of the Torah, the idea that such gentiles were to be accepted on equal terms within the community of believers in Christ would have been more problematic. Although Jewish believers in Christ were not necessarily insisting that all Jews within the Jewish community join them in accepting gentile believers as equals, at the very least their own acceptance of those gentiles as their equals within the *ekklēsia* would have raised some eyebrows. As noted above, if Jewish believers in Christ entered into full fellowship with uncircumcised gentile believers, the existence of such a fellowship would have made it necessary for those Jews who were not believers in Christ to make a decision as to whether they would join Jewish believers in accepting those gentile believers on equal terms. If they did, it would appear that they were erasing or disregarding the traditional distinctions between Jews and non-Jews and thus calling into question the value and validity of their law and customs on the basis of which such distinctions had been established. If those Jews who did not believe in Christ did not accept gentile believers in Christ on equal terms within their community, they would not only have rejected full fellowship with those gentiles themselves but at times would also have had to reject full fellowship with Jewish believers in Christ, since fellowship with the Jewish believers would require fellowship with the gentiles to whom those believers had joined themselves as well. In addition, under certain circumstances Jewish believers in Christ would be forced to decide whether to relate more closely to their fellow Jews or instead to their fellow believers in Christ who were not Jews. Needless to say, tensions, conflicts, and divisions would arise almost inevitably.

As we have also noted above, these problems would become exacerbated if large numbers of gentile believers in Christ came to participate in gatherings of Jews in Jewish synagogues or places of prayer. Those gentile believers might be seen as taking over a Jewish space that did not belong to them, especially if they eventually became a majority there. Furthermore, because the community of believers in Christ was defined and viewed as a community that was distinct from the Jewish community at large, sooner or later the communities of Jesus' followers would want to procure meeting places that they could call their own rather than continuing to depend on the hospitality of those who did not form part of their community. Once those communities began gathering separately for their own meetings in order to give expression to their faith in Christ, it would not be long before some type of "parting of the ways" took place, at least to some extent. Even if they continued to meet in Jewish gathering places and participate in the activities there, they must have come to meet separately at different times for their own activities as well, including especially baptisms and the celebration of the Lord's Supper. Undoubtedly, some Jews and perhaps even non-Jews might continue to participate in both communities, yet each community would schedule, organize, and lead its own activities.[84] If at some point those who did participate in both communities were pressured to define their primary identity in terms of belonging to one group or the other, whatever parting of the ways came about would be even more pronounced. Those Jews who opted to identify first and foremost with the community of believers in Christ would almost certainly face some type of criticism among their fellow Jews who were not believers in Christ. At some point, they might even be regarded as having abandoned or rejected the Jewish community. Those who instead identified more strongly with the Jewish community would be seen as lacking the type of commitment necessary to be full members of the *ekklēsia*.

While the formation and consolidation of the communities of believers in Christ as a distinct entity would almost certainly have generated at least some tension and conflict in relation to the Jewish community at large, it would be a mistake to suppose that any parting of the ways between the two communities would necessarily be acrimonious, antagonistic, or violent. In principle, there was no reason why the two communities could not coexist peacefully and amicably, even when they began to gather in different spaces or at different times. Those who wished to form part of both communities might continue to be welcomed by members of each, though of course there would be times when they would need to opt for one or the other, especially if both communities were planning a gathering on the same day at the same time. At times the members of one community might invite members of the other to gather together for some shared activity. A person who belonged to both groups might also invite members of both communities to gather simultaneously at that person's home or property for the same

---

84. The simple fact that the leaders of the communities of believers in Christ founded by Paul and others were not appointed by the Jewish community at large and did not ultimately regard themselves as accountable or subject to the leaders and authorities of the Jewish community would justify the conclusion of Wayne A. Meeks that Paul and his associates "had created an organized movement that was entirely independent of the Jewish communities in the cities of the northeastern Mediterranean basin" ("Breaking Away: Three New Testament Interpretations of Christianity's Separation from the Jewish Communities," in *"To See Ourselves as Others See Us": Christians, Jews, "Others" in Late Antiquity*, ed. Jacob Neusner and Ernest S. Frerichs, SPSH 9 [Chico, CA: Scholars Press, 1985], 93-115 [107-8]). Every indication is that the *ekklēsiai* were self-funded, self-governing, and autonomous in other ways as well.

purpose. In principle, there would be no reason why each community might not go its own way to some degree without divorcing itself entirely from the other so as no longer to enjoy friendly and cooperative relations with it.

At some point, however, the conflicting truth claims made by each of the two communities would have led to tensions between them. As we have seen in Chapter 1 of this study, Jews who did not believe in Christ would have regarded the God being proclaimed by those who did as distinct from the God whom they had always worshiped. By its very nature, the proclamation that God had raised his Son Jesus Christ from the dead and seated him at his right side in heaven over all things and all people would have been divisive at least to some extent, since such a claim was of central and primary importance to the belief system of Jesus' followers rather than being secondary or incidental. The claim that as God's Son Jesus stood above the Torah would also be extremely controversial. Of course, all of these beliefs had important ramifications for daily life as well, especially because those who believed in Jesus were expected to regard nothing in life as more important than their relation to him as their Lord (Phil 3:7-9). Thus the claims made by Jesus' earliest followers did not lend themselves to being met with apathy, indifference, or impartiality. Instead, those claims easily incited passions and sooner or later required those who heard them to take a stand either with or against Jesus and his community of followers.

As scholars such as Paula Fredriksen have argued, the proclamation of a man who had been crucified by Rome as a Messiah, king, Lord, or savior figure would also have been regarded as problematic and dangerous. Because those crucified by Rome were considered Rome's enemies, such a proclamation would naturally be regarded as subversive among those non-Jews loyal to Rome. However, even those Jews who identified more with Jerusalem than with Rome might have found that proclamation troublesome for the reasons mentioned by Fredriksen:

> [T]he enthusiastic proclamation of a Messiah executed very recently by Rome as a political troublemaker—a *crucified Messiah*—combined with a vision of the approaching End *preached also to Gentiles*—this was dangerous. News of an impending Messianic kingdom, originating from Palestine, might trickle out via the ekklesia's Gentiles to the larger urban population. It was this (by far) larger, unaffiliated group that posed a real and serious threat. Armed with such a report, they might readily seek to alienate the local Roman colonial government, upon which Jewish urban populations often depended for support and protection against hostile Gentile neighbors. The open dissemination of a Messianic message, in other words, put the entire Jewish community at risk.[85]

If the Jewish community feared reprisals of a formal or informal nature for accepting within its ranks a group that proclaimed such a subversive

---

85. Fredriksen, "Judaism," 556.

message, it would have been natural for it to wish to manifest publicly its rejection of such a message by distancing itself from that group and either asking it to withdraw from its midst or obliging it to do so. Once again, however, this process would not necessarily have to be acrimonious or violent. The Jewish community might simply and calmly ask the community of believers in Christ to meet elsewhere and not to identify itself as part of the Jewish community. In that case, the community of believers in Christ might comply willingly with that request out of respect and consideration for those who up to that point had shown them the kindness of allowing them to gather in their space.

For all these reasons, it is by no means impossible that followers of Jesus such as Paul continued to relate amicably to Jews who did not accept their proclamation regarding Jesus. Rather than condemning those Jews, they might simply hold out the expectation that at some point in time they would discover the truth of his message, as Paul did. In fact, Paul seems to reflect precisely that type of attitude in Romans 9–11, where he claims that at present the hearts of those who have not accepted the gospel have been hardened yet holds out hope that some day they will come to be saved through Christ. Just as many people today maintain with great conviction truth claims that are strongly at odds with the beliefs of others while nevertheless enjoying harmonious and peaceful relations with them, often even within the same immediate family or circle of friends, so also was it possible for people in Paul's day to do the same. Likewise, the same Jews who were diligent in the practice of their own faith yet at the same time made generous contributions to the temples of their gentile neighbors could have related to believers in Christ in the same way, independently of whether those believers were Jewish or not.

CHAPTER 7

Redefining Righteousness

Among Jews in antiquity, righteousness was defined primarily on the basis of the Torah. The righteous were those who were committed to living in obedience to the commandments that God had given to Israel. While uncircumcised gentiles might attain some degree of righteousness by observing the basic moral principles found in the Torah, that righteousness was not believed to be comparable to that of those faithful Jews who strove to live fully in accordance with the Torah.

When we look to Paul's epistles, however, we encounter a reality that is very different. According to those epistles, uncircumcised gentiles who come to faith in Christ and live in that faith are just as righteous in God's sight as the circumcised and law-observant Jews who share that same faith. While Paul seems to have expected Jewish believers in Christ to continue to observe the law and encouraged them to do so, he insists that such observance does not make them any more righteous than gentile believers who do not submit to that law.

Naturally, such a view lent itself to generating tension between those Jews who believed in Christ and those who did not. While Paul might insist that he did not abolish the law, as he does in Rom 3:31, his claim that through Christ people could attain the righteousness God demanded of all out of love for them independently of their observance of the Torah seemed to call into question the value of such observance. For this reason, Paul repeatedly found it necessary to clarify his views regarding the Mosaic law and the righteousness and justification of believers in Christ.

RIGHTEOUSNESS AND THE TORAH IN
SECOND TEMPLE JUDAISM

In ancient Jewish thought, it was widely recognized that the life of righteousness God desired to see in all was from beginning to end a gift of God. God had made that righteousness possible by graciously giving Israel the guidance and instruction of the Torah, and when the people failed to live in accordance with his commandments, God graciously acted in various ways to attempt to bring them back into conformity with those commandments. Of course, it must be stressed once more that God desired and commanded that his people obey the commandments he had given them *for their own sake* rather than for his. Because of the intrinsic relation between obedience to the commandments of the Torah and the people's well-being, they could enjoy the blessings God desired for them only if they strove to obey those commandments. God thus commanded and demanded that the people practice justice and righteousness—which in both Hebrew and Greek were understood as being the same thing (*tsedaqah; dikaiosynē*)—out of love for them.

As E. P. Sanders argued in his 1977 work *Paul and Palestinian Judaism*, it was generally recognized that no one could fulfill the Mosaic law perfectly.[1] The law itself made provisions for this by prescribing means by which those who violated it might seek God's forgiveness and thereby remain within the community of the righteous.[2] At the same time, most Jews believed that it was possible for people to grow and increase in their obedience to the Torah and for greater numbers of Jews to do so. Many of those who expected God to redeem Israel from its present plight appear to have believed that both of these things had to happen before that redemption might come. However, God's people were to look to God in faith not only for that redemption itself but also for the obedience that was necessary for it to take place. All that God could expect of his people was that they trust in him by committing themselves to living as best they could in accordance with the commandments he had given them out of love for them. Even if they went astray, he would do everything in his power to bring them back in obedience to those commandments. As long as they continued to keep their eyes fixed on God and depend fully on him, therefore, God would be active to bring about in them the obedience and righteousness he desired to see in them for their own good.

For that reason, most Jews would have agreed wholeheartedly with Paul's claim that righteousness and justification were *by faith*.[3] By definition, no

---

1. See E. P. Sanders, *Paul and Palestinian Judaism: A Comparison of Patterns of Religion* (Philadelphia: Fortress, 1977), 137-38, 204-5, 346, 420-22. Of course, perfection can be defined in different ways, so that there is a sense in which those who are fully committed to living in accordance with God's law can be said to obey it perfectly, even though they still fall into sin; see Kent L. Yinger, *God and Human Wholeness: Perfection in Biblical and Theological Tradition* (Eugene, OR: Cascade, 2019), 11-22, 65-69, 104-21.

2. See Sanders, *Paul and Palestinian Judaism*, 422.

3. See, for example, the discussion in Nijay K. Gupta, *Paul and the Language of Faith* (Grand Rapids: Eerdmans, 2020), 5-7, 161-62.

one could live righteously in accordance with God's will without believing in God and believing that he had given the commandments of the Torah for the good of all. To believe and trust in God was inseparable from living in the way he had commanded in the Torah, since those who refused to live in accordance with those commandments were not truly believing and trusting in the God who had given them. Righteousness was therefore inseparable from faith and was regarded as the result or fruit of faith.

At the same time, righteousness and justification were said to depend on one's works or behavior. However, as Sanders also argued in *Paul and Palestinian Judaism*, contrary to many Christian caricatures of Judaism, the notion that one might *earn* one's salvation through one's works was foreign to ancient Jewish thought.[4] All who lived as God's people depended on his grace not only for forgiveness but also for the ability to do what he had commanded. The reason why God examined one's works when judging human beings was that they revealed what was in one's heart. If one was committed to doing God's will, that commitment would inevitably be manifested in actions that were in conformity with that will. Conversely, the absence of such a commitment would be reflected in a lack of the works or deeds that God desired to see. As Kent Yinger has shown, in Second Temple Jewish thought, "when it is said that individuals will be recompensed or judged 'according to their deeds,' this presumes a holistic or unitary view of human works. It is not a deed for deed inspection, but rather one's entire pattern of life is in view, one's 'way'. . . . It is the standard Jewish expectation that one's outward behavior (one's *works* or *way*) will correspond to, and be a visible manifestation of, inward reality."[5] Obedience to God's commandments was therefore not understood "as sinless perfection, but as a consistent and wholehearted conformity to God's will."[6]

When God declared a person to be righteous, therefore, that declaration was based on that person's way of thinking and living. Because no one could obey God's commandments perfectly, an element of forgiveness was always involved when God judged someone to be righteous. Those justified or declared righteous by God were never thought to be sinless or guiltless, nor was God believed to be pronouncing them innocent or acquitting them of wrongdoing when he justified them. Rather, by virtue of their commitment to living in conformity with God's will, God simply overlooked their sin, since that commitment would be manifested in the type of life God desired to see in all out of love for them. In other words, even though they were not perfect and were constantly in need of forgiveness, God declared them righteous because they were committed to living righteously and

---

4. See Sanders, *Paul and Palestinian Judaism*, 126, 181-82, 293, 371, 517-18.

5. Kent L. Yinger, *Paul, Judaism, and Judgment according to Deeds*, SNTSMS 105 (Cambridge: Cambridge University Press, 1999), 284, 290.

6. Yinger, *Paul*, 181.

because that commitment manifested itself in the type of life he desired to see in them for their own good and that of others.

God's purpose in judging people was therefore to determine whether or not they were committed to living in a manner that would make it possible for them and others to enjoy the well-being and shalom that God intended for all. Such an understanding of God's judgment precluded the idea that one might earn God's grace and favor through one's works, since what mattered was not simply attaining God's approval but living the type of life that enabled one to experience the well-being that was an intrinsic consequence of obedience to God's will. In fact, God's approval could be attained only by living such a life, looking to God and his gift of the Torah for knowledge, strength, and guidance. God judged human beings for *their* sake rather than for the sake of his own holiness or justice, since his judgment was aimed at overcoming sin and evil and liberating the faithful from those whose way of life impeded and destroyed their well-being.

The belief in a final judgment responded to the same concerns. If God was to judge all people at the end of the present age, this was because only in that way could the world to come be free of the sin and injustice that made it impossible for people to live in peace and enjoy God's blessings, unmolested by those who refused to practice justice and righteousness. Therefore, it was necessary for God to determine which people were committed to living in conformity with his will, since the very nature of the life of the age to come required such a commitment on the part of all who would come to partake of that life.

As we have seen previously, this understanding of God and his will was fundamentally different from the understanding of the gods and their will that Jews associated with gentile beliefs. Those gods were thought to make demands of human beings for their own sake and not out of any concern for human beings themselves. This made it necessary for human beings constantly to be inquiring as to what those gods wanted in order to satisfy their needs, desires, and demands, which were often capricious and egotistical. What mattered was simply gaining their favor and averting their wrath. In the case of Israel's God, however, there was one thing alone that could obtain his favor and avert his wrath: the practice of justice and righteousness.

Curiously, many Christian interpretations of God present him as behaving in essentially the same way that the gods of the nations were believed to do. According to those interpretations, God desires and demands the practice of justice and righteousness, *not for the sake of human beings but for his own sake.* Ultimately, what matters to him is not that people in general actually obey him, live righteously, and practice justice, but that he receive from someone—be it human beings themselves or Christ as their substitute—the perfect obedience, righteousness, and justice that his holy nature demands.[7] Thus, while the content of God's demand is said to be different from that of other gods in that what he demands is justice and righteousness, he is just like those gods in that his concern is ultimately for himself and his own nature rather than the well-being of human beings. If he gets from human beings the righteousness he wants and demands, he is satisfied, no matter who gives it to him. If he does not, he becomes irate and inflicts punishment. As long as human beings have Christ to give God what he requires and satisfy his demands in their place, they can live in peace, unbothered by him.

PAUL AND THE RIGHTEOUSNESS OF FAITH

Rather than constituting a departure from Jewish thought, Paul's understanding of justification, righteousness, and faith is in full continuity with the Jewish beliefs just considered.[8] What distinguishes Paul's teaching on justification from that which we find in Second Temple Jewish literature in general is his understanding of the will of God. Because it is Christ rather than the Mosaic law alone that defines God's will, the faith that leads to the righteousness that God desires to see in all is not merely faith in the God of Israel, but faith in Christ as his Son as well.

Traditional Interpretations of Paul's Doctrine of Justification

Since the period of the Protestant Reformation, it has been customary to claim that in Paul's thought there are two grounds for the justification of believers: Christ's death and their faith.[9] Supposedly, Christ's death was

---

7. John M. G. Barclay notes with regard to John Calvin's interpretation of Paul, for example: "It is characteristic of Calvin that he will not allow God's mercy and grace to suggest any diminution in God's just demand for perfect righteousness" (*Paul and the Gift* [Grand Rapids: Eerdmans, 2015], 129). Similarly, N. T. Wright ascribes to Paul the idea that "the task of the Messiah, bringing to its appointed goal the single-plan-through-Israel-for-the-world, was to offer to God the 'obedience' which Israel should have offered but did not" (*Justification: God's Plan and Paul's Vision* [Downers Grove, IL: InterVarsity, 2009], 104).

8. On what follows, see David A. Brondos, *Jesus' Death in New Testament Thought*, vol. 2: *Texts* (Mexico City: Theological Community of Mexico, 2018), 665-68, 724-33.

9. Simon J. Gathercole, for example, claims that for Paul justification is "*on the basis of faith*" and "on the basis of trust in Christ," while at the same time claiming: "The atoning death of Christ is, for Paul, the ground of the justification of the ungodly" ("Justified by Faith, Justified by his Blood: The Evidence of Romans 3:21–4:25," in *Justification and Variegated Nomism*, vol. 2: *The Paradoxes of Paul*, ed. Donald A. Carson, Peter T. O'Brien, and Mark A. Seifrid, WUNT 2/181 [Tübingen: Mohr Siebeck, 2004], 169-84 [161, 183]). Often those who interpret Paul's doctrine of justification in this way make a distinction between the *ground* or *basis* for the justification of believers, which is Christ's atoning death, and the *means* by which they are justified, which is faith in Christ and his death; see, for example, George Eldon Ladd, *A Theology of the*

necessary in order for God to forgive sins and declare sinners righteous. While in principle the sins of all human beings are forgiven by virtue of Christ's death, it is still necessary for them to come to faith in order to make that forgiveness theirs. The content of that faith is generally said to be the efficacy of Christ's atoning death to take away sins.[10] In order to be justified by God, that faith is sufficient. While good works should follow upon such faith, they do not constitute the basis for one's forgiveness and justification. Salvation and justification are by grace alone and through faith alone, and for that reason, those who have faith can have full assurance that they are forgiven and justified, independently of any works on their part. Justification is also forensic in that it involves a declaration on God's part that someone is righteous rather than a recognition on God's part that one actually *is* righteous on the basis of one's conduct, works, or way of life.

Such an understanding of Paul's teaching on justification is highly problematic for a number of reasons. By positing faith as a second basis or condition for justification, it reduces Christ's death to a formality that does not actually obtain the forgiveness of sins for anyone, since no one is ultimately forgiven on account of his death unless they *believe* that they are forgiven on account of his death. Faith in the efficacy of Christ's death tends to be seen as the one work necessary in order to be justified, and it is not clear why good works and a sanctified life must necessarily follow from one's justification. If those who have been justified by faith do not come to produce good works as they should and instead continue to live in sin, the question arises as to whether their justification is thereby nullified. If one answers that question affirmatively, then even if justification is initially by faith alone, subsequently it depends on one's works. In that case, ultimately it is *not* by faith alone. If one instead answers that one's ongoing condition of being justified does *not* depend on one's works, then those works become unnecessary and superfluous for one's justification and salvation.

For centuries, those who defend this traditional understanding of justification have attempted to get around these problems, yet in reality they admit of no satisfactory solution. For that reason, proponents of this view inevitably fall into contradictions. Thus, for example, Leon Morris, who was renowned as one of the most capable and ardent defenders of the view of justification just considered, maintained that "Christ has really put our sins out of the way, effectively and finally," yet at the same time affirmed: "There

---

New Testament, rev. ed. (Grand Rapids: Eerdmans, 1993), 490. As long as faith is considered an indispensable condition for justification, however, in reality it also becomes a basis or ground upon which one is declared righteous by God, since without it one is *not* justified.

10. According to Ladd, for example, "Faith means acceptance of this work of God in Christ, complete reliance upon it, and an utter abandonment of one's own works as the grounds of justification" (*Theology*, 490).

is a divine wrath against every evil thing and when that has been put away by what Christ did we must have a due horror of arousing it again."[11] Here it is clear that, if one can arouse God's wrath again, it has *not* been put away "effectively and finally" by Christ's death. Believers must still live obediently in order to remain free of that wrath.

This interpretation of Paul's thought also seems to run contrary to some of the affirmations Paul makes in his epistles. In particular, Paul states that all people will be judged by their works.[12] In Rom 2:13, he even affirms that "it is the doers of the law who will be justified." This verse is so problematic for the traditional interpretation of Paul's teaching on justification that some Pauline scholars have claimed that Paul is here alluding to Jewish teaching rather than expressing his own thought.[13] Scholars often respond to these difficulties by claiming that judgment is by works only because one's works provide evidence of one's faith.[14] Yet this raises the question of how many works are necessary to demonstrate that one has saving faith. Rather than having full assurance of salvation because of their faith, believers must constantly be examining their works to see if they provide sufficient evidence that they do indeed possess the faith God requires of them in order for them to be justified and saved.

The problems associated with this forensic understanding of Paul's doctrine of justification have led many Pauline interpreters to follow Sanders in claiming that Paul's soteriology is primarily *participatory*. According to Sanders, "the prime significance that Christ's death has for Paul is not that it provides atonement for past transgressions (although he holds the common Christian view that it does so), but that, by *sharing* in Christ's death, one dies to the *power* of sin or to the old aeon, with the result that one *belongs to God*. . . . The transfer takes place by *participation* in Christ's death."[15] In this case, believers are forgiven and justified because through faith they participate in Christ's death. It has also become common for adherents of this participatory soteriology to claim that when Paul speaks of the faith of Christ or *pistis Christou*, rather than referring to faith *in* Christ, he is speaking of Christ's own faith or faithfulness. Supposedly,

---

11. Leon Morris, *The Cross in the New Testament* (Grand Rapids: Eerdmans, 1965), 6; *The Atonement: Its Meaning and Significance* (Downers Grove, IL: InterVarsity, 1983), 204.

12. See Rom 2:6-16; 14:10-12; 2 Cor 5:10; 1 Thess 4:1-6; cf. 1 Cor 1:8; 4:3-5; 6:12-13; 2 Cor 11:15; Phil 1:9-10; 1 Thess 3:13; 5:23.

13. E. P. Sanders, for example, claimed that Rom 2:13 must have been taken from a synagogue sermon from the Jewish diaspora, since it runs contrary to the thought of Paul (*Paul, the Law, and the Jewish People* [Philadelphia: Fortress, 1983], 126-29).

14. Herman Ridderbos, for example, writes that "works are indispensable as the demonstration of the true nature of faith" (*Paul: An Outline of His Theology*, trans. John Richard de Witt [Grand Rapids: Eerdmans, 1975], 180).

15. Sanders, *Paul and Palestinian Judaism*, 467-68; cf. 447-511.

Christ's faith or faithfulness is salvific in that people may now participate in it.[16] As we have noted in Chapter 3 of this study, the notion of participation has often been understood in ontological terms: in some mysterious fashion, believers in Christ become united to him in a real and literal sense and even come to constitute one person with him, in addition to participating in the event of his death on the cross.[17] Paul's allusions to dying and being buried with Christ in baptism in Romans 6 and his repeated use of the phrase "in Christ" are interpreted on the basis of these ideas. This participatory understanding of justification also focuses primarily on salvation from sin *as a power* rather than from "sins" in the plural.[18]

Precisely what scholars mean when they speak of Paul's understanding of participation in Christ and his death is by no means clear. Those who affirm that Paul understood such participation in a literal, ontological, or "real" sense are generally forced to admit that it is impossible for us today to grasp adequately Paul's thought in this regard.[19] Evidently, we are incapable today of conceiving of something that was perfectly clear and comprehensible to people in Paul's day.

The most serious problem with these interpretations of Paul's thought, however, has to do with the concepts of God and salvation associated with them. As just noted above, according to forensic interpretations of Paul's thought, if God wishes to forgive and save human beings, his nature requires that his justice first be satisfied. His perfection requires that human beings be perfect in their conduct in order for him to accept them, yet because this is impossible for them, God's Son had to become human and live a perfect and sinless life before dying on the cross in order that his perfection might be reckoned to others or accepted by God in their stead. In

---

16. Svetlana Khobnya, for example, speaks of "the universal consequences of Christ's faithfulness" in Paul's thought: "Through Christ's obedience many will be made righteous because Christ overcomes not only Israel's unfaithfulness but all human unrighteousness and sin. This opens up a possibility for believers to participate in Christ's faithfulness" (*The Father Who Redeems and the Son Who Obeys: Consideration of Paul's Teaching in Romans* [Eugene, OR: Pickwick, 2013], 165).

17. So, for example, Sanders, *Paul and Palestinian Judaism*, 453-72, 519-23; Stanley K. Stowers, "What is 'Pauline Participation in Christ'?," in *Redefining First Century Jewish and Christian Identities: Essays in Honor of Ed Parish Sanders*, ed. Fabian Udoh et al. (Notre Dame: University of Notre Dame Press, 2008), 352-71. For further references to these ideas, see Brondos, *Jesus' Death*, 2:674-84.

18. On this point, see Simon Gathercole, "'Sins' in Paul," *NTS* 64 (2018): 143-61.

19. See, for example, Sanders, *Paul and Palestinian Judaism*, 522-23; Troels Engberg-Pedersen, *Paul and the Stoics* (Louisville: Westminster John Knox, 2000), 27; Richard B. Hays, "Crucified with Christ: A Synthesis of the Theology of 1 and 2 Thessalonians, Philemon, Philippians, and Galatians," in *Pauline Theology*, vol. 1: *Thessalonians, Philippians, Galatians, Philemon*, ed. Jouette M. Bassler (Minneapolis: Fortress, 1991), 227-46 (242).

this case, God does not care *who* lives a perfect life, but merely demands that *someone* do so—whether Christ or human beings. What matters is not that sinful people actually *become* righteous but that God be able to *reckon* them to be righteous without compromising his perfect righteousness. The idea that believers must participate in Christ's faith or faithfulness in order to be saved also implies that, due to the perfection of his own nature, God requires a perfect faith or faithfulness on the part of human beings. Because they cannot attain that perfection on their own, through Christ's life and death a perfect faith or faithfulness must be brought about first in Christ so that others may come to participate in it and thereby fulfill God's just demand.

Such interpretations fail to take into account the intrinsic relation between the faith of human beings and their salvation. In biblical thought, faith in God leads to the well-being and wholeness of human beings (*sōtēria*) because it brings them to live in conformity with what God has commanded, not for *his* sake, but for *theirs*. In and of itself, such a life enables them to experience the well-being that God desires for all people. God's concern is not to be able to declare human beings righteous, as if this were all that were necessary for them to be saved, but to enable human beings to practice the righteousness that will allow them to be saved by being made whole. In the thought of Paul, the reason why God sent his Son and calls human beings to faith is not that he must satisfy some need found in his own nature before he can forgive or save them. Instead, it is the nature of the well-being that God desires for all people out of love for them that requires that they be brought to think and live in a way that makes that well-being possible. According to Paul, this is what takes place through Christ and faith.

Faith, Obedience, and Righteousness in Paul's Thought

A proper understanding of the intrinsic relation between faith and righteousness is indispensable for understanding Paul's teaching regarding justification by faith. As scholars such as Teresa Morgan have argued, for Paul faith is primarily *trust in God* rather than the mere belief that certain propositions are true: "he sees *pistis* as predominantly an exercise of trust which involves heart, mind, and action. Like all trust, it is intimately connected with belief, on which it depends and which depends on it."[20] In other words, one will only trust in God if one believes certain truths concerning God and his activity in human history, yet what saves human beings is not simply belief in those truths but the life of trust in God that is *based* on those truths. If one truly trusts in God and his love, one will obey him and practice

---

20. Teresa Morgan, *Roman Faith and Christian Faith: Pistis and Fides in the Early Roman Empire and Early Churches* (Oxford: Oxford University Press, 2015), 261.

naturally the righteousness he desires and commands of all for their own good. Thus, *in and of itself*, faith in God leads one to live righteously as God desires. In contrast, any who refuse to live as God desires and commands for the good of all are not truly trusting in God and therefore cannot rightly be said to have faith in him.

As Paul argues in Romans 4, the clearest illustration of this relationship between faith and righteousness is the life of Abraham. According to Gen 15:6, Abraham was accepted as righteous by God before he had done anything other than believe in God's promises (Rom 4:3-12). The reason for this, however, was that his faith and trust in God would lead him to do all that God commanded of him so that the promises he had made to Abraham might be fulfilled. Had Abraham not obeyed out of faith, the fulfillment of those promises would not have come to pass. Throughout Romans 4, Paul seems to presuppose that his readers are acquainted with the story of Abraham. If so, they would have known that, from the moment God revealed himself to Abraham and told him to leave his own land for another one, Abraham had obeyed. Obviously, he had done so because he believed God and trusted in the promises God had made to him. The readers of Romans would have been acquainted with the story of the binding of Isaac or *Akedah* in Gen 22:1-19, which was considered by most Jews in Paul's day to be one of the most important passages in the Hebrew Scriptures.[21] There Abraham demonstrates that he is willing to obey God no matter what God asks of him, even if this involves putting to death the son that God had miraculously given him. It must have seemed to Abraham that the death of his son would make it impossible for the promises that God had made to him to be fulfilled. Nevertheless, "hoping against hope," throughout his life Abraham believed in God and did not waver or weaken in his faith and trust in God (Rom 4:18-20). He remained "fully convinced that God was able to do what he had promised" (4:21). Thus, while it was solely on account of his faith that Abraham was accepted by God as righteous (Rom 4:1-12; Gen 15:6), *there was a reason for this*: Abraham's faith inevitably led him to obey God in everything so that God might accomplish his gracious will and purposes in and through Abraham.

For Paul, then, faith and obedience to God are inseparable. On this point, Paul is in full agreement with the Hebrew Scriptures and Second Temple Jewish thought. Where Paul differs, however, is in his understanding of God's will. Whereas in the Hebrew Scriptures and Second Temple Jewish thought righteousness was defined primarily on the basis of the Torah, in Paul's thought righteousness and obedience to God cannot be

---

21. As Joshua Jipp notes, several Second Temple Jewish writings as well as the Epistle of James associate the story of the binding of Isaac in Genesis 22 with Gen 15:6 ("Rereading the Story of Abraham, Isaac, and 'Us' in Romans 4," *JSNT* 32 [2009]: 217-42 [223-24]).

reduced to observance of the Torah or simply equated with such obser-vance. According to Paul, by virtue of his faith and trust in God, Abraham was regarded as righteous by God independently of any observance of the commandments of the Torah, which had not yet been given. For Paul, faith and trust in God are now to take the form of believing "in him who raised from the dead Jesus our Lord" (Rom 4:24). Those who truly believe in that God will live in accordance with his will as it has now come to be defined through Jesus. For that reason, like Abraham, gentile believ-ers can be declared righteous simply by virtue of their faith in the God of Abraham and Jesus.

Elsewhere in his epistles Paul ties faith to obedience and righteousness explicitly. In Rom 1:5 and 16:26, he states the purpose of his ministry in terms of bringing about the "obedience of faith" (*hypakoē pisteōs*) among the gentiles or nations (cf. Rom 15:18). What Paul seeks is not simply that others come to faith, as if that were an end in itself, but that they come to practice the "obedience that leads to righteousness" by becoming "obedi-ent from the heart" to the form of teaching committed to them (Rom 6:16-17). Through faith they become "slaves of obedience" and "slaves of righteousness" (Rom 6:16, 18-19). Because by definition faith is constantly "active through love" (Gal 5:6), it leads believers to live righteously in the way that God desires for their own good. In Rom 10:10, Paul affirms that "with the heart one believes unto righteousness" (*eis dikaiosynēn*). For Paul, then, by its very nature, faith results in a life of love, righteousness, and obedience to God.[22]

The idea that righteousness is the result of faith is reflected especially in Paul's use of the Greek phrase *ek pisteōs*, which appears over fifteen times in Romans and Galatians. While this phrase is generally translated as "by faith," it literally means "out of faith." It thus designates something that *arises* out of faith, *originates* in it, or has faith as its *source*.[23] In Rom 1:17 and Gal 3:11, Paul quotes Hab 2:4, which can be translated in two differ-ent ways: either "the righteous one will live out of faith" or "the one who is

---

22. James Dunn captures well the relationship between faith and obedience in Paul's thought when he writes: "faith means total and unconditional reliance on God. . . , complete trust in God, total reliance on God's enabling. That is the root of obedience for Paul: unless obedience springs from that, it is misdirected. The 'obedience of faith' is that obedience which lives out the sort of trust and reliance on God which Abraham demonstrated" ("'The Law of Faith,' 'the Law of the Spirit' and 'the Law of Christ,'" in *Theology and Ethics in Paul and His Interpreters: Essays in Honor of Victor Paul Furnish*, ed. Eugene H. Lovering Jr. and Jerry L. Sumney [Nashville: Abingdon, 1996], 62-82 [68]).

23. It can therefore be said, as Don B. Garlington does, that when Paul speaks of the obedience of faith, he has in mind "a twin idea: the obedience consisting in faith and the obedience arising out of faith" (*Faith, Obedience, and Perseverance: Aspects of Paul's Letter to the Romans*, WUNT 79 [Tübingen: Mohr, 1994], 72).

righteous as a result of faith will live."[24] According to the first of these two translations, those who live out of faith will be righteous in the sense that their faith will constitute the basis for all they do in life. According to the second, those who are righteous as a result of their living out of faith will attain life. In either case, faith is the source of the righteous way of life that makes one righteous.

Particularly significant is Paul's use of the same phrase in Rom 14:23, where he writes: "Everything that is not 'out of faith' (*ek pisteōs*) is sin." Here Paul's idea is that whatever does not proceed from faith or have faith as its source is sinful. Obviously, for Paul everything that one does in life is to be grounded in faith in some way. This passage is also significant in that it demonstrates that for Paul the righteousness that is brought about *ek pisteōs* does not merely consist of a forensic standing before God but involves a way of life and conduct. Just as the sin that results from *not* living out of faith involves an *activity* or *behavior* rather than a *status*, so also the righteousness that results from faith is not merely a forensic standing but the righteous way of thinking, being, and behaving that is the consequence of living out of faith. There is therefore an *intrinsic relation* between faith and righteousness: in and of itself, faith leads to the righteous way of living that God desires to see in all people. Undoubtedly, faith also results in a forensic standing before God in which he accepts one as righteous, yet that standing is based on the fact that such a faith will invariably lead one to live righteously in accordance with God's will.

It is important to stress that, for Paul, to be righteous is not to be perfect or entirely innocent of sin. In this regard, Paul once again reflects the same thought we find in the Hebrew Scriptures and Second Temple Jewish writings. Undoubtedly, the God of Paul and the Hebrew Scriptures would like believers to be perfect in their conduct, yet this is not possible. In fact, in principle believers themselves would also like to be perfect in their righteousness, since they know that sinful behavior does them great harm and prevents them from experiencing fully the wholeness that God desires for them and that they desire for themselves. When they fall into sin, it upsets them just as much as it upsets God, since they know that sin undermines and destroys their well-being. While at times Paul speaks of believers being "blameless," this word should be understood in a relative sense rather than a categorical one.[25] As in Jewish thought, for Paul one is righteous and

---

24. On these two readings of Hab 2:4, which he labels "adverbial" and "adjectival," see Arland J. Hultgren, *Paul's Letter to the Romans: A Commentary* (Grand Rapids: Eerdmans, 2011), 78-79.

25. See 1 Cor 1:8; Phil 1:10; 2:15; 1 Thess 3:13; 5:23. On this understanding of blamelessness, see Yinger, *God and Human Wholeness*, 22-23, 126-28. On the idea of perfection in Paul's thought, see 93-137.

blameless, not because one has never sinned, but because one is truly committed to living as God desires out of love for all.

Righteousness as a Gift

In Rom 5:17, Paul speaks of "those who receive the abundance of grace and the free gift of righteousness" through Christ. These words have traditionally been understood primarily or exclusively in a forensic sense: in his grace, God graciously reckons believers to be righteous, despite the fact that they are not truly righteous but sinful.[26] God's basis for doing so is supposedly both Christ's death and their faith in Christ and his death. In reality, however, there is no reason to regard the righteousness of which Paul speaks in Rom 5:17 as purely forensic. Through faith, which is itself a gift of God, God graciously brings about in believers the new life of obedience and righteousness that he desires for all out of love for them. It is this new life, which believers receive by God's grace alone through faith alone, that constitutes the basis upon which God also forgives them their sins and accepts them as righteous. Rather than being limited to his forgiveness, God's grace is *all* of his activity in relation to believers—past, present, and future—, which is aimed at enabling them to live in the way that makes it possible for them to attain the wholeness and well-being he desires for them. That grace is not, however, something that God infuses into believers. Instead, it is a way of relating to human beings.

While in some of the passages in which he speaks of the righteousness of believers Paul undoubtedly has in mind a forensic standing, in numerous passages from his epistles righteousness clearly has to do with activity, actions, or conduct on the part of believers. In Romans 6, for example, Paul calls believers "slaves of righteousness" and exhorts them to present their members to God as "instruments" or "weapons of righteousness" (*hopla dikaiosynēs*; Rom 6:13, 18-20). He uses this latter phrase in 2 Cor 6:7 as well, where he speaks of having "the weapons of righteousness (*hopla tēs dikaiosynēs*) for the right hand and for the left."[27] In 2 Cor 9:10 and Phil 1:11, Paul alludes to the "fruit" or "harvest" of righteousness that is produced in believers.[28] In Rom 8:4, Paul uses the term *dikaiōma* to refer to

---

26. Thus, for example, Leon Morris comments: "That *righteousness* is a *gift*... shows plainly that Paul is thinking of it as a status, a standing; the term is forensic. We often use the word to denote an ethical quality, but such a quality cannot be given" (*The Epistle to the Romans* [Grand Rapids: Eerdmans, 1988], 237).

27. As Paul Barnett notes, the phrase "weapons of righteousness" in 2 Cor 6:7 should be understood as referring to an ethical rather than a forensic righteousness (*The Second Epistle to the Corinthians*, NICNT [Grand Rapids: Eerdmans, 1997], 330).

28. Ben Witherington III rightly stresses that, when Paul speaks of the "fruit of righteousness" in Phil 1:11, he is not referring to a forensic righteousness (*Paul's Letter to the Philippians: A Socio-Rhetorical Commentary* [Grand Rapids: Eerdmans, 2011], 66).

the righteousness of the law being fulfilled in believers. The fact that in Rom 5:17 Paul contrasts "the free gift of righteousness" with "one man's trespass" indicates that in both cases he has in mind something that people *do* rather than a status they possess. In all of these instances, then, it is clear that when Paul speaks of righteousness he is referring to *righteous activity or behavior* and not merely to a forensic standing. Of course, as in Jewish thought, for Paul the righteous way of living brings with it a forensic standing of righteousness before God. Therefore, even when Paul has in mind this forensic standing, it is not divorced from the life of righteousness that leads to that standing.

Furthermore, contrary to many traditional interpretations of his thought, for Paul the life of righteousness is not the *result* of one's forensic standing of righteousness before God but rather its *basis*. Temporally, of course, God's declaration that one is righteous on the basis of one's faith may precede the life of righteousness that follows upon that faith, yet as noted above, the reason that God declares those who have faith to be righteous is precisely because that faith will lead to the life of righteousness that he wants all to lead for their own sake. Such was the case with Abraham, whom God regarded as righteous merely because he believed, prior to any "working" on his part (Rom 4:3-8). Yet, as we have seen above, the reason why Abraham's faith led God to account him as righteous was that it would lead Abraham to do whatever God asked him to do, thereby making it possible for God to accomplish his purposes through Abraham. Thus, even though the "working" would be *subsequent* to faith, that working, together with the faith that would lead to it, can still be seen as the basis upon which God declared Abraham righteous—not because those works would merit God's favor or his forgiveness, but because they would consist of the righteous way of life that God desired Abraham to live for his own good and that of others.

The key to grasping this understanding of justification, then, is precisely the notion that God desires and commands that human beings live in conformity with righteousness and justice *for their sake and not for his*. According to most traditional views of justification, the ultimate objective of human beings must consist of fulfilling a requirement that God has deemed necessary in order to grant them his approval, forgiveness, and acceptance, whether this be faith alone or some type of work as well. The condition for them to be justified and saved is derived from God's righteous nature and therefore must be fulfilled *for the sake of God himself and his nature*. However, once it is understood that in biblical thought God commands human beings to practice justice and righteousness *for their own sake rather than his*, then the focus and objective of human beings must be *to live in a manner*

In 2 Cor 9:10, Paul's allusion is probably to the fruit that is produced by righteousness rather than righteousness itself as a fruit; see Murray J. Harris, *The Second Epistle to the Corinthians*, NIGTC (Grand Rapids: Eerdmans, 2005), 643-44.

that makes their wholeness and well-being possible. This alone can please and satisfy God and obtain his approval. Through faith, by means of his Son, his Spirit, the gospel, and the community of believers in Christ, God makes it possible for believers to live in such a manner out of pure grace. As they look to God in faith, God uses those means to bring about in believers the just and righteous way of life that enables them to experience the good that God desires for them out of love for all. On that basis, they are accepted by God as righteous. What God calls on all to do, therefore, is simply to look to him in faith and trust, depending entirely on him to bring about in them the way of life necessary for them to attain the well-being he desires for all. Those who do so are pleasing to him because they are doing what he wants, namely, living in a way that makes it possible for God to make them whole (*sōzein*). God also forgives them the sins that they continue to commit *contrary* to their own will by virtue of the fact that through Christ they are being brought to live in the way he desires for their own good and that of others.

In Rom 9:30–10:10 and Gal 2:16-21, Paul contrasts the righteousness that is the result of faith (*ek pisteōs*) with the righteousness that comes from the law (*ek nomou*) or from the works it prescribes (*ex ergōn nomou*). For Paul, to base one's life on the law alone is not to live out of faith: "For the law is not *ek pisteōs*" (Gal 3:10). In and of itself, obedience to commandments does not lead to the righteous way of living God desires to see in all. Instead, such a way of life is brought about by looking to God's love and promises in Christ: "For through the Spirit, *ek pisteōs*, we anxiously await the hope of righteousness" (Gal 5:5). According to Rom 9:30-32, even though the gentiles did not pursue it, they have received righteousness—that is, the righteous way of living God desires to see in all—*ek pisteōs* (v. 30). In contrast, "Israel, pursuing a law of righteousness, did not arrive at that law. Why? Because they did not pursue it *ek pisteōs* but as if it were *ex ergōn*. They have stumbled over the stumbling stone" (vv. 31-32). A few verses later, Paul claims that those of Israel sought to establish their own righteousness rather than looking to that which is from God, evidently because they thought that the righteousness God desired was brought about by law-observance rather than by looking in faith to the fulfillment of God's promises in Christ, who is the end or goal of the law for all who believe (Rom 10:3-4). In contrast to the righteousness that is *ek tou nomou* of which Moses spoke, the righteousness that is *ek pisteōs* looks to Christ, who has risen from the dead after descending into the abyss, so as now to be Lord of all and save those who call upon him (Rom 10:5-13). In that way, the righteous way of life that the law anticipated but could not bring about is now given to believers as a free gift.

When Paul speaks of the works of the law, it is quite likely that he has in mind things such as circumcision, regulations regarding purity, and the observance of the Sabbath.[29] If so, there is no reason to think that he rejected the value of obedience to such commandments among his fellow Jews or believed that Jewish believers in Christ should no longer observe them. Rather, what Paul apparently wished to stress is that in itself the observance of such commandments does not make one righteous. On this point, in fact, the vast majority of his fellow Jews would have agreed with him.

Once it is recognized that in Paul's thought righteousness involves a way of living or behaving that makes it possible for one to experience the well-being and salvation God desires for all, it becomes clear why he insists that righteousness is not brought about by the law or its works. For Paul, righteousness has to do with things such as those he mentions in passages such as Rom 12:1-21, 2 Cor 6:6-7, Gal 5:22-23, and Phil 2:1-5: love, kindness, goodness, patience, and similar ways of relating to others. Ultimately, as we have seen in Chapter 4 of this study, these are the things that God desires to see in human beings. Such behaviors are not brought about merely by observing commandments regarding circumcision, the Sabbath, and the distinctions between clean and unclean, even though in Jewish thought the observance of commandments such as these was thought to help promote righteous behavior. For that reason, for Paul it is good and proper for Jews to observe them. To impose the observance of such commandments on non-Jewish believers in Christ, however, is not only pointless but cruel. It is pointless in that they have no need for such observances in order to lead the kind of life that God desires to see in them, and it is cruel in that those observances would be a tremendous burden for non-Jews, who were not accustomed to them. Of course, this is particularly the case with regard to circumcision, which is the primary focus of Paul's argument in Galatians, since for non-Jewish adult males to undergo circumcision would be extremely painful for them.

In this regard, it is significant to note that Paul's language of righteousness is found primarily in the letters and passages in which he is engaged in discussions and debates regarding Jewish concerns and the Jewish law. Around forty of the approximately forty-five instances of the word *dikaiosynē* in Paul's epistles occur in Romans (especially chapters 3-10), in Galatians, and in Phil 3:2-9, where he is contrasting the righteousness of faith with the righteousness of the law in order to argue that it is those who live out of faith who are righteous. The fact that Paul speaks of righteousness primarily in these contexts, which are to some extent polemical in nature, suggests that he is adopting and using the language of his opponents in order to refute

---

29. On this discussion, see especially Matthew J. Thomas, *Paul's 'Works of the Law' in the Perspective of Second Century Reception*, WUNT 2/468 (Tübingen: Mohr Siebeck, 2018), 39-61; Serge Ruzer, "Paul's Stance on the Torah Revisited: Gentile Addressees and the Jewish Setting," in *Paul's Jewish Matrix*, ed. Thomas G. Casey and Justin Taylor, StJC (Mahwah, NJ: Paulist, 2011), 75-97 (78-83).

their arguments. At the same time, he is framing his own views in terms that they will readily understand and that are pertinent to the debate in which he is involved. Similarly, Romans and Galatians account for twenty-five of the twenty-nine instances in which the noun "justification" and the verb "to justify" appear in Paul's letters, and outside of those two epistles Paul uses the adjective *dikaios* ("just" or "righteous") only in Phil 1:7 and 4:8.

In contrast, the word "love" appears some eighty-four times in Paul's epistles and is much more evenly distributed among them.[30] The most convincing explanation for this is that Paul prefers the language of love to that of righteousness. If one were to summarize in a word the many different qualities, attitudes, and behaviors that Paul commends throughout his epistles, that word would unquestionably be "love." Nevertheless, the term "righteousness" would also be fitting, as long as it is stressed that to practice righteousness or that which is right is by definition to practice love as well. Any behavior that is not loving and does not seek the well-being of others is not righteous, just as any behavior that is unjust and unrighteous must be regarded as unloving.

According to Paul, it is God who produces in believers both love and righteousness as a gracious gift through Christ and the Holy Spirit. Throughout his epistles, Paul stresses time and again the idea that God himself brings about in believers the new life he desires to see in them. After thanking God for the grace given the Corinthian believers in Christ and for having enriched them in all speech and knowledge so that they are "not lacking in any gift," Paul speaks of them "awaiting eagerly the revelation of our Lord Jesus, who shall also confirm you to the end, blameless in the day of our Lord Christ. God is faithful, through whom you were called into fellowship with his Son, Jesus Christ our Lord" (1 Cor 1:4-9). The verb *bebaioun* used here by Paul means not only to confirm but to strengthen and sustain. Elsewhere Paul writes that God has given Christ to believers as the one who is for them "wisdom and righteousness and sanctification and redemption *from God*" (1 Cor 1:30). When he chides the believers in Corinth for boasting, he asks them: "What do have that you did not receive? But if you did receive it, why do you boast as if you had not received it?" (1 Cor 4:7). After telling the Corinthian believers that whoever is in Christ is a new creation, he affirms that "all of this comes from God" (2 Cor 5:17-18). It is God who makes believers "the righteousness of God" in and through Christ (2 Cor 5:21). In 2 Cor 1:21-22, Paul uses the verb *bebaioun* once more to affirm that God establishes believers in or through Christ, in addition to anointing and sealing them by giving them his Spirit in their hearts as a pledge. Believers are controlled or constrained by the love of Christ

---

30. On the centrality of love in Paul's thought, see Wolfgang Schrage, *The Ethics of the New Testament*, trans. David E. Green (Philadelphia: Fortress, 1988), 211-17.

(2 Cor 5:14-15), and through Christ they are strengthened and empowered to do all things (Phil 4:13). In Phil 1:9-11, Paul prays that God make his love abound "more and more" in the believers to whom he writes and that God enable them to be "filled with the fruit of righteousness which comes through Jesus Christ." Here the idea that both love and righteousness are graciously brought about in believers by God is particularly clear. Even more explicit is Paul's affirmation in Phil 2:13 that "it is God who is at work in you so that you may both desire and carry out what is well-pleasing to him." The idea that God remains at work in believers is stressed from the very outset of the same letter, where Paul tells the believers in Philippi: "I am confident of this very thing, that the one who began a good work in you will bring it to completion at the day of Jesus Christ" (Phil 1:6).

In 1 Thessalonians, Paul speaks of God's word performing its work in the Thessalonian believers (1 Thess 2:13). He tells the readers: "may the Lord cause you to grow and increase in love for one another and for all people, just as we also do for you, so that he may establish your hearts blameless in holiness before our God and Father at the coming of our Lord Jesus with all of his angels" (3:11-13). Paul also reminds them that they have been "taught by God to love one another" (4:9). He ends his letter with the petition that God sanctify them entirely and preserve complete their spirit, soul, and body so that they may be "without blame at the coming of our Lord Jesus" (5:23). In all of these passages, Paul makes it clear that it is the task *of God* to produce love, holiness, and righteousness in believers and preserve them blameless until the end. All that believers can do is trust in God by looking to God in the same way that Paul does, asking him to confirm, strengthen, and sustain them in the work he has begun in them until the coming of Christ.

Other passages from Paul's epistles speak of God graciously giving believers the Holy Spirit or the Spirit of his Son.[31] Through that Spirit, God works to transform believers, producing in them the knowledge, holiness, gifts, and fruit he desires to see in them.[32] In Rom 15:13, Paul presents both God and the Holy Spirit as being active in believers: "Now may the God of hope fill you with all joy and peace in believing, so that you will abound in hope by the power of the Holy Spirit." It is God who "works all things in all persons" through that Spirit (1 Cor 12:6). As noted above, God gives believers the "hope of righteousness through the Spirit by faith" (Gal 5:5). The Holy Spirit also creates the obedience God desires to see in believers by guiding them, filling them with knowledge, and enabling them to put to death the deeds of the flesh.[33] Paul even affirms that the Holy Spirit helps believers in their weakness by interceding to God for them, since they are

---

31. See Rom 8:14-17; 1 Cor 12:7-13; 2 Cor 5:5; Gal 4:6.

32. See Rom 8:2, 13-14, 26; 15:16; 1 Cor 2:12-13; 12:3-11; Gal 3:5; 5:22-23.

33. See Rom 8:13-14; 1 Cor 2:10-14; Gal 5:16-18, 25.

not capable of praying as they should without the Spirit's assistance (Rom 8:26-27). Most importantly, in Rom 5:5 Paul affirms that the love of God has been poured out in the hearts of believers by means of the Spirit whom God has given to them.

In Jewish thought, of course, it was believed that the Torah was capable of producing in those who followed it almost all of the same qualities Paul repeatedly mentions, including especially love, knowledge, wisdom, holiness, and righteousness.[34] For Paul, however, the law is not able to bring about the same righteousness that is given to believers in Christ as a gift.[35] Paul's clearest statement of this belief is found in Rom 8:3-4, where he writes: "For what was impossible for the law, in that it was weak through the flesh, God has done by sending his own Son in the likeness of sinful flesh and for sin: he has condemned sin in the flesh, so that the just requirement (*dikaiōma*) of the law might be fulfilled in us, who walk not according to the flesh but according to the Spirit." These verses must be viewed in the context of Paul's argument in chapters 7 and 8 of this epistle, where he claims that the sin that dwells in human beings and the flesh that characterizes their existence in the present age do not allow them to do what is good and live in righteousness as God desires out of love for them. According to Paul, the law is incapable of overcoming this "sin in the flesh"; only Christ and God's Spirit can accomplish that task (Rom 7:14–8:13). As we have seen previously, in Rom 8:29 Paul defines God's objective in terms of bringing people to be conformed, not to the Torah, but to "the image of his Son." This involves bringing them to practice the same type of love that Paul identifies with Christ, that is, a love that cannot be brought about merely by commandments and legal prescriptions. Instead, what has made it possible for that type of love to become a reality in the lives of believers is that God sent his Son and handed him over to death rather than sparing him when his efforts to bring into existence a community in which all would live in that love led to the threat of death and the cross.

---

34. According to Bruce Chilton and Jacob Neusner, in rabbinic thought, "God gives the Torah, the antidote to sin, its laws intended to 'purify the heart of man,' which is what God most craves. For rabbinic Judaism, therefore, the Torah is the answer to the question of the fall of man from grace...." (*Classical Christianity and Rabbinic Judaism: Comparing Theologies* [Grand Rapids: Baker Academic, 2004], 67-68). Elsewhere they add: "Through Torah God educates the heart of humanity to love, which cannot be coerced. The Torah purifies the heart of humanity, the commandments are media of regeneration and sanctification.... The rabbinic sages leave no doubt that Torah study changes disciples, producing humble persons prepared to love the Lord our God with all our heart, soul, and might" (106-7). There is good reason to suppose that similar ideas characterized the thought of many Jews in the Second Temple period as well.

35. See especially Rom 3:9-24; 7:7–8:4; 9:30–10:10; Gal 2:15–3:25; Phil 3:9.

The Righteousness of God and Christ-Faith

In the same contexts in which he speaks of righteousness as resulting from faith, Paul uses two genitival phrases whose meaning has been debated a great deal among Pauline scholars: the righteousness of God (*dikaiosynē theou*) and the faith of Christ (*pistis Christou*). For centuries, it was common to understand these phrases primarily as objective genitives.[36] The righteousness of God was interpreted as alluding to the forensic status of righteousness that believers attain before God through faith, while the faith *of* Christ was generally translated as "faith *in* Christ." Since then it has become common among many New Testament scholars to understand both of these phrases as *subjective* genitives: God's righteousness is his saving activity or faithfulness to his covenant, whereas the faith of Christ is the faith or faithfulness to God that Christ displayed throughout his life and especially in his passion and death.

Many of those who have argued that *dikaiosynē theou* should be understood as a subjective genitive do so in large part due to their rejection of the notion that Paul has in mind a righteousness that is entirely forensic when he uses the phrase. There can be little doubt that Paul uses the phrase as a subjective genitive in Rom 3:5-6, where he insists that, even though "our unrighteousness demonstrates the righteousness of God," God is not unrighteous to bring his wrath upon human beings when judging the world. Here, however, rather than referring to God's "faithfulness to his covenant with Israel" or to his "faithfulness to his own person and word,"[37] Paul clearly has in mind God's dealing with the world in general by acting through judgment to deliver it from sin, evil, and injustice. While it is possible to make sense of Paul's words in the other passages in which he uses that phrase by interpreting it as a subjective genitive, when those passages are viewed in light of what we have seen above, it seems more likely that in most of them it should be understood as a righteousness that comes from God or is given by him, as well as the righteous way of living that is truly in accordance with his will.[38] Nevertheless, this righteousness should not be understood as something that God communicates to believers or imparts to them as

---

36. For summaries of the scholarly discussion on these two phrases, see Hultgren, *Romans*, 605-15, 623-61; Barry D. Smith, *The Meaning of Jesus' Death: Reviewing the New Testament's Interpretations* (London: Bloomsbury T & T Clark, 2017), 77-97; Matthew C. Easter, "The *Pistis Christou* Debate: Main Arguments and Responses in Summary," *CurBR* 9 (2019): 33-47.

37. See respectively N. T. Wright, *Paul and the Faithfulness of God*, vol. 4 of *Christian Origins and the Question of God* (Minneapolis: Fortress, 2013), 800; Douglas J. Moo, *The Epistle to the Romans*, NICNT (Grand Rapids: Eerdmans, 1996), 190.

38. As John A. Ziesler insists, however, "we cannot accept that there is any one meaning of 'righteousness of God'. It is not a formula in the sense of a recognised phrase for a consistent notion, having a specific and unchanging content" (*The Meaning of*

a *iustitia infusa*, but rather as a way of life that God brings about in them through the gospel, Christ, the Holy Spirit, and the community of believers. According to this understanding of the righteousness of God, when Paul speaks of the righteousness of God, he has in mind righteousness as it is *defined* by God as well as righteous *activity* or *conduct*, as proponents of the subjective genitive interpretation of the phrase claim.[39] However, the activity or conduct of which Paul is speaking in most of the passages in which he uses that phrase is not that of God but that which is to characterize the lives of *believers*.

Such, in fact, is the meaning of the phrase in the two passages in the New Testament outside of Paul's epistles in which it appears. These are Matt 6:33, where Jesus tells his disciples to "seek first the reign of God and his righteousness," and James 1:20: "For the wrath of a man does not work the righteousness of God."[40] In these passages, the righteousness of God is something that one is to *do* and actively *seek*. In Phil 3:9, Paul speaks of wanting to be "found in Christ, not having a righteousness of my own that comes from the law (*ek nomou*), but the righteousness that comes through the faith of Christ, that is, the righteousness that comes from God by faith" (*tēn ek theou dikaiosynēn*). Here, just as the righteousness of Paul's own involves a way of living and behaving that is grounded in the law, so also the righteousness that comes from God through faith in Christ should be understood as a righteous way of living that is given by God through faith. The reason that Paul would have referred to the righteousness of which he speaks as the "righteousness *of God*" is to stress not only that this righteous conduct is brought about by God but also that it is in conformity with his will as he has now defined or redefined that will *through Jesus*. Paul also appears to use the phrase "righteousness of God" to distinguish that righteousness from other conceptions of righteousness, such as the righteousness he associates with the observance of the Mosaic law.

Righteousness in Paul: A Linguistic and Theological Inquiry, SNTSMS 20 [Cambridge: Cambridge University Press, 1972], 186).

39. As most scholars recognize, such is the normal meaning of righteousness in both the Old and New Testaments. Wright, for example, comments: "The word *tsedaqah/dikaiosynē* and its cognates in the Israelite scriptures seem to have the primary meaning of 'right behavior'" (*Paul and the Faithfulness of God*, 796). Cf. Ziesler, *Meaning of Righteousness*, 18-28.

40. In his extensive study on the subject, Benno Przybylski writes: "God's righteousness in [Matt] 6:33 must be understood as a norm for man's conduct. It is 'righteousness of life in agreement with the will of God'" (*Righteousness in Matthew and his World of Thought*, SNTSMS 41 [Cambridge: Cambridge University Press, 1980], 90). Przybylski rightly notes that the same idea is present in James 1:20 (90), yet because he assumes that in Paul's thought righteousness is primarily a forensic term, he concludes that Matthew and Paul understand righteousness in two conflicting ways rather than recognizing the essential agreement between the two (105-6, 123).

The same understanding of the righteousness of God seems to be evident in Rom 10:3, where Paul uses the phrase twice when speaking of those who belong to Israel: "For because they were unaware of the righteousness of God and sought to establish their own righteousness, they did not submit to the righteousness of God."[41] When Paul speaks of these two forms of righteousness, he has in mind not merely a righteous status before God but the way of life that *leads* to that status and constitutes its *basis*. This is the righteousness of God that Israel sought by observing the law but did not attain, since that righteousness is brought about through Christ and faith rather than merely by observing the commandments of the law. According to Paul, the righteousness of God is now defined primarily by God in Christ rather than through the law alone. Because that righteousness is brought about by living out of faith in the way that gentile believers now do rather than by practicing the works of the law, whoever does not live out of faith does not submit to the true righteousness of God or attain that righteousness.

This understanding of the righteousness of God would also explain what Paul means in Rom 1:17 when he affirms that the righteousness of God has been revealed as being *ek pisteōs eis pistin*, which can be translated literally "*out of* faith *into* faith." Pauline interpreters have disagreed greatly regarding the meaning of this phrase, yet if it is viewed in light of the idea that the righteous way of life God desires and commands of all for their own good is brought about by living "out of faith," then the meaning of this phrase becomes obvious: when people—including both Jews and gentiles—come to know that the righteousness that God demands of all out of love for them is a gracious gift produced by living *out of* faith (*ek pisteōs*), they consequently come *to* faith (*eis pistin*) so as to receive and attain that righteousness.[42] This is the righteousness of which Hab 2:4 speaks when the prophet affirms that the one who is righteous shall live out of faith or that the one who is righteous as a result of faith shall live. As those who are brought to faith as a result of that knowledge come to live out of faith, they

---

41. As Smith comments with regard to this passage, "Because it stands in contrast to 'their own righteousness', the genitive phrase 'righteousness of God' can only be a genitive of origin: it is a righteousness that has its origin with God, the very opposite of self-righteousness through the Law" (*Meaning of Jesus' Death*, 81). Nevertheless, in Paul's thought, this righteousness that has its origin in God is not merely a righteous status or standing before God but the righteous way of life that results in that standing.

42. Curiously, this interpretation of Rom 1:17 is not even considered by commentators who survey the common scholarly interpretations of the passage; see, for example, Charles L. Quarles, "From Faith to Faith: A Fresh Examination of the Prepositional Series in Romans 1:17," *NovT* 45 (2003): 1-21; C. E. B. Cranfield, *A Critical and Exegetical Commentary on the Epistle to the Romans*, 6th ed., ICC (Edinburgh: T & T Clark, 1975), 1:99-100; Richard N. Longenecker, *The Epistle to the Romans: A Commentary on the Greek Text*, NIGTC (Grand Rapids: Eerdmans, 2016), 176-78.

attain the righteousness of God. Here and elsewhere, Paul specifies that the righteousness of which he speaks is the righteousness *of God* in order to distinguish that righteousness from other forms of righteousness, in particular that which is based on the law alone.

At the same time, it might be said that those Jews who lived according to the law were also living out of faith in the sense that they believed that God had given Israel the law and had commanded his people to live out that belief and to trust in him by obeying that law. For this reason, Paul may have used the phrase *pistis Christou* to make a distinction between the general faith in God that characterized all who believed in the God of Israel and the faith that revolved around Christ as the Son of God.[43] While the faith out of which all were now to live was undoubtedly faith *in* Christ, it was also much more than that. The object of that faith was not merely Christ, but the God who had intended for human beings to be conformed to the image of his Son from the start and to that end had sent his Son in the likeness of human flesh, given him up to death, raised him from the dead, exalted him to his right hand, poured out on believers his Spirit, and established the *ekklēsia* as his body.[44] While Paul does speak of believing *in* Christ (Gal 2:16), for the most part he calls on others to believe not only in Christ but in *all* of the things God has done and will continue to do in and through Christ.

For this reason, the best translation of *pistis Christou* may simply be "Christ-faith."[45] In that case, it can be understood as a genitive of content. This is in fact how Paul uses the genitive in many other phrases, such as "the word of Christ" (Rom 10:17), "the witness of Christ" (1 Cor 1:6), "the revelation of Jesus Christ" (Gal 1:12), "the hope of our Lord Jesus

---

43. In the words of Francis Watson, "The 'faith' in question pertains to Christ, differentiating it from non-Christian varieties of faith while leaving the precise nature of that pertinence unspecified" (*Paul and the Hermeneutics of Faith*, 2nd ed. [London: Bloomsbury T & T Clark, 2016], xliii-xliv).

44. See Rom 4:25; 5:5; 8:3, 9, 29, 32; 1 Cor 12:27; Gal 4:4.

45. A growing number of Pauline interpreters seem to be proposing a third alternative to the understandings of *pistis Christou* as either "faith in Christ" (objective genitive) or "the faith(fulness) of Christ" (subjective genitive), often claiming that the genitive *Christou* is best taken as simply referring to the faith that pertains to Christ in some way. See, for example, Francis Watson, *Paul, Judaism, and the Gentiles: Beyond the New Perspective* (Grand Rapids: Eerdmans, 2007), 243-44; Ryan S. Schellenberg, "οἱ πιστεύοντες: An Early Christ-Group Self-Designation and Paul's Rhetoric of Faith," *NTS* 65 (2019): 33-42 (40-41); Michael Wolter, *Paul: An Outline of His Theology*, trans. Robert L. Brawley (Waco, TX: Baylor University Press, 2015), 75-77; Benjamin Schliesser, "'Christ-faith' as an Eschatological Event (Galatians 3.23-26): A 'Third View' on Πίστις Χριστοῦ," *JSNT* 38 (2016): 277-300; Garwood P. Anderson, *Paul's New Perspective: Charting a Soteriological Journey* (Downers Grove, IL: InterVarsity, 2016), 149-50; Gupta, *Paul*, 171-76.

Christ" (1 Thess 1:3), and "the knowledge of Christ Jesus" (Phil 3:8). All of these phrases are clearly objective genitives and refer to the word, witness, revelation, and hope *concerning* Christ that revolves around him as God's Son. Likewise, "the proclamation (*kērygma*) of Jesus Christ" (Rom 16:25) is clearly the proclamation *concerning* Christ, just as "the gospel of Christ" is the gospel *about* Christ.[46] Of course, such an understanding of these phrases does not exclude the possibility that Paul also had in mind a subjective genitive when he used them, since he no doubt believed that the word, witness, revelation, hope, knowledge, proclamation, and gospel that he shared with the world were the same ones that Christ himself had shared with all in his own lifetime. In fact, part of the gospel proclamation was that Christ had indeed remained faithful and obedient to God throughout his life all the way to his death (Rom 5:19; Phil 2:6-8). For Paul, however, the way in which Christ's faithfulness and obedience to God all the way to his death have led to the salvation of others is not that others have come to participate in that faithfulness and obedience in some mystical or mysterious fashion or simply through imitation. Rather, that faithfulness and obedience led God to raise Christ and exalt him as Lord so as to bring about through him the *ekklēsia*, in which all are now committed to living under Christ's lordship in the same faith, faithfulness, love, obedience, and righteousness seen in him.

When Paul speaks of "the righteousness of God through the faith of Jesus Christ for all who believe" in Rom 3:22, he probably has in mind the righteous way of living in conformity with God's will that is brought about in believers as a result of their faith regarding all that God has done and will continue to do through Christ. God justifies those who are *ek pisteōs Iēsou* (Rom 3:26; Gal 2:16) in the sense that he regards as righteous those who base their lives on that same "Jesus-faith," which constitutes the source or origin of the new righteous way of living that God graciously brings about in them as a gift.[47] The means by which people are led to live in the way God desires and commands so as to be declared righteous and forgiven by him is thus not their submission to the Mosaic law but their faith concerning Christ as the one in whom all of God's promises are fulfilled (Gal 2:16; 3:21-22). In Paul's thought, then, the righteousness of God is brought about through Christ-faith.

---

46. See Rom 15:19; 1 Cor 9:12; 2 Cor 9:13; Gal 1:7; Phil 1:27; 1 Thess 3:2.

47. Thus Wolter, for example, affirms that Paul interpreted "the central mark of Christian identity, 'Christ-faith,' as a 'behavior' on the basis of which God declares a person *just*" (*Paul*, 396).

Justification and God's Judgment

On the basis of what we have seen in this chapter, Paul does not understand justification in terms of acquittal. When God justifies believers, he does not declare them to be sinless, innocent, or free of guilt but merely acknowledges that they are committed to living in conformity with his will and on that basis overlooks their sins. At the same time, God himself is active to bring about that conformity to his will and righteousness as a gift, and he does so through the faith which he also graciously gives to believers by creating it in them. From beginning to end, their salvation as well as all that God brings about in them is a free gift of God rather than anything they obtain through their own merits or efforts. They are "justified as a gift by his grace through the redemption that is in Christ Jesus" (Rom 3:24) in that, through Christ and by pure grace, God redeems them both from their previous way of living and from the condemnation that results from that way of living so as to bring about in them the new life of righteousness that is in accordance with his will. Justified as a result of the life that proceeds from their faith (*ek pisteōs*), they now have peace with God through Christ and obtain access to God and his grace through that faith (Rom 5:1-2). Because this life of righteousness is the work of God in them rather than their own work, they can have full assurance of their salvation as long as they look to God alone to bring about the way of life necessary for them to attain the well-being and wholeness God desires to see in them for their own good. Rather than depending on their own efforts or strength, they put their faith, trust, and confidence solely in God, knowing that because he loves them and desires their salvation he will accomplish in them the transformation necessary to make that salvation a reality.

In Paul's thought, therefore, to be justified is simply to be *declared righteous*. While of course God also brings believers to live righteously and in that sense can be said to *make* them righteous, when Paul speaks of justification, for the most part he has in mind not the process of transformation that takes in place in believers but rather the result of that process, namely, God's acceptance of those who are undergoing that transformation.[48] For the same reason, it is not necessary to use terms such as "rectify," "rightwise," or "righteous" as verbs to translate the Greek verb *dikaioun*, since the meaning of this verb is expressed perfectly well by the English verb "to justify" in the sense of "to accept as righteous."[49]

---

48. This point is rightly stressed by Stephen Westerholm: "One is dikaios ('righteous,' 'upright'; Gk. *dikaios*) when one does dikaiosness—when, in other words, one lives as one ought and does what one should. To be dikaiosified (*dikaiousthai*) is, in effect, to be given the treatment appropriate to one who is dikaios...." (*Perspectives Old and New on Paul: The "Lutheran" Paul and His Critics* [Grand Rapids: Eerdmans, 2004], 272).

49. On the use of these verbs as replacements for the verb "to justify," see Michael F. Bird, *The Saving Righteousness of God: Studies on Paul, Justification, and the New Perspective,*

Once it becomes clear that God's gift to believers consists not only of faith and the forgiveness of sins but the righteous way of living that he brings about in them *through* the faith he creates in them, most of the difficulties commonly associated with Paul's teaching that all will be judged on the basis of their works disappear. In accordance with Jewish thought, the reason why Paul maintains that God will judge all by their works is that those works reveal what is in their heart. Paul himself mentions this idea when describing God's judgment. In Rom 2:6-16, where he affirms that God will "repay to each according to one's deeds," he contrasts "those who have sought glory and honor and immortality by persevering in doing what is good" with "those who act out of selfishness and do not obey the truth but instead persist in injustice" (vv. 7-8). If gentiles are able to "do instinctively what the law requires," it is because by nature what the law commands is written on their hearts, conscience, and thoughts (vv. 14-15). According to Paul, God "will judge through Jesus Christ the hidden secrets of all people" (v. 16). Several verses later, Paul adds that it is those Jews who keep the law, live as Jews inwardly, and possess the spiritual circumcision of the heart who obtain commendation from God (Rom 2:27-29). Paul's idea, then, is that what God sees when he looks at the hearts and the works of people makes it evident to him whether they are committed to doing what is good and right in accordance with his will as he has made it known in the law.[50]

Other passages from Paul's epistles reflect the same idea. When he thanks God that the Roman believers have become obedient to the teaching given them, he stresses that they have become "obedient *from the heart*" (Rom 6:17). In Rom 8:27, he speaks of God as "the one who searches the hearts of human beings." Similarly, after alluding to Christ's judging activity and his second coming in 1 Cor 4:3-5, Paul adds that Christ "will bring to light the things now hidden in darkness and will disclose the purposes of the heart. Then each one will receive commendation from God." In 1 Thess 3:13, he expresses to the believers in Thessalonica his desire that God and the Lord Jesus "strengthen your hearts so that they may be blameless in holiness before God our Father at the coming of our Lord Jesus with all his holy ones." Here it is not the *behavior* of believers that is blameless but their *heart*. Of course, as Paul also states here, it is God and Christ who graciously give believers such a heart and strengthen it in them. It is therefore not something that believers produce in themselves on their own but rather something produced in them by God and Christ through faith.

PBM (Milton Keynes: Paternoster, 2007), 6; E. P. Sanders, *Paul: The Apostle's Life, Letters, and Thought* (Minneapolis: Fortress, 2015), 505-7; J. Louis Martyn, *Galatians: A New Translation with Introduction and Commentary*, AB 33A (New York: Doubleday, 1997), 249-50.

50. On this point, see Yinger, *Paul*, 158-61, 181, 289-91.

Once again, however, it is important to stress the intrinsic relation between faith, righteousness, and salvation in Paul's thought. The reason why faith enables believers to be righteous and attain the salvation promised by God is that such faith is the cause, origin, basis, and source of the type of life that makes wholeness, well-being, and salvation possible. Such faith *produces* and *generates* all of the different behaviors that Paul exhorts his readers to make their own as its fruit (2 Cor 9:10; Phil 1:11). These behaviors in turn make it possible for believers to experience the righteousness, peace, and joy that Paul associates with God's reign (Rom 14:17). Only those whose lives are characterized by such behavior can experience the well-being and wholeness that will exist in the life to come.

Conversely, when Paul affirms that those who practice the types of behavior he condemns cannot inherit God's reign, it is important to capture his logic.[51] Paul's idea is not simply that those who practice such things *will* not inherit that reign because God will condemn them, but more importantly that they *cannot* inherit that reign because their behavior would make it impossible for them and others to experience the justice, peace, and joy that will characterize that reign. In Paul's thought, the reason that God will condemn those who refuse to submit to his will is not located in his own righteous nature per se but rather in the nature of the world to come: God condemns them, not because his righteous nature does not let him tolerate them on account of their sinfulness and impurity, but rather because the nature of life in the world to come does not allow for the kind of behavior that is contrary to the well-being of all. Paul's idea, therefore, is not so much that salvation depends on God's approval but rather that God's approval of people depends on his seeing in them the way of life that makes their salvation possible.[52]

Thus, just as there is a *reason* why faith saves, for Paul there is also a reason why unbelief prevents people from being saved. Faith in God leads to the righteous way of life necessary for people to live in the type of relation with God and others that will allow them to experience the blessings of the world to come. In contrast, those who do not live out of faith and trust in

---

51. See 1 Cor 6:9-10; Rom 1:18, 32; 2:2-4; 8:8; Gal 5:19-21; 6:7-8; 1 Thess 4:3-6.

52. To affirm that in Paul's thought this way of life "makes their salvation possible" is by no means to claim that he believed that it was *impossible* for God to save human beings without Christ or his death, as later Christian theology came to affirm. Like other Jews of his day, Paul would have maintained that nothing is impossible for God. For that reason, the later theological discussions among Christians regarding the necessity of Christ and his death for human salvation would probably have seemed extremely odd to Paul. When Paul states that, by sending his Son, God has accomplished through him what was "impossible for the law" (Rom 8:3-4), there is no reason to suppose that he intended this impossibility in a categorical sense, as if the sending of his Son had made it possible for God to do something that he could not have done otherwise or in some other way.

God will not live the type of life that will allow them to experience those blessings. It is therefore not unbelief in itself that prevents people from being saved and leads God to condemn them, but the life of sin and injustice that results from unbelief. If the world to come is to be characterized by things such as justice, righteousness, joy, peace, well-being, harmony, wholeness, and everlasting bliss, those who insist on living and behaving in ways that destroy these things cannot be admitted into that life. How can love and harmony coexist with hatred and enmity? How can communion and fellowship coexist with strife, envy, bitterness, arrogance, deceitfulness, rivalry, or aggressive and abusive behavior? Or in the words of Paul himself, "What fellowship can there be between righteousness and wickedness? Or how can there be communion between light and darkness? What harmony can exist between Christ and Beliar? Or what can a believer have in common with an unbeliever?" (2 Cor 6:14-15). The idea that Paul expresses here is not that there *should* not be fellowship, communion, and common ground between light and darkness or Christ and Beliar, but rather that these things *cannot* exist together. Where light shines, darkness does not exist. Where there is belief, there cannot be unbelief at the same time. By definition, those who are committed to righteousness cannot also be dedicated to sin and injustice, just as those who are dedicated to sin and injustice cannot by definition be committed to righteousness and justice.

In Paul's thought, it is this commitment to righteousness that the law demands for the good of all. On this basis he can affirm that "it is not those who merely hear the law who are accepted as righteous by God but those who do the law who will be justified" (Rom 2:13). To do the law is to practice righteousness, and this righteousness constitutes the basis upon which people are justified, even though it is not of course perfect.

As Paul himself states in Phil 3:4-9, where he claims to have lived blamelessly according to the law and speaks of having attained a certain type of righteousness by doing so, there is a kind of righteousness that one can attain through observance of the law, even though this righteousness is not the same as that which comes through Christ-faith (*pistis Christou*).[53] Paul also refers to "the righteousness that results from the law" in Rom 10:5. In fact, in Gal 5:3-4, Paul seems to affirm that such a righteousness can also lead to justification. There he tells the Galatians: "I witness again to all who submit to circumcision that they are under obligation to do the whole law. Those of you who would be justified through the law have cut yourselves off from Christ; you have fallen away from grace." It is commonly claimed that, when Paul speaks here of the possibility of being justified by means of the law, he regards such a possibility as existing only in theory. The

---

53. As Sanders observes with regard to Paul's thought in Phil 3:6-11, for Paul righteousness by the law "is possible and is a good thing in and of itself...." (*Paul: The Apostle's Life*, 610).

Galatians may *seek* to be justified by means of the law, but they will not succeed.[54] However, such an interpretation raises difficulties for Paul's affirmation that those who submit to circumcision are under obligation to do the whole law. In light of what we have seen previously, Paul cannot mean that once circumcised they must then observe the rest of the commandments of the Mosaic law in order to be justified and saved, since for Paul such observance is not a condition for the justification and salvation of either Jewish or gentile believers in Christ. It therefore seems more likely that Paul means that, by submitting fully to the observance of the law, including the commandment to be circumcised, the Galatians may attain a certain righteousness that may even enable them to be justified, but that righteousness will be only that which comes from observing the law rather than that which God gives by grace through Christ-faith, namely, the righteousness of God of which Paul speaks. The distinction between these two forms of righteousness would therefore be the same that Paul mentions in passages such as Rom 9:30–10:10 and Phil 3:9, where he recognizes that there is a righteousness that can be attained through the law. In Gal 5:4, Paul's idea may also be that those who submit to circumcision are under obligation to do the whole law, not in order to be declared righteous by God, but rather to gain the acceptance they seek within the Jewish community.

While Paul repeatedly insists that the righteousness that God desires to see in all is brought about through Christ rather than the law, however, nowhere does he ever affirm explicitly that only those who believe in Christ will be saved in the end. In fact, his words in Rom 2:6-16 suggest that there are both Jews and gentiles who will attain the glory, honor, and peace of the life of the age to come simply by doing good, avoiding evil, and obeying the truth rather than wickedness (vv. 7-10). In Paul's thought, people who live in that way can be received into the life of the world to come even if they do not know Christ or believe in him, because their commitment to what is good, right, and just will enable them to share in that life without destroying the well-being of others. Paul may have believed that at the *eschaton* those who had lived in that way independently of faith in Christ will come to acknowledge Christ's lordship and live under that lordship, as Phil 2:9-11 implies. The reason why he proclaims the gospel concerning Christ, therefore, is not that only those who believe in Christ and the gospel can be saved, but that it is through Christ and the gospel that the wholeness, well-being, and righteousness that God desires

---

54. Thus Martinus C. de Boer, for example, argues that *hoitines en nomō dikaiousthe* should be translated: "You are seeking to be justified," since in light of Gal 3:11 "Paul clearly does not mean to suggest that the Galatians are in fact being justified in the realm of the law. . . ." (*Galatians: A Commentary*, NTL [Louisville: Westminster John Knox, 2011], 314).

for all is given in its fullness.[55] As Paul insists in Phil 3:7-9, there are other forms of righteousness in the world, but none can compare to that which comes through Christ. While like many Jews Paul probably believed that all people who live righteously will in the end be saved by God, at the same time he was convinced that those who did not come to faith in Christ would never know in this life the peace, joy, and wholeness that he had found in Christ. In his words, "But whatever things were gain to me, these I now consider loss on account of Christ. More than that, I regard everything as loss because of the surpassing value of knowing Christ Jesus my Lord, on whose account I have suffered the loss of all things and consider them rubbish in order that I may gain Christ" (Phil 3:7-8).

When Paul rejects the notion that one can be justified by works of the law, therefore, he is not rejecting the idea that people can attain a certain level of righteousness in life by observing the law and on the basis of such a life be declared righteous by God in the end. Rather, what he is rejecting is the idea that simply doing the works that the law prescribes without living in faith makes one righteous and constitutes sufficient grounds for justification. In other words, the mere observance of commandments regarding things such as circumcision, the Sabbath, and the distinctions between pure and impure does not make one righteous or enable one to be justified, even though the observance of those things may help promote a life of righteousness that can lead to one's justification, as long as such observance is grounded in true faith.

In that case, what Paul denies in passages such as Rom 3:20, 28, and Gal 2:16-17 is not that the observance of the law can help promote a life of righteousness or that such a life can constitute the basis for one's justification, but rather that simply observing commandments in itself without living out of the faith of which he speaks constitutes righteousness and leads to justification. In other words, one is justified by faith apart from the works of the law because true righteousness is brought about by faith in God rather than by works of the law independently of such faith. On this point, Paul would be in agreement with traditional Jewish teaching rather than contradicting it. There is no reason to suppose that Paul believed that his fellow Jews who did not come to faith in Christ yet were nevertheless committed to practicing justice and righteousness in their daily life as a result of their faith in the God of Israel were not regarded by God as righteous or were condemned by God as unrighteous simply because they did not believe in Jesus. Nor is there any reason to think that Paul would have denied that Jews who did not believe in Jesus could nevertheless believe in

---

55. If salvation is understood in this way (see above, Chapter 2), then the desire Paul expresses in Rom 10:1 would be that in the end his fellow Israelites attain through Christ the well-being and wholeness God desires for all. Such would also be the expectation he mentions in Rom 11:26 (cf. 11:14).

God and entrust their lives to him so as to live in ways that pleased him. The same could be said of non-Jews as well. Paul no doubt knew many Jews and non-Jews who lived righteously and would meet the criteria he mentions in Rom 2:6-16 in order to be justified and saved when the end came. When Paul insists that people will be justified through Christ-faith and not by works of the law, therefore, he is not questioning the idea that works of the law are good and can help promote righteous living. Instead, he is simply insisting that gentiles who live out of Christ-faith can be righteous without observing the works that the Mosaic law prescribes, since it is not those works but a life of faith that leads one to live righteously and on that basis be accepted by God as righteous.

CHAPTER 8

Redefining the Basis for God's Forgiveness

Because in Second Temple Jewish thought not even the righteous could live entirely without sin, it was necessary for all of God's people continually to acknowledge their sinfulness, repent of it, and ask God for forgiveness. The basis upon which they were thought to attain that forgiveness was their renewed commitment to living in accordance with God's will as he had made it known through the Torah. At the same time, the Torah prescribed sacrificial rites through which those who had sinned might manifest their repentance and seek God's forgiveness.

According to many reconstructions of Second Temple Jewish thought, it was believed that under normal circumstances atonement for sins was always necessary in order to obtain God's forgiveness. While atonement could be made through the sacrifices for sin prescribed by God in the Mosaic law, the sufferings and death of a righteous person could also atone for the sins of others. These beliefs supposedly led Jesus' earliest followers to interpret his death as sacrificial and to claim that his sufferings, death, and blood had made atonement for the sins of human beings collectively. It is widely accepted that this interpretation of Jesus' death is found in numerous passages from Paul's epistles, which affirm that Jesus died for others and for their sins, thereby redeeming them from those sins and reconciling them to God.[1]

When we take a close look at the relevant texts from antiquity, however, it soon becomes evident that many of the ideas upon which the traditional interpretations of those texts are based are in reality foreign to them and have mistakenly been read back into them. Rather than ascribing some type of atoning power or effect to suffering, death, and sacrifice, those texts reflect the common Jewish idea that suffering, death, and sacrifice are

---

1. See Rom 3:24-25; 4:24-25; 5:6-11; 1 Cor 15:3; 2 Cor 5:14-21; Gal 1:4; 2:20; 3:13.

salvific and obtain God's acceptance and forgiveness only when they are the consequence or expression of a firm and sincere commitment to doing God's will and seeking to bring others to do the same.

ATONEMENT AND FORGIVENESS IN SECOND TEMPLE JEWISH THOUGHT

While many passages from the Hebrew Scriptures and Second Temple Jewish literature allude to the sacrificial rites prescribed in the Torah through which the people of Israel were to seek forgiveness and atonement, nowhere do those writings offer any explanation as to how those rites were believed to work. Nevertheless, rather than asking whether the authors of those writings did in fact believe that those sacrificial rites worked in some way, Jewish and Christian scholars have assumed that those who composed and read those writings had a fairly clear understanding of what is often called the *modus operandi*, "mechanics," or "mechanism" of sacrifice, but for some reason never explained what that understanding was.[2] This assumption has led them to overlook much of what those writings do say regarding the meaning and purpose of the sacrificial worship that they describe.

Several passages from the same writings are also thought to relate atonement or the forgiveness of sins to the suffering and death of the righteous. The most important of these passages is generally considered to be Isaiah 53, which we have already examined in Chapter 3 of this study. Two others are found in the book of 4 Maccabees, which uses sacrificial language to speak of the sufferings and death of certain Jews at the hands of the Seleucid king Antiochus IV Epiphanes.[3] Numerous scholars have also argued that Hellenistic and Roman writings of the Second Temple period reflect an understanding of vicarious death that influenced the thought of Jews such as Jesus' first followers either directly or indirectly.

The Meaning and Purpose of Sacrifices for Sin in Ancient Hebrew and Jewish Thought

Despite the many problems associated with it, among Christians the most common view of the manner in which the sacrifices for sin offered by Jews

---

2. On the use of terminology such as this to refer to Hebrew and Jewish sacrifice, see Jacob Milgrom, "The *Modus Operandi* of the *Ḥaṭṭā't*: A Rejoinder," *JBL* 109 (1990): 111-17; Christian Eberhart, "Opfer, Sühne und Stellvertretung im Alten Testament," in »... *mein Blut für Euch*«: *Theologische Perspektiven zum Verständnis des Todes Jesu heute*, ed. Michael Hüttenhoff, Wolfgang Kraus, and Karlo Meyer, BTS 38 (Göttingen: Vandenhoeck & Ruprecht, 2018), 40-55 (46-48); Stephen Finlan, *The Background and Content of Paul's Cultic Atonement Metaphors*, AcBib 19 (Atlanta: SBL, 2004), 190; James D. G. Dunn, *The Theology of Paul the Apostle* (Grand Rapids: Eerdmans, 1998), 218-19.

3. See 4 Macc 6:27-29; 17:20-22.

in antiquity were believed to make atonement for sin has been that which is based on the notion of penal substitution. While there are several variations of this view, the central idea is that the animals that were sacrificed to God endured in the place of those who offered them the suffering or death to which the offerers were subject on account of their sins, thereby freeing them from having to endure the penalty or consequences of their sins themselves.[4] Generally, it is claimed that when those who offered up an animal as a sacrifice for sin laid their hands upon the animal prior to the sacrifice, they were transferring to it their sins or guilt. The blood of the slaughtered animal was subsequently sprinkled or poured out before God to demonstrate that the necessary penalty had been inflicted upon it in the place of the guilty.[5] In this way, God's wrath at the sin committed was propitiated.[6] The ritual with the goat for Azazel prescribed for the Day of Atonement in Lev 16:20-22 is interpreted in the same basic manner. By laying his hands on the goat as he confessed the sins of the people, the high priest transferred those sins to the goat. When the goat was then led out to the desert to die, it took with it the sins that had been laid upon it.[7] Supposedly, in this way, atonement was made for those sins, which were borne away by the goat.

These interpretations of the sacrificial rites for sin prescribed in the Mosaic law raise numerous problems. They suggest that God had established the sacrificial system primarily so that his sinful people might be delivered from the punishments they deserved on account of their sins. In reality, such an idea is foreign to biblical thought. In the Torah, those who were subject to some type of punishment on account of their wrongdoing, including the death penalty, are never given the option of presenting a sacrifice in order to be spared that punishment. Nor were those who had sinned but failed to present a sacrifice for sin regarded as being subject to the death penalty due to that failure. In Hebrew and Jewish thought, God was always free to chastise or forgive sins whenever he saw fit in accordance with his

---

4. See, for example, Gordon J. Wenham, *The Book of Leviticus*, NICOT (Grand Rapids: Eerdmans, 1979), 62; Jay Sklar, *Sin, Impurity, Sacrifice, Atonement: The Priestly Conceptions*, HBM 2 (Sheffield: Sheffield Phoenix, 2005), 169-74; Allen P. Ross, *Holiness to the LORD: A Guide to the Exposition of the Book of Leviticus* (Grand Rapids: Baker Academic, 2002), 85-95, 131.

5. So, for example, Leon Morris: "what is ritually presented to God is the evidence that a death has taken place in accordance with his judgment upon sin" (*The Cross in the New Testament* [Grand Rapids: Eerdmans, 1965], 219).

6. According to Jarvis J. Williams, for example, behind the sacrificial rites prescribed in Leviticus is the idea that "bloody sacrifice actually satisfied God's wrath" (*Maccabean Martyr Traditions in Paul's Theology of Atonement: Did Martyr Theology Shape Paul's Conception of Jesus' Death?* [Eugene, OR: Wipf & Stock, 2010], 39-40).

7. So, for example, Roy Gane, *Cult and Character: Purification Offerings, Day of Atonement, and Theodicy* (Winona Lake, IN: Eisenbrauns, 2005), 243-46.

purposes, independently of whether or not any sacrifices were offered to him. Numerous passages from the Hebrew Scriptures speak of God forgiving people their sins without receiving any sacrifice.[8] The sacrificial system was therefore not regarded as a means for being spared divine punishment or penalties for one's sins. Nor do the prescriptions regarding sin offerings in the Torah ever speak of those offerings propitiating God's wrath.

According to Lev 5:11-13, those who were poor could offer up to God a measure of flour rather than an animal victim when making a sacrifice for sin. Those who did so were hardly thought to be inflicting on the flour the punishment that their sins deserved. In addition, if atonement could be made through a flour offering, then sacrificial death or blood was not necessary to make atonement for sins. Equally foreign to the prescriptions regarding sacrifice in the Torah is the notion that sin or guilt was transferred to the sacrificial animals to be presented to God. There is nothing in Leviticus 16 to suggest that the rite with the goat for Azazel was anything more than a symbolic act. Furthermore, the goat was not offered up as a sacrifice. Most of the sacrificial offerings presented to God, in fact, were not sacrifices for sin and thus did not have the objective of seeking forgiveness from God or making atonement.

More importantly, however, both the Hebrew Scriptures and the Jewish literature of the Second Temple period repeatedly insist that no sacrifice is pleasing or acceptable to God unless it is offered up with a pure heart and a sincere commitment to practicing the justice and righteousness that God commands in his law.[9] Unlike other gods in antiquity, the God of Israel did not need sacrifices or depend on them in any way and thus was not interested in simply receiving meat, fat, or other parts of the animal from those who offered sacrifice. Sacrifices for sin were acceptable to God only if they were offered up in a spirit of sincere and heartfelt repentance. It was universally acknowledged that those who had sinned deliberately and had no intention of repenting and living in obedience to God could not make

---

8. Gane, for example, notes that in the Hebrew Scriptures, "YHWH was able to forgive people apart from the sanctuary cult before it began to function (e.g., Exod 34:6, 7) and while it was in operation (e.g., 2 Sam 12:13; 2 Chr 33:12-13; cf. 30:18-19)" (*Cult and Character*, 316). Among the passages from the Hebrew Scriptures and Second Temple Jewish literature that speak of God forgiving sins without exacting punishment on people or receiving sacrificial offerings, see Num 11:1-2; 2 Chron 32:24-26; Prov 16:6; Isa 27:9; Dan 4:27; Jonah 3:8-10; Sir 3:3; 35:1-10; 48:10; Tob 12:9; Bar 2:7-14; Pss. Sol. 3:9; Sib. Or. 4:215; 1QS 3.7-10; 9.4-6.

9. See, for example, Ps 40:6-8; 50:7-18, 23; 51:16-19; Hos 8:11-13; Mic 6:6-8; Jdt 16:16; Sir 7:9-10; 35:1-9, 14-15; 2 En. 45:3; Philo, *Moses* 2.106-8; *Spec. Laws* 1.67-70, 171, 196-97, 203, 257-60, 269-86, 293; 2.35, 42; *QG* 1.61; 2.52; *Unchangeable* 8-9. On this point and what follows, see especially David A. Brondos, *Jesus' Death in New Testament Thought*, vol. 1: *Background* (Mexico City: Theological Community of Mexico, 2018), 125-201.

atonement and receive forgiveness for their sins by offering up the sacrifices for sin commanded by God, no matter how costly or lavish those sacrifices were.[10] In fact, sacrifices for sin that were not offered up with a repentant heart were thought to provoke God to wrath, since they could only be seen as an attempt to bribe God or manipulate him in order to obtain his forgiveness and blessings.[11] In passages such as Isa 1:11-17, Jer 7:1-15, and Amos 5:21-25, God is presented as refusing to accept the sacrifices of his people and even despising their sacrifices when they persistently practiced injustice and oppression.

For this reason, it is contrary to ancient Hebrew and Jewish thought to maintain that sacrifices were thought to "work" by virtue of some type of *modus operandi*. The only thing that could obtain God's forgiveness, make atonement, or put away God's wrath at sins was a renewed commitment to living in conformity with God's will. Where that commitment was not present, no sacrifice could please God or obtain his favor and forgiveness. Conversely, those who were truly repentant of their sins and approached God with a sincere heart and a renewed dedication to doing his will were always thought to be acceptable to God and attain his forgiveness, independently of whether or not they offered up a sacrifice for sin.[12] Naturally, it was expected that they do so if they were able, but only as an expression of the sincerity of their repentance and their commitment to obeying what God had commanded.

In Jewish thought, therefore, God had not established sacrifice as a means by which people might obtain forgiveness and make atonement for their sins simply by carrying out certain rites that would produce some salvific effect in and of themselves when accompanied by faith and repentance. Nor had God commanded the offering of sacrifice to satisfy a need on his part to receive some type of payment or inflict some type of penalty upon sinners, as if his holiness, justice, or righteousness prevented him from forgiving sins without such a payment or penalty.[13] The obstacle to God's forgiveness was thought to lie *not in God* but *in human beings themselves*, that is, in their refusal and failure to live in conformity with God's good will. What God sought in his holiness, justice, and righteousness was not that some type of penalty be inflicted on sin, as if this might set things right and solve the

---

10. On this point, see Jacob Milgrom, "Atonement in the OT," *IDBSup* 78-82 (79-81).

11. See, for example, 1 Sam 15:22-23; Prov 15:8; 21:27; Jer 11:14-15; 14:10-12; Mal 1:7-14; 2:13-15; Sir 34:23-24; 2 En. 46:1; Josephus, *Ant.* 6.147-48.

12. See, for example, Philo, *Moses* 2.108; *Spec. Laws* 1.271-72; Josephus, *Ant.* 6.149.

13. Such an idea is commonly defended on the basis of the notion that "the holiness of God cannot coexist with what is unholy, what is impure or 'unclean'" (Jo Bailey Wells, *God's Holy People: A Theme in Biblical Theology*, JSOTSup 305 [Sheffield: Sheffield Academic Press, 2000], 79).

problem of sin, but that his people return to him in obedience, righteousness, and love when they had sinned. Because only God could determine if such obedience, righteousness, and love were present in the hearts of those who approached him asking for forgiveness, sacrifices in themselves had no power to effect atonement. God had not placed himself under the obligation to forgive sins when sacrifices for sin were offered, since in each case it was necessary for him to determine whether those who offered such sacrifices were truly repentant and sufficiently committed to doing his will.

Many biblical scholars, of course, have proposed other understandings of the way in which sacrifices for sin were believed to make atonement for sins in ancient Jewish thought.[14] While it is neither possible nor necessary to review all of those proposals here, the same general observations would apply to them as well. Ultimately, what was thought to atone for sins was not the offering of sacrifice itself but the spirit of repentance and the renewed commitment to living in accordance with God's will that those who offered sacrifices for sin manifested by means of their sacrificial offerings. This rules out the possibility that some type of mechanics or *modus operandi* was thought to be involved, since even when sacrifices were offered to God with the proper spirit and inner disposition, neither sacrificial blood nor death in themselves were thought to effect some change in God, the status of those who offered them, or the places and objects involved in the rites.

Rather than seeing sacrifices for sin as something that God had prescribed because he was unable to forgive sins or accept sinners without such sacrifices, there is clear evidence that Jews in antiquity believed that God had prescribed sacrifice in order to promote the attitudes and conduct he desired to see in them for their own good. As we have seen in Chapter 2, such was thought to be the purpose of sacrifice in general. In the case of sacrifices for sin, by prescribing such sacrifices, God brought his people to examine and reflect upon their conduct, acknowledge their wrongdoing, and commit themselves anew to living in accordance with his commandments, *not for his sake*, but *for theirs*. The offering of sacrifice thus contributed to their well-being by promoting among them the way of life that was in their own best interest and leading them to leave behind the destructive attitudes and conduct that God had prohibited out of love for them.

Sacrifices for sin were therefore thought to take away sin by virtue of the change that they helped bring about in the hearts and lives of God's people. In addition to promoting repentance and the way of life God desired to see in them for their own good, those sacrifices served as means by which his people could manifest in visible and tangible ways their desire to be forgiven by God and their renewed commitment to living in the way he

---

14. See Brondos, *Jesus' Death*, 1:130-36, 172-85.

had commanded out of love for them. The sacrificial rites enabled them to reflect on the seriousness of their sins, to offer God a gift as a concrete and palpable expression of what was in their heart, and to be reassured that the God who had prescribed those rites for their benefit received them favorably whenever they approached him with a contrite spirit and a pure heart, offering themselves up to him by means of their sacrificial gifts.

It is also important to stress once more that sacrifices were first and foremost *embodied prayers*.[15] They were means by which people conveyed concretely the earnestness and sincerity of their petitions before God. Sacrifices for sin were therefore petitions that God forgive and accept once more those who presented them or those on whose behalf they were offered, looking favorably on their renewed commitment to live in accordance with his will. While offerings for sin might be thought to put away God's wrath, this was not because those offerings themselves were thought to placate him but rather because they served as means by which his people manifested the type of spirit and commitment to God's will that God desired and demanded of all for their own good. The sincere intention to return to a life of loving obedience to God was the only thing that could ever please and appease God when one had fallen into sin.

Vicarious Suffering and Death

Many scholars have claimed to find in various Jewish writings from antiquity the idea that the sacrificial suffering and death of a righteous person could make atonement for the sins of others. Chief among these writings is 4 Maccabees, which describes the tortures inflicted on the Jewish priest Eleazar, seven Jewish brothers, and their mother at the hands of Antiochus Epiphanes in an effort to bring the Jews in his reign to abandon their laws and adopt Hellenistic customs.[16] Rather than transgressing the Jewish law, all of these figures remain faithful in the midst of those tortures and ultimately suffer a violent death as a result of their refusal to submit to Antiochus's tyranny.

What is often overlooked by interpreters of 4 Maccabees is the purpose that the author ascribes to the afflictions of which the book speaks.[17] Those afflictions are not merely retribution for the people's sins. In fact, the only sin mentioned at the beginning of the book is that of the Jewish high priest Jason, who is said to have aroused God's anger by altering the customs

---

15. See Brondos, *Jesus' Death*, 1:145-55.

16. On the background and date of 4 Maccabees, see Jan Willem van Henten, "Datierung und Herkunft des Vierten Makkabäerbuches," in *Tradition and Re-Interpretation in Jewish and Early Christian Literature: Essays in Honour of Jürgen C. H. Lebram*, ed. Jan Willem van Henten et al., StPB 36 (Leiden: Brill, 1986), 136-49; David A. deSilva, *4 Maccabees* (Sheffield: Sheffield Academic Press, 1998), 11-32.

17. On what follows, see Brondos, *Jesus' Death*, 1:241-56.

and way of life of the Jewish people and abolishing the sacrificial worship offered to God at the Jerusalem temple.[18] Nevertheless, because the book repeatedly states that the perseverance of Eleazar, the seven brothers, and their mother in the midst of their sufferings strengthened the people's obedience to the law, it presupposes that the people needed to be brought into greater conformity with God's will as he had made it known in the law. This is what these figures are said to have accomplished through their perseverance unto death. The author praises Eleazar by telling him: "You, father, strengthened our loyalty to the law through your glorious endurance" (4 Macc 7:9). In the final chapter, the author once again points to the willingness of Eleazar, the brothers, and their mother to give up their lives for the sake of the law so as to affirm: "Because of them the nation achieved peace, and by renewing observance of the law in the homeland, they ravaged the enemy" (18:4; cf. 6:18-22; 16:14-25).[19]

These passages make it clear that, in the thought of the author of 4 Maccabees, God had allowed Antiochus to inflict such suffering on the figures he mentions in order to strengthen the people's resolve to observe the law. The author's argument is that their perseverance inspired other Jews to be willing to resist Antiochus as well since it demonstrated their unshakeable faith in the law's goodness and gave witness that it was better to die than to abandon the law. Clearly, it was this perseverance, faith, and witness that pleased God and led him eventually to deliver Israel from Antiochus's tyranny. Such an idea is stated explicitly in 4 Macc 9:23-24, where one of the brothers says: "Imitate me, brothers; do not abandon your post in my struggle or renounce the courage that is ours as brothers! Fight the sacred and noble battle for our godly way of life, through which the righteous providence of our ancestors will become merciful to our nation and take vengeance on the accursed tyrant!" According to these verses, what brings God to be merciful to his people and deliver them from Antiochus is the willingness of the brothers to remain steadfast in their struggle against Antiochus by refusing to give in to his demand that they abandon their observance of the law. The sufferings and death of those whom Antiochus had tortured and killed would hardly have been pleasing to God. Rather than appeasing his wrath, such deaths would have aroused his anger even more, though that anger would have been directed at Antiochus rather than at the figures whom he tortured and put to death.

---

18. On this point, see Jan Willem van Henten, *The Maccabean Martyrs as Saviours of the Jewish People: A Study of 2 and 4 Maccabees*, JSJSup 57 (Leiden: Brill, 1997), 185.

19. Because of this, while in one sense it can be said that the author of the book "hardly pays attention to the notion of disciplinary suffering," as van Henten does (*Maccabean Martyrs*, 140), in another sense the people's suffering undoubtedly has the purpose of bringing about in them a greater obedience to the law.

These ideas must be kept in mind when considering the two passages in which the author speaks of the deaths of Eleazar, the seven brothers, and their mother as vicarious. In 4 Macc 6:27-29, he ascribes to Eleazar the following words: "You know, O God, that rather than choosing to be saved from burning torments, I have elected to die for the sake of the law. Show mercy to your people by letting our suffering on their behalf suffice. Make my blood their purification and receive my life in exchange for theirs (*antipsychon autōn labe tēn emēn psychēn*)." In effect, what Eleazar is asking God here is that what he and others have suffered "suffice," not in the sense of satisfying God's justice or exhausting God's wrath, but in the sense of demonstrating to God that his purposes among the people had been accomplished so that he might put an end to Antiochus's tyranny in the land. Eleazar's perseverance not only served as sufficient evidence of the willingness of God's people to obey his law but would also inspire in others the same type of unbending obedience.[20] If that was the case, it was now pointless for God to allow Antiochus to continue to inflict suffering and torture on those who remained firm in their obedience to the law. Of course, because God alone could determine if what he had done was sufficient to bring about the obedience he desired to see in his people, Eleazar does not make any type of demand upon God but simply places himself in submission to God's will and phrases his desire as a petition, leaving it up to God to respond as he sees fit. Thus Eleazar and others are viewed as suffering on behalf of the people, not in the sense that their suffering in itself led God to put away his wrath or satisfied his justice, but in the sense that their faithfulness to the law in the midst of that suffering strengthened the obedience of others to the law for their own good.[21] Only this could appease God and satisfy his justice.[22]

Similarly, when Eleazar asks God to make his blood the purification of others, he is not asking that by virtue of his death God declare all the Jews in the land to be pure and free of sin. Eleazar was not praying that God accept his righteousness in the stead of others, nor would God have responded favorably to such a petition, since what God wanted was that *all*

---

20. In this regard, David Seeley writes: "By inspiring others to re-enact their resistance they create an implacable barrier to Antiochus's efforts, sending him finally on his way" (*The Noble Death: Graeco-Roman Martyrology and Paul's Concept of Salvation*, JSNTSup 28 [Sheffield: JSOT, 1990], 93).

21. The idea that the law is good is especially stressed in 4 Macc 5:22-26, where the author argues that the law teaches and promotes things such as self-control, courage, endurance, justice, and what is most suitable for their lives. It is therefore an expression of God's compassion toward his people.

22. As Sam K. Williams notes, "the most significant aspect of the martyrs' endurance unto death is the author's assertions concerning the *effects* of that endurance" (*Jesus' Death as Saving Event: The Background and Origin of a Concept*, HDR 2 [Missoula, MT: Scholars Press, 1975], 167).

of his people practice righteousness for their own good, not that a single individual do so in the place of others. The purification of the people that Eleazar sought should also not be seen as merely forensic, as if Eleazar were asking God simply to *accept* others as pure without their *becoming* so. This is clear from the way in which the author uses the language of purification both at the beginning of the book and at its end. In the book's introduction, the author says of the figures who remained faithful in the midst of tortures and death: "For when they had won the admiration of all the people, including even their torturers, for their courage and endurance, they became the cause of the downfall of tyranny over the nation, conquering the tyrant through their endurance. In that way, their native land was purified through them" (4 Macc 1:11). Near the end of the book, the author says of the same figures: "These, therefore, having consecrated themselves for the sake of God, have been honored not only with this honor but also in that, because of them, our nation was not overcome by its enemies, but the tyrant was punished and the native land was purified" (17:20-21).

In both of these passages, the purification of which the author speaks involves the reestablishment throughout the land of the observance of the law together with the virtues it promotes (1:7-19; 17:8-24).[23] Of course, the land was also purified from the presence of the people's enemies, yet the author makes it clear that God drove Antiochus and his army out of the land on account of the endurance of those who persevered in their obedience to the law. Eleazar's petition that God make his blood the purification of others, therefore, should be understood in the sense that he is asking God that his willingness to suffer and die a cruel death for the sake of the law not be in vain, but instead bring God to put an end to Antiochus's persecution and drive him out of the land so that its inhabitants might be able to live in peace, practicing faithfully what God had commanded in his law now that their obedience had been demonstrated and strengthened.[24]

Eleazar's petition that God receive his life in exchange for that of the people or as their *antipsychon* should be understood on the basis of these same ideas. In the mind of the book's author, what interested God was not

---

23. Brian J. Tabb rightly points out that the author of 4 Maccabees "employs the cultic terms *purification* (καθάρσιος) and *purify* (καθαρίζω) to indicate the reversal of Israel's moral and ceremonial uncleanness" (*Suffering in Ancient Worldview: Luke, Seneca, and 4 Maccabees in Dialogue*, LNTS 569 [London: Bloomsbury T & T Clark, 2017], 111).

24. Sam Williams rightly stresses that 4 Maccabees sees Antiochus's departure from the land as "a result of the martyrs' *endurance* (not their spilled blood)" (*Jesus' Death*, 176). It should also be stressed, however, that when the author of the book refers to the blood of Eleazar in 6:29, he has in mind his endurance unto death rather than the shedding of Eleazar's blood per se, since it is Eleazar's endurance that leads to the purification of which the author speaks.

the taking of the life of Eleazar as retribution for the people's sins, as if God merely sought to exact punishment and satisfy his wrath by inflicting death on Eleazar as the people's substitute. Rather, what God sought was that the people be strengthened in their obedience to the law. Because it was for that purpose alone that he had subjected them to suffering, nothing but the accomplishment of that purpose could have brought him to put an end to that suffering. Thus Eleazar is said to present his life to God asking that in return or in exchange for his life—or rather, strictly speaking, in response to his faithfulness unto death to God's good commandments—, God spare his fellow Jews any more cruel sufferings and agonizing deaths such as the one that he is enduring. His hope is that God will react to his willingness to give up his life for the law by putting an end to the people's afflictions at the hands of Antiochus so that their lives may be spared from his tyranny. The reason why God will react in that way is not that he has satisfied his wrath and justice by taking Eleazar's life but rather that Eleazar's death will be sufficient for God's objectives among the people to be accomplished. Eleazar asks God, therefore, that in response to his willingness to give up his life, God intervene to put an end to the afflictions he had imposed on his people in order to chastise and correct them. Only in that sense is there any type of exchange.

The same ideas are behind the observations that the author makes in 4 Macc 17:22. After affirming that Antiochus was overcome and the land was purified by means of those who gave up their lives out of obedience to the law (17:20-21), the author continues: "It was as if they had given up their lives in exchange for the sin of the nation (*hōsper antipsychon gegonotas tēs tou ethnous hamartias*). And by virtue of the blood of these pious persons and the propitiation (*hilastērion*) that they made in their death, the divine providence rescued Israel from what it had been suffering previously" (4 Macc 17:20-22). In this passage, which is extremely difficult to translate into English, the author once again refers to those who endured suffering on account of their faithfulness to God's law as an *antipsychon*. This term is often translated as "ransom," yet such a translation supposes that their lives constituted a payment made *to* someone—in this case God—in order to free others. Nothing in the passage or the book in general, however, suggests that God was demanding the lives of those tortured and killed as payment for the liberation of the people, in exchange for the people's lives, or as punishment for their sins. What satisfied God was not the deaths of those who remained faithful to his law but rather the renewed obedience that would exist in the land as a result of the faithfulness of those who had died for the law once Antiochus had been driven out.

The author's idea, therefore, is that those who gave up their lives for the sake of the law obtained in exchange (*anti-*) for their faithfulness and perseverance the deliverance of the people from the plight that they were suffering on account of their sin. Once again, however, what concerned God was not that the people's sin receive its due punishment but that they be strengthened and renewed in their commitment to obeying his law. Only this could satisfy him. In other words, what those who gave up their lives for the law obtained from God for the people in exchange for their lives was not the forgiveness of the people's sins per se, but the deliverance of the people from the plight to which God had subjected them in an attempt to bring them to put away their sins. And what led God to deliver them from that plight was not the death or blood of those who died, but the renewed commitment to his will that the death or blood of those who died made possible among the people. What God is interested in receiving from Eleazar, the brothers, and the mother was not their life, death, or blood, but rather their unbending faithfulness to the law, since that faithfulness would bring others to be faithful to the law in the same way for their own good.[25]

Interpreters have debated whether the word *hilastērion* in the final verse of this passage should be translated as "expiation" or "propitiation."[26] If the first of these translations is preferred, the idea is that, through their perseverance in remaining faithful to the law, those who gave up their lives cleansed or purified their people from their sinfulness so that God might deliver them from the suffering to which he had subjected them in an effort to strengthen them in their obedience to his law. If God came to *accept* them as clean or pure, it was because the willingness of their fellow Jews to give up their lives for the law served to demonstrate that the people were indeed committed to living in the type of purity God desired to see in all and would help to bring about in the people that same pure way of life. If *hilastērion* is instead understood in the sense of propitiation, then what must be seen as having appeased God's wrath at the people's sins was not the blood or death of Eleazar, the brothers, and their mother per se, but their faithfulness to the law even to the point of being willing to suffer and endure a violent and bloody death for it. The *hilastērion* that put away God's wrath and led to the purification of the people was not their *death* but their *faithfulness unto death.*

Perhaps the simplest way to demonstrate that it was not the sufferings and death of the figures who endured torture at the hands of Antiochus that made atonement for the people's sins or brought God to forgive them is to consider whether God would have delivered the people from the suffering

---

25. This point is rightly stressed by Francis Watson, who notes that the book's argument does not revolve around the suffering of the Jewish people or atonement for sin, but the strengthening of the people's obedience to the law ("Constructing an Antithesis: Pauline and Other Jewish Perspectives on Divine and Human Agency," in *Divine and Human Agency in Paul and His Cultural Environment,* ed. John M. G. Barclay and Simon J. Gathercole [London: T & T Clark, 2006], 99-116 [108-15]).

26. On this discussion, see Sam Williams, *Jesus' Death,* 39-46.

that he had brought upon them through Antiochus if those figures had not remained faithful to the law all the way to their death. If all that concerned God was that the people's sins be punished, then it would not have mattered to God if Eleazar, the brothers, and their mother had transgressed the law in the midst of their tortures, because even if they had, God's demand that the people's sins receive their due punishment would still have been satisfied by their torments and death. Such is clearly not the thought of the author of 4 Maccabees. Similarly, even if Eleazar, the mother, and her sons had remained steadfast and faithful to the law all the way to their death, their death would not have attained God's forgiveness for the people if the people themselves had refused to turn away from their sin and had instead persisted in disobeying God and his law. It is therefore a grave misrepresentation of Jewish thought to affirm on the basis of these passages, as Howard Marshall does, that "when people fall into sin and apostasy they arouse the wrath of Yahweh. He proceeds to punish them, and on the completion of the punishment his anger is satisfied and he is reconciled to the people."[27] If that were the case, then simply inflicting death on people as punishment for their sins would put away God's wrath and satisfy his justice, independently of whether or not any of them came to live in the way God commanded and desired for their own good. Like a pagan deity, God would simply be venting his wrath for his own sake rather than attempting to bring about a change in his people by chastising them.

Neither of these passages from 4 Maccabees, then, provides any basis for the claim that in ancient Jewish thought suffering and death could atone for sins or put away God's wrath.[28] In ancient Hebrew and Jewish thought, reconciliation is never brought about by punishment alone, since by definition only those who live in a way that makes peace possible can be reconciled to God and one another. Suffering and death only appeased God's wrath and obtained his forgiveness when they served as means by which people were brought to return to God in obedience and righteousness, yet even then it was that obedience and righteousness rather than the suffering or death of anyone that pleased God and brought him to grant his forgiveness. Similarly, only a renewed commitment to live in conformity with God's will could atone for sins.

A number of Greco-Roman sources with which many Jews in antiquity would have been acquainted also allude to vicarious suffering and death.[29]

---

27. I. Howard Marshall, "The Meaning of Reconciliation," in *Unity and Diversity in New Testament Theology: Essays in Honor of George E. Ladd*, ed. Robert A. Guelich (Grand Rapids: Eerdmans, 1978), 121.

28. For a discussion of other passages from ancient Jewish sources that speak of vicarious death, see Brondos, *Jesus' Death*, 1:231-40, 256-77.

29. For references, see especially Martin Hengel, *The Atonement: The Origins of the Doctrine in the New Testament* (Philadelphia: Fortress, 1981), 6-28; van Henten,

In some cases, what is actually vicarious and benefits others is what we have just seen in 4 Maccabees: the willingness of someone to suffer and die in order to bring others to value and adhere to certain principles, values, or laws that are in accordance with what is good, right, and just. The example *par excellence* of this type of death is that of Socrates, who took his own life not only for the purposes just mentioned but also to avoid any kind of violent uprising in his defense that might result in the death of many.[30] This kind of death, of course, did not atone for anyone's sins. In other cases, those sources speak of persons sacrificing their lives for others or suffering and dying for them in the context of a battle or struggle against an oppressive enemy. Once again, such sacrificial sufferings and deaths had nothing to do with atonement for sins, but were simply aimed at obtaining victory over the enemy and liberating the oppressed from their oppressors.

There are numerous examples in ancient Greco-Roman literature, however, of persons offering up their lives to certain gods in the place of others in order to fulfill some demand being made by those gods, obtain their favor, or appease their wrath at something that the people had done or failed to do. As we have seen previously, however, Israel's God was believed to be fundamentally different from those gods. In Jewish thought, the only thing that could please God was that the people practice goodness, justice, and mercy, caring especially for the oppressed and those in need. In contrast, the gods of the nations desired and demanded sacrificial offerings for their own sake and at times even demanded the life of human beings to satisfy their selfish impulses and whims. Unlike Israel's God, they often took pleasure in seeing human beings suffer and die, and therefore at times the death of one individual as a substitute for others was acceptable to them. In those cases, what interested them was simply receiving a human life or human blood, independently of whose life or blood it might be. Furthermore, what angered and offended those gods was not injustice and oppression but the failure of human beings to give them what they wanted or needed for their own sake. Such gods were very different from Israel's God, not merely because nothing but the practice of what was good, right, and compassionate could satisfy and appease him, but also because he abhorred and prohibited the sacrifice of human life and took no pleasure whatsoever in the suffering and death of any human being, including those who were sinners (Ezek 18:23, 32).

Maccabean Martyrs, 145-46, 156-59, 213-24, 245-50; Henk S. Versnel, "Making Sense of Jesus' Death: The Pagan Contribution," in *Deutungen des Todes Jesu im Neuen Testament*, ed. Jörg Frey and Jens Schröter, WUNT 181 (Tübingen: Mohr Siebeck, 2005), 213-94 (227-53). On what follows, see Brondos, *Jesus' Death*, 1:226-31.

30. On the ways in which Jesus' death and that of Socrates may have been compared to each other among Jesus' earliest followers, see Greg Sterling, "*Mors Philosophi*: The Death of Jesus in Luke," *HTR* 94 (2001): 383-402.

PAUL AND JESUS' DEATH

According to many traditional interpretations of Paul's thought, he understood the human plight primarily in terms of the need to obtain from God the forgiveness of sins in order to be delivered from the condemnation to which all are subject on account of those sins.[31] Supposedly, because human beings could not attain the level of perfection they needed in order to merit God's forgiveness, it was necessary for Christ to merit or obtain that forgiveness for them by means of his death on a cross.[32]

Such an understanding of salvation and the work of Christ is problematic for a number of reasons. It locates the problem that must be resolved in God rather than in human beings. While undoubtedly their sin prevents human beings from being saved, supposedly the obstacle that must be overcome is not their sinfulness but God's inability to forgive them that sinfulness without compromising his perfect holiness and justice. Christ's task is therefore not to bring them to put away their sin but to make it possible for God to forgive and overlook that sin so that he may save them. It is this that Christ's death was designed to accomplish. While of course the result of the forgiveness that believers receive through Christ's death produces a change in them, it is not that change that constitutes the basis for their forgiveness but Christ's death alone, as well as their faith in the atoning efficacy of his death.

As we have just seen above, however, in Hebrew and Jewish thought, what satisfied God's justice and put away his wrath was not the punishment of sin or the inflicting of suffering and death on sinners but the return of his people to him and his commandments in love, obedience, and righteousness. If this did not take place, nothing that human beings could do or offer God could bring him to be reconciled to them and forgive them their sins, nor could God's punishment of their sins reconcile him to them or them to him. Just as in Jewish thought sacrifices, suffering, or death in themselves could not atone for sins or obtain his forgiveness, so also in the thought of Jesus' first followers the sacrificial suffering and death of Christ in itself had neither made atonement for human sins nor obtained God's forgiveness for those sins. Only a commitment to living in accordance with God's will as God had now made that will known through Jesus could accomplish those things.

Of course, for centuries biblical interpreters have claimed that the idea that Jesus' death or blood atoned for human sins is found in a number

---

31. Stephen Westerholm, for example, summarizes Paul's thought thus: "Certainly he saw humanity's plight as desperate: divine judgment looms over wayward humankind" (*Perspectives Old and New on Paul: The "Lutheran" Paul and His Critics* [Grand Rapids: Eerdmans, 2004], 358). See further his discussion on 352-407.

32. So Westerholm: "through Christ God declares the guilty innocent, clearing while cleansing them of their sins, thereby initiating a reconciliation with sinners. Those who respond to his kerygma with faith enter the community of the saved" (*Perspectives*, 366).

of passages from Paul's epistles.[33] A close look at these passages, however, reveals that in every case they consist of brief formulas that by their very nature lend themselves to having a wide variety of ideas read back into them. What Paul actually says is that Jesus died for others and for their sins, that believers are justified through his blood, and that through Jesus' death believers have been reconciled to God.[34] Nowhere do any of these passages or others from Paul's epistles affirm explicitly the idea of penal substitution. Nevertheless, because for centuries they have been read on the basis of that idea, many find it virtually impossible to interpret them in any other way.

In order to make sense of Paul's formulaic allusions to Jesus' death, some type of narrative background is necessary. In principle, the penal substitution interpretation of Jesus' death can provide such a background, yet because Paul never affirms any of the ideas that constitute the basic elements of that interpretation, it can be attributed to Paul only by reading it back into the formulas he uses to speak of the salvific significance of Jesus' death. Thus, for example, nowhere does Paul ever argue that Jesus had to die because God could not forgive sins without his death or claim that only by having Jesus endure the punishment that human sins deserved could God enable human beings to be spared from that punishment.

Of course, many Pauline scholars would argue that Paul never presents any type of narrative regarding Jesus and his death in his letters.[35] While in a sense that is true, it is nevertheless possible to reconstruct in broad terms the narrative Paul told on the basis of the allusions he makes to Jesus' death and his activity on behalf of others throughout his letters. A brief summary of this narrative can therefore provide the background necessary to consider the significance that Paul ascribes to Jesus' death in the passages in which he alludes to it, as well as his understanding of the manner in which Jesus' death relates to the forgiveness of sins.

Jesus' Death in the Context of the Narrative Told by Paul

As we have seen in previous chapters, for Paul the narrative concerning Christ began long before his birth. Not only do all things exist through him (1 Cor 8:6), but from the start God intended for human beings to be conformed to his image (Rom 8:29). Figures such as Adam and Abraham and events such as the exodus from Egypt and Israel's sojourn in the wilderness

---

33. Chief among these passages are Rom 3:24-25; 5:6-10; 8:3; 1 Cor 15:3; 2 Cor 5:21; Gal 1:4; 3:13.

34. See Rom 4:24-25; 5:6-10; 14:15; 1 Cor 8:11; 15:3; 2 Cor 5:14-15, 21; Gal 1:4; 2:20; 1 Thess 5:9-10.

35. Francis Watson, for example, questions the idea that any type of narrative or story of Jesus runs throughout Paul's letters ("Is There a Story in These Texts?," in *Narrative Dynamics in Paul: A Critical Assessment*, ed. Bruce W. Longenecker [Louisville: Westminster John Knox, 2002], 231-39).

pointed forward to what would take place through Christ, as did the Scriptures of Israel in general.[36]

When the appointed time arrived, God sent his Son into the world to bring both Jews and gentiles back to himself as his own and to condemn in them the power of sin so that they might be able to fulfill the righteousness of which the law speaks.[37] In obedience to his Father's will, in love the Son emptied himself to take human form and was even willing to endure a type of death reserved for slaves so that a community characterized by his same love, affection, compassion, solidarity, humility, and concern for others might be brought into existence through him (Phil 2:1-8). Out of love for others and for their sake, he was willing to become poor so that they might become rich (2 Cor 8:9).

Paul's understanding of the purpose of Christ's coming as well as the significance of his life and death becomes evident when we look at the exhortations he makes in his letters. Because Paul considers himself a servant or slave of God and Christ and is dedicated to doing their will, the objectives he pursues in his own ministry constitute the objectives of God and Christ as well.[38] Among these objectives was that people might come to present themselves to God rather than being conformed to this world, living as members of the body of Christ and ministering to one another with the gifts God would give them (Rom 12:1-7). Believers would be enabled to "lay aside the works of darkness" so as to "live respectably as in the day" (Rom 13:12-14). They would also walk in Jesus' same love and "pursue what contributes to peace and mutual upbuilding," seeking to please their neighbor.[39] Jesus' objective had been that others come to live in unity, harmony, and fellowship with him and one another, sharing the same mind and purpose as they received one another in the same way that he would receive them (Rom 15:5, 7; 1 Cor 1:9-10). By means of the gospel, many were to be brought to share of themselves and their possessions generously and to live a life worthy of that gospel, struggling alongside one another on its behalf (2 Cor 9:13; Phil 1:27). Within the community of believers, all would live in accordance with the "law of Christ" by bearing one another's burdens and serving one another in love (Gal 5:13-14; 6:2). They would live in his same compassion, constantly increasing in love and producing the fruit of righteousness through him (Phil 1:8-11; 1 Thess 3:12). Those who would live under Christ's lordship would practice kindness and value what is true,

---

36. See Rom 5:14-19; 16:25-26; 1 Cor 2:7-8; 10:1-11; Gal 3:16.

37. See Rom 8:3; Gal 4:4. As Hans Dieter Betz notes, the phrase "the fullness of time" in Gal 4:4 should probably be read in light of 4:2, "the time fixed by the father" (*Galatians: A Commentary on Paul's Letter to the Churches in Galatia*, Hermeneia [Philadelphia: Fortress, 1979], 206).

38. See Rom 1:1; 1 Cor 3:5; 4:1; 2 Cor 6:4; Gal 1:10; Phil 1:1.

39. See Rom 14:15, 20; 15:2; 1 Cor 10:23-24; 14:1.

honorable, right, pure, agreeable, praiseworthy, virtuous, and commendable (Phil 4:5, 8). Rather than exploiting others or repaying evil with evil, they would encourage and help one another and show love to those outside of their community as well.[40] If these are all things that Paul seeks as an apostle or envoy of God and Christ and as God's ambassador for Christ, they must be things that God and Christ sought as well.[41]

In a number of passages, Paul associates a number of these attitudes and behaviors with Christ's death. Perhaps the most important of these is Phil 2:1-8, just mentioned above, where Paul describes in detail the type of love that is to exist within the community of believers in Christ. In 2 Cor 5:14-15, Paul affirms that Christ died for all so that all might be constrained by his same love and "live no longer for themselves but for him who died and was raised for them." According to Paul, the reason why believers do not live or die to themselves is that Christ himself died and lived again to be Lord on their behalf (Rom 14:7-9). All are to walk in love and avoid anything that might injure or destroy their brothers and sisters because Christ died for each member of the community, including especially the weak (Rom 14:15; 1 Cor 8:11). Believers are also to please their neighbors and build them up because Christ did not strive to please himself but was willing to endure the insults of others (Rom 15:2-3).[42] They are to show consideration for one another and live as one rather than being divided into factions and failing to be attentive to the needs of others because it was that type of community that Christ sought to establish when he spoke of giving his body and blood for others in the night of his betrayal (1 Cor 11:17-34). Like a Passover lamb, he had been sacrificed so that the old leaven of malice and wickedness might be replaced with the unleavened bread of sincerity and truth among believers (1 Cor 5:6-8). Jesus had given up his life and died to sin so that others might put away their old self and dedicate their lives to God as his obedient servants, living as slaves of righteousness rather than slaves of sin and unrighteousness (Rom 6:3-20; 15:18). In love Jesus had given himself up for those such as Paul who would come to believe in him so that they might be crucified to the world like him and no longer live their own lives but rather his (Gal 2:20; 6:14).

In Paul's thought, all of these things constituted the objective of Christ in life and death. He had sought to make others his own and had been willing to pay the price necessary for that to happen.[43] The goal of both Christ

---

40. See Rom 12:17-18; 1 Thess 4:6, 12; 5:11-15.

41. See Rom 1:1, 5; 1 Cor 1:1; 2 Cor 1:1; 5:20; Gal 1:1; 1 Thess 2:7.

42. As Leander E. Keck notes, whether or not Paul is presenting Christ as the implied speaker of the words he cites from Ps 69:9 in Rom 15:3, he is able to apply those words to Christ because they "fit an already known image of Christ's demeanor and so can validate him as the paradigm of not pleasing oneself" (*Romans,* ANTC [Nashville: Abingdon, 2005], 351).

43. See Rom 12:11; 16:18; 1 Cor 3:23; 6:19-20; 7:23; 2 Cor 10:7.

and his Father had been that others come to belong to Christ as his slaves or servants so as to be betrothed to him and live their lives clothed in him.[44] Christ had sought to become the foundation of a new construction and to enable others to be born anew and refashioned as a new creation.[45] His desire was that others might come to live as members of his body, the "body of Christ," so that they might build up one another there.[46] If these are the things that Christ set out to accomplish, then they must have constituted his objective not only in life but also in death. Similarly, these must have been the same things God had been seeking when he sent his Son, gave him over to death, and subsequently raised and exalted him as Lord.

Although Paul never speaks of Jesus offering up any type of petition to God in his death, he must have believed that Jesus had gone to his death seeking at least three things from God. The first of these was that all of the things just mentioned be brought to pass through him. These included both the new reality that would come to exist among believers in the present world as well as their salvation in the age to come. The second was that God raise and exalt him as Lord, not merely for his own sake, but so that he might remain active from heaven to bring to pass all that he had sought for others in life and death until those things might be fully consummated. The third was that God not only enable the community of believers to be established and strengthened but also that God accept and receive the members of that community in spite of their sins and imperfections. While Paul never states these three things explicitly, they are clearly presupposed throughout his letters.

Paul does, of course, speak of Christ interceding on behalf of believers from God's side in Rom 8:34. He does not specify the content of that intercession, yet it is likely that he believed that it involved asking God not only to strengthen and confirm those on behalf of whom he intercedes but to forgive and accept them as well. In the same context he affirms that the Holy Spirit helps believers in their weakness by interceding to God on their behalf in accordance with God's will (Rom 8:26-27). It is reasonable to think that he understood Christ's heavenly intercession on behalf of believers in much the same terms. If Paul believed that Christ intercedes on behalf of believers in the present, he almost certainly would have thought as well that during his life and as he went to his death Christ had interceded on behalf of all those who would come to believe in him so as to form part of his community of followers. The idea that Christ carries out a mediating task on behalf of believers in relation to God is also suggested in Rom 5:1-2, where Paul affirms that believers now have peace with God through

---

44. See Rom 13:14; 14:18; 2 Cor 11:2; Gal 3:27-29; 5:24.
45. See 1 Cor 3:11; 2 Cor 5:17; Gal 4:19; 6:15.
46. See Rom 12:4-5; 1 Cor 6:15-17; 12:4-27.

Christ,[47] and in 2 Cor 3:4, where Paul mentions the confidence that believers have through Christ in relation to God.[48]

In accordance with his Father's will, Christ had also given up his life and sought to be raised and exalted so that he might become the source of new life for others and continue to carry out his saving activity on their behalf in the present. By sending his Son, handing him over to death when his ministry led to the threat of the cross, and raising him from the dead, God has made it possible for him to be the source of power, wisdom, righteousness, holiness, and redemption for believers.[49] Through his Son's faithfulness unto death to the task given him, God has brought believers to live in peace and friendship with himself by practicing the righteousness he desires.[50] In his risen condition, Christ can now be the source of grace, peace, and love for others as well.[51] This was what he had sought in life and death: that he might be able to be at work in others as he is presently in order to confirm, comfort, strengthen, and establish them and to serve as the foundation for the community of which they would come to form part.[52] Christ remains at work in them to make them increase in love for their sisters and brothers in the faith and all people in general (1 Thess 3:11-12). Because Christ has been raised, believers are able to call on his name and intercede to him for healing, as Paul does (1 Cor 1:2; 2 Cor 12:8). They also live as one Spirit with Christ, who dwells in them as they also live in him.[53] The risen Christ continues to guide Paul, speak through him, and work through him to win obedience from the gentiles.[54] If Christ does these things on behalf of others at present, he must have sought to be enabled to do them when he offered up his life to God. And when God responded to Christ's self-offering by raising him from the dead, he made it possible for Christ to continue to be active on behalf of believers in all of these ways.

Ultimately, of course, in Paul's thought Christ must also have given up his life seeking that he be raised and exalted so as to be able to bring about the consummation of all that he had sought in life and death. His resurrection and exaltation make it possible for him to come in power some day to rid the world of evil as judge of all, saving believers from God's wrath

---

47. On the likelihood that Paul is alluding to the mediatorial role of the risen Christ in Rom 5:1-2, see James D. G. Dunn, *Romans 1-8*, WBC 38A (Dallas: Word, 1988), 247.

48. If Paul is referring to the presence and activity of the risen Christ in 2 Cor 3:3, as Chris Tilling has argued, it is likely that in 3:4 he has in mind the risen Christ as well (*Paul's Divine Christology*, WUNT 2/323 [Tübingen: Mohr Siebeck, 2012], 246-48).

49. See 1 Cor 1:24, 30; Rom 3:24; 10:4-16.

50. See Rom 5:1, 10-11; 2 Cor 5:18-21.

51. See Rom 1:7; 5:2; 2 Cor 13:3; Gal 1:3; Phil 1:2.

52. See 1 Cor 1:8; 3:11; 2 Cor 12:9-10; Phil 4:1, 7, 13; 1 Thess 2:13.

53. See 1 Cor 6:17; 2 Cor 13:5; Gal 2:20.

54. See Rom 15:18; 1 Cor 4:19; 2 Cor 13:3; 1 Thess 3:11.

against all those who suppress the truth through the injustices they commit.[55] Jesus' objective was to be able to bring others to share in the life of the age to come by raising up believers from the dead and transforming their bodies to be like his own.[56] Ultimately, he sought to reign as Lord so that he might subject all things to himself and then hand over all things to God so that God may be "all in all" (1 Cor 15:24-28).

In Rom 14:9, Paul writes: "For to this end Christ died and lived again, so that he might be Lord of both the dead and the living." Here Paul clearly affirms that Christ died seeking to be raised and exalted as Lord.[57] The same idea is suggested in Phil 2:5-11, which speaks of God raising Christ as a result of his obedience unto death, and in 1 Thess 5:9, where he writes that Christ "died for us so that whether we are awake or sleep we may live with him." When viewed in their context, these passages conceive of Christ's lordship as something that he sought for the sake of others and now exercises on their behalf. He sought to be raised and exalted precisely so that he might carry out all of the activity on behalf of others just mentioned, both in relation to believers and in relation to God on their behalf.

If Paul thought that Jesus had been seeking to establish the *ekklēsia* as he went to his death and to bring about in others the new life of love and righteousness that God desired to see in all, he must also have thought that Jesus sought that God receive favorably the members of that community. In other words, Jesus must have sought that God accept as righteous or justify those who would live as members of his community under his lordship. As Paul tells the Romans, Jesus "was raised for our justification" (Rom 4:25). Because believers would not yet be entirely righteous, however, this justification would involve an element of forgiveness, not only for their past sins, but also for the sins that they would inevitably continue to commit contrary to their will as they lived under Christ. By virtue of their relationship to Christ their Lord and the new life that would result from this relationship, however, God would accept and forgive them so that they might have peace with him and be reconciled to him.

When viewed against the background of these ideas, Jesus' resurrection and exaltation would be understood as God's implicit acceptance of all that Jesus had sought from God as he went to his death. By raising and exalting Jesus, God had made it possible for Jesus to continue to serve others as their Lord so that God's purposes in them might be accomplished. However,

---

55. See Rom 1:18; 2:16; 5:9; 2 Cor 5:10; 1 Thess 1:10.

56. See Rom 6:23; 1 Cor 15:21, 45; Phil 3:20-21; 1 Thess 4:14-17; 5:10.

57. As James Dunn observes with regard to Rom 14:9 and other passages, "It is characteristic of Paul's Christology and soteriology that he sees the primary thrust of Christ's death and resurrection as directed toward his becoming lord of all things, including dead as well as living. . . ." (*Romans 9-16*, WBC 38B [Dallas: Word, 1988], 808).

in Jesus' resurrection and exaltation God would also be seen as having responded positively and in definitive fashion to Jesus' petition on behalf of the salvation of all who would form part of the *ekklēsia* so as to be transformed through Jesus, the Holy Spirit, and the gospel. Because their faith in Christ would enable them to live in the way God desired for their own good, God would overlook the sinful past of believers and receive them as his own. They could have certainty of God's acceptance and approval because God had raised Jesus as their Lord precisely so that he might continue to be active on their behalf until the day when he would come again to bestow upon them the resurrection life and deliver them from the wrath of God, by means of which the world would be liberated from sin and evil. Their confidence that through Christ God would receive them favorably in the future also gave believers full assurance that God received them favorably even now as they lived as his children under the lordship of his Son.

While Christ would therefore be seen as having given up his life so that the members of his community might be forgiven and accepted by God as righteous and delivered from his wrath, it would not be his death in itself that would attain these things on behalf of believers. Rather, the basis for their forgiveness and acceptance by God would be the new life of love and righteousness that would be brought about by them through Christ and the gospel. Nevertheless, because that new life was now possible only because Christ had dedicated himself fully to doing what was necessary for it to become a reality in them and had given up his life so that it might be theirs, it would be said that he had attained their salvation, justification, and reconciliation with God by means of his death. His death was thus not the *basis* for their forgiveness and acceptance by God but the *means* by which he had attained God's forgiveness and acceptance for them by virtue of the new life that was now theirs as a result of all that he had done and continued to do on their behalf in obedience to his Father.

Because Jesus had offered up his life to God seeking that God accept, forgive, and save others through him, it would not have been long before his followers would come to use sacrificial language and imagery to allude to the salvific significance of his death. Just as those who offered up sacrifices to God sought his acceptance and forgiveness not only for themselves but for others as well, so also in his death Jesus had offered himself up to God seeking that God accept and forgive all those who would form part of his community of followers. Just as God received favorably the sacrificial offerings of those who approached him with a pure heart and a commitment to live in accordance with his will, he now had received favorably Jesus' self-offering on behalf of others by granting him once and for all time what he had sought for those who would live under him, precisely because through him they too would approach him with a pure heart, fully committed to doing his will as he had made it known through his Son.

In broad terms, then, this is the narrative that lies behind Paul's formulaic allusions to the salvific significance of Jesus' death. Because all believers in Christ were well-acquainted with this simple and basic narrative, Paul could confidently assume that the formulas he uses when speaking of Jesus' death would be easily understood by his readers, including even those who were not acquainted with him personally, such as those to whom he addressed his Epistle to the Romans. In fact, his readers probably employed the same type of formulas themselves. Because they were so brief and concise, such formulas enabled those who used them to express with only a few words all of the ideas associated with their interpretation of the significance of Jesus' death and to encapsulate in its entirety the narrative they told regarding what God had done in Christ to bring about the new reality they had now come to experience through their faith in him.

Jesus' Death for Others in the Thought of Paul

Once we have grasped Paul's narrative regarding Jesus and the significance that Jesus' death has for him in the context of that narrative, the formulas that Paul employs to allude to the salvific significance of Jesus' death become readily comprehensible. The simplest of these is that Christ died or gave himself "for us" (*hyper hēmōn*). In 1 Thessalonians, which is probably the earliest of Paul's extant letters, Paul writes that "God has not destined us for wrath but for obtaining salvation through our Lord Jesus Christ, who died for us so that whether we remain awake or fall asleep we might live together with him" (1 Thess 5:9-10). According to Paul's words here, Christ's ultimate goal was that others be brought to live together with him, especially in the age to come, though Paul may have in mind life in the present age as well. Paul's idea would be that Christ had given up his life seeking that those who would come to form part of the community whose salvation he had sought in life and death might some day be brought to live together with him. Because through him they would be brought to live in accordance with God's will, they would not come under God's wrath on the day in which that wrath would be manifested. When God raised Christ from the dead and exalted him as Lord in response to his faithfulness unto death in seeking the salvation of all who would live as his own under his lordship, in effect he granted Christ what he had sought for them when he gave up his life. Now risen and exalted, he would be able to bring them to live together with him as he had desired. Paul alludes to these same ideas in the previous chapter of his letter, where he writes that "if we believe that Jesus died and rose, in the same way through Jesus God will also bring with him those who have fallen asleep" (1 Thess 4:13). This will take place when Christ returns from heaven to raise the dead and take them to himself (4:15-17). In Paul's thought, Jesus must also have asked to be given the power and authority to do these things when he gave up his life seeking the salvation of others.

Paul uses the same Greek phrase in Rom 8:32, where he writes that "he who did not spare his own Son but delivered him up for us all (*hyper hēmōn pantōn*), will he not also give us all things together with him?" While here Paul no doubt has in mind primarily Jesus' death, it must be remembered that his death was the consequence of his being sent by God to bring into existence the community of believers in which they would live in the type of love and righteousness that God desired to see in all. When his dedication to that task led to the threat of death on a cross, Jesus did not back down or shy away from such a death, since he knew that to do so would mean that the type of community he had sought to establish would never become a reality through him. For the same reason, rather than intervening to spare his Son the death of the cross, God had handed him over or delivered him up to such a death.

According to the logic of Paul's thought here, both God and his Son had embraced the cross, not because nothing but Jesus' death on a cross would make it possible for God to forgive human beings their sins, but because only by giving themselves to and for human beings fully to the very end and holding nothing back could God and his Son expect and call on human beings to give of themselves to and for one another in the same way. If in the face of the cross God had not given up his Son and Jesus had not given up his life, Paul could never have written that neither hardship, distress, persecution, peril, death, life, the present, the future, nor anything else can ever separate believers from the love of Christ and the love of God in Christ (Rom 8:35-39). The reason for this is that God's refusal to give up his Son and Jesus' refusal to give up his life would have shown such an affirmation to be untrue. The hardship, pain, suffering, and death of the cross *would* in fact have separated human beings from the love of Christ and his Father, because those things would have led both Christ and God to hold back their love and stop giving themselves to and for human beings. Paul would also have had no basis for claiming that God will now give believers all things together with Christ, since there would have been something that God himself was unwilling to give up for human beings, namely, the life of his Son. Of course, because God had gone to such lengths in order to bring human beings to live as his own in his same love, there could be no doubt that he would also receive favorably all those who through faith in Christ now came to live in that way. Among the things that God will now give to those who live under Christ his Son as their Lord, of course, is the forgiveness of sins. As Paul tells the Romans, "If God is for us, who is against us? . . . Who will bring any charge against God's elect? It is God who justifies. Who is to condemn?" (8:31, 33-34).[58]

---

58. As Timothy Milinovich stresses, when Paul speaks of what God has done for believers through Christ in Rom 8:31-34, he has in mind not only Jesus' death but all that God has done on their behalf from even before time and down to the present,

In Romans 14 and 1 Corinthians 8, where he is discussing the need for believers to show concern for those who are weak, Paul exhorts his readers to refrain from doing anything that might harm a brother "on whose behalf Christ died" or "on account of whom Christ died" (Rom 14:15; 1 Cor 8:11).[59] In Paul's thought, Christ had died seeking that both Jews and non-Jews be brought to form part of the community that he had dedicated his life to establishing so that, as they lived in his same love and righteousness under him, they might attain salvation through him. Everyone who through faith in him came to form part of that community, therefore, could be referred to as one on whose behalf or for whose sake Christ had died.[60] This was not because Christ's death in itself had fulfilled some requirement that God had established as a condition for their salvation, however. What was necessary was that people come to walk in love in the way that God commanded for their own good (Rom 14:15). It was to this objective that Christ had dedicated himself fully, even to the point of giving up his life so that through him both that new life and the salvation that would result from that life might become a reality for all who would come to live under him as members of his community. The Roman and Corinthian believers were therefore to remember that Christ had attained the salvation of everyone who came to form part of that community at a great price, the price of his life. They were to consider of supreme value each member of the community in the way that Christ had, including especially those who were weak, since Christ himself had shown a special concern for the weak. In a sense, of course, *all* people might be considered weak and as the object of Christ's love, as Paul affirms in Rom 5:6: "For while we were still weak, at the right time Christ died on behalf of the ungodly." In another sense, however, there were many within the community of believers who remained weak and for that reason needed to be shown special consideration by their sisters and brothers in the faith (Rom 14:1–15:6; 1 Cor 8:9-13).

Immediately after affirming that Christ died on behalf of the weak and the ungodly in Rom 5:6, Paul continues:

---

when he guides them to new life and resurrection by means of the Spirit ("Once More, with Feeling: Rom 8,31-39 as Rhetorical *Peroratio*," *Bib* 99 [2018]: 525-54 [537-40]). For Paul, therefore, God's handing his Son over "for us" is part of a whole that embraces much more than Christ's death.

59. In Rom 14:15, Paul uses the phrase *hyper hou Christos apethanen*, while in 1 Cor 8:11, the phrase he uses is *di' hon Christos apethanen*. The difference in meaning between these two phrases is probably not significant.

60. Heinrich Schlier rightly points out that Paul's affirmations in Rom 14:15 and 1 Cor 8:11 that Christ died for the brother or sister who is weak presuppose that the brother or sister now belongs to Christ and thus lives for him (*Der Römerbrief*, HThKNT 6 [Freiburg im Breisgau: Herder, 1977], 414). In Paul's thought, therefore, Christ had died in order to attain that end.

For one will hardly die for a righteous person, although perhaps one might dare to die for a good person. But God demonstrates his love toward us in that, while we were still sinners, Christ died for us. Much more then, having now been justified by means of his blood, shall we be saved through him from the wrath. For if while we were still enemies we were reconciled to God through the death of his Son, now that we have been reconciled, how much more shall we be saved by means of his life. And not only this, but we also glory in God through our Lord Jesus Christ, through whom we have now received the reconciliation (Rom 5:7-11).

Everything Paul says here can easily be understood on the basis of the same narrative considered in the previous section. Christ had died as a result of his efforts to bring into existence a community in which all would leave behind their sinful ways so that those who would come to form part of that community might live as God's own and attain the life and salvation God desired for all. By affirming that those who have now through faith come to form part of that community were previously weak, ungodly, and sinners and lived at enmity with God, Paul stresses that none had done anything to deserve such love on the part of Christ.[61] This point is particularly important in the context of Paul's argument that those who lived under the law as Jews were no more righteous in God's sight than those gentiles who had come to faith in Christ without submitting to the law. Both Jews and gentiles had previously been under sin equally (Rom 3:9). Therefore those of both groups were also equally weak, ungodly sinners and equally in need of the love and grace God has now shown them by sending his Son and giving him over to death in order that they might attain God's righteousness and salvation by living as members of the community that Christ had given up his life to establish.

For this reason, Paul can also say that believers have been justified by means of Christ's blood. As we have seen in Chapter 7 of this study, when Paul speaks of justification through Christ, he has in mind the idea that God accepts as righteous those who live out of faith or Christ-faith. In accordance with the narrative considered above, when Paul alludes to Jesus' blood he must be referring not merely to his death per se but especially to the dedication to the transformation and salvation of others that had led him to be willing to give up his life for them. He had gone to his death seeking what he had sought throughout his ministry, namely, that others might be saved by being brought into conformity with God's will as that will would come to be defined through him and his love for others. When God raised his Son from the dead and exalted him as Lord over all, God in effect accepted as righteous all who would come to live under his lordship, because

---

61. By reminding his readers that they too were "weak," Paul may also have wished to promote greater solidarity with the "weak" or "stumbling" of whom he speaks in Romans 14–15; see Mark D. Nanos, *The Mystery of Romans* (Minneapolis: Fortress, 1996), 144.

by definition to live under his lordship is to be committed to living in the same love and righteousness that he manifested in life and especially in death. The reason Paul speaks of Jesus' blood here rather than referring simply to his death is probably that he wishes to emphasize what it cost Jesus to accomplish what he did, that is, the price Jesus paid in order to bring about in others the type of love and righteousness that now leads God to declare them righteous or justify them. It is therefore not Jesus' blood or death per se that enables believers to be justified, but rather the new life of righteousness that he and his Father are now able to bring about in believers as a result of Jesus' willingness to give up his life. Similarly, it is not Jesus' blood or death per se that brings about in them that new life of righteousness, but *all* that God has done and continues to do through his Son.

According to Paul, if both Christ and his Father were willing to pay such a high price in order to bring into existence the community that now lives under Jesus as Lord, there can be no question that God will ultimately forgive and accept all who come to live as part of that community. For this reason, they can be certain that they will be saved from God's wrath in the end, when God comes to judge all people through Christ (Rom 2:16).[62] Paul's point in Rom 5:9, therefore, is that neither Christ nor his Father would have given up so much to bring about that community only then to reject those who would come to belong to it.

Paul stresses God's grace and love once more in this passage when he adds that, by means of Christ's death, those who once lived as God's enemies have now been reconciled to him (Rom 5:10). The logic behind Paul's words is that, thanks to Christ's dedication to the end to bringing others to be enabled to put away their enmity toward God and live in the way God desired so as to enjoy peace with him, what Christ sought in life and death has now become a reality. The righteous way of life that God has brought about in them through his Son now allows them to be reconciled to God, yet because that way of life is a gift rather than something that they produce in and of themselves, Paul can speak of reconciliation with God as something that believers simply receive (Rom 5:11).[63] That righteous way

---

62. It is incorrect to affirm, as Ben Witherington III does, that in Rom 5:9 "rescue from wrath is said to come by Christ's blood, which surely favors the view that Christ's death is what assuaged and propitiated that wrath" (*Paul's Letter to the Romans: A Socio-Rhetorical Commentary* [Grand Rapids: Eerdmans, 2004], 138). While Paul says that believers have been justified through Jesus' blood in Rom 5:9, he speaks of the salvation of believers from God's wrath in 5:10 as something that will come about through Christ *in the future*.

63. To affirm that, because of Jesus' "atoning sacrifice" in his death, "God has overcome and ended from his side the hostility which prevailed between sinners and himself," as Peter Stuhlmacher does, gravely misrepresents Paul's thought in Rom 5:9-10 (*Paul's Letter to the Romans: A Commentary*, trans. Scott J. Hafemann [Louisville: Westminster John Knox, 1994], 82). Paul's allusions to the coming wrath of God in these same

of life is now a reality in them precisely because Christ was willing to pay the ultimate price of his own life in order to make it possible for everything that he had sought for others to come to fruition. Now that he has been raised as a result of his dedication to that task, believers can be certain that they will be "saved by means of his life." In other words, now that he is alive and enthroned as Lord, there can be no doubt that he will bring to pass everything for which he had lived and died in accordance with the will of his Father.

In 1 Cor 6:20 and 7:23, Paul once again stresses the high price that both God and Christ paid to make believers their own when he tells the Corinthians: "You were bought with a price." There is no reason to interpret Paul's words here in the sense that Christ's death constituted a payment made *to* someone, such as the devil or God himself, in order to liberate human beings from their bondage or from a penalty to which they were subject.[64] Rather, the metaphor is that of paying a high price in order to accomplish something, such as victory in an athletic competition or a military battle. As Paul writes in 1 Cor 9:22-27, athletes must subject their body to strict discipline in order to bring it into submission, yet only by paying such a price can they win the competition. In the case of God and Christ, the price that both had paid in order to obtain the new community in which believers now live as God's own and Christ's possession was the death of Christ on a cross. Yet both God and his Son were willing to pay that price because it was the only way in which that objective could be accomplished in the way God desired. The members of that community no longer regard themselves and their lives as their own but instead live as slaves of God and of Christ, doing God's will as he has now made it known in Christ rather than their own will (1 Cor 6:19; 7:22). Of course, those who live as God's own are acceptable to him and are therefore forgiven by him as well.

The idea that Christ paid a price in order to make believers his own seems to be reflected as well in Gal 3:13-14. According to a literal translation of Paul's words there, "Christ bought us out from under the curse of the law, having become a curse for us, since it is written, 'Cursed be everyone

---

verses and elsewhere in Romans make it clear that for Paul God's wrath against those who persistently refuse to abandon their sinful, destructive ways and "repress the truth with injustice" (Rom 1:18) remains firmly in place until the end (see Rom 2:5, 8; 3:5; 4:15; 12:19). God's wrath therefore has *not* been put away by Christ's death, though believers can be confident that they will be spared that wrath when it is manifested.

64. As Hans Conzelmann comments, Paul does not speak of anyone receiving payment in 1 Cor 6:20 or 7:23: "The metaphor is not developed. The point is merely that you belong to a new master. Beyond this the metaphor should not be pressed" (*1 Corinthians: A Commentary on the First Epistle to the Corinthians*, Hermeneia [Philadelphia: Fortress, 1975], 113).

who is hung upon a tree,' so that the gentiles might obtain the blessing of Abraham through Christ Jesus, in order that through faith we might receive the promise of the Spirit." This passage has generally been understood in the sense that Christ endured the same curse that the law pronounced on believers so as to deliver them from that curse, as if what God's justice demanded was simply that the law's curse be inflicted on someone, whether on human beings themselves or on Christ as their substitute.[65] Besides the fact that nothing in Paul's epistles or the New Testament as a whole ever suggests such an idea, it is important to note that Paul speaks of two different curses in Gal 3:13: Christ endured the curse pronounced by the law on those who are hung on a tree in order to save believers from a different curse, namely, the one that the law pronounced on those who do not abide by all the things written in the law (Deut 21:23; 27:26; Gal 3:10).[66]

Paul's words in Gal 3:13 should instead be understood on the basis of the same narrative considered above. Those who lived under the law could be said to be under a curse because it pronounced a curse on those who did not observe it and perhaps because it confined and constrained them as well (Gal 3:10, 23-24). In Gal 6:13, Paul states explicitly that there is a sense in which even those who live under the law do not actually keep it.[67] What Christ sought was to deliver others from the law's curse by bringing them to live out of faith or Christ-faith as God's sons and daughters so that they might receive the blessing of the Spirit through faith and thereby come to practice the righteousness of God so as to be justified (Gal 3:14, 22-27). According to Paul, it was for this same purpose that God had sent his Son (Gal 4:4-7). Yet the price that Christ had to pay in order to achieve that objective was that of dying a type of death that the law associated with a curse. His willingness to endure that death has made it possible for believers now to be delivered from the curse that Paul associates with the law. This is not because Christ's death in itself accomplished something on

---

65. According to Cilliers Breytenbach, for example, in Gal 3:13 "Christ is depicted as the one who took the place of Paul and those he includes in his 'we'. . . . He was cursed by God. . . . His crucifixion as a cursed person is understood to be in place of those under the curse of the law, in order for them to be freed from the curse placed on those who have transgressed the law" ("The 'For Us' Phrases in Pauline Soteriology: Considering their Background and Use," in *Salvation in the New Testament: Perspectives on Soteriology*, ed. Jan G. van der Watt, NovTSup 121 [Leiden: Brill, 2005], 163-85 [169]).

66. On this point, see David A. Brondos, "The Cross and the Curse: Galatians 3.13 and Paul's Doctrine of Redemption," *JSNT* 81 (2001): 3-32 (22-23).

67. As Mark Nanos argues, Paul's affirmation in Gal 6:13 can be understood in the sense that those attempting to influence the uncircumcised Galatian believers to become circumcised are transgressing the law in the sense that, contrary to the spirit of the Torah, they are pursuing personal interests rather than acting out of a genuine concern for the welfare of others, that is, the Galatians (*The Irony of Galatians: Paul's Letter in First-Century Context* [Minneapolis: Fortress, 2002], 226-29).

their behalf or delivered anyone from the law's curse, however, but because only by being willing to endure the consequences of his efforts to bring into existence the community in which all would obtain the blessing of Abraham and the promise of the Spirit could that community become a reality and take the shape it has. Because all those who form part of that community are now his own and live under him rather than under the law as a *paidagōgos*, Christ can be said to have acquired them at the price of his life.

A similar idea seems to be present in Rom 7:4-6, where Paul tells the Roman believers:

> You were brought to die to the law through the body of Christ in order that you might come to belong to another, to him who was raised from the dead so that we might bear fruit for God. For when we were in the flesh, the sinful passions that are aroused by the law were at work in our members in order to bear fruit for death. But now we have been released from the law and are dead to that which held us captive, since we serve in the newness of the spirit rather than the oldness of the letter.

It is not entirely clear whether Paul is here referring to the physical body of Christ or to the community of believers when he speaks of the body of Christ.[68] In either case, in Paul's thought Christ gave up his life as well as his body to bring that community into existence and thereby make it possible for many to live as his own as members of that community, which may also be called his body. Those who now form part of that community therefore live under Christ their risen Lord and are subject to him and the Spirit rather than to the law, which had previously kept them captive or under restraint, as Paul argues here and in Gal 3:23–4:6. In this way, as they live as Christ's own, they are able to live in the newness of the spirit and bear fruit for God. By giving up his life, then, Christ had made it possible for believers to be free from sin and the confinement of the law.

The same logic appears to be behind Paul's words in Gal 2:19-21, where he writes: "For I through the law have died to the law, so that I might live to God. I am crucified together with Christ, and it is no longer I who live but Christ who lives in me; and what I now live in the flesh, I live in the faith of the Son of God, who loved me and gave himself for me. I do not nullify the

---

68. While it is possible that in Rom 7:4 Paul is referring to Christ's physical body that was crucified, one should not discount the possibility that Paul has in mind the *ekklēsia* on the grounds that such an interpretation would involve "introducing an ecclesial consideration into the text that otherwise lacks any reference to it," as Joseph A. Fitzmyer does (*Romans: A New Translation with Introduction and Commentary*, AB 33 [New York: Doubleday, 1993], 458). The simple fact that Paul is using the second person plural to address the Roman believers as his sisters and brothers in itself suggests an "ecclesial consideration." Of course, Paul may intentionally be speaking of the body of Christ in both of those senses.

grace of God; for if righteousness were through the law, then Christ died in vain." As we have noted previously, Paul's affirmation that he has died *to* the law *through* the law should probably be understood in the sense that the law itself leads one to Christ by pointing to him as the one in whom it finds its fulfillment and goal or purpose (Gal 3:24; cf. Rom 10:4). Because they now live under Christ as their Lord, they no longer live under the law in the way they did previously. The type of righteousness that the law commanded but could not bring about in people is now brought about by God through Christ as believers look to him in faith so as to live in the same love that he manifested for all in his death. That love sought to form a community in which all would be committed to practicing the righteousness of God by loving others in the same way he did. His death was therefore the means by which both that community and the love and righteousness that are its primary characteristic have become a reality. However, as Paul affirms here, if that same righteousness could have been brought about by the law independently of Christ, it would have been pointless and unnecessary for Christ to have given up his life seeking to make that righteousness a reality. He would therefore have died for no reason, since he would have attained nothing that was not already available through the law.

Dying with Christ

According to many of those who ascribe to Paul the idea of participation in Christ and his death, his allusion to being crucified with Christ in Gal 2:19 should be understood in a literal or ontological sense rather than a metaphorical one. Supposedly, Paul believed that in some mysterious fashion he actually had been and continued to be crucified with Christ and that Christ now lived in him. While in theory it is possible to claim that Paul's language here and elsewhere reflects such an idea, a careful examination of his letters reveals that in reality there is nothing in them to indicate that he thought in those terms.[69] On the contrary, his repeated use of metaphor throughout his letters suggests that his language in passages such as Gal 2:19 is metaphorical.[70]

Paul's language in passages such as Gal 2:19 should be understood on the basis of the ideas that form part of the story Paul tells regarding Jesus and the *ekklēsia.* By acknowledging and confessing Christ as Lord, believers such as Paul identify fully with the love that characterized him not only in life but especially in death. As they do so, they reject the behaviors and values of

---

69. See David A. Brondos, *Paul on the Cross: Reconstructing the Apostle's Story of Redemption* (Minneapolis: Fortress, 2006), 151-89.

70. On Paul's extensive use of metaphor, see Raymond F. Collins, *The Power of Images in Paul* (Collegeville, MN: Liturgical Press, 2008); David J. Williams, *Paul's Metaphors: Their Context and Character* (Peabody, MA: Hendrickson, 1999).

the world so as to refuse to be conformed to that world and instead become transformed in their way of thinking (Rom 12:2; Gal 6:14). At the same time, they come to live to God rather than living to sin, unrighteousness, or the flesh. The result of such a life is the same type of persecution and rejection that Christ endured. Because in the face of that persecution and rejection Christ chose to remain firm in his love for others and his commitment to bringing them to love in the same way, he was crucified. He thus preferred to die rather than to be conformed to the world, since only in that way could he hope to bring others to live in the same type of love. Even though God raised him from the dead as a result of his perseverance and faithfulness to the task given him, according to a tradition that is reflected elsewhere in the New Testament and appears to have been passed down to Paul, in his risen condition Christ continues to bear the scars of his crucifixion on his body.[71] In 1 Cor 1:23 and 2:2, Paul uses the perfect tense to speak of Christ as the one who not only *was* crucified but *remains* crucified even in his risen condition. He also uses the perfect tense to speak of himself being crucified with Christ in Gal 2:19 and to affirm that he is crucified to the world in Gal 6:14.[72]

Therefore, because believers identify fully not only with Christ but also with the way he related to God, to others, to sin, and to the world, they too can be said to be crucified with Christ in a metaphorical sense. When they came to faith, they renounced sin and the flesh and committed themselves to living in accordance with God's will as it is now defined through Christ. In their baptism, they manifested this commitment in the presence of others who had also assumed the same commitment in relation to Christ. In that sense, they were "baptized into his death" and have been "united with him in a death like his" (Rom 6:3, 5). On the basis of that commitment, they can be said to have died and been buried with Christ (Rom 6:4, 8). In other words, the old persons that they were previously no longer exist. Through their faith in Christ and their subjection to him as their Lord, they now live as new persons or a "new creation" (2 Cor 5:17; Gal 6:15). The persons they were prior to coming to faith have disappeared and now lie forever dead and buried, just as Christ in his risen condition remains forever dead to sin because he lives to God (Rom 6:9-11). Because believers identify fully with Christ and everything that he and his death represent, they can be said not

---

71. See John 20:20, 25-27; Gal 6:17.

72. When Paul uses the perfect tense to speak of being crucified with Christ, there is no reason to think that he saw himself as "still hanging on the cross," contrary to what James Dunn affirms (*The Theology of Paul's Letter to the Galatians*, NTT [Cambridge: Cambridge University Press, 1993], 120). Both Matthew and Mark use the same perfect participle *estaurōmenos* to allude to the risen Christ as one who was and thus *remains* forever crucified, even though he does not continue to hang on a cross (Matt 24:5; Mark 16:6).

only to have died and to have been crucified and buried but also to have died and to have been crucified and buried *together with Christ.* They come to belong to Christ so as to crucify their flesh with its passions and desires (Gal 5:24).

These ideas provide the background necessary to understand Paul's words in Gal 2:19-20, as well as in Rom 6:1-14, 2 Cor 5:14-15, and Gal 6:14-17. When Paul writes that believers in Christ have died and been buried with Christ in their baptism, he is not affirming that some type of mysterious transformation took place in them when they were baptized that should now constitute the basis for a new way of life on their part. In Paul's thought, the imperative "consider yourselves dead" is not based on the indicative "you have died."[73] Rather, from the moment that believers came to faith in Christ so as to live under his lordship, they already considered themselves or their old persons dead to sin and alive to God together with Christ. When Paul says that believers were buried and crucified with Christ in their baptism, he is referring to the fact that in their baptism they manifested their commitment to putting away their old person in order to identify fully with Christ in their way of thinking and living so as to "walk in newness of life" (Rom 6:4). Their "body of sin" is destroyed in that their body and its members are no longer dedicated to sin and unrighteousness, as they were previously (Rom 6:6, 13, 16, 19).[74] Instead, believers now present their members "as slaves to righteousness for sanctification" (Rom 6:18-19). In part, the reason that Paul uses the passive voice to say that they were buried with Christ in baptism and were joined with him in the likeness of his death in Rom 6:4-5 is that baptism was not an act that believers performed upon themselves but rather something to which they submitted at the hands of

---

73. On the indicative-imperative distinction in Pauline studies and the criticisms that have been made of the ways in which that distinction has been understood, see Ruben Zimmermann, *The Logic of Love: Discovering Paul's "Implicit Ethics" through 1 Corinthians*, trans. Dieter T. Roth (Lanham, MD: Lexington/Fortress Academic, 2018), 13-21.

74. When Paul speaks of the "body of sin" in Rom 6:6, the context indicates that he is not referring to some collective entity in which all participate, but rather to the body of each believer. He uses the singular "body" in similar fashion in v. 12 to tell the Romans: "Do not let sin reign in your mortal body" (*en tō thnētō hymōn sōmati*). Here he is clearly referring to the body of each believer rather than some collective body in which all share. With respect to the phrase "body of sin," Arland J. Hultgren notes: "In this context and others Paul does not refer specifically to the anatomical body as such. The term refers to the physical-social-spiritual identity of a person. The understanding presupposed is that human life has many aspects (physical, social, spiritual) that cannot be reduced to any one alone. By 'the body of sin' in this context Paul refers to the life of the Christian prior to baptism, a life that has now been put to death through baptism into the death of Christ" (*Paul's Letter to the Romans: A Commentary* [Grand Rapids: Eerdmans, 2011], 249).

another believer. They were therefore baptized into Christ's death in the sense that they came to identify fully with everything that Christ's death represented, namely, his love for others and his commitment to living to God and rejecting sin. It was this to which believers joined themselves rather than to the actual event of Jesus' death, which now lay in the past and remained there, like all historical events from the past.

In Romans 6, therefore, Paul is reminding believers of what they had already done in baptism, when they put off their old self so as to become dead to sin and alive to God together with Christ, and exhorting them to continue to do these things. At the same time, he insists that the reason that they will not live to sin is that in their baptism they manifested in definitive fashion their commitment to living to God together with Christ and therefore died to sin once and for all (Rom 6:1-2). Rather than "becoming what they are," therefore, they are to continue in the same commitment that they made when they were baptized. The indicatives "we have died with Christ" and "you were buried with Christ" are therefore based on the fact that in their baptism they came to regard themselves as dead and buried by identifying with Christ crucified, who now lives for God as they do.

Because of his own commitment to living under Christ as his Lord, in Gal 6:14 Paul uses the perfect tense to affirm that through Christ's cross he has been crucified with Christ to the world. The world is also crucified to him in that he identifies with everything that the cross represents and symbolizes rather than identifying with that which the world values.[75] Due to his work as an apostle of Christ and the opposition of the world to that work, he has come to have on his body the same type of scars that Christ bears on his risen body as a result of the opposition that his own work on behalf of the salvation of others generated (Gal 6:17).[76] Paul expects all those who are dedicated to the same purpose to identify with Christ's cross in the same way so as to be willing to endure whatever is necessary to bring others to live under that gospel rather than seeking their own interests or backing down from their efforts to see that objective accomplished in the face of persecution.[77]

In 2 Cor 5:14-15, Paul states explicitly the purpose for which Christ had died: "For the love of Christ constrains us, because we are convinced of this: that one died on behalf of all; therefore all have died. And he died on behalf of all, so that those who live might no longer live for themselves but for him who died and was raised for them." Christ's objective in life and

---

75. For this understanding of Gal 6:14, see Jeff Hubing, *Crucifixion and New Creation: The Strategic Purpose of Galatians 6.11-17*, LNTS 508 (London: Bloomsbury T & T Clark, 2015), 229-45.

76. See Martinus C. de Boer, *Galatians: A Commentary*, NTL (Louisville: Westminster John Knox, 2011), 409.

77. See Gal 5:11; 6:12; Phil 3:18-19.

death was that all come to be constrained by his same love, living not for themselves but for God and others as he did and together with him. His dedication and commitment to that objective led to his being put to death but also to his being raised from the dead by his Father. He died on behalf of all in the sense that he sought to bring about in them the type of life that would enable them to experience God's salvation and forgiveness. What leads them to live that type of life now is their conviction that God raised Christ after he had given his life seeking that all come to live in his same love. That conviction brings them to live for him, since they know that if they do so he will bring them to live *with* him some day. His love constrains them in the sense that, as they acknowledge him as their Lord who gave his life for them so that they too might come to give their life for others, they can do nothing else but live in that way.[78]

Christ's Death for Sins

In three passages from his epistles, Paul uses short formulas to speak of Jesus dying for the sins of others. In 1 Cor 15:3, he tells the Corinthians: "For I passed on to you as of first importance that which I also received: that Christ died for our sins in accordance with the scriptures." Many scholars believe that Paul is also citing a traditional formula in Rom 4:25, where he writes that Jesus "was delivered up on account of our transgressions and was raised for our justification." At the outset of his letter to the Galatians, Paul similarly states that Christ "gave himself for our sins to set us free from the present evil age in accordance with the will of our God and Father" (Gal 1:4).

Due to the influence of penal substitution interpretations of Paul's thought, all three of these passages have traditionally been understood in the sense that Jesus died to obtain for others the *forgiveness* of their sins. This presupposes that without Jesus' death it was impossible for God to forgive sins. As we have seen above, however, the idea that suffering or a sacrificial death was necessary for God to forgive sins is foreign to Jewish thought. Likewise, the idea that God could not forgive sins without Jesus' death appears nowhere in Paul's epistles, the New Testament as a whole, or any Christian writing until the Middle Ages.[79] Furthermore, none of the three passages just cited mentions forgiveness. While Rom 4:25 refers to the justification of believers, it relates that justification to Jesus' resurrection rather than his death.

---

78. On the possible meanings of the verb *synechein* in 2 Cor 5:14, see Margaret E. Thrall, *A Critical and Exegetical Commentary on the Second Epistle to the Corinthians*, ICC (Edinburgh: T & T Clark, 1994), 1:408-9.

79. The first Christian theologian to affirm and develop such an idea explicitly was Anselm of Canterbury (1033-1109); see David A. Brondos, *Fortress Introduction to Salvation and the Cross* (Minneapolis: Fortress, 2007), 76-87.

In reality, these three passages can be readily understood by looking instead to the narrative regarding Jesus and his death considered above in order to interpret them. According to that narrative, the purpose for which God sent his Son and gave him up to the death of the cross was not to make it possible for him to forgive human beings their sins without compromising his perfect justice, but rather to bring into existence through his Son a community in which people might come to live in the way that God desired for their own good so that they might experience his blessings of salvation both in this world and in the world to come. What prevented them from attaining that life was precisely their sinful way of life, that is, the sins in which they lived. And the way in which God intended to save them from those sins was by sending his Son to bring them to live under his lordship as members of his community of followers so that they might thereby be conformed to his image, practicing the righteousness that God would bring about in them as a free gift by pure grace and having God's love poured into their hearts.

When Jesus' dedication to that task led to conflict and the threat of the cross, in obedience to his Father's will, he gave up his life rather than seeking to save it, since only in that way could he and his Father hope to accomplish their objective. Had Jesus refused to give up his life in the face of the cross and instead turned in on himself, he would have ceased to love others in the way that God loves them, with a love that holds nothing back. In that case, he could never have become the type of Lord that he is now, a Lord fully dedicated and consecrated to the salvation of others out of love for them. Nor could he have presided over a community in which all would love one another in the same way, since he would never have laid the basis for such a community. Neither he nor his Father could expect to bring into existence a community such as the one Paul describes in Phil 2:1-5 and elsewhere throughout his epistles had Jesus not given of himself to and for others to the very end, even to the point of dying the death of a slave on the cross (Phil 2:7-8). As noted above, had God withheld his Son when his activity led to the threat of the cross rather than giving him up, the community whose defining characteristic would be the type of love of which Paul speaks in Rom 8:31-39 would never have been established.

Rather than giving up his life in order to make it possible for God to forgive sins, therefore, Jesus had died for the sins of others in the sense that he had given up his life so that what he had sought on behalf of others might come to pass, namely, that they might be brought to leave behind their sins and thereby be delivered from the destructive consequences of those sins. It was thus his commitment to saving them from their sins—that is, their sinful life—that had led to his death. Paul's words in 1 Cor 15:3 suggest that when Jesus' earliest followers were asked why God had allowed his Son to die on a cross, they responded by saying that he had died for the same reason that the servant of Isaiah 53 had died: he had entered into the midst of a sinful people seeking to save them from their sins by bringing them to abandon those sins.[80] Although his efforts to accomplish that objective had cost him his life, his faithfulness to that objective and his willingness to give up his life for it had also made it possible for it to be achieved, as it now was in the community of his followers. Of course, by bringing about such a change in those who would come to form part of his community, at the same time Jesus had attained their acceptance and forgiveness by God. Therefore his death would be said to have been "for their sins" in that sense as well.

There were thus several senses in which the affirmation that Jesus had given up his life and been handed over for the sins and transgressions of others could be understood. He had died as a result of his commitment to saving others from their sins in the sense of bringing them to put away those sins so as to be delivered from their destructive consequences. Their sins had necessitated Jesus' coming to carry out a ministry aimed at enabling them to leave behind those sins, and the consequence of Jesus' dedication to that ministry had been his death. He had of course also died on account of the sins and transgressions of others in that his death had been brought about by the sins and transgressions of those who opposed him and wished to silence him. By saving others from their sinful ways and the intrinsic consequences of their sins, however, he had also saved them from God's wrath and judgment at their sins. When God came to judge the world in order to do away with sin, evil, and injustice, those who through faith in Christ had been brought to leave behind their sins so as to live to God would be saved from that judgment. Christ had therefore given up his life so that this too might take place. And because he had given up his life for the sins of others in obedience to the will of his Father (Gal 1:4), it could be said that he had been "delivered up" by God for their transgressions as well (Rom 4:25; 8:32).

The narrative regarding Christ's death considered above also provides the basis necessary for understanding what Paul affirms in 2 Cor 5:21, where he writes that God "made him who knew no sin to be sin for our sake, so that we might become the righteousness of God in him." Interpreters have debated whether Paul's affirmation that God made Christ sin is an allusion to Christ's coming into the world or instead refers to his death, yet it is possible that Paul had both of these things in mind.[81] If Paul ascribes some type of preexistence to Christ, then Paul's idea is that prior to coming

---

80. It is possible that Jesus' earliest followers initially appealed to Isaiah 53 in response to the accusation that he had died for his own sins; see Peder Borgen, "'In Accordance with the Scriptures'," in *Early Christian Thought in its Jewish Context*, ed. John Barclay and John Sweet (Cambridge: Cambridge University Press, 1996), 193-206 (197-99).

81. On this discussion, see Thrall, *Second Corinthians*, 1:439-42.

into the world, Christ knew no sin. Because the world is dominated by sin, to come into the world involved being "made sin" in some sense. At the same time, the consequence of Christ's efforts to bring others to practice the righteousness of God of which Paul speaks was the threat of the cross. Rather than sparing his Son the cross, God gave him up to death and in that sense can be said to have "made him sin," since God treated him as if he were a sinner by not intervening to spare him such a death. According to Jewish thought, God does not answer the prayers of sinners, and thus by abandoning Jesus to death on a cross, God appeared to have treated Jesus as a sinner and "made him sin." Nevertheless, because Jesus had not lived in sin, Paul can say that he "knew no sin" not only prior to coming into the world but also in the course of his life. When God had sent his Son to dedicate himself to the very end to the task of bringing others to leave behind their sin and instead live to righteousness, in a sense his death became inevitable, since his dedication to that task would ultimately lead to his death. Yet for the reasons just considered above, by giving up his Son and "making him sin," God had made it possible for believers to be brought into a community in which they now become the "righteousness of God" by identifying fully with that righteousness.[82]

Only a few passages from Paul's epistles use language taken from the realm of sacrifice to speak of Jesus' death. In 1 Cor 5:7, Paul writes that "Christ our Passover lamb has been sacrificed." Because Passover lambs were not offered up as sacrifices for sins or regarded as expiatory in any sense, here Paul is not relating Jesus' death to the forgiveness of sins. Rather, his idea instead appears to be that Christ's death fulfills typologically the sacrifice of Passover lambs, which prefigured the way in which Christ's life would be offered up so that through him others might come to be liberated from their bondage and slavery to sin.

In 1 Cor 10:16-18, Paul speaks of sharing in the blood and the body of Christ by partaking of the cup of blessing and the bread that were used when believers celebrated the Lord's Supper. In the following chapter, he recalls Jesus' words over the bread and cup at the Last Supper, when he referred to the bread as "my body for you" and to the cup as "the new covenant in my blood" (1 Cor 11:24-25). Here Paul presents Jesus giving up his life—that is, his body and blood—on behalf of others, thereby establishing a new covenant with them. Neither of these two passages relates Jesus' death to the forgiveness of sins explicitly. Because of the intimate link between

---

82. On the difficulties of interpreting Paul's affirmation that believers in Christ become the righteousness of God in 2 Cor 5:21, see Morna D. Hooker, "On Being the Righteousness of God: Another Look at 2 Cor 5:21," *NovT* 50 (2008): 358-75 (369-75). Hooker is probably correct in affirming that, for Paul, the phrase should be understood in terms of "living righteously" and "serving as instruments of God's righteousness" (373-74).

sacrifice and prayer in Jewish thought, however, these passages imply that Jesus had offered himself up to God seeking that God accept and receive all those who would come to identify with his self-offering on their behalf. This identification would involve committing themselves to loving others and sharing their lives with them in the same way that Jesus had as members of the community that would live under his lordship, yet also seeing themselves as those on whose behalf Jesus had offered himself up to God, seeking that God accept and receive them. This acceptance would undoubtedly be understood in terms of the forgiveness of their sins as well. The basis upon which God would accept, receive, and forgive believers, however, was not Jesus' death itself but the new life that they would come to lead as they lived under him and the new covenant established through his death.

Because the Greek phrase *peri hamartias* that Paul employs in Rom 8:3 is used in the Septuagint to refer to sacrifices for sin, many interpreters have claimed that in that passage Paul is affirming that God sent his Son as a sacrifice for sin.[83] This presupposes that God sent his Son primarily for the purpose of offering up his life as a sacrifice. As we have seen above, however, sacrifices for sin were not understood in terms of inflicting on a sacrificial victim the punishment or condemnation to which others were subject on account of their sins. Nor were sacrifices for sin thought to deal with the power of sin in the flesh of those on whose behalf they were offered. Rather, they were merely means by which God's people expressed to him their sincere repentance and petitioned him for forgiveness. Above all, it must be stressed once more that in Jewish thought God did not need sacrifices in order to forgive sins. To affirm that God sent Christ to offer himself up to God as a sacrifice for sin so that God might forgive human beings their sins would be to maintain that God sent Christ to die because God needed Christ's death in order to do something that he could not do otherwise, namely, forgive sins. Such an idea must be considered as foreign to Paul's thought as the idea that God could not forgive sins without a sacrificial death or sacrificial blood was foreign to ancient Jewish thought.

Paul's words in Rom 8:3-4, therefore, should instead be understood against the background of the narrative considered above. According to that narrative, God had sent his Son to bring people to live in conformity with his will. God's objective had not been that his Son die, but that he enable the "sin in the flesh" that made it impossible for people to practice the righteousness of which the law spoke to be condemned so that they might be enabled to fulfill that righteousness by walking according to the Spirit. As this takes place, of course, they are also freed from the condemnation that results from living subject to sin's power (Rom 8:1), yet the basis upon

---

83. See, for example, N. T. Wright, *The Climax of the Covenant: Christ and the Law in Pauline Theology* (Edinburgh: T & T Clark, 1991), 220-25.

which they are delivered from this condemnation is not Christ's death per se but his activity in liberating them from the body of sin and death that holds them captive (Rom 6:6-13; 7:24). Christ came "for sin" (*peri hamartias*), then, in the sense that God sent him to free those who were subject to sin from its power. Undoubtedly, Christ died as a result of his dedication to that task, yet according to Paul it is not his death itself that enabled that objective to be accomplished but rather all that God has done through Christ and his Spirit.

The passage in which Paul almost certainly relates Jesus' death to a sacrifice for sins is Rom 3:24-26, which is also among the most difficult passages from Paul's epistles to translate and interpret.[84] There Paul applies to Christ the same term *hilastērion* that is found in 4 Macc 17:22. According to a literal rendering of Paul's words in the passage, he speaks there of "the redemption that is in Christ Jesus, whom God put forward as a *hilastērion*-through-faith by means of his blood in order to make known his righteousness on account of the previous passing-over of sins in the forbearance of God, for the purpose of making known his righteousness in the present time, so that he might be righteous and the one who justifies the one who lives out of Jesus-faith." Most Pauline scholars agree that, even though Paul adds the words "in" or "by means of his blood" (*en tō haimati autou*) immediately after the word "faith" (*pistis*) in 3:25, he is not referring there to faith in Christ's blood—an idea that appears nowhere else in the letters attributed to Paul or the New Testament as a whole—but of God's putting Christ forward or displaying Christ as a *hilastērion* by means of his blood or death.[85] Yet Christ is a "*hilastērion*-through-faith" in the sense that he serves as *hilastērion* for all those who live "out of Jesus-faith" (*ek pisteōs Iēsou*, 3:26).

It is important to note that Paul does not speak here of *Jesus' death* as the *hilastērion*, but of *Jesus himself* being put forward by God as a *hilastērion* by means of his blood. Because the Septuagint uses the term *hilastērion* to refer to the mercy seat that stood in the Holy of holies upon which sacrificial blood was sprinkled on the Day of Atonement, many interpreters have claimed that Paul is affirming that in some sense God put Jesus forward as a new mercy seat in his death. Other interpreters, however, argue that *hilastērion* should be understood in the sense of expiation or propitiation.[86] In reality, any of these interpretations is possible when the passage is understood on the basis of the narrative regarding Christ's death outlined above.

---

84. On the many difficulties involved in translating Rom 3:24-26, see especially Richard N. Longenecker, *The Epistle to the Romans: A Commentary on the Greek Text*, NIGTC (Grand Rapids: Eerdmans, 2016), 392-94.

85. On this understanding of the phrase "through faith in his blood," see Robert Jewett, *Romans: A Commentary*, Hermeneia (Minneapolis: Fortress, 2007), 297-98.

86. On this discussion and its history, see especially Finlan, *Background and Content*, 123-62.

It must be remembered, however, that sacrifices for sin such as the one offered up by the high priest on the Day of Atonement were in essence petitions for God's forgiveness and that God responded favorably to such petitions and the sacrificial blood offered up to him only when they were a sincere expression of the people's commitment to living in accordance with his will.

Of course, when Jesus offered himself up to God seeking that God accept and forgive all those who would come to live under him as members of his community, they had not yet been brought to leave behind their sinful life and commit themselves to living in accordance with God's will. However, both Jesus' self-offering as well as the implicit petition he would be seen as having offered up on their behalf would have presupposed that those whose acceptance and forgiveness he sought from God would come to live in the way God desired and commanded. If they instead were simply to continue unrepentantly in their sins, they would not be acceptable to God and would not obtain his forgiveness by virtue of Jesus' intercession on their behalf. Of course, in that case neither could they be said to live in the "Jesus-faith" of which Paul speaks.

When Paul refers to Jesus as a *hilastērion*-by-faith by means of his blood, therefore, he would have had in mind the idea that Jesus went to his death seeking that God accept and forgive all who would come to live in faith under him. God responded favorably to that petition when he raised Jesus from the dead and exalted him so that he might be Lord over the community of believers. If *hilastērion* is understood in the sense of expiation, Paul's idea would be that all who would come to live out of Jesus-faith would become acceptable to God by being cleansed of their sins, not only in a forensic sense but also in the sense that they would no longer live in those sins so as instead to live in accordance with God's will. By being cleansed from their sinful life, they would be cleansed in God's sight as well, though they would also remain in need of God's forgiveness because they would not be able to live entirely free of sin. In spite of this, God would accept them as pure by virtue of their relationship to Christ through faith, since that relationship ensured that they would come to live as God desired and commanded out of love for all.

For the same reason, it could be said that in his death Jesus had put away God's wrath at the sins of those who would come to live under him. Nevertheless, it was not Jesus' death or blood that put away God's wrath, but rather the fact that as a result of Jesus' death many would be able to be transformed in the way God desired through their faith in Jesus as their Lord as they came to live as members of his community. It was to that end that God had sent his Son and given him over to death. All those who now looked to Jesus in faith so as to live out of that faith could therefore be assured that they were no longer under God's wrath. Nevertheless, the purpose for which God had put Jesus forward as a *hilastērion* was not that he put away God's wrath at sin, but rather that through his death he might bring into existence a community of people who would be able to enjoy peace with him and experience his forgiveness by virtue of their relation to Jesus as their Lord. Because under Jesus they would no longer live in ways that destroyed their own lives and those of others, they would no longer fall under God's wrath.

If Paul is instead referring to Jesus as a mercy seat in his death, his words can be interpreted in the sense that God sent his Son and gave him over to death so that he might be the one through whom believers can now draw near to him to find forgiveness and acceptance. Once again, however, the reason for this would be that through Jesus they would be brought into conformity with God's will and therefore be able to approach him through Jesus confidently, knowing that he would receive them favorably in spite of the fact that they were not entirely without sin.

Given the context of Rom 3:25, Paul may have alluded to Jesus in the way he does there to stress that, by pure grace and at the cost of the life of his Son, God had given both Jews and gentiles the same means of access to him, given that previously only those who lived under the Torah could approach him through sacrificial means to experience his acceptance and forgiveness. By God's grace alone, it was now through Christ rather than through the Torah independently of Christ that believers could find redemption and be declared righteous as they practiced the righteousness of God to which the Torah and the prophets had pointed (Rom 3:21-24).

Interpreters of Rom 3:24-26 have debated whether the allusions to God's righteousness that appear in these verses should be understood as objective or subjective genitives. They have also disagreed as to whether God's "passing-over" of sins alludes to the forgiveness of sins given through Jesus or instead to something God did prior to making him a *hilastērion*.[87] In reality, any of these interpretations are possible and can be regarded as being in full accordance with what we have seen above. God may be said to have shown himself to be righteous, not in the sense that he has shown in Christ's death that he punishes sin rather than tolerating it, but in the sense that he is fully committed to bringing about in human beings the righteousness that he desires to see in all. This is what he has done in Christ. Furthermore, once it

---

87. Opposition to the idea that in Rom 3:25-26 Paul speaks of God passing over sins freely independently of Christ's death and prior to it is based on the presupposition that God's strict justice makes it impossible for God to forgive sins without the sacrificial death of Christ. C. E. B. Cranfield, for example, comments that "for God simply to pass over sins would be altogether incompatible with his righteousness" (*A Critical and Exegetical Commentary on the Epistle to the Romans*, 6th ed., ICC [Edinburgh: T & T Clark, 1975], 1:211-12). For reasons we have seen, however, such an idea must be considered foreign to Paul's thought.

is understood that it is not Christ's death that serves as the basis for the forgiveness of believers but the new life of righteousness that God graciously brings about in them through Christ, it can be said that God overlooks and forgives both the past and the present sins of all people on the condition that they come to live in faith under Christ as their Lord so that in that way they may become the people God wants them to be for their own good. As they live out of Jesus-faith, God's righteousness is manifested in and through them, both because they come to *practice* that righteousness and because, on that basis, God *accepts* them as righteous. In his forbearance God had thus passed over the sins of human beings in anticipation of the time when, in spite of that sin and out of pure grace, they might be brought to live in his righteousness by means of his Son.

Paul appears to have the same ideas in mind in 2 Cor 5:18-19, where he writes: "All this is from God, who has reconciled us to himself through Christ and given us the ministry of reconciliation; that is, in Christ God was reconciling the world to himself, not taking into account their trespasses, and entrusting to us the word of reconciliation." Here Paul attributes the reconciliation of believers with God to all that God has done through Christ rather than to his death alone. He also seems to have in mind the proclamation of the gospel through Paul and other "ambassadors of Christ" as the means by which the reconciliation of which he speaks is brought about. When Paul affirms that God does not take into account the trespasses of human beings, his words should be understood once more in the sense that God is willing to overlook the sins of the past as long as people come to live in harmony, friendship, and peace with him through Christ by accepting the "word of reconciliation" proclaimed to them. Ultimately, it is this that he desires out of love for them.

CONCLUSION

No matter what date one may assign to any "parting of the ways" between Judaism and Christianity, what we have seen in this study makes it clear that a "parting of the Gods" between those Jews who believed in Jesus as the Christ and those who did not had taken place by Paul's day. In fact, there can be little doubt that the key elements in the gospel that we find in Paul's epistles go back to a time prior to his experience on the road to Damascus, some seventeen years before he wrote his Epistle to the Galatians.[1] By then, the belief that God had raised Jesus from among the dead had already led Jesus' earliest followers to the conviction that God had also exalted him to his right hand as Lord and Christ and that Jesus was God's Son in a way that set him apart from all other human beings, including the great figures from Israel's past. From the moment in which that conviction was in place, the God being proclaimed by Jesus' followers was no longer simply the God of Israel or the God of Abraham, Isaac, and Jacob. He was first and foremost the God of Jesus Christ, the same God whom we encounter throughout Paul's epistles. And from the perspective of those Jews who were not persuaded by the claims that Jesus' followers were making about him, the God of Israel was *not* the God of Jesus Christ, nor was the God of Jesus Christ the God of Israel. In effect, Jesus' followers were proclaiming a God that most Jews would have found strange, new, and unrecognizable, a God who had sent his Son into the world, handed him over to death on a cross, and then raised him from the dead three days later before exalting him at his side in heaven. This was not the God in whom Jews had always believed.

What set the God of Jesus Christ apart from the God in whom Jews had traditionally believed, however, was not simply that he was inseparable from Jesus as his Son. If what Jesus' followers were proclaiming about God was true, it was necessary to rethink many of the most basic tenets of the Jewish faith. In order to discern God's will for their lives, God's people were now to look to Jesus rather than to the Torah alone. In order for God's purposes to be accomplished among them, it was not enough for people simply to live in accordance with the Torah. Uncircumcised gentiles who lived as

---

1. See Gal 1:18; 2:1.

followers of Jesus but did not form part of Israel and did not observe the Torah were now to be accepted on equal terms with those who did, since God himself had accepted them on those terms. The righteousness that God desired to see in all was to be defined on the basis of faith in Christ or Christ-faith and could be brought about independently of the observance of the Torah. God now wanted people to relate to him through Jesus and to address Jesus as Lord in much the same way that they addressed God as Lord.[2] God also desired that Jews and gentiles together live under a new or renewed covenant that he had established through Jesus. All of these points were central to Paul's proclamation of the gospel, and there is every reason to believe that they also constituted an integral part of the message proclaimed by the other apostles of Jesus, including James and Peter, who gave to Paul "the right hand of fellowship" in support of his ministry to the gentiles (Gal 2:9).

Yet while the God proclaimed by Paul and other apostles was in many ways different from the God in whom Jews had traditionally believed, in other ways he was the same. As the sovereign and omnipotent creator of all things, he needed nothing from human beings and did not depend on them in any way. In his love, he desired above all else that human beings enjoy his blessings of shalom and well-being. For that reason, he called on all to live according to his will, not for *his* sake, but for *theirs*. His judgments were aimed at doing away with evil and rooting out those who insisted on aligning themselves with evil so that what is good, right, and just might prevail and all might attain the wholeness he desired for human beings, both in this world and the world to come. He therefore declared his acceptance of those who committed themselves to living in conformity with his good will, while at the same time warning those who refused to do so of the consequences of such a refusal. The basis upon which he justified people, therefore, was their commitment to practicing justice, righteousness, and love. Of course, because such a commitment could be brought about only by faith in him and his word, it could be said that justification was by faith. Any who truly believed in God would live in the way he desired and commanded out of love for all, since any who refused to commit themselves to living in that way could hardly be said to be living in faith or truly believing and trusting in God. That commitment was also the basis upon which God forgave people the sins they had committed in the past and inevitably continued to commit in the present. God did not demand perfection, which was impossible for human beings to attain, but simply that all look to him in faith to receive as a gift the life of righteousness that he brought about in those who believed and trusted in him by pure grace and not because of any merit or works on their part.

---

2. See especially Rom 10:9-13; 14:9; 1 Cor 1:2; 8:6; 12:3; 2 Cor 5:5; Phil 2:9-11.

On all of these points, those Jews such as Paul who believed in Jesus as the Christ and those Jews who did not were in full agreement. The difference between the two was that believers in Jesus defined God's will primarily by looking to Jesus, while those Jews who did not believe in Jesus continued to look to the Torah independently of Jesus to define God's will. Yet even among believers in Christ it was never questioned that the observance of the Torah among Jews was a good thing, although in light of their faith in Christ his followers who were Jewish seem to have understood the purpose and significance of such observance in a manner that was in some ways distinct from other Jews.

On the basis of these observations, however, it is also necessary to speak of a second "parting of the Gods." This parting of the Gods took place, not in the first century, but in later centuries with the development of Christian theology. It involves a parting of the Christian God away from the Jewish God that Paul had in common with his fellow Jews, including those who did not believe in Jesus. This parting of the Gods is especially evident in Western Christian thought since the time of Anselm of Canterbury (1033-1109). What distinguishes the God of traditional Western Christianity from the Jewish God of Paul and first-century Judaism is the belief that God's perfectly holy, just, and righteous nature places limits on God and thus presents an obstacle to the salvation of human beings.[3] Because salvation is equated with the forgiveness of sins and it is maintained that it would be contrary to God's justice for God simply to forgive sins freely, it is claimed that God's Son had to become human in order to make satisfaction for human sins to God or God's justice through his death on the cross. Only in that way could human beings be delivered from the punishment to which they were subject on account of their sins.

Despite the fact that it is based on philosophical and theological arguments regarding the nature of God that are foreign to the thought world of the Hebrew Scriptures, ancient Judaism, Paul, and the New Testament as a whole, for centuries such an understanding of God has simply been assumed and read back into the biblical texts by biblical scholars and theologians. More than anything else, it is this assumption that has not only obscured the interpretation of Paul's epistles but has also generated

---

3. In Eastern Christian thought, since the time of the church fathers, the obstacle to human salvation has also been defined on the basis of a particular understanding of the nature of God as well as that of human beings: because their human nature prevents human beings from sharing in the divine nature so as to be united with God, it was necessary for God's Son to become human in order to unite human nature with the divine and thereby save it. On the problems of such an understanding of Christ's saving work as well as the problems raised by the thought of Anselm and the Reformers discussed throughout the remainder of this chapter, see David A. Brondos, *Fortress Introduction to Salvation and the Cross* (Minneapolis: Fortress, 2007), 49-115.

discussions and debates that continue to plague biblical interpretation and Christian thought.

While there is no need to enter into those discussions and debates in detail here, it is important to stress just how alien such an understanding of God is both to the thought of Paul and to first-century Judaism in general. Among Jews in antiquity, it was not the God of Israel but the gods of the nations who were subject to the limitations of their own nature. The one true sovereign creator God knew no such limitations and was always free to do anything he willed or desired. Nothing in his nature prevented him from forgiving sins or holding back his wrath against sins if he so desired. In his love, what concerned him was not that human sins receive their due punishment but that human beings be delivered from their sinful and destructive ways so that they might not perish as a result of that sinfulness.

More importantly, when God is made subject to his own righteous nature, his activity in human history is regarded as ultimately being motivated by an inner need intrinsic to his being that must be satisfied. Ultimately, he acts not for the sake of human beings but for *his own* sake. He gives the law and demands that human beings obey it, not for *their* sake out of love for them, but for the sake of his own righteousness, which must be upheld, preserved, satisfied, and safeguarded. The law is then seen as an onerous burden imposed on human beings by a holy God rather than a gracious gift that promotes human well-being and shalom, as in the Hebrew Scriptures and ancient Jewish thought. Similarly, God is said to demand obedience—and in most cases an obedience that is *perfect*—, not for the good of human beings, but for his own sake, because his just and righteous nature requires it. Like the gods of the nations, what concerns this God is not the effect that the behavior of human beings has *on them* but the effect that it has *on him*. He condemns certain behavior as sinful, not because of the ways in which that behavior harms human beings, but because of the manner in which it displeases, offends, and aggravates *him* due to his perfectly holy and righteous nature.

When God is understood in this fashion, in essence he becomes analogous to a pagan god who must be satisfied or appeased by means of offerings. In order to be delivered from his wrath and judgment, the human beings who have offended him must offer him whatever he demands. According to the Western Christian teaching that developed out of Anselm's thought, because human beings are unable to present God with the perfect offering that his justice requires due to their sinfulness and imperfection, God himself accomplishes this task, placating his own wrath and satisfying the demands of his inflexible justice by means of his Son's death on the cross. Supposedly, in that way he manifests his love for human beings without compromising his just and righteous nature.

While such an understanding of God seemingly explains why Jesus' death was necessary for human salvation, it implies that all human beings without exception should be saved and forgiven on account of Jesus' death, since that death is said to have made sufficient satisfaction for the sins of humanity as a whole. Because a universal salvation of that type is considered contrary to biblical thought, however, it is maintained that Christ's death alone was *not* actually sufficient for human salvation and that a second condition must be fulfilled by human beings in order for them to be saved. The debate then becomes precisely what this second condition is. While a number of passages from Paul's epistles and the New Testament affirm that all people will be judged by their works,[4] in other passages Paul insists that justification is by faith and not by works of the law.[5]

On the basis of these latter passages, Protestant theologians since the time of the Reformation have claimed that faith alone is sufficient for salvation and have condemned the notion that salvation depends on one's works.[6] This latter position is characterized as "works-righteousness" and is attributed to Roman Catholicism and Judaism. Both of these traditions are then represented as denying God's grace and burdening human beings with the impossible task of earning their own salvation by producing on their own the good works God demands. While this in itself is oppressive, it also leaves believers in perpetual uncertainty and anxiety as to whether they have accumulated the sufficient number of works to be saved. Conversely, critics of the Protestant claim that justification and salvation are by faith alone repeatedly point out that it renders any type of obedience to God's law or the performance of good works superfluous and ends up constituting faith as the one "work" that must be fulfilled in order to attain justification and salvation. This debate rages on with no end in sight, precisely because it admits of no satisfactory solution. Most Christians ultimately resolve it by affirming that faith alone is the *initial* basis upon which one is justified and forgiven, but that subsequently one must live in the way God commands in order to *continue* to be justified and forgiven and remain free of God's wrath. In effect, this involves positing works as the basis for one's ultimate justification, though Protestant theologians do their best to avoid stating such a conclusion explicitly. In the Reformed tradition, it is common to attempt to resolve the difficulty by appealing to the doctrines of election and limited atonement, yet these doctrines raise other serious problems.

In both cases, the claim that there is a second condition in addition to Christ's death that must be fulfilled in order for human beings to be forgiven,

---

4. See, for example, Matt 7:1-2; 25:31-46; John 5:28-29; Rom 2:6-16; 14:10-12; 2 Cor 5:10; Rev 20:12-13.

5. See Rom 3:20, 27-30; 4:6; 5:1; Gal 2:16; 3:10-12, 24.

6. On what follows, see David A. Brondos, *Redeeming the Gospel: The Christian Faith Reconsidered*, SLHT (Minneapolis: Fortress, 2011), 51-150.

justified, and saved—whether this condition be works or faith alone—is once again grounded in an understanding of God that is foreign to ancient Jewish thought. Nothing compels God to establish this second condition for salvation, since in principle he could establish any condition he pleases or no additional condition at all. In principle, by virtue of Christ's death, which has satisfied his justice, God could forgive and save anyone he wishes independently of how they live or what they believe, yet for some unknown reason he has determined to demand of human beings either faith alone or faith together with works as a second and necessary condition for their salvation. There is no intrinsic reason why faith or works should enable human beings to be saved. The only reason that faith in Christ and perhaps works as well are required for salvation is that in his sovereignty God has decided that it should be so.

Furthermore, when works are said to be necessary in addition to faith, then the reason that human beings must do those works is not because those works are good in themselves or promote human well-being, but merely because in his righteousness and holiness God has decided to demand them. God is presented as a heavenly lawgiver and judge who, for no necessary reason, requires that human beings do the works he prescribes simply because it pleases him or satisfies his nature. Like a pagan god, in his law he commands human beings to do certain things and avoid others for *his* sake rather than *theirs* and promises to bless all who give him what he demands but to punish any who do not by pouring out his wrath upon them. Human beings are thus placed in the position of constantly having to placate this God and obtain his favor by subjecting themselves obediently to his will.

Thanks in large part to the influence of E. P. Sanders's work *Paul and Palestinian Judaism* and the work of other biblical scholars, it is now widely recognized that many of these ideas are foreign to ancient Jewish thought. Yet while Sanders and others questioned the notion that one needed to *earn* one's salvation by dedicating oneself tirelessly to accumulating the works necessary to appease God, they kept in place the same Western Christian concept of God and continued to attribute that concept of God to Paul and the New Testament in general. For no good or necessary reason, this God has supposedly decided that salvation should now be by Christ's death and faith in Christ rather than the law.[7] It is thus by no means clear precisely what Paul found wrong with Judaism, except that it is not Christianity.[8] In

---

7. E. P. Sanders, *Paul and Palestinian Judaism: A Comparison of Patterns of Religion* (Philadelphia: Fortress, 1977), 442-47.

8. See Sanders, *Paul and Palestinian Judaism*, 548-52. In his more recent work, Sanders has continued to make the same claim: "According to Paul's argument in Rom. 10:1-4, *what is wrong with the Jews is that they are not Christian; what is wrong with Judaism is that it does not accept Christianity*" (*Paul: The Apostle's Life, Letters, and Thought* [Minneapolis: Fortress, 2015], 681).

addition, discontent with the traditional Protestant understanding of Jesus' atoning death and the forensic view of justification associated with it has led Pauline scholars to attribute to Paul other ideas that were just as foreign to Second Temple Jewish thought in order to explain his understanding of the manner in which Jesus' death leads to salvation. These include especially the idea that persons can participate in Jesus and his death through some type of mystical or ontological union. Such an explanation of Paul's thought leaves unanswered the question of why God should have determined that human beings are now to be saved in that way, since there is no intrinsic reason why salvation should require such a participatory union.

What must be recognized, therefore, is that at the root of all of these problems and debates is an understanding of God that was as foreign to Paul as it was to Judaism and the Hebrew Bible in general. At the heart of the biblical understanding of God is the idea that behind all of God's activity in the world and in human history is a deep love for human beings and a profound concern for their well-being and wholeness. According to this understanding, God created a good world for *their* sake, just as he prohibited them from practicing sin, evil, and injustice for *their* sake rather than his own. When they persisted in sin, he elected Abraham so that through him and his descendants he might bless all the families of the earth. He established his covenant with Israel and gave his people the Torah out of love for them and those who would come to know him through them, since in and of itself the Torah promotes shalom and well-being for all. Like creation itself, the Torah is thus consistently seen as something that is very good, an instrument of blessing given by God out of love rather than an onerous burden imposed on people by a tyrannical, semi-pagan God out of a concern for his own holiness, justice, and righteousness. On all of these points, Paul was in full agreement with the traditional Jewish understanding of God.

Similarly, the reason that the God of Paul, the Jewish tradition, the New Testament, and the Hebrew Scriptures judges people is not to satisfy an inner need to condemn sin that is inherent to his righteous nature. He judges human beings, not for *his* sake, but for *theirs*, in order to establish and promote peace, justice, and well-being among them. For that reason, in biblical thought God's judgments are considered an expression of his *love*, since they are aimed at doing away with sin, injustice, oppression, and the evil that brings suffering. In the present world, God's judgments were thought to have the additional purpose of disciplining and correcting people out of love for them. Of course, the biblical writings and Second Temple Jewish literature also claim that, in order to accomplish his good purposes, at times God must inflict pain, suffering, death, and even destruction on the human beings he loves when judging evil in order to do away with it. In a sinful and chaotic world, at times God is thought to have no choice but to let the innocent suffer with the guilty. Such considerations make the problem of suffering, evil, and divine judgment an extremely complex one, not only in biblical thought but also for those who struggle with such questions today.

While it is not possible to address those questions here, it is important to stress that both in biblical thought and in Second Temple Judaism God's act of judging human beings was seen as *rooted* in his love and concern for human beings rather than being *contrary* to his love. The problem that had to be addressed was found, not in *God's* nature, but in the nature of *human beings*. And what was needed was not merely *forgiveness*, which for God was not a problem, but the transformation of human hearts and minds. To forgive human beings their sins while they persisted willfully and unrepentantly in those sins would benefit no one. In fact, simply to forgive and overlook their destructive behavior without attempting to bring them to change their ways would only make things worse. Forgiveness would therefore be contrary not only to God's justice but also to his love, since it would involve overlooking and ignoring the problem rather than acting to solve it.

Both Paul and his Jewish contemporaries understood the human plight or problem in these same terms. Where they parted ways was in their understanding of the solution to that plight. In Jewish thought, the solution to that problem was the Torah, since the Torah provided God's people with the guidance and knowledge they needed to live in ways that enabled them to enjoy the wholeness and well-being God desired for them. This wholeness and well-being would be the result of practicing the justice and righteousness prescribed in the Torah and brought about graciously by God in his people through the Torah as a gift.

For Paul, however, while the Torah was undoubtedly of great help in dealing with the problem of human sinfulness, it could not resolve that problem in the way God desired or accomplish God's purpose of bringing about among human beings from all nations the type of community he sought to create. Paul makes this clear especially in Romans 7–8 and Galatians 3. For Paul, the law is incapable of overcoming sin in the flesh and producing the kind of life God intended for people from the very beginning, a life in which all would be "conformed to the image of his Son so that he might be the firstborn among many sisters and brothers" (Rom 8:29). The Mosaic law had never been designed for that purpose. Instead, it was to lead people to Christ.

In particular, there are two reasons why the law as Paul understood it could not accomplish God's purpose of enabling human beings to attain the wholeness and well-being God desired for all. First, the type of genuine love, commitment, and dedication necessary for human beings to attain that wholeness and well-being cannot be brought about by commandments, prohibitions, rewards, and punishments. It can only be brought about in the context of a community in which all are able to experience that love first-hand and have their lives filled with it. According to Paul, it is this that God now accomplishes through Christ rather than the law, which had never been able to lead to the full realization of that objective, although it had undoubtedly enabled it to be attained in part among many Jews within their communities of faith.

Second, the law of Moses was given to Israel alone. Whether or not God ever intended other nations to come to observe it, it had obviously not produced that result. History had made it evident that as long as things in the world remained as they were, the nations were never going to be brought to live under the Jewish law. It could therefore not serve as an instrument to bless all of the families of the earth. However, by establishing through his Son a community of communities in which all could live in love, justice, righteousness, peace, and solidarity independently of the Torah, God had now made it possible for all people, including both Jews and gentiles, to live as one and enjoy the same blessings, not only in this life but in the life of the age to come. The Torah had not been able to accomplish this objective due in large part to the distinctions it made between Israel and the other nations. This was not because there was anything wrong with those distinctions. According to Paul, they were good and necessary to accomplish God's purposes in history and could still contribute to those purposes even after Christ's coming and the establishment of the *ekklēsia*, especially by pointing people to Christ as the fulfillment of the promises made in the Torah. However, those distinctions could not bring about the type of community that God had now created through his Son.[9]

Of course, when Paul speaks of believers being freed from sin and the flesh and enabled to practice the righteousness that God desires of all, at times he points to God's Spirit rather than Christ as the one through whom this objective is accomplished.[10] Contrary to many interpretations of Paul, however, this was not because Paul understood the solution to the human plight in terms of the need for God to produce some type of mysterious ontological transformation in human beings by infusing some power or "stuff" into them, altering their genetic makeup, or uniting them to his divine substance or nature through Christ or the Holy Spirit.[11] There is

---

9. Paul never refers to the idea that "Torah" would go out to the nations from Zion (Isa 2:3), nor does he comment explicitly on the notion that God would write his Torah on his people's hearts (Jer 31:33). In both cases, however, he could have understood Torah generically rather than as an allusion to the law of Moses: what God would send out from Zion and write upon human hearts was not the Mosaic law per se but his guidance and instruction.

10. See especially Rom 8:1-13; Gal 5:5, 16-25; 6:8.

11. Commenting on Paul's thought, for example, Matthew Thiessen speaks of "the gene therapy that the infusion of Christ's *pneuma* into gentile flesh provides" (*Paul*

no reason to read such ideas back into Paul's thought. Rather, for Paul the Holy Spirit acts upon the hearts and minds of believers by using various means to lead them to see, understand, think, and behave in the ways that God desires for their good in much the same way that one human person leads another to do these things.[12] In particular, the Spirit brings them to have the "mind of Christ" and to be conformed to the image of Christ as God's Son.[13] The work of the Spirit thus depends on what God has done in and through Christ.

In the thought of Paul, the reason why Jesus' coming and death had been necessary was not that without Jesus' death it would have been impossible for God to forgive human beings or produce some type of mysterious ontological change in them. Rather, the purpose for which God had sent his Son was to form the *ekklēsia*, that is, the type of community of which Paul speaks repeatedly throughout his epistles, a community in which all would be brought to live in love, communion, and solidarity, giving themselves to and for one another within that community and also sharing the same love with those outside of that community. It was to this objective that Jesus had dedicated himself in life and death. According to Paul's logic, the reason that Jesus had had to die in order to accomplish that purpose had nothing to do with God's nature or any type of righteous demand on God's part. Rather, in a sinful, unjust, and oppressive world that stands opposed to God's loving purposes, Jesus' efforts to establish that type of community inevitably led to conflict and the threat of a violent death. Had Jesus backed down from his efforts to bring about that community in the face of the cross, such a community could never have come into existence through him, since by definition it requires that one give oneself fully to and for others in love. In Paul's thought, only by giving up his life rather than seeking to save it could Jesus have expected to form a community in which all would be willing to give of themselves fully in order to seek the well-being of one another and others together with their own. Similarly, had God intervened to spare his Son the cross rather than giving him up, he could never have

---

and the Gentile Problem [Oxford: Oxford University Press, 2016], 15). Similarly, Paula Fredriksen attributes to Paul the idea that Christ's *pneuma* is "infused" into gentile believers in Christ (*Paul: The Pagans' Apostle* [New Haven: Yale University Press, 2017], 120). Stanley K. Stowers maintains that in Paul's thought *pneuma* "is a refined, qualitatively higher substance with its own power of movement and intelligence" and attributes to Paul the idea that "those who are in or of Christ actually possess as part of them the stuff of Christ, a portion of his pneuma" ("What is 'Pauline Participation in Christ'?," in *Redefining First Century Jewish and Christian Identities: Essays in Honor of Ed Parish Sanders*, ed. Fabian Udoh et al. [Notre Dame: University of Notre Dame Press, 2008], 352-71 [355, 362]).

12. See, for example, Rom 8:5-6, 15-16; 1 Cor 12:8-11; 2 Cor 1:22; 12:13; Gal 5:16-18, 22-25; Phil 1:19; 2:1; 1 Thess 1:6.

13. See Rom 8:26-29; 1 Cor 2:10-16; Phil 2:1-8.

expected to establish the same type of community in which all would love one another with a love that would know no limits or bounds and be willing to pay the price for loving others in that way.

RETHINKING PAUL, JUDAISM, AND CHRISTIANITY

The understanding of Paul's thought just considered makes it possible to address on a different basis many of the questions regarding Christianity and Judaism that have been the subject of a great deal of debate in recent decades. It has been common, for example, to ask what Paul thought was "wrong with Judaism."[14] To phrase the question in that way is problematic from the start. Nothing in Paul's letters indicates that he ever thought that there was anything "wrong" with Judaism. On the contrary, for Paul Judaism was something good and wonderful, something to be appreciated and celebrated. While he claims to have found in Christ something that he values much more highly than his life in Judaism alone, it is not because Judaism was not good. If one is very happy living in one community but then finds another community in which one discovers even more joy and satisfaction, that does not make the first community bad or suggest that there was something "wrong" with it. In fact, one will probably wish to continue living as part of both communities, as Paul did. One may also wish to bring those two communities together or keep them united to one another, especially if one grows out of the other. This is what Paul sought.

To continue the analogy, it would be a mistake to think that for Paul the *ekklēsia* replaces or supersedes Israel or the Jewish community. As Paul indicates in his epistles, he considered Israel "according to the flesh" his natural family due to his birth and lineage.[15] The *ekklēsia* was in essence his "adopted" family.[16] Just as a person who joins a Christian community today does not generally need to stop living as a member of his or her natural family in order to do so, especially if that family is itself a part of the same community, so Paul did not have to abandon his natural family in order to form part of the adopted family he called the *ekklēsia*. However, neither did those who did not form part of the Jewish family need to abandon their own natural family and kinspeople in order to come to belong to the *ekklēsia* as their adopted family. In fact, Paul was strongly opposed to such an idea, and therefore insisted that gentiles should not become Jews and submit to circumcision in order to form part of the *ekklēsia*. In the case of both Jewish and gentile believers in Christ, therefore, membership in the *ekklēsia* did

---

14. On this discussion, see especially Daniel Boyarin, *A Radical Jew: Paul and the Politics of Identity*, Contraversions 1 (Berkeley: University of California Press, 1994), 39-56.

15. See Rom 9:3; 11:1; 2 Cor 11:22; Phil 3:4-5.

16. See Rom 8:15-16; 9:8; Gal 3:23–4:7; 4:21-31. Paul's repeated allusions to believers as his sisters and brothers reflects this same idea.

not replace or supersede their previous identity but preserved and presupposed it. The *ekklēsia* did not take the place of any other entity, including Israel, but simply incorporated people from a wide variety of social groups and ethnic communities into a new and broader entity.

Of course, if one's natural family prohibited one from joining the *ekklēsia* as one's adopted family, it would be necessary for one to decide in which of the two families one preferred to live. In principle, however, one would hope that one's natural family would not force one to make such a choice. One might even attempt to persuade them to join the same adopted family, as Paul did. At the very least, one would do whatever was possible to encourage both one's natural family and one's adopted family to get along well with one another and accept one another rather than living at enmity with each other. Again, this is precisely what we see in the ministry of Paul.

For similar reasons, it is misleading to claim that Paul thought that there was something wrong with the Jewish law or that it was bad in some way. That law had not been given to people of all nations but only to Israel. While it was a much better law than the laws of other nations, especially because it had been given by the one true God who was the creator of all, that God had not left other people without laws but had graciously written his law in their hearts and made known his will to them in general terms.[17] In that sense, it could be said that people of other nations had received from God a good law as well.

As we see in our world today, there are laws of many different types, including laws that regulate human interaction and behavior in local communities, cities, states or provinces, and entire countries. There are also international laws that regulate the ways in which different nations and countries relate to one another. Each of these laws addresses a particular group of people at a certain level and in a certain context. The law of a state or province does not invalidate, replace, or supersede the local law of a particular city, town, or community, but instead complements it and builds upon it. To attempt to establish the law of a local town or community as the law over an entire country or over the countries of the world in general would be not only foolish but entirely implausible. Local ordinances are not designed to be applied on a national or international level. In a similar manner, for Paul the Mosaic law was not designed to govern all people, and to attempt to make it do so was foolish, implausible, and even cruel, especially in that it would require subjecting males to the painful procedure of circumcision for no good reason or purpose.

At the same time, it would be a mistake to insist that local laws applying to towns and communities be abolished and replaced by national and

---

17. See Rom 1:19-21, 32; 2:14-15. Cf. 1 Cor 5:1, where Paul suggests that in their own laws and customs non-Jews uphold some of the same basic principles as Jews do in theirs.

international laws that were not designed to address issues related to life on a local level. In the same way, Paul would have regarded it as foolish and implausible to claim that the law of Moses should be abolished and replaced by the "law of Christ" or the "law of the Spirit of life in Christ Jesus" (1 Cor 9:21; Gal 6:2; Rom 8:2). Whatever he meant by these phrases, he understood the general principles he associated with the law of Christ and his Spirit—things such as love, kindness, gentleness, and care and concern for others—as something that transcended the laws of particular peoples and nations, such as the law of Israel. While most of those laws also prescribed love for others, Paul regards the love God has shown in Christ as unique in many ways. If there was anything "wrong" with the Mosaic law, it was simply that it had not been designed for a reality such as the *ekklēsia*, in the same way that local laws are not designed to be applied on a national or international level. The law of Christ and his Spirit was of a very different nature and order than the laws that governed particular nations in the way that the law of Moses governed Israel.

Although Paul speaks of a new covenant in Christ, there is no reason to think that he believed that this covenant replaces or supersedes God's previous covenant with Israel. Each of those covenants or pacts applied to different people and contexts. A pact or agreement established among a variety of nations, for example, does not generally nullify, render obsolete, or replace a pact or agreement previously made at a local or regional level within one particular nation. Undoubtedly, in 2 Cor 3:5-18 Paul affirms that the giving of the covenant established through Moses led to death and condemnation and states that its splendor pales in comparison to that of the new covenant that he associates with Christ and the Spirit. He also writes that the covenant made through Moses can only be fully understood on the basis of the new covenant given through Christ. None of these affirmations, however, imply that the covenant made through Moses should be abolished or replaced, any more than a pact that prohibits injustice and prescribes punishments for wrongdoings in one particular region or nation is abolished or replaced by a new pact established on an international level that is aimed at conferring great privileges and benefits upon people of many different countries in some way. The latter may be much more glorious, but that does not mean that there was anything wrong with the former pact, which fulfills its own good purpose in a different way within a particular context, even though it pales in scope and comparison to the newer pact, which transcends that context.

Similarly, from Paul's perspective, the new covenant that he associates with Christ is greater and broader than the covenant that God had previously made with Israel and affords greater blessings and glory, but that does not mean that there was anything wrong with the covenant given through Moses. The Mosaic covenant had simply not been designed to accomplish the same purposes or apply to the same reality as the covenant established through Christ. The Sinai covenant may have led to death and condemnation in that it prescribed penalties and punishments for violations of its precepts and stipulated that God would act to discipline his people when they strayed from his commandments, yet as Paul insists with regard to the law in Romans 7, the problem was not that covenant itself but human sin. Because the covenant made through Moses had also laid a foundation for the new covenant, which in some sense continued to depend on the previous covenant, it was a good thing. Nevertheless, in the thought of Paul, the old covenant could be understood properly only when it was viewed from the perspective of the new.

The same type of logic should be seen as underlying Paul's insistence that the righteousness that God desires to see in all comes through "Christ-faith" rather than through the Mosaic law and the works it prescribes. In itself, there is nothing wrong with that law and the works prescribed in it. In Paul's thought, however, the law had simply not been designed to bring about the same type of righteousness that God gives through Christ in the context of the community of believers. For that reason, Paul never claims that his fellow Jews should abandon the law or no longer do the works it prescribes. On the contrary, he values the law highly and considers what it commands to be "holy, just, and good" (Rom 7:12). It is therefore not to be abolished or replaced but preserved as a very good thing among those to whom it was given, namely, God's people Israel. Life in the community of believers in Christ, however, both requires and affords a righteousness of a different sort.

Of course, in addition to insisting that the Mosaic law should not be imposed on people in a way that runs contrary to its purpose, Paul insists that all are to have freedom with regard to its interpretation and observance rather than being confined by it or enslaved to it. According to Paul, the law is to be interpreted in the light of Christ, through whom the freedom to observe it in a way that is not confining or constraining is given. Jewish believers in Christ may not be under the law in the same way that they were previously, but that does not mean that they are to dispense with it. To develop the analogy that Paul himself uses in Gal 3:22–4:3, when children who have grown into adulthood continue to live alongside their siblings and parents as part of the same family, they are expected to observe many of the same rules that were in place when they were younger, treating one another with respect and showing special consideration for the will of their parents. Nevertheless, as adults they do so voluntarily and with freedom and maturity rather than being obliged by the use of force and the imposition of punishments. The kinds of rules and respect that characterized their lives previously remain a good thing without confining or constraining them in the way that they did when they were children. In a similar manner, in

Paul's thought it is a good thing for God's people Israel to continue to live under the Torah, as long as they interpret and observe it with freedom and maturity rather than being enslaved to it. The manner in which Paul views, interprets, and observes the law has changed in light of his faith in Christ and sets him apart from those Jews who are led by the letter of the law alone and not by the spirit or Spirit of which he speaks (Rom 7:6; 8:15-17; 2 Cor 3:5-6). For Paul, only that kind of observance allows for the close fellowship with gentile believers in Christ that he values so highly. Paul would surely have agreed, however, that one does not need to be a believer in Christ in order to interpret and observe the law in a similar manner, focusing on its spirit rather than being confined by its letter in the way that he claims to have been prior to knowing Christ.

When Paul speaks of the works of the law in his epistles, it is likely that he is referring primarily to things such as circumcision, regulations concerning food and purity, and observance of the Sabbath and other Jewish holy days. If so, his insistence that one is not justified by those works would have been entirely *in accordance* with Jewish thought rather than *contrary* to it. All faithful Jews knew that the mere literal observance of commandments such as those was not sufficient and did not in itself constitute a life of righteousness, since true law-observance went beyond the mere fulfillment of legal prescriptions. When Paul insists that justification is not by works of the law, therefore, he was simply repeating something that Jews in general knew and acknowledged in order to develop his argument concerning life in Christ. The same must be said of the idea that justification is by faith. In Jewish thought, what made one righteous and pleasing to God was that one live "out of faith" (*ek pisteōs*) in the same way that Abraham had, dedicating oneself to obeying God in all that he commanded, motivated by the same kind of trust in God that Abraham had shown.

Paul's understanding of the intrinsic relation between human well-being and a life of faith and obedience to God's will is behind Paul's hope that his fellow Jews might come to believe in Jesus as God's Son and live under him as their Lord. For Paul, that hope was grounded in his desire that they find the same joy and wholeness that he had found in Christ. It is that joy and wholeness of which he speaks in Phil 3:4-9, where he says that he regards all that he valued most in his former life as "loss" and "rubbish" in comparison to the surpassing value of knowing Christ as Lord. In Rom 9:1-3 and 10:1, Paul expresses the great sorrow and unceasing anguish he feels in his heart for his kinspeople according to the flesh and his wish that he might be accursed if only that might allow them to attain the wholeness that he had found in Christ. These words reflect a sincere and profound love for his fellow Jews rather than any desire to see them condemned. They also reflect the same concept of God, that is, a God who longs for his people to find in his Son the wholeness that he desires for them. In Paul's thought, rather than condemning or rejecting his people, God continues to seek only their wholeness and well-being. Such a God stands in stark contrast to the type of pagan or semi-pagan god who is aroused to anger, not out of love for others, but because he has been wronged, offended, and slighted by human beings and thus demands that they pay a high price for having aggrieved him.

Unfortunately, it is precisely this pagan or semi-pagan conception of God that has led so many Christians to condemn, vilify, and inflict violence of many different kinds upon the Jewish people over the centuries. Supposedly, God is offended that they have rejected and even crucified his Son and thus wants to see them suffer for their unbelief and disobedience, motivated solely by a desire for vengeance. Such a God stands in stark contrast to the God of Paul, who out of love for the sinners and the ungodly who lived as enemies was willing to give up even his own Son to reconcile them to himself.[18] Nowhere in the epistles attributed to him does Paul ever condone any kind of violence toward those Jews who do not come to faith in Christ or toward anyone else, for that matter.[19] On the contrary, believers in Christ are to love all people deeply and seek to live in peace with everyone, including even those who might wish them ill or harm.[20]

Throughout his epistles, what Paul does condemn are things such as hatred, evil, injustice, and oppression, as well as the violence that results from these things, not only among Jews but among all people, and especially believers in Christ. While he maintains that those who insist on practicing such things are under God's wrath, nowhere does he ever affirm that people are condemned by God or subject to his wrath simply because they do not believe in Jesus as his Son. The reason for this is that which we have seen above: the God of Paul is not a semi-pagan God who has arbitrarily established faith in Christ as the condition upon which he will save human beings simply because, for some unknown and unnecessary reason, it has pleased him to establish that condition rather than some other one. Rather, just as God had previously given the Torah and called on his people to obey it out of love for them due to the *intrinsic consequences* of such obedience, so also for the same reason he now calls on all to believe in his Son out of love for all on account of the *intrinsic consequences* of such a faith. For Paul, faith in Christ saves because it leads to a way of life that enables people to experience the wholeness and well-being God desires for all, thereby making it possible for them to experience God's blessings both in this life and the life to come. Of course, faith in Christ is not the *only* way to attain that

---

18. See especially Rom 5:6-10.

19. Even the problematic passage of 1 Thess 2:14-16 does not call on believers in Christ to exercise any type of hatred or violence toward "the Jews" of whom it speaks, whoever they may have been. Rather, faithful to Jewish thought, the passage leaves judgment up to God.

20. See especially Rom 12:9-21.

type of life. As Paul knew very well, the Mosaic law is also capable of bringing about a life of justice, righteousness, and love that leads to wholeness and well-being. In the thought of Paul, however, neither the Mosaic law nor anything else can enable one to attain and experience such a life to the same extent and in the same degree as the faith in Christ that brings one to live as part of the community established through him. It was this conviction that led Paul to proclaim the gospel to Jews and gentiles alike out of a profound love for them and a heartfelt desire that they too find what he had found in Christ.

Undoubtedly, Paul regarded unbelief as disobedience to God, yet he condemned that unbelief because in his mind it did not enable one to be made whole in the way that God desires, not because it was an offense or affront to a holy and righteous God who demanded that all submit to him for his own sake. It is contrary to Paul's thought, therefore, to claim that God condemns people and excludes them from the life of the age to come simply because they do not believe in Christ. As we have seen at the end of Chapter 7 of this study, for Paul the criterion upon which both Jews and non-Jews will be judged is their commitment to practicing what is good and right in accordance with God's will as this commitment is reflected in their deeds and present to God's sight in their heart (Rom 2:6-16).

Paul apparently had no problem understanding why his proclamation of a crucified Messiah constituted a stumbling-block to Jews and foolishness to gentiles (1 Cor 1:23). Nevertheless, as Rom 11:23-27 suggests, Paul held out hope that when the "deliverer from Zion" would appear, his fellow Jews who had not come to faith in Christ would finally be brought to acknowledge the truth of the gospel he proclaimed. In this regard, his hope was similar to that of many Jews who anticipated the day when God would manifest himself in glory to the world so that people of other nations might come to believe in him and live in accordance with his will for their own blessing and happiness. On the basis of hopes such as these, both Paul and his fellow Jews—whether believers in Christ or not—would simply have proclaimed that at present the God in whom they believed called on all people to put away sin, evil, and injustice and practice the type of love, justice, and righteousness that promoted wholeness and well-being in the world. Then, when the end came, it would become clear to all who God really was and whether or not Jesus was truly his Son and his anointed one.

All of this is not to say, of course, that Paul found nothing wrong with the Judaism of his day. In this regard, however, he would have been no different from other Jews, who would have been critical of the Judaism of their day in the same way in which people of all faith traditions are critical of many things within their own tradition. As we have seen in Chapter 5 of this study, Paul believed that one of the things that needed to change in Judaism was that it was necessary for it to be redefined and resignified in the light of Christ. To criticize something, however, is not the same as condemning it outright or affirming that it should disappear. Thus, rather than condemning his fellow Jews who did not believe in Christ for their unbelief, through his proclamation of the gospel Paul hoped to convince them to come to understand and resignify Judaism in the way that he did in the light of faith in Christ.

Paul may also have been critical of the way in which some Jews conceived of God's election of Israel if they understood that election to imply that God loved Israel more than people of other nations. Undoubtedly, Paul regarded God's love for Israel as special and unique, yet that does not mean that he considered it to be greater than his love for the nations, who in Christ might also come to live as God's beloved (Rom 9:25). For this reason, the idea commonly associated with Christian supersessionism, according to which "the Christian church has superseded the Jews in the affections of God" and the Jewish people "have been replaced by Christians in the affections of God," has no place in Paul's thought.[21] The reason Paul would have rejected such an idea, however, is not that he believed that God loved Israel more than other nations but because of his conviction that God's love for all of the people and nations he had created was limitless and unconditional, as was his love for Israel. For this reason, God now sent out his apostles such as Paul to all nations and not to Israel alone.[22]

If by Paul's day it had become common among many Jews to view Judaism as a religion in the sense in which that word is commonly used today, Paul would also have been critical of such an understanding of God's will for his people. Neither the God of Israel nor the God of Jesus Christ was interested in people simply practicing a religion, submitting to certain doctrines, rituals, commandments, customs, and authorities, as if these were the things that were truly important. What God wanted was not that his people live as adherents of a religion but that they practice love, justice, and righteousness. The observance of the law and the commandments he had given was a means to that end rather than an end in itself. For this reason, while Paul proclaimed a new faith that revolved around Christ and the gospel, he was not out to establish a new religion, just as Jesus himself had never intended to found any type of religion.

For the same reason, if the term "Christian" is associated with the faith Paul proclaimed rather than a religion, it is by no means inappropriate or anachronistic to speak of Paul as a Christian. Undoubtedly, that designation has many connotations today that it would not have had in the first century, yet the same is true of the term "Judaism," which has come to refer

---

21. Bruce Longenecker, "On Israel's God and God's Israel: Assessing Supersessionism in Paul," *JTS* 53 (2007): 26-44 (26, 35). In both of the passages cited here, Longenecker is summarizing the views of others rather than expressing his own views.

22. See Rom 1:5; 10:14-20; 15:15-21; 2 Cor 5:18-20.

to the rabbinic form of Judaism that has survived over the centuries rather than any of the many other forms of Judaism that existed in antiquity. For that reason, it can be just as misleading to speak of Paul as a Jew as it can be to refer to him as a Christian. Just as there is a sense in which Paul was not a Christian, so also is there a sense in which Paul was not a Jew in the modern sense of the word, even though he spoke of himself as a *Ioudaios*, since the term "Jew" has many connotations today that do not apply to Paul. Whether or not either of these terms is applied to Paul, however, he certainly would have rejected the idea that Judaism and Christianity are two mutually exclusive religions or faiths and that one cannot be a faithful *Ioudaios* and a believer in Christ at the same time. On the contrary, Paul would almost certainly have agreed that those who follow Christ are in some sense "living Jewishly," as Mark Nanos has argued, and thus can be considered "Jewish" even if they are not actually Jews.[23]

In the end, even though Paul and his fellow believers in Christ proclaimed a God who was in important ways distinct from the God in whom most of his fellow Jews believed, in what matters most, those two Gods remained one and the same. Both sought to bless and save not only Israel but people of all the nations of the world by bringing them to live in ways that might make it possible for them to experience the well-being and wholeness he desires for all in his love. Whether one regards the God of Israel and the God of Jesus Christ as two different Gods or as one and the same, therefore, ultimately what matters is the conviction that only those who share passionately that same desire and strive zealously to see it achieved can rightly be said to be living as God's people. There are good reasons to think that, on this point, Paul and his fellow Jews would have been in full agreement.

---

23. See Mark D. Nanos, *Reading Paul within Judaism*, vol. 1 of *Collected Essays of Mark D. Nanos* (Eugene, OR: Cascade, 2017), 128-32.

Abbreviations

<table>
<tr><td>AB</td><td>Anchor Bible Commentary</td></tr>
<tr><td>AcBib</td><td>Academia Biblica</td></tr>
<tr><td>AGJU</td><td>Arbeiten zur Geschichte des antiken Judentums und des Urchristentums</td></tr>
<tr><td>AJEC</td><td>Ancient Judaism and Early Christianity</td></tr>
<tr><td>ANRW</td><td>Aufstieg und Niedergang der römischen Welt: Geschichte und Kultur Roms im Spiegel der neueren Forschung. Part 2, Principat. Edited by Hildegard Temporini and Wolfgang Haase. Berlin: de Gruyter, 1972– .</td></tr>
<tr><td>ANTC</td><td>Abingdon New Testament Commentaries</td></tr>
<tr><td>ASBT</td><td>Acadia Studies in Bible and Theology</td></tr>
<tr><td>AYBRL</td><td>Anchor Yale Bible Reference Library</td></tr>
<tr><td>BECNT</td><td>Baker Exegetical Commentary on the New Testament</td></tr>
<tr><td>BETL</td><td>Bibliotheca Ephemeridum Theologicarum Lovaniensium</td></tr>
<tr><td>Bib</td><td>Biblica</td></tr>
<tr><td>BibInt</td><td>Biblical Interpretation</td></tr>
<tr><td>BibSem</td><td>Biblical Seminar</td></tr>
<tr><td>BJS</td><td>Brown Judaic Studies</td></tr>
<tr><td>BNTC</td><td>Black's New Testament Commentaries</td></tr>
<tr><td>BTS</td><td>Biblisch-theologische Schwerpunkte</td></tr>
<tr><td>BZNW</td><td>Beihefte zur ZNW</td></tr>
<tr><td>CBET</td><td>Contributions to Biblical Exegesis and Theology</td></tr>
<tr><td>CBQ</td><td>Catholic Biblical Quarterly</td></tr>
<tr><td>ConBNT</td><td>Coniectanea Biblica New Testament Series</td></tr>
<tr><td>CRINT</td><td>Compendia Rerum Iudaicarum ad Novum Testamentum</td></tr>
<tr><td>CurBR</td><td>Currents in Biblical Research</td></tr>
<tr><td>ECC</td><td>Eerdmans Critical Commentary</td></tr>
<tr><td>ECL</td><td>Early Christianity and its Literature</td></tr>
<tr><td>EI</td><td>Edition Israelogie</td></tr>
<tr><td>EKKNT</td><td>Evangelisch-katholischer Kommentar zum Neuen Testament</td></tr>
<tr><td>ESEC</td><td>Emory Studies in Early Christianity</td></tr>
<tr><td>FAT</td><td>Forschungen zum Alten Testament</td></tr>
<tr><td>HBM</td><td>Hebrew Bible Monographs</td></tr>
<tr><td>HCS</td><td>Hellenistic Culture and Society</td></tr>
<tr><td>HdO</td><td>Handbuch der Orientalistik</td></tr>
<tr><td>HDR</td><td>Harvard Dissertations in Religion</td></tr>
<tr><td>HNTC</td><td>Harper's New Testament Commentaries</td></tr>
<tr><td>HThKNT</td><td>Herders Theologischer Kommentar zum Neuen Testament</td></tr>
<tr><td>HTR</td><td>Harvard Theological Review</td></tr>
<tr><td>HUCA</td><td>Hebrew Union College Annual</td></tr>
</table>

ICC	International Critical Commentary on the Holy Scriptures of the Old and New Testaments
IDBSup	*Interpreter's Dictionary of the Bible: Supplementary Volume*. Edited by Keith Crim. Nashville: Abingdon, 1976.
ISACR	Interdisciplinary Studies in Ancient Culture and Religion
IVPNTC	InterVarsity Press New Testament Commentary
JCPS	Jewish and Christian Perspectives Series
JBL	*Journal of Biblical Literature*
JBLMS	*JBL* Monograph Series
JJMJS	*Journal of the Jesus Movement in Its Jewish Setting*
JPSEJS	Jewish Publication Society Essential Judaism Series
JSJSup	Supplements to the *Journal for the Study of Judaism in the Persion, Hellenistic, and Roman Periods*
JSNT	*Journal for the Study of the New Testament*
JSNTSup	*JSNT* Supplement Series
JSOT	*Journal for the Study of the Old Testament*
JSOTSup	*JSOT* Supplement Series
JTS	*Journal of Theological Studies*
LCL	Loeb Classical Library
LNTS	Library of New Testament Studies
LSTS	Library of Second Temple Studies
LXX	Septuagint
MT	Masoretic Text of the Hebrew Bible
NCBC	New Century Bible Commentary
NCC	New Covenant Commentary
NICNT	New International Commentary on the New Testament
NICOT	New International Commentary on the Old Testament
NIGTC	New International Greek Testament Commentary
NovT	*Novum Testamentum*
NovTSup	Supplements to *NovT*
NTAS	New Testament after Supersessionism
NTL	New Testament Library
NTS	*New Testament Studies*
NTTS	New Testament Tools and Studies
NTT	New Testament Theology
PBM	Pasternoster Biblical Monographs
PCNT	Paideia Commentaries on the New Testament
PNTC	Pillar New Testament Commentary
RevExp	*Review and Expositor*
RIBLA	*Revista de interpretación bíblica latinoamericana*
SBT	Studies in Biblical Theology
ScEs	*Science et esprit*
SHJ	Studying the Historical Jesus
SJLA	Studies in Judaism in Late Antiquity
SJT	*Scottish Journal of Theology*
SLHT	Studies in Lutheran History and Theology
SLTHS	Siphrut, Literature, and Theology of the Hebrew Scriptures
SNTSMS	Society for New Testament Studies Monograph Series
SNTW	Studies of the New Testament and its World
SPSH	Scholars Press Studies in the Humanities

StJC	Studies in Judaism and Christianity
StPB	Studia Post-Biblica
STDJ	Studies on the Texts of the Desert of Judah
TENTS	Texts and Editions for New Testament Study
THNTC	Two Horizons New Testament Commentary
TynBul	*Tyndale Bulletin*
VTSup	Supplements to *Vetus Testamentum*
WBC	Word Biblical Commentary
WUNT	Wissenschaftliche Untersuchungen zum Neuen Testament
ZNW	*Zeitschrift für die neutestamentliche Wissenschaft und die Kunde der älteren Kirche*

BIBLIOGRAPHY

PRIMARY SOURCES

Biblia Hebraica Stuttgartensia. Edited by K. Elliger and W. Rudolph. Stuttgart: Deutsche Bibelstiftung, 1977.

Novum Testamentum Graece. Edited by Barbara and Kurt Aland et al. 28th ed. Stuttgart: Deutsche Bibelgesellschaft, 2012.

The Old Testament Pseudepigrapha. Vol. 2: *Expansions of the "Old Testament" and Legends, Wisdom and Philosophical Literature, Prayers, Psalms and Odes, Fragments of Lost Judeo Hellenistic Works.* Edited by James H. Charlesworth. Garden City, NY: Doubleday, 1985.

Philo of Alexandria. *Works.* Edited by F. H. Colson, G. H. Whitaker, J. W. Earp, and R. Marcus. 12 vols. LCL. Cambridge, MA: Harvard University Press, 1929–1953.

Septuaginta. Edited by Alfred Rahlfs. 2nd rev. ed. edited by Robert Hanhart. Stuttgart: Deutsche Bibelgesellschaft, 2006.

SECONDARY SOURCES

Ådna, Jostein. "The Servant of Isaiah 53 as Triumphant and Interceding Messiah: The Reception of Isaiah 52:13–53:12 in the Targum of Isaiah with Special Attention to the Concept of the Messiah." Pages 189-224 in *The Suffering Servant: Isaiah 53 in Jewish and Christian Sources.* Translated by Daniel P. Bailey. Edited by Bernd Janowski and Peter Stuhlmacher. Grand Rapids: Eerdmans, 2004.

Agersnap, Søren. *Baptism and the New Life: A Study of Romans 6.1-14.* Aarhus: Aarhus University Press, 1999.

Alexander, Philip S. "Torah and Salvation in Tannaitic Literature." Pages 261-303 in *The Complexities of Second Temple Judaism.* Vol. 1 of *Justification and Variegated Nomism.* Edited by Donald A. Carson, Peter T. O'Brien, and Mark A. Seifrid. WUNT 2/140. Tübingen: Mohr Siebeck, 2001.

—————. "Predestination and Free Will in the Theology of the Dead Sea Scrolls." Pages 27-49 in *Divine and Human Agency in Paul and his Cultural Environment.* Edited by John M. G. Barclay and Simon J. Gathercole. London: T & T Clark, 2006.

Allen, David L. "Substitutionary Atonement and Cultic Terminology in Isaiah 53." Pages 171-89 in *The Gospel According to Isaiah 53: Encountering the Suffering Servant in Jewish and Christian Theology.* Edited by Darrell L. Bock and Mitch Glaser. Grand Rapids: Kregel, 2012.

Allison, Dale C., Jr. *The End of the Ages Has Come: An Early Interpretation of the Passion and Resurrection of Jesus.* Philadelphia: Fortress, 1985.

Amaru, Betsy Halpern. "The Killing of the Prophets: Unraveling a Midrash." *HUCA* 54 (1983): 153-80.

Amit, Yairah. "The Jubilee Law—An Attempt at Instituting Social Justice." Pages 47-59 in *Justice and Righteousness: Biblical Themes and Their Influence.* Edited by Henning Graf Reventlow and Yair Hoffman. JSOTSup 137. Sheffield: JSOT, 1992.

Anderson, Garwood P. *Paul's New Perspective: Charting a Soteriological Journey.* Downers Grove, IL: InterVarsity, 2016.

Aulén, Gustav. *Christus Victor: An Historical Study of the Three Main Types of the Idea of Atonement.* Translated by A. G. Hebert. New York: MacMillan, 1969.

Badenas, Robert. *Christ the End of the Law: Romans 10.4 in Pauline Perspective.* JSNTSup 10. Sheffield: JSOT, 1985.

Baird, William. *History of New Testament Research.* Vol. 1: *From Deism to Tübingen.* Minneapolis: Fortress, 1992.

Barclay, John M. G. *Obeying the Truth: A Study of Paul's Ethics in Galatians.* SNTW. Edinburgh: T & T Clark, 1988.

—————. "Do We Undermine the Law? Study of Rom 14:1–15:6." Pages 287-308 in *Paul and the Mosaic Law.* Edited by James D. G. Dunn. WUNT 89. Tübingen: Mohr, 1996.

—————. "Snarling Sweetly: Josephus on Images and Idolatry." Pages 73-87 in *Idolatry: False Worship in the Bible, Early Judaism, and Christianity.* Edited by Stephen C. Barton. London: T & T Clark, 2007.

—————. *Paul and the Gift.* Grand Rapids: Eerdmans, 2015.

Barnett, Paul. *The Second Epistle to the Corinthians.* NICNT. Grand Rapids: Eerdmans, 1997.

Barrett, C. K. *A Commentary on the First Epistle to the Corinthians.* HNTC. New York: Harper & Row, 1968.

—————. *A Commentary on the Second Epistle to the Corinthians.* HNTC. New York: Harper & Row, 1973.

Betz, Hans Dieter. *Galatians: A Commentary on Paul's Letter to the Churches in Galatia.* Hermeneia. Philadelphia: Fortress, 1974.

Bird, Michael F. *The Saving Righteousness of God: Studies on Paul, Justification, and the New Perspective.* PBM. Milton Keynes: Paternoster, 2007.

—————. *An Anomalous Jew: Paul among Jews, Greeks, and Romans.* Grand Rapids: Eerdmans, 2016.

Blenkinsopp, Joseph. *Isaiah 40-55.* AB 19A. New York: Doubleday, 2002.

Bloomquist, L. Gregory. *The Function of Suffering in Philippians.* JSNTSup 78. Sheffield: JSOT, 1993.

Bockmuehl, Markus. "Halakhah and Ethics in the Jesus Tradition." Pages 264-78 in *Early Christian Thought in its Jewish Context*. Edited by John Barclay and John Sweet. Cambridge: Cambridge University Press, 1996.

—————. *The Epistle to the Philippians*. BNTC 11. Peabody, MA: Hendrickson, 1998.

Boecker, Hans Jochen. *Law and the Administration of Justice in the Old Testament and Ancient East*. Translated by Jeremy Moiser. London: SPCK, 1980.

Bond, Helen K. *Caiaphas: Friend of Rome and Judge of Jesus?* Louisville: Westminster John Knox, 2004.

Borgen, Peder. "Philo of Alexandria." Pages 233-82 in *Jewish Writings of the Second Temple Period: Apocrypha, Pseudepigrapha, Qumran Sectarian Writings, Philo, Josephus*. Edited by Michael E. Stone. CRINT 2. Philadelphia: Fortress, 1984.

—————. "'In Accordance with the Scriptures'." Pages 193-206 in *Early Christian Thought in its Jewish Context*. Edited by John Barclay and John Sweet. Cambridge: Cambridge University Press, 1996.

Boyarin, Daniel. *A Radical Jew: Paul and the Politics of Identity*. Contraversions 1. Berkeley: University of California Press, 1994.

Breytenbach, Cilliers. "The 'For Us' Phrases in Pauline Soteriology: Considering Their Background and Use." Pages 163-85 in *Salvation in the New Testament: Perspectives on Soteriology*. Edited by Jan G. van der Watt. NovTSup 121. Leiden: Brill, 2005.

Brondos, David A. "The Cross and the Curse: Galatians 3.13 and Paul's Doctrine of Redemption." *JSNT* 81 (2001): 3-32.

—————. *Paul on the Cross: Reconstructing the Apostle's Story of Redemption*. Minneapolis: Fortress, 2006.

—————. *Fortress Introduction to Salvation and the Cross*. Minneapolis: Fortress, 2007.

—————. *Redeeming the Gospel: The Christian Faith Reconsidered*. SLHT. Minneapolis: Fortress, 2011.

—————. *Jesus' Death in New Testament Thought*. 2 vols. Mexico City: Theological Community of Mexico, 2018.

Broshi, Magen. "Predestination in the Bible and the Dead Sea Scrolls." Pages 235-46 in vol. 2 of *The Bible and the Dead Sea Scrolls: The Second Princeton Symposium on Judaism and Christian Origins*. Edited by James H. Charlesworth. Waco, TX: Baylor University Press, 2006.

Bruce, F. F. *The Epistle to the Hebrews*. Rev. ed. NICNT. Grand Rapids: Eerdmans, 1990.

Brueggemann, Walter. "Election." Pages 61-64 in *Reverberations of Faith: A Theological Handbook of Old Testament Themes*. Louisville: Westminster John Knox, 2002.

Bultmann, Rudolf. *Theology of the New Testament*. Translated by Kendrick Grobel. 2 vols. New York: Scribner, 1951/1955.

Campbell, William S. "Perceptions of Compatibility between Christianity and Judaism in Pauline Interpretation." *BibInt* 13 (2005): 298-316.

—————. *Paul and the Creation of Christian Identity*. London: T & T Clark, 2008.

—————. "Covenantal Theology and Participation in Christ: Pauline Perspectives on Transformation." Pages 41-60 in *Paul and Judaism: Crosscurrents in Pauline Exegesis and the Study of Jewish-Christian Relations*. Edited by Reimund Bieringer and Didier Pollefeyt. LNTS 463. London: T & T Clark, 2012.

——————. *Unity and Diversity in Christ: Interpreting Paul in Context. Collected Essays.* Eugene, OR: Cascade, 2013.

Capes, David B. *The Divine Christ: Paul, the Lord Jesus, and the Scriptures of Israel.* ASBT. Grand Rapids: Baker Academic, 2018.

Carraway, George. *Christ is God over All: Romans 9:5 in the Context of Romans 9–11.* LNTS 489. London: Bloomsbury T & T Clark, 2013.

Carson, Donald A. "Mystery and Fulfillment: Toward a More Comprehensive Paradigm of Paul's Understanding of the Old and the New." Pages 393-436 in *The Paradoxes of Paul.* Vol. 2 of *Justification and Variegated Nomism.* Edited by Donald A. Carson, Peter T. O'Brien, and Mark A. Seifrid. WUNT 2/181. Tübingen: Mohr Siebeck, 2004.

Charlesworth, James H. "From Messianology to Christology: Problems and Prospects." Pages 3-35 in *The Messiah: Developments in Earliest Judaism and Christianity. The First Princeton Symposium on Judaism and Christian Origins.* Edited by James H. Charlesworth. Minneapolis: Fortress, 1992.

——————. "Did They Ever Part?" Pages 281-300 in *Partings: How Judaism and Christianity Became Two.* Edited by Hershel Shanks. Washington, DC: Biblical Archaeological Society, 2013.

Chilton, Bruce. *The Temple of Jesus: His Sacrificial Program within a Cultural History of Sacrifice.* University Park: Pennsylvania State University, 1992.

Chilton, Bruce, and Jacob Neusner. *Classical Christianity and Rabbinic Judaism: Comparing Theologies.* Grand Rapids: Baker Academic, 2004.

Christiansen, Ellen Juhl. "The Consciousness of Belonging to God's Covenant and What It Entails according to the Damascus Document and the Community Rule." Pages 69-97 in *Qumran between the Old and New Testaments.* Edited by Frederick H. Cryer and Thomas L. Thompson. JSOTSup 290. Sheffield: Sheffield Academic Press, 1998.

Church, Philip. *Hebrews and the Temple: Attitudes to the Temple in Second Temple Judaism and in Hebrews.* NovTSup 171. Leiden: Brill, 2017.

Ciampa, Roy E., and Brian S. Rosner. *The First Letter to the Corinthians.* PNTC. Grand Rapids: Eerdmans, 2010.

Cohen, Shaye J. D. *The Beginnings of Jewishness: Boundaries, Varieties, Uncertainties.* HCS 31. Berkeley: University of California Press, 1999.

——————. "The Temple and the Synagogue." Pages 298-325 in *The Early Roman Period.* Vol. 3 of *The Cambridge History of Judaism.* Edited by William Horbury, W. D. Davies, and John Sturdy. Cambridge: Cambridge University Press, 1999.

——————. *From the Maccabees to the Mishnah.* 2nd ed. Louisville: Westminster John Knox, 2006.

Collins, John J. "What Was Distinctive about Messianic Expectation at Qumran?" Pages 71-92 in vol. 2 of *The Bible and the Dead Sea Scrolls: The Second Princeton Symposium on Judaism and Christian Origins.* Edited by James H. Charlesworth. Waco, TX: Baylor University Press, 2006.

—————. "What Is Apocalyptic Literature?" Pages 1-16 in *The Oxford Handbook of Apocalyptic Literature*. Edited by John J. Collins. Oxford: Oxford University Press, 2014.

Collins, Raymond F. *The Power of Images in Paul*. Collegeville, MN: Liturgical Press, 2008.

Condra, Ed. *Salvation for the Righteous Revealed: Jesus amid Covenantal and Messianic Expectations in Second Temple Judaism*. AGJU 51. Leiden: Brill, 2002.

Conzelmann, Hans. *1 Corinthians: A Commentary on the First Epistle to the Corinthians*. Translated by James W. Leitch. Hermeneia. Philadelphia: Fortress, 1975.

Cranfield, C. E. B. *A Critical and Exegetical Commentary on the Epistle to the Romans*. 2 vols. 6th ed. ICC. Edinburgh: T & T Clark, 1975.

Crossley, James G. *Why Christianity Happened: A Sociohistorical Account of Christian Origins (26-50 CE)*. Louisville: Westminster John Knox, 2006.

Das, A. Andrew. *Solving the Romans Debate*. Minneapolis: Fortress, 2007.

Daube, David. *The New Testament and Rabbinic Judaism*. London: University of London Press, 1956.

Davies, Philip R. *The Damascus Covenant: An Interpretation of the "Damascus Document"*. JSOTSup 25. Sheffield: JSOT, 1982.

Davies, W. D. *Torah in the Messianic Age and/or the Age to Come*. JBLMS 7. Philadelphia: SBL, 1952.

—————. *Paul and Rabbinic Judaism: Some Rabbinic Elements in Pauline Theology*. 4th ed. Philadelphia: Fortress, 1980.

de Boer, Martinus C. *Galatians: A Commentary*. NTL. Louisville: Westminster John Knox, 2011.

Deibert, Richard I. *Second Corinthians and Paul's Gospel of Human Mortality: How Paul's Experience of Death Authorizes His Apostolic Authority in Corinth*. WUNT 2/430. Tübingen: Mohr Siebeck, 2017.

Deines, Roland. "The Social Profile of the Pharisees." Pages 111-32 in *The New Testament and Rabbinic Literature*. Edited by Reimund Bieringer et al. JSJSup 136. Leiden: Brill, 2010.

deSilva, David A. *4 Maccabees*. Sheffield: Sheffield Academic Press, 1998.

Di Mattei, Steven. "Paul's Allegory of the Two Covenants (Gal 4.21-31) in Light of First-Century Hellenistic Rhetoric and Jewish Hermeneutics." *NTS* 52 (2006): 102-22.

Donaldson, Terence L. *Paul and the Gentiles: Remapping the Apostle's Convictional World*. Minneapolis: Fortress, 1997.

—————. "Jewish Christianity, Israel's Stumbling and the *Sonderweg* Reading of Paul." *JSNT* 29 (2006): 27-54.

—————. *Jews and Judaism in the New Testament: Decision Points and Divergent Interpretations*. London: SPCK, 2010.

—————. "Paul within Judaism: A Critical Evaluation from a 'New Perspective' Perspective." Pages 277-301 in *Paul within Judaism: Restoring the First-Century Context to the Apostle*. Edited by Mark D. Nanos and Magnus Zetterholm. Minneapolis: Fortress, 2015.

—————. "Supersessionism and Early Christian Self-Definition." *JJMJS* 3 (2016):1-32.

Dunn, James D. G. *Christology in the Making: A New Testament Inquiry into the Origins of the Doctrine of the Incarnation.* London: SCM, 1980.

—————————. *Romans 1–8.* WBC 38A. Dallas: Word, 1988.

—————————. *Romans 9–16.* WBC 38B. Dallas: Word, 1988.

—————————. *Jesus, Paul and the Law: Studies in Mark and Galatians.* Louisville: Westminster John Knox, 1990.

—————————. *The Partings of the Ways between Christianity and Judaism and their Significance for the Character of Christianity.* London: SCM, 1991.

—————————. *A Commentary on the Epistle to the Galatians.* BNTC 9. Peabody, MA: Hendrickson, 1993.

—————————. *The Theology of Paul's Letter to the Galatians.* NTT. Cambridge: Cambridge University Press, 1993.

—————————. "Jesus Tradition in Paul." Pages 155–78 in *Studying the Historical Jesus: Evaluations of the State of Current Research.* Edited by Bruce Chilton and Craig A. Evans. NTTS 19. Leiden: Brill, 1994.

—————————. "Judaism in the Land of Israel in the First Century." Pages 229–61 in *Historical Syntheses.* Part 2 of *Judaism in Late Antiquity.* Edited by Jacob Neusner. HdO 1.17. Leiden: Brill, 1995.

—————————. "'The Law of Faith,' 'the Law of the Spirit' and 'the Law of Christ'." Pages 62–82 in *Theology and Ethics in Paul and His Interpreters: Essays in Honor of Victor Paul Furnish.* Edited by Eugene H. Lovering Jr. and Jerry L. Sumney. Nashville: Abingdon, 1996.

—————————. *The Theology of Paul the Apostle.* Grand Rapids: Eerdmans, 1998.

—————————. "The Question of Anti-Semitism in the New Testament Writings of the Period." Pages 177–211 in *Jews and Christians: The Parting of the Ways A.D. 70 to 135. The Second Durham-Tübingen Research Symposium on Earliest Christianity and Judaism.* Edited by James D. G. Dunn. Grand Rapids: Eerdmans, 1999.

—————————. "Did Paul Have a Covenant Theology? Reflections on Romans 9.4 and 11.27." Pages 287–307 in *The Concept of the Covenant in the Second Temple Period.* Edited by Stanley E. Porter and Jacqueline C. R. de Roo. JSJSup 71. Leiden: Brill, 2003.

Easter, Matthew C. "The *Pistis Christou* Debate: Main Arguments and Responses in Summary." *CurBR* 9 (2019): 33–47.

Eberhart, Christian. "Opfer, Sühne und Stellvertretung im Alten Testament." Pages 40–55 in »*... mein Blut für Euch*«: *Theologische Perspektiven zum Verständnis des Todes Jesu heute.* Edited by Michael Hüttenhoff, Wolfgang Kraus, and Karlo Meyer. BTS 38. Göttingen: Vandenhoeck & Ruprecht, 2018.

Eisenbaum, Pamela. *Paul Was Not a Christian: The Original Message of a Misunderstood Apostle.* New York: HarperOne, 2009.

Elliott, Mark Adam. *The Survivors of Israel: A Reconsideration of the Theology of Pre-Christian Judaism.* Grand Rapids: Eerdmans, 2000.

Elliott, Neil. *Liberating Paul: The Justice of God and the Politics of the Apostle.* Minneapolis: Fortress, 2006.

Elmer, Ian J. *Paul, Jerusalem and the Judaisers: The Galatian Crisis in Its Broadest Historical Context*. WUNT 2/258. Tübingen: Mohr Siebeck, 2009.

Engberg-Pedersen, Troels. *Paul and the Stoics*. Louisville: Westminster John Knox, 2000.

Erlemann, Kurt. "Der Geist als ἀρραβών, 2 Kor 5,5." *ZNW* 83 (1992): 203-9.

Evans, Craig A. "Aspects of Exile and Restoration in the Proclamation of Jesus and the Gospels." Pages 263-93 in *Jesus in Context: Temple, Purity, and Restoration*. Edited by Bruce Chilton and Craig A. Evans. AGJU 39. Leiden: Brill, 1997.

——————. "Jesus' Action in the Temple: Cleansing or Portent of Destruction?" Pages 395-439 in *Jesus in Context: Temple, Purity, and Restoration*. Bruce Chilton and Craig A. Evans. AGJU 39. Leiden: Brill, 1997.

——————. "Isaiah 53 in the Letters of Peter, Paul, Hebrews, and John." Pages 145-70 in *The Gospel according to Isaiah 53: Encountering the Suffering Servant in Jewish and Christian Theology*. Edited by Darrell L. Bock and Mitch Glaser. Grand Rapids: Kregel, 2012.

Fee, Gordon D. *Philippians*. IVPNTC 11. Downers Grove, IL: InterVarsity, 1999.

——————. *Jesus the Lord according to Paul the Apostle: A Concise Introduction*. Grand Rapids: Baker Academic, 2018.

Ferguson, Everett. "Spiritual Sacrifice in Early Christianity and its Environment." Pages 1151-89 in *ANRW* 2.23.2.

Finlan, Stephen. *The Background and Content of Paul's Cultic Atonement Metaphors*. AcBib 19. Atlanta: SBL, 2004.

——————. *Problems with Atonement: The Origins of, and Controversy about, the Atonement Doctrine*. Collegeville, MN: Liturgical Press, 2005.

Fitzmyer, Joseph A. *Romans: A New Translation with Introduction and Commentary*. AB 33. New York: Doubleday, 1993.

——————. *First Corinthians: A New Translation with Introduction and Commentary*. AB 32. New Haven: Yale University Press, 2008.

Flemington, W. F. "On the Interpretation of Colossians 1:24." Pages 84-90 in *Suffering and Martyrdom in the New Testament: Studies Presented to G. M. Styler by the Cambridge New Testament Seminar*. Edited by William Horbury and Brian McNeil. Cambridge: Cambridge University Press, 1981.

Flusser, David. *Judaism of the Second Temple Period*. Vol. 1: *Qumran and Apocalypticism*. Translated by Azzan Yadin. Grand Rapids: Eerdmans, 2007.

Förster, Werner. *Palestinian Judaism in New Testament Times*. Translated by Gordon Harris. Edinburgh: Oliver & Boyd, 1964.

Fowl, Stephen E. *Philippians*. THNTC. Grand Rapids: Eerdmans, 2005.

Fredriksen, Paula. "Judaism, the Circumcision of Gentiles, and Apocalyptic Hope: Another Look at Galatians 1 and 2." *JTS* 42 (1991): 532-64.

——————. "Paul, Purity, and the *Ekklēsia* of the Gentiles." Pages 205-17 in *The Beginnings of Christianity: A Collection of Articles*. Edited by Jack Pastor and Menachem Mor. Jerusalem: Yad Ben-Zvi, 2005.

——————. "What Parting of the Ways?: Jews, Gentiles, and the Ancient Mediterranean City." Pages 35-63 in *The Ways that Never Parted: Jews and Christians in Late Antiquity and the Early Middle Ages*. Edited by Annette Yoshiko Reed and Adam H. Becker. Minneapolis: Fortress, 2007.

—————————. "Judaizing the Nations: The Ritual Demands of Paul's Gospel." *NTS* 56 (2010): 232-52.

—————————. "The Question of Worship: Gods, Pagans, and the Redemption of Israel." Pages 175-201 in *Paul within Judaism: Restoring the First-Century Context to the Apostle*. Edited by Mark D. Nanos and Magnus Zetterholm. Minneapolis: Fortress, 2015.

—————————. *Paul: The Pagans' Apostle*. New Haven: Yale University Press, 2017.

—————————. "Paul and Judaism." Pages 633-37 in *The Jewish Annotated New Testament*. Edited by Marc Brettler and Amy-Jill Levine. 2nd ed. New York: Oxford University Press, 2017.

—————————. *When Christians Were Jews*. New Haven: Yale University Press, 2018.

Frey, Christofer. "The Impact of the Biblical Idea of Justice on Present Discussions of Social Justice." Pages 90-104 in *Justice and Righteousness: Biblical Themes and Their Influence*. Edited by Henning Graf Reventlow and Yair Hoffman. JSOTSup 137. Sheffield: JSOT, 1992.

Frick, Peter. "Monotheism and Philosophy: Notes on the Concept of God in Philo and Paul (Romans 1:18-21)." Pages 237-58 in *Christian Origins and Hellenistic Judaism: Social and Literary Contexts for the New Testament*. Edited by Stanley E. Porter and Andrew Pitts. TENTS 10. Leiden: Brill, 2012.

Fuller, Michael E. *The Restoration of Israel: Israel's Re-gathering and the Fate of the Nations in Early Jewish Literature and Luke-Act*s. BZNW 138. Berlin: de Gruyter, 2006.

Furnish, Victor Paul. *II Corinthians: Translated with Introduction, Notes, and Commentary*. AB 32A. Garden City, NY: Doubleday, 1984.

—————————. "The Jesus-Paul Debate: From Baur to Bultmann." Pages 17-50 in *Paul and Jesus: Collected Essays*. Edited by Alexander J. M. Wedderburn. JSNTSup 137. Sheffield: Sheffield Academic Press, 1989.

Gadenz, Pablo T. *Called from the Jews and from the Gentiles: Pauline Ecclesiology in Romans 9–11*. WUNT 2/267. Tübingen: Mohr Siebeck, 2009.

Gager, John G. *Reinventing Paul*. Oxford: Oxford University Press, 2000.

Gane, Roy. *Cult and Character: Purification Offerings, Day of Atonement, and Theodicy*. Winona Lake, IN: Eisenbrauns, 2005.

Garland, David E. *1 Corinthians*. BECNT. Grand Rapids: Baker Academic, 2003.

Garlington, Don B. *Faith, Obedience and Perseverance: Aspects of Paul's Letter to the Romans*. WUNT 79. Tübingen: Mohr, 1994.

Gathercole, Simon J. "Justified by Faith, Justified by his Blood: The Evidence of Romans 3:21–4:25." Pages 147-84 in *The Paradoxes of Paul*. Vol. 2 of *Justification and Variegated Nomism*. Edited by Donald A. Carson, Peter T. O'Brien, and Mark A. Seifrid. WUNT 2/181. Tübingen: Mohr Siebeck, 2004.

—————————. "'Sins' in Paul." *NTS* 64 (2018): 143-61.

Goldenberg, Robert. *The Nations that Know Thee Not: Ancient Jewish Attitudes towards Other Religions*. BibSem 52. Sheffield: Sheffield Academic Press, 1997.

Goldingay, John, and David Payne. *A Critical and Exegetical Commentary on Isaiah 40-55*. 2 vols. ICC. London: T & T Clark, 2006.

Goodman, Martin. *The Ruling Class of Judaea: The Origins of the Jewish Revolt against Rome, A.D. 66-70*. Cambridge: Cambridge University Press, 1987.

——————. *A History of Judaism*. Princeton: Princeton University Press, 2018.

Gowan, Donald E. *Eschatology in the Old Testament*. Philadelphia: Fortress, 1986.

Grabbe, Lester L. *Judaism from Cyrus to Hadrian*. Vol. 2: *The Roman Period*. Minneapolis: Fortress, 1992.

——————. *An Introduction to First Century Judaism: Jewish Religion and History in the Second Temple Period*. Edinburgh: T & T Clark, 1996.

——————. *An Introduction to Second Temple Judaism: History and Religion of the Jews in the Time of Nehemiah, the Maccabees, Hillel and Jesus*. London: T & T Clark, 2010.

——————. *A History of the Jews and Judaism in the Second Temple Period*. Vol. 3: *The Maccabean Revolt, Hasmonean Rule, and Herod the Great 175-4 BCE*. LSTS 95. London: T & T Clark, 2020.

Gräbe, Petrus J. *New Covenant, New Community: The Significance of Biblical and Patristic Covenant Theology for Contemporary Understanding*. Waynesboro, GA: Paternoster, 2006.

Gray, Rebecca. *Prophetic Figures in Late Second Temple Jewish Palestine: The Evidence from Josephus*. Oxford: Oxford University Press, 1993.

Greene, G. Roger. *The Ministry of Paul the Apostle: History and Redaction*. Lanham, MD: Lexington/Fortress Academic, 2019.

Grindheim, Sigurd. "Election and the Role of Israel." Pages 329-46 in *God and the Faithfulness of Paul: A Critical Examination of the Pauline Theology of N. T. Wright*. Edited by Christoph Heilig, J. Thomas Hewitt, and Michael F. Bird. Minneapolis: Fortress, 2017.

Gupta, Nijay K. *Paul and the Language of Faith*. Grand Rapids: Eerdmans, 2020.

Häggland, Fredrik. *Isaiah 53 in the Light of Homecoming after Exile*. FAT 2/31. Tübingen: Mohr Siebeck, 2008.

Hansen, G. Walter. *The Letter to the Philippians*. PNTC. Grand Rapids: Eerdmans, 2009.

Harker, Christina. *The Colonizers' Idols: Paul, Galatia, and Empire in New Testament Studies*. WUNT 2/460. Tübingen: Mohr Siebeck, 2018.

Harris, Murray J. *The Second Epistle to the Corinthians*. NIGTC. Grand Rapids: Eerdmans, 2005.

Harvey, Graham. *The True Israel: Uses of the Names Jew, Hebrew and Israel in Ancient Jewish and Early Christian Literature*. STDJ 70. Leiden: Brill, 2008.

Hay, David M. *Glory at the Right Hand: Psalm 110 in Early Christianity*. SBLMS 18. Nashville: Abingdon, 1973.

Hays, Richard B. "Crucified with Christ: A Synthesis of the Theology of 1 and 2 Thessalonians, Philemon, Philippians, and Galatians." Pages 227-46 in *Thessalonians, Philippians, Galatians, Philemon*. Vol. 1 of *Pauline Theology*. Edited by Jouette M. Bassler. Minneapolis: Fortress, 1991.

Hengel, Martin. *Victory over Violence*. Philadelphia: Fortress, 1973.

—————. *The Atonement: The Origins of the Doctrine in the New Testament*. Philadelphia: Fortress, 1981.

—————. "The Interpenetration of Judaism and Hellenism in the Pre-Maccabean Period." Pages 167-228 in *The Hellenistic Age*. Vol. 2 of *The Cambridge History of Judaism*. Cambridge: Cambridge University Press, 1989.

—————. "The Effective History of Isaiah 53 in the Pre-Christian Period." Pages 75-146 in *The Suffering Servant: Isaiah 53 in Jewish and Christian Sources*. Translated by Daniel P. Bailey. Edited by Bernd Janowski and Peter Stuhlmacher. Grand Rapids: Eerdmans, 2004.

Heschel, Susannah. "From Jesus to Shylock: Christian Supersessionism and 'The Merchant of Venice'." *HTR* 99 (2006): 407-31.

Hogeterp, Albert L. A. *Expectations of the End: A Comparative Traditio-Historical Study of Eschatological, Apocalyptic, and Messianic Ideas in the Dead Sea Scrolls and the New Testament*. STDJ 83. Leiden: Brill, 2009.

Holloway, Paul A. *Philippians: A Commentary*. Hermeneia. Minneapolis: Fortress, 2017.

Hooker, Morna D. "On Being the Righteousness of God: Another Look at 2 Cor 5:21." *NovT* 50 (2008): 358-75.

Horbury, William. "The Temple Tax." Pages 265-86 in *Jesus and the Politics of His Day*. Edited by Ernst Bammel and C. F. D. Moule. Cambridge: Cambridge University Press, 1984.

Horn, Friedrich Wilhelm. "Paulus und der Herodianische Tempel." *NTS* 53 (2007): 184-203.

Horsley, Richard A. "High Priests and the Politics of Roman Palestine: Contextual Analysis of the Evidence in Josephus." *JSJ* 17 (1986): 23-55.

—————. "'Messianic' Figures and Movements in First-Century Palestine." Pages 276-95 in *The Messiah: Developments in Earliest Judaism and Christianity. First Princeton Symposium on Judaism and Christian Origins*. Edited by James H. Charlesworth. Minneapolis: Fortress, 1992.

—————. *Jesus and the Spiral of Violence: Popular Jewish Resistance in Roman Palestine*. Minneapolis: Fortress, 1993.

—————. "The Dead Sea Scrolls and the Historical Jesus." Pages 37-60 of vol. 3 of *The Bible and the Dead Sea Scrolls: The Second Princeton Symposium on Judaism and Christian Origins*. Edited by James H. Charlesworth. Waco, TX: Baylor University Press, 2006.

Hubbard, Moyer V. *New Creation in Paul's Letters and Thought*. SNTSMS 119. Cambridge: Cambridge University Press, 2002.

Hubing, Jeff. *Crucifixion and New Creation: The Strategic Purpose of Galatians 6.11–17*. LNTS 508. London: Bloomsbury T & T Clark, 2015.

Hultgren, Arland J. *Christ and His Benefits: Christology and Redemption in the New Testament*. Philadelphia: Fortress, 1987.

—————. *Paul's Letter to the Romans: A Commentary*. Grand Rapids: Eerdmans, 2011.

Hurtado, Larry W. *Lord Jesus Christ: Devotion to Jesus in Early Christianity*. Grand Rapids: Eerdmans, 2003.

—————. "Jesus' Death as Paradigmatic in the New Testament." *SJT* 57 (2004): 413-33.

—————. *How on Earth Did Jesus Become a God?: Historical Questions about Earliest Devotion to Jesus*. Grand Rapids: Eerdmans, 2005.

—————. *Ancient Jewish Monotheism and Early Christian Jesus-Devotion: The Context and Character of Christological Faith*. Waco, TX: Baylor University Press, 2017.

Jewett, Robert. *Romans: A Commentary*. Hermeneia. Minneapolis: Fortress, 2007.

Jipp, Joshua. "Rereading the Story of Abraham, Isaac, and 'Us' in Romans 4." *JSNT* 32 (2009): 217-42.

Johnson Hodge, Caroline. *If Sons, Then Heirs: A Study of Kinship and Ethnicity in the Letters of Paul*. Oxford: Oxford University Press, 2007.

—————. "The Question of Identity: Gentiles as Gentiles—but also Not—in Pauline Communities." Pages 153-73 in *Paul within Judaism: Restoring the First-Century Context to the Apostle*. Edited by Mark D. Nanos and Magnus Zetterholm. Minneapolis: Fortress, 2015.

Kaminsky, Joel S. "Did Election Imply the Mistreatment of Non-Israelites?" *HTR* 96 (2003): 397-425.

—————. *Yet I Loved Jacob: Reclaiming the Biblical Concept of Election*. Nashville: Abingdon, 2007.

Käsemann, Ernst. *Commentary on Romans*. Translated by Geoffrey W. Bromiley. Grand Rapids: Eerdmans, 1980.

Keck, Leander E. *Romans*. ANTC. Nashville: Abingdon, 2005.

Kensella, Sean Edward. "The Transformation of the Jewish Passover in an Early Christian Liturgy: The Influence of the Passover *Haggadah* in the *Apostolic Tradition*." *ScEs* 52 (2000): 215-28.

Khobnya, Svetlana. *The Father Who Redeems and the Son Who Obeys: Consideration of Paul's Teaching in Romans*. Eugene, OR: Pickwick, 2013.

—————. "'The Root' in Paul's Olive Tree Metaphor (Romans 11:16-24)." *TynBul* 64 (2013): 257-73.

Klawans, Jonathan. *Purity, Sacrifice, and the Temple: Symbolism and Supersessionism in the Study of Ancient Judaism*. Oxford: Oxford University Press, 2006.

Knight, George A. F. *A Christian Theology of the Old Testament*. Richmond, VA: John Knox, 1959.

Kraftchick, Steven J. "Death's Parsing: Experience as a Mode of Theology in Paul." Pages 144-66 in *Pauline Conversations in Context: Essays in Honor of Calvin J. Roetzel*. Edited by Janice Capel Anderson, Philip Sellew, and Claudia Setzer. JSNTSup 221. London: Sheffield Academic Press, 2002.

Krause, Andrew R. *Synagogues in the Works of Flavius Josephus: Rhetoric, Spatiality, and First-Century Jewish Institutions*. AJEC 97. Leiden: Brill, 2017.

Kwon, Yon-Gyong. "Ἀρραβών as Pledge in Second Corinthians." *NTS* 54 (2008): 525-41.

Ladd, George Eldon. *A Theology of the New Testament*. Rev. ed. Grand Rapids: Eerdmans, 1993.

Lambrecht, Jan. "The nekrōsis of Jesus: Ministry and Suffering in 2 Corinthians 4,7-15." Pages 309-33 in *Studies on 2 Corinthians*. Edited by Reimund Bieringer and Jan Lambrecht. BETL 112. Leuven: Leuven University Press, 1994.

Lampe, Peter. "Das korinthische Herrenmahl im Schnittpunkt hellenistisch-römischer Mahlpraxis und paulinischer Theologia Crucis (1 Kor 11,17-34)." *ZNW* 82 (1991): 183-213.

Lee, Aquila H. I. *From Messiah to Preexistent Son: Jesus' Self-Consciousness and Early Christian Exegesis of Messianic Psalms*. WUNT 2/192. Tübingen: Mohr Siebeck, 2005.

Levine, Baruch A. *In the Presence of the Lord: A Study of Cult and Some Cultic Terms in Ancient Israel*. SJLA 5. Leiden: Brill, 1974.

Lieu, Judith M. "Self-Definition vis-à-vis the Jewish Matrix." Pages 214-29 in *Origins to Constantine*. Vol. 1 of *The Cambridge History of Christianity*. Edited by Frances M. Young and Margaret M. Mitchell. Cambridge: Cambridge University Press, 2006.

Lim, Kar Yong. *'The Sufferings of Christ are Abundant in Us' (2 Corinthians 1.5): A Narrative Dynamics Investigation of Paul's Sufferings in 2 Corinthians*. LNTS 399. London: T & T Clark, 2009.

Lindgård, Fredrik. *Paul's Line of Thought in 2 Corinthians 4:16–5:10*. WUNT 2/189. Tübingen: Mohr Siebeck, 2005.

Lohr, Joel N. *Chosen and Unchosen: Conceptions of Election in the Pentateuch and Jewish-Christian Interpretation*. SLTHS 2. Winona Lake, IN: Eisenbraums, 2009.

Longenecker, Bruce. "On Israel's God and God's Israel: Assessing Supersessionism in Paul." *JTS* 53 (2007): 26-44.

Longenecker, Richard N. *The Christology of Early Jewish Christianity*. SBT 2/17. London: SCM, 1970.

—————. *Galatians*. WBC 41. Dallas: Word, 1990.

—————. *Paul: Apostle of Liberty*. 2nd ed. Grand Rapids: Eerdmans, 2015.

—————. *The Epistle to the Romans: A Commentary on the Greek Text*. NIGTC. Grand Rapids: Eerdmans, 2016.

López, Mercedes, and Carlos Mesters. "Codicia, corrupción, pecado estructural en la Carta a los Romanos." *RIBLA* 78 (2018): 103-12.

Lull, David J. "Salvation History: Theology in 1 Thessalonians, Philemon, Philippians, and Galatians. A Response to N. T. Wright, R. B. Hays, and R. Scroggs." Pages 247-65 in *Pauline Theology*. Vol. 1: *Thessalonians, Philippians, Galatians, Philemon*. Edited by Jouette M. Bassler. Minneapolis: Fortress, 1991.

Luther, Martin. "On the Jews and Their Lies." Pages 121-306 in vol. 47 of *Luther's Works*. Edited by Helmut T. Lehmann. Philadelphia: Fortress; St. Louis: Concordia, 1971.

Mackie, Scott D. "The Two Tables of the Law and Paul's Ethical Methodology in 1 Corinthians 6:12-20 and 10:23–11:1." *CBQ* 75 (2013): 315-34.

Marcus, Joel. "'Under the Law': The Background of a Pauline Expression." *CBQ* 63 (2001): 72-83.

Marshall, Christopher D. *Beyond Retribution: A New Testament Vision for Justice, Crime, and Punishment.* Grand Rapids: Eerdmans, 2001.

Marshall, I. Howard. "The Meaning of 'Reconciliation'." Pages 117-32 in *Unity and Diversity in New Testament Theology: Essays in Honor of George E. Ladd.* Edited by Robert A. Guelich. Grand Rapids: Eerdmans, 1978.

Martin, Brice L. *Christ and the Law in Paul.* NovTSup 62. Leiden: Brill, 1989.

Martin, Michael Wade, and Bryan A. Nash. "Philippians 2:6-11 as Subversive *Hymnos*: A Study in the Light of Ancient Rhetorical Theory." *JTS* 66 (2015): 90-138.

Martin, Ralph P. *2 Corinthians.* WBC 40. Waco, TX: Word, 1986.

Martyn, J. Louis. *Galatians: A New Translation with Introduction and Commentary.* AB 33A. New York: Doubleday, 1997.

Mason, Steve. "Pollution and Purification in Josephus's *Judean War.*" Pages 183-207 in *Purity, Holiness, and Identity in Judaism and Christianity: Essays in Memory of Susan Haber.* Edited by Carl S. Ehrlich, Anders Runesson, and Eileen Schuller. WUNT 305. Tübingen: Mohr Siebeck, 2013.

Matera, Frank J. *Romans.* PCNT. Grand Rapids: Baker Academic, 2010.

McCready, Wayne O., and Adele Reinhartz. "Introduction: Common Judaism and Diversity within Judaism." Pages 1-10 in *Common Judaism: Explorations in Second Temple Judaism.* Edited by Wayne O. McCready and Adele Reinhartz. Minneapolis: Fortress, 2008.

McKnight, Scot. *A Light among the Gentiles: Jewish Missionary Activity in the Second Temple Period.* Minneapolis: Fortress, 1991.

McLaren, James S. *Power and Politics in Palestine: The Jews and the Governing of their Land, 100 BC–AD 70.* JSNTSup 63. Sheffield: JSOT, 1991.

Meeks, Wayne A. *The First Urban Christians: The Social World of the Apostle Paul.* New Haven: Yale University Press, 1983.

—————. "Breaking Away: Three New Testament Interpretations of Christianity's Separation from the Jewish Communities." Pages 93-115 in *"To See Ourselves as Others See Us": Christians, Jews, "Others" in Late Antiquity.* Edited by Jacob Neusner and Ernest S. Frerichs. SPSH 9. Chico, CA: Scholars Press, 1985.

Meier, Johann. "The Judaic System of the Dead Sea Scrolls." Pages 84-108 in *Historical Syntheses.* Part 2 of *Judaism in Late Antiquity.* Edited by Jacob Neusner. HdO 1.17. Leiden: Brill, 1995.

Milgrom, Jacob. "Atonement in the OT." Pages 78-82 in *IDBSup.*

—————. *Studies in Cultic Theology and Terminology.* SJLA 36. Leiden: Brill, 1983.

—————. "The *Modus Operandi* of the *Ḥaṭṭāʾt*: A Rejoinder." *JBL* 109 (1990): 111-17.

Milinovich, Timothy. "Once More, with Feeling: Rom 8,31-39 as Rhetorical *Peroratio.*" *Bib* 99 (2018): 525-54.

Moo, Douglas J. *The Epistle to the Romans.* NICNT. Grand Rapids: Eerdmans, 1996.

Morgan, Teresa. *Roman Faith and Christian Faith: Pistis and Fides in the Early Roman Empire and Early Churches.* Oxford: Oxford University Press, 2015.

Morland, Kjell Arne. *The Rhetoric of Curse in Galatians: Paul Confronts Another Gospel.* ESEC 5. Atlanta: Scholars Press, 1995.

Morris, Leon. *The Cross in the New Testament.* Grand Rapids: Eerdmans, 1965.

——————. *The Atonement: Its Meaning and Significance.* Downers Grove, IL: InterVarsity, 1983.

——————. *The Epistle to the Romans.* Grand Rapids: Eerdmans, 1988.

Murphy, Catherine M. *Wealth in the Dead Sea Scrolls and in the Qumran Community.* STDJ 40. Leiden: Brill, 2002.

Nanos, Mark D. *The Mystery of Romans: The Jewish Context of Paul's Letter.* Minneapolis: Fortress, 1996.

——————. *The Irony of Galatians: Paul's Letter in First Century Context.* Minneapolis: Fortress, 2002.

——————. "What Was at Stake in Peter's 'Eating with Gentiles' at Antioch?" Pages 282-318 in *The Galatians Debate.* Edited by Mark D. Nanos. Peabody, MA: Hendrickson, 2002.

——————. "Paul's Relationship to Torah in Light of His Strategy 'to Become Everything to Everyone' (1 Corinthians 9:19-23)." Pages 106-40 in *Paul and Judaism: Crosscurrents in Pauline Exegesis and the Study of Jewish-Christian Relations.* Edited by Reimund Bieringer and Didier Pollefeyt. LNTS 463. London: T & T Clark, 2012.

——————. "Was Paul a 'Liar' for the Gospel? The Case for a New Interpretation of Paul's 'Becoming Everything to Everyone' in 1 Cor 9:19-23." *RevExp* 110 (2013): 591-607.

——————. "The Question of Conceptualization: Qualifying Paul's Position on Circumcision in Dialogue with Josephus's Advisors to King Izates." Pages 105-52 in *Paul within Judaism: Restoring the First-Century Context to the Apostle.* Edited by Mark D. Nanos and Magnus Zetterholm. Minneapolis: Fortress, 2015.

——————. *Reading Corinthians and Philippians within Judaism.* Vol. 4 of *Collected Essays of Mark D. Nanos.* Eugene, OR: Cascade, 2017.

——————. *Reading Paul within Judaism.* Vol. 1 of *Collected Essays of Mark D. Nanos.* Eugene, OR: Cascade, 2017.

——————. *Reading Romans within Judaism.* Vol. 2 of *Collected Essays of Mark D. Nanos.* Eugene, OR: Cascade, 2018.

Neusner, Jacob. *The Rabbinic Traditions about the Pharisees before 70.* Part 1: *The Masters.* Leiden: Brill, 1971.

——————. *The Rabbinic Traditions about the Pharisees before 70.* Part 3: *Conclusions.* Leiden: Brill, 1971.

——————. *Torah: From Scroll to Symbol in Formative Judaism.* Philadelphia: Fortress, 1985.

——————. *Judaism When Christianity Began: A Survey of Belief and Practice.* Louisville: Westminster John Knox, 2002.

——————. *The Emergence of Judaism.* Louisville: Westminster John Knox, 2004.

Newton, Michael. *The Concept of Purity at Qumran and in the Letters of Paul.* SNTSMS 53. Cambridge: Cambridge University Press, 1985.

Nickelsburg, George W. E. *Ancient Judaism and Christian Origins: Diversity, Continuity, and Transformation.* Minneapolis: Fortress, 2003.

Nielsen, Jesper Tang. "The Lamb of God: The Cognitive Structure of a Johannine Metaphor." Pages 217-56 in *Imagery in the Gospel of John: Terms, Forms, Themes, and Theology of Johannine Figurative Language.* Edited by Jörg Frey, Jan G. van der Watt, and Ruben Zimmermann. WUNT 200. Tübingen: Mohr Siebeck, 2006.

Orlinsky, Harry M. *The So-Called "Servant of the Lord" and "Suffering Servant" in Second Isaiah.* VTSup 14. Leiden: Brill, 1967.

Oropeza, B. J. *1 Corinthians.* NCC. Eugene, OR: Cascade, 2017.

Oswalt, John. *The Book of Isaiah: Chapters 40-66.* NICOT. Grand Rapids: Eerdmans, 1998.

Paget, James Carleton. *Jews, Christians, and Jewish Christians.* WUNT 251. Tübingen: Mohr Siebeck, 2010.

Park, Young-Ho. *Paul's Ekklesia as a Civic Assembly: Understanding the People of God in their Politico-Social World.* WUNT 2/393. Tübingen: Mohr Siebeck, 2015.

Paul, Shalom M. *Isaiah 40-66: Translation and Commentary.* ECC. Grand Rapids: Eerdmans, 2012.

Pitre, Brant. *Jesus, the Tribulation, and the End of the Exile: Restoration Eschatology and the Origin of the Atonement.* WUNT 2/24. Tübingen: Mohr Siebeck, 2005.

Pollefeyt, Didier, and David J. Bolton. "Paul, Deicide, and the Wrath of God: Towards a Hermeneutical Reading of 1 Thess 2:14-16." Pages 229-57 in *Paul's Jewish Matrix.* Edited by Thomas G. Casey and Justin Taylor. StJC. Mahwah, NJ: Paulist, 2011.

Porter, Stanley E., and Jacqueline C. R. de Roo, eds. *The Concept of the Covenant in the Second Temple Period.* JSJSup 71. Leiden: Brill, 2003.

Przybylski, Benno. *Righteousness in Matthew and his World of Thought.* SNTSMS 41. Cambridge: Cambridge University Press, 1980.

Puech, Émile. "Messianism, Resurrection, and Eschatology in Qumran and in the New Testament." Pages 235-58 in *The Community of the Renewed Covenant: The Notre Dame Symposium on the Dead Sea Scrolls.* Edited by Eugene Ulrich and James VanderKam. Notre Dame: University of Notre Dame Press, 1994.

Quarles, Charles L. "From Faith to Faith: A Fresh Examination of the Prepositional Series in Romans 1:17." *NovT* 45 (2003): 1-21.

Reed, Annette Yoshiko, and Adam H. Becker. "Introduction: Traditional Models and New Directions." Pages 1-33 in *The Ways that Never Parted: Jews and Christians in Late Antiquity and the Early Middle Ages.* Edited by Annette Yoshiko Reed and Adam H. Becker. Minneapolis: Fortress, 2007.

Regev, Eyal. *The Temple in Early Christianity: Experiencing the Sacred.* AYBRL. New Haven: Yale University Press, 2019.

Richards, Earl J. *First and Second Thessalonians.* SP. Collegeville, MN: Liturgical Press, 1995.

Richardson, Peter. *Herod: King of the Jews and Friend of the Romans.* Columbia, SC: University of South Carolina Press, 1996.

Ridderbos, Hermann. *Paul: An Outline of His Theology*. Translated by John Richard de Witt. Grand Rapids: Eerdmans, 1975.

Riesner, Rainer. *Paul's Early Period: Chronology, Mission Strategy, Theology*. Translated by Doug Stott. Grand Rapids: Eerdmans, 1998.

Roetzel, Calvin J. *Paul: The Man and the Myth*. Minneapolis: Fortress, 1999.

Rogers, Trent A. *God and the Idols: Representations of God in 1 Corinthians 8 and 10*. WUNT 2/427. Tübingen: Mohr Siebeck, 2016.

Ross, Allen P. *Holiness to the LORD: A Guide to the Exposition of the Book of Leviticus*. Grand Rapids: Baker Academic, 2002.

Rudolph, David J. *A Jew to the Jews: Jewish Contours of Pauline Flexibility in 1 Corinthians 9:19-23*. WUNT 2/304. Tübingen: Mohr Siebeck, 2011.

Runesson, Anders. "The Question of Terminology: The Architecture of Contemporary Discussions on Paul." Pages 53-77 in *Paul within Judaism: Restoring the First-Century Context to the Apostle*. Edited by Mark D. Nanos and Magnus Zetterholm. Minneapolis: Fortress, 2015.

Ruzer, Serge. *Mapping the New Testament: Early Christian Writings as a Witness for Jewish Biblical Exegesis*. JCPS 13. Leiden: Brill, 2007.

—————. "Paul's Stance on the Torah Revisited: Gentile Addressees and the Jewish Setting." Pages 75-97 in *Paul's Jewish Matrix*. Edited by Thomas G. Casey and Justin Taylor. StJC. Mahwah, NJ: Paulist, 2011.

Saldarini, Anthony J. *Pharisees, Scribes and Sadducees in Palestinian Society: A Sociological Approach*. Wilmington, DE: Michael Glazier, 1988.

Sampley, J. Paul. "The Weak and the Strong: Paul's Careful and Crafty Rhetorical Strategy in Romans 14:1–15:13." Pages 40-52 in *The Social World of the First Christians: Essays in Honor of Wayne A. Meeks*. Edited by Michael L. White and O. Larry Yarbrough. Minneapolis: Fortress, 1995.

Sandelin, Karl-Gustav. *Attraction and Danger of Alien Religion: Studies in Early Judaism and Christianity*. WUNT 290. Tübingen: Mohr Siebeck, 2012.

Sanders, Boykin. "Imitating Paul: 1 Cor 4:16." *HTR* 74 (1981): 353-63.

Sanders, E. P. "The Covenant as a Soteriological Category and the Nature of Salvation in Palestinian and Hellenistic Judaism." Pages 11-44 in *Jews, Greeks and Christians: Essays in Honor of William David Davies*. Edited by Robert Hamerton-Kelly and Robin Scroggs. SJLA 21. Leiden: Brill, 1976.

—————. *Paul and Palestinian Judaism: A Comparison of Patterns of Religion*. Philadelphia: Fortress, 1977.

—————. *Paul, the Law, and the Jewish People*. Philadelphia: Fortress, 1983.

—————. "Jewish Association with Gentiles and Galatians 2:11-14." Pages 170-87 in *The Conversation Continues*. Edited by Robert Fortna and Beverly Gaventa. Nashville: Abingdon, 1990.

—————. *Judaism: Practice and Belief, 63 BCE–66 CE*. Philadelphia: Trinity Press International, 1992.

—————. *Paul: The Apostle's Life, Letters, and Thought*. Minneapolis: Fortress, 2015.

——————. *Comparing Judaism and Christianity: Common Judaism, Paul, and the Inner and Outer in the Study of Religion*. Minneapolis: Fortress, 2016.

Sapp, David A. "The LXX, 1QIsa, and MT versions of Isaiah 53 and the Christian Doctrine of Atonement." Pages 170-92 in *Jesus and the Suffering Servant: Isaiah 53 and Christian Origins*. Edited by William H. Bellinger Jr. and William R. Farmer. Harrisburg, PA: Trinity Press International, 1998.

Savage, Timothy B. *Power through Weakness: Paul's Understanding of the Christian Ministry in 2 Corinthians*. SNTSMS 86. Cambridge: Cambridge University Press, 1996.

Schaper, Joachim L. W. "The Pharisees." Pages 402-27 in *The Early Roman Period*. Vol. 3 of *The Cambridge History of Judaism*. Edited by William Horbury, W. D. Davies, and John Sturdy. Cambridge: Cambridge University Press, 1999.

Schellenberg, Ryan S. "Does Paul Call Adam a 'Type' of Christ?" *ZNW* 105 (2014): 54-63.

——————. "οἱ πιστεύοντες: An Early Christ-Group Self-Designation and Paul's Rhetoric of Faith." *NTS* 65 (2019): 33-42.

Schiffman, Lawrence H. "Jewish Law at Qumran." Pages 75-90 in *Theory of Israel*. Vol. 1 of *The Judaism of Qumran: A Systemic Reading of the Dead Sea Scrolls*. Part 5 of *Judaism in Late Antiquity*. Edited by Alan Avery-Peck, Jacob Neusner, and Bruce Chilton. HdO 1.56. Leiden: Brill, 2001.

Schlier, Heinrich. *Der Römerbrief*. HThKNT 6. Freiburg im Breisgau: Herder, 1977.

Schliesser, Benjamin. "'Christ-faith' as an Eschatological Event (Galatians 3.23-26): A 'Third View' on Πίστις Χριστοῦ." *JSNT* 38 (2016): 277-300.

Schnabel, Eckhard J. *Law and Wisdom from Ben Sira to Paul: A Tradition Historical Enquiry into the Relation of Law, Wisdom, and Ethics*. WUNT 2/16. Tübingen: Mohr Siebeck, 1985.

Schrage, Wolfgang. *The Ethics of the New Testament*. Translated by David E. Green. Philadelphia: Fortress, 1988.

Schreiner, Thomas R. *Romans*. 2nd ed. BECNT. Grand Rapids: Baker, 2018.

Schüssler Fiorenza, Elisabeth. *In Memory of Her: A Feminist Reconstruction of Christian Origins*. New York: Crossroads, 1983.

Schwartz, Daniel R. *Studies in the Jewish Background of Christianity*. WUNT 60. Tübingen: Mohr, 1992.

Schweitzer, Albert. *The Mysticism of Paul the Apostle*. Translated by William Montgomery. Baltimore: Johns Hopkins University Press, 1998.

Seeley, David. *The Noble Death: Graeco-Roman Martyrology and Paul's Concept of Salvation*. JSNTSup 28. Sheffield: JSOT, 1990.

Segal, Alan F. *The Other Judaisms of Late Antiquity*. BJS 127. Atlanta: Scholars Press, 1987.

——————. *Paul the Convert: The Apostolate and Apostasy of Saul the Pharisee*. New Haven: Yale University Press, 1990.

Setzer, Claudia J. *Jewish Responses to Early Christians: History and Polemics, 30-150 C.E.* Minneapolis: Fortress, 1994.

Silva, Moisés. *Philippians*. BECNT. Grand Rapids: Baker Academic, 2005.

Simon, Marcel. *Verus Israel: A Study of the Relations between Christians and Jews in the Roman Empire 135–425.* Translated by H. McKeating. Oxford: Oxford University Press, 1986.

Sklar, Jay. *Sin, Impurity, Sacrifice, Atonement: The Priestly Conceptions.* HBM 2. Sheffield: Sheffield Phoenix, 2005.

Slee, Michelle. *The Church in Antioch in the First Century CE: Communion and Conflict.* JSNTSup 244. London: Sheffield Academic Press, 2003.

Smart, James D. *History and Theology in Second Isaiah: A Commentary on Isaiah 35, 40–66.* Philadelphia: Westminster, 1965.

Smit, Joop F. M. *"About the Idol Offerings": Rhetoric, Social Context and Theology of Paul's Discourse in First Corinthians 8:1–11:1.* CBET. Leuven: Peeters, 2000.

Smit, Peter-Ben. "In Search of Real Circumcision: Ritual Failure and Circumcision in Paul." *JSNT* 40 (2017): 73-100.

Smith, Barry D. *The Meaning of Jesus' Death: Reviewing the New Testament's Interpretations.* London: Bloomsbury T & T Clark, 2017.

Smith, Daniel A. *The Post-Mortem Vindication of Jesus in the Sayings Gospel Q.* LNTS 338. London: T & T Clark, 2006.

Smith, Morton. "The Troublemakers." Pages 501-68 in *The Early Roman Period.* Vol. 3 of *The Cambridge History of Judaism.* Edited by William Horbury, W. D. Davies, and John Sturdy. Cambridge: Cambridge University Press, 1999.

Sohn, Seook-Tae. *The Divine Election of Israel.* Grand Rapids: Eerdmans, 1991.

Spence, Stephen. *The Parting of the Ways: The Roman Church as a Case Study.* ISACR 5. Leuven: Peeters, 2004.

Stanton, Graham N. "The Law of Moses and the Law of Christ." Pages 99-116 in *Paul and the Mosaic Law.* Edited by James D. G. Dunn. WUNT 89. Tübingen: Mohr, 1996.

Stegemann, Ekkehard W., and Wolfgang Stegemann. *The Jesus Movement: A Social History of its First Century.* Translated by O. C. Dean Jr. Minneapolis: Fortress, 1999.

Stegemann, Hartmut. *The Library of Qumran on the Essenes, Qumran, John the Baptist, and Jesus.* Grand Rapids: Eerdmans, 1998.

Stendahl, Krister. *Paul among Jews and Gentiles, and Other Essays.* Philadelphia: Fortress, 1976.

Sterling, Greg. "*Mors Philosophi*: The Death of Jesus in Luke." *HTR* 94 (2001): 383-402.

Stökl Ben Ezra, Daniel. *The Impact of Yom Kippur on Early Christianity: The Day of Atonement from Second Temple Judaism to the Fifth Century.* WUNT 163. Tübingen: Mohr Siebeck, 2003.

Stowers, Stanley K. *A Rereading of Romans: Justice, Jews, and Gentiles.* New Haven: Yale University Press, 1994.

—————. "What is 'Pauline Participation in Christ'?" Pages 352-71 in *Redefining First Century Jewish and Christian Identities: Essays in Honor of Ed Parish Sanders.* Edited by Fabian Udoh et al. Notre Dame: University of Notre Dame Press, 2008.

Stuhlmacher, Peter. *Reconciliation, Law, and Righteousness: Essays in Biblical Theology.* Translated by Everett R. Kalin. Philadelphia: Fortress, 1986.

——————. *Paul's Letter to the Romans: A Commentary.* Translated by Scott J. Hafemann. Louisville: Westminster John Knox, 1994.

Sumney, Jerry L. "Paul and Christ-believing Jews Whom He Opposes." Pages 57-80 in *Jewish Christianity Reconsidered: Rethinking Ancient Groups and Texts.* Edited by Matt Jackson-McCabe. Minneapolis: Fortress, 2007.

Tabb, Brian J. *Suffering in Ancient Worldview: Luke, Seneca, and 4 Maccabees in Dialogue.* LNTS 569. London: Bloomsbury T & T Clark, 2017.

Taylor, Joan E. *The Immerser: John the Baptist within Second Temple Judaism.* SHJ. Grand Rapids: Eerdmans, 1997.

Taylor, N. H. "Popular Opposition to Caligula in Jewish Palestine." *JSJ* 32 (2001): 54-70.

Tellbe, Mikael. *Paul between Synagogue and State: Christians, Jews, and Civic Authorities in 1 Thessalonians, Romans, and Philippians.* ConBNT 34. Stockholm: Almqvist & Wiksell, 2001.

Theissen, Gerd. *Social Reality and the Early Christians: Theology, Ethics, and the World of the New Testament.* Translated by Margaret Kohl. Minneapolis: Fortress, 1992.

Thiessen, Matthew. *Paul and the Gentile Problem.* Oxford: Oxford University Press, 2016.

——————. "Paul's So-Called Jew and Lawless Lawkeeping." Pages 59-83 in *The So-Called Jew in Paul's Letter to the Romans.* Edited by Rafael Rodríguez and Matthew Thiessen. Minneapolis: Fortress, 2016.

——————. "Paul, the Animal Apocalypse, and Abraham's Gentile Seed." Pages 65-78 in *The Ways that Often Parted: Essays in Honor of Joel Marcus.* Edited by Lori Baron, Jill Hicks-Keeton, and Matthew Thiessen. ECL. Atlanta: SBL, 2018.

Thiselton, Anthony C. *The First Epistle to the Corinthians: A Commentary on the Greek Text.* NIGCT. Grand Rapids: Eerdmans, 2000.

Thomas, Matthew J. *Paul's 'Works of the Law' in the Perspective of Second Century Reception.* WUNT 2/468. Tübingen: Mohr Siebeck, 2018.

Thompson, Marianne Meye. *The Promise of the Father: Jesus and God in the New Testament.* Louisville: Westminster John Knox, 2000.

Thompson, Michael B. *Clothed with Christ: The Example and Teaching of Jesus in Romans 12.1–15.13.* JSNTSup 59. Sheffield: Sheffield Academic Press, 1991.

Thrall, Margaret E. *A Critical and Exegetical Commentary on the Second Epistle to the Corinthians.* 2 vols. ICC. Edinburgh: T & T Clark, 1994.

Tilling, Chris. *Paul's Divine Christology.* WUNT 2/323. Tübingen: Mohr Siebeck, 2012.

Tolmie, D. Francois. "Salvation as Redemption: The Use of 'Redemption' Metaphors in Pauline Literature." Pages 247-69 in *Salvation in the New Testament: Perspectives on Soteriology.* Edited by Jan G. van der Watt. NovTSup 121. Leiden: Brill, 2005.

Tomson, Peter J. *Paul and the Jewish Law: Halakha in the Letters of the Apostle to the Gentiles.* CRINT Section 3: Jewish Traditions in Early Christian Literature 1. Assen: Van Gorcum; Minneapolis: Fortress, 1990.

——————. *Studies on Jews and Christians in the First and Second Centuries.* WUNT 418. Tübingen: Mohr Siebeck, 2019.

Tucker, Brian J. *Reading Romans after Supersessionism: The Continuation of Jewish Covenantal Identity.* NTAS 6. Eugene, OR: Cascade, 2018.

Turnage, Marc. "Jesus and Caiaphas: An Intertextual-Literary Evaluation." Pages 139-68 in *Jesus' Last Week*. Vol. 1 of *Jerusalem Studies in the Synoptic Gospels*. Edited by R. Steven Notley, Marc Turnage, and Brian Becker. JCPS 11. Leiden: Brill, 2006.

Udoh, Fabian E., et al., eds. *Redefining First-Century Jewish and Christian Identities: Essays in Honor of Ed Parish Sanders*. Notre Dame: University of Notre Dame Press, 2008.

Unterman, Jeremiah. *Justice for All: How the Jewish Bible Revolutionized Ethics*. JPSEJS. Philadelphia: Jewish Publication Society, 2017.

van Buren, Paul M. *According to the Scriptures: The Origins of the Gospel and of the Church's Old Testament*. Grand Rapids: Eerdmans, 1998.

van der Horst, Pieter Willem. "'I Gave Them Laws that Were Not Good': Ezekiel 20:25 in Ancient Judaism and Early Christianity." Pages 94-118 in *Sacred History and Sacred Texts in Early Judaism: A Symposium in Honour of A. S. van der Woude*. Edited by J. N. Bremmer and F. García Martínez. CBET 5. Kampen: Kok Pharos, 1992.

VanderKam, James C. *An Introduction to Early Judaism*. Grand Rapids: Eerdmans, 2001.

van Henten, Jan Willem. "Datierung und Herkunft des Vierten Makkabäerbuches." Pages 136-49 in *Tradition and Re-Interpretation in Jewish and Early Christian Literature: Essays in Honour of Jürgen C. H. Lebram*. Edited by Jan Willem van Henten et al. StPB 36. Leiden: Brill, 1986.

——————. *The Maccabean Martyrs as Saviours of the Jewish People: A Study of 2 and 4 Maccabees*. JSJSup 57. Leiden: Brill, 1997.

VanLandingham, Chris. *Judgment and Justification in Early Judaism and the Apostle Paul*. Peabody, MA: Hendrickson, 2006.

Vermes, Geza. *Jesus the Jew: A Historian's Reading of the Gospels*. Philadelphia: Fortress, 1973.

Versnel, Henk S. "Making Sense of Jesus' Death: The Pagan Contribution." Pages 213-94 in *Deutungen des Todes Jesu im Neuen Testament*. Edited by Jörg Frey and Jens Schröter. WUNT 181. Tübingen: Mohr Siebeck, 2005.

Vlach, Michael J. *The Church as a Replacement of Israel: An Analysis of Supersessionism*. EI 2. Frankfurt am Main: Peter Lang, 2009.

Wakefield, Andrew H. *Where to Live: The Hermeneutical Significance of Paul's Citations from Scripture in Galatians 3:1-14*. AcBib 14. Leiden: Brill, 2003.

Wassen, Cecilia. "Do You Have to Be Pure in a Metaphorical Temple? Sanctuary Metaphors and Construction of Sacred Space in the Dead Sea Scrolls and Paul's Letters." Pages 55-86 in *Purity, Holiness, and Identity in Judaism and Christianity: Essays in Memory of Susan Haber*. Edited by Carl S. Ehrlich, Anders Runesson, and Eileen Schuller. WUNT 305. Tübingen: Mohr Siebeck, 2013.

Watson, Francis. "Is There a Story in These Texts?" Pages 231-39 in *Narrative Dynamics in Paul: A Critical Assessment*. Edited by Bruce W. Longenecker. Louisville: Westminster John Knox, 2002.

——————. "Constructing an Antithesis: Pauline and Other Jewish Perspectives on Divine and Human Agency." Pages 99-116 in *Divine and Human Agency in Paul and His Cultural Environment*. Edited by John M. G. Barclay and Simon J. Gathercole. London: T & T Clark, 2006.

—————————. *Paul, Judaism, and the Gentiles: Beyond the New Perspective*. Rev. ed. Grand Rapids: Eerdmans, 2009.

—————————. *Paul and the Hermeneutics of Faith*. 2nd ed. London: Bloomsbury T & T Clark, 2016.

Webb, Robert L. "John the Baptist and his Relationship to Jesus." Pages 179-229 in *Studying the Historical Jesus: Evaluations of the State of Current Research*. Edited by Bruce Chilton and Craig A. Evans. NTTS 19. Leiden: Brill, 1994.

Wedderburn, Alexander J. M. "Paul and Jesus: Similarity and Continuity." Pages 117-44 in *Paul and Jesus: Collected Essays*. Edited by Alexander J. M. Wedderburn. JSNTSup 137. Sheffield: Sheffield Academic Press, 1989.

Wedderburn, Alexander J. M., and Andrew T. Lincoln. *The Theology of the Later Pauline Letters*. NTT. Cambridge: Cambridge University Press, 1993.

Wells, Jo Bailey. *God's Holy People: A Theme in Biblical Theology*. JSOTSup 305. Sheffield: Sheffield Academic Press, 2000.

Wells, Kyle B. *Grace and Agency in Paul and Second Temple Judaism: Interpreting the Transformation of the Heart*. NovTSup 157. Leiden: Brill, 2015.

Wenham, David. *Paul: Follower of Jesus or Founder of Christianity?* Grand Rapids: Eerdmans, 1995.

Wenham, Gordon J. *The Book of Leviticus*. NICOT. Grand Rapids: Eerdmans, 1979.

Werman, Cana. "The Concept of Holiness and the Requirements of Purity in Second Temple and Tannaic Literature." Pages 163-79 in *Purity and Holiness: The Heritage of Leviticus*. Edited by Marcel J. H. M. Poorthuis and Joshua Schwartz. JCPS 2. Leiden: Brill, 2000.

Westerholm, Stephen. *Perspectives Old and New on Paul: The "Lutheran" Paul and His Critics*. Grand Rapids: Eerdmans, 2004.

Westermann, Claus. "Peace (Shalom) in the Old Testament." Pages 16-48 in *The Meaning of Peace: Biblical Studies*. Edited by Perry B. Yoder and William M. Smartley. Louisville: Westminster John Knox, 1992.

Whybray, R. N. *Isaiah 40-66*. NCB. London: Oliphants, 1975.

Wicks, Henry J. *The Doctrine of God in the Jewish Apocryphal and Apocalyptic Literature*. London: Hunter & Longhurst, 1915.

Williams, David J. *Paul's Metaphors: Their Context and Character*. Peabody, MA: Hendrickson, 1999.

Williams, Jarvis J. *Maccabean Martyr Traditions in Paul's Theology of Atonement: Did Martyr Theology Shape Paul's Conception of Jesus' Death?* Eugene, OR: Wipf & Stock, 2010.

Williams, Sam K. *Jesus' Death as Saving Event: The Background and Origin of a Concept*. HDR 2. Missoula, MT: Scholars Press, 1975.

Wilson, Todd A. *The Curse of the Law and the Crisis in Galatia: Reassessing the Purpose of Galatians*. WUNT 2/225. Tübingen: Mohr Siebeck, 2007.

Winger, Michael. "The Law of Christ." *NTS* 46 (2000): 537-46.

Wisdom, Jeffrey R. *Blessing for the Nations and the Curse of the Law: Paul's Citation of Genesis and Deuteronomy in Gal 3.8-10*. WUNT 2/133. Tübingen: Mohr Siebeck, 2001.

Witherington, Ben, III. *Paul's Letter to the Romans: A Socio-Rhetorical Commentary*. Grand Rapids: Eerdmans, 2004.

—————. *Paul's Letter to the Philippians: A Socio-Rhetorical Commentary*. Grand Rapids: Eerdmans, 2011.

Wolff, Christian. "Humility and Self-Denial in Jesus' Life and Message and in the Apostolic Existence of Paul." Pages 145-60 in *Paul and Jesus: Collected Essays*. Edited by A. J. M. Wedderburn. JSNTSup 37. Sheffield: Sheffield Academic Press, 1989.

Wolter, Michael. *Die Brief an der Römer*. 2 vols. EKKNT 6. Ostfildern: Patmos, 2014/2019.

—————. *Paul: An Outline of His Theology*. Translated by Robert L. Brawley. Waco, TX: Baylor University Press, 2015.

Wright, N. T. *The Climax of the Covenant: Christ and the Law in Pauline Theology*. Edinburgh: T & T Clark, 1991.

—————. *The New Testament and the People of God*. Vol. 1 of *Christian Origins and the Question of God*. Minneapolis: Fortress, 1992.

—————. *Justification: God's Plan and Paul's Vision*. Downers Grove, IL: InterVarsity Academic, 2009.

—————. *Paul and the Faithfulness of God*. Vol. 4 of *Christian Origins and the Question of God*. Minneapolis: Fortress, 2013.

—————. *Pauline Perspectives: Essays on Paul, 1978-2013*. Minneapolis: Fortress, 2013.

—————. "Yet the Sun Will Rise Again: Reflections on the Exile and Restoration in Second Temple Judaism, Jesus, Paul, and the Church Today." Pages 19-80 in *Exile: A Conversation with N. T. Wright*. Edited by James M. Scott. Downers Grove, IL: InterVarsity Academic, 2017.

Yinger, Kent L. *Paul, Judaism, and Judgment according to Deeds*. SNTSMS 105. Cambridge: Cambridge University Press, 1999.

—————. *God and Human Wholeness: Perfection in Biblical and Theological Tradition*. Eugene, OR: Cascade, 2019.

Young, Edward J. *The Book of Isaiah: The English Text, with Introduction, Exposition, and Notes*. 3 vols. NICOT. Grand Rapids: Eerdmans, 1965-1972.

Zeitlin, Irving M. *Jesus and the Judaism of His Time*. Oxford: Basil Blackwell, 1988.

Zetterholm, Karin Hedner. "The Question of Assumptions: Torah Observance in the First Century." Pages 79-103 in *Paul within Judaism: Restoring the First-Century Context to the Apostle*. Edited by Mark D. Nanos and Magnus Zetterholm. Minneapolis: Fortress, 2015.

Ziesler, John A. *The Meaning of Righteousness in Paul: A Linguistic and Theology Inquiry*. SNTSMS 20. Cambridge: Cambridge University Press, 1972.

Zimmermann, Ruben. *The Logic of Love: Discovering Paul's "Implicit Ethics" through 1 Corinthians*. Translated by Dieter T. Roth. Lanham, MD: Lexington/Fortress Academic, 2018.

Index of Ancient Sources

Index of Subjects

Abraham, 18, 31, 38, 40, 43-44, 147, 186,
202, 213, 215, 222-23, 284, 297-98, 327
children of, 39-40, 79, 81-82, 188,
198, 215, 226-27
election of, 48-50, 81-82, 319
faith of, 21, 26, 75, 88, 126, 215, 246-
47, 250
Adam, 18, 154, 171, 186, 284
Akedah, 246
Anselm of Canterbury, 303, 315-16
antipsychon, 277-79
atonement, 3, 5, 60, 104-5, 112, 118-19,
243, 269-83

baptism, 7, 37, 40, 186, 212, 224, 233
as dying/being buried with Christ,
139, 191, 244, 300-302

Caiaphas, 178, 192
Calvin, John, 241
Christ. *See also* Jesus; Jesus' death
as crucified, 7, 32, 35, 86, 97, 123, 138,
141, 225, 234, 298-302, 329
blood of, 44, 87, 90-91, 110, 119,
138-39, 187, 192-93, 224-25, 269,
283-84, 286, 294-95, 306-9
body of, 22-23, 86, 104, 138-39, 209,
224-25, 259, 285-87, 298, 306
dying/being buried with, 28, 87, 139,
160-61, 191, 225, 244, 298-302
faith in, 5-8, 23, 45, 82, 88-89, 159-
60, 187-94, 237, 241-42, 292-93,
300, 308, 314-15, 327-29
faith/faithfulness of, 109, 111, 117,
119, 152, 194, 243-45, 256-60,
264-65, 267, 288, 291, 294, 297,
300, 305, 309, 311, 314, 326

law of, 22, 101, 159-60, 223-24, 285,
325
love of, 23, 76, 106-11, 120-23, 137-
39, 141-45, 225, 255, 285-86,
292-96, 299-304
participation in, 87-93, 96-97, 100, 109
preexistence of, 12, 36-37, 136-37, 305
relation to the God of Israel, 20-38,
44-45, 243-45, 260, 299, 319
salvation through, 5-7, 9-11, 86-90,
122-23, 265-66, 290-97, 302-5
Spirit of, 23, 25, 35-36, 148, 155, 254-
55, 325
Christus Victor idea, 88
church. See *ekklēsia*
circumcision, 42, 74, 81-82, 126, 138, 144,
160-63, 168, 180, 199-201, 209-10,
212-22, 229, 251-52, 264-66, 323-24,
327
covenant. *See* Israel, covenant with; new
covenant

David, 16, 25-27, 31-33, 44, 85, 87, 171-
72, 222-23
Day of Atonement, 60, 190-92, 271,
308-9
divine judgment, 19, 21, 33, 41, 53, 55,
68-69, 77-79, 133, 172, 239-40, 243,
256, 261-67, 295, 305, 314, 317-20,
329
divine plan/purposes, 21, 34, 37, 51, 134-
35, 148, 246, 250, 313, 320-23
divine punishment/chastisements, 18, 41,
57-58, 68-69, 83, 87, 113-14, 117,
128, 149-51, 153, 191, 241, 271-72,
279-81, 283-84, 310, 315-16, 318,
325-26